# ETHICS WITH
# ARISTOTLE

# ETHICS WITH ARISTOTLE

SARAH BROADIE

New York    Oxford
OXFORD UNIVERSITY PRESS
1991

Oxford University Press

Oxford   New York   Toronto
Delhi   Bombay   Calcutta   Madras   Karachi
Petaling Jaya   Singapore   Hong Kong   Tokyo
Nairobi   Dar es Salaam   Cape Town
Melbourne   Auckland

and associated companies in
Berlin   Ibadan

Published by Oxford University Press, Inc.,
200 Madison Avenue, New York, NY 10016

Oxford is a registered trademark of Oxford University Press

Library of Congress Cataloging-in-Publication Data
Broadie, Sarah Waterlow.
Ethics with Aristotle / by Sarah Waterlow Broadie.
p.   cm.
Includes bibliographical references.
ISBN 0-19-506601-4
1. Aristotle—Ethics.   2. Ethics, Ancient.   I. Title.
B491.E7B7   1991
171'.3—dc20          90-33456   CIP

2 4 6 8 9 7 5 3 1

Printed in the United States of America
on acid-free paper

This book is dedicated
to
Frederick Broadie
who set the field

# Foreword

I had intended, originally, to cover in one work all the ethical topics that have come down to us from Aristotle, but was unable to make room here for some that certainly deserve a place. Hence the absence of what I would have had to say about Aristotle on the individual moral virtues, on friendship, on justice and on the foundations of politics. I have likewise had to postpone for the time being any systematic attempt to situate Aristotle's views in relation to contemporary ethics or in the history of philosophy itself. My main concern here was to make as clear as I could what has registered with me as crucial for the understanding of Aristotle's ethics.

Although the *Eudemian Ethics* is still much less well known than it deserves, I have followed tradition in treating the *Nicomachean Ethics* as the principal text, including, of course, the common books V–VII (= *EE* IV–VI). I have, however, gone to the *EE* for general support throughout, as well as for the special light it sheds on the contingency of the voluntary, the structure of rational choice and the virtue of nobility. I agree with those who identify the *EE* as the first home of the common books, but nonetheless take it that Aristotle himself would have sanctioned placing them in the Nicomachean context. None of my arguments depends on assigning a Eudemian or a Nicomachean origin to any given passage in the common books. Nor have I had to presuppose any particular order of composition as between the two treatises.

Except where it is otherwise stated, I have used the *Revised Oxford Translation* when quoting from Aristotle.

*Hamden, Connecticut*                                              S. B.
*August 1990*

# Acknowledgements

I thank the John Simon Guggenheim Foundation for honouring me with a fellow-ship taken in 1986. The fellowship period included my first semester on the faculty of Yale University, and I thank the Yale administration for permitting me leave of absence during that time.

*Ethics with Aristotle* was completed too soon for me to take account of Richard Kraut's *Aristotle on the Human Good* (Princeton, 1989). But since my work was read by him for Oxford University Press and provoked pages of thoughtful comments, I have benefited from his views, if not in one way then in another, and I wish to thank him for that.

I am grateful to Celene Abramson for her help with the indices; to Glena Ames for superb secretarial assistance; and to Cynthia Read and her staff at Oxford University Press, New York, for their care and dispatch in seeing this book through the printing.

And here it is appropriate for me to express deep thanks for the unfailing support of Kate Thuillier, who helped from whichever side of the Atlantic whenever she could be most effective.

# Contents

## Works Cited    439

## Name Index    445

## Subject Index    449

## Index Locorum Aristotelis    453

# ETHICS WITH
# ARISTOTLE

# CHAPTER 1

# Happiness, the Supreme End

### I. Presuppositions of the Question

What is the best, the happiest, the most worthwhile sort of life for human beings? Is it a life of honourable achievements: of pleasures and excitements; of service in one's community: of material productiveness: a life marked by happy personal relationships: by luxury and splendid belongings: by love of beauty: by culture of intellect and imagination: or whatever else might come to mind as we learn more about the possibilities of human nature? How are we to decide, and on what principle? Aristotle's *Ethics* begins and ends with this question of the best life, since the task of ethics, as he conceives it, is to seek a systematic answer.

Why should we be interested in such an inquiry? Because it is abstract philosophy, and we have a taste for that? If this were the only motive, it would make no practical difference what answer we found, or whether we found one at all. We might be convinced in advance that no answer can be better than another to a question of this kind, yet still be curious to see a philosopher trying to solve the insoluble. As connoisseurs it may interest us to compare Aristotle's performance in ethics with those of others. In that case, we should not think it a fruitless enterprise for him either, since he like us must enjoy the intellectual exercise.

But according to Aristotle himself, it would be a vain inquiry for all concerned unless a well-grounded answer is possible. Philosophical ethics is practical. 'The end is not knowledge but action' (*NE* 1095 a 5–6; cf. *EE* 1216 b 21–25). We seek to know what the good life is so as to live better. The sheer desire to understand the nature of this life, unburdened by concern for the practical benefits of the knowledge, is not an attitude that Aristotle countenances in the *Ethics.*[1] If there are or might be practical benefits, it is hardly human not to take an interest in them. Hence someone who studies ethics with no eye to a practical end must really believe that the study can make no practical difference, either because philosophers' conclusions cannot influence behaviour or because no conclusion is possible. Yet whoever really believes this should not bother with ethics except perhaps in quotation marks, as a cultural curiosity. For if ethics is supposed to be practical but cannot be, serious attention to ethical arguments is a waste of time. There are better ways of being practical, and if we want to exercise our intellects there are more rigorous disciplines than ethics for that.

On similar grounds, we should not linger over ethics if we are confident of already possessing satisfactory answers to its questions. Learning new arguments for the practical answers which we already have cannot affect what we do. And how would knowing those answers in a reflective articulate way be of any practical advantage? Indeed, reflection might be positively harmful, for once we start to think and to discuss the good, we can make intellectual mistakes about it and be led off the right practical track. It may be that for fallible human beings ethical self-reflection is a luxury which we cannot safely afford.

But in any case for countless numbers of human beings it could never have made any personal difference what philosophers conclude about the best life. Such discussions are unreal for those in no position even to imagine enjoying the freedom to implement such general conclusions. For them, existence is a struggle: however a philosopher would describe and rank their lot against other "alternatives", the individuals concerned are stuck with having to get on with it as best they can for themselves and their children, under conditions which no one would choose. People so situated lack leisure for even thinking about ethics. Hence if we find ourselves asking abstract questions about the good life, this can be only because we have space to modify our lives in the light of possible answers. But whoever is thus free to, had *better* design his life in accordance with an aim, or he will waste it:

> First then about these things we must enjoin every one that has the power to live according to his own choice to set up for himself some object for the good life to aim at (whether honour or reputation or wealth or culture), with reference to which he will then do all his acts, since not to have one's life organized in view of some end is a mark of much folly. (*EE* 1214 b 6–11)

Yet Aristotle is far from suggesting that all we need is to follow some single direction, no matter what. On the contrary, he continues by saying that we should 'define to ourselves' what it is to live well and what are the conditions required (1214 b 14). And he says that we should take careful thought on this, and not rush to a conclusion, presumably because there is a correct answer, but it is not easy to find.

For in supposing, as Aristotle does, that ethics can be to our practical advantage, one is bound to suppose that some one answer to the question of the good and happy life is more on the mark than others. Or perhaps we need only suppose some answers are better than others though none is necessarily best. If the question cannot be answered well or badly and is just a matter of opinion, then although coming up with a particular answer might lead us to adopt different courses of action, these would not be superior to other possibilities although we may then be convinced that they are. But if we were better off only in our own opinion, and other opinions were equally true, we might as well have stayed with whatever views we had in the first place. And logically it should not worry us if our original opinions about how to live were uncertain or switched about as we moved into different stages of life or met different people and encountered new practical pressures. For if every opinion is equally respectable, it is logical (whether or not psychologically possible) to be happy with each as it settles on us and for as long as it chooses to stay.

Philosophers who argue that ethical views are subjective cannot believe that ethical inquiry makes any practical difference for the better. Of course it may make people alter their lives and try to alter the lives of others, but not for either worse or better. Those philosophers might argue that at least we can learn the rationality of being tolerant towards those of contrary opinions, and that tolerance is better than dogmatic crusades to suppress or convert. But an opposite moral can equally be drawn. If every passing view is allowed to make itself felt in practice (and these are, after all, views about how to live), there would be chaos in our lives and in society. Hence it is better to stick to some one position and impose it if necessary by force, even doing violence to the dissenting voices within ourselves in the interests of unity. This is not to be castigated as the stifling of criticism, because there was never any chance of improvement through criticism if every opinion is right.

But the judgment that order of whatever kind is better than chaos—since chaos is no kind of human life at all—is already a judgment of value. Is it no better than the contrary judgment, even if it only amounts to the claim (modest or ambitious is not easy to say) that a recognisably human existence is to us more worth aiming for than death or other kinds of destruction? But if we hold, as to live at all we must, that each of us is more than subjectively right in at least that claim, and right in thinking that there is something wrong with anyone who does not agree (he must be insane or has not understood the words), then it may be possible to achieve the same measure of objective truth with regard to more specific and more controversial values.

We are committed to all this by taking part in ethical inquiry at all, if, as Aristotle holds, the purpose of the inquiry is practical. For whatever our original motive for taking part, once we do, we accept the inquiry on its own terms, which includes accepting its purpose. Given that the purpose is practical, the inquiry is worth our while only on the above assumptions. And by taking part with Aristotle, Aristotle's audience must accept that the purpose of ethics is indeed as he represents it to be. For how can it make sense to attend his lectures if, from no authoritative position of their own, they are going to reject one of his first and most fundamental statements? And how can it make sense to attend while refusing to enter into the spirit of the lectures? The learner who knows better than the teacher what the subject is really all about should be off somewhere teaching others, if he can find others more teachable than himself.

All these assumptions (some of which had already been explored in earlier Greek philosophy, notably by Plato in the *Theaetetus*) must be taken on board by the members of Aristotle's audience. Aristotle's audience, for present purposes, may be taken to include not only those whom Aristotle knew he was addressing, but anyone who takes himself or herself to be addressed by Aristotle. The relation is impersonal in the sense that the parties need not be mutually acquainted, but it is such that the listener takes himself as an instance of a universal 'You' spoken by the speaker. (Aristotle is not in the habit of apostrophising his audience with an explicit second person plural, but the absence of vocatives is perhaps a sign of confidence that he holds their attention and does not need to arouse it.)

But this set of assumptions need not be accepted by the 'we' who study Aristotle's *Ethics* almost from a different world. We may examine his ethical doctrines and read and write books about them in order to understand and explain what he is saying. This is not the same as joining him in his ethical inquiry, because those who study him in this way want to know about Aristotle's arguments, whereas Aristotle wants to know about the good life. Hence we need not share his presuppositions otherwise than in the fictional sense in which we 'assume' somebody's point of view the better to understand what he says. But of course one possible reason for our wishing to understand Aristotle's arguments is that they may help in a similar inquiry of our own. Aristotle, I imagine, would have regarded this as the best and perhaps as the only good reason for studying his or anyone else's *Ethics,* and he would not have been at home with someone whose interest is purely academic, even though such scholars are at home with him or his texts.

One of the assumptions which we must share or pretend to share is that among competing answers to the question 'What is the best life?' there must be better and worse. Having accepted this much we might naturally suppose that just one answer is best. If at some stage of the inquiry there appeared to be two (say) equally good answers, so that anyone who shaped his life by one would seem to be missing out on a genuine and equally important value represented by the other, it would be rational to look out for a yet better single answer in which these or their essentials would be reconciled. In advance of inquiry taking off from the point of apparent conflict, one could not know reconciliation not to be possible. For the two answers would initially present themselves as contraries, not contradictories, and whether they were really in conflict would depend on whether they could be modified into consistency. It is interesting that even if in some sense they might be "really" reconcilable although no one ever finds out how to reconcile them, from a practical point of view they will tend towards irreconcilability until they are reconciled. For as long as we see them as competing alternatives, we shall, if we act by one or the other, make choices that speak more loudly for the respects in which our preferred direction differs from its rival than for those respects which unite them; and the differentiating aspects, by being put into exclusionary practice, will come to stand for the whole of which the common aspects were also parts. This is a practical analogue to the process of logical abstraction, but unlike logical abstraction it leaves us having to live with the existentially real result. Ethical reflection, being not yet action, keeps alive the possibility of reconciliation; thus it is not unreasonable that Aristotle starts his reflections by assuming that a single answer to his question will emerge the winner.

We can wrap this up logically by noting that the question itself presupposes that the definite description 'the best life' is satisfied. (Its being satisfied amounts to this: amongst the objectives at which it could make sense for us to aim, one indisputably fits the description.) But the logical point overlooks a difference between ways of presupposing. One may, for instance, merely hold the working assumption that there is something to which the question refers, and continue to inquire on that basis as long as there is no reason to conclude to the contrary. Launching the question does not require us to assume in advance that a unique answer is available whether found or not, but only that nothing yet rules one out. Alternatively, one could start from the fixed and categorical position that there is a best life. This carries a comforting certainty that ethics has a real question to answer: a certainty especially welcome in view of the actual variety of current opinion. This includes the opinion that the three most desirable kinds of things in life—the noble, the beneficial and the pleasant— tend not to go together; so that the best life, in which they would converge, is not a coherent practical possibility.

That view worried Aristotle enough for him to place it as a target for refutation at the very beginning of the *Eudemian Ethics:*

> The man who stated his own[2] judgement in the god's precinct in Delos made an inscription on the propylaeum to the temple of Leto, in which he separated from one another the good, the beautiful [or: the noble], and the pleasant as not all prop- erties of the same thing; he wrote, 'Most beautiful is what is most just, but best is health, and pleasantest the obtaining of what one desires.' But let us disagree with him; for happiness is at once the most beautiful and best of all things and also the pleasantest. (1214 a 1–8)

'The man' was the well-known poet Theognis, whose verses, many of them addressed to a youth, are full of ethical reflections. Aristotle quotes from him on several occa- sions, usually by name and with approval. But to mention his authorship here would lend the lines even more weight than they already possessed through having been inscribed on the wall of one of the grandest and most visited sanctuaries of the ancient world. Hence Aristotle stresses that the maxim was only the writer's *own* opinion. However, at this point we see Aristotle offering nothing more than *his* own flat rejection.

Among the multitude of views tossed about on a question 'on which judgment seems to all easiest, and the knowledge of it in the power of any man' (1215 b 15– 16), many are not worth taking seriously. We need not even consider the views them- selves but only notice from whom they arise:

> To examine then all the views held about happiness is superfluous, for children, sick people, and the insane all have views, but no sane person would dispute over them; for such persons need not argument but years in which they may change, or else medical or political correction—for medicine, no less than whipping, is a correction. Similarly we have not to consider the views of the multitude (for they talk without consideration about almost everything, and most about happiness); for it is absurd to apply argument to those who need not argument but experience. (1214 b 28-1215 a 3)

Only the opinions of the wise need be examined.[3] But even the *wise* have conflicting views. It would be somewhat presumptuous to take this as the sign that a fresh inquiry is needed; for why should Aristotle's efforts to give an undisputable answer fare better? And how long can one sustain a merely *working* assumption that such an answer is possible, when the reflections of others whom one respects collectively fail to uphold it?

But as with insurance and all sorts of practical calculations, the amount reasonable to invest depends on the magnitude of the issue as well as on the probability of a given outcome. In matters theoretical we can often afford to set aside some question as undecidable even if it has not been so proved. Thus it might be with 'What is the best life?' if this were only theoretical. But since in fact no question could make a greater difference, the truly practical philosopher is justified in pushing ahead with it even when there are grounds for pessimism. This handily illustrates the unity, which Aristotle will expound in detail, of practical rationality with moral soundness. For the pushing ahead is rational according to the insurance principle; and yet when it happens it seems to say more about character than intellect.

But how much better, in the light of all this, if we could start from a more than merely methodological assumption that the basic question of ethics is a question about *something*. Aristotle, we shall now see, finds a way to secure this premiss in advance. He sets about it in the first two chapters of the *Nicomachean Ethics*.

## II. The Statesman's Objective

According to one not uncommon interpretation of the opening lines of the *Nicomachean Ethics*, we must start by lowering our expectations of Aristotle as logical thinker. It is charged that in his anxiety to justify the view that there is a supreme good for human beings, he begins by committing a gross fallacy, this being the move ($M_1$) from 'Each thing aims at some good' to 'There is some good at which each thing aims'. Here is the celebrated opening: 'Every art and every inquiry, and similarly every action and choice, is thought to aim at some good; and for this reason the good has rightly been declared to be that at which all things aim' (1094 a 1–3).

A glance over the next page or so of the text should allay suspicions of that fallacy. True, it is not obvious what the reasoning is in the few lines just quoted, but we can, I think, be sure that if they did embody the fallacy, Aristotle would not have proceeded as he then does. For a little further on he writes as if he had not yet asserted but had only hypothesised the proposition that there is a supreme end. For example, at 1094 a 18–22 that proposition is treated as virtually equivalent to the proposition that there is an ultimate end; at which point (lines 20–21) we find Aristotle arguing for the truth of the latter. This suggests that he regards the former as not yet firmly established. But that would be scarcely possible for anyone misled by the fallacy allegedly contained in the opening sentences. Such a step parades as a purely logical argument; if it were valid it would be as decisive as the correct inference with which it might have been confused, namely ($M_2$) from 'There is some good at which all things aim' to 'Each thing aims at some good'. No one who accepted the premiss of $M_2$ would remain in doubt about its conclusion; and the same applies to $M_1$, given its premiss, for anyone who considered it formally valid in the same way. There is no place for doubt or further persuasion concerning the conclusion in such a case.

Now the premiss stated in Aristotle's first sentence does figure as evidently true, being for him a virtual tautology; to say (I) that every craft etc. aims at some good is really to say that every craft etc. has some aim or end, the achievement of which would constitute an exercise of the craft etc. an effective performance.[4] We could hardly say less. With the second sentence, I believe, we pass to a tacit hypothetical: namely, (II) '*The* good (i.e. the supreme good)—if there is such a thing—has rightly been characterised as that at which all things aim.' The reason for regarding this as hypothetical is simply that what I here present as its antecedent is later felt to stand in need of argument. Had Aristotle been guilty of the alleged fallacy, the second sentence would really have been the categorical that it appears on the surface to be.

Aristotle's actual move from (I) to (II) is not formally valid, but unlike $M_1$ it does not pretend to formal validity. Hence it cannot be written off as erroneous without ado. What is the logic of this passage of thought? Let us be clear what it is intended to establish. It is intended to establish a certain definition of *the* good, a definition in terms of 'aiming.' The logic is this: every distinct craft, inquiry, purpose, action aims—each one—at *some* sort of good. That is, each aims at what we may call a limited good: a good which does not include or presuppose the goods aimed at by each of the other activities. Now none of the limited goods is entitled to be called '*the* good', since none, as a limited good, is unique: either uniquely desirable or uniquely satisfying. *The* good, then, supposing such an end were recognised at all, would not be the object of just another activity—one activity among many. If it were, so to say, only partially aimed at, i.e. aimed at by an activity that is only a *part* of life, it would be only a partial good. Hence *the* good (if there were such a thing) would be a universal objective. In sum, whether or not there really is a supreme good, for an end to be the supreme good is for it to be an absolute and unqualifed end: which means not in relation to some activities and not others, but in relation to all. Only such an end could rightly be termed '*the*—as distinct from *some* (limited kind of)— good'.

Well, is there a universal end? This is what Aristotle now seeks to establish. But first let us pause briefly over the sense or senses of 'end' relevant here. According to the position to be put forward, every art, inquiry, purpose, action has, in a way, two ends. For each aims at *some*—i.e., some limited—good; but also, if Aristotle is right, each aims at *the* good, which is an end common between it and all the others. Now for Aristotle the limited good at which each activity aims determines the character of that activity, since it belongs to the definition of the activity that it is directed towards that good. (Examples: health and the practice of medicine; houses and the activity of building; etc.) In this sense, no two different sorts of activity have the same end. It follows that *the* good is not an end of any of those activities in the same sense as that in which, for each, its defining end is an end. How are these ends related? That is to say, what is the relation between *the* good (always supposing that this concept has application) and, say, health, such that medical science, in aiming (as by definition it does) at health, can also be said to aim at *the* good?

But are we right to be thinking of these as two ends; for is it not really a matter of two descriptions of the same end? Medical science aims at health, and health is a good; so, broadly stated, the objective of medical science is *good*. And so in a sense this objective is the same as, e.g., the objective of navigation, namely safe passage at sea, since that is good too. This is to say that *good* is the formal object of aiming, much as *visible* is the formal object of seeing. It is not to say that either activity has a further end, called 'good,' beyond the specific end which defines it.

But it is precisely this, namely a universal end "beyond" the specific or partial ones, that occupies Aristotle here. He is clear that if what he is talking about exists—which is to say, if such an end really is recognised in practice—then it, one and the same objective, functions as a practical point of convergence in relation to all activities and projects. Thus it is very far from being nothing but health, or nothing but safety at sea, each considered under a generic description 'good'. (Here the same word 'good' applies to both, but it does not signify the same good or one and the same end. Just so, a man and a horse are not the same animal merely because the same generic term 'animal' applies to both.)

Our question, then, is: How is *the* good, which is the end of all activities, related to the special ends of each of these considered singly? In this connection we should also consider the meaning of 'good' here. In a way it is a tautology that every craft etc. aims at some good, but in another way it is not. If 'some good' is taken to mean the same here as 'some end', or (which perhaps adds something) as 'something that figures as good to those who pursue it in practising the relevant craft'—then the proposition is a tautology. This is shown by that fact that it is necessarily true even of nonexistent or purely imaginary crafts and activities. If there were a craft of painting on water, or if there were still the craft of fashioning stone arrowheads, they would have their defining objectives. They may be said (indicatively) to *have* them, in the way in which one says: 'The phoenix *is* a bird.' What is not a tautology is the claim that in any of these cases the good, in the sense of the end aimed at, is in fact good, desirable, valuable, so that it is or would be worth aiming at under real conditions. And clearly some activities are not practised (either never, or are now obsolete) because the ends at which they definitively aim are not considered to be goods in the second sense; i.e., are not considered to *be* of value or to *be* worth the exercise.

Does Aristotle, then, begin his work on ethics with the purely conceptual point that every activity etc., has some end—which is all that is meant by 'aims at some good' in the first sense? It is not likely. For how would such a formal observation by itself open the way to the discussion which he wants to hold of *the* good, and of what is actually good, and of how we should in fact live in order to live well? The conceptual point applies to all conceivable activities, including those to which no actual agent sets his hand. Let us now take it that Aristotle's practical ethical orientation focuses not on this class of conceivables, but on actual activities, crafts which are practised, inquiries which are engaged in, undertakings which are pursued in the real world now. And his interest in them is in them as aiming, each, at some *actually* valuable objective. Now, how can he be so sure that each existing activity does aim at some good in the second, the substantial, sense?

The point, surely, is this: it is a necessary fact about *existing* crafts, activities, etc., that they are directed towards ends that *are* of value. They are carried on because, in one way or another, they justify themselves, earning their places in the real world of human society through each achieving something desirable. Otherwise no one would encourage the practice of them, whether by legal or market sanctions, and ultimately they would not be practised or would never have been invented. This is not a conceptual truth grounded in the concept of an activity pure and simple; it is grounded, rather, in the idea of an activity actually engaging the energies of people having to live by (and with the results of) what they and their fellows do.

This opens the way to the notion of *the* good, and to Aristotle's conclusion that there *is* such a supreme end. For if we ask why the narrow ends aimed at by the crafts etc. are good, in no case will the answer rest simply with a description of the product or the activity itself. An illuminating reply will show how in each case the use or enjoyment contributes to something that is not, and is not the product of, any one of them—namely the *good life*. Moreover, most of these various goods, those severally aimed at by the various activities, would be of no value at all unless at least some of the others were also provided. What value in houses, if disease has killed the population? Thus each of those ends is not merely, by itself, a *partial* good at best, so that other goods, too, are needed if life is not to be deficient; but each of those ends by itself would be of *no* value at all; and the craft or activity which aims at providing it might just as well not exist for all the actual *good* it would achieve.

Already, then, Aristotle's initial reference to the various specific activities in society, and to the special goods which are their ends, implies a reference to some less easily classifiable good which is other than they but related. So far we know nothing about it except that any end aimed at in a specific activity would have no value but for its relation to this other good. But from this we also know that the other good is not just an empty concept. The specific ends are goods, or the activities aiming at them would be pointless. But these activities are engaged in by serious intelligent beings. Hence the specific ends *are* good, which is to say that they *are* worthwhile ends. Therefore any further good on which their goodness depends must likewise be good in the same categorical sense.

But we are not yet entitled to conclude to a supreme good. A 'further good' would be supreme only if (1) it underpins the goodness of every one of the specific ends; (2) it is unique in having this function; (3) there is nothing on which it in turn depends for its value as others depend on it.

Aristotle's next move is to show that the various activities mentioned at the start can be collected under just a few ends, so that the multiplicity confronting us at the beginning is already severely reduced. After remarking that some ends are activities, others products external to productive activities, he points out that activities are hierarchically related to other activities, and ends to ends:

> Now, as there are many actions, arts, and sciences, their ends also are many; the end of the medical art is health, that of shipbuilding a vessel, that of strategy victory, that of economics wealth. But where such arts fall under a single capacity—as bridle-making and the other arts concerned with the equipment of horses fall under the art of riding, and this and every military action under strategy, in the same way other arts fall under yet others—in all of these the ends of the master arts are to be preferred to all the subordinate ends; for it is for the sake of the former that the latter are pursued. It makes no difference whether the activities themselves are the ends of the actions, or something else apart from the activities, as in the case of the sciences just mentioned. (1094 a 9–18)

Let us dwell for a moment on this notion of hierarchies of crafts as a device for showing how some ends are subordinate to others (and then—perhaps—how all but one are subordinate to that one). Contrast this idea with what may seem a more obvious method of making the point: namely, the sort of argument that starts by

referring to something (A, or B) which (for whatever reasons) is held to be of unde-
rived value (an 'end in itself'), e.g., pleasure. The next step is to point out things (X,
Y and Z) which, it is assumed (for whatever reason), are not of value in themselves;
and then the conclusion is drawn that these should be pursued only for the sake of a
contribution which they make to achieving A or B. Notice that in this type of argument, well known to utilitarians, the proposition that X, Y and Z are subordinate to
(should be pursued only for the sake of) A or B is not put forward as a given: rather,
it is a conclusion from first premises consisting of value-judgments to the effect that
A or B is of value in itself, and that X, Y and Z are not. By contrast, on the Aristotelian approach based on the idea of the craft-hierarchy, the relations of subordination are given. For instance, it is an observable social fact that the spear-maker's
expertise is subordinate to that of the general; and there are very many such facts.
The primary meaning of 'subordination' here is that (e.g.) the general qua general
has authority to give orders to the spear maker qua spear maker. From this we *infer*
that the end, i.e. the product, of the spear-maker's craft is subordinate to, in the sense
of to be pursued for the sake of, the end that characterises the art of the general,
namely victory (1094 a 9).

The point to which I would call attention is that this relation of subordinacy in
which spears stand to military victory has been identified without our having had to
make any prior judgment about what is of value in itself. In the present instance, the
relation can be seen to hold regardless of whether military victory is valuable per se,
or as a means to something else, or in both these ways. That is just the sort of point
on which poeple's ethical attitudes differ, but they can agree on the relation of victory
to spears. By contrast, on the line of argument indicated above, a hedonist, say, and
a nonhedonist would not be able to agree on what is subordinate to what; for the
principle by which the hedonist decides, e.g., that virtue is for the sake of pleasure,
is precisely the principle that defines him as a hedonist. What distinguishes Aristotle's
approach is the focus on subordination-relations that are, so to say, objectively there
for people of very different ethical attitudes. The self-indulgent person (as Aristotle
regards him) who makes physical pleasure his leading priority, no less than the person devoted to duty, can see that spears are for the sake of military victory. Hence
these subordination-relations, obvious to anyone who understands how the various
activities in society are organised, are not matters of opinion but factual data from
which to build an ethical argument: for instance, an argument showing that there is
some single ultimate end.

Even so, Aristotle cannot pass directly to that conclusion. It is clear that many
activities have ends which are subordinate to one or another of a small number of
ends; but it needs more than that to show that there is one under which all others
fall. Aristotle argues next that unless we have some *ultimate* end for the sake of which
we pursue 'the others', but which itself is pursued for its own sake, our desire would
be 'empty and futile', since the pursuit would go on to infinity (1094 a 18–22). By
itself this is not a satisfactory argument on two counts. (1) To establish that some
end is ultimate and derives its value from nothing else, Aristotle should have said
that it is desired for its own sake and *only* for its own sake; but perhaps this is to be
understood. (2) He is not entitled to speak of an ultimate end as that for the sake of
which we pursue '*the* others', as if everything else must be subordinate to it. To claim

the ultimacy of some end is to claim no more than that *some* things are pursued for the sake of an end which is desired only for its own sake. This is compatible with a situation in which other things are pursued for the sake of a different ultimate end.

But does the point about the infinite regress show that there has to be even one ultimate end? What would be wrong, logically or in any other way, with our pursuing something for the sake of something which in turn was for the sake of something else, without end? Suppose that the ends and activities were related in such a way that in pursuing end $E_1$ we were also effectively pursuing $E_2$, and thereby $E_3$ and so on. Thus in saying 'Yes' I express affirmation, in expressing affirmation I answer your question, in answering your question I give you certain information, in giving you that information I enable you to draw a certain conclusion, and so on. If we had a series of ends that were different but not strung out at spatial or temporal intervals, could not they all be accomplished in accomplishing the first, even if the series were infinite?

To meet this objection on Aristotle's behalf, we need not, it seems to me, engage with the thorny issue of his rejection of an 'actual infinite'. Even if by a single stroke here and now I can bring about an actual infinity of consequences causally related in such a way that each could reasonably be seen as the means to the next in the series, I could not *know* all that I was bringing about, and consequently I could not *aim for* each member of the series. My desire must settle at some point because until it does I do not actually desire anything for the sake of which I then desire the things through which I can accomplish it. If I shift along the series discarding each as an ultimate objective in favour of the next, then not only do I form no desire for a particular objective, but my general desire *for good* (whatever the good may be) is 'empty and futile'—not because it cannot be implemented to the maximum, but because it cannot be implemented *at all* unless I fix on some given objective as good, and set about acting for the sake of it. Now in settling on some objective O, I take O to be good and worth pursuing because I am doing or am about to do other things, perhaps troublesome things, for the sake of it. But suppose that I believed that any objective on which I settle is not good in itself, but only because of its relation to some other good which cannot be my objective, since it lies beyond the horizon of what I am able to consider when I settle on the first. In that case, I should believe that the end on which I had settled was pointless in itself, just as the nearer objectives would be pointless but for it. I might somehow assure myself that the one on which I have settled is not in fact pointless, on the ground that it is related to some unknown further thing which gives it its point and in turn has point because of something else. For I might just believe that this is so, although I cannot even name these objects. Hence I might be sure that the one which I have fixed upon as my end (and which I do know) is in fact worth pursuing, but I could not ever know why. But however matters lay within myself, I should seem foolish if I were questioned by another who doubted (as we have seen can easily happen) the worthwhileness of my objective, for I could only say that I am sure that it is worthwhile, but do not know why.

But apart from the desirability of being able to make sense of oneself to others (a fundamental dimension of the good life for human beings who, if Aristotle is right, are essentially social, and the formal nature of whose good is currently being spelt out by him in terms of hierarchies within society), there is the further question of whether we can or ought to be satisfied with an objective which to us is ultimate, but whose value we cannot begin to understand. For if we cannot know why something which is known to us is good, but only *that* it is, then we can never come to value it for what about it makes it valuable, and so we can never value it in the appropriate way. And this can make an ethical difference. For instance, we look askance at those who pursue material possessions as if merely having them were good in itself. But perhaps it would be more charitable to say of such people that they pursue possessions not in the belief that having them is good in itself (does anyone explicitly think this?), but because they do not know (perhaps being too busy to give it any thought) what they are good for. But on the hypothesis being considered, no one would be better off than anyone else on this score. The person who pursues whatever it is that he thinks material goods should be used for will be pursuing that end as if he believed it good in itself, since otherwise he has no business taking a high moral line with those who pursue what he clearly sees as not good in itself as if it were; but this person's values would be no less off key than those of the others whom he criticises.

To return to Aristotle's argument: from the consideration that desire is empty and futile unless some end is ultimate, he seems to pass to the immediate conclusion that what is ultimate is '*the* good and the *best*' (1094 a 21–22). But this does not follow immediately, because logically there might be more than one ultimate end, in either of two ways: some activities might lead to one and be worthwhile accordingly, and some to another; or all might lead to each of several ultimate ends, and be rendered worthwhile by each independently. In either case, what is ultimate is not uniquely supreme, but this seems logically and ethically harmless. In the first case there could be conflict not resoluble by argument, since it might not always be possible to act for the sake of one end without passing up an opportunity to act for the sake of the other. But this does not have to spell anarchy or the imposition of arbitrary decisions, for it is possible for rational beings to take steps to avoid situations in which different ends become rivals. And a plurality of ultimate ends does not do away with the need for philosophical ethics, for it is still necessary to determine what those ends might be. What is more, it could be argued that the basic topic of ethics is unitary even on these conditions. For the topic is the best and happiest life, and from the assumption of different ultimate ends it does not follow that no life is the best, but that the best is one which combines the ultimate ends.

However, Aristotle is about to justify his passage at 1094 a 18–22 from 'There is an ultimate end (or desire would be vain)' to 'There is one ultimate end at which everything aims—*the* good and the best'. He postpones the justification briefly, in order to raise a question which at this moment he is not yet entitled to raise: What is *the* good and best? The question is so important that (he implies) we should lose no time in trying to answer it even if only in outline (22–25). And then he points to an answer. But can the question '*What* is the best?' be so important that we are right to ask it even before knowing *that* there *is* a best? Aristotle need not halt for this possible objection, because in proceeding to sketch the nature (or *what*) of the supreme end, he makes clear beyond doubt that such an end is real. To get a grip on what it might be, he asks what sort of practical knowledge or aptitude would aim at the supreme end (25). Now an answer to this might not tell us very much about the nature of the supreme end, for as a rule we derive our understanding of what some branch of knowledge is, or what sort of capacity some capacity is, from what we already know about the objects of that branch of knowledge or the activity or product which the capacity is a capacity for.[5] But here, for once, Aristotle wants us to identify the knowledge or skill first in order to identify its object or end. And in particular, I think, he wants to turn us away from the argument: 'No one can say what the End of ends is; so surely there is no such End.' For even if no one can say what it is, suppose we can name and vaguely conceive the kind of rational activity that would be correlative to that end, as medical practice to health; and suppose it is clear to everyone that that activity *is* carried on in real life (however imperfectly understood, even by its practitioners): then at last we know that there *is* an End of ends, in the sense that there is such a real objective.

Thus roughly to characterise the supreme end, should there be such, Aristotle says this: 'We must try, in outline at least, to determine what it is, and of which of the sciences or capacities it is the object. It would seem to belong to the most author-itative art and that which is most truly the master art. And politics appears to be of this nature' (1094 a 25–29). People do involve themselves in government. Hence there is such an activity, and its end is real. And the status of this activity vis à vis other activities will tell us the status of its end vis à vis other ends.

> It is this that ordains which of the sciences should be studied in a state, and which each class of citizens should learn and up to what point they should learn them; and we see even the most highly esteemed of capacities to fall under this, e.g. strategy, economics, rhetoric; now, since politics uses the rest of the sciences, and since, again, it legislates as to what we are to do and what we are to abstain from, the end of this science must include those of the others, so that this end must be the good for man. (1094 a 28–b 7)

Statecraft dictates terms to all other activities in society and none dictates terms to it. Its ultimacy is unique, because there is no other activity to which the few 'most highly esteemed' skills are subordinate in this way. Its end, therefore, is the supreme end.

Thus Aristotle's conclusion that there is a supreme end, and that it is an actual objective of human life, is not spun from sheer analysis of the concepts *ends, activity, aiming for,* but from what is not the less a datum of human experience because of being a necessary condition for so much of that experience: the fact that human soci-eties exist and are organised, and that this organisation is not instinctive or mechan-ical like that of a biological system (for then we should not need to know about it, since its operation would not depend on our knowing about it), but depends on a rational or would-be rational activity of government which cannot escape the notice of those who engage in it or are affected by it. *The* good at which 'all things aim' has been identified as the objective of those who govern; it is the objective of the *politikos* or statesman.[6]

But then how is *the* good related to the aims and choices of *individuals?* And whose good is it that is the object of the statesman? Is it that of the statesman himself, the citizens in general, or the community considered as some single entity? (This last, as a distinct possibility, can be set aside. For the good, so far as ethics is concerned, is happiness, and [aside from God] happiness can be ascribed only to human individuals.[7]) Now Aristotle's argument does not presuppose that political leaders have a monopoly of concern for the supreme good in any sense that would rule this out of bounds for the so called ordinary citizen. The difference between governors and governed is conceptual: they need not be distinct classes (cf. *Politics* 1277 b 8–22). And so far as the ordinary citizen accepts the end of government as overriding, it is *his* end. The argument is designed so that it does not matter that no one concerned has a clear idea of the nature of this end; a clear idea would obviate the need for Aristotle's philosophical inquiry. However, the argument naturally draws attention to the statesman or politician in the narrow and familiar sense of 'leader'. For in the leader's case the political activity is at its most visible, which is what the argument requires.

As for the question of whose good is the supreme good at which the statesman aims, Aristotle surely expects his audience to remember a lesson from Plato's *Republic:* the ruler's objective is the good of the citizens as such, and his own so far as he is included among them. A cobbler as such makes shoes, which are good for anyone who needs shoes—not merely shoes for himself and his family. If he served only the latter, this would be because there was no wider market or because these are the clients closest at hand. Although Aristotle of course thinks that every individual is especially concerned for his own happiness, this opening argument of the *Nicomachean Ethics* neither proves nor presupposes that an individual can or should pursue only his own good. Whether a person achieves it for one man or for a cityful, the difference is in quantity. To achieve it even for one person is no mean thing, although it is more splendid to benefit a whole community (1094 b 7–10); but either way the end is the same in kind, and the kind of activity is fundamentally the same.

We should notice that the argument itself does not operate with the notion of a human self whose interests might conflict with the interests of another, or of the citizens at large. The dramatis personae of this argument are not you, I, we or they, but rôles or functions. The *aiming* which is the central notion of the argument is not intending, seeking, or purposing in a psychological sense. Only human individuals can 'aim' in that sense, and the aim may vary depending on the motive. But Aristotle's argument attaches aims and ends to those abstract entities crafts, activities, practices, projects. *They* cannot have motives, and the 'aim of' each is defined by the end whose achievement is the mark of *success* for that kind of craft, activity, etc. The status of health as the end of medicine is the same whatever one's motive for engaging in the practice of medicine.

Since the statesman's function is defined as aiming at a good of a certain *nature,* Aristotle's conceptualised ordinary citizen easily merges with the statesman. One ordinary citizen is concerned about *the* good for his own family and friends, another for his, and the men in office for the good of citizens in general. Their ends are the same in kind, and Aristotle's task in the *Ethics* is to explain what this kind of good is. By comparison, questions of who should receive, at whose hands, that and other kinds of good, or how goods in general or the opportunities for them should be distributed, are not the fundamental questions of ethics. Similarly, the concept of statesman or state as that whose function it is to ensure respect for individuals' rights to goods, is not, from this perspective, a fundamental concept. If that is how we essentially view the statesman, Aristotle's argument does not make sense.

For we may agree that the statesman or state is the ultimate authority, yet on the view just mentioned we shall reject the proposition that his or its function is to achieve the highest good of citizens. The highest good of citizens will be the business of the citizens themselves in their private capacity, and the business which defines the state is to provide conditions protecting the individual in his personal pursuit of the good. The collective need for conditions which can be provided only by collective action is the ground of the state's authority. Hence in this picture the state's authority does not derive from its definitively aiming at the supreme good, if the supreme good is individual human happiness. For the conditions for the pursuit of happiness, which it is the state's duty to provide or protect, are a lesser good than happiness.

It follows (on such a theory of the state) that the existence of the state, and the state's authority, provide no argument at all for the thesis that there is such a thing as *the* supreme good. These facts prove only that people need to be governed and protected, and some quite new argument would have to be adduced to show (if it can be shown) that one kind of good, and one kind of life, is objectively best. The 'happiness' which individuals are said to pursue under the protection of the state and within limits laid down by law may (so far as this picture goes) be one thing for one person and something quite else for another. So it may not be the business of universal philosophy to determine what this precious happiness is, since it is now not clear that it makes sense to look for a single answer.

### III. Method and Starting Points

In the first two chapters of the *NE* Aristotle has declared and argued for the ambitious thesis that there is a single supreme end, the objective of statecraft *(politikē)*. We are now set to begin discovering what the nature of this might be. But in Chapter 3 he sounds a strong note of caution about the coming investigation. He is not promising precision or certainty in ethics.

> Our discussion will be adequate if it has as much clearness as the subject-matter admits of; for precision is not to be sought for alike in all discussions, any more than in all the products of the crafts. Now fine and just actions, which political science investigates, exhibit much variety and fluctuation, so that they may be thought to exist only by convention, and not by nature. And goods also exhibit a similar fluctuation because they bring harm to many people; for before now men have been undone by reason of their wealth, and others by reason of their courage. We must be content, then, in speaking of such subjects and with such premises to indicate the truth roughly and in outline, and in speaking about things which are only for the most part true and with premises of the same kind to reach conclusions that are no better. In the same spirit, therefore, should each of our statements be *received;* for it is the mark of an educated man to look for precision in each class of things just so far as the nature of the subject admits: it is evidently equally foolish to accept probable reasoning from a mathematician and to demand from a rhetorician demonstrative proofs. (1094 b 11–27; see also 1104 a 1–9)

In ethics we have to be content with generalisations true only for the most part. What is fine and just varies with the circumstances—a fact taken by some to show that these predicates apply only 'by convention', never 'by nature'. The contrast suggests that such judgments are never really true or apposite rather than not. Aristotle rejects that implication, pointing out that what is good or beneficial varies too, even though it is obviously not just a matter of convention that things such as wealth are beneficial—when they are. What the variation shows, as his account of practical wisdom will explain, is that the truth or aptness of an ethical judgment varies with the situation in which it is made. That at any rate is so for judgments whose content is specific enough to guide action one way rather than another.

But in this passage Aristotle is not just reminding his audience that day-to-day practical judgments are rough and ready and will always prove to have exceptions if we try to universalise them. He is also, and primarily, making a statement about method in ethical philosophy. And as such, his remarks are questionable. Ethical philosophy will study, amongst other things, the nature of day-to-day practical judgments; but does this entail that the philosopher's conclusions share the variability of this subject matter? On the contrary: this very point that true practical judgments are true only for the most part must be intended by Aristotle as simply true, without qualification and universally. And in the *Ethics* he puts forward many other propositions, as for instance that 'excellence of character is a mean', which are meant as universal.[8] Indeed, in that instance he undertakes a lengthy case-by-case survey for the purpose of showing that there are no exceptions.

It would seem, then, if we distinguish between the subject matter of philosophical ethics and the philosophical analysis of that subject matter, that the conclusions of the analysis can (though Aristotle seems to deny it) possess the universality and exactness of mathematical truths. After all, pure mathematics is not itself undermined in those respects by the fact that the physical objects to which it may be applied are perhaps never exactly spherical, or equal, or unequal by any exact amount. But the analogy is misplaced. It is not intrinsic to the nature of any branch of pure mathematics that it be applicable (even approximately) to concrete objects. Its success as that kind of intellectual discipline does not depend on this, but on internal rigour and theoretical explanatory power; and the mathematician who takes no interest in concrete applications has not missed the point of his discipline.

But ethics is practical. To investigate the human good for the sake of intellectual exercise alone would be a kind of perversion. Since the question 'What is the best life?' is pursued with a view to making the answer make a practical difference, some propositions of philosophical ethics will resemble ordinary practical judgments in being only roughly true. This may hold for the answer to the principal question, and for some of its premisses.[9] Thus Aristotle here prepares us to accept that even his own carefully pondered answer may be subject to later qualification (cf. 1098 a 20–26). After all, this answer of his, as he never tries to conceal, is itself reached by elaboration of views already held by philosophers or embedded in the ordinary moral consciousness.

Now in this last respect Aristotle's conclusions             ble his conclusions in metaphysics, which is a theoretical inquiry can          own sake only. For there, too, he seeks truth by carving it out of exist          often transforming the latter beyond recognition). The qualifications, distinctions and regroupings which mark the advance of *theōria* depend on the contributions, at different stages, of historic thinkers. On the other hand, their activity and the activity which builds on theirs does not reflect (so Aristotle believes) and is not limited by their external (in the sense of nonintellectual) circumstances. This is where ethics differs from theoretical philosophy, and the difference arises not from the fact that ethics develops, but from the fact that it is practical. A practical truth, however deep and far reaching, depends for its actual practicality on externals. A simple example, which will be relevant again later, concerns the use of leisure. For people with leisure, a condition which depends on the social and economic background, the answer to the question about the best life is not exactly the same as for people stretched to the limit by practical urgencies. The latter, as we remarked earlier, cannot even ask the question on their own behalf; but for them the answer which applies to the leisured is not only not yet known to be true: it is not even true. For if this kind of truth is essentially practical, it arises only where it can make a practical difference; and that may depend on conditions not necessarily present.

However, revision or correction in accordance with changing conditions does not apply to all the propositions of an ethical system, even if it applies to all those which express value judgments or recommendations. For these rest in part on logical distinctions, psychological analyses and conceptual structures which Aristotle would certainly not consider vulnerable to the changes that affect practice. And perhaps even we do not consider them directly vulnerable to such change. So far as Aristotle's ethics is based, as it firmly is, on a conception of human nature, his findings must be intended as universal and necessarily applicable. But even so, the practical character of the enterprise must colour our attitude to the invariant elements in the picture. In this connection, his strictures on method in the last quoted passage amount to a warning not to pursue precision, even with regard to *universal* truths of ethics, beyond the point of ethical illumination. Even exceptionless generalisations may be rough, in the sense that they fail to display the structure of their subject matter with the sharpness it would be right to demand in a theoretical investigation. It is inappropriate to be moved by intellectual curiosity or by the perfectionist desire to reduce everything to clear and distinct ideas, even if it were possible in this area. To take a modern example: if it makes no practical difference at all whether ethical judgments are classified as indicatives or imperatives, the question should not be pursued in ethics.[10] Likewise, it is not automatically legitimate (simply because we are engaged in a rational inquiry) to look for explanations,[11] definitions, and perspicuous foundations:

> For a carpenter and a geometer look for right angles in different ways; the former does so in so far as the right angle is useful for his work, while the latter inquires what it is or what sort of thing it is; for he is a spectator of the truth. We must act in the same way, th      all other matters as well, that our main task may not be subordinated to          s. Nor must we demand the cause in all matters alike; it is enough         that the *fact* be well established, as in the case of the first principles; the t.          ary thing or first principle. (1098 a 29–b 3)

Hence even if an exact theoretical science of human nature is possible, philosophical ethics should not hold fire until theory has become revealed.

All this carries implications about the sort of person one must be if one is going to profit from a course on ethics (which Aristotle now freely calls 'political science', since the aim is the same as that of the statesman).

> Now each man judges well the things he knows, and of these he is a good judge. And so the man who has been educated in a subject is a good judge of that subject, and the man who has received an all-round education is a good judge in general. Hence a young man is not a proper hearer of lectures on political science; for he is inexperienced in the actions that occur in life, but its discussions start from these and are about these. (1094 b 27–1095 a 4)

In learning mathematics it helps to put contingent experience on one side. One cannot understand or believe in infinite divisibility or the incommensurability of the diagonal if one's concepts are loaded with sensory imagery. But in ethics the good learner must be a person of practical experience and ready to integrate that experience with the generalities taught in ethics. This is not only because this gives them meaning, but because they cannot otherwise affect his practice for the better. From his own experience he will recognise exceptions and find ways of qualifying or extending the general principles so that exceptions are covered. Ethics deals in abstractions, but its purpose is defeated unless someone translates those abstractions into concrete terms. There are, however, no firm rules of translation.

Experience and the sense of how to bring it to bear are qualities of mind or cognition; but to profit from the study of ethics the student must also be of a certain moral character. He must be free from the childishness of living by impulse:

> And further, since [a young person] tends to follow his passions, his study will be vain and unprofitable, because the end aimed at is not knowledge but action. And it makes no difference whether he is young in years or youthful in character; the defect does not depend on time, but on his living and pursuing each successive object as passion directs. For to such persons, as to the incontinent, knowledge brings no profit; but to those who desire and act in accordance with a rational principle knowledge about such matters will be of great benefit. (1095 a 4–11)

An incontinent person is one who has rationally decided what he should do in a particular situation but lets impulse take him in a different direction. Here Aristotle implies that unless we have learnt to master impulse, philosophical ethics will not help us even in forming good particular decisions, let alone in carrying them out. Lectures on ethics cannot substitute for moral discipline. Aristotle has contemptuous words for those who think they can make progress that easy way:

> But most people do not [engage in the right actions], but take refuge in theory and think they are being philosophers and will become good in this way, behaving somewhat like patients who listen attentively to their doctors, but do none of the things they are ordered to do. As the latter will not be made well in body by such a course of treatment, the former will not be made well in soul by such a course of philosophy. (1105 b 12–18)

'Most people' here (i.e., 'the many') is not just a quantitative expression. Aristotle is saying that it is not intellectual refinement but positive vulgarity to be handling ethical arguments in the belief that the true benefit of such arguments costs no more than the mental effort of following them.

So 'desiring and acting in accordance with reason' is not something which Aristotle promises to his hearers if they listen; it is a required precondition. Hence 'reason' here does not refer to philosophical illumination gained only by systematic study of ethics, but to an already active interest in the good life. This interest is 'rational' not because it is founded in an intellectual grasp of principles, but because the good life, whatever it consists in, is a kind of good which can be attained only if we are prepared to subordinate some desires to others: which latter therefore constitute *reasons* for choosing what we do and rejecting what we may have felt like doing. That the good life is attainable only in this way is proved by the fact of our engaging in this inquiry at all. If we could win our supreme good by following impulse (and that we cannot is a remarkable fact, since other animals are guided by impulse alone, and flourish by it given health and the right surroundings—conditions towards which impulse itself tends to lead them), the inquiry would be pointless, since we could gain no advantage by trying to think clearly about the nature of the good life.

This follows from the assumption that the advantage to be gained is practical, and the same assumption gives a moralising edge to Aristotle's warning not to expect the accuracy of mathematics. He is not so much trying to save his theoretically minded students from disappointment, or (conversely) to reassure theoretically untrained members of the audience that they will not be expected to follow complicated chains of proof. He is implying that whoever expects mathematical accuracy in ethics is only playing at ethics. For practical knowledge cannot meet that standard, and does not need to in order to be effective.

So much for ways in which personality qualifies or disqualifies people for approaching ethics in the first place. But having approached, and knowing something in general about what to expect, how do we make a start? Aristotle raises the question by recalling Plato's distinction between movement from and movement to starting points (1095 a 30–b 1). We seek out the first principles of a discipline, and then we move in reverse from them as starting points. In the former movement we begin from obvious but unexplained data for which we hope to find deep principles; in the latter, we return to the data in the light of the principles which now explain them. The principles, in Aristotle's parlance, are better known 'in themselves' or 'by nature' than the initial data, but the data are better known 'to us' (*Posterior Analytics* 71 b 33–72 a 1).

Where do we start in ethics? It has been shown that there is a supreme good; the question now is what it is. Some may think that the answer can be given straightaway by referring to whatever could explain the goodness of familiar good things whose nature we already know. Thus Plato identified the highest good with the Form or Idea of Good which is the metaphysical source of the goodness of all other good things through their participation. Since Plato's highest good is a principle in this way, it would seem that for him we attain knowledge of it only by an upward movement *from* the derivative goods familiar to us. Thus in a chronological sense the inquiry starts with them. Schematically this is what Plato's picture implies, but if we look more closely we see that the reality is different. For the Platonic Form of the Good has no character other than to be good. And the good things which derive their goodness from it are all (it is implied) good in the same way—by participating in the Form, or mirroring it. From this it follows that we need not examine the specific characters of those familiar good things. We need only know that there are mundane good things, whatever they are and however different in other respects from each other, and this one premiss assures us that there is the Form which is nothing but what it logically has to be: namely, good or the Good. And so in fact we can start at once with the Form, since the various natures of the lower goods, the ones 'better known to us', can tell us nothing. And the same start might be made, and the same destination reached in the Form, even by people whose values we do not accept; for strictly all that they need is the formal recognition that something or other is good.

Aristotle on the contrary says that in ethics we must start from what is known to us, and really start from this, not skip over it (1095 b 2 ff.). In other words, we must take account of *what* we ordinarily take to be good in all its variety. Aristotle can insist on this because he has arguments, some of which he will give in *NE* I.6, against the very notion of Plato's Form of Good. One of the less technical arguments is that ordinarily recognised goods such as honour, intelligence and pleasure have 'distinct and diverse accounts, just in respect of their goodness insofar as they are goods. The good, therefore, is not something common answering to one Idea' (1096 b 23–26). Another is that Plato's Form, whose nature is to be good and nothing but good, is not something that we can pursue in action or possess. For anything that we can bring about or coherently aim to bring about must be *something* that is good, even if it is the highest good. We could not aim at a good that was describable only as 'good', for there would be nothing to determine our aim in given direction. But ethics is concerned with a highest good that is humanly practicable; hence it is not concerned with the Form (1096 b 32–35; cf. *EE* 1217 b 23–25).

We start, then, with the things known to us, which is to say the goods we ordinarily recognise as such, and in all the shapes in which we know them. To make a start we do not need to know why they are good (1095 b 6–7). But we do need, Aristotle says, to have been brought up in good ways of feeling and acting (1095 b 4–6). We must have sound values, because our actual values afford the only possible ethical starting points, and unless they are sound the starting points will be false.

How can Aristotle's hearers know whether they are well brought up? They have only the upbringing itself to assure them. But Aristotle makes no space for this question. If it seems to us that his unsupported starting point needs a foundation in something else, we should be prepared to indicate what that might be. To his audience, it would have to be more certain than their initial values. In the absence of any such prior foundation, Aristotle and his audience will proceed without it, especially since accepting those values as starting points is not an absolute commitment that forbids critical reassessment along the way. The value data of ethics, like the perceptual data from which natural science starts, can be modified and corrected, but only against *each other* and in the light of deductions for which some of *them* must serve as premisses.

The parallel with science is helpful only up to a point. The aim of science is to construct theories which will explain the phenomena or provide a framework within which phenomena fall into order, however that be judged. Aristotle will seek to show how the things which we ordinarily value are related to the supreme end in ways that make it clear why they are worth valuing. But his principal purpose is not to explain our basic value judgments or to order them in relation to the supreme end for the sake of an intellectually harmonious picture. Nor is it even to show that we are justified in holding them, since this he assumes from the start and expects us to share the assumption if we wish to engage in ethical inquiry. Rather, his aim in that ordering is to show the goods which we initially value in such a light that we shall end by valuing them only as they ought to be valued. Thus he will argue for instance that pleasure is a good, and good in itself, but not to be sought without restriction, since pleasure takes its worth from the particular activity which it attends. His developing account of the supreme end will conform to our original intuitions, but by setting them in perspective it will also refine them, and thereby perhaps enable us to identify ethical possibilities previously unrecognised but nonetheless contained in the familiar material of the starting point.

It should be clear from these considerations that Aristotle does not introduce the conception of the supreme end in order to provide us with a motive for valuing those things which well-brought-up people value. In particular, in arguing as he will that this highest good in a sense consists in morally virtuous action, he cannot be seeking to cast morally virtuous action in such a light that his listeners will be more disposed to engage in it than if they did not know of this argument. Already he has declared that argument cannot make that kind of difference. Those for whom the investigation is intended are by upbringing committed to moral goodness. But what, in that case, do they gain by having philosophy show them that the life they are already prepared to lead is itself the highest good? For they are now virtually in possession of that good. But it is one thing to be virtually living the sort of life that is best, and another to make the most of that best and be able to pass it on uncorrupted. Aristotle's inquiry assumes that to make the best of the best which we already have, we must reflect on it philosophically.

I have already indicated ways in which Aristotle might be going to show how reflection is necessary for making the best of the good which we already have in advance of reflection, and it may turn out helpful later to bring them to mind at the start. With regard to the values to which we are already committed (which cannot but include, as object of commitment, the very form of life that values such values), there is the question of whether our accepting them without reflection necessarily ensures that we shall value them as they should be valued; and there is also the question whether our prereflective commitment can expose us to all the good ethical possibilities implicit (though only as possibilities) in the form of life just mentioned. These questions will not be taken up again until the last chapter of this study, where we shall see that for Aristotle the answers are linked. There is, however, a further consideration which can be brought to bear straightaway. Holding an inquiry presupposes that some ethical positions are more acceptable than others, and that participants do not know in advance which the more acceptable are. So it is not at the start impossible that the participants and others like them should reach or be led to the wrong conclusions. In short, good upbringing does not necessarily protect against false reflective views. One need not suppose that correct reflection improves sound prereflective practice in order to find practical value in correct ethical reflection, since it is enough to suppose that sound prereflective practice can be undermined by false reflection. Aristotle says that good arguments do not make us good people, but it does not follow that bad ones might not help to make us bad.

If so, then once people start to reflect (or, worse still perhaps, once they start to enjoy without reflection the leisurely conditions under which reflection is possible), true reflection may be necessary to protect a good status quo. But as Aristotle's *Ethics* draws to an end, and especially his *Nicomachean Ethics,* we see him holding (or so I shall argue) that once the conditions for reflection take hold, the good status quo cannot in fact survive in its original form, but is preserved only by becoming the basis of a life-style centered on an altogether different kind of good; and that this becomes apparent (so as to be acted on) only through ethical reflection. But following this dénouement presupposes having followed Aristotle from the start of his investigation into the supreme good, and this beginning of his is where we now stand.

### IV.  What Is Happiness?

Then what is the supreme good? There is no agreement except on a word. Everyone, the ordinary man and the person of refinement, talks about 'happiness'[12] *(eudaimonia),* and takes it that living well and doing well are the same as being happy (1095 a 17–20). But here consensus ends.

> For the [many] think it is some plain and obvious thing, like pleasure, wealth, or honour; they differ, however, from one another—and often even the same man identifies it with different things, with health when he is ill, with wealth when he is poor; but, conscious of their ignorance, they admire those who proclaim some great thing that is above their comprehension. (1095 a 22–26)

For example, the Platonists (1095 a 26–28).

However, if we attend to how people live their lives rather than to what they say (1095 b 14 ff.), it seems that common and coarse people identify happiness with pleasure and would be satisfied with a life of gratification. But two other kinds of life, as well as the life of pleasure, are mooted as possible ideals by people who talk about these things. One is 'political', the other 'theoretic'. Now the life of pleasure, as common people understand it, is fit only for cattle. To choose it shows a slavish mentality, although the choice gets a semblance of respectability from the fact that people with power and leisure, in a position (opposite of slavish) to live as they prefer, give themselves up to sybaritic pleasures. People of quality seem to live for honour. But honour, Aristotle says, cannot really be happiness, because it is a surface phenomenon: it is how the agent is reflected by others, whereas happiness, the supreme good, must be something that belongs to us in ourselves. Those who pursue honour do so really because they want the assurance that they are good, for they desire the respect of people whose judgment carries weight, and who respect them for their virtue or personal excellence, not anything else. This shows that excellence is better than honour. But even excellence cannot be happiness. It falls short because it is a disposition not an activity, and because it is consistent with extreme misfortunes. Good people still count as good even when asleep or in trouble, but in the real world a life of inactivity or suffering would never be called happy, even if in schoolrooms people sometimes defend the position that a good man can be happy while terribly afflicted (cf. 1153 b 19–21). The theoretic life will be considered later (in Book X), and Aristotle says nothing more about it here (1096 a 4–5). As for the life of money-making, this is carried on under the constraint of need, whereas happiness (he implies) is free and unburdened. In any case, its goal is obviously not the supreme good, since wealth is good merely because it is useful for other things (5–8).

These short arguments are very characteristic of Aristotle's approach. It is in keeping, for instance, with his earlier remarks about the imprecision of ethics that here he says that people's values are shown in how they live.[13] An action carries a value-judgment to the effect that what is pursued is worthwhile in proportion to the *practical* importance it holds for the individual. The fact that such actional judgments-in-practice are inarticulate and nebulously bound up with irrelevant particulars does not affect their status as evaluative *claims*. For even the verbally stated propositions of philosophical ethics are infected with indeterminacy. No doubt judgments-in-practice are made partly in response to the person's circumstances (as when the sick equate happiness with health, the penurious with wealth), but this does not place them beyond rational criticism. Thus honour, wealth and excellence do not make sense as supreme objectives, even if people sometimes act as if they did. At the same time, such action is not simply irrational, because in each case that higher thing in terms of which honour, or excellence or wealth is shown up as less than supreme is closely bound up with the illusory end. Judgments-in-practice carry many meanings which the agent himself need not have distinguished. If I am desperate to earn a living or the respect of others, do I consider whether I am seeking this for its own sake or for the sake of something else which makes sense of wanting prosperity or respect? What I have to do to obtain them is the same in either case, and on the level of action the difference need not have crystallised. Thus the behaviour is neither rational nor irrational but potentially either, and only reflection can disengage right from wrong ways of valuing those things.

This matters, because the claim embodied in the behaviour is a large one. Aristotle is considering various standardly classified lives or life-styles, each of which is typified by pursuit of a certain goal. In this context, the pursuit amounts to the claim that the life which it typifies is good or best, not merely that the goal is best on that occasion. Thus each of those lives contains, if successfully lived, not only that accomplishment or possession which is supposedly the source of happiness, but also the agent's lived judgment that this kind of life is best. There is thus no radical discontinuity between ground level human living and philosophical reflection on how to live. For any life, by means of its representative actions, is logically self-referential even if not self-consciously so.

Whereas Aristotle's arguments against honour, excellence and wealth depend on conceptual analysis of the facts of each case, his argument against vulgar pleasure also shows the influence of "good upbringing". He and his intended listeners find such a life contemptible for free persons. Its adherents are classed as the coarsest kind of people, whereas those who seek honour are classed as 'refined' by comparison

(1095 b 22). This is not merely the reflex of a certain kind of upbringing, since a reason is given for the condemnation. The vulgar pleasure seekers set no store on what is distinctively human: what these human beings judge best is to spend their time like cattle. There is something close to logical incoherence here. For how can it make sense to prefer a life which, lived to the full, would require one, in effect, to have ceased to be, since one could not both thoroughly live it and be what one essentially is, namely human? Still, so far as incoherence is concerned, the pleasure seekers seem no more gravely confused than those who pursue honour as if it were an end per se, or those who pin everything on excellence, as if a mere disposition could be more desirable than the living use of it. Yet Aristotle evidently regards the pleasure seekers as worse than merely conceptually confused, and hence as worse than the others. What has this moral attitude of his, presumed shared by his audience, to do with the question of the nature of happiness? Simply that we cannot accept a proposed definition of happiness (even if the proposal were to harbour no logical flaw) that finds practical expression in the behaviour of people of a sort we ourselves could not wish to be—even though, if we were of that sort, we should no doubt be contented to be who we were.

It is necessary now, for the sake of clarity, to register the fact that Aristotle's discussion swings between the notion of the supreme good as *a certain sort of life,* and the notion of it as *some element within a life* which may dominate that life in the logical sense of typifying it. For no one is seriously suggesting that the happy life could consist of nothing but pleasure or nothing but honour or excellence or excellent action or theoretic activity; and perhaps everyone will agree that any kind of life that claims to be happy will contain some measure of several of these goods, as well as other good things such as health, prosperity, friends. The difference between the kinds of life surveyed in the preceding discussion lies, rather, in the centrality of one or another of those narrower goods. They are narrower in the sense that they cannot be literally omnipresent. But in some sense they shed a light that is omnipresent. The central good of a life is the one which, if that life were rightly regarded as happy, would be the source of its being a happy life. Thus in any life that is not haphazard, but has a centre, what occupies the position of 'central good' is that which the subject (by his actions) affirms to be what would make his life happy and him a happy person. I say only that his central good is seen by him as what *would* make his life happy, because Aristotle insists that a happy life, to *be* happy, requires more than its central good. This is partly because it requires other things to be a life at all, and also because the central good cannot be fully enjoyed unless other things make this possible. Thus straightaway after offering his own definition of the central good, he says: 'But it must be in a complete life. For one swallow does not make a spring, nor does one day; nor similarly does one day or a short time make us blessed or happy' (1098 a 18–20). This implies that the happy life must be of a decent span, long enough for its potential to become actual; and that it must contain a variety and a sufficiency of goods other than the central. For spring is not made by mere repetition, either, of swallows and days, but by the many different marks of spring which do not all come on one day.

According to this passage, a happy person is one who has a happy life (which is not to say that he is necessarily happy all his life, for a person and his life can cease to be happy: cf. *NE* I.10). Thus the happiness (1) of the happy *person* (the abstract quality of his being happy) logically depends on his having a happy life. On the other hand, 'happiness' can also mean (2) a happy life (which is something concrete), as when we wish happiness to a newly wedded pair. But these are not the only meanings of the word. It can also connote (3) the abstract quality of happiness which all particular happy *lives* have in common. Now happiness in this third sense (the happiness of a happy life) logically depends on a life's containing as central the specific narrow good which above all others ought to be central, whatever the nature of that good may be. That good is the source or principle whereby the happy life and the happy person are happy. And Aristotle, on logical and metaphysical grounds inherited from Plato, equates the primary significate of a term 'T' with the source, in those things which are commonly described as 'T', of their deserving the description. Hence for him 'happiness' strictly signifies (4) the good that is central to the happy life.[14] Similarly when he speaks of 'the supreme good' or 'the highest end'. These phrases may sometimes refer to the best sort of life, but in his usage they generally refer to the good which is the inner focus of the best life.[15]

We shall now consider how to make sense of the notion, just now taken for granted, that some one specific good is, so to speak, *the* good in the good or happy life. For given that such a life must include many other things and many other goods (what some of them are, Aristotle will explain later, and why), how can we claim that one is preeminently *the* good of that life when each is necessary for its being happy? No one of them is more necessary than the others, since the absence of any renders the life less than happy; hence none is closer than another to being sufficient for the happy life. Did we not learn from John Stuart Mill that any sine qua non of an event can equally be called its cause, depending on our interest?

The language of sufficient and necessary conditions flattens logical distinctions that cannot be captured in terms of 'if . . . then';[16] for example, the difference between the determinant of what kind of thing something is and the factors necessary for its being or occurring as whatever it is. The distinction is perhaps easier to apply in biology than in modern (as distinct from Aristotelian) physics. Genes determine *what* a living creature develops as; that its development *occurs* is due to environmental factors. Now the central good is the one which the agent values most and without which the other goods would be pointless to him. And that is enough to establish its logical preeminence. For in general the kind of life a person leads (and the kind, too, of the person living it) is typified by the object of principal value. This does not merely provide a label for the type of life, but renders the actual life a life of that kind.

This does not strictly imply (although Aristotle sometimes writes as if it does) that the agent values the other good things only as means to whatever for him is central. In fact, he may recognise some of them as good because of what they themselves are, and not because of something else which they make possible. But the agent may also recognise that without the central one he would not *want* any of the others. On that condition, they would not be goods or ends for him at all, whether for themselves or as useful for something else. In that sense the central good gives the others their point. Consequently, a life in the large which includes them all owes its goodness and happiness to, above all, the central good. The latter is as it were the essence[17] or substantial form of the happy life; because of this it is called '*the* good' and 'happiness' according to the metaphysical usage mentioned above.

The other goods enter the good life in, broadly speaking, either of two ways: as means to, preconditions for or substructure of, the central informing good; and as consequential on the latter's being realised. Health, prosperity, power, dispositions and capacities fall on the side of preconditions; pleasure is consequential, and so (under the appropriate social conditions) are honour and friendship. These may be regarded as perfecting the central good, and as perfections they, like it, should be prized for themselves. And in Aristotle's view, that central good, which he identifies with virtuous activity, must itself enter into the perfections which follow upon it; thus the pleasure is pleasure in that activity, and the friendship friendship of the actively virtuous.

This construction enables Aristotle to explain why there are so many conflicting views on the nature of happiness: a fact which, unless explained, casts doubt on the possibility of settling the question. Not only is it the case that the *presence* of each of the other goods in the good life is explained by its relation to the central good, some being for the sake of it and others flowing from it; but each of the others is *good* because of its relation to the centre. And the generic possibility of that relation casts a glow on the kind of good in question, so that even when it is wrongly valued on its own, or not properly organised in a good life, valuing it still makes a sort of sense, just as a gesture towards a disjoint and even outlying part of X may be read as a clumsy attempt to pinpoint X.[18] Thus we have a natural orientation towards those goods, even if not always in precisely the form in which they would figure in the good life, just as we have a natural physical orientation towards foods suitable for human beings. So it is not surprising that people confuse one or another of the peripheral goods with the essence of happiness.

The construction also enables Aristotle to save the grain of truth in the Platonic notion of the Form of good—that a rational unity runs through our various uses of the word.[19] Platonism as Aristotle depicts it in *NE* I.6 tried to account for this by postulating a universal one-over-many which is present in the same way in each of its instances without so to say touching the specific nature of any one. (In fact, in the *Republic* Plato seems to hold the more sophisticated view that a particular thing is good if good of its kind, and is good of its kind so far as it approximates to the Form of that kind. The Form of Good pervades all the kind-Forms—it is their substance and source of being; thus good things such as this good horse and that good man connect with the Form of Good via their specific kinds.[20] Such a theory, however, does not apply to the goods which Aristotle cites in I.6 [1096 b 17–18]: honour, certain pleasures, seeing, and wisdom; for these are not each good of a kind, but simply good.) After arguing against this single flat universal, Aristotle asserts that it cannot be by chance homonymy that 'good' applies to the different goods (1096 b 26–27), and he goes on: 'Perhaps they are homonymous by all being derived from a single source or by all referring to a single focus. Or perhaps instead they are homonymous by analogy; for as sight is good in the body, so understanding is good in the soul, and other things are good in other cases' (27–29). The first sentence may refer to the categorial diversity of goods which is a major problem for the theory of the Platonic universal.

> Good is spoken of in as many ways as being is spoken of. For it is spoken of in [the category of] what-it-is as god and intelligence; in quality, as the virtues; in quantity, as the measured amount; in relative, as the useful; in time, as the opportune moment; in place as the [right] situation. Hence it is clear that the good cannot be some common [nature of good things] that is universal and single; for if it were, it would be spoken of in only one of the categories, not in them all. (1096 a 23–29)

Although the exact interpretation is disputable, the main suggestion of this is clear. Just as the being of qualities, quantities, relations, etc. derives from the primary being of substance, so the goodness of the goods in the various categories derives from a primary and independent good which figures in relation to them as substance. That is to say: it and some connection with it must be mentioned in explaining why each of the others is good. Thus although ethics is centrally concerned with the central good, it will have systematic things to say about other goods. We can claim that ethics is about all the human goods without risk of implying that the subject matter of ethics is just a heap of different topics. In the same way Aristotle elsewhere shows how metaphysics, the study of being, is a unified science despite (and because of) the different categories of being (see *Metaphysics* IV.2).

If we lean on the obscure passage just quoted, it seems that 'God' and 'intelligence' refer to the central human good. Are they then names of the same thing? And what can it mean to say that the central human good is God? Aristotle holds that mind is something divine or godlike, and that our highest good is the activity of intelligence.[21] But that this is his position does not become clear until we reach the end of the *Ethics.*

From now on Aristotle will use the term 'happiness' *('eudaimonia')* interchangeably with such expressions as 'the best' and 'the ultimate end'; and as a rule he will mean by them the primary and central good of the best life.[22] What is gained by this equivalence of 'happiness' and 'the best'? Not a substantial answer to the question, What is the highest good? in the sense in which 'pleasure' and 'honour' might be meant to answer it. That this good is *eudaimonia* or happiness does not give information which would lead us to act in one way rather than another.[23] (Thus 'happiness' here does not mean what it means in ordinary English when people say, e.g., that one should value duty or righteous action above happiness. That this makes perfectly good sense shows that 'happiness' is not a snug translation for *'eudaimonia',* a term which, in Aristotle's use at least, is virtually synonymous with 'what one should value most'.)

Purely formal though it is, the equivalence provides more than verbal variation. It helps Aristotle's argument in two ways. First, it supports his opening contention that there really is a supreme end, the objective of *politikē.* (It makes no difference whether in that opening argument he thinks of the supreme end as the best life or as the supreme good of the best life, for there cannot be a best life unless there is a best good at its centre.) The support comes from the fact, as he takes it, that people really do take themselves to be desiring and aiming for happiness, even when they scarcely know what it is. One may sometimes doubt whether there is a single end of statecraft, or even whether statecraft really is a rationally structured activity with its own proper end like familiar crafts such as medicine. Political leaders cannot tell us clearly what they ultimately aim for; they cannot teach their "craft", and they usually know no better than the rest of us what they should be aiming for. If we distance ourselves from these leaders, the initial argument for a supreme end looks fragile. Where even those who are supposed professionally to aim at it do not know what it is, surely it is an empty concept. Aristotle can battle with this difficulty only by taking it into our own camp. As long as aiming at some overriding end which no one can identify looks like somebody else's problem (that of the high-ups in government), we can afford to say that there is no such end, and that the officials concerned (or rather, perhaps, the philosophers who expect too much from them) are under the illusion that they aim at something of the sort. But once the notion of happiness is introduced we see that we are in the same case as the statesman. We seek happiness, and happiness is the goal that matters more than anything else. Perhaps not everyone cares about being happy, but we do not think much of those who do not. They have given up, we say. They are not bothering or are not able to be fully alive. It may not be out of indifference to happiness but because they believe it not possible for them. But if we have not given up, we seek happiness. At any rate we see ourselves in those terms. And our not knowing what happiness is makes no difference. But it does affect our right to doubt whether an end whose nature is nebulous is really an aimed for end.

The second advantage of the equivalence lies in the special nuance of the word 'eudaimonia' ('happiness'). Etymology points to the notion of a favourable divinity steering a person's destiny. To be happy is to be blessed (makarios), and the happy are said to be loved by the gods, though whether this is cause or effect of their happiness may not be clear (cf. 1099 b 9–18; cf. 1179 a 22–32). However, the gods themselves are said to be happy and blessed, as are those immortalised pure souls whose abode is the Isles of the Blest. Perhaps because of this connotation of divine perfection, nonhuman animals cannot be said to seek eudaimonia, although they certainly pursue their good. Eudaimonia strictly speaking cannot be ascribed to children either, according to Aristotle (1100 a 2). These considerations make it easier for him to argue, as he will, that our central good consists in rational activity. For he now has a word for that good—'eudaimonia'—which cannot apply to creatures lacking in reason or only potentially rational, and which therefore invites us to focus on what it is that those creatures lack (cf. 1099 b 32–1100 a 4; 1139 a 20; 1178 b 27–28).

However, he has to establish that equivalence. For even if we agree that everyone seeks happiness, it does not follow that happiness is the uniquely ultimate good. He begins by stressing that goods are ends (telē) of human action, and goes on to observe that if there is a single end of everything we do, then 'the good we are seeking' (1097 a 15) would be that end, and if there are several, it would be those several (22–24). Now we do seem to have many ends, but some of these are sought only for the sake of others, so they are not final[24] (teleios): for example, wealth and all kinds of instruments. So the highest good must be a final end, and if there are several final ends, it must be the most final. One end is more final than another if it is pursued for its own sake, and the other only for the sake of something else, or if it is pursued only for its own sake whereas the other is pursued for itself and also for something else (30–34). Now on these grounds happiness seems most final of all, for we pursue it only for its own sake, whereas other things, such as honour, pleasure, intelligence, and all kinds of excellence, we pursue each for its own sake ('for if nothing resulted from them we should still choose each of them'), but also for the sake of happiness, 'judging that through them we shall be happy' (1097 a 30–b 6). That is to say, we can pursue those things unreflectively, without thinking that through them we shall be happy, even though, if we considered the question of happiness, we might then pursue them for the sake of happiness. By contrast, no one could seek to acquire what he knew to be an instrument without at the same time knowing that it is to be used for something else, or undertake what he knew to be an unpleasant course of medical treatment without, again, knowing it to be for a further end.

At the opening of his first chapter, Aristotle stated that the end of every activity is a good of one sort or another. Here, it seems to me, the emphasis is reversed. Goods are *ends;* i.e., by and large they are to be had or maintained or made possible only through purposeful effort. Anyone who understands this, and who holds something to be good, automatically gears himself to efforts and sacrifices in its regard. Thus Aristotle tends to say that holding something to be happiness or the highest good is being prepared to do everything else for the sake of it (e.g. 1140 b 18–19). This implies a substantial difference between pursuing honour for its own sake (or as an intrinsic good) and pursuing it for the sake of happiness (if 'happiness' means 'the central good').[25] Pursuing honour 'for the sake of happiness' can be taken in two ways: (1) I identify honour with happiness or the central good; (2) I see honour as a condition for obtaining whatever it is that I identify as the central good. In the latter case I am not pursuing honour for itself—because it is what it is. In the former case, I pursue it as just what it is in itself, but as one who is prepared to do everything for it. This is much more than simply pursuing it for its own sake. I might have many separate unintegrated interests, each focused on something which I want for itself, but I would not be pursuing each of these goals for the sake of happiness. For sense (2) does not apply, since I seek each for itself, and sense (1) does not apply to a multiplicity of goals. If I identify any one of these goods with happiness, I cannot so identify the others; and if I identify one of them with happiness, I cannot see myself as pursuing my other goals except for the sake of happiness in sense (2). For I cannot have one goal for the sake of which I am prepared to do everything, and also be seriously pursuing, i.e. doing things for, another goal without considering the latter as a condition for the first. Perhaps I need not consider it a positive means to the first, but at least I must be asking whether my pursuing or obtaining it is a condition that would undermine my pursuit of the first, and, if the answer is 'Yes', be prepared to give up this other goal. But what if I identify happiness (still considered as the central good in life) with a compound of things each of which I previously valued for its own sake? Is it not the case that I value a multiplicity of things each for its own sake, and also value them each for the sake of happiness? Presumably the answer is that I do *not* now value them each for its own sake, but for the sake of the whole which they compose.

This set of positions is difficult to assess, because Aristotle does not explain how we are to take the crucial expression 'for the sake of *(heneka)* happiness'. To make his claims plausible, we have to stretch this to mean 'having regard to happiness'. Thus the central good functions sometimes as a constraint rather than a goal in the ordinary sense of a positively aimed for objective. I would stop doing what might adversely affect it, even if I was not doing that thing *in order to* obtain it. But even with this allowance, it may seem intolerably artificial to hold that, if we make one good central in our lives, then *every* other is viewed in relation to it. However, the position does not imply that we can never, for instance, admire, delight in, love, take an interest in, something else just for what it is. (This would be as much as to say that everything in life but the central value would or should be flat and insipid. But Aristotle wants people to be brought up from youth delighting in many good things for themselves, so can hardly expect that when a well-brought-up agent makes one of them central, which comes about only when a person can organise his life, the others will lose their charm.) Although the attitudes of love, admiration and so on may lead to action, they are not themselves activities of practical pursuit. Aristotle only means that when we take *practical* steps towards any object, we should do so having regard to the central good.

In the *Eudemian Ethics* he makes the point in a manner logically less stringent than the 'for the sake of' formula on its narrow interpretation (in terms of a positive goal rather than a constraint). He speaks there of happiness (or what a person considers to be happiness) as that in life for the sake of which one is glad to have been born rather than not (1215 b 30; 1216 a 11–14; cf. 1215 b 15–22).[26] This implies, I think, that it is also that without which one would rather not have been born.[27] Now a person may pursue many things for themselves, and yet there may be just one thing in his life without which pursuing the others would lose all interest. This would not necessarily be because of a change traceable to some particular relation in which those other things stood to the central good, but simply because nothing is worthwhile without at least its possibility. But the practical attitude towards this central good need consist in no more than doing nothing that would endanger it. Life to Orpheus was meaningless without Eurydice, but it does not follow that everything which he did while she was on earth was done for her sake in the narrow sense.

It is important for Aristotle to stress that happiness is an *end* for us, in the sense of a practical objective, because this blocks the possible suggestion that, being divine in some way, it is beyond our power to achieve. Thus he takes seriously the question whether it comes to us only as a divine gift, or else by luck (*NE* 1099 b 10–13; *EE* 1214 a 22–25; cf. *EE* VIII.2), and argues that there are reasons why something may be said to be godlike even if it is not sent from outside by God (*NE* 1099 b 14–18). However, in the argument showing that happiness is the supreme end he also plays on other senses of finality or end-hood: senses which underwrite the logical affinity of human happiness with God, since they have to do with completeness and perfection. These meanings are behind the following thought: 'From the point of view of self-sufficiency the same result seems to follow; for the complete good is thought to be self-sufficient. . . . The self-sufficient we now define as that which when isolated makes life desirable and lacking in nothing; and such we think happiness to be' (1097 b 6–16). Aristotle takes care to say that by 'self-sufficiency' here he means what applies not to a person living an unnatural solitary life, but to one living in the midst of family, friends and fellow-citizens, since by nature we are social. His point seems to be that happiness (anyway for mortals) consists in whatever it is which, added on its own to the conditions necessary for it, makes a social being want nothing more out of life.[28] (Strictly, what makes me want nothing more out of life is what counts *for me* as happiness by my being thus contented by it. Whether it *is* happiness depends on whether it is right to be contented by it, which for Aristotle depends on whether it is good to be the sort of person who is thus contented.) One could value some good more than anything else, having regard to it in all one's dealings, yet still feel incomplete even though one could not imagine anything better. In that case the most valued good would not, from the agent's point of view, be his happiness.

The next point is similar:

> And further we think [happiness] most desirable of all things, without being counted as one good thing among others—if it were so counted it would clearly be made more desirable by the addition of even the least of goods; for that which is added becomes an excess of goods, and of goods the greater is always more desirable. Happiness, then, is something complete [*teleion*] and self-sufficient, and is the end of action. (1097 b 16–21)

That 'happiness is complete' means, here, that whatever happiness is, it is what perfects or rounds off the good life. Happiness (that which we identify as happiness) cannot be counted as one among many goods: for, in that case, just as it when added to other goods produces a better aggregate, so some further good added to it plus the others would make a better aggregate still. So what we are calling 'happiness' cannot be happiness, for nothing deserves the title 'happiness' unless it is such that adding it creates a result that cannot by further addition be enhanced or improved.[29]

This analysis of happiness in terms of finality, completeness and self-sufficiency is really an account of what it is for something to figure as happiness for an agent. Such an attitude, we have just seen, involves a categorial or functional distinction between whatever good is termed 'happiness' and the other goods.[30] The former is seen or felt as completing the latter much as a line is completed by its end-point. And no being is capable of happiness unless it is capable of comprehending its own life in this way. It is clear why nonrational animals are incapable of happiness, although of course they are capable of flourishing according to the norm for the species: they have no sense of life as a whole, or of that categorial distinction.

It is debatable whether these formulations are all equivalent, and whether each would pick out just one good. More than one thing in life can be crucial to being glad that one was born. And features such as *being distinctively human, being sought only for its own sake, being such that whoever has it seeks nothing further* may serve to eliminate certain candidates, but (even jointly) they fail to guarantee no more than one. Nor, in allowing for several possibilities, do they guarantee that these could be combined in a single life. Aristotle may be overconfident about the uniqueness of the good that makes life happy; but all the same, the arguments so far reviewed do succeed in pointing us toward a unified topic which concerns, it would seem, not merely that good itself, but the nature of the being whose good and happiness it is. This is the *practical agent,* since happiness is here considered above all as an end of practice. Something counts as happiness to an agent only so far as he or she subordinates other things to it by practical choice. Thus what counts as happiness to a person typifies that person as a practical agent of that kind. And no one can achieve what counts as happiness unless something does so to him or her. But, as we know, such judgments are not infallible, and some are false. So, since it is good to be happy, it would be good to be a practical agent of the kind, whichever it is, whose typifying happiness-judgment is true. But—since we do not yet know what ought to count as happiness—how are we to know which kind judges truly?

We can ask this question as if by means of it we were also asking 'Which kind of practical agent would it be good to be?—as if we do not know (just as we do not yet know what happiness is). But Aristotle will not allow his audience to assume this posture. He has reminded them that they are reared in the right values. Therefore they *already* have some quite firm views about what sort of practical agent it is good to be. Since they grasp what sort it is good to be, they have access to knowing what happiness is. For happiness is whatever happiness is taken to be by the sort of person who judges right on such a matter, and this is the sort which we can already identify as good to be. In other words, it is the person of virtue or excellence, who is soon to become the principal topic of Aristotle's *Ethics*.

## V. Happiness Defined

Aristotle's discussion of the formal features of happiness (the central good of the happy life) seems to leave him satisfied that there will be just one genuine claimant to the title. The question now is the substantial one of identity. Aristotle states his answer in terms of the 'function of man':

> Presumably, however, to say that happiness is the chief good seems a platitude, and a clearer account of what it is is still desired. This might perhaps be given, if we could first ascertain the function of man. For just as for a flute-player, a sculptor, or any artist, and, in general, for all things that have a function or activity, the good and the 'well' is thought to reside in the function, so would it seem to be for man, if he has a function. Have the carpenter, then, and the tanner certain functions or activities, and has man none? Is he naturally functionless? Or as eye, hand, foot, and in general each of the parts evidently has a function, may one lay it down that man similarly has a function apart from all these? (1097 b 22–33)

The question is only rhetorical. But the argument itself may seem to us rhetorical rather than logically compelling. It looks at first like an inductive argument or an argument by analogy. Those other beings have functions; therefore everything has a function, therefore man qua man has one. Or: those other beings have functions; man is in some way analogous to them; hence man too has a function. These reasonings are dismally weak; should we accept that everything has a function from a small number of hand-picked cases of things that obviously do? Why should we accept that man is analogous to them in a way that supports the desired conclusion?

But the thought is not so foolish. Aristotle connects the function of a thing with the good at which it characteristically aims. The carpenter's deed or function *(ergon)* is the specific thing which he is skilled to produce, or his productive activity. He aims at making both product and activity as good as they should be. And his good or perfection as carpenter is in doing this successfully; so that in a sense he aims also at his own good. Again, the perfection of an organ is measured by whether it does its job well, and the job itself is useful or good for the well-being of the whole organism.

Craftsmen and bodily organs have each a function correlative to their end. But human beings have an ultimate end or good—this (it is assumed) we already know; they are capable of excellence or of being good themselves; and they reach their good, in the sense of human perfection, through attaining their end. It is therefore conceptually impossible for Aristotle that man as such should lack a function—a typifying deed or activity.

The function expresses the distinctive nature of a thing; hence the function itself is distinctive.

> What, then, could this [sc. the human function] be? For living is apparently shared with plants, but what we are looking for is the special function of a human being; hence we should set aside the life of nutrition and growth. The life next in order is some sort of life of sense perception; but this too is apparently shared, with horse, ox and every animal. The remaining possibility, then, is some sort of practical life of the part of the soul that has reason. (1097 b 33–1098 a 4)[31]

In rational functioning we are alive in the way special to human animals, with a grade of life that presupposes life on the levels which we share with other creatures.[32] But what if there were other rational animal species? Should we then consider our distinctive characteristic to be something other than reason, and so be led to redefine our function and our good accordingly? Then does Aristotle's *Ethics* rest on the fragile empirical claim that we alone of mortal beings are rational?[33] It seems intolerable that the truth of claims about the good life for man should depend on the truth of a proposition that might be overturned one day.

Perhaps, however, the assumption that we are the only rational animals expresses not so much an empirical belief about other animals as the sense that in rational activity we are most truly *whatever* we are. Thus in several places Aristotle identifies the self with mind or intelligence (1168 b 34–1169 a 4; 1178 a 2–7). This would not be overturned by the discovery of rationality in another biological species. The question then would be whether we could see them as 'other selves' and interact with them as such. If so, the biological difference might not appear important enough for us to regard them as of a different essence or species.[34] In short, ethics would have its own conception of the species to which 'we' belong: a conception not determined by biological criteria.

The more than empirical force, then, of the claim that reason is our essence springs, it would seem, from the value-judgment that reason is our ethically most important characteristic. In the context this is not arbitrary. Aristotle has already taken us along with him in a series of moves whose reiterated message is that the highest good whose nature we investigate in ethics is essentially a *practicable objective.* Only practical beings could have as their good such a good; but being practical is a form of rationality. If we were not essentially rational, we should not be essentially practical either, and a good that is essentially practicable would be of concern only to a nonessential layer of ourselves. The good pertaining to what we most centrally are would in that case have to present itself to us under a different guise than that of being practicable. But there could be no point in our inquiring about its nature *in order better to attain it,* for then already we would be approaching it as something practicable, and would connect with it as practical beings and not as what (on this hypothesis) we essentially are. In short: Aristotle's premiss that we are essentially rational rests not on a dubious empirical fact, but on the assumption that our fundamental good, which this investigation is about, is a good for us *as* beings who (among other things) investigate and seek it rationally. It might be difficult to reject this assumption, yet still engage in the present inquiry.

The downside of this approach is that it throws into the background aspects of human nature not capable of standing up for themselves in logical argument, since that is not their way. Besides being rational, we are spiritual beings, responsive to beauty, imaginatively creative, capable of humour, pride and compassion, and of who knows what else that must be ethically relevant, as well as being uniquely ours so far as we know. Some of these sides of human nature are largely unexplored in Aristotle's philosophy. But we should not draw conclusions from this without also bearing in mind that reason to him is not (as for instance to Hume) a narrowly calculative or demonstrative faculty. It includes the capacity for language (*Politics* 1253 a 9–15), the sense of past and future (*On the Soul* 433 b 5–10), and reflectiveness in general.[35]

However, Aristotle defines the distinctively human grade of life not merely as rational, but as 'some sort of *practical* life of the part of the soul that has reason' (1098 a 3–4). The qualification 'practical' implies that our happiness or central good is in practical functioning. But what grounds the qualification, since reason operates in many modes, and notably for Aristotle in theoretic as well as practical activity? True, practical rationality has been central to his argument so far, as well as being what in the context is central in the person who follows the argument in order to benefit from it; but this was because the highest good is assumed practicable—which is not the same as practical. Theoretic activity is practicable, since we can bring it about, or bring about conditions under which it would naturally arise; but it is not practical, because it intends to make no changes in the world; not even such as might have to be made to facilitate its own occurrence. And in *NE* X theoretic activity is said to be the highest good. But in the present passage, where Aristotle first defines happiness, he says nothing about theoretic activity; and he even seems to exclude it from happiness when he says that happiness is some sort of *practical* life of reason.[36] And this seems to leave theoretic activity very much out on a limb, since if it is a good, this cannot be because it forwards practical activity, or is a species or dimension or concomitant of practical activity, because none of these things is true. It would not be unreasonable to infer that it is not a good, yet Aristotle, we all know (unless we are reading the *Ethics* for the first time), far from holding this, holds in *NE* X that theoretic activity is the supreme good.

Whether he has changed his mind between there and here, and how, if not, the positions are reconcilable, are questions which I leave until my final chapter. Meanwhile, the best way, I suggest, to advance our present understanding is to ask why, at this crucial juncture where he leaves behind the formal features of happiness and says for the first time what it substantially is, Aristotle points to the area of *practice*. This is not the same as asking why he does not point to the area of theoretic activity, for the thought of theoretic activity does not grow out of the present stage of his argument. *We* think of it now because we have read ahead to the end of the *Ethics,* but there is no reason why a first-time audience should be wondering about it now, or why Aristotle should want them to have it in mind at all at this point.

That they should have practice in mind when considering where to locate happiness is a result for which he has already prepared the way by a passing remark earlier that people equate living well and *doing* well with being happy (1095 a 18–19), but more especially by his opening argument that the highest good is the statesman's objective. While this was intended to show only that there is a supreme good, it could not fail to adumbrate the nature of that good, since unless we have some rough idea of what a statesman is and what he is supposed to aim for, the term 'statesman' is meaningless. Now according to the received wisdom, popular and philosophical (for the latter see especially Plato's *Laws*), the main focus of statecraft is 'making the citizens to be of a certain character, viz. good and capable of noble acts *(practikous tōn kalōn)*' (1099 b 29–32; cf. 1094 b 14–15; 1102 a 7–10). 'Noble acts' here means noble *conduct*. In other words, the argument which shows that there is one ultimate good forces us to accept that this good consists in acting well in a *practical* way. For it would certainly have seemed very strange to Aristotle's audience to be told that the main job of the statesman is to produce fine theoretical thinkers.

To pursue this we must stay with the argument about the function of man. Having said that the function is rational and practical, Aristotle emphasises that it lies in active exercise, not mere possession, of rational vitality (1098 a 5–7). He then goes on:

> Now if the function of man is an activity of soul in accordance with, or not without, rational principle, and if we say a so-and-so and a good so-and-so have a function which is the same in kind, e.g. a lyre-player and a good lyre-player, and so without qualification in all cases, eminence in respect of excellence being added to the function (for the function of a lyre-player is to play the lyre, and that of a good lyre-player is to do so well): if this is the case, and we state the function of man to be a certain kind of life, and this to be an activity or actions of the soul implying a rational principle, and the function of a good man to be the good and noble performance of these, and if any action is well performed when it is performed in accordance with the appropriate excellence: if this is the case, human good turns out to be activity of soul in conformity with excellence. (1098 a 7–17)

Now taken out of the context of those to whom it is addressed, this conclusion is a formal statement which conveys no more information than such earlier formal statements as 'Happiness is that for the sake of which we do everything else', or 'that which renders life complete and lacking in nothing'. This is because an *excellence* or *virtue,* as Plato and Aristotle understand that concept, is nothing but a characteristic which makes the difference between functioning and functioning well (cf. 1106 a 15–24). The passage just quoted makes that clear. The excellence of a knife is to be sharp, of an eye to be clearsighted, of a harpist to be skilled at playing. So in general, unless we already know what the function is we cannot identify the empirical qualities in which the excellence consists. And unless we know the purpose or end, we cannot know the function. Thus, in the case of man as such, if we antecedently knew that the human end or good is to tyrannize over others, or to indulge physical appetites, then we should know that the main human excellence or virtue is ruthless ambition, or a strong constitution coupled with an uninhibited attitude to physical satisfactions. Anything could be an excellence depending on how we understand the end. The present argument is supposed to tell us what the end *is;* yet, by the logic of 'excellence', it cannot do so by stating that the end is to function in accordance with excellence, since the term is not a name for any specific quality or set of qualities, but a variable whose value varies with the value assigned to 'end'.

Perhaps in every other kind of case we identify the excellence by first identifying the end. Here, however, we do not know the human end, since it is still our object of inquiry; but we *can* identify many human excellences or virtues. We are able to do so because we who take part in the inquiry are also the *persons* we are. We know bravery, justice, generosity, wisdom, temperance, truthfulness to be human virtues, because upbringing has taught us to value them as the qualities of a fine human being—someone it is good to be. We know this, because we have learnt certain attitudes and ways of expressing them.[37] An individual with these qualities we call 'good' without qualification, and one of opposite qualities we call 'bad' in the same way; whereas an adept rider is called 'a good rider', an effective doctor 'a good doctor', and we do not allow the inference from 'good rider/doctor etc.' to 'good' without qualification.

The philosopher can explain this as follows: since we are essentially human beings, the primary use of 'good' (when used by us as a predicate of human individuals) will be that in which it signifies 'good as a human being'. And the use which signifies this, being primary, will also be a logically unqualified use. Hence 'Callias is good', said without qualification, means 'Callias is a good man (or person)'. It follows that qualities of Callias which ground the unqualified predication are excellences of a human being as such (since 'excellence' is another name for 'goodness'). And once philosophers have made clear the analytic truth that the excellence of an F, for whatever F, is the quality by which something functions well as an F, and that functioning well is nothing other than functioning which reflects the excellence, we automatically find our own way to the substantial conclusion that functioning well as a human being is living the life of a just, courageous, temperate, and in all familiar respects decent person and citizen according to the standards we absorbed before ever starting to do academic philosophy. And those standards in Aristotle's day, as in the present, were such that a person who is wise about practical life—who can advise well, make good decisions—counts as a good human being; whereas one who is a master of metaphysics or mathematics or natural science is a good philosopher or theoretician, but not on that account necessarily a good human being. What this means is that even if theoretical activity at its best is indeed the most perfect mode of human functioning (we shall see much later how Aristotle argues that it is) he cannot expect his audience to form for themselves or accept from him that conclusion here so close to the start of the *Ethics,* where so far all they have to go on are the values in which they were raised, together with some purely formal intuitions evoked by the philosopher.

These are the only resources on which Aristotle can draw at this stage, but his procedure manifests confidence that they *are* there to call upon. For not long after delivering his definition of the human end as 'the soul's activity according to excellence', which is true on any interpretation of 'excellence', he starts to use the term 'excellence' to refer specifically to such qualities as justice and generosity (1099 a 18–20), without having argued in the interim or anywhere else that when we are talking about human beings as such, *these* qualities must count as virtues. Aristotle can do this, not because there is a logically immediate connection between the uninterpreted meaning of 'excellence' and this particular range of interpretations, but because he can take it for granted that his hearers have supplied the interpretations themselves.

Even so, immediately after stating the definition, Aristotle adds a detail which possibly paves the way to modifications for which his audience is currently unprepared. He says: 'And if there are more than one excellence, [the good will be] in conformity with the best and most final' (1098 a 17–18). And later on, speaking of the 'best activities' he says: 'These [activities], or one—the best—of these, we identify with happiness' (1099 a 29–31). The first of these passages has sometimes been taken to mean that the good of man is activity expressing the complete (and in this sense 'finished') set of human excellences. For obviously there are many such qualities: we have listed several already—and obviously a good which embraces them all is better than one in which some excellence or other is lacking (cf. *EE* 1219 a 35–39; 1220 a 2–4; 1248 b 14–16). On the other hand, the second passage shows Aristotle envisaging one excellence as the best of all and uniquely related to happiness. This suggests that in the first passage, too, he has it in mind that one is superior to the others, and therefore more 'final' in the sense of more perfect.[38] Since happiness is that ingredient in the good life which above all perfects it humanly speaking, it is logical to equate happiness with activity expressive of the most perfect excellence if there is an excellence more perfect than the others. It seems to me that at this stage the statements pointing to a single superlative excellence are not intended to refer to one (as yet unspecified) quality, but to hold the ring for whichever quality will emerge preeminent as the argument of the *Ethics* progresses. The first-time audience remembering these remarks later on in the inquiry may be expected to fill the slot differently at different stages. Thus when they get to the analysis of practical wisdom (*NE* VI) and learn that the virtue of practical wisdom in a way includes all the other practical virtues without being crudely identical with the set of them, they may conclude that the single most final excellence must be practical wisdom. But when they get to the discussion of theoretic activity in Book X, they will then conclude, if Aristotle's argument there seems successful, that the best excellence is not practical at all, but is a quality expressed in *theōria*.

Whether that final position represents a radical shift away from the definition of happiness as a *practical* activity must mainly be decided by examining the arguments of X in their context. For now we need only ask whether the present definition in terms of practice could be consistent with the final equation of happiness with theoretic activity. It would *not* be consistent if the definition when first proposed is proposed as a complete explication of happiness. For at this point, as Aristotle very well knows, a definition incorporating the unqualified notion of 'excellence' will be taken by his audience to refer to such traits as courage, justice, temperance: practical virtues. Hence if the proposed definition is already complete under the interpretation natural at this initial stage, it does not allow for theoretic excellence, and consequently excludes any idea of happiness as consisting in the exercise of that. On the other hand, these two positions—the initial and the final accounts of happiness in the *Nicomachean Ethics—would* be consistent if the theoretic happiness of the final chapters could be understood as somehow necessarily embedded in a context of good practical functioning which—again, somehow—continues to deserve the name 'happiness' even though it is not the same as *theōria*.[39] This requirement might be satisfied if, for example, it turned out that we or Aristotle's audience could not come to understand why theoretic activity is happiness unless it is first firmly established that happiness is good practical activity in some sense not contradicted by the final theoretic equation, but carried over into it. However, this possibility entails that the earlier, practical, definition was not complete at its first appearance, even if it was as good as it could be at that stage.[40]

If this is correct, then at no stage of the *Ethics* should phrases such as 'the best of the excellences' be taken to single out their referent to the exclusion of familiar and obvious practical virtues such as justice and generosity. Rather, they should be taken as directing attention to their referent, whatever it is, within a context which assumes the latter. But the word 'somehow' as used in the previous paragraph indicates that introducing this hypothesis in these sketchy terms is a very different thing from giving it clarity and substance. This will be attempted in the last chapter, but for now we can point to an auspicious sign. After defining happiness as excellent practical activity, Aristotle issues a warning not to regard this as the final word: 'Let this serve as an outline of the good; for we must presumably first sketch it roughly, and then later fill in the details. But it would seem that any one is capable of carrying on and articulating what has once been well outlined, and that time is a good discoverer or partner in such a work' (1098 a 20–24). It may be easy later to fill in the details; but this is consistent with its not being even possible to fill them in now before the implications of the outline have been thoroughly explored, which takes both work and time.

But in any case, it is already staring us in the face that this definition as it stands is incomplete. If Aristotle's listeners are 'well brought up', they already are or are on the way to being fine practical agents. Thus happiness according to the definition already figures in their lives, or is round the next corner of natural development to maturity. But as a result of the definition they *know* this, which they could not have known in a principled way before, or the inquiry would not have been necessary. Yet how can they not be better off, hence happier, for knowing what happiness is, even if the knowledge is incomplete (and perhaps even if it were to make no practical difference)? Reflection even at this early point shows a paradox true: although happiness was agreed to be something final (complete and perfect), it is possible to have happiness in one's life—that is, to have in one's life the good which deserves the title of 'happiness'—without its actually being complete happiness. The agreement that it was 'final' served to exclude popular claims such as that it is wealth or honour; but even if by successively eliminating alternatives our inquiry led to the uncontrovertible conclusion that happiness is X, this would still fall short of a complete identification of complete happiness; for complete happiness (what perfects existence for rational beings) can scarcely be supposed not to include recognition of itself as such. But it would be a mistake to rewrite on that account the conclusion of inquiry as 'Happiness is X along with the knowledge of what happiness is'. For then in effect the definiens will be 'X along with the knowledge that happiness is X along with the

knowledge that happiness is X along with the knowledge that . . .'—an endless formula. But how can the human end of ends be attainable in practice if the formula
saying what it is cannot reach an end? It may be replied that the necessary incom-
pletion of the *formula* does not imply that happiness itself is beyond full realisation.
But even if this is so and happiness is practicable, a formula that forever outruns our
grasp is hardly a helpful instrument for pursuing anything. Yet it was Aristotle who
said at the outset that we have a better chance of hitting our target if we know what
it is (1094 a 24–25). Supposing that we continue with him to accept this assumption,
we shall also accept its implication: that if the nature of happiness cannot be completely expressed except by an infinite formula, it is better (at least while we hope to
make rational progress) to be satisfied with a finite formula that expresses it incom-
pletely but nonetheless does succeed in setting up a definite mark at which the statesman should aim. This is not at all to say that we cannot know all that it concerns us
to know about the nature of happiness. Rather, it is to say that not everything which
it concerns us to know can be packed into an explicit definition. Aristotle expects his
audience to supply for themselves, whether now or in the light of later developments,
what the formula fails to say. He relies on their own reflectiveness to complete his
message, just as he relies, we also saw, on their upbringing.

## VI. Taking Stock of the Definition

Aristotle has argued that human happiness, the central good of a happy human life,
is rational practical excellent activity; and he has let it be understood that the excellence in question covers the qualities which we ordinarily take to be human virtues.
The connection between happiness here and excellent activity is as close as the word
'is' can convey. Aristotle does not view qualities like fairness and generosity as causing happiness in the modern sense of 'cause', as if happiness were something distinct.
His definition rests on the classic conception of the excellence of a thing as the quality
whereby it functions well according to its kind or essential nature; but 'whereby' is
not causal here. The difference between possessing and not possessing the excellence
is simply the difference between functioning well and not always so well, whenever
an occasion arises for active functioning. Hence if (another classic position) fulfilment of one's nature, or happiness, is functioning well, the fulfilment just *is* excel-
lence-in-action, not any distinguishable effect of excellence. It is true that excellence
considered as a characterisation of the person is not the same as the action expressing
it, since we do not think that, e.g., someone's generosity evaporates when there is no
occasion for being actively generous, any more than we think that the carpenter loses
his skill when he knocks off work (cf. *Metaphysics* 1046 b 36–1047 a 4). But the
difference is not such as to make sense of saying that the excellence 'produces' the
excellent activity called 'happiness'. For if excellence produces something, excellence
is already active and making a difference in the world, and this productive activity
of excellence is itself what is meant by 'happiness', so that happiness cannot be what
is produced. In short, the difference between excellence and happiness which has to
be assumed if the former is to count as a cause of happiness in the modern sense of

'cause' holds only when excellence is inactive and not causing anything at all, including even happiness!

It follows from this construction that the notion of *happiness* in Aristotle cannot serve to explain why qualities like justice and generosity should count as human virtues or excellences, nor to justify our regarding them as such.[41] On the contrary, the empirical content of the notion *happiness* is drawn from the standard virtues, whose status as such is not called into question. Now Aristotle may be entitled to proceed in this way with his audience, who are supposed already to have absorbed the usual values; but does this entitle him to proceed as if these values had never been seriously questioned? They had been—especially justice—as we know from the *Republic* and the *Gorgias;* and Plato had had to struggle to meet the challenge. It was never questioned that virtues are qualities by which we function well and realise in ourselves the human good, but not everyone accepted that *justice* is such a quality. According to some quite plausible theories of human nature, just behaviour is not an intrinsic enhancement of the agent, but an unwelcome though necessary bargain which we make with others so as to avoid the worse evil of being victims of their injustice. This is rooted in the thought that true happiness would consist in exercising power to do and take what one pleased regardless of rights, rights being merely a net of human conventions woven by the inferior many to entangle the superior few and hold them trapped on the level of mediocrity lest they realise their power and gain the upper hand. But Aristotle, by contrast with Plato, does not engage such theories in argument. For his famous dictum that man is by nature (i.e., not by convention) a social animal is a statement more than an argument (1097 b 11; 1169 b 18; *Politics* 1253 a 2ff.).

But perhaps it is too much to expect that he treat 'Justice is a human virtue' otherwise than as a starting point. Enough people agree in this attitude to justify building on it even if it cannot be justified itself. How could it be, in any case? There seems little chance of finding an independent or neutral theory of human nature in which to ground it, for we cannot help starting with some idea of what happiness is, or some idea of which qualities it is good to have, and the account we give of human nature will be partly determined by those values. I shall return to this question in the next chapter after examining Aristotle's theory of the way in which the virtues are developed, since that may shed some light on the status of justice.

These considerations focus on that part of Aristotle's definition which represents happiness as *excellent* activity. Later in this section I shall consider something of what is implied by his defining it as *rational* activity. But now I pass to some questions which arise from his categorising happiness as *activity* at all. This means action or activity as distinct from capacity or disposition. The point is worth stressing, because Plato in the *Republic* spent so much time on the structure and disposition of the virtuous soul, but he did not conduct an analysis of virtue-in-action.[42] By itself, however, the word 'activity' says nothing about the type of activity that happiness is. For instance, at the opening of the *NE* Aristotle distinguished activities which have ends beyond themselves, and activities which are themselves the ends of those who engage in them (1094 a 3–5). Under which of these headings falls the activity of happiness?

In *NE* VI Aristotle will maintain that virtuous activity is not productive in the sense in which craft-activities are. By this he means that it is not technical. It is not governed by rules; it is not directed to producing one single specific type of result; and its success is not measured by the quality of some product. Given that happiness is virtuous activity, these positions of course entail that happiness is not a technical craft-activity. They are, however, compatible with holding that happiness or virtuous activity is productive in the broad sense of manifesting on any given occasion an intention or decision to bring about this or that state of affairs, depending on the circumstances. And in this broad sense virtuous activity is certainly productive, because it is practical. The agent aims to make various differences in the world, and shows wisdom, courage, honesty, generosity, in his making them. Theoretic activity, by contrast, aims at nothing beyond itself (1177 b 19–20).

These seem simple strokes, but they have been obscured by misinterpretations, especially of the opening passage of Book I:

> Every art and every inquiry, and similarly every action and choice is thought to aim at some good; and for this reason the good has rightly been declared to be that at which all things aim. But a certain difference is found among ends; some are activities, others are products apart from the activities that produce them. Where there are ends apart from the actions, it is the nature of the products to be better than the activities. (1094 a 1–6)

This has been taken to imply (1) that the activity of the soul which is happiness cannot be productive, because if it were the product would be better, yet nothing is better than happiness; and (2) that the activities said here to be ends themselves are, or constitute, happiness.[43] But both implications create difficulties, and I question both.

As to (1): taken in one way (a), it implies that happiness cannot be a practical activity, which flatly contradicts Aristotle's definition; taken in another (b), it calls into question any contrast he might wish to draw between happiness and technical productive activity. On interpretation (a), if someone does A in order that the distinct result S should come about, his doing A with that intention is not an instance of the activity called 'happiness'. Thus fighting in the breach against odds in order that others should have time to escape is courageous action, but is not an instance of that good which is happiness. By using similar examples from other practical virtues we could destroy all connection between practical virtue and happiness, on this interpretation. On interpretation (b) we think of the action not as *staying in the breach,* but as *staying-in-the-breach-in-order-that-others-can-get-away.* Someone might do this for no further end, and he would be acting as a fine human being. But similar alternative descriptions can be offered of anything, with similar results. The physician applies this ointment for a further end, the patient's recovery. He also applies-ointment-for-the-recovery-of-the-patient, and as physician he has no further end in view, since it is not qua physician that he hopes to make a living or do good in society: these are aims which he has qua human being, but qua doctor he is ultimately concerned with health. The fact that technical productive activity can be described so as to refer to no further product does not begin to qualify such activity for the status of

Aristotelian happiness; and the fact that virtuous practical activity can be described so as to refer to an ulterior end does not disqualify it.

As to (2): if we take bridle-making and medical practice as standard examples of activities which aim at a further product, we can see that many actions or activities are not like this: listening to music, playing games, chatting with a friend are standardly not, and likewise theoretic activity. Is each of these the central good called 'happiness'? Are they all? Is each a 'part of happiness'? How is this consistent with Aristotle's assumption that happiness (in the sense of the central good) is a unified activity? Of course, if by 'happiness' we mean 'a happy life', then many different things are parts of happiness, but 'parts of happiness' in this sense will also cover activities engaged in not for their own sake, such as money making, since these are parts within (not external means to) an ongoing happy life. Such are the difficulties if we accept implication (2).

The division of ends at 1094 a 4 into activities and products may be meant to provide a contrast that paves the way for Aristotle's later announcement that happiness is an activity (hence by implication not a thing or state of a thing or product). However, I am inclined to think that at 1094 a 4 ff. he is preparing to make a different point. The point comes at lines 14–18, and it is that every end has a place in some hierarchy, and that a higher end is to be preferred to an end below it. He wishes to stress that these relations hold whether the ends are products or activities. This is in case it be thought that ends which are products are always subordinate to ends which are activities, as some of Aristotle's examples might seem to suggest. (For instance, at 10–11 he speaks of bridle-making as subservient to riding.) Now, the difference between an end which is a product and one which is an activity is as follows. In both cases there is an activity A, but where the end is a product, A is other than the end. However, in each case the end (i.e., its realisation) is what we look at to judge the excellence or success of an instance of A. If someone undertakes to make a million in six months, we look at the results at the end of the time to judge the success of the intervening enterprise. But in some cases the excellence of an activity is decided by observing the activity as it occurs. A horseman's performance is judged by the performance itself, and the agent considered as horseman has no end beyond the riding, even though this activity may as a matter of fact exist only to subserve some further end. Thus horsemanship may be encouraged in society only for military purposes. In that case, it falls under the 'art of generalship' in the hierarchy, and the general's requirements determine what will count as good horsemanship. (Should speed be stressed or ability to manoeuvre in a confined space?) So while riding is an activity, and is itself the end of the rider as such, it is also every bit as much for *use* as the potter's pots and the bridle maker's bridles. (Thus a product [bridles] can fall under an activity [riding], but an activity [riding] can fall under a product [victory, the general's product].)

In those opening lines, as often elsewhere, Aristotle uses 'end' and 'good' as interchangeable terms. Hence the statement 'where there are ends apart from the actions, it is the nature of the products to be *better* than the activities'. He means that the product is more of an end than the activity. That is to say, it makes more sense in the case of production to judge success by looking at the product than by looking at the activity. It also makes more sense to aim at having the product if one could have it without the activity than to engage in the activity without any assurance that it would result in the product. None of this entails that the product is *better* than the activity in any sense entailing 'superior', 'more worthy of respect', 'more admirable'. The potter's activity, even when cut off short, is of course in that sense 'better' than any pot, since living skill and intelligence are in the activity, not in the pot.

The act of courage was intended to save lives, and in acting bravely for this end the agent achieved happiness according to Aristotle's definition (though whether also in a whole happy life depends on other circumstances). Safety, a great good, was the goal of the action, but this end was not better than the brave action itself. That is, safety (of whomever and however many) is not a nobler or finer thing than someone's acting bravely. (Nor is it finer than someone's brave but unsuccessful attempt to save lives.) In this comparison we consider the deed as an enacted performance. But that is not what is seen from the point of view of the agent rationally deciding what to do. For him the safety of those who concern him is obviously preferable to taking risky and possibly unsuccessful action if the former could be secured without that risk. For the prospective agent his comrades' safety was more of an end than his facing danger for its sake. But the action done for the sake of that end was *ethically* superior to its end.

I have just argued that it is a fallacy to suppose that happiness, for Aristotle, logically cannot consist in actions which aim at an ulterior result. Now another, more insidious, confusion arises from the fact that in the *Nicomachean Ethics* he operates on two levels, using similar language on both. He begins by arguing that the supreme good is the statesman's objective, and goes on to investigate the nature of that objective. This second stage continues through the rest of the work, but in Book I it culminates in the definition of happiness as virtuous or excellent activity. Now this activity is distinct from that of the statesman as such. The statesman aims, we are told, at making excellent citizens; but his ultimate aim, the measure of his success, is the excellent activity of individual citizens—which is to say their happiness. The statesman's own happiness does not figure at either stage, although we can infer that his fulfilment as statesman lies in achieving his goal as such. This is the happiness of citizens, which in relation to them is not their product but their activity (though, being practical, it will consist in the bringing about of changes in the world). But in relation to *him* their happiness is not his activity, but more like a distinct product or result. ('Result' is perhaps the better word, since the citizens' activity is not a thing or state of a thing like a pot or safety or health, and the statesman's action is not an action of making or bringing into being the citizens' virtuous activity. This is because an activity has being only through being engaged in by the one whose activity it is. It cannot be made by another or passed from hand to hand. Strictly, then, the statesman can only make or bring to be the *conditions* of others' virtuous activity. But since he shapes the conditions precisely to make such activity possible in many individuals, the activity is the ultimate end to which he looks—an end separate from his own activity, and in this respect like a product.)

Failure to recognise the difference of levels has resulted in major confusions. For instance, it is often supposed that Aristotle equates the ordinary individual's happiness with an ulterior objective aimed for in that individual's own virtuous action: this is because it is falsely assumed that the good at which all things are said to aim in *NE* I.1 is there being considered from the logical perspective of the individual subject of happiness, not from that of the statesman who is agent of its conditions. The latter's activity is indeed distinct from the good which he aims to make possible, namely individuals' happiness. Noticing that happiness here figures as a result beyond the activity, and not noticing that the activity in question is not that of the individual subject of happiness as such, readers are led to the conclusion that Aristotelian happiness is an external product aimed for in individual virtuous activity. Since this directly contradicts the definition of happiness as identical with virtuous activity, Aristotle stands out as incoherent. Again, he seems incoherent on the question of my own versus others' happiness. Someone may be said to 'pursue' an activity by engaging in it. Only I can engage in my activity, and I cannot engage in anyone else's. If the activity in question is of the sort which Aristotle identifies with happiness, I engage in and 'pursue' my happiness, and logically cannot in this sense pursue anyone else's. In itself, this position is easy to reconcile with the view, which of course Aristotle holds, that the virtuous person is often actively concerned about the happiness of others. In the best kind of friendship, he says, we love the other for his own sake and take an interest in his happiness (1156 b 6–11). There is no contradiction, for in such a case the happiness sought is not my own current activity but its ulterior objective. I *engage* in the activity which is necessarily no one's happiness but mine, but what I *seek* through so engaging is someone else's. But there seems to be a conflict of doctrines here if we mix the two levels and suppose that my own happiness stands to my activity as the statesman's objective to his. For if we also absorb the point that in some sense only *I* can 'pursue' only *my* happiness, it will follow (1) that happiness is always an ulterior end, and (2) that for me this ulterior end can be only my own happiness.[44]

Confusion of the levels is not surprising, since the difference between 'statesman' and 'ordinary individual' is more conceptual than real. Aristotle's ethical inquiry is meant to educate the statesman about his proper goal. So far as any of us partakes in such an inquiry with a view to making its conclusions tell in our own lives and the lives of those around us, we too are 'statesmen'. But while the human individual's happiness, considered as a universal, is indeed a topic for the statesman's practical reflection, an instance of happiness-activity is not in the same way a *topic* for its particular individual agent at the moment of enactment. However, that activity may be consciously directed to producing conditions for further such activity, one's own or others', and this consciousness may be illuminated by an understanding of the nature and supreme worth of this kind of activity. In such a case, the activity identical with happiness has as its conscious ulterior goal the happiness that is a topic for ethics. But, we shall see, it need not have such a goal.

Because ethics is practical, happiness as a topic for ethics figures as a goal or *practicable* end, rather than as a fait accompli. But when actualised in a given instance, happiness is an end or completion in the different sense of actually perfecting (on this occasion) a particular individual's existence. We gain philosophical understanding of the practicable end by reflection on our experience of particular achieved instances. There is therefore a basic level of virtuous activity and happiness which is logically and often chronologically prior to such reflection. On that basic level the good practical agent[45] has not articulated to himself a single specific goal which in general he equates with happiness. For many people this may be the only level. It has to come first because whatever one reflectively decides that happiness is—pleasure, honour, fine action—that which it is must first occur and be a familiar element in human life before it can be grasped as a universal and become a topic.

Hence on what I am calling the basic level, the virtuous individual, acting day to day in response to particular situations, aims at this, that and the other goal, short-term and long: to get his harvest in, to educate his children, to help a friend in difficulties, to run for office, prepare himself for a military campaign etc., etc. He might, if asked on any occasion, acknowledge that, yes, he pursues his various ends 'for the sake of happiness' (it would be odder to say 'No' than 'Yes'). This does not mean that he equates any one of them with happiness in a universal definition, or that he equates them all (a questionable totality, in any case) with happiness in that way. Nor does it mean that he defines happiness to himself as something else specific to which all these others are means. 'For the sake of happiness' in this context is, I would say, a logically unitary phrase from which the word 'happiness' cannot be detached so as to create space for substituting an equivalent. The phrase expresses the bare bones of practical rationality without benefit of philosophical instruction: namely, the agent's awareness of each of his actual and possible projects as unfolding within his own life, hence as having to be mutually adjusted, where possible, so that the achievement of any one of these goods would not render itself harmful or futile: for instance by destroying his chances for a greater good, or by undermining conditions for enjoying or using the first. This ground-level rationality issues in thought and action that not only uses and aims at the various goods which occupy our practical attention, but upholds their very title as 'goods' by using and aiming in the right way. And ground level rationality is also the universal human potential from which can grow, given experience and conditions of reflection, the abstract ethical thinking which aims to break up that unitary adverbial expression and fix in definitional isolation that which, on the *political* level, we should be acting for the sake of if we act for the sake of happiness.

Does this distinction between the ground-level activity *of* happiness and the enlightened statesman's logically superior activity *towards* happiness, compel the conclusion that the latter is better than the former, so that the former would be not happiness but something inferior (since 'happiness' is the name of the supreme good)? It depends on what we mean by 'better'. The statesman is perhaps more accomplished, and in that sense more perfect. He is useful, too, on a wider front, if he is successful. But it is not at all clear that he deserves more credit than the ground-level agent, or that his activity is that of a better human being. If Aristotle squarely thinks that it is, then we should expect him to restrict the possibility of happiness to enlightened statesmen. In fact he takes no such logically straightforward line. At 1100 b 18 ff. he seems willing to call happy a person of steadfast good character who responds with dignity even to straitened circumstances. Aristotle mainly has in mind external or physical conditions which the agent would not have chosen, but he might also have mentioned conditions of culture and knowledge. Most human beings have lived, and live, under conditions in which an articulate reasoned vision of the good was not available. But the practical virtues (including the virtue of Aristotelian practical wisdom), are possible under these conditions, and so therefore is the happiness which is their exercise.[46]

The distinction of levels demands a comparable distinction between senses in which happiness is the 'central good' of the happy life. If the happy life is considered as the statesman's ultimate objective, then happiness, whatever it is defined as, lies at the centre of his objective: it is the bull's eye of his target. But if happiness is considered as an activity of the subject of the sort of life that the statesman aims to make possible, then happiness cannot be to its subject as the bull's eye of his target: once it becomes so, it is future happiness or other people's happiness, and he is operating as statesman. So is there any sense in which the subject's own happiness is his central good? Yes, if we allow that conduct is a kind of value judgment. For if we examined the life of the sort of person whom Aristotle deems happy, we should say that although for him different targets loom at different times, each presenting itself as his current goal, what he really cares about more and more constantly than he does about any of these is conducting himself well. For, if we judge by behaviour, he puts more into that than into anything else.

The rationality, then, which is active in the rational activity of happiness, is, I take it, the basic organising attitude expressed by the integral phrase 'for-the-sake-of-happiness'. It may be, but need not be, illuminated by articulate views concerning happiness. However, rational activity is not happiness according to Aristotle's definition unless it is also good. Now the goodness is not an additional feature that might just as well have been mentioned first. Just as the good harpist is good *as* a harpist (1098 a 8–12), so the good rational agent is good *as* a rational agent. His is the goodness of practical reason as such. Aristotle will explain this in his analysis of the virtues, for they are defined with reference to 'right reason'. But this general approach raises a question to which we shall return when discussing his account of practical wisdom.[47] There he argues that the rational organising activity is good only if the agent's various ends are good and are pursued in a good way. But how can this goodness be goodness of reason as such? A bad man who pursues wrong ends may be just as rational in his pursuit of them: just as logical, intelligent, sound in his calculations and grasp of empirical facts. But if the good man is not, on account of being good, more rational, how can his goodness be the goodness of reason?[48]

This question is worth raising in the context of a discussion of Aristotle's definition of happiness, because it helps us take the measure of his claim that happiness *is* (good) rational activity. The question belongs with a view which sees reason as the means or equipment by which we obtain what we desire or feel to be good. The equipment is the same though the ends vary according to ideals, taste and character. Some ends are bad (perceived by others as undesirable), but the agent's rational equipment may be as good by rational standards as anyone else's. From this point of view it would seem that the supreme good is not the rational activity by which we obtain ends at a practical distance from us, since that activity is only a means to the good.

Aristotle can reply: while it is true that *through* rational activity we bring about many goods, including the supreme good, it does not follow that the supreme good should be viewed as just another objective of rational activity attainable by means of it. Rather, it *is* the activity of rationally reaching out for (in the first instance) lesser goods. *By* rationally reaching out we realise both the other goods and the supreme good, but 'by' signals a different relation in each case. Just so, by seeing we become aware of many objects, and we also (Aristotle holds) are aware of seeing them; but this is not because we are aware of our seeing by seeing it, as we might be aware of someone else's seeing by watching him (cf. *On the Soul* 425 b 11 ff).

A general metaphysical consideration sustains the view that our supreme good is a rational reaching out towards lesser goods. A modern contrast may serve to introduce it briefly. It is often held that purposeful or end-directed activity is properly ascribed only to beings with minds and, derivatively, to artifacts designed by such beings. Other things—living creatures and their organs—seem to lend themselves to being spoken of in such terms, but the most respectable or scientific way of describing them would make reference only to antecedent causes. Now if something is an end only so far as there is a mental reaching out towards it, and is an end only for those to whom it is a mentally presented objective, their mental reaching cannot in the first instance be an end for them, because it is the precondition of anything's being for them an end at all. (It might become an end for them if they cease to take it for granted and begin to worry about ensuring future conditions for its continued operation. This is like visually observing someone else seeing something.) But according to Aristotle's science and metaphysics, all living things, including mindless plants, have a good or an end proper to their species towards which they naturally tend to develop from a formless or potential state. Thus 'having an end' does not in general depend on desiring or having the end as a conscious objective. On the contrary, it is more likely that beings like ourselves, who naturally have various conscious objectives, have them because the end proper to our species is or involves the having of conscious objectives.

Against this general metaphysical background it is not plausible to say that practical reason is *useful* for attaining our good—our good being something beyond the activity of practical reason. Every creature, unless maimed from birth, is naturally endowed with what it needs for efficiently attaining its good. And for most species, orderly development towards the good takes place without reflective reason. So if reflective reason were simply a superb natural instrument for achieving a nonrational good, why are we the only species possessed of reflective reason? The others all lack it even though, on the hypothesis, they each resemble humankind in having a nonrational sort of good. Are they all by nature underequipped with means? An absurd supposition. On the other hand, viewing the actual success of plants and nonrational animals, we might sooner think that if our good were like theirs and not intrinsically rational, we should be better off with instinct alone and not reason, since reason gives rise to many distractions and often points us in false directions (for it points us in many, and they cannot all be true). If reason is an instrument, it is a poor one.[49] But in that case our own species would be universally defective. And that too is absurd. On general principles of natural teleology, the human possession of reason makes sense only if some sort of rational activity is indeed our *end*. So those principles fill a gap in Aristotle's ethical argument; for from his premiss that we are uniquely rational animals, it does not follow that rational activity is (at its best) our end: reason would still distinguish us even if reason were only our special instrument.

We can enjoy Aristotle's *Ethics* as an intellectual system or study it as a piece of cultural history: we may also find him saying many true and wise things about ethics. If we value the *Ethics* for that, a word of caution may be in order in the light of the foregoing considerations. So far as his findings depend on the thesis that good rational activity is the supreme human end, we lack one of Aristotle's fundamental reasons for accepting those results if we reject Aristotelian natural teleology. Perhaps some other metaphysical position could be rolled into place to perform the same function in the argument. But any position of similar breadth is unlikely not to carry some consequences alien to the spirit of Aristotle's ethics.

If good rational activity is our end in the sense sanctioned by natural teleology, such activity is our *natural* end. In that case why do we not for the most part naturally develop to the point where this end emerges in its prefigured perfection, as happens with other creatures and their natural ends? It seems that virtue and happiness should be as common as speaking a language for human beings, and false values and wrong actions as rare as birth defects. On the contrary, such mistakes are a sign of our rationality, not only because many errors are backed by reasons, but more especially because human rationality is the power to get things right which we by our failure could have got wrong. Without significant space for failure, there is no space for reason. It has to be possible for genetically normal individuals to fail, and to fail in respect of the most important ends. This is why our nature leaves us genetically underendowed from the point of view of ethical development, so that we do not just grow into virtue and rationality. Only so is there space for major tasks of human reason: for instance, development of virtue in the young by deliberate measures directed towards control of their genetically grounded impulses.

Virtue has to be cultivated, and happiness depends on that cultivation. Hence happiness does not depend on divine favour or on fortune. It would sound a false note, Aristotle says, to entrust what is greatest and noblest to fortune (1099 b 20–25); and in fact, he implies, it would be self-contradictory. It is *better,* he says, to be happy through care and training than by chance. Hence if happiness is to be the *supreme* good, it must represent an investment of human thought and effort. This investment, on one level, is the process of moral training, the next main topic of *Ethics.* On another level, it is the inquiry of ethical philosophy itself, which is necessary because our nature marks us out for an end which we are born not knowing but able to aim for before we know what it is, since our very seeking to know it is one way of pursuing that good for which we seek. This is because whatever the best turns out to be for the fallible rational beings we are, it cannot be such as to be achieved to full perfection except in and through our coming to know what it is by our own efforts.

## VII. On the Other Goods and the Scope of 'Happiness'

For some time now I have used the term 'happiness' a ser     'ch is artificially circumscribed if one judges it by standards of ordinary English, but which reflects Aristotle's use of his corresponding term to refer to the good that is principal ingredient of a good and happy life. Happiness in this sense is iden . ied as a certain activity carried on well, and logically therefore it could be said to belong to or be enjoyed by someone (on the ground that he is engaged in the good activity) without its implying that he is happy *(eudaimōn)* in the ordinary sense. In the latter sense someone is happy only if he is living a happy life, and for that to be true (or for it to be reasonably taken as true) goods are needed besides some particular passage of the activity, or even many such passages. Necessary, too, according to Aristotle, is a 'complete life' (1098 a 18), by which he probably means no particular period such as seventy years, but a life affording opportunities for a full range of human action and experience.[50]

Why and to what extent he thinks the other goods are necessary is difficult to determine, because of shifts in meaning and evaluative criteria.[51] Aristotle regularly uses 'happiness' *('eudaimonia')* as a synonym for 'the best' or 'the highest good'; but how are we to think of the best and the highest? The superlative may, in good metaphysical style, be made the label of the prime principle or source of the good life's goodness. (Then the implied comparison between the bearer of the label and any of the other goods is not so much in respect of goodness—so that the former is *better* than any of the latter—but rather in respect of entitlement to be called 'good'.) In that case, 'the best' refers to virtuous activity. On the other hand, it is hard not to think of the best as (1) *that which is most desirable,* or as (2) *that which it makes most sense to pursue or promote or cultivate.* But a fully happy *life* is obviously (1) more desirable than just the central activity, or just this activity carried on in a life cut short, or under the barest necessary conditions. Now it might seem that the happy life, rather than the activity, is (2) that which it makes more sense to pursue, since the former is more desirable. But for rational beings this is not necessarily so. In theory and practice we try to go first for essentials. If the essence of the happy life is the exercise of the human virtues, then it makes sense to secure that first (with the minimal conditions necessary)[52], and the rest should generally follow. By this argument, the virtuous activity is what we should call 'the best', not the life.

Aristotle's use of the statesman figure at the beginning of the *Nicomachean Ethics* imposes yet another (and semitechnical) sense on 'the best' and 'the highest good'. The best is that which is aimed at by the supreme authority. Thus conceived, the best is a certain *kind* of life for the citizens, just as health considered as the goal of medicine is a kind of benefit. In this context 'the best' does not refer to this or that individual's happy life or activity. Here, the superlative implies a comparison of ends in a hierarchy of authority, and the comparison is between kinds. It follows that two concrete individuals may instantiate the best, i.e. both afford all round examples of what the statesman should aim for, yet one is better or better off than the other, being an even finer or a more successful person.

Happiness, then, both includes and does not include some measure of other goods besides the leading activity, depending on whether by 'happiness' we mean the happy life; the activity as actually carried on; or the activity in the abstract. And it is both supreme in kind and surpassable in individual cases. These are logical distinctions. But it is not merely the word's fault that it is used in these several senses. Their association is not an fact it is a fact about the activity which Aristotle identifies as happiness that it tends to generate happy lives. The activity is intelligent, fair, sober, enterprising action in and upon a material and social environment. In general, such admirable action conduces to the health, safety, prosperity of all concerned.

These are ingredients of the happy life affording means and occasions for more such activity: not merely basic conditions but opportunities for new kinds of excellent action and admirable achievement. These opportunities are not uniformly distributed, and the ethical quality of a person's activity may show itself only in modest effects. In one sense, then, two individuals may both instantiate the best (each makes the best possible personal contribution to the situation), yet one is so situated as to live much better than the other.

One can therefore be less fortunate, and even much less fortunate, than someone else, and rightly be counted happy. This is because (1) the happiness of a happy life stems from virtuous activity, and (2) it is of the nature of human virtue to value its own activity above all else. Human excellence, Aristotle holds, is incomplete without the virtue of *greatness of soul:* that is to say, the good man's sense of the incomparable worth of his goodness (*NE* IV.3; *EE* III.5). This attitude carries the implicit claim that life would be worth living just for the sake of excellent action. Hence the good person will be fundamentally undisturbed by changes in his material and physical circumstances and in his external relations. For he will not feel that he or his life is a failure if he is not successful in those respects, nor that he is more what he values being if on these fronts he flourishes.

> No function of man has so much permanence as excellent activities (these are thought to be more durable even than knowledge), and of these themselves the most valuable are more durable because those who are blessed spend their life most readily and most continuously in these. . . . [Permanence], then, will belong to the happy man, and he will be happy throughout his life; for always, or by preference to everything else, he will do and contemplate what is excellent, and he will bear the chances of life most nobly and altogether decorously, if he is 'truly good' and 'foursquare beyond reproach'. (1100 b 12–22; cf. 32–33)

This is not a picture of indifference. The happy person as here conceived may suffer grief and disappointment, as long as the affliction does not spoil the vigour of his agency or deprive him of the means to exercise it. Even under severely diminished circumstances the good person's life may count as happy, if *he,* even by living it as best he can (1101 a 1–5), endorses it as a good and worthwhile life (a life good enough for the best kind of person). For, as Aristotle constantly tells us, in ethical matters the good and wise person is the standard, and his judgment must be accepted as right (e.g., 1113 a 25–33). It is as if by his attitude this agent legislates it true that his reduced life is a happy one, and we, brought up to respect such a person, cannot but heed his declaration.

Above we saw the central activity of excellence bringing in its train an abundance of other goods. Now we see it as shrugging them off, all but the necessary minimum, and drawing tighter the boundaries of the happy life so as to exclude them from having to belong. Virtue gives rise to both these developments, and we should not expect that Aristotle would see himself forced to choose between them, nor that he would be caught unawares by shifts in the demands of concepts such as *self-sufficiency.* The combination of the two 'dynamics of virtue'—increase in prosperity and an increasing sense of the insignificance of prosperity as compared with personal

merit and its expressions in thought, feeling and action—sets a challenge for ethics
and politics to which perhaps there are many responses worth trying. Aristotle's
answer, as I understand it, finds practical virtue inadequate to solve the problem
which it generates, and from this deficiency it derives an ethical justification of *theōria*. However, that solution remains in hiding until the end of the *Ethics* (*NE* X.6–
8; *EE* VII.15; see Chapter 7 below).

But notwithstanding his occasional reminders of the inwardness of happiness,
Aristotle is very far from holding that the rightminded person desires no more than
virtuous striving, or than inner tranquillity, or than a good conscience or unshaken
sense of one's own worth. Aristotle never loses sight of the fact that even if the good
man labouring under difficulties is not necessarily to be denied the accolade 'happy',
the agent would be better off if such difficulties were removed, and of course should
take steps to that end where possible. Not to care at any level about having the 'natural goods' such as health, abilities, security, wealth, opportunities—having them so
as to use them in all sorts of ways—is inhuman not only by ordinary standards but
certainly by Aristotle's, since it implies the rejection of his starting point. For it
implies that human well-functioning is not *practical* well-functioning, and that the
practical virtues, so called, should not count as virtues. For if they really are virtues,
the exercise of them in virtuous striving cannot alone be the ultimate good, even if
it is the source of that good, since the exercise of practical virtue has to look beyond
itself by taking seriously the practical aim of getting things done which it rightly
judges call for being done. Such an attitude cannot but care about actual success: not
only about the agent's own part in it but also about the aspects that depend on causes
beyond his control. Misfortune can nullify the projects of the best of agents, either
by frustrating their purposes or, worse still, by leading them blindly into dénoue-
ments where they live to regret their *not* having failed at what it turns out they were
doing, or (worst of all) their very possession and use of whatever fine qualities it took
to frame and execute the action.

Happiness, then is more than the exercise of virtue: it is *eupraxia* or faring well
(1098 b 22). Here we have the ideal combination: human excellence *achieving* an
end worthy of itself under circumstances that harbour no reason why the agent, later,
should unwish his excellence or its success, or why those who love him should regret
that he deserved their congratulations. The complexity of this notion of 'faring well'
*(eu prattein)* highlights a conclusion reached earlier: that Aristotle relies on his listeners' common sense to interpret 'human excellence'. For if the interpretation were
fixed by the abstract truism that excellence is the attribute, simple or complex, by
which a thing functions well, then (since functioning well for a human being is faring
well in accordance with the ideal of *eupraxia*) we should logically expect human
excellence to include freedom from ill luck and the possession of external means to
success, as well as the more personal qualities commonly called 'virtues'. But in
actual fact we do not consider one worthy individual a better (as distinct from happier) man than another on the ground that the first is better placed to succeed. Aristotle says that people do not consider external goods and bodily goods to be goods
in the strictest and primary sense, but reserve that status for actions and activities of
the soul (1098 b 9–16). The ground of this remark is, I think, that it is only on
account of this last category that we in our culture call someone a good human being

or person. Thus the possession of a measure of external and physical goods is not a part of *human virtue* but a necessary condition of the successful exercise which is happiness (*EE* 1214 b 11–27). The fact that Aristotle's audience accepts this distinction, with its implication that a human virtue is a quality only of the *soul* (cf. 1098 b 12–20), will make it easier, when the moment arrives, to commend to them as a truly human virtue some quality or set of qualities whose exercise depends on nothing external, and which neither makes nor is meant to make any practical difference to anything.[53]

## Notes

1. Cf., however, *Politics* 1279 b 12–15.
2. That the opinion was only his own is not brought out by *The Revised Oxford Translation* (Solomon).
3. On some readings, this or a similar thought appears in the text at 1215 a 1–2. See Dirlmeier [1] ad 1215 a 1; Woods [1], 200.
4. For the analytic connection of 'good' and 'end', see e.g. *Metaphysics* 983 a 31; 1013 b 25–27.
5. See, e.g., *On the Soul* 415 a 16–22.
6. For the shape of the argument, cf. Irwin [7], 359. Joachim ad 1094 a 1–b 11 takes it the other way round; i.e., as an inference from the proposition that there is a supreme end to the architectonic status of *politikē*.
7. At *Pol.* 1264 b 15–21 Aristotle allows that a *polis* can be reckoned happy, but only on the ground that its citizens are.
8. Cf. Barnes [2], 20–22.
9. This is well discussed by Cooper [3]. See also Devereux [2].
10. Aristotle shows no interest in this question.
11. But see a different position at *EE* 1216 b 35–39, where Aristotle says that even in an inquiry about ethics we should 'look for the cause'. This is probably because, if we hold the right ethical positions for the wrong reasons, our values and practice are in the end affected.
12. For a vigorous defence of this translation, see Kraut [2].
13. Cf. Kenny [2], 193.
14. Cf. Cooper [3]. J. L. Austin (in Moravcsik) implies that, primarily, a certain kind of *life* is happiness, and that equating a good *within* a life (e.g. pleasure or wealth) with happiness is 'loose language' (279–81). He seems to ascribe this view to Aristotle. In fact, Aristotle's strict use is Austin's loose one, and it is strict not by standards of ordinary usage but in accordance with an ideal and technical use designed to reflect the metaphysical priorities.
15. The central good is meant at, e.g., 1095 a 20–25; b 14–15; I.7 passim; 1098 b 32; 1099 a 25; 1100 a 14; 1102 a 5; X.6–8 passim. The happy life is meant at, e.g., 1100 b 9; 1101 a 18; and possibly 1100 b 2 and 1101 a 9.
16. Even when this is a stronger-than-material conditional.
17. Cf. Devereux [1].
18. Aristotle thinks that there is 'some truth' in all the opinions he mentions. He shows what in each case it is, in *NE* I.8. On the general attitude, cf. *EE* 1216 b 30–35; *Meta.* 993 a 30–b 8; *Rhetoric* 1355 a 15–18. See Barnes [4], and Dahl, 72–73.
19. On Aristotle's need (more marked in *EE* than in *NE*) to provide an account of *the good* that satisfies certain Platonic expectations, see D. Robinson.
20. Cf. Hare.
21. *Kai* is epexegetic in *ho theos kai ho nous,* 1096 a 24–25.
22. There is a possible source of confusion in the fact that Aristotle identifies happiness ( =

the central good) with an activity *(energeia)*. This concept is metaphysically cognate to that of life in the sense of vitality *(zoē)*. But the life made happy by the central good is a life in the biographical sense *(bios)*. (The happy *bios* and the happiness-activity fully coincide only in the case of God.) The ambiguities of 'happiness' and 'life' surely help explain the indecisive nature of much of the recent debate over the comprehensiveness or exclusiveness of Aristotelian happiness. The happy life 'includes' many goods (some intrinsic, many instrumental); it is 'dominated' by the one good which is happiness in the strict (or 'exclusive') sense. Cf. Heinaman [2].

23. This is brought out well by Engberg-Pedersen, Ch. 1. See also McDowell [3].

24. *The Revised Oxford Translation* misleadingly says 'complete'.

25. *Pace* e.g. Ackrill [2], who regards 'for the sake of happiness' as virtually synonymous with 'for its own sake'. This does not fit well with 1097 b 2–5, where *men . . . de* and *kai . . . kai* in 3–4 indicate different (and possibly incompatible) ways of choosing pleasure, honour etc. Choosing X (where X is not happiness) for its own sake and choosing X for the sake of happiness are perhaps compatible if happiness is a multiplicity of intrinsic goods (cf. Urmson [5], 10–11). But in Aristotle 'happiness' refers either to a single activity, or to a life *(bios)* which contains many goods that are instrumental as well as others that are intrinsic.

26. Korsgaard, in an interesting discussion, makes this the basis of Aristotle's eventual elevation of *theōria.*

27. This seems to clash with *NE* 1100 b 22–1101 a 13. Here Aristotle envisages a virtuous person's loss of happiness, but there is no suggestion that the person automatically comes to regret having been born. (I owe this observation to Richard Kraut.) However, there is no discrepancy if one allows for wider and narrower senses of 'happiness', one referring to the activity of virtue, which is what the good person lives for, and the other involving extraneous goods as well. See Section VII of this chapter.

28. The interpretation is problematic. 1097 b 8–11 says that what is self-sufficient for someone (i.e., what renders him self-sufficient) is what suffices for him *and* his family, friends etc. Since happiness here is identified with what makes someone self-sufficient, it would seem that a person's happiness consists in a multiplicity of goods shared by him and his group. But lines 14–15, by contrast, imply that what makes someone self-sufficient is a single good which completes an otherwise acceptable life. A dense crop of commentary has grown up round this passage in the last generation; this is because, depending on the interpretation, it has seemed to provide crucial evidence on whether Aristotle adheres to an inclusive or monistic notion of happiness. In my view, however, this dispute is solved by attending to the ambiguity of 'happiness' (see above, n. 22); hence the precise interpretation of 1097 b 8–15 makes little difference.

29. This is argued in Kraut [3].

30. Cf. Wedin on the modal sense in which *eudaimonia* is 'final'. In so far as happiness is what makes life worth living, it is to the happy life as soul to living organism; thus other goods are analogous to the body or its parts. Consequently, happiness cannot be counted as one along with those other goods, any more than the form of a metaphysical concrete is an item additional to its material components (cf. *Meta.* 1041 b 11 ff.).

31. The translation here is by J.A.K. Thomson. Ross's translation (retained in *The Revised Oxford Translation*) of 1098 a 3–4 as 'an *active* [instead of *practical*] life of the element that has a rational principle' misrepresents the text. 'Activity' does not enter Aristotle's discussion until line 6.

32. Kraut [1] stresses that the comparison class in the function argument is the class of physical living things; and that Aristotle neither shows nor attempts to show that rational activity is uniquely our function. It is not, since God is rational.

33. For him, of course, it could not seem such a fragile claim, since the earth and its immediate environs are the only possible home for mortal living things.

34. Is Zeus called 'father of gods and men' because men and gods have (anyway) so much in common; or are men and gods represented as having much in common because it is ante-

cedently supposed that they have a common ancestor? Aristotle, I think, would take the former view, as should we.

35. Cf. Clark, 21–25; Irwin [7] 338–39.

36. At *Pol.* 1325 a 16 ff. Aristotle contends that *theōria* should count as a sort of *praxis.* Does he expect his Nicomachean audience to take this into consideration? Possibly; *tis* in line 3 might indicate as much. If he does expect this, it could only be on the basis of their having been exposed to an argument like that of *Pol.* 1325 a 17 ff. For there an argument is certainly felt to be needed to justify stretching the extension of *praxis;* hence Aristotle cannot expect his Nicomachean audience to supply this point entirely of themselves.

37. Cf. MacIntyre [1], 147–49. See Monan [1], N. P. White and Gomez-Lobo on the point that Aristotle has no antecedently established notion of happiness on which to base a 'deduction' of the virtues.

38. Alternatively, take 'final' in the sense indicated at 1097 a 30–34. In that case 1098 a 17–18 speaks of 'the excellence which is pursued only for its own sake'. This presumably refers to the nonpractical excellence of theoretic wisdom. Cf. Cooper [3].

39. The question is not whether theoretic activity must necessarily be embedded in a context of good practical activity (for it is obvious that although some *praxis* is necessary, it need not be all that good); but whether theoretical activity could count as *happiness* except in a setting of practical excellence. See below, Chapter 7, Section IX.

40. On the incompleteness of the definition, see the excellent discussion by Cooper [3].

41. In particular, Aristotle's notion of happiness is not designed to answer the question 'Why should I be moral?' *pace* Prichard.

42. Cf. Gauthier and Jolif, Vol. II, Part 1, ad 1096 a 2. Speusippus and Xenocrates are also Aristotle's targets here. Cf. Burnet ad 1098 b 31, and his Introductory Notes to Book I (Section 4).

43. Thus Joachim ad loc. finds here the distinction between theoretical and practical (including technical) activity. This is supposed to prepare us for the identification of happiness with *theōria* in *NE* X. Ackrill [2] followed by Urmson [5], 10–11, takes the distinction to be between things done for their own sake and things done for the sake of something else; this is supposed to pave the way for a notion of happiness whereby something's being done for its own sake *is* its being done for the sake of happiness.

44. Another confusion from the same source has to do with *pursuing virtue.* The ground level agent exercises virtue and need not see himself as doing so, or as 'pursuing' it. The statesman in his rôle as educator pursues, i.e. deliberately tries to promote, virtue in the community. The point is touched on by Allan [3].

45. I am assuming that this agent has practical wisdom. For further discussion of the 'ground level *phronimos*' see Chapter 4.

46. See below, Chapter 7, Section XI on the life that is 'happiest in a secondary sense'.

47. See Chapter 4, Section X ad fin.

48. This point is strongly put by Siegler [1]; see also Dahl, 55 and 111–112.

49. As, e.g., Kant points out, pp. 62–63.

50. Thus the happiness, in one sense, of noble activity culminating in self-sacrifice on the battle field is certainly compatible with a life cut short, *pace* Hardie [1].

51. On this entire topic, see Cooper [2].

52. This is the task of the statesman.

53. From an ethical point of view, practical action 'is regarded not as a contribution to the world's welfare, but as a case of spiritual activity or self-expression'. The words are those of Stocks (p. 80), whose own ethical conception of action is very close to Aristotle's. See especially Stocks, Chapters 1 and 4.

# CHAPTER 2

# Virtues and Parts of the Soul

### I. Why an Ethics of Virtue?

Human virtue is the central topic of Aristotle's *Ethics,* and it is worth considering why this should be so. Aristotle's supreme good is the well functioning of the human being qua human; functioning well is nothing other than 'activity in accordance with virtue (or excellence)'; and this he interprets so that practical virtue (as ordinarily understood) becomes the focus of attention. So of course Aristotle's *Ethics* is concerned mainly with virtue and the virtues and would not be what we know as Aristotle's *Ethics* otherwise.

But to illuminate his preoccupation, let us not take for granted, as if it were a fact of nature, that Aristotle's is a 'virtue-oriented' ethics. Why this perspective? It is not enough to say that he follows Plato, since in many things Aristotle goes his own way. The topic at hand provides an example. Both philosophers hold personal excellence to be of the essence of human well-being and both regard it as a state of the soul; but these similarities come with a striking difference. Aristotle constantly reminds his readers that happiness is activity: it is virtue in action, not virtue unused. And virtue as a state of the soul is of value only for the activity which it makes possible (cf. 1098 b 30–1099 a 7). Plato, by contrast, writes in the *Republic* as if that harmonious internal state which he calls 'justice' were something good and beautiful in itself apart from the external actions through which it is expressed. Thus he is able to reach a position which Aristotle decisively rejects, namely that *virtue,* as distinct from virtuous activity, is the supreme good for man.

The Aristotelian emphasis on activity is well to the fore in that early passage where the term 'virtue' first appears as an element in the definition of happiness (1098 a 7–18). Leaning on the flute-playing example, Aristotle rewrites 'acts (or functions) *well*' as: 'acts (functions) *in accordance with excellence (or virtue)*'. Is the rewriting justified? What is the point of it, justified or not? We must take up these questions now, since from here on in the text the Aristotelian connection between happiness and virtue will be doctrinally established.

I have shown how Aristotle can rely on his listeners' upbringing to interpret 'human virtue' in terms of justice, courage, generosity and the others. This applies mutatis mutandis to cognate adverbial phrases such as 'in accordance with virtue' and 'well'. My emphasis in that discussion was on the difference between the formal conception, whether nominal or adverbial, and its interpretation. Here I am concerned with the shift of formal focus from adverb to noun; or, more precisely to begin with, from the simple 'well' to the complex adverbial phrase 'in accordance with excellence' by which Aristotle replaces it. The replacement is logically justified, of course, only if the new expression introduces no idea not already implied by the first.[1] Since these are natural-language expressions, there is no rule for deciding that question. But whether or not their information content is the same, their force is not, since they suggest different lines of subsequent investigation. If one were to pursue the inquiry concerning happiness in the light of a definition formulated in terms of the simple adverb 'well', the next question would be 'What is it to act (or function) well?' If, on the other hand, one accepts the formulation 'activity in accordance with excellence', one is thereby granted an opportunity to dissect the previously monosyllabic (in Greek, too) adverbial concept. In particular, it is now possible to isolate the embedded term 'excellence', so that under this formulation of the definition of happiness, the next question for a methodical inquirer is sure to be: and what is excellence? Not surprisingly, this is just the question to which Aristotle turns at the start of his next main stage of argument/'Since happiness is an activity of soul in accordance with complete [or perfect] excellence, we must consider the nature of excellence; for we shall thus see better the nature of happiness' (1102 a 5–7).

But this passage of attention from 'acting well' to 'excellence' is by no means logically mandatory, nor would it necessarily occur to everyone. It makes sense to ask for the point of this transition. What is the advantage for Aristotle of approaching an understanding of happiness by considering what excellence or virtue is, rather than by directly considering what it is to act or function well?

A virtuous person is one who is *such as to*, who is *disposed to*, act well when occasion arises. And so far as 'acting well' implies not merely causing certain changes in the world, but doing so in the right frame of mind or with the right motive, a disposition to act well is also a disposition to act in the right frame of mind. 'Action' means the agent's involvement, not merely his body's. But now, given Aristotle's emphasis on happiness as live action by contrast with mere capacity or disposition, we may wonder why virtue, or the attribute of *being such as to act well*, should figure so large in his ethical thinking/

Partly, of course, it is because no one is happy on account of some isolated good action or stretch of good activity. Indeed, it is not clear that it even makes sense to describe someone as acting well only sporadically rather than, in Aristotle's phrase, from 'a settled disposition' (1105 a 33). The craftsman's same skill is behind his every skilful move, though the moves vary in response to different situations. So with the good man's good actions/ This much, however, would be common ground between Aristotle and ethical philosophers less insistent than he that the purpose of ethics is not to increase our knowledge, but to achieve a better life. This practical concern gives a further clue to Aristotle's preoccupation with virtue.|

Let us recall that in the *Nicomachean Ethics* the supreme good for man was characterised as the goal of *politikē,* the craft of politics. This, we saw, is implied by the very terms of Aristotle's initial proof that there is such a supreme good. Now this conception of the summum bonum as the objective of *politikē* is not quite easy to integrate with subsequent developments in which he firstly identifies it with happiness, and secondly defines happiness as a kind of *activity.* If happiness is what the practitioner of *politikē* ultimately aims to realise, then it is this practitioner's intended effect, whether to be effected for few or many (cf. 1094 b 7–10). The often-used model of the physician, whose goal is the patient's health, suggests a logical and generally also a factual distinction between being the agent who effects happiness, and being the subject or beneficiary in whom this effect is realised. But if happiness is essentially an activity of or by whoever "has" it, happiness cannot be the effect of a possibly external agent in the manner envisaged above. Does this mean that Aristotle cannot logically retain the definition of happiness as good activity without abandoning his conception of it as object of *politikē?* Hardly; what is needed is the distinction between an effect or product, and the actual use for which it is intended. Strictly speaking, the practitioner of *politikē* can only effect the conditions or substructure for the activity of happiness. In the same way, the physician cannot directly make happen the healthy *use* of the limb he has healed: only the user can be agent of that. But just as the use or exercise of a healthy body is the end to which the physician looks, since what he does is with a view to this, so with happiness and the *politikos.* Happiness is the end to which the *politikos* looks in aiming to bring about, not that end, but its conditions.

I use the word 'condition' broadly to refer not only to external conditions, physical and social, necessary for the well-functioning of human beings, but also to the personal dispositions, 'dispositions of the soul', whereby someone is *such as to* make good use of external conditions. Since such dispositions or virtues are not a constant of basic human nature but acquired through training, their development is crucial for happiness. And given that our proper concern with happiness is practical, a good definition or account of its essence should reflect its practicability. Aristotle's definition, 'activity of reason in accordance with excellence', does just this. It throws into relief the concept of virtue, which is nothing other than the concept of that which the practitioner of *politikē* must directly aim to produce in those whose happiness is his ultimate concern. Thus the passage last quoted continues as follows:

> The true student of politics, too, is thought to have studied this above all things; for he wishes to make his fellow citizens good and obedient to the laws. As an example of this we have the lawgivers of the Cretans and the Spartans, and any others of the kind that there may have been. And if this inquiry belongs to political science, clearly the pursuit of it will be in accordance with our original plan. (1102 a 7–13)

There is, however, a further ground for the importance to Aristotle of the concept of virtue, which appears when one considers his views about the impossibility of making accurate generalisations in ethics. The following passage is typical:

> Since, then, the present inquiry does not aim at theoretical knowledge like the others (for we are inquiring not in order to know what excellence is, but in order to become

good, since otherwise our inquiry would have been of no use), we must examine the
nature of actions, namely how we ought to do them. . . . Now, that we must act
according to right reason [*orthos logos*] is a common principle and must be
assumed—it will be discussed later, i.e. both what it is, and how it is related to the
other excellences. But this must be agreed upon beforehand, that the whole account
of matters of conduct must be given in outline and not precisely, as we said at the
very beginning that the accounts we demand must be in accordance with the subject-
matter; matters concerned with conduct and questions of what is good for us have
no fixity, any more than matters of health. The general account being of this nature,
the account of particular cases is yet more lacking in exactness; for they do not fall
under any art or set of precepts, but the agents themselves must in each case consider
what is appropriate to the occasion, as happens also in the art of medicine or of
navigation. But though our present account is of this nature we must give what help
we can. (1103 b 26–1104 a 11)

He then proceeds to introduce his famous conception of virtue 'as a mean'. That
conception represents his offer of help in the unsatisfactory situation in which he has
left his audience. If they (we) are as serious and practical as he demands, then even
if not exactly a surprise, it must come as something of a disappointment to be told
that not even the wisest moralist can firmly lay down general rules for good or right
action, since only the agent in each case can know then and there what is best. There
is no recipe for 'functioning well'. It is functioning in accordance with right reason
or the *orthos logos*,[2] but no one can say in advance what the *orthos logos* for a particular situation would be.

Now, although in the passage just quoted Aristotle says that he will return to the
question of what the *orthos logos* is, this is not a promise to provide later on a rule
or general criterion for determining how to act well. If he thought he could provide
this, why would he not set about doing so now? And when, in *NE* VI he does return
to the subject, it is still not to give the sort of guidance that his hearers might have
been hoping for. But might it not be that here in Book II he promises to do just that
because he imagines that after further investigation he will be able to deliver the
goods eluding him now, only to find out afterwards that they continue elusive? This
is to misunderstand the present passage. Here Aristotle clearly says that exact rules
of action are not possible: not that he has not yet got them at his fingertips. The
clinching point comes in the 'offer to help'. This is offered *instead* of the illusory
rules, not as prelude to a subsequent revelation of them.

From the standpoint of the *politikos* the difficulty now is this: even if, per impossible, he could bring about the well-functioning of others as if it were a product
directly under his control, no one operating at such a practical distance from the
circumstances of that functioning could know what form it should take on any occasion. He could not know *what* to try to bring about, if his task were to try to bring
about that. He must therefore have recourse to what would seem like a second best
if the other were not wholly impracticable: namely, to the goal of training others so
that they become *such as to* act in accordance with the *orthos logos,* whatever particular shape it happens to assume for any of the indefinitely varying situations an
agent might find himself facing. We might say that even if one were concerned only
that right or good actions get done, and attached no value to their being the free

expressions of autonomous agency, still in the end it could only be by allowing such autonomy that one would increase the incidence of right action. Such an expectation would assume, of course, that the available agents are indeed *such as to* act according to the *orthos logos*. And (also of course) the project of trying to develop such personalities makes sense only if the property of *being such as to* is more determinate (anyway in advance) than the property of *actually acting in accordance with the* orthos logos. The first must be determinate enough to set a recognisably approachable goal for the *politikos*. Merely being definable does not ensure this, for *actually acting according to the* orthos logos may well be definable in the sense that an analysis of the concept can be given. What is necessary, if there is to be any sense in aiming to make people *such as to* act in that way, is that we formulate this objective in an account with enough substantial content to enable us to decide whether some particular training or mode of development tends in that direction or not. It is just such an account that Aristotle hopes to provide in his famous doctrine of virtue as a mean. Whether he is successful is a question for later, when we consider the doctrine in detail. Meanwhile, having shown that his equating of 'well-functioning' with 'functioning in accordance with virtue' is by no means a trivial move, but indeed indispensable to his essentially practical inquiry, let us look more closely at the nature of human virtue.

## II. Division of the Soul (I)

What, then, is that virtue or excellence whereby a man functions well qua man? It is an excellence of soul, not body, since the functioning that concerns us is an activity of soul (1098 b 14–16). So the *politikos* ought to know something of psychology (1102 a 18 ff.). However, Aristotle continues, a detailed study of the soul is not necessary for this purpose. In fact, he says, we need only take account of an apparently already familiar division of the soul into a rational (or *logos*-having) part and a nonrational part. In the present context we can pass by metaphysical questions about the ontological status of these different sides of the soul. For instance, could they exist separately from each other? Is the whole soul a continuous something that can be divided as can the body? Are the so-called parts different aspects of something that integrally entails both, like the convex and concave sides of a curve? These questions are irrelevant for ethics (1102 a 28–32). All that concerns us now is a division between functions of the soul. To speak of the soul as if it were partitioned is simply a way of registering a difference of functions, and of capacities and types of excellence corresponding to those functions.

Aristotle's ethical psychology[3] is certainly not burdened with complexity. On the contrary, as we try to make sense of his account of the different kinds of virtue, we may well come to think that his anxiety to avoid academic questions of psychology may have led him to ignore distinctions significant for ethics. Indeed, what many have considered the most fundamental of all distinctions in ethics, that between judgments of fact and judgments of value, seems to have passed over Aristotle's head. True, there are passages in which his division between the two parts of the soul seems to reflect the modern distinction between those types of judgment; but we shall also find passages to warn us that if he did accept that distinction, he accepted it in such a confused way that it is more reasonable to regard him as not having recognised it at all.

Our immediate concern, however, is with the question 'What is it to be such as to function well as a human being?' And this, in effect, is the same as the question 'What is it to be such as to act in accordance with the *orthos* ( = right) *logos?*' It is unilluminating, Aristotle implies, to speak of rational functioning, and excellence of rational functioning, as if these were monolithic. In one sense, the phrase 'rational soul' refers to two types of function, both special to human beings. One of these is rational in a strict sense, whereas the other by contrast hardly seems to deserve the title 'rational' at all. It is clear, however, that a soul that was purely rational only in the strict sense, whatever it would be like, would not be that of a human being. Thus ethics must take account of the nonrational soul, too. Yet it would be a mistake to suppose that ethics should be concerned with all nonrational psychic functions. For instance, there is the function common to us and all living things: the body-animating activity which Aristotle calls 'growth and nutrition'. This biological level of life is not specifically human. It is a topic for physiology, not political reflection. For it is not on account of our body's ability to digest or to repair its tissue that we are considered good or bad human beings (1102 a 33–b 12). On the other hand, such assessments are not reserved for our purely intellectual performance. They apply to us as agents. And from this point of view, we are assessed not only as thinkers (since practical thinking is an aspect of agency), but as subjects of desires and feelings which issue in action.

Now this sensitive, desiderative and emotional part of the human soul is not strictly rational; but Aristotle insists that it is not simply nonrational either. Its function, he says, is to 'listen to reason'. Thus it 'partakes of reason in a sense' (1102 b 13–14). Despite the Platonic associations of this phrase, he is not saying that it is rational by weakly imitating the strictly rational part, so that its functioning would be a kind of shadow of the strictly rational exercise. He means that in human beings the functioning of the desiderative part is to be defined by reference to its relation to the strictly rational function. In this respect it differs from the human soul's nutritive part, and also from the desiderative part of nonrational animals. The human nutritive faculty is human only in the sense of being essential to all life, and therefore to human life. But it is not defined by its relation to any specifically human faculty, and so it may be said to be formally the same in human and subhuman organisms. Now, in a sense desire, too, is common to a wider class of creatures than man, for according to Aristotle's biological classification, sense perception and desire are universal in animals. But according to the division of the *Ethics,* the fact that dogs, fishes and human beings may all be described as desiderative creatures does not entail that they share something formally the same. For the essence of human desideration is different, it being defined in terms of a functional relationship possible only for creatures rational in the strict sense.

〔 Ethics, then, for Aristotle is concerned with the well-functioning of the rational side of the soul, 'rational' being meant broadly so that not only the strictly rational part, but also the reason-responsive part, is dignified by the title. The virtues to be investigated are the qualities whereby each of these functions as it should. This conception of a complex whole in which one part is not reason, but is essentially related to reason as that to which it should respond, lies at the heart of Aristotle's ethics. So far, however, the difference and relation of these parts have been only schematically indicated. We should now turn to the ambiguities of Aristotle's more concrete presentation.

He introduces the difference between the two ethical parts of the soul by pointing to the fact of conflict. We often have impulses going contrary to reason, and this is the basis of continence and incontinence (containing the impulse or surrendering).

> We praise the reason of the continent man and of the incontinent, and the part of their soul that has reason, since it urges them aright and towards the best objects; but there is found in them also another natural element beside reason, which fights against and resists it. For exactly as paralysed limbs when we choose to move them to the right turn on the contrary to the left, so is it with the soul; the impulses of incontinent people move in contrary directions. But while in the body we see that which moves astray, in the soul we do not. No doubt, however, we must none the less suppose that in the soul too there is something beside reason, resisting and opposing it. In what sense it is distinct from the other elements does not concern us. Now even this seems to have a share in reason, as we said; at any rate in the continent man it obeys reason—and presumably in the temperate and brave man it is still more obedient; for in them it speaks, on all matters, with the same voice as reason (1102 b 14–28).

And in case anyone should think that this is an intellectual 'listening to reason', he says: 'The appetitive and in general the desiring element in a sense shares in [reason], in so far as it listens to and obeys it; this is the sense in which we speak of paying heed to one's father or one's friends, not that in which we speak of 'the rational' in mathematics' (1102 b 30–33). But this allusion to respect for paternal authority quickly ceases to be metaphor. Aristotle points to the actual exercise of authority in family or community as providing further evidence that there exists a part of the soul capable of listening to reason: 'That the non-rational element is in some sense persuaded by reason is indicated also by the giving of advice and by all reproof and exhortation' (1102 b 33–1103 a 1). The reference to *every* sort of reproof etc. cancels any suggestion that he has in mind only *self*-admonition, *self*-reproach and the rest. He is squarely considering paradigm cases where the parties are distinct individuals. But what, except metaphorically, has this to tell us of a relation *within* the soul of a single person? And how can the literal material of the metaphor 'indicate' that what the metaphor illustrates is true?

A tangle of considerations lies behind this transition, and they do not all pull in the same direction. There is the need to represent the soul as capable of moral development; there is also a need to justify the proposed account of what the goal of such development should be. The child's obedient response to parental admonition is, in a sense, of identical nature with the response made to internal reason by the nonrational rational part of the mature soul. For the first is *potentially* the second: which is a closer relation than that of mere analogy. It is also a more important relation from the practical point of view. That a virtuous soul *can be developed* is the presupposition of Aristotle's whole inquiry, but as yet he has said nothing about how it develops, or from what. The internal conflicts of continent and incontinent individuals may prove the soul's dual nature, but they shed no light on the question of how to attain that virtue which is less like continence or incontinence than they are like each other. For virtue is a harmony of right reason and desire, but both continence and incontinence involve desire at odds with reason. That this dissension can happen at all may lead us to suppose the desiderative part incapable not only of moderating itself, but even of falling in with reason though the message of reason is perhaps quite vividly present. So how can there be a source *within* the individual soul from which virtue could develop? But if virtue arose spontaneously from within, the virtuous would all have become so by nature, given the luck of unimpeded development. The facts, however, tell the opposite story. We are brought up to be good by others: our elders and (for the time being) betters. So at least there is something in us capable of accepting their authority. And that something must be the same or at least continuous with that in us which later accepts the precepts of our own internal reason. For how, unless by supposing this identity or continuity, how can we make sense of the fact that adult virtue has its roots in childhood training?

What is more, it would show a misunderstanding of 'externality' to insist that a guardian's relation to an immature person is only a metaphor for the relation between the two parts of the adult soul, on the ground that in the one case the prescription comes from outside, and in the other from within. While there are obvious reasons for calling the parent or guardian an 'external authority', he or she is also *not* external in the sense in which this term, when applied to relations, suggests a connection between distinct metaphysically complete individuals. In Aristotle's ontology, a child or childlike member of the species is not a complete human substance; it could no more ethically exist apart from guardian or guide than a foetus physically could from the mother-animal.

There is, I suggested, more than one consideration prompting Aristotle to declare that our amenability to *external* admonition proves the existence, *within* the soul, of a nonrational element capable of responding to reason. Now, with regard to his concern for the possibilities of ethical development, any identification (via the concept of potentiality) of virtuous adult with obedient child must allow for just those differences in the child which the development is supposed to overcome. We may also, however, see the declaration as an attempt to defend his bipartite division in its application to the morally develop*ed* soul. And from this point of view any relevant differences between the autonomous reason-heeding capacity of the mature agent, and the child's responsiveness to parental authority, are likely to be ignored. This is because, for Aristotle, the duality of the human soul is not simply the symptom or result of its imperfection. On the contrary, human virtue, when achieved, is precisely an excellence of reason and feeling in partnership. Analytically, then, human virtue breaks down into two coordinated kinds of excellence, one for each part. Thus the acme of moral development is not a state in which one part has been sloughed off or has merged into the other. Nothing could be further from the truth as Aristotle saw it. Yet just such a view had been put forward by Socrates or the early Plato, and even though Plato himself broke away, the type of view holds perennial attraction. According to it, the best soul is one in which everything but reason or intellect has been effaced. As Socrates said in the *Phaedo,* it is as if the person, if so he can be called, had already taken his departure from the world of emotion and sense. After all, Socrates was not looking forward to his own biological death as such, since bodily existence in itself is neither bad nor good; he, the philosopher, was pleased to die because the biological connection feeds the activity of the desiderative and emotional part of the soul, and this obstructs the best life, which is the life of reason.

This outlook, of course, makes the huge assumption that feeling and emotion cannot stand in a good relation to reason: if present at all, they disrupt. Surely, then, it is easy to dismiss that Socratic ideal of intellectual activity disengaged from most of what makes us human, on the ground that we are not compelled to grant its premiss. But this is not so easy, as Aristotle must surely have realised, when the main if not only argument for diversity within the soul consists in an appeal to the fact that sometimes we desire the contrary of what reason prescribes. Plato had used this powerful argument in the *Republic,* and Aristotle is happy to use it again. But it is logically disturbing to realise that in this case, as perhaps in no other, our conception of a so and so (in this case, a human soul) is drawn largely from consideration of degenerate instances of so and so. For as Aristotle says, in a *virtuous* soul the nonrational part 'speaks, on all matters, with the same voice as reason' (1102 b 28). But this means that if we were to examine the perfectly integrated functioning of a virtuous soul, we should never from that be able to tell that it is an integration of distinct elements rather than a uniform unity. So now the way is open for someone to object that any argument for psychic complexity based on the phenomena of continence and incontinence falls short of proving anything more than that imperfect souls of conflicted people are complex. More particularly, these phenomena provide no defence against the suggestion that the virtuous soul has achieved its unity simply by eliminating one party to the conflict. And if this were so, effective moral education would not be at all the kind of process that Aristotle understands it to be.

Much, then, hangs on being able to show that a relationship can exist between reason and something to which reason addresses its precepts that has the following features: (1) addresser and addressee are clearly other than each other; (2) they are clearly in harmony. This pair of conditions is seen to be fulfilled by the relationship between *external* authority and *willingly obedient* respondent. The possibility of such a relationship shows that there is in human beings something capable of heeding reason though not itself the rational source. And so we now have no ground for refusing to accept that such a distinct capacity is present and operative even when the source of reason lies within the same self, and that self is in self-harmony.

As I noted above, the force of these considerations depends on our attention's being confined to points actually common between the two cases. For instance, it would be a mistake, from the present point of view, to suggest that the child may be only potentially, or only imperfectly, in harmony with its guardian, for this would throw us back against the objection that perhaps the inner distinction between guide and guided is inapplicable except in cases of incomplete coordination.

In effect, then, we must, in this context, forget all but those cases of external authority in which orders are given to a person already totally identified with the rôle of one who does as he is told. But now it seems that the ideal relation of the parts of the soul is not at all like that of child and parent; it is more like that of a general and his troops or a craftsman and his instrument. The latter relation is (or is akin to) *using,* whereas the parental relation is that of *being in charge of.* But this goes unnoticed as long as one is content to employ such abstract terms as 'prescribe', 'control' and 'authority' to explain indifferently various potential and actual relations between elements of the soul or elements of society. In fact, these terms make distinct points depending on whether the relation meant is that of controlling in the sense of 'determining', or controlling in the sense of 'bringing under control'. On the one hand, we have the supplying of definite direction to some element which in itself takes no initiative but is ready to follow or fall in with any that authority indicates. On the other hand, and at the opposite end of the scale of ethical development, there is the authority of the parent or guardian who in getting its charge to behave in a certain way not only guides its behaviour into this new direction but thereby teaches, or, as Aristotle might prefer to say, 'persuades', the other to *accept* such guidance at all. And the authority may further intervene so as to reinforce such acceptance. Such a move, like the initial move of bringing under control, is logically excluded from taking place between the parts of the soul of the virtuous agent.

The difference shows itself both in the state (one might almost say, the contents), of the nonrational partner in each case, and in the manner in which the authoritative partner operates. A child can be brought to a state of obedient attention from the midst of 'wild' activity whose direction follows his natural presocialised needs and impulses. He is told to behave himself in a certain way, and in complying he stops or refrains from doing what he otherwise would. The command moreover is presented in such a way as to elicit *willing* attention. Thus what Aristotle calls 'persuasion' is in order, by which he means something which is neither reasoned argument, nor the application of force, nor, I believe, the straightforward association of pain or pleasure with noncompliance or compliance. Of this more later, but to give some slight indication, such time-honoured (surely in all cultures) encouragements as 'Do it—for me' and 'Be a good boy (girl) and do it' would be examples. And admonition, exhortation and reproof have their place on this level, together with the gamut of familiar feelings and gestures surrounding these transactions on either side.

But with the harmonious virtuous individual, such persuasion and exhortation, even in their self-reflexive versions, are no part of the picture, because the nonrational element, ideally at least, is never not immediately at the ready to fall in with and lend its energy to any project prescribed by the internal analogue of authority. Carrying out the prescription does not involve an initial calling to heel, a dislodging from some already definite ongoing trajectory dictated by the more primitive side of human nature. For in the virtuous person's case the nonrational element is already listening *for* some change of direction by reason, even before there are specific instructions which it can listen *to.* It is as if the nonrational part is, from itself, a practical tabula rasa. This is not to say that it is not the scene of sensations and emotions often identical with those felt by the merely continent individual who does have to bring himself to order, or by the incontinent one, or even on occasion, perhaps, by the untrained child. But in the virtuous person such feelings appear only as feelings and not as incipient actions. In the absence of *rational* opposition to the projects prescribed by reason, it is enough for performance if reason merely articulates those projects: it does not need to bang the board. Indeed, reason as such can *only* articulate, and in this respect its function is not at all like that of a parental authority. In itself it has no power to bring to order or get itself heard from being unheard within the soul. As Aristotle puts it:

> Now if arguments were in themselves enough to make men good, they would justly, as Theognis says, have won very great rewards, and such rewards should have been provided; but as things are, while they seem to have power to encourage and stimulate the generous-minded among the young, and to make a character which is gently born, and a true lover of what is noble, ready to be possessed by excellence, they are not able to encourage the many to nobility and goodness. For these do not by nature obey the sense of shame, but only fear, and do not abstain from bad acts because of their baseness but through fear of punishment; living by passion they pursue their own pleasures and the means to them, and avoid the opposite pains, and have not even a conception of what is noble and truly pleasant, since they have never tasted it. What argument would remould such people? It is hard, if not impossible, to remove by argument the traits that have long since been incorporated in the character. (1179 b 4–17)

### III. Division of the Soul (II)

We have been examining some of the ambiguities surrounding Aristotle's attempt to conceptualise the relation of reason to nonreason in the ethical soul in terms of an authority relation. So far the difficulties have mainly involved his notion of the nonrational, reason-responsive element. We must now turn to the role of reason in all this. And the first point to note as we look again at Aristotle's willingness to invoke the phenomena of continence and incontinence in order to argue that the soul is complex, is the way in which, on this view, we are precluded from seeing reason in anything but a good light. The only psychic malfunctioning mentioned in the passages which we have examined is the disorder resulting from feeling's recalcitrance to reason. Aristotle writes here as if all is well when reason is in full control: we then have true virtue such as courage and temperance (1102 b 27–28). But that is so only if reason's directions are not merely followed without murmur but are the right directions. Taken alone, these passages give the impression that Aristotle uses 'having reason' or 'strictly rational' to label a part of the soul that is infallible in its moral or practical choices.

Later, however, and especially in the detailed discussion of incontinence in *NE* VII, Aristotle makes it clear that the prescription in the soul may be misguided, reflect the wrong values; and that this is a worse fault even than the unruliness of incontinence. And *NE* VI, too, makes it clear that a bad or wicked prescription may be as ingeniously *reasoned* as a blameless one. Once we see this we start to raise questions which the early model of wise authority scarcely allows. For instance: if the rational prescriber within the soul can be misguided, but nonetheless is still properly called 'rational', what is the difference between its being misguided and not? However one tries to answer that question, the prescriptive part of the soul is going to be revealed as internally complex, since it would seem that the good and the bad cases have a common rational structure but different moral content.

To pursue these complexities in the necessary detail would take us too far from Aristotle's own order of exposition. But a sketch is useful at this point, for the following reason. We are about to follow him into his examination of the virtues of the nonrational but reason-responsive part of the soul. This way of dividing up the subject-matter gives the impression that the excellences of the rational part will be the topic of a different inquiry. And indeed this other inquiry, concerning practical wisdom, is held in *NE* VI. But in the course of reading Book VI, and not before, we discover that a discussion of virtues belonging to the so-called rational part, as this first figures in Book I, has started a long way back. It has already started with the inquiry in Book II into the virtues of the *responsive* part. For it turns out that the rational prescriber within the soul is a locus of two sorts of virtues: one of these sorts is properly called 'intellectual'; but the other, or its various species, go by the same names, and are inculcated by the same means, as the virtues of the part that is nonrational but responsive.

This is because the rational prescriber is more than pure reason. It is the faculty of deliberation and decision: that by which we can consider what to do as distinct from acting on impulse. One has reasons for a decision, and can justify and explain the action to others by communicating the reasons. This is evidently 'rational' activity by contrast with the mere having of feelings, reacting to stimuli, being carried by impulse. But this practical rational activity is no more purely rational or intellectual than is the rational activity of theorising about the empirical world. Just as the latter combines empirical and contingently given elements with formal and a priori elements, so practical reasoning applies structures of argument to experiential matter. Were it not for this, no rational prescription could be formed to *be* either smoothly obeyed or chafed against by the reason-responsive element. Now, the relevant content, in this, the practical, case, is partly experience of the way things are, but partly also our interests, moral concerns and values. The prescription issued reflects the agent's evaluative priorities, or it would not be a practical prescription at all. And it is above all in respect of their evaluations, as distinct from the more purely ratiocinative side of the rational-practical process, that good people differ from bad. The question of how to generate sound values is consequently of vital concern to Aristotle's *politikos*. So, of course, is the question of how to generate the obedience that willingly executes reasoned decisions reflecting those values. Considered in terms of psychic functions these two practical questions seem to be concerned with quite different types or levels of virtue. But it seems that the *politikos* can kill two birds with one stone. For the qualities whereby the prescribing part of the soul prescribes in the light of proper values, and the qualities whereby the supposedly responsive part responds without trouble to prescription, are cultivated by the self-same process of upbringing (see Section X below). Thus from the practical standpoint which asks 'How do we produce them?' the two sets of qualities are identical. These are the qualities known as the virtues of character or 'moral' virtues: courage, temperance, justice and the like.

So what Aristotle has called the rational part of the soul 'strictly speaking', has two aspects: one, the yet more narrowly rational ratiocinative side, while the other, the evaluative, shows kinship with what has been termed the nonrational but reason-responsive part. We should not be surprised to find Aristotle shifting his terminology to accommodate this distinction. For example, at 1102 b 30–31 he uses the word 'desiderative' *(orektikon)* to mark off the reason-responsive part from the prescriptive. But in *NE* III and VI, where he analyses the rational prescription itself, 'desideration' is an element in its definition, and 'reason' or 'thought' now means not the entire faculty of prescription, but one distinguishable aspect of it.[4]

What, however, one would not expect is that Aristotle should fail to distinguish between the two distinctions, or, if one prefers, between the two relations: (1) that of prescriber to respondent, and (2) that of ratiocination to evaluation within the prescriber. Yet just on the verge of launching his account of the development of the virtues, he speaks as if these relations are the same. Summing up the divisions of the soul, he recalls the primary distinction between what is and what is not rational in the broadest sense, which excludes as nonrational only the nutritive faculty. He then repeats that this broadly speaking rational part in turn consists of two parts related as parent to child: 'That which has reason also will be twofold, one subdivision having it in the strict sense and in itself, and the other having a tendency to obey as one does one's father' (1103 a 1–3). He then immediately continues:

> Excellence too is distinguished into kinds *in accordance with this difference;* for we say that some excellences are intellectual and others moral, philosophic wisdom and understanding and practical wisdom being intellectual, liberality and temperance moral. For in speaking about a man's character we do not say that he is wise or has understanding but that he is good-tempered or temperate. (1103 a 3–8; italics mine)

From the modern point of view the entire passage presents a disconcerting combination of ideas. On the one hand, the famous division of virtues, along with the corresponding division of soul into intellect (or mind) and character, seems intended to correspond to the distinction between reason and desire. Here, then, Aristotle seems to be reaching towards the Humean contrast of reason and sentiment and, through this, towards the correlative contrast of judgments of fact with judgments of value. On the other hand (as Hume clearly saw), from this point of view reason-as-an-authority-figure, i.e. reason as represented by an evaluative prescription, no more deserves the title 'reason' than does the lowly respondent which, when good, is represented by the equally evaluative *acceptance* of that prescription.

Taken by itself, Aristotle's division of virtues into virtues of character and those of intellect seems to be a move in the direction of clarity. It is also, we should note, a move that saves the purely theoretical intellect from falling outside the bounds of ethics.[5] For if 'reason' and 'intellect' were to go on being used to refer to that which rationally prescribes some course of conduct, then for the purpose of ethics theoretical reason will fail to count as 'reason' at all, and its excellence is no more a matter of proper concern to the *politikos* than the health of the digestive system. Perhaps Aristotle would prefer to avoid this conclusion even at the cost of compromising what previously seemed a satisfactory division. So at 1103 a 4–6 'intellect' now comes to mean intellect as such. On these terms, practical reason enters the picture no longer as the rational prescriber considered *in concreto,* but as the intellectual side of this considered in abstraction.

Now it probably seems obvious to us that one cannot logically adopt the new division without giving up the old; and in particular, that shifting to the new one requires abandoning the image of the nonrational part of the soul as that which is supposed to listen to *reason as to a father*. For according to the new conception of reason, or intellect, the 'father' is *not* reason just to the extent that his prescription has a specific evaluative content. But in the passage last quoted, the child-versus-father image is not only retained: as the italicised words in the passage show, it is *equated with* the new concept of character as contrasted with intellect. This is disturbing. Can we expect coherent results from Aristotle's inquiry into the nature of virtue, when the starting point here is as confused as we have just seen it to be?

I would respond by saying in the first place that it is helpful for the purpose of analysis to present the thought of the above passage as if it had resulted from the superimposition of one conceptual scheme upon another. That such an analysis is possible also helps to explain why the interpretation of Aristotle's ethical psychology has proved as deeply problematic as the vast quantity of commentary testifies. Secondly, however, reflection may lead us to a perspective from which Aristotle turns out to be less confused than the above exposition would suggest. It is possible to interpret the shift of focus just analysed as much less radical than it is bound to appear to anyone approaching this topic from a grounding in classical modern ethics, and above all the ethics of Hume. Here I shall touch briefly on points to which I shall return in more detail later when examining Aristotle's full discussions of practical reason and incontinence.

From Hume's point of view, Aristotle, following Plato, begins by making the classic mistake of assuming that reason and desire are a pair which it makes sense to treat as possibly *opposed*. According to Hume, reason is concerned only with causal and logical reasoning and the holding of factual and logical beliefs; and whereas belief can be contrary to belief, desire to desire, no belief can be contrary to a desire. However, it then appears that Aristotle changes course within a very short space: his division of the virtues into those of character and those of intellect suggests that he now demarcates reason in a way which Hume would approve. Unfortunately, though, it then appears that far from having seen the light, Aristotle compounds his original blunder by equating it with the new, correct, position.

Let us now sketch a different approach, starting from what is admittedly an oversimple analysis of what I have been calling the 'rational prescription'. The rational prescription is a system of three elements: (1) a practical interest in some end; (2) a picture of the particular factual situation as the self-prescribing agent sees it; (3) a grasp of logical and causal connections relating the realisation of the end to some action possible for the agent in the factual situation as pictured by him. Thus a prescription to do X is not the flat imperative 'Do X!': it is a prescription to do X given that the end is S, the situation is T, and the world (as the agent understands it) is such that in T, S is more likely to result if X is done. Now let us also suppose that in addition to the prescription, there also arises in the agent (4) an impulse or emotion whose natural expression in action would, under the circumstances, preclude his doing X.

Hume sets (2) and (3) together on one side over against (1), and having effected this isolation of (1) from the other components of the prescription, he argues that whereas (1) may be said, under the circumstances, to be opposed to (4), this cannot be said of (2) and (3). His ground for treating (4) as sufficiently similar in nature to (1) for it to make sense to say that they are opposed is that (1) and (4) share the very abstract characteristic of being tendencies towards action. Both are desires or 'passions', although he has to concede that (1) by contrast with (4) might be a 'calm passion'.

The Aristotelian view, on the other hand, ranges (1), (2) and (3) together, uniting them through the shared possibility of their forming a whole at odds with (4). From this point of view, (1), (2) and (3) have more in common with each other than any of them has with (4).

To understand this unity of such disparate items as (1), (2) and (3), we must take it that the psychological faculties exercised in agency form a system of organically related parts teleologically geared to action. It is hardly surprising that Aristotle should hold such a view. One implication is that if, through (4), the agent fails to execute his self-prescription, then not only is (1) opposed and defeated, but (2) and (3) (or the corresponding faculties) are also in a sense *frustrated.* The capacity to attend to logical and causal connections as applied to particulars, and to work out ways and means, exists so that ends be achieved that could not be otherwise. The capacity to notice the particulars themselves exists for the same general purpose. If the agent fails to enact the prescription, all its elements are alike in vain and wasted.

Not only can (4) frustrate (render pointless the actual functioning of) the capacities represented by (2) and (3); it can also obstruct their functioning. In general, an agent's grasp of connections and particular circumstances is a grasp by someone out to realise some end. But if an emotion or desire for immediate satisfaction takes hold of his interest, he will not be fully alive to facts and connections relevant to achieving a more distant end, unless, of course, they happen also to be relevant to satisfying the immediate drive. But the more the object of the drive appears to be immediately obtainable, the less will the agent controlled by this drive take cognitive note of anything in his situation apart from the object itself.[6] Thus (4) equally threatens (1), (2) and (3) by threatening the very possibility of a prescription analysable into these elements. From this point of view, the resemblance of (1) and (4) which so struck Hume (they are both desires) seems insignificant, as does their common difference from (2) and (3). This, I think, helps explain why Aristotle does not fuss over the difference between what to us look like two importantly different distinctions.

To summarise crudely, so as to be brief: Aristotle divides the soul into a non-rational desiderative part which is supposed to be responsive to reason and a rational part which prescribes to the former. He also divides the virtues into virtues of character and virtues of intellect. These distinctions do not coincide, although, as we have seen, Aristotle at one point writes as if they do (1103 a 1–15) and nowhere brings it to our attention that they do not. Coincidence fails because the prescriptive part turns out to be desiderative in its own right, as well as cognitive and ratiocinative. The virtues of character are virtues of the desiderative: that is to say, they are virtues of the reason-responsive part of the soul, but also of the prescriptive part qua desiderative. Consequently, any strictly distinct and contrasting virtues of mind or intellect would have to do with the latter's ratiocinative and cognitive aspects only.[7] They would not belong to the prescriptive part as a whole, so to speak, and virtues of character do not belong only to the responsive part. Hence the distinctions' failure to coincide. But now if we look at things with a Humean eye, the basic dualism is between intellect (as in 'virtues of intellect') and desire. From this point of view it seems extraordinary that a philosopher should tend to conflate the distinctions. For that is like conflating a compound (the prescription) of desiderative and cognitive-intellectual with the so to speak purely cognitive-intellectual. How could this happen if (as the view implies) an item such as (1) above has no more natural affinity with items such as (2) and (3) than (4) has with (2) and (3)? But on Aristotle's view, (1), (2) and (3) are in a sense made for each other, so (4) is their common enemy. It is therefore less surprising that he speaks of the whole that they form as 'reason' or as 'intellect'—terms which strictly refer to just one aspect of that whole.

## IV. Preliminaries on the Development of Virtue

We have already had occasion to emphasise that the point of view from which Aristotle considers the virtues is that of practical concern for their development and preservation. It is hardly too much to say that, for him, the question of what the virtues are is at least in part the question of how they may be inculcated. Thus we should be ready to treat an account of their origin as by no means an external causal statement. Aristotle sees himself as already beginning to say what the virtues essentially are when he opens the inquiry about them with these words:

> Excellence, then being of two kinds, intellectual and moral, intellectual excellence in the main owes both its birth and its growth to teaching (for which reason it requires experience and time), while moral excellence [ēthikē aretē] comes about as a result of habit [or usage; ēthos], whence also its name is one that is formed by a slight variation from the word for 'habit'. (1103 a 14–18)

For the rest of this chapter we shall be specifically concerned with the excellences of character, so called: courage, temperance, gentleness and the like. Even etymology seems to support the point that the nature of these qualities reflects the process by which they are inculcated (although one can accept the point without accepting the etymology). Hence it would seem that our first question should be: What is that process, having to do with *habit* (or *usage* or *custom*), which gives rise to the virtues of character?

Aristotle's account of the process seems true as far as it goes, but it leaves important questions unanswered. In summary, he says that we become brave or just by behaving as the brave or the just person would behave (1103 a 31ff.). What he does not make clear is *how* by engaging in the behaviour we come to develop the virtuous disposition expressed by that sort of behaviour. This means that his conception of the virtuous disposition is open to different interpretations, depending on how we think he conceives of the process through which it arises.[8] Is it that by doing brave things we get better and better at doing them, in the same way as we acquire skills—through practising? Or is it that by doing brave things enough times, we acquire a habit of doing them automatically? In other words, is the brave man an *expert,* so to speak, at performing brave actions? Or is it more as if he is *addicted* to performing them? Aristotle has a few remarks suggesting each of these interpretations, but he also makes it clear that neither skill nor habit has all the features of ethical virtue. What are the features? As I have indicated, his sketch of how such virtue is acquired is presumably intended to explain in part what it is; but in fact it sheds very little light on that question. Really the case is the other way round: we need to take an independent survey of what (for Aristotle) virtue of character *is* in order to fill in some of the gaps in his account of the process of *acquiring* it.

But first let us see what can be gathered from the contrast with 'teaching', the name which Aristotle gives to the process that develops virtues of intellect. If this were clear it would be of some help in interpreting the other member of the contrast. Unfortunately, it is not all that clear. This is partly because we are not told whether he has in mind mainly the teaching of theoretical science, of technical accomplishments, or of some kind of nontechnical subject matter especially connected with practical life. Nor is it easy to interpret his remark that since virtue of intellect arises from teaching it needs time and experience. Coming where it does in the passage, this seems to be intended as a point of contrast with virtue of character. But the contrast can hardly be that the learner needs time and experience *as a learner* to acquire the virtues of intellect. For Aristotle would surely agree that it takes time and experience to acquire the virtues of character. So his meaning must be that for virtues of intellect, time and experience are needed *before that instruction can begin* by which those qualities are developed. This suggests that Aristotle has in mind practical wisdom (and perhaps nonformal theoretical skills), since elsewhere he says that young persons may shine in mathematical studies, whereas practical wisdom needs experience (1142 a 12–15). At any rate, on this interpretation of the 'need for time and experience' we have a clear contrast with virtues of character: the implication is that *they* are such that from earliest youth no time should be lost before inculcation begins.

The purpose and methods of the teaching that develops the virtues of intellect must remain obscure as long as it is not stated what sorts of things are taught. But we can say this much about any process that Aristotle would call 'teaching': its purpose is that the learner should not only learn to give the right answers or construct the desired product, but should understand the reasons why the moves are correct, be able to apply any principles he learns to new kinds of case, and also himself know how to explain these things, giving reasons. And reason-giving is not only part of the result at which teaching aims, it is essential to the method of teaching. But the training of character, as Aristotle understands it, aims to create dispositions to *act* properly. The ability to understand why what is right is right is not an essential part of that goal, which will have been achieved if the subject comes to have such dispositions whether or not he can also explain to himself and others why what is right is right. Similarly, such reason-giving is not a necessary part of the training process.

This may give the impression that Aristotle's brave or temperate person is one who does not know, and does not consider, why he should do as he does, but simply does it, devotedly, or even, as some say, blindly. We shall return to this question when considering Aristotle's remarks about the frame of mind in which the virtuous agent acts. At present it is enough to say that whereas acting from courage is certainly not inconsistent with understanding why the action is right, this understanding or ability to give a reason is itself not an aspect nor an expression of courage.

But Aristotle would not contrast the methods of inculcating the different types of virtues if he did not also see much in common. First, for instance, neither type belongs to us by nature, since were this so we should not need teaching or training. Second, not only are they not part of the genetic endowment, but they are not just haphazardly picked up either, as a child may pick up the language of those round it without directed efforts on either side. This may be true of various *bad* qualities, whether of character or intellect, but not of the virtues any more than of skills or branches of theoretical knowledge. Third, the virtues are not simply acquisitions or adjuncts to our nature, present in us as qualities of a determinate substance. When a substance comes to have some new quality, this is because it has been altered; which is to say that a new quality has been acquired in place of a previous one. Although alteration presupposes the prior absence of the quality changed to, the change is not primarily from not having to having a certain quality, but from one quality positively conceived to another. Acquiring a virtue, on the other hand (or, for that matter, a skill or a theoretical mastery), is not an alteration, but a perfecting or completing of our nature (1103 a 25). What the new state replaces is not a positive contrary of itself, but only the potentiality for the positive new state. Fourth, even if it is not precisely the aim of teaching to produce new teachers, a pupil's attaining the point where he in turn can teach the same things is the sign that his own teacher has succeeded. Similarly, those who rear children in the moral virtues are aiming to produce a generation of autonomous moral agents capable of relaying the same values to their own children.

## V. Virtue of Character and the *Orthos Logos*

To the question 'What is excellence of character?' Aristotle gives a concentrated answer in his famous definition:

> Excellence . . . is a state concerned with choice, lying in a mean relative to us, this being determined by a *logos* and in the way in which the man of practical wisdom would determine it. Now it is a mean between two vices, that which depends on excess and that which depends on defect; and again it is a mean because the vices respectively fall short of or exceed what is right in both passions and actions, while excellence both finds and chooses that which is intermediate. (1106 b 36–1107 a 5)

In the discussion which follows I shall focus mainly on the three terms *logos* (or, as often elsewhere, *orthos logos*); 'concerned with choice'; and 'mean'.

Let us begin by taking it that an excellence of character, such as courage, is the property of being *such as to* respond well or appropriately to a certain sort of situation: e.g., a dangerous situation. Now, a good or appropriate response is not necessarily an excellent one. Excellence or virtue, like skill or expertise, distinguishes its possessor from the common run; hence an appropriate response would not indicate virtue in the subject if it was easy or straightforward or to be taken for granted; or if anyone would or could make it. Thus situations in which excellence is actually manifested have two sets of features: (1) those on account of which the appropriate response is in fact appropriate, and (2) those whose presence makes the giving of the appropriate response something of an achievement. Among the features belonging under (2) are ones likely to cause, let us say in the average person, emotions and impulses that would naturally tend to block an appropriate response or to undermine its effectiveness. Virtue of character is a disposition such that those emotions and impulses either do not arise or do not have their normal effect when this would endanger the proper response. A number of excellences may be distinguished—e.g., courage and temperance—corresponding to the different kinds of potentially obstructive feelings: fear, physical appetites and so on.

The response need not be strictly practical. Aristotle, of course, treats the virtues as dispositions to act and behave, but he is equally interested in them as dispositions to *feel* appropriately. Partly this is because feeling often directly issues in action, which is then the focus of judgments of appropriateness. But Aristotle is also concerned with appropriate and inappropriate feeling on its own account. In this he would surely be right, since feeling and lack of feeling manifest character no less than action and failure to act. It would be absurd to draw the boundaries of the concept of morally significant response so narrowly that our reactions to the conduct of agents beyond our control, or our feelings about some course of action which we had to decide not to take, say nothing about us morally. This carries an important implication concerning the ethical value of action. Let us roughly characterise the difference between an action and a "mere" feeling by stating that action essentially makes changes in the external world, some of them intended by the agent. Now if feelings have ethical significance, it would seem that actions are of ethical significance not because of their external effects, but because of the difference it makes regarding the *agent* that he so acts. The action, like the feeling, matters as expressing *him* in response to his situation, and to be someone who responds appropriately is per se desirable, whether the response be in action, feeling or thought.

It may be objected to Aristotle that we cannot be fairly assessed on the basis of our feelings but only of our actions, since we cannot will to feel or cease feeling something, whereas we can will to act or not act. A full discussion would take us into the topic of the voluntary, Aristotle's complex treatment of which is the subject of the next chapter. Meanwhile, we can say that if by 'willing' is meant 'choosing between envisaged alternatives' then even on the level of action not everything is willed, and moral assessment is not confined to what is. In this sense of 'will', neither the surge of angry feeling nor the angry blow is willed, and although in general it may be possible to will to deliver a blow, it may not have been possible for the angry agent.

In explaining that excellence is a *state* (or disposition), Aristotle focuses on its relation to *feeling:*

> Since things that are found in the soul are of three kinds—passions, faculties, states—excellence must be one of these. By passion I mean appetite, anger, fear, confidence, envy, joy, love, hatred, longing, emulation, pity, and in general the feelings that are accompanied by pleasure or pain; by faculties the things in virtue of which we are said to be capable of feeling these, e.g. of becoming angry or being

pained or feeling pity; by states the things in virtue of which we stand well or badly with reference to the passions, e.g. with reference to anger we stand badly if we feel it too violently or feel weakly, and well if we feel it moderately; and similarly with reference to the other passions. (1105 b 19–28)

He goes on to argue that since a virtue is neither a feeling nor a capacity for feeling, it must be a state whereby we feel as is right or proper to feel; for instance, neither too intensely nor too weakly.

Then what sort of response is appropriate? There seems to be no kind of feeling, e.g. loving or hating, nor any kind of action, say helping or hindering, that is always the right response, and its contrary always wrong:

both fear and confidence and appetite and anger and pity and in general pleasure and pain may be felt both too much and too little, and in both cases not well; but to feel them at the right times, with reference to the right objects, towards the right people, with the right consequences and in the right way, is what is both intermediate and best, and this is characteristic of excellence. Similarly with regard to actions also ... (1106 b 18–23)

It does not follow, of course, that if some kind of object is specified, or some kind of consequence, a universal rule would not result. Thus it may be held that though killing is not always wrong, killing a parent always is (Aristotle, at one point, comes close to saying just this [1110 a 26–29]); or that even though killing is only sometimes right, killing for the sake of the greatest happiness is always right. However, Aristotle holds, as we have seen, that there are no definitive rules; thus no general description of the action or feeling, even if filled in with general descriptions of its object and its circumstances, provides a model to be reliably followed. All that Aristotle can say in general about the appropriate response is that it is whatever response would be given by the 'man of practical wisdom' apprised of the situation in all its particularity (cf. 1141 b 14–16).

For the moment we are not concerned with the problem of defining or even recognising the man of practical wisdom. The point is that he figures in the *Ethics* as the personification of that ungeneralisable *orthos logos* that is the form of an appropriate response. How should we understand this phrase—never neatly trans- latable, because almost always more than one of its related meanings is operative at a time? One pertinent meaning (to start with) is 'right proportion', since Aristotle tends to group all faulty responses under the heading of 'too much or too little'. Extrapolating from the category of quantity, we may then say that the *orthos logos* is the set of correct determinations of an abstractly considered action or feeling; i.e., its determinations in respect of object, time, place, circumstances etc. However, *'orthos logos'* may also refer to a good reason that might be given to explain or justify one's reaction. 'Why angrier with *him* than with him?' 'Because *he* had encouraged me to trust him, the other had not'. We see from this that the ungeneralisability of the *orthos logos* into a rule does not entail that it cannot be articulated by means of statements employing general terms. It is a *logos,* after all. What cannot be relied upon to hold good beyond the present case is its *orthotēs,* its correctness. That a person who offends me had encouraged me to trust him is not necessarily a reason for such anger on another occasion, even if now it is.[9]

The close connection between the concepts of the *orthos logos* and the person of practical wisdom may lead us to overlook the relevance of a point which surfaced earlier. A given response may be informed by an *orthos logos* yet not be an exercise of the virtue of practical wisdom. For sometimes it is easy to get things right, and simply to be one who gets things right when it is easy is not to be virtuous or excellent, whether in character or intellect. A person has practical wisdom only if he or she is such as to hit on the *orthos logos* when perhaps many or most would not. We must, however, be more specific about the kind of difficulty (as it would be to an inferior person) that marks those cases in which the virtue of practical wisdom can be seen to be exercised. For the present, let us accept Aristotle's initial division of the virtues according to which practical wisdom is an excellence of intellect as distinct from character (1103 a 6–7). Since practical wisdom is prescriptive, this is not, we have seen, a neat distinction, and in *NE* VI Aristotle will elaborate on the contribution of character to practical wisdom. But if for the moment we treat practical wisdom as an intellectual quality, we can see that the relevant type of difficulty is to do with thought, not feeling. The difficult situation, in this regard, is not one likely to cause obstructive passions in morally ordinary people; rather, it is, for instance, one whose morally relevant features are complex: where many distinctions would have to be made, and many relations correctly taken in and compared, for a correct response to be possible. Or, to use examples involving different sorts of virtues of thought, it might be necessary to think with unusual speed; or to interpret some perceived fact in terms of experience which few people have had, or few have remembered; or to calculate chances of success or failure of some project even though the situation is not a usual one.

However, at this stage of our study of Aristotle's theory of human excellence, we are not concerned with the nature of practical wisdom in itself, nor even with the *orthos logos* which it is the nature of practical wisdom to be able to deliver even when discerning it is difficult, but with the nature of character-virtue. Since, by Aristotle's own formulation, the concept of virtue of character makes essential reference to the *orthos logos* (and to the man of practical wisdom simply as representing this formal aspect of the appropriate response), our question now is: How are we to understand the relationship between the *orthos logos* and virtue of character?

Let us begin with an unashamedly teleological thesis: excellence of character, or moral virtue *(ēthike aretē),* exists in order to make possible the effective exercise of the *orthos logos.* But this is an ambiguous statement, since the question of effective exercise arises on at least two levels. On one, what is effective is the agent's ability in general to hit upon the *orthos logos*—his capacity for forming a correct judgment. On another level, we are concerned with the practical effectiveness of the determinate judgment once it is formed. We can apply the Aristotelian distinction between *what* and *that,* as follows: a virtuous agent is such as to respond appropriately, in general, to his or her situation; *that* appropriate responses in general *occur* is due to virtue of character; that the responses are *what* they are so as to be appropriate, is to the credit of judgment, the ability to discriminate correctly through feeling and through action.

It may seem as if the distinction between *what* and *that* simply corresponds to the difference between *forming* a correct judgment and *executing* it. In fact, the distinction even applies to the very act of forming. For in many situations the proper response is a discriminating emotional reaction or a no less immediate discriminating behavioural reaction. In such cases, moral virtue has the undivided role of making possible the reaction's formation. It holds the ring against potentially unbalancing impulses, so *that* a patterned response has the chance to crystallise, the response being fully instantiated as soon as formed. Elsewhere, by contrast, the appropriate response is such that it cannot be immediately completed. For instance, it is the judgment that one should do a certain thing, where doing it takes time or has to await an occasion. We can look on this judgment as an incipient action, or on the action as a continuation of the same affirmation of value expressed in the judgment. Either way, the time interval with its possibilities of interference lays an extra burden on moral virtue. It is not enough that a person should be in a state, with regard to impulses and feelings, such that the *orthos logos* is permitted to form in him: he must also, if this formation is not itself an already complete response, see the completion through in practice in the same unobstructed spirit. Otherwise, he may be incontinent or continent, but he is not morally virtuous.

## VI. 'A Prohairetic State'

It is natural at this point to turn to another key-term of Aristotle's statement of the essential nature of moral virtue: moral virtue (and likewise moral vice) is a state of the soul 'concerned with choice' (Ross) or 'involving choice' (Ostwald), or a state of the soul 'that decides' (Irwin). The word is *'prohairetikē'*. There are two items for translation. The first is the chief cognate term, *prohairesis.* Some say 'choice', some 'decision', some 'preference', some 'reasoned choice' or 'reasoned preference', some 'purpose'. In this book I have settled for 'rational choice' (or sometimes just 'choice'), although I shall often stay with the Greek word. The second is the adjectival ending *'-ikē'*. Translators who render it as 'concerned with' or 'involving' (e.g. 'concerned with choice') may be overcautious. In general, the *'-ikos'* ending is causative, though it speaks of a tendency or ability to cause, rather than of actual causing. Thus the meaning of 'prohairetic' may be found somewhere among the following: 'tending to give rise to a *prohairesis*'; 'formative of a *prohairesis*'; 'contributing to a *prohairesis*'; 'promoting a *prohairesis*', 'tending to result in . . .', 'expressed in . . .'.

What are we to make of *'prohairesis'* itself as it occurs in this context? It may seem that the answer lies in seeing how the concept figures elsewhere, especially in the major discussions of *NE* VI and VII. But this procedure leads to difficulties. If we go to Books VI or VII for an understanding of *prohairesis,* we are likely to come away with a notion too narrow, or in some other way not adequate, to provide a satisfactory interpretation of what Aristotle means when he says that a moral quality is a 'prohairetic state'.

For example, in *NE* VI (and also III) a *prohairesis* is said to be a practical judgment arrived at through deliberation (1113 a 2 ff.; 1139 a 23 ff.). If 'deliberation' means a temporal process in which alternatives are envisaged and their merits weighed, it is reasonable to say that moral quality is expressed in a *prohairesis,* but it is not clear why this should be singled out as definitive of moral quality. For if a *prohairesis* is the product of deliberation in the above sense, then many a morally significant response is not a *prohairesis,* nor is it accompanied by one. For example, friendliness is an Aristotelian virtue: it is the quality of knowing how to be, and of being, pleasant to others (not necessarily only one's friends) to the right extent and in the proper way; the contrast is with the ingratiating person who makes up to everyone, and the churlishness of the person who 'cares not a whit about giving pain' (1126 b 15–16). Such a virtue is displayed most often—and surely most purely—in unpremeditated moment-to-moment exchanges. Then there is a point which earlier seemed to make sense, namely that an appropriate and virtuous response might consist in a *feeling* not expressed in action; but this notion is absurd, if virtue is defined as expressed in a deliberate judgment. For we deliberate on what to do, not on what to feel about something.[10]

Similar problems arise if we draw our concept of *prohairesis* from the discussion of Book VII. Whereas in Books III and VI the emphasis is on *prohairesis* as the endpoint of deliberation, in VII it is on *prohairesis* as the starting point of action which may or may not be carried out in accordance with the *prohairesis.* The focus is on the incontinent person who fails to execute his *prohairesis.* Here it is not insisted that the *prohairesis* is the product of deliberation; but the gap now envisaged between *prohairesis* and its realisation makes this conception as unsuitable as the deliberative one for providing a general analysis of the notion of morally significant response.

Leaning on the connection of *prohairesis* with deliberation, should we perhaps see Aristotle as saying not that every morally significant response is a deliberated judgment, but that deliberated judgment is the response most typical of a moral characteristic? It may be that virtue, of character as well as intellect, plays a larger, more noticeable, part where deliberation is necessary. Not only is finding the right decision something of an achievement of intellect, but where deliberation takes time, and time is also needed to execute the decision, virtue of character has a more extensive area to defend from disruptive impulses than if the response were instantaneous. But while it is understandable that Aristotle should focus on cases like these as especially instructive examples, it does not follow that he means them as examples of virtuous response at its most essential. That would be to imply that where deliberation is lacking, the morally virtuous response is not virtuous in the strictest or most proper sense. But we deliberate only when we do not know straight off what the right response would be. If, as often happens, we know at once and so immediately that the knowledge itself is already the response, this unhesitant expression of our moral nature must be at least as perfect (as an expression of *moral* nature) as if it had been reached through deliberation.

These difficulties have led many commentators to the view that 'deliberation' in Aristotle really refers not to a psychological process but to the structure of reasoned explanation which is at least potentially present in the rationale of the agent's response. The agent can, if pressed, say why he did or felt this rather than some alternative without its being the case that he considered other options or needed to think how to react. In the same way, a tennis player ex post facto can analyse why he moved to the net. Alternatively, it may be suggested that although Aristotle's discussions in Books III and VI undeniably exhibit a *prohairesis* as resulting from a conscious process of deliberation, it would have been natural for him to extend the concept so that it relates to situations which psychologically (or phenomenologically) differ from deliberation, but which exemplify the sort of logical and explanatory structure that deliberation exemplifies.[11]

These are attractive suggestions, since each allows us to see a more or less unitary conception of *prohairesis* at work in all the various contexts.[12] One or the other should be taken on board for the present, and the difference between them need not concern us now. So far, then, our result is this: a moral characteristic is a prohairetic state, and a prohairetic state is one that issues in reason-structured responses. Such responses may be good or not, and the prohairetic state is a virtue only if the responses are good. No doubt every prohairetic response seems to the agent to be right—to express the *orthos logos* and the mean between excess and deficiency—but some agents are, as Aristotle puts it, corrupted in their vision (1144 a 29–36), and what seems right to them is wrong. Virtue, then, is a state issuing in correct reason-structured responses, those which the person of practical wisdom would actually endorse.[13]

Is this an adequate account of Aristotle's definition of moral virtue? No, because it has failed to extract the full meaning of 'prohairetic state'. We have just focused on the fact that a prohairetic state issues in a reason-structured response, and a good such state in a good response. But not every state that issues in a good reason-structured response is a moral virtue. For example, a skill is such a state and so is theoretical knowledge. From these, too, come justified responses, according to the relevant canons of justification, but in Aristotle's usage these are not *prohairetic* states. In fact, he has coined that phrase precisely to distinguish the kind of 'getting it right' that uniquely typifies the moral virtues from other types of 'getting it right'. Correspondingly, the *orthos logos* which it is the function of moral virtue to render effective in the different ways sketched earlier is, distinctively, a *prohairesis*. But what is the difference?

Aristotle will treat this question at length in *NE* VI, to which Chapter 4 of this book is devoted. There he is concerned with the good *prohairesis* considered as the product of practical wisdom exercising itself in good deliberation. At present, however, his concern is with good *prohairesis* as rendered possible and effective by the moral virtues: qualities of the nonrational part of the soul, even though, as has already been indicated, they also in some way inform the good person's rational prescription. Now the connection with *moral* virtue sheds, in my view, more light on Aristotle's concept of *prohairesis* than does the famous connection with deliberation. For *deliberation* does not differentiate a prohairetic response from the deliberated—or as if deliberated—decisions of a craftsman. So while Aristotle proposes to define moral virtue (and, by implication, vice) in terms of *prohairesis*, modern readers will find it easier to grasp *'prohairesis'* by means of what they already understand of the former. Nor would Aristotle necessarily disapprove, since he expects us to know something of the human virtues and virtue in general before we embark on the inquiry, and he can hardly expect us not to use this knowledge along the way.[14]

A set of clues is afforded by themes figuring large in Aristotle's account of the moral virtues but not explicit in the official definition, which I quote again: 'Excellence is a prohairetic state, lying in a mean relative to us, this being determined by a *logos* and in the way in which the man of practical wisdom would determine it' (1106 b 36–1107 a 2). One of those themes not mentioned here has already been noticed: the intimate connection between moral character and feelings *(pathē)* such as 'appetite, anger, fear, confidence, envy, joy, friendly feeling, hatred, longing, emulation, pity, and in general the feelings that are accompanied by pleasure and pain' (1105 b 21–23). Another is the connection with pleasure and pain in general (whether accompanying feelings or actions). Aristotle emphasises that good character is a matter of being pleased and pained by the right things, in the right way, on the right occasions etc. (1106 b 16–23). A person's moral quality is typified by the pattern of his pleasure and pain responses. This is so important to Aristotle that one is surprised not to find it included in his definition of moral virtue in addition to, if not instead of, the reference to prohairetic state, which (unless we suppress the connection with deliberation) inevitably focuses on action rather than pleasure and pain.

These oddities are resolved, however, if we suppose, as I now shall, that Aristotle's reference to the prohairetic state is by implication a reference to those very emotions, urges, pleasures and pains which seem to be left out of the definition[15]—the relation being this: what characterises a prohairetic state (as distinct from, say, a skill) is that it shows itself in the agent's acting and failing to act *because of his feelings.* Fear might prevent the craftsman from functioning properly as a craftsman; it might hinder his dexterity or warp his judgment in some way; but if we know the situation we shall not assess his *skill* on the basis of that response. Conversely, if we do assess someone as a bad performer on the basis of a performance which we know fell short because of fear, lust or anger, then we are assessing his quality as a prohairetic agent. Emotional excitements, like physical handicaps, tend to excuse the craftsman, in the sense that his skill is not impugned by performances spoilt by these conditions. But while the prohairetic agent may be thus excused by physical handicaps, he is not as a rule by emotions, pleasures and pains. It is not in general the proper business of the builder as such to have made sure that he is not so upset that he cannot operate, any more than it is his business qua builder to make sure that his body is healthy. But it is, Aristotle thinks, the proper business of the prohairetic agent to be in whatever emotional condition is necessary for him to function well.

This connects with something which we already know about the qualities currently under consideration by Aristotle: temperance, justice, courage etc. Because of these a person is called a good human being, and also good without qualification, whereas the skills for which someone is called a good doctor or lawyer do not license the unqualified accolade 'good', since the virtues of a doctor and lawyer are not *human* virtues (see Chapter I, Section V). Now the unqualified goodness of the human virtue is reflected in the categorical nature of the evaluative responses which express that state of the person. He responds as a human being, which is what for good or ill he essentially is, and not as the expert in some particular field which he might or might not have become, and whose products or services may or may not be worth pursuing, depending on circumstances. The *orthos logos* prescribed by a craft does not rationally demand to be acted on, even by the individual who frames it, for what he frames is his expert opinion that if the goal were being pursued, this would be the thing to do. There may be good reason not to do it and not to pursue the goal. But the *orthos logos* (whether really correct or apparently) of one who responds as a human being cannot be set aside for any good reason. That is to say, the prohairetic agent cannot both identify with his response as correct and also recognise reasons for ignoring it. The term 'prohairetic' indicates the categorically practical nature of this *logos.*

So it is not surprising that the state which issues in such a *logos* should be a disposition with regard to the basic feelings and impulses which everyone has, and with regard to the pleasures and pains of resisting or going along with them. For these feelings, and the pleasures and pains themselves embody what we may think of as primitive categorical judgments of value: they imply desires and aversions tending towards actions. Hence the part of the soul that issues in such impulses is a naturally suitable vehicle for the categorical *orthos logos.* But unless the impulses fall in with it, they will figure as peculiarly irrational. These emotions and feelings of pleasure and pain, and the objects giving rise to them, can certainly be cited as providing reasons (even good reasons) for not taking action on the *orthos logos* of some craft. They cannot, however, ground *reasons* for overriding a *prohairesis* (an ethical judgment of what is best), although they can of course *cause* it to be overridden, because of the unqualified or categorical nature of their own claims for practical attention. Hence unless they are allies, they are competitors and enemies of the prohairetic *orthos logos,* which can therefore be characterised as the type of *logos* whose formation and execution is potentially supported or threatened by just these entities: the most salient denizens of what Aristotle calls the nonrational part of the ethical soul. It is the business of moral training to reduce the threat and strengthen the support. The other kinds of *orthoi logoi* such as the technical and the theoretical do not (for different reasons) directly depend on an accommodation with this emotional material; which is why training in the disciplines relevant to them is not primarily a training of potentially recalcitrant feelings.

## VII. Conditions of Virtuous Action

In the light of the foregoing let us look at the difficult passage in *NE* II.4 where Aristotle tries to explain the difference between doing what a virtuous person would do and acting virtuously. He has to show how these differ, because he holds that we become brave, just etc. by doing actions of kinds characteristic of those virtues. But we do not become virtuous at a jump, by acting once in the relevant way. We engage in those actions while still on the way to virtue, when as yet they are not expressions of virtue itself.

Thus truly virtuous activity arises from what is a sort of imitation of itself, although the person engaged cannot be said to know what he is imitating. Later we shall consider this process of development as Aristotle describes it, but for the moment we are concerned with the end-result and with ways in which it differs from earlier stages where the visible behaviour is the same. Aristotle points out that the same sort of question arises in connection with skills. We acquire skills, too, by practising the relevant actions; thus we perform the actions before being proficient in the skills.

The question might be asked, what we mean by saying that we must become just by doing just acts, and temperate by doing temperate acts; for if men do just and temperate acts, they are already just and temperate, exactly as, if they do what is grammatical or musical, they are proficient in grammar and music. Or is this not true even of the arts? It is possible to do something grammatical either by chance or under the guidance of another. A man will be proficient in grammar then, only when he has both done something grammatical and done it grammatically; and this means doing it in accordance with the grammatical knowledge in himself. Again, the case of the arts and that of the excellences are not similar; for the products of the arts have their goodness in themselves, so that it is enough that they should have a certain character once they have been produced. (1105 a 17–28)

This last point is odd if it means that the product's[16] being in the right condition is sufficient evidence of skill in the (immediate) producer, since Aristotle has just said that the product could be correct through chance or someone's instruction. Instead he must mean that we are satisfied with things which are normally produced by art or skill provided they are up to standard, even when they were produced by someone without skill. If we assess what such a doer has done by *what he has made,* we can say that what he has done is good. The lack of skill implies no defect in what he has done on this occasion, and it might reasonably be claimed that the skill is of value only because whoever possesses it is more likely to produce acceptable articles. Aristotle's point is that it is not like this with virtue and right actions (hence, he implies, virtue is too different from skill for one to be justified in drawing conclusions about virtue from premisses about skill[17]). If someone does what is called a brave or just action, but not from virtue but by accident or reluctantly at the instigation of another, then what he has done (a deed, not a product) is *not* as good as such deeds should be. Had it been done from virtue it would have been better, although (we may add) not necessarily more useful or socially acceptable. Thus the value of possessing a virtue does not lie in the fact that it increases an agent's chances of giving rise to good doings the goodness of which can be independently specified and which he might have given rise to (though it was not likely) in all their goodness even before he acquired the virtue. For what is done from virtue is at its best only when done from virtue.

What, then, is lacking when the just deed is not done from justice? Before we follow Aristotle in his attempt to spell this out, there is a point which is obvious but can easily fall out of focus. A just man's deed is not just merely because it "expresses his virtue of justice". As this entire passage implies, a deed is just only if it conforms to a certain description, and this it may do even if it fails to evince the virtue of justice. In other words, the deed cannot be reckoned just unless it fits what would be the *orthos logos* for that situation, even if the agent is not interested in it from that point of view, or if the *logos* reflects someone else's judgment of what should be done, not his. The judgment which is that *orthos logos* is made on grounds having to do with the empirical situation: this money was borrowed, this person needs assistance, so many days have passed, and so on. The *orthos logos* is a wise person's judgment about what the correct response would be, given the facts: it is not a judgment about the spirit in which that response should ideally be made, nor is it itself a spirit in which someone responds. There has to be some content to the correct response whereby it is correct before we can raise questions about the ideal spirit in which it should be made.

These considerations show how crucial was the quiet step by which Aristotle, in defining happiness in *NE* I.7, moved from saying that happiness is nothing other than 'functioning *well*' to saying that it is nothing other than 'functioning *in accordance with virtue*' (1098 a 14–17). It might have seemed reasonable to gloss the former with 'doing what is right', or (given the definition) 'doing what it is right that a rational being should do'. Animals are functioning well when they are doing whatever creatures of their species naturally should be doing, and if we want to say that a well-functioning animal functions 'in accordance with the excellence of its kind' we may mean no more than that it is functioning healthily and effectively at this moment and can be reliably expected to do so at other moments. We may also imply the theory that its functioning well at all those moments is rooted in a single set of continuing empirical properties, which we may think of as constituting the relevant excellence. But this way of thinking could easily be misleading, for we should not be entitled to assert that at a given moment the animal's functioning is only fully good *because* it has and will continue to have the properties by which it functions well at this and other moments. Those properties (on the theory) make causally possible the functioning that is good, but their presence is not what makes it *good* functioning. By contrast, the human virtues, on Aristotle's account, do not stand to human good functioning as a set of properties that make causally possible a functioning whose goodness can be explained as complete without reference to them. On the contrary, the functioning is both possible and, by external standards, correct and good without virtue standing behind it, but is not in any instance completely good (hence not an instance of happiness) except when it issues from virtue.

Phrases such as 'issues from virtue' are dangerous, however, because they suggest that a human virtue is a distinct causal basis for some kind of behaviour regarded as wholly independently desirable, like the hardness of the steel whereby a knife cuts cleanly. Yet it is difficult to manage without such phrases, because it now appears that a virtue is more than a trend (so to speak) of acting well on particular occasions. For talk of such a trend or tendency is consistent with the view that each individual action would still be as good as it can be even if it were not a member of a class of similar actions—a class numerous enough to justify speaking of a 'trend'. Thus in predicating a virtue of someone we do not merely predicate a rough set of good actions (some of them actual, some of them expected); but neither do we predicate an actual property which, it is hoped, would causally explain those various good actions under the various circumstances.[18]

So Aristotle's elliptical remarks face us with the question 'What is a human virtue, if it is not a tendency and not the causal basis of a tendency to act in desirable ways?'—a question which he probably would not have considered germane to practical ethics. More germane is the intuition (which should influence the *politikos* in his choice of educational programmes), that the happiness of human beings consists not simply in their generally *doing* what is good or right to do (any more than it consists in their merely *being such as to* do what is good or right to do), but in their *doing* what is right *as agents who are themselves such as to;* or, alternatively, in their activity as agents who are such as to do what is right. This means that the *politikos* whose goal is his citizens' happiness should not opt for programmes intended to turn out citizens of whom it is merely true that they generally do what is right. Earlier it was pointed out that in the absence of hard and fast rules for proper behaviour, owing to the infinitely various demands of particular situations, the best way of ensuring good behaviour in advance is to rear citizens who will respond appropriately to their own unforeseeable situations through being themselves such as in general to respond appropriately. But now it is clear that even if advance conditioning were possible, or if it were possible to have most people doing the right thing under orders all the time, this would be a less desirable goal than that which Aristotle in fact lays down for the *politikos,* since it falls short of the citizens' happiness, given that happiness is activity *in accordance with virtue.* One is inclined to say that far from being happy (which only gods and human beings can be; cf. below, Chapter 7, Section VIII) they would not even be human; and beings less godlike would be hard to imagine. It is therefore by a fortunate arrangement of *rerum natura* that the particularity of things is such that the general automation of good behaviour is not possible; if it were, such is society's need for general good behaviour that the *politikos* (himself, somehow, a free being?) would find it hard not to prefer robotic agents around him to the uncertainties of the autonomous activity called 'happiness'.

Let us return to Aristotle's explanation of the difference between doing that which a virtuous person would do and acting virtuously oneself; e.g., between doing what is just or temperate, and acting, oneself, as a just or temperate person. (The differences which he finds would also distinguish doing what a dishonest or greedy person would do from acting greedily or dishonestly oneself.) The flow of ideas is not entirely straightforward, because he is concerned not only to explain the difference just mentioned, but also to show how acting from virtue is different from acting from skill, despite the fact that both virtue and skill develop through practice.

> The case of the arts and that of the excellences are not similar; for the products of the arts have their goodness in themselves, so that it is enough that they should have a certain character once they have been produced; but if the acts that are in accordance with the excellences have themselves a certain character it does not follow that they are done justly or temperately. The agent also must be in a certain condition when he does them; in the first place he must have knowledge, secondly he must choose [*prohairoumenos*] the acts, and choose them because of themselves,[19] and thirdly his action must proceed from a firm and unchangeable state [or disposition]. These are not reckoned in as conditions of the possession of the arts, except the bare knowledge; but as a condition of the possession of the excellences, knowledge has little or no weight, while the other conditions count not for a little but for everything, i.e. the very conditions which result from often doing just and temperate acts. (1105 a 26–b 5)

On the first requirement: if the just or temperate act is A, then for A to be done from justice or temperance the agent must obviously know what he is doing in the sense in which Oedipus did not know what he was doing when he killed his father. Thus a person does not exercise temperance in refusing one enjoyable drink too many if he supposes the drink to be something disgusting. But framed as it is in terms of 'knowledge', this is a tricky point, since one might be exercising temperance if one mistakenly thought the drink enjoyable. However, Aristotle is starting from a situation in which external observation (which is presumed correct) identifies the act as, e.g., refusing a pleasant drink, which is the sort of thing that a temperate person would do. The temperate person, then, must know himself to be doing this. But if that is what Aristotle means, why does he say that knowledge counts less towards the ascription of virtue than towards the ascription of craft? Perhaps the point is that the craftsman has a more precise and detailed knowledge of the factual nature of his action than a layman would have who engaged in a similar action; whereas the difference between the virtuous and nonvirtuous performance of an action does not lie in that sort of knowledge.

I turn to the second requirement for 'acting from virtue'. A few lines back, Aristotle has said that one is not yet exercising the skill of writing if one writes correctly by chance or under someone's guidance (1105 a 22–26). This suggests that the main part of the second condition ('from *prohairesis* or choice') says the same about virtue. If so, we have a new nuance to the concept of a *prohairesis:* it is not only a reasoned response, and one that is categorically practical, but it expresses the agent himself. This, too, is tricky, because the last is true of the skilled agent, as the example about writing makes plain. The difference is that the skilled agent's autonomy is not to be called 'prohairetic'; this is because the autonomy of skill is not categorically practical. The craftsman as such knows from himself *what* a craftsman should do, but it is not as such that he actually does it, since there have to be reasons from beyond the field of the craft why it should be exercised at all or on this occasion. The actual doing awaits the go-ahead of a more authoritative kind of agent than the craftsman as such, namely, the *politikos* (who of course may be the same individual).

For ease I have spelt this out in terms of actions, but we must try to accommodate this material to the fact that for Aristotle emotional responses are equally expressions of moral character. In their case there is an analogue to the autonomy condition: no doubt one cannot feel because one is instructed to, but one can be caught up in an emotion merely because others around one are full of it, and afterwards be quite unable to say why one felt such hatred or enthusiasm. An emotional response would count as 'prohairetic' if it is from oneself.

'Autonomy' must not be taken in an extreme sense so as to imply that no one can be acting virtuously if he acts under somebody else's orders. The brave soldier need not himself have decided that this is the place and time to scale the rampart, and it often belongs to practical wisdom to accept someone else's authority on what should be done.[20] Even if the decision is not a decision for experts, it may simply not be one's business to make it. This is obvious to anyone with the slightest experience of cooperative enterprise. I think that what we should say on Aristotle's behalf is this. He is concerned here with the virtues of character, not directly with practical wisdom. A particular right action can be an exercise of temperance or courage without exhibiting any special practical wisdom on the part of the brave or temperate agent. He cannot act entirely without judgment, but he need not be the one who determined what was right to do. There are two ways in which one may need external guidance towards doing what one ought to do. In the first, what a person lacks is intellectual knowledge: he lacks some of the facts, or is not well placed to interpret them correctly. He might be about to act from an erroneous conception but for another's intervention. In the second way, he is drawn by emotion or appetite towards doing what he should not, but is checked by someone else. In the former case one needs *direction* from another party; in the latter, one needs *control.* The second, not the first, kind of lack of autonomy is inconsistent with moral virtue, which is above all a capacity to deal, oneself, with one's feelings. This can also be explained as the difference between needing direction and needing *encouragement.* The agent who only needs direction is already of himself actively willing to do what he should. Encouragement by contrast, is not just getting someone to do what he would not have done for himself; it is also evocation of the elementary willingness to do the thing he is supposed to.

Aristotle's second condition for acting virtuously is: 'he must choose the acts, and choose them because of themselves' *(di'hauta).* This is difficult. Some commentators take the 'and' as epexegetic, so that the whole condition is 'he must choose them because of themselves? It is then supposed that the contrast is with the craftsman who (it is suggested) 'chooses' (i.e. has a *prohairesis* concerning) his actions not because of themselves but because of their products. On this interpretation, the craftsman too has a prohairetic response. This cannot be correct. How, if it were, could Aristotle propose to *define* moral virtue as prohairetic and as concerned with a mean determined by the *orthos logos?* For all these things would be equally true of craft.

In my view, the 'and' in the second condition heralds something new. Virtue has already been distinguished from craft on the ground that the former is prohairetic, the latter not; and the new point concerns the difference between actions done from virtue and outwardly similar actions done from a different ethical condition. After all, Aristotle's principal question in our passage as a whole is not the difference between deeds of virtue and deeds of skill, but between acting *like* a person of virtuous (or, it might be, vicious) character, and acting *as* one. This difference is captured as follows: the action is done from (say) justice or temperance only if the description 'A' under which it is deemed the sort of thing that a just or temperate person would do is the primary description of the action for the agent. In other words, the agent is virtuous only if the action which observers describe as 'A' is done by him as A or *because it is A.* That is what is meant by 'doing it because of itself'. If someone eats no more than is good for him now in preparation for enjoying a binge tomorrow, then *what* he is now doing is preparing for tomorrow's binge, and this is not the description of a temperate act.

What we have here is not a general contrast between good and inferior moral agents, as if the latter never do what they do 'because of itself', but between a good agent and an agent who (in a sense) does the same thing, but with a different intention.[21] Of course bad agents too do what they do 'because of itself'; i.e., the description under which the action would be classed as, e.g., intemperate can indeed be that under which the agent intends it, as in the above example. Suppose that an action strikes an observer as greedy (he sees it as A, when A is what would be intended by a greedy person); it is not actually done from greed unless the observer's preferred description is that under which the agent primarily intends it; otherwise it may even be virtuous. In such a case, a *virtuous* agent would be said by Aristotle to 'choose the action but not because of itself'.

The 'because of itself' qualification has caused special difficulty, because when Aristotle discusses *prohairesis* in the context of deliberation, he emphasizes (e.g., *EE* 1227 b 36), that a *prohairesis* is *of* some action *for the sake of* something else. Thus it seems that what a person chooses *(prohaireitai)* is never chosen 'because of itself', according to certain central passages. There is not a straightforward contradiction, however, since choosing to do A for the sake of B is not quite the same as choosing to do what an observer would describe as 'A', but choosing it under the different description 'B'. The contrary of this second situation is *choosing A under the observer's description 'A',* which is not necessarily the same as *choosing A with no further end in view.* It is the former, not the latter, which Aristotle means to establish at 1105 a 32.[22]

However, the situation is immensely complicated by the fact that it is true of some actions (as the observer would describe them) and not of others that they evince a virtue only if done with no further end in view. Repaying one's debt is an expression of the virtue of justice only if done as *that,* and not as a means of avoiding unpleasantness or to make a good impression. Aristotle may have had such cases mainly in mind when writing the passage which we are examining; but if so, this was unfortunate, since in very many cases the observable action is virtuous only if done for one end rather than another. Thus in our example, simply refraining from a dish of food now is not in itself an expression of any sort of moral quality: it proves temperance if done, say, with an eye on health and greed if done for the sake of future overindulgence. If 'with no further end in view' applies to this type of case, it can be only because the observer sees the action under the description 'refraining from *too much* food'. We can certainly say that temperance is exercised in choosing the action under *that* description; but then this may be because 'too much' refers to what would be excessive from the point of view of health. Thus there is, after all, a reference to a further end. (Other interpretations are possible: e.g., the dish might be 'too much' because taking it would deprive others of their share.) An additional difficulty is that if the agent refrains through calculations of greed, the description under which he chooses to refrain is in a verbal sense identical with the one that strikes the observer. The latter sees the action as refraining from *too much* food, and so does the greedy agent, since for him it is *too much* from the point of view of maximum future enjoyment. To avoid the conclusion that this greedy agent fulfils Aristotle's second condition for acting from temperance, 'too much' must be allowed to have different implications depending on what it is too much for; thus there has to be a reference to that further end.

I think it a mistake to suppose that Aristotle's phrase 'chooses it because of itself' is backed by a theory in which the concepts of prohairesis, *doing something under a certain description* and *doing something for the sake of something else* stand to each other in clearly worked out relations.[23] In the passage, he appeals to our rough (but firm) sense of a difference between doing what in fact is right and doing it in the right spirit. This probably resolves into a number of kinds of difference from the point of view of the theory of action, but it is not clear how far these differences matter for ethics. Aristotle's statement, in my view, simply ignores the distinction between (1) choosing the action which the virtuous person would choose (refraining from this dish), but not for the reason for which (under the description under which) the virtuous person would choose it; and (2) choosing, for an ulterior reason, the action (paying his debt) which the virtuous person would choose for no ulterior reason.

Similarly, I think it profitless to try to bring the use of *'prohairesis'* in this passage into strict line with those where Aristotle says that a *prohairesis* is of something for the sake of something else. In the present context he would, I suspect, be happy to say any and all of the following: the just agent chooses *(prohaireitai)* to *pay his debt,* with no further end in view; he also chooses to *sell some property* for the sake of paying the debt; the unjust one chooses to *pay his debt* for the sake of avoiding unpleasantness; the latter also chooses to *pay-his-debt-for-the-sake-of-avoiding unpleasantness.* (The fourth choice, like the first, is not made with a view to anything further.) This is a rough notion of *prohairesis,* which is elsewhere refined and made more technical by being linked to the idea of a conclusion of deliberation. The technical development makes sense if we take it that what is essential to *prohairesis,* roughly conceived, is its practical ultimacy (i.e., its categorical nature) as well as its having a rational structure (which is not necessarily the same as being grounded on an external reason). With this stress on practical ultimacy, which is what distinguishes an ethical judgment of what to do from judgments of skill, it is not surprising that in contexts (the present passage is not among them) where Aristotle focuses on the fact that to bring about C we have to do B first, and to do B, we have to do A, he should come to identify *the* object of *prohairesis* proper with that point within the whole of what is done (the bringing about of C) which is the source of its *being done*—i.e., with the point at which the agent's *doing* gets applied. This is what is shown in the conclusion of deliberation; it is the action "nearest to" the agent, which he does for the sake of the "further" end.

I now turn to Aristotle's third condition for virtuous action: the agent must act from a 'firm and unchangeable state'. He must be such as not to be easily put off by difficulties, temptations or the persuasion of others. He does not act idly (as when one makes an idle remark) but is prepared to stand by what he does, which means not merely that by doing it he gives us to understand that this is something which he *would* stand by, but that he would stand by it in fact. Putting it forth as something he would stand by is acting prohairetically, but engaging in prohairetic action at one moment is consistent with being tempted astray the next. The third condition also distinguishes moral qualities from skills: as we have seen, it says nothing against a person's skill if he fails to exercise it in the face of distractions or with someone begging him not to.

Similarly, it says nothing against the quality of a skill if its possessor voluntarily lets it go or decides to give it up as no longer worth the exercise. But it is not consistent with virtue that virtue voluntarily be allowed to slide (or 'be forgotten'; cf. 1100 b 17). For a prohairetic response is an unselfconscious assertion by the agent that the sort of person who responds like that is good and a sort of person it is good to be. This is an absolute assertion. For there is no more fundamental point of view from which he could rightly assert that although this is a kind of *person* it is good to be, it is not good (or not always good) to *be* a good person, on the ground that being a good person sometimes conflicts with being a good something else that is more fundamental in the sense (for instance) in which being a person is more fundamental than being some kind of craftsman. Nothing is more fundamental, since he is essentially a person, whether he is glad of it or not. Having no standpoint to fall back on from which he can reasonably make light of the value of being a good person, he has to value this if he is rationally to value anything else at all. Hence he cannot be rationally willing, while remaining a person in his own eyes, to let go of qualities which he thinks essential to a good person; and this is so even if he holds a mistaken view of what those qualities are. Thus every prohairetic response expresses (to put it starkly) an absolute refusal to cease being the kind of being to respond like that. Hence every such response at the same time carries the claim that under no manageable circumstances would one voluntarily act otherwise than *as the one who in this particular case responds like this.* The claim does not assume knowledge of how one would act in other circumstances, but it does assume that a response different from the present one would be different for a reason, or in a way, that would not make nonsense of the present one.

Now for a person actually to *be* of the moral character which his prohairetic response on some occasion proclaims it good to be, it is not enough that he thereby so to speak affirms that he would in general so act; for the affirmation must be *true.*[24] However, this is a case where the truth of the affirmation (which has something in common with a promise) is not entirely independent of the affirmer's affirming it. For he must now mean what he affirms (since this affirmation is not in words, but is a prohairetic response), hence he cannot but care now that it be true. And whether it is elsewhere upheld and not falsified is largely or entirely up to him. But his now caring that it should be upheld is, of course, not enough to ensure that he never would waver on other relevant occasions. If that were so, accepting the conclusion of a wise practical argument would be enough to make us act accordingly whenever the situation calls for it, and incontinence would be impossible.

## VIII. 'With Pleasure' and 'for the Sake of the Noble'

Before we turn to the doctrine of the mean, there remain to be considered two further connected features of moral virtue, neither of which, for some reason, appears in Aristotle's definition. One is that the agent acts 'with pleasure'; the other, that he acts 'for the sake of the noble' (or 'the fine').

Pleasures and pains enter the theory not only as accompanying basic impulses and emotions which need controlling if the person is to act well and become virtuous, but also as dimensions of correct response.

> We must take as a sign of states the pleasure or pain that supervenes on acts; for the man who abstains from bodily pleasures and delights in this very fact is temperate, while the man who is annoyed at it is self-indulgent, and he who stands his ground against things that are terrible and delights in this or at least is not pained is brave, while the man who is pained is a coward. For moral excellence is concerned with pleasures and pains; it is on account of pleasure that we do bad things, and on account of pain that we abstain from noble ones. Hence we ought to have been brought up in a particular way from our very youth, as Plato says, so as both to delight in and to be pained by the things that we ought; for this is the right education. (1104 b 3–13)

Just as we cannot use the concept of *prohairesis* to elucidate the notion of virtue, even if this is Aristotle's intention, but rather have to move from the latter to understanding the former, so we cannot use these remarks about pleasure and pain as if they were clear premises, but must interpret them in the light of the sort of conclusion we already know we are supposed to find. A satisfactory interpretation (which I shall not attempt comprehensively) would have to distinguish types and levels of pleasure and pain so as to overcome such problems as the following. (1) Virtue is sometimes expressed in our being pained at things at which we should be pained (e.g., someone else's vile action): how is this consistent with taking pleasure ('delighting') in one's morally correct response? (2) How can it realistically be held that fighting until one is cut to pieces is pleasant or even, as Aristotle says above, 'not painful'?

On the second question we can say, first, that the pleasure with which the virtuous person acts must be distinguished from his enjoying or finding enjoyable what he does. Doing it with pleasure must be doing it freely, unreluctantly, ungrudgingly, hence in this sense gladly. It may also be taking satisfaction in doing it. All this is consistent with its being an unpleasant or painful thing to do (as Aristotle recognises at 1117 a 29 ff., in his detailed account of courage). Second, it might be argued that the battlefield hero is 'not distressed' by his sufferings on the ground that his distress is 'merely potential' in the following sense: it is not actually expressed in avoidance behaviour or in any tendency towards avoidance. His brave action does not go against the *practical* grain. This is consistent with his *feeling* all kinds of pain. Similarly, he acts 'fearlessly' even though he may experience fear as a feeling (1115 b 10–19). It is possible that Aristotle's practical orientation leads him to write as if these feelings were literally unreal once their normal connection with avoidance action is broken, as in the courageous agent it is.[25]

The virtuous person 'takes pleasure' in his virtuous acts because they do not go against the grain; and because they express his moral nature, which is metaphysically anxious (so to speak) to be expressed in action.[26] This is not his basic biological and psychological nature, but the 'second nature' (1152 a 30–33) into which he has been formed by upbringing and practice. Now, if this is all, it should follow that the constitutionally bad person also in this sense takes pleasure in his characteristic actions. But Aristotle does not say so. The reason may be that, though much of what he says about virtue is generically true of vice as well, he is less concerned to spell out the nature of vice. The statesman need not know in detail what it is in order to aim away from it. On the other hand, if 'doing the virtuous deed with pleasure' implies 'doing it with *satisfaction*', there is ground for holding that a vicious person cannot take pleasure in action in the way in which his virtuous counterpart does.

This is because in many cases vicious persons focus on inferior goods. They live as if the acme of happiness were experiencing physical pleasure or owning large possessions or wielding power over others etc. All these things may be good in their place, but *the* good is acting virtuously. Now, everyone thinks that he acts well and makes the right response to his situation. Vicious people hit, in their own view, the *orthos logos*. The coward sees the brave man as rash, the hothead thinks him a coward, each treating himself as the norm (1108 b 19–26). And their response is engaged in gladly, in the sense of uninhibitedly, since it voices their second nature. Their action proclaims that it is good to be the sort of person who acts like this. But those who live as if happiness were something quite other than acting well cannot consistently draw satisfaction simply from the doing of what they deem appropriate. For much of what they deem appropriate seems so to them because and only because it leads to an end other than acting well as such. They may consider themselves to be acting or faring well when they are actually enjoying the ulterior end; but they must also see themselves as acting well when they pursue that end effectively. They cannot, then, value acting well entirely for its own sake, since at times they value it only because it leads to what they do value for its own sake. As soon as they take satisfaction in the effectiveness as such of their own approach to the end—and hence in the rightness of their own action, since in their eyes it is right if it is effective—they no longer at that moment wholeheartedly believe that happiness is something altogether else, such as physical pleasure or receiving honours and awards.

It is natural to human beings to take joy in doing things well (as they think) and getting things right, and this is nowhere clearer than in craft-activity. It is so natural that people set up all sorts of trivial ends in order to have the satisfaction of achieving them correctly. It is therefore difficult to live consistently, in all one's feelings and practice, the life of someone for whom happiness lies in something quite other than getting things right. Hence it is difficult thoroughly and firmly to be this kind of faulty character, and difficult for such a character to stay on good terms with itself.

Now let us consider acting 'for the sake of the noble' *(to kalon)*. The following passages are typical:

> Now the brave man is as dauntless as man may be. Therefore, while he will fear even the things that are not beyond human strength, he will face them as he ought and as the *logos* directs, and he will face them for the sake of the noble; for this is the end of excellence. (1115 b 10–13)

> Now excellent actions are noble and done for the sake of the noble. Therefore the liberal man, like other excellent men, will give for the sake of the noble, and rightly; for he will give to the right people, the right amounts, and at the right time, with all the other qualifications that accompany right giving; and that too with pleasure or without pain; for that which is excellent is pleasant or free from pain—least of all will it be painful. (1120 a 23–27)

The noble or fine is connected with what is fitting, appropriate or in the broad sense just, and is standardly contrasted with the useful and the pleasant (see e.g., 1104 b 30–32). It can also be equated with what is admirable and therefore outstandingly or conspicuously good. But 'for the sake of the noble' can also cover cases in which the agent acts simply because it would be disgraceful (ignoble) not to. The notion can refer to actions or their results: such and such an action or state of affairs is seen as noble on account of being the kind of action or state of affairs it is. In this case, that it is noble would figure as a reason for doing it or bringing it about.[27] But more fundamentally, I think, 'for the sake of the noble' refers to a spirit in which the person does whatever he has independent reason to think it right or good to do. Thus he may decide to do A, some mundane action, because it would be useful, and this might be sufficient reason for choosing A as the right thing to do. But the *doing* of A could still count as noble or fine. This would especially be so if the circumstances are such that doing it is difficult, hence something of an achievement, even though by its general description A is a mundane action. 'For the sake of the noble' captures what we might think of as the sense of owing it to oneself to do what is right or best even when this is costly. Aristotle would more naturally see it as the sense of being enhanced by the doing. The agent who does A because it is noble to do it does A as one who, by the doing of this independently right action, renders *himself* noble or fine.[28]

This spirit is not restricted to virtuous or to morally mature agents. It would play a large part in the life of someone who cares too much about honour and admiration; and it is important for Aristotle's theory of moral education that subjects not yet established in their prohairetic attitudes can act for the sake of the noble. This is a spirit that requires to be educated, since misdirections are possible. Those who are ambitious for honour, reputation and rank, act for the sake of the noble, but as often as not what they consider noble are these external goods themselves, and they measure the excellence of their actions by their success in achieving these ends. But according to Aristotle, what is truly noble are good actions or activities (or engaging in them); the dispositions for these; and the persons who have those dispositions (see especially *EE* VIII.3, and Chapter 7, Sections III–IV below). Thus the person in love with honour is mistaken: he ranks having honour as a finer thing than the fine actions through which he earns it.

Aristotle's standard contrast between the noble and the *pleasant* must be read to accommodate the thesis that a virtuous agent characteristically 'delights in' his virtuous actions. Thus the acting for pleasure that is excluded by acting for the sake of the noble has to do with logically *antecedent* pleasure. Someone who does A simply because he feels like it or feels he would enjoy it (these are not the same, but Aristotle tends to merge them) is not doing A for the sake of the noble. Again, if he chooses to do A on the ground that it is pleasant or would lead to something pleasant, doing it is not acting for the sake of the noble. This, I think, is so even when it is quite right (as it sometimes may be) to choose to do A on grounds of pleasure. Doing or moving towards what one anyway finds pleasant affords little opportunity for the exercise of moral virtue, which is most clearly shown in the setting aside of antecedent pleasures and pains. (It may be right to give oneself over to some pleasure or relaxation, but it is not shameful not to.) It is true, of course, that an agent who sets great store on some kind of pleasure might face moral challenges in pursuit of it. But the more he is willing to sacrifice for that pleasure, the more he appears as someone who equates having that pleasure with happiness. Hence even though in pursuing it he does what, in terms of his values, is right and proper, and does it under difficulties, he is in the same position as the person who equates happiness with honour: he treats what is really noble (doing what is right when this is a challenge) as no more than useful. And Aristotle would certainly condemn this agent for setting such store on a pleasure, at any rate if the pleasure is physical.

So when Aristotle says that the temperate person delights or takes pleasure in temperate actions, meaning that they are engaged in gladly and with satisfaction, he is referring to an attitude *consequential* upon seeing the action as good or proper and as what it would be noble to do or shameful not to; whereas pleasures that can clash with the noble are felt to be pleasures independently of the rightness of pursuing them.

'For the sake of the noble' refers to the manner of an immediate and particular response. It may be that an agent who responds in this spirit will generally respond in this spirit, but on no occasion does this manner of response depend per se on the agent's seeing himself at the time as one who generally responds in this way, or on his seeing himself as 'exercising a virtue'. Clearly he must take himself to be doing what is appropriate, and in some sense he knows that he cares about that. He, after all, is the one who would say, if asked, that he did what he did because it would have been shameful not to. But his knowledge in each case need refer to no more than his particular action on that occasion. Virtue entails the general disposition to act in this way, and with this knowledge, in particular cases. But to have this disposition, it is not necessary that one think of oneself as having it; and to exercise it, one need not see oneself as exercising it, or value one's action as the exercise of a virtuous disposition.

So in making 'for the sake of the noble' a condition of virtuous activity, Aristotle is not committed (as many interpreters suppose) to the distasteful view that a person cannot act from virtue unless he sees himself as acting from virtue. (Of course, such a view may be uncontroversial if 'sees himself' is sufficiently diluted. Commentators sometimes write as if an Aristotelian courageous action must be done from the thought: 'Courage demands that I do this'. Whether this is objectionable or unrealistic partly depends on what counts as 'doing something from the thought that . . .'. If there is a useful sense in which the artist can be said characteristically to paint from the thought 'My gift of composition demands that I place this here', then in this sense no doubt the courageous man characteristically acts with the above thought.) The agent in action must focus on the objects and circumstances of his action, in a manner that cares that his response to them is right. This is different from focusing on his own engagement in virtuous activity. What concerns him at the time is to act appropriately in the particular situation, and if he is virtuous this sort of concern is dispositional. But caring about acting appropriately on this occasion, even when it manifests a disposition to care about acting appropriately, does not entail caring about acting from a disposition so to care.[29]

I have, however, suggested that a prohairetic response declares it good to be the sort of person who under the circumstances responds like that. It is a sort of proclamation about what counts as human virtue, and so about what counts as happiness. Others may immediately focus on this message sent by the action, but the agent need not be attending to it. Just so, a person's verbal utterances proclaim his beliefs and linguistic capacities to others without necessarily being *about* himself or his beliefs and his language. Aristotle, realistically, thinks it quite difficult for a good person in action to see himself as exercising virtue; in a well-known passage he argues that one reason why good people in order to be happy need good friends is that otherwise they are likely to lack the pleasure a good person gets from perceiving virtue-in-action, since it is easier to see this in others who are close than in oneself (1169 b 30–1170 a 4).

Nevertheless, if acting from a *prohairesis* is taking a practical stand, anyway on this occasion, as to the goodness of acting so, then presumably the stand includes a recognition, in some sense, of the goodness of the disposition for such action. No doubt this self-referring feature of prohairetic action fosters the idea that Aristotle's virtuous agent in action sees himself as exercising virtue. (The agent, of course, assumes that he is acting well in the sense of doing what is right or appropriate, but 'acting well' in that sense is not synonymous with 'acting virtuously' or 'exercising virtue'.) However, the implicit claim, made in acting like *this,* that a good sort of person acts like *this* (in this situation), is impersonal and universal (apart from the reference to *this*). The action is a sort of ostensive definition of what it is to be a fine (or at any rate acceptable) person, and a definition does not ascribe the definiendum to any subject in particular.

Against this it might be argued that if we venture on this path of construing actions as claims or implicit claims about what a good person does, then it is only reasonable to interpret an agent's *engagement in* an action as indeed a claim about *himself,* to the effect that he, the agent, is doing what (as he proclaims it to be by doing it) a good person would do.[30] This, however, still falls short of ascribing to the agent the claim-in-action that he himself is a good or virtuous person, or is exercising virtue. For the latter involves not only a value judgment that this is what a good person would do, but also the additional factual judgment that he himself has and is acting from a firm and unchanging disposition so to act (Aristotle's third condition). And it still remains true that the agent need not (and very likely does not) act as he does *in order to* do what a good person would do, any more than a speaker, who presumably takes it that what he is saying is what those who speak the truth about the matter at hand would say, makes his statement *in order to* say the same as those who would say the truth. Thus the agent does not (or need not) identify his action to himself as the doing of what a good person would do in the way in which someone who puts on the kettle in order to make tea must be able to identify what he does as 'making tea'. He is taking care that by his actions he fulfils the description 'making tea', and he already knows (at least roughly) what making tea consists in. Thus he knows what to aim for. But his assumption that what he does is what a good person would do is not grounded in an aim to conform his action to an antecedently held picture of what the good person would do. *From* his own beliefs he discovers (if he is reflective) what he thinks true believers believe; and *from* his own action he discovers what he thinks a good person, thus placed, would do.[31]

## IX. The Status of the Mean

We come now to the doctrine of the mean, which Aristotle regards as an important contribution, to judge by the solemnity with which he introduces it and the many pages where he strains over the details of its application. Yet the doctrine often gets a disappointed reception. It seems at first to offer special illumination, but in the end, according to its critics, it only deals out truisms together with a questionable taxonomy of virtues and vices.

There is a Janus-quality to Aristotle's conception of excellence of character or moral virtue. This excellence is the source of the mature individual's own responses to his particular situations. It is the basis, too, of the autonomous well-functioning which is the acme of human existence. But at the same time, it is the reflection in the individual of the community in which he was reared. From that point of view excellence of character is the product and goal of a development initiated and largely guided by others. This duality of approach is a main source of difficulty in interpreting Aristotle's doctrine of moral virtue as a mean. Some of the trouble is due to his use of similar language from both perspectives. The notion of 'mean' is applied on those two fronts, sometimes to qualities of character, sometimes to particular responses. We cannot be sure that Aristotle himself is always apprised of his shifts. If he is not, that might help to explain any lack of fit between different things which he says in this area, and, in particular, any discrepancy between what the doctrine of the mean seems to promise and what it seems to deliver.

The central ambiguity is clearly marked in the definition of excellence as

> a prohairetic state, lying in a mean relative to us, this being determined by a *logos* and in the way in which the man of practical wisdom would determine it. Now it is a mean between two vices, that which depends on excess and that which depends on deficit; and again it is a mean because the vices respectively fall short of or exceed what is right in both passions and actions, while excellence both finds and chooses that which is intermediate. (1106 b 36–1107 a 6)

Here the idea of a *mean* figures in two ways. First we are told that excellence (or a kind of virtue such as courage or temperance) is a state which can be classified as occupying a midpoint between a vice of excess and a vice of defect. We are then told that it is a mean for the additional reason ('and again') that it, by contrast with the vices, 'finds and chooses that which is intermediate'. Here, what is 'found and chosen' is presumably a particular response, consisting in feeling, action or judgment, and this response is intermediate between responses that would have been 'found and chosen' by the vices.

This latter statement summarises the previous chapter (II.6), which is concerned with excellence as the source of good deeds and good functioning. The chapter begins:

> every excellence both brings into good condition the thing of which it is the excellence and makes the work of that thing be done well; e.g. the excellence of the eye makes both the eye and its work good; for it is by the excellence of the eye that we see well. . . . Therefore, if this is true in every case, the virtue of man also will be the state of character which makes a man good and which makes him do his own work well [i.e., function well as a human being]. (1106 a 15–24)

Aristotle then broaches the abstract quantitative concepts that underlie any notion of a mean: 'In everything that is continuous and divisible it is possible to take more, less, or an equal amount, and that either in terms of the thing itself or relatively to us; and the equal is an intermediate between excess and defect' (1106 a 26–29). Next he explains the distinction between the absolute mathematical mean, and the mean relative to us—that which is, so to say, 'equal to' the needs or requirements of any given occasion. This is illustrated by the varying amounts of food that a gymnastic trainer judges proper for individuals of different physiques. Aristotle then continues:

If it is thus, then, that every art does its work well—by looking to the intermediate and judging its works by this standard . . . and if, further, excellence is more exact and better than any art, as nature also is, then it must have the quality of aiming at the intermediate. I mean moral excellence; for it is this that is concerned with passions and actions, and in these there is excess, defect and the intermediate. For instance, both fear and confidence and appetite and anger and pity and in general pleasure and pain may be felt both too much and too little, and in both cases not well; but to feel them at the right times, with reference to the right objects, towards the right people, with the right motive, and in the right way, is what is both intermediate and best, and this is characteristic of excellence. Similarly with regard to actions also there is excess, defect and the intermediate. Now excellence is concerned with passions and actions, in which excess is a form of failure, and so is defect; while the intermediate is praised and is a form of success; and both these things are characteristics of excellence. Therefore excellence is a kind of mean since it aims at the intermediate. (1106 b 8–28)

Here it is the appropriate feelings and actions that are neither too much nor too little of whatever it may be, and the disposition that gives rise to such intermediate responses is called intermediate itself because of its effects. And so with the relevant vices: they would be called excesses or deficiencies after responses that go too far or not far enough. However, the definitional passage 1106 b 36 ff. implies that excellence is a mean between vices of excess and defect for some other reason as well: a reason that does not derive the intermediacy of the character trait from that of the responses. We can trace this other reason to an earlier passage where the notion of excellence as a mean appears in a very different light:

let us consider this, that it is the nature of such things to be destroyed by defect and excess, as we see in the case of strength and of health (for to gain light on things imperceptible [sc. such as states of the soul] we must use the evidence of sensible things); both excessive and defective exercise destroys the strength, and similarly drink or food which is above or below a certain amount destroys the health, while that which is proportionate both produces and increases and preserves it. So it is too, then, in the case of temperance and courage and the other excellences. For the individual who flies from and fears everything and does not stand his ground against anything becomes a coward, and the individual who fears nothing at all but goes to meet every danger becomes rash; and similarly the man who indulges in every pleasure and abstains from none becomes self-indulgent, while the one who shuns every pleasure, as boors do, becomes in a way insensible; temperance and courage, then, are destroyed by excess and defect, and preserved by the mean. (1104 a 11–27)

Here excellence is said to be, or to lie in, a mean, and the vices to lie in excess and defect, because the former owes its existence to intermediate behaviour, while the latter owe theirs to behaviour that is extreme one way or the other. As before, excellence itself is intermediate only derivatively, through a relation to something else that is primarily intermediate; but this time the something else is the behaviour that generates and preserves the excellence, not the behaviour that manifests it when already securely present. Thus the concept of excellence as a mean is here linked to what, in effect, is a practical prescription to parents, guardians, or community leaders on how to breed good moral qualities: do not let your charges shrink from everything alarming; do not let them rush aggressively into everything; do not let them have every pleasure that appeals to them; do not rule out pleasures altogether. In other words, teach them in a practical way that no one kind of thing is always right or always wrong; and at the same time get them through practice to learn not to be mechanical in their responses, so that when they acquire the wisdom or experience to be able to discriminate a correct response, they will already be endowed with the emotional flexibility to translate that finding into practice without let or hindrance.

In two ways, then, moral excellence is a mean state, and in each because of its connection with actions or particularised responses. But on one side this is because it is a state that gives rise to responses considered individually as appropriate, and therefore as median or mean by contrast with possible wrong particular responses. On the other side, however, the concepts of excess and defect are applied on a frequentative basis, i.e. to a set of responses all of which, or none of which, are of a certain type, while what is said to be mean is a mixed set; each set gives rise to a state of the soul which in turn is called 'median', 'excessive' or 'deficient' after its cause. An appealing but possibly misleading symmetry suggests itself between the set of responses (in early life) that cause the moral state of the soul, and the set of those that are its output; for it is natural to think that someone who becomes a coward by avoiding every danger will express his cowardice in continual avoidances. Correspondingly, the set of responses that spring from virtue will be a mixed set, like the one which is supposed to have produced the state. Since these effect-sets of responses are presumably of similar efficacy to the sets that originally caused the state, it follows that moral states are not only manifested in behaviour like the behaviour by which they were acquired, but are also preserved, reinforced and transmitted by the behaviour in which they are manifested. As Aristotle remarks: 'That excellence, then, is concerned with pleasures and pains, and that by the acts from which it arises it is both increased and, if they are done differently, destroyed, and that the acts from which it arose are those in which it actualizes itself—let this be taken as said' (1105 a 13–16). This self-propagating power of the moral qualities in individuals mirrors the passing on of a community's moral culture from one generation to the next.

However, this symmetry of what for convenience we may label the cause-sets and the effect-sets (in relation to a moral state of the soul) must not divert us from a fundamental difference. If a member of a cause-set of responses can be said at all to be 'median', 'excessive' or 'deficient', this is only because it *belongs to a set,* whose membership is mixed or homogeneous in one of two contrary ways. But a member of an effect-set bears one or other of those predicates because of *its own* quality of being just right or else wrong in one or another way. If we wish to identify the wrongnesses with excess and deficiency in some kind of continuous quantity of which the particular just-right response is or expresses a median amount, the quantity in question cannot be *frequency of occurrence,* which applies only to *types* of response considered as multiply instantiated. Aristotle seizes on any likely candidate, depending on the context, for this role of continuum of nonfrequentative quantity; thus it may be the action of *giving,* instances of which are said to be excessive, deficient etc. if too much etc. is given; or it may be the feeling of *anger,* where the instances differ in intensity. And since the predicates 'excessive' etc. are applied to individual responses in virtue of their being or not being appropriate in their particular circumstances, the application does not depend on a mechanical comparison with other cases. Thus if a response is held to be excessively angry, this is not because the anger is more than what was found right for some other situation. On the contrary, what is excessive anger for this situation might have been too little for that other, so that the median in one case exceeds what would be excessive in the other.

Thus this notion of the appropriate response as the median response does not entail that it is always appropriate to respond moderately. If, in a given case, it is right to be moderately angry, this is not because the moderate as such is right; in a different case that moderate anger might be beyond or below what is called for. However, this holds good only if we compare cases of anger in the abstract. If, instead, we compare instances of anger in relevantly similar situations, it becomes reasonable to complain that this demonstration was excessive, or that one deficient, on the ground that the first was more intense. Such evaluative comparisons will, of course, include not merely the same individual's different responses to similar situations, but different individuals' responses to the same one: 'Why was it all right for you to take it quietly, whereas he hit back?' And as well as a principle of fairness—'Treat like cases the same'—we also recognise a principle of proportionality which takes account of possible, even unlikely, cases as well as the actual. Thus it may be complained that someone is excessively angry on the ground that if it is right to be as angry as this for *this* reason, the degree of anger appropriate if something really outrageous were to happen would be beyond human capacity. 'Save extreme reactions for extreme situations' is a principle that nudges in the direction of moderation, partly because what counts as extreme counts so in relation to what is usual, so that common situations by definition are not extreme; and partly because the wise person bears in mind that often even when things are going worse than was previously imagined possible, worse is possible still.

However, Aristotle's position is clearly not that the *moderate* response is always appropriate, since the whole tenor of his ethics is that no one kind of response is right for all situations. A more subtle mistake would be to identify appropriate with *proportioned* response. This may seem plausible if we assume that bad conduct is undiscriminating behaviour. Aristotle may seem to suggest this when he says that children who are allowed to shrink from everything frightening become cowards, while those who always rush in become foolhardy. But he does not say, and the words do not imply, that these bad characters, when established, mindlessly always react in the same way. This no more follows than it follows that because virtue is fostered by an early diet of mixed behaviour, the virtuous person mindlessly rushes in on 50 per cent of the occasions and runs away on the others. Virtue is not intermediate between vices because it is a mixture of the vices! But then is it intermediate because its responses are more discriminating? They may be more discriminating than those of a nature less mature. But many vices are marked not by a brutish absence of priorities, but by intelligently selective pursuit of wrong ones. We have no warrant to interpret Aristotle's notion of vice as necessarily excluding the proportionality of response that is a mark of any sort of rational coherent behaviour. For example, a devotee of physical pleasure would surely roughly measure the worthwhileness of this or that effort in terms of quantity of pleasure, cost, duration, certainty, and whatever other dimensions have seemed to make plausible the idea of an hedonic calculus.

We must ask, then, what point is made by calling right responses 'intermediate', if it is not that they are moderate, nor that they are in proportion to other comparable responses, seeing that these properties may be shared by wrong responses. Let us recall the context of this question. Aristotle has two grounds for calling the excellences 'mean' or 'intermediate' dispositions. One is the factual intermediacy, or mixed nature, of the class of actions by which (in his view) virtue is inculcated. Virtue, then, is likewise a factually intermediate disposition because of its relation to that class of actions. On this basis one might also go on to say that individual virtuous responses are (factually) intermediate, meaning that they are expressions of a disposition that is termed 'intermediate' on the grounds just mentioned. In this mode of speaking, the intermediacy of the responses has to do with their origin and is not primarily a feature of their individual *appropriateness* to the situation. But this is not how Aristotle applies the concept of intermediacy to a virtuous response. He works the other way about, treating the good responses as intermediate per se; and because of this (his other ground), the disposition giving rise to them is said to be intermediate derivatively. Thus our question regarding the point of his calling the responses 'intermediate' is also a question about the validity of this latter ground for applying the term to moral virtue.

Is the alleged intermediacy of right responses supposed to guide a prospective agent, so that he should consider what would be an intermediate reaction and enact it? There are passages where Aristotle seems to say this, as for instance when he compares virtue to 'an art that does its work well by looking to the intermediate and judging its works by this standard' (1106 b 8–9). This suggests that one could discover that such and such a possible response would be intermediate independently of knowing that it would be right, and from this deduce that it would be right. But there seems to be no independent sense of 'intermediate' such that every response is right to which that sense applies. We saw this point in connection with 'moderate' and 'proportioned'. And even if being moderate and being proportioned were necessary features of virtuous response (and the first certainly is not), we should still lack firm guidance on what actions to avoid; for although some wrong responses are wrong because they are too high or too low on some scale or other, not all wrong responses can be faulted in such a way, unless metaphorically. What does a person do too much or too little of when he agrees to sell secrets to a foreign power? He may act with insufficient loyalty or from excessive desire for wealth, but neither of these is the treacherous response itself which the example is about. And the person who says 'No' to the enemy agent's suggestion probably does not do so because accepting it would be going too far or not far enough on some scale: such a reason may be nowhere near his mind.[32]

We also have statements such as this:

> both fear and confidence and appetite and anger and pity and in general pleasure and pain may be felt both too much and too little, and in both cases not well; but to feel them at the right times, with reference to the right objects, towards the right people with the right aim, and in the right way, is what is both intermediate and best,

and this is characteristic of excellence. Similarly with regard to actions also . . . (1106 b 18–24)

Here, 'intermediate' seems virtually a synonym for 'right' and it includes every category of rightness, with no special emphasis on the quantifiable. One could hardly take what is intermediate in this sense as an independently discernible standard by which to determine what would be best. Now it is not easy to understand why, if 'intermediate response' simply means 'right response', Aristotle clings to the term 'intermediate' and the associated language of excess and defect. The explanation must lie not in the presumed intermediacy in any substantial sense (for none applies) of the right response itself, but rather in some sort of intermediacy belonging to the disposition that gives rise to right responses.

We have seen how this disposition may be said to be intermediate because it is inculcated by intermediate (mixed) behaviour. But it is also intermediate in another sense: a virtuous person is dispositionally neither too fearful nor too cautious, cares about wealth, pleasure, the opinion of others etc. neither too much nor too little, *to* make the right responses in particular situations. It is not that the right responses themselves are intermediate, although Aristotle, as we have seen, falls into this way of thinking at times; but rather that virtue itself is a disposition such that whoever has it is protected from excesses and deficiencies of feeling and impulse that *lead to* faulty particular responses. In an obvious sense, then, virtue is intermediate between the temperaments typified by such excesses and deficiencies. It may seem to follow, although in fact it does not, that responses manifesting, respectively, the excessive, deficient and intermediate temperaments are themselves to be viewed as too much, too little or the right amount of something. Perhaps that is why Aristotle, instead of saying only that virtue is an intermediate disposition that 'aims at the right or appropriate response', says instead, at moments, that virtue is a disposition that 'aims at the intermediate—which is the right—response'.

This notion that virtue '*aims at* the intermediate' betrays, I believe, a confusion on his part between the two perspectives distinguished at the beginning of this section. The ground-level virtuous person, on any particular occasion, may be said to aim to respond well; but he does not necessarily look for the intermediate response, unless this means only that he seeks to do what is right and proper for the situation. Encouraging a prospective agent to aim at the intermediate is not helpful even as a metaphor. On the other hand, within the framework of Aristotle's ethical theory there certainly exists a figure whose proper function it is to aim at the balanced *temperament,* and for whom a prescription in these terms might be a guide of sorts. This is the *politikos,* which is to say any mature member of the community in his or her capacity of helping form or develop moral qualities in others. On this level it is useful to point out that a balanced temperament is much less likely to be achieved either through a training that forces people to face, or through one that allows them to evade, everything fearful or unpleasant. Yet even on this level no exact recipes are possible, since it is not as if one could mix (or weave) a desirable temperament out of definite quantities of emotional ingredients according to formula. But if Aristotle did not always distinguish the different levels of his investigation, he could be deceived into thinking the doctrine of the mean useful in ways in which in fact it is not. This may be what happens in *NE* II.2, where he bewails the impossibility of giving exact rules for correct particular *responses* (1104 a 5–9); then says that he must give what help he can (1104 a 10–11); and then goes on to discuss, not *responses,* but *dispositions.*

While the doctrine of the right response as intermediate is of no practical use to the prospective agent, it does make an important statement on the level of ethical theory,[33] and here the metaphor though obvious is not idle. The theory is that no kind of natural[34] response, neutrally described, as e.g. being afraid, hitting back, eating, grieving, is either right or wrong in itself; this depends always on the particulars which further determine the case. The proposition that the particular right response is 'intermediate' amounts to this: in every case a description of the right response (and similarly for wrong ones) can be analysed into (1) a term representing some general response-type, whether action or feeling, and (2) a set of specifications of particular determinants such as objects, time, place, manner, degree of intensity, attendant circumstances etc. With different determinants the same sort of response can be right and wrong, and wrong in different ways. Granted that the possible responses appropriate for any situation are few compared with the faulty ones, the image is not inept of a target whose position defines a pair of much larger areas as the fields of 'too far' and 'not far enough'.

This view clearly bears on the theory and practice of moral education, and on moral attitudes in general. If no type of natural response is as such wrong, there is none which the educator ought to try to suppress or eradicate. And if in some case he were to try, as likely as not he would be destroying (supposing it feasible) the possibility of some range of good particular responses as well as bad. Moreover, if the difference between good and bad response is in the particular determining circumstances, there is no reason not to hold, as indeed Aristotle does, that good and bad persons share or began by sharing the same basic capacities for response. They are of common emotional stock even if their developed prohairetic attitudes differ too sharply to permit compromise, mutual respect or even toleration. This confirms the view that we are not good or bad by nature, and that training makes the difference.

The position is not indisputable. For instance, envy *(phthonos)* appears in one of Aristotle's lists of basic types of response supposed neither good nor bad per se. But it would not be ridiculous to hold it always wrong to envy, no matter whom, for what, how much, etc. It would not be an obvious mistake to try to eradicate envy altogether, whereas only a lunatic would try to do away with fear. If one accepted that envy as such is wrong, one could only maintain an Aristotelian view of human nature by ousting it from the list of basic natural types of response and analysing any particular case of 'envy' as a logical complex containing (1) a term that denotes some more basic and universal feeling such as 'longing' (also on Aristotle's list), along with (2) specifications in respect of object, circumstances, etc. The example shows that within Aristotle's framework a value-free theory of 'basic' human nature is impossible.[35] For he would not be willing to include as part of our basic natural equipment any propensity that he judged to be bad as such.[36] If such were part of the normal endowment, the development of virtue would be against the natural grain. Virtue could be achieved only by altogether overriding some part of our nature. But then virtue could not be achieved, since Aristotle holds on general grounds that nothing can be kept in a state contrary to its nature for indefinite time and stably; yet virtue is above all a stable disposition. It cannot be true that 'the heart of man is evil from his youth', for in that case human virtue and the human good would be not *humanly* practicable.

## X. How We Learn to Be Good

Our topic now is Aristotle's conception of moral training. How does a person become morally good? Not by 'teaching', which is a business of words, reasons and explanations, but by a process called *'ēthismos'*, which is to say, the inculcation of *ĕthē*. *Ĕthē* are habits, customs, mores, accepted ways of behaviour, usages. No one of these English terms always gives the right nuance: I shall vary them as exposition demands. Most translators have decided on 'habit', to which they stick. Whichever term is appropriate, it is always understood that *ĕthē* are not part of the natural endowment. Nor are they simply the results of interaction between the physical environment and some element in human physical nature. Screwing up one's eyes is not universal, but it is not on that account an *ĕthos* of those who dwell where vision has to be shielded from glare.

Moral qualities are *ēthē* in Greek, a word which, as Aristotle remarks, differs only slightly from *'ĕthē'*. Whatever the actual etymological relation, this fact provides him with an a priori ground for asserting what in any case experience shows: that moral dispositions are formed by *ĕthismos*. Our values prove their practical reality in action and response to particular situations; and when the attitudes are genuinely our own we are at home with ourselves as responding like that, and find it natural. As the poet Evenus said, *'ĕthos'* (custom, habit) ends by becoming nature for human beings' (1152 a 31–33). And a person's *ĕthē* (moral qualities) are also a sort of nature which he acquires through upbringing and sustains by his own practice. If we ask concerning someone who cares about justice or honesty why he behaves fairly and honestly, the answer is: that it is his way, or he is that sort of person. But this is of the same structure as what we say about physical things when no further explanation of their behaviour can be forthcoming. It is not because of some further feature of the stone that the stone falls downwards: the stone is a substance of a nature to behave in this way unless impeded. In science we classify things in accordance with what we think each kind is such as to do and show itself being. Similarly, human beings can be classified according to their ethical natures, and this nature, good or bad, is the ethical essence or substance. Thus although the *Categories* (8 b 25 ff.) gives goodness and badness as examples of *qualities,* acquired through alteration to a substance already in being, the process by which a person comes to be of a determinate moral character can also, and more suggestively, be viewed as the process by which there comes into being a particular ethical substance.

In what does the process consist?

of all the things that come to us by nature we first acquire the potentiality and later exhibit the activity (this is plain in the case of the senses; for it was not by often seeing or often hearing that we got these senses, but on the contrary we had them before we used them and did not come to have them by using them); but the excellences we get by first exercising them, as also happens in the case of the arts as well. For the things we have to learn before we can do, we learn by doing, e.g. men become builders by building and lyre-players by playing the lyre; so too we become just by doing just acts, temperate by doing temperate acts, brave by doing brave acts. This is confirmed by what happens in states; for legislators make the citizens good by forming habits in them [*ĕthizontes*] and this is the wish of every legislator; and those who do not effect it miss their mark, and it is in this that a good constitution differs from a bad one ... by doing the acts that we do in our transactions with other men we become just or unjust, and by doing the acts that we do in the presence of danger, and by being habituated to feel fear or confidence, we become brave or cowardly. The same is true of appetites and feelings of anger; some men become temperate and good-tempered, others self-indulgent and irascible, by behaving in one way or the other in the appropriate circumstances. Thus, in one word, dispositions arise out of like activities. (1103 a 26–b 22)

Let us take it that experience bears this out, and also shows no other more effective method of moral development. From a practical point of view that may be all that needs to be known by the budding *politikoi* in Aristotle's audience. Even so, it is remarkable that he has almost nothing to say about *how* or *why* by acting in a certain way we acquire the corresponding moral disposition. That skills, too, are acquired only through practice makes it no less remarkable. It is not our business, perhaps, to build a theory of this on Aristotle's behalf; yet we shall not ignore such clues as he does provide.[37]

The only doubt which Aristotle himself anticipates is levelled at the view that moral qualities are *consequent* on the relevant behaviour. Surely someone who does just or temperate things is just or temperate already (1105 a 16–21)? Aristotle replies, we have seen, by pointing to differences between doing just things and doing them as the just person would. But the more he stresses the differences, the more one is entitled to wonder how merely performing the actions leads to moral character.

He has already implied a partial answer: we are of a nature to be able to receive the virtues, but are completed by them only through *ĕthos* (1103 a 25–26). From the start we have the capacity for prohairetic activity, but this capacity is necessarily indeterminate, since without the *ĕthē* of a specific upbringing it cannot issue in *prohaireseis* of any determinate sort. The indeterminate capacity could be said to be looking for determination, since we shall be incomplete until we exercise it, and we cannot exercise it unless determinately. Thus ours is a nature that takes to *ĕthismos* and could even be said to be rushing to form set ways of prohairetic behaviour. And although Aristotle speaks mainly of virtue, we are in a sense equally completed if the definite state thus acquired is vicious. Looked at in this way it is not at all surprising that from morally formless we become firmly prohairetic beings. It ought to be equally unsurprising that the development takes place through *ĕthismos* and through practising the relevant actions. But on some accounts of this process, it is a mystery that the result comes about.

Abstractly conceived, the purpose of moral education is to render the nonrational part of the soul amenable to autonomous rational prescription. Our question is how this is done. Or, rather, since we already know from experience that it is done by accustoming the young, through practice, to behaving in certain ways which do not come naturally in the first place, our question is: How is this result achieved by that method? Let us approach by recalling what 'amenability to reason' entails. Two levels were distinguished earlier (by an analytic distinction not necessarily reflected in psychologically discernible phases). On the one hand, the nonrational part is to be made (1) receptive so that it actually 'listens to reason'. Since 'listening to reason' is a practical listening, this means a readiness to execute the prescription smoothly. So the nonrational part must be brought to a state of detachment from the emotions and drives natural to it. Alternatively, we can think of this as a state in which the nonrational part will, on any occasion, assume directions, proportions and intensities necessary for conformity to the prescription. On this level, we are thinking of the nonrational part as having to be 'brought to order' in a general sense, so that it then cooperates with any particular order (in the sense of 'instruction'). The model for this is child and parent; the latter represents the rational prescription, but it also represents something else: a moving cause whereby the prerational agent is called to order or heedfulness of *whatever* prescription is issued. The acts of communication (gesture, speech, whatever) by which a child is encouraged to do X, or checked for doing Y, have two aspects: (a) they get the child's attention and, it is hoped, thereby get him into an attitude of practical receptiveness for what is to come, and (b) they express specifically what he is to do. One reason why it is confusing to apply this model within the one soul is that the act by which an internal rational prescription is formed within the soul is *not* at the same time an act of quelling noise from the nonrational part and getting it to stand at attention. If we speak of a faculty of reason, its competence extends only to the production of rational judgments of whatever kind, and it makes no sense to ascribe to *reason* a power or an effort to induce their acceptance.

Hence where the rational prescription is internal, 'amenability to reason' denotes not only the executive readiness described above, but also (2) a reflective state in which it is possible for a rational prescription to form in the first place. If the nonrational part is absorbed in its own impulses, there is no space in which a prescription can even take shape, for *within* the soul there is no equivalent to the case of a parent formulating an instruction to an as yet completely unheeding child. (An inner prescription, once it has been formulated in the necessary atmosphere of obedient receptiveness, may later cease to be heeded, if execution takes time or has to be deferred: the interval allows for distractions.) In other words, the reflective space enabling reason to form a direction at all is identical with that distance between responsive part and its impulses that allows the response, so formed, to go forward into the world as an actual event. In a practical sense the impulses are absent to the extent that the rational response *does* take place: they fade into nonbeing, even if the scene of their might-have-been practical presence is marked by traces of pure feeling.

Thus the process whereby an untrained soul becomes receptive and obedient to external authority is identical with the process whereby it comes to be morally in a state to be able to form its own judgments of what is right, or to mediate its behavioural and emotional response by its own rational perception. But now what about the *content* of this reason-mediated response, which for convenience I shall continue to speak of as the 'rational prescription'? Aristotle, we have seen, distinguishes *within* the prescriptive faculty a desiderative from a more purely intellectual component. These are by no means automatically good; there are virtues and defects corresponding to each. Now the virtues that ensure the soundness of a prescription's desiderative content are virtues of character *(ēthikai aretai)*, which he also assigns to the 'listening' part of the soul. The arrangement, as we saw in Section III of this chapter, seems messy, even incoherent. Why does Aristotle not postulate three types of human virtue: one, a set of intellectual virtues; two, the virtues that ensure the goodness of the desiderative side of a rational prescription; and three, the virtue of amenability to this two-sided prescription?

It is because notwithstanding their functionally quite different contributions to the occurrence of a particular right response, dispositions of the second and third types are educationally identical: they are goals of the same process, whose name *'ēthismos'* invites us to apply the seemingly cognate term *'ēthikē'* to both its kinds of result. The etymology helps Aristotle reach this position, but the position itself does not depend on that, but on the fact that the general method of *ĕthismos* does not distinguish the goals since the method is identical for each. True, if we focus on already developed individuals, we see some striking cases in which serious defects of the second type coexist with virtues of the other two. 'The person's values are wrong', we say, 'though nothing is wrong with his intellect and his self-discipline.' But, of course, if his values carry forward those of whoever brought him up, then from the latter's point of view he is a total success and an unqualified triumph of training. Aristotle's division of the virtues into two instead of three types is a remarkable example of his practical approach to philosophical ethics: the division reflects the producer's perspective on virtue, not that of a judge or biographer of the product.

The virtues of character account, then, for both the *that* and the *what* of particular *orthoi logoi* (these being the ultimate goal of the educator): for the fact that they are formed and substantiated in an actual response, and for the desiderative concerns expressed in them. How is this so? Because the basic impulses and emotions are got under control in children by encouraging them to engage in other kinds of activity, which are kinds that get a chance to take hold only in agents not wholly given up to basic impulses. Aristotle divides the nonrational desires into two broad categories: appetites *(epithumiai)*, which are commonly exemplified by physical urges,[38] and impulses of temper *(thumos)*, of which the most obvious example is anger. Desires expressed[39] in a rational prescription are a third kind, which he calls *'boulēsis'*, usually translated 'wish' and often glossed as 'rational desire'[40] (1111 b 11; *EE* 1223 a 27; b 26–27; 1225 b 25). A *boulēsis* is a desire for something conceived of as good (by contrast with an appetite, which desires its object qua pleasant; cf. e.g. 1113 a 15–24; 1111 a 32–33). But perhaps it is more to the present point that a *boulēsis* is a desire for something at a distance. The distance may be such that the object is not practicable at all; thus we can wish that something in the past had been different (cf. 1139 b 8–9), or we can wish for something to happen over which we know we have no control (1111 b 22–24). However, some wishes are for things that can come about through us, so in what way are these objects at a distance? They are objects such that the mere desiring of them does not automatically carry with it instinctive action of a sort that would tend to satisfy the desire. This is by contrast with the appetites and temper, which are typically aroused by the presence or imagined presence of the appropriate object or occasion, as e.g. food or drink or a sexually attractive individual, or an insult, obstacle or act of aggression. The desire to take or otherwise engage is expressed straightaway in typical movements immediately linked to perception of the object or the triggering circumstance. Hence it is characteristic of these desires automatically to tend to their own satisfaction without mediation by reflective thought:[41] if the tempting drink is before me, I reach for it, or my body does, without my having to think how, any more than I have to think how to feel towards that object. But there are objects towards which we have no inbuilt mechanism of effective and appropriate reaction. When one of these is desired, the desire leads to action only if I can separately identify a means (or presumed means) to realize it. And whatever means I identify, I identify it *as* a means to the desired end; hence I conceive of the latter as the future effect of my present action. The knowledge of the means is verbal and articulate (at least potentially), and above all the knowledge is acquired. These are connected features, for I can teach others the means to something, either by words or in some way pointing out a causal process distinct from the desired end. In this sense I myself hardly know *how* I reach for a drink or duck a blow; but I do not need to know how in order to do it effectively, and I do not need to teach others how, since basic nature has equipped them, too, with the necessary mechanism.

A *boulēsis,* then, is properly called 'rational desire', not because its objects are discerned as good by some kind of intellectual vision which intuits the goodness as we intuit a proportion between numbers, but because they are such that only a reflectively rational being can take an appropriate interest in them. It is not necessarily inappropriate to wish that the past had been different, but for this one has to have a sense of the past and an understanding of why things would have been better had it been different. No one could wish for no reason that Troy had not been taken (Aristotle's example) in the way in which one can *just want* a drink of water or to return a blow. And when the wish is an interest in obtaining something regarded as obtainable, it does not remain appropriate unless it takes practical form; thus appropriate interest is possible only for beings capable of devising and understanding *ways* of achieving the object.[42]

Now moral training is not only a matter of first curbing nonrational impulses and thereby eliciting a more structured attitude, for the process can work in either direction. One way to detach the child from an impulse or fit of emotion is *by* arousing interest in a more distant objective. ('More distant' still means that one cannot even see the objective as actual or possible unless one sees past the immediacy of the situation. Thus the interest in it becomes causally structured the instant it becomes practical.) This is how values and priorities begin to be cultivated—values and priorities which will be expressed in future prohairetic responses. The human ability to see things in other and wider terms is such that a child's interest in a mundane objective like finishing the food on his plate or getting dressed or helping a younger child to dress can easily at the same time be an interest in doing something neatly, getting something right, getting something right *oneself,* not disgracing the family, being responsible for someone else, preparing now for the future, not being wasteful, respecting others by using properly what they have made, being helpful, doing something because it is worthwhile even though one does not feel like it.[43] And his interest in the same mundane objective can also be an interest in being superior to someone else, in lording it over someone else, in showing that *he* does not need to be told what to do, and so on. Here we have the potential for many virtues and for not a few vices, since some of the learned good traits, if carried further, lead to meanness, vanity, arrogance, stubborness. But just as one learns in a practical way very quickly that the appropriate thing to do is not necessarily what one feels like doing, so one is in a position to learn from the start, and continually reconfirm, that the appropriate thing to do is not necessarily what seems obvious at first even to a more cultivated eye. Thus earliest training, which is a training away from appetite and impulse, already contains seeds of the general openness that should save one from mechanical adherence even to higher values.

Having seen what virtue of character is, and how the same virtues that make possible the prescription and its execution are cultivated by the same processes as those that ensure its excellent content, let us return to the question: How simply by *doing* just and temperate deeds does one acquire the virtues of justice and temperance? Is it Aristotle's idea that the normal child starts with an indeterminate desire or willingness to do what is fine and right, and through specific doing under guidance by others he acquires knowledge of what to do when? Or is it rather that in the doing he also acquires that willingness? Should we think of him as learning, by doing, to enjoy the doing; or should we think of him as developing moral muscle through repeated action, so that what was initially hard comes easily? The latter metaphor is misleading so far as it suggests that mere repetition has the desired moral result. However many times he does it against his will or under threat of punishment, he will not end by identifying himself with the action in the way characteristic of virtue. Nor is it clear from Aristotle's words whether the sameness of the repeated actions matters more, or their difference. If we focus on sameness in a narrow sense, we are probably gripped by the model of drill which softens up initial resistance like gymnastic exercise. Some detect this thinking in the following passage:

> it is plain that none of the moral excellences arises in us by nature [or contrary to nature]; for nothing that exists by nature can form a habit contrary to its nature. For instance the stone which by nature moves downwards cannot be habituated to move upwards, not even if one tries to train it by throwing it up ten thousand times . . .
> (1103 a 18–22)

However, this may only mean that it makes sense to try again with a recalcitrant human being, but not with a stone. We need not take the passage to say (what would be illogical as well as unrealistic) that because sheer repetition cannot train a stone, therefore similar sheer repetition does train a human being to virtue. If the young person is trained to justice by getting him to perform just actions again and again, these may be physically and psychologically quite different though they have it in common that they are just.[44] This, too, is something which we have to learn if we are going to have the virtue of justice ourselves, so that practice should cover all sorts of cases, in which the just action is sometimes a giving, sometimes a withholding, sometimes treating people alike, sometimes differently and so on.

*Habits* of doing what is usually desirable are important, not least because at any level they free the agent to reach for special achievement on a higher level. Forming a habit is connected with repetition, but where *what* is repeated are (for example) just acts, habituation cannot be a mindless process, and the habit (once formed) of acting justly cannot be blind in its operations, since one needs intelligence to see why different things are just under different circumstances.[45] So far as habit plays a part, it is not that of autopilot, where we take for granted that we know (without special monitoring) *what* to do to get to the destination; rather, the moral habit is one by which it can be taken for granted *that* whatever we are going do, it will be what we find appropriate. Now how does doing and repeated doing generate this habit?

It engenders concrete experience of very general things: being an agent, trying, succeeding through trying, concentrating against distractions, looking for what is relevant. It generates the knowledge that one can rise to an occasion, as well as pride in having so risen. It seems no more possible to know without personal experience what these moments of action are like than to absorb the quality of sounds and tastes solely from someone's description. But we not only learn about our own possibilities as agents in carrying out the actions which test our agency, they having been pointed out by someone else as right; for at a basic stage we also learn, by doing, that the things which we are encouraged to do are indeed what *are to be done;* and by doing we also learn to do them 'for the sake of the noble'.[46] For we become aware of the unconditional nature of the response expected of us from the fact that those in charge at the beginning, if they carry out their function, will not let us get away with not doing what they make it clear we should. Why should the child accept that A is the proper response if he thinks that the parent in saying so does not mean it, and why should he think that the parent means it if the latter is not firm about compliance?

It is not that the child's doing A teaches him that A is what he is supposed to do; in a sense he already has this information from the parental instruction. Rather, it is that being *got to do A* teaches him that what you are supposed to do is indeed what you *do.* He becomes aware that his own not anyway wanting to do it is not a consideration for the parent. (It would not occur to him to think that the parent insists only because he or she is unaware of his, the child's, reluctance!) Learning that there are things which one is expected to do even when all concerned are aware that one does not feel like doing them is perhaps the only way we have of learning from scratch that there are things worth doing and aiming for which are not immediately pleasant. This is our way into an active sense of 'noble'. We do not need to know why the enjoined things are good, and we may be incapable of understanding the reasons. We learn by practice that they are good, because by our practice we accept that the authority who says so means it; we also thereby learn that these things are good in a way which belongs to a world beyond the world of impulse, since their claim overrides what we feel like; and from this we know that the things which we immediately felt like doing could never be good in that way. Our sense of the goodness of the former is the sense of their being worth rising to; but the things whose drawing us consists in our naturally finding them pleasant cannot be risen to, since desires for them are the point from which we start.

Thus the noble (at least for human beings) presupposes a departure point in what is not noble. Our original nature prepares us to be at home with the noble and with reason and structured agency; otherwise we could never come to completion as autonomous prohairetic beings. But the original preparedness is only general and indeterminate, and it remains a potentiality until specific direction is provided: a distanced focus on a specific object. This cannot come from our own impulse; on the contrary, the prevalence of impulse within the untrained soul entails that the focus must be generated from outside. In short, the logic of our natural bent for the noble is such that we begin by being utterly dependent on others for our development to autonomous nobility. It is, of course, human nature to tend to accept (even if against the immediate grain) those others' authority, since otherwise our nature has no chance of becoming actually human.

## XI. A Basis for Justice

We have traced Aristotle's conception of human virtue from its basis in the perfectly general truism that the virtue of a thing is that whereby it functions well according to its nature, through specific determinations relating to *human* nature. The field of human excellence and defect was labelled 'rationality', and rationality was explained in terms of the prescriptive and obedient parts of the soul. The detailed expounding of the natures of these parts and their virtues has centred mainly on the correlative concepts of rational choice or *prohairesis,* and the prohairetic state that makes a *prohairesis* possible and effective. We have only begun to comb this complex array of topics, since Aristotle has yet to give his account of the intellectual process of arriving at a *prohairesis;* and he still has to face the logical problems which arise when we try to classify the condition (incontinence) of someone who for no good cause abandons his formed *prohairesis.*

It is clear, though, that these further investigations will be carried on within the area already outlined, and that they will contribute to what will continue to be a formal inquiry into the virtues and defects of the ethical soul. Thus we should not expect the discussion, either now or at a later stage, to yield grounds for deducing any substantial conclusions to the effect that this or that set of empirically described general ways of acting and feeling is or is not virtuous. The doctrine of the mean, with its postulate of different types of continua (whether of feeling, action or type of situation) defines each of the moral virtues as a disposition to light on the mean in the relevant continuum. But the analytic proposition (as we today would view it) that courage lights on the mean in the fear-confidence dimension, does not justify Aristotle's or anyone else's judgments about which actions and types of personality are in fact courageous. This is because what counts as the mean in any given case depends on what the *orthos logos* would be in that case: on what practical wisdom would perceive as the right or proper response. Thus to risk one's life for what practical wisdom would see to be an unworthy end is not an act of courage.

Aristotle takes it for granted that the *orthos logos* is objectively correct. Perhaps the coward considers the courageous person rash, and the rash considers him timorous, each regarding his own response as the standard for the mean (1108 b 15–26); but they are simply mistaken. We need not look far or deep to see how Aristotle can legitimately take this to be so. No one would need to deliberate if every passing practical impression were as good as any other. And it is obvious to the slightest intelligence that 'man is by nature social' (1097 b 11), which squarely rules out private worlds of value no less than private worlds of fact. That Aristotle spends no time on this is only to be expected.

But what does call for consideration is whether he gets away too easily with the assumption that the human virtues really are those qualities which we, or his hearers, ordinarily regard as virtues. Granted that some such assumption is a necessary starting point for everyone concerned with ethics, should not the assumption be paid for somewhere along the way? For in any case the starting points (in general) of this type of inquiry are not axiomatic premises to be held rigidly under the same interpretations (truth automatically preserved, therefore) all along the line. However, to bring forward for discussion, even by way of defence, ordinary views about what qualities are virtues might be deemed idle troublemaking if the original assumption had never been seriously questioned. 'If it ain't broke, don't fix it'. But as Aristotle and his hearers very well know, this is not the case in the present instance. For they are all familiar with the first two books of Plato's *Republic*.[47]

Since a virtue is a disposition for good, right, appropriate response, what counts as a virtue depends on what responses are counted good, appropriate etc. While no rules can be given that would automatically justify particular practical findings, the findings are nonetheless influenced by values whose validity is ordinarily never in question, though the detail of their application may often be. One, and many would say, the main such value, is that of justice in the broad and informal sense in which justice is the theme of the *Republic*. To rate an action 'just' in this sense is to say that it manifests regard for the rights and interests of others and for law and society in general. The concern of course may stem from various motives, one of which could be self-interest. But the circumstances grounding our judgment that a given response is 'just' frequently do not include the fact that the response would be to the agent's own interest as this is usually conceived. Thus if someone believes that by doing the just thing he will gain some personal advantage of a kind that he can specify and knowingly look forward to as an effect of his action, then this may explain why he chooses in general or (which is not quite the same) generally chooses to do what is just; but the personal advantage which his belief presumes is not in general any part of the reason for describing his behaviour as 'just'. Now Aristotle does not consider someone morally virtuous who does what in fact is right and proper, but only incidentally. Hence to the extent that what is right and proper is determined by considerations of justice in the broad sense indicated, a person is not virtuous unless he cares about doing what is just because what is just is as such right and proper. Moreover, since Aristotle on the whole endorses ordinary notions of the right and proper, he certainly holds that what is right and proper is decided largely, if not exclusively, by reference to the claims of justice in that broad sense. It follows that Aristotle's morally virtuous person is one who actually cares to do what is just simply because that is what it is; and this attitude pervades the life of the virtuous person, being reflected in all his responses regardless of which of the various moral virtues is especially evinced in a given response. Thus Aristotle says:

in one sense we call those acts just that tend to produce and preserve happiness and its components for the political society. And the law bids us do both the acts of a brave man (e.g. not to desert our post or take to flight or throw away our arms), and those of a temperate man (e.g. not to commit adultery or outrage), and those of a good-tempered man (e.g. not to strike another or speak evil), and similarly with regard to the other excellences and forms of wickedness, commanding some acts and forbidding others; and the rightly-framed law does this rightly, and the hastily conceived one less well. This form of justice, then, is complete excellence—not absolutely, but in relation to others. And therefore justice is often thought to be the greatest of excellences and 'neither evening nor morning star' is so wonderful; and proverbially 'in justice is every excellence comprehended'. (1129 b 17–30)

Now by what right does Aristotle inject this standard attitude into the *Ethics*? We can see that he might not welcome a challenge in this direction, because the statesman argument from which the *NE* starts locks him into the assumption. (He is not in the same way locked into it in the *EE,* which does not depend on the statesman argument, but here, too, the assumption is never in question.) The argument was that there must be a supreme good for human beings, because the statesman is supremely authoritative, and this makes sense only if there is a supreme good for him to aim at. It then quickly became clear that the statesman aims at producing (the conditions for) excellent people. This is as much as to define the supremely important kind of excellence (as distinct from, e.g., the excellence of carpenter or navigator) as the kind which the statesman works to foster. In this context, 'excellence' or 'virtue' is sure to be understood as entailing 'justice', since the statesman as such cannot but be concerned with the cooperative law-abiding dimension of human excellence, even if this is not his sole concern. If we were to construct a notion of human excellence and a corresponding notion of happiness or excellent functioning in which justice did not figure, a discussion could certainly be held on whether this is a coherent and, if so, true conception of the human good. But it would be utterly implausible to identify the human good thus conceived with the *statesman's* definitive goal, since the statesman's definitive goal continues to be the existence of a good political community. Now, to subscribe to a justiceless notion of the supreme good is not necessarily to deny a rôle to the statesman. We could still say that his proper concern is with the socially desirable characteristics; but then for consistency we should have to say that these are not intrinsic to human virtue and happiness, but are means to happiness (in the same way as, for Aristotle, physical strength and material possessions are only means).[48] In that case we should have to abandon (if we ever held it) the position that the goal which defines the statesman is the supreme good. And from this it follows that the idea of the statesman and the statesman's proper objective cannot be taken as a basis for showing that there is such an end as the one supposedly referred to by the title 'the supreme good'.

So if we accept the way in which, at the opening of the *NE,* Aristotle establishes the nonemptiness of the concept 'supreme human good', and thereby establishes the existence of a unified field of ethical inquiry (since everything now converges on determining the nature and provenance of that good), we cannot question whether justice is a dimension of virtue and just activity a dimension of happiness. This may explain why Aristotle does not engage with that question; but is he entitled to a starting point which relieves him of this burden of engagement? He might be, if the statesman argument gave the only available ground for the claim that there is a supreme good or, alternatively, if other grounds for the claim all entailed that the supreme good includes justice. But Aristotle's other, much more noticed, proof that there is an end of ends—namely, that man like everything else must have a characteristic good functioning, which in the case of man is called 'happiness'—shows only that the supreme good is virtuous functioning and sets no constraints on what should be considered a virtue.

That justice is a dimension of human virtue cannot be derived from 'Man is by nature social', because this obvious truth can be and has been interpreted in such a way that man's social nature and the bonds to which it gives rise are not positive factors in happiness and excellence, but the unwelcome consequence of human weakness. We have to live with others, and by and large we have to observe their rights in order to avoid the yet more undesirable condition where we are each the victims of everyone else's unlimited greed and aggression. But the best life, which is not to be aspired to except by individuals extraordinary for their ruthless intelligence, would be that of taking and enjoying whatever one wanted, whenever one wanted it, regardless of others' claims. That is the truly happy life, and the rest of us, the herd, must make do with a second best, which is the fulfilling of as many of our desires as we dare under the shadow of the usual sanctions. So Glaucon supported by Adimantus, with Thrasymachus in the background (*Republic* I and II). In this situation it is wise to do just things as a rule, and wisdom of course is a virtue; but caring about justice for its own sake is not wisdom but the foolishness that mistakes means for ends. Those who, as a necessary evil, pay their outward respects to the rights of others under no illusion that this is of any but instrumental value are not lacking in the *virtue* of justice, if justice is an attitude that values justice as such, since on this theory justice is not a virtue (cf. *Republic* 348 d). But they certainly exercise a virtue which, like justice, can be understood only by reference to other people. The quality in question is a judicious mixture of cunnings: the cunning of the hunter and the cunning of the hunted, where the other term of each relation is constituted by members of the same human community.

This position was put forward as an objective theory of the human good which most people are mistaken in not realizing to be the truth. The mistake is of course deliberately fostered by those in the know, since if most of us endorse justice for its own sake we are easier prey. Thus the account is able to account for its own failure to be generally believed. Plato took it seriously enough to respond with that massive construction, the *Republic*. How can Aristotle reasonably step out of the obligation to respond? Is it that he rests satisfied with Plato's response? We can hardly suppose this, given his open divergence from Plato on many fundamentals of ethics.

I take it to be common ground to all disputants in this area—Thrasymachus, Glaucon, Adimantus, Plato and Aristotle—that every being, in some sense of 'pursues', is always and in all that it does pursuing its own good and well-functioning; and that the virtues of a being are the qualities by which it functions well. The question, then, is why justice should belong with human virtue. The problem as it concerns these ancient philosophers is not the supposed logical problem: how, in seeking one's own good, can one be concerned about others for their own sake? As has often been pointed out, there is nothing logically abhorrent in conceiving of an individual's own good as consisting or partly consisting in altruistic activity. The question is whether this is a true conception of anyone's own good. For obviously it is possible to pursue one's good under a mistaken notion of what it is.

Now Aristotle, I shall argue, is under no necessity to stage an elaborate defence of justice in the broad sense in which we are still considering it. For he has, and must suppose it obvious that he has, the elements of a powerful answer which is independent of his formal equation of the supreme good with the statesman's objective. This becomes clear if we consider the following.[49] True happiness, according to the kind of view believed in by Thrasymachus, and ably stated by the unbelieving collaborators, Glaucon and Adimantus, is getting and enjoying whatever one wants unconstrained by law and morality. But such an end, it is made very clear in the *Republic*, is not practicable except by magic: Gyges' ring of invisibility, which is later translated into what has to be considered a virtually superhuman talent to deceive (without being physically invisible) one's fellows as well as to disarm the gods, should it be the case that there are gods misguided enough to demand that the intelligent among mortals no less than the stupid, value justice for its own sake. If the gods can make that foolish demand, then even if they have the power to punish the noncompliant, they are weak and foolish enough to be cajoled into accepting the mere appearance of compliance. But in the real world, to accomplish these manoeuvres even with regard to one's fellow citizens, one would need to be almost divinely ingenious, and divinely fortunate. So the genuinely human practicable good turns out to be an uneasy compromise in which the indulgence of one's desires is heavily constrained by the fear of all sorts of sanctions. That the best for us in our actual condition is not at all what it would be if we were as independent and invulnerable as gods, is hardly an objection to the theory. This constrained best, then, *is* the human best. But is even *it* practicable?

Human beings are not born effectively practical, any more than physically independent; how do we become practical, even if only practical rational egoists, if not by learning from others, through precept and example? Given no other way, it follows that our earliest (and it is tempting to say, our core) conception, however inchoate, of our good, must be of a good the practical knowledge of which is capable of being learnt and being imparted. Now if every creature is by nature reaching towards its own good without knowing initially, or in many cases ever, what the correct description of that good would be, then anything that the creature freely does is done under the assumption made, so to speak, by its nature and manifested in its action, that this doing is for its good. On the rational level, then, I shall not teach another the ways of virtue and happiness if, according to my conception of these, he at his best would observe my interests only so far as it suited some independent private interest of his which he always puts first. On those conditions, to rear him successfully is to rear a potential enemy, so I will not rear him, but will keep him sleepy and amenable. So how did *I* achieve the position from which I exercise such uncommon sense? By the same argument, I could not have been reared, or not by anyone as intelligent as I am now. If I was reared but not reared to *be* stupid, then I was stupidly reared by stupid people; so how do I know that I am not now stupid, being of stupid stock, and wrong in my egoist views about virtue and happiness? Yet I must have been reared, since I did not spring fully armed from the head of a god.

If, when others were rearing me and showing me how to be and behave, I had already been able to exercise reason, I might have reasoned that I ought not to absorb their lessons and examples unless I could see that accepting these would conduce to what I saw to be my own good; and I might have cautioned myself to be vigilant about this, on the ground that the others would be imparting those lessons only to forward their own advantage and not for the sake of mine at all except incidentally. But as things actually were, I could engage in and act on no such reasonings, partly because I was too unformed to be under my own rational control, and partly because I had no sustainable conception of my own good independent of what I gained by simply accepting to do what I was encouraged by others to do. Of course, I may have tended to equate my good (it need not have been an articulate equation) with the satisfaction of whatever my immediate inclination happened to be. This, however, is not a sustainable because not a viable "conception" of the good; with this as guide, I could not survive. Consequently, when I was encouraged, say, to 'respect the rights of others' with no reason given, and put through my paces in this regard in various concrete situations, by falling in with this I in effect accepted that this sort of conduct is part of my own well-being and well-functioning. Since I am a creature that like all others seeks its own well-functioning, the content of my conception of my own well-being is shown in what (under the final description) I voluntarily do. If, for instance, in giving something to someone I keep a promise for no further reason, then that shows that keeping promises as such enters into my conception of the best way to live for me. If my early training results in my practical acceptance that it is good, for no further reason, to keep a promise, to speak the truth, to respect the peace and possessions of others, then to that extent my conception of my good, and of the sort of person it is good for me to be, is now determinate. What has determined it is not the training but my acceptance of the training. However, I can only accept what training is offered, and according to the argument of the last paragraph, no training will be offered in a surviving community that does not include the elements of justice.

As one who started life amongst others unable to reason on my own behalf, I was unable to regard others as either means or obstacles to ends of mine that looked beyond ends of theirs. Consequently, I lacked the capacity to see others in their dealings with me as working through me, round me or past me towards ends that are theirs and in no way mine. On the contrary, if I absorbed their teaching at all, a kind of practical natural logic will have sustained me in the trust that what they impart to me they seek to impart for my own good. In accepting what is imparted I accept it as being for my good. But I also accept it as what others of my kind intend me to accept. If as yet I am incapable of forming the thought that the difference which they intend to make to me is other than, and hides behind, the difference I knowingly take on, then I can hardly suppose that they intend to make their difference in any but the same spirit as that in which I accept it, namely for the sake of *my* good.[50] Of course I do not regard them as treating me as an "end in myself" so far as this is understood by contrast with treating me or anyone else as a means, since this conception is beyond my grasp. But I cannot, in accepting the initial training, regard its author as exploiting or manipulating me, any more than I can see him or her as *my* tool or instrument. The latter is ruled out because whatever my good may be, I cannot develop to it unless by accepting some others as wise and benevolent authorities. For the undeveloped self, they have to play the rôle of internal prescriptive reason in the mature agent. But the external authority cannot be regarded by me for whom it is an authority as a possible instrument through which I might pursue an end that is mine but not its. To suppose this would be like supposing that an autonomous agent could use his own faculty of prescriptive reason as an instrument for achieving an end his but not its; which would be possible only if there were another prescriptive faculty to prescribe the use of the first. Perhaps, in the end, despite the difficulties of the analogy (see above, Section II), Aristotle was right to model the ethical soul on the relation of parent and child. For in order to develop as a human being at all, the child trusts the parent or guardian as the latter trusts, say, herself; and the latter trusts herself, having as a child trusted not herself but whoever reared her to be the one she and the child trust now.

Parents may think that they have a double responsibility: to teach the child to know and care about its own welfare, and to teach it to respect the rights and interests of others. This familiar division invites the question of the *Republic:* what has what you learn when you learn the second to do with what you learn when you learn the first? According to the present argument, the materials of which are present in Aristotle's *Ethics,* once we take account of the universal conditions under which the first is *learned,* it becomes clear that the two projects cannot be dissociated. For a being which in all things seeks its own good logically cannot accept or act on any directive without thereby implicitly affirming, through the deed itself, that it is to its own good to do this, even if the directive never mentions its own good. This practical affirmation is not, of course, a judgment that the behaviour in question is to its good, if by 'judgment' we mean a conclusion in accordance with an independent standard. For the acceptance is a case of learning what might be thought of analytically as a practical (and partial) definition of 'my good' by one who is ready to be directed towards such a definition precisely because he has formed no independent standard.

To be effective, the delivery of the directive should also take practical form: the form of example. If children see discrepancies between precept and parental behaviour, they are more likely to draw their lesson from the behaviour (cf. 1172 a 34–b 7). When behaviour conflicts with precept, the former is not deliberately aimed at the child as an example to follow, but nonetheless it will be taken to express the adult's authoritative view of his own good. It is as if the nature of the child divines a truth fundamental to Aristotle's ethics: that our happiness consists in *practical* activity. What another *does* shows in what he takes to be his own good, and the child's tendency to imitate can be thought of as mediated by another piece of natural logic (which is no more articulate than it need be to be acted on): 'What is good for him is good for me, since we are of the same kind'. Or it can be seen as equivalent to a direct assumption on the part of the child that adult action is in general meant as a model for the child to follow for his own good. This assumption is sometimes mistaken if interpreted to refer to the adult individual's intention. But from the Aristotelian point of view it is not absurd to say that in the case of a species whose members develop by learning from each other, and whose learning involves a good measure of imitation, nature does indeed "intend" the behaviour of the mature as a model for the immature, whatever the particular purposes of the individuals concerned. Thus elders are taken as models whether or not they choose to be, and models are what they naturally are. Hence it might be argued that the good of a human being cannot consist in activities which depend as a rule on concealment for their success. We are natural exhibitionists. Since nature made us learners of how to live only from our own kind, it must have made us natural communicators too, so as not to have made us learners in vain (cf. *Poetics,* 1448 b 5 ff.).

This is a nuclear Aristotelian model, according to which human values are necessarily transmissible between generations, and the conditions of transmission require that some modicum of good will, trust, trustworthiness and mutual respect be part of what is transmitted. However, the relation of parent or guardian to child is only the earliest instance of a general principle. Since there are no definite rules about how to act and how to live well, which is the same as how to be happy, one is never a complete master of this trade but must always be ready to learn. We continue to fashion ourselves by others, as they by us. We seek advice, and advice given is a model in words of how the adviser would act in our situation. Often the adviser himself only discovers this, hence discovers something about the particular form which his own good would have to take if he were so placed, when he sets himself to think on our behalf. His willingness to concern himself for my good assumes that my good, as I interpret it, will not be to his own destruction; but might not the assumption just as well be false as true? No, it will rather tend to be true, because if what I need and must generate through dealings with others is the concrete knowledge of how to be and flourish *as a person,* then in general it is better for me to *be* what you trust me to be, rather than only to *seem* it; for if I wear with you a complicated façade necessary to conceal unscrupulous intentions, then the side of you which relates to me, in which my nature hopes to read something for its own good, will be activated by the *apparent* me, so that the lessons I read there will be suited more to the person I only pretend to be than to the one I am. Again, if I trust the intelligence of others, then I would rather know what they really think I should do for my own good than what they want me to believe they think I should do, assuming this to be different.

Not only is it to my interest to be such that those others, from whose selves I can learn, have reason (though they may not need to reflect on it) to be willing to open themselves to me. It is also a logically more fundamental interest of mine (of the human being that I am) that there should actually *be* those others doing and faring well. For I need the model itself, not just the conditions of communication under which it is presented. Hence it belongs to my nature, so far as I am not defective, to tend to promote what the model requires in order to exist. Thus it is to the interest of the human being that I am to help protect the welfare of those others, for instance by defending them in their possession of the external goods which are necessary conditions for a life of effective and recognizable excellence (cf. 1178 a 28– b 1).

Let me now take stock of these implications in the light of the original question. In the first place, it should be said straight out that they do not yield rules of equity and fairness. More fundamentally, they cannot by themselves ground a system of rights and duties, because they supply no principle for determining who should fall within the circle of those with whom the ethically developing individual stands in the relationships on which the present argument relies. The argument only shows that benevolence, affection, candour, trust and trustworthiness—qualities which perhaps give life and soul to rules and systems of rights although they do not provide a logical foundation—are woven into the fabric of our individual well-being. But this is enough to answer the array of positions developed by Thrasymachus, Glaucon and Adimantus, according to which justice is not a human virtue because the mutuality of human beings at their best is a mutuality of fear and exploitation. In the end, what is wrong with this view is not that it offends the moral sensibilities developed in us by upbringing, but that it could hold true only of beings who need no upbringing to be at their best.[51]

The Aristotelian reply also provides what most of us would intuitively find a more attractive answer than the one forged by Plato in the *Republic,* according to which the members of the ideal community, from cobblers to rulers, indeed respect one another, but what they respect is the pursuit by each of his professional vocation. This is the source of the communal harmony which Plato denominates 'justice.' The account fails as a theory of man's social nature, though it may forward Plato's other great purpose, which is to give a model of the individual soul. For it says nothing to explain the human value of our being together not merely as well-working functionaries but as excellent individual persons.

## Notes

1. Joachim ad 1098 a 12–16 notes that the move cannot be taken for granted.
2. I have tended to keep this expression (sometimes abbreviated by Aristotle to 'the *logos*') untranslated. Some render it 'reason' (or 'right reason'), but this is often misleading so far as it suggests the faculty of reason; some, 'right rule' or 'rational principle'; but Aristotle's whole point is that there can be a rational finding that lacks the generality of a rule or what would nowadays be called a 'principle'.
3. I agree with Fortenbaugh [2] that the distinction between rational and reason-responsive parts of the soul is expressly made for the purpose of ethics; that it is not the same as the *On the Soul* distinction between intellect and sense (on this, see especially Fortenbaugh [2] 26); and that these distinctions serve different purposes and are not mutually exclusive.
4. Similarly, *boulēsis* (wish) is usually associated with the prescriptive part (the concept of *boulēsis* is used to elucidate deliberation and *prohairesis*), but at *Pol.* 1334 b 21–24 it is associated with the potentially responsive part. See below, note 40.
5. Cf. Natali [1].
6. See Leighton [1] for documentation of Aristotle's thinking on ways in which the emotions affect judgment.
7. Thus practical wisdom, being the virtue par excellence of the prescriptive part qua prescriptive, is not a 'strictly distinct' quality of intellect, as Aristotle shows clearly in *NE* VI. This is by contrast with the intellect's 'proper excellence' (cf. 1177 a 17); i.e., theoretic wisdom.
8. See below, Section X.
9. Because another occasion may differ from this one in some relevant respect which I would not be able to envisage until I am in it.
10. This problem is raised by Kosman [2].
11. Cf. Cooper [1], 5–10. Emphasis on the explanatory structure permits extending the notion

of *prohairetic response* to cover emotional reactions, since we have reasons for feeling as well as for acting. Cf. *On the Soul* 432 b 30–31, where the heart is said sometimes to beat faster 'even though the mind does not enjoin the emotion of fear'. The implication is that fear sometimes has the sanction of reason (and in the well-conditioned agent would occur accordingly). However, debate about the deliberative process and its relation to *prohairesis* cannot get far until we decide (a) what are our criteria, and (b) what are Aristotle's, for 'deliberative process'. On (2) see the excellent discussion by Mele [3]. Aristotle calls deliberation a 'seeking' (1112 b 20; 1142 a 31 ff.). It may be helpful to distinguish two cases (not that he does): (1) I ask myself the question that defines the seeking (e.g., What shall I do about so and so?) and consciously reason my way to an answer, in the light of beliefs, assumptions, interests etc. which register with me at the time. (2) I ask the question and an answer presents itself. I then see reasons why it is a good one (or not). Whatever we mean by 'conscious', both (1) and (2) should count as conscious seeking (if question and answer are conscious). Both should count as processes, too, since there is a temporal interval. Commentators (encouraged by Aristotle's examples) generally think of deliberation as (1). But if it is also typically (2), then the phenomenon of it, in some cases, is not all that different from when (3) I react without pause for reflection, but afterwards can explain or justify it on request.

12. By contrast, Ross [1] 198–200, and Aubenque 119 ff., separate *prohairesis* as it figures in the definition of moral virtue from *prohairesis* as upshot of deliberation, on the ground that the latter is only 'of means', while the former is a commitment even to the ultimate values expressed in action. Aubenque distinguishes two 'senses'. I prefer to see here two facets of one concept, especially as the allegedly separate senses occur close together in a single stretch of argument at *EE* 1227 b 38–1228 a 5. For further discussion see Chapter 4 below.

13. In characterising the right response as that which would be made by the person of practical wisdom, Aristotle is not committed to holding that every such response is a *display* of practical wisdom. Cf. Fortenbaugh [2] 74. (It is unhelpful that some interpreters write as if *phronēsis* [practical wisdom] in Aristotle were a faculty rather than a virtue. Perhaps they are misled by a supposed parallel with *'nous'*, which names both the faculty of intellect and the virtue of intelligence.) In view of the close connection in Aristotle between *moral virtue* and *prohairesis, prohairesis* and *deliberation, deliberation* and *practical wisdom,* it may be as well to mark some easily obscured points about their real life connections. (1) A good or right *prohairesis* (rational choice) may or may not be reached through actual deliberation, (2) If it is not so reached, it may still show wisdom. (3) If it is so reached, it may still fail to show wisdom on the part of the deliberator, since it may be such that an average person would have reached it as easily as a wise person, or such that a wise one would have reached it without deliberating.

14. *Prohairesis* is prior in definition, hence for Aristotle prior 'in being' to *virtue* and *vice,* but not on that account prior in the order of our knowledge.

15. In the parallel passage of *EE* (1222 a 6–17), the determination 'having to do with choice' *('prohairetikē')* does not appear, and the mean is specified as a mean in *pleasures and pains.*

16. 'Product' in this context is not restricted to physically independent products; thus it may refer to a musical performance. See Chapter 4, Section V.

17. The argument weaves about in a manner not uncharacteristic of Aristotle. The first sentence, posing the problem, assumes (1) that virtues are analogous to skills; (2) that doing what is grammatical is a sufficient condition for being proficient in grammar. Aristotle responds by denying (2), which is all that he needs for his main point; but then as if to be on the safe side he takes this opportunity to argue against (1).

18. *Pace* Ross as quoted by Hardie [4] 108–9. If a virtue (or a vice) were an actual property P which, under relevant circumstances, regularly gave rise to, e.g., just (unjust) actions: and if 'gave rise to' is interpreted in a modern sense, then P would have to be specifiable in some terms other than 'whatever gives rise to just/unjust actions'. In that case it would be

logically contingent that the virtue of justice gives rise to just actions: it might, still being justice, have given rise to murderous actions or to gardening or to flute playing.

19. 'Because of themselves' is the literal translation; *The Revised Oxford Translation* has 'for their own sakes'.

20. Cf. Fortenbaugh [2] 70–73.

21. See also the parallel passage 1144 a 13–20. It is often assumed that Aristotle is contrasting doing what is right 'for its own sake' (i.e., because it is right) and doing it from an ulterior motive. (On this view, the first limb of the contrast is virtually the same as *acting for the sake of the noble* [to be discussed below].) See, e.g., Hutchinson, 93 ff. (especially the phrase 'purity of choice').

22. See Ackrill [4] for close discussion of this and connected points.

23. This seems also to be Ackrill's conclusion; see Ackrill [4].

24. If this is taken strictly, then any claim that someone acted from genuine virtue on a given occasion would have to be withdrawn if later the person were to make a morally wrong choice (or failed to live up to his right choice) in the area of the virtue in question. Cf. Hutchinson 106–7. However, Aristotle does seem to allow, sometimes, that it is possible to lose a virtuous (or a vicious) disposition. The passages which speak of firmness (e.g., 1100 b 11 ff., *Categories* 8 b 27–35) say only that moral qualities are the *firmest* psychic characteristics. But when he stops short of saying that they are absolutely unchangeable, this may not be because he is willing to allow for the case where a person manifests virtue at $t_1$ and misbehaves (freely, etc.) at $t_2$. Rather, it may be because of the thought that through sickness or age a person may simply cease to function as a moral agent or may function as one at a reduced level.

25. Cf. Pears on the 'behavioural use of "courage"', and Fortenbaugh [2] 79–81.

26. Is the courageous man happy even when wounded or dying? The answer is not straightforward. He may not live long or fully enough to be ascribed (1) a *happy life*. But his particular courageous deed is an instance of (2) *well-doing* in the purely moral sense; and, if it achieves something of its intended result (holding the pass until help arrives etc.), it is a case of (3) *well-doing* in the more comprehensive sense entailing *success* (see Chapter 1, Section VII). Aristotle is willing to call (3) and even (2) 'happiness' in the quasi-technical sense in which the term means 'source of a happy life's being happy'. But it seems that a further condition must be met; namely, that the ordeal does not involve *submission to humiliation* (that it is painful in the ordinary sense is irrelevant). Otherwise, why would Aristotle say flatly that it is nonsense to call a good man happy who is being tortured on the wheel (1153 b 19–21)? He is probably guided by the thought that even if it is right to undergo the torture, and even if this does some good, a good person would reasonably wish he had died before undergoing it or that he had not been born.

27. *Rhetoric* 1366 b 25 ff. gives a long list of things deemed noble. Actions done for the sake of others or the community are salient examples, but are far from exhausting the extension of the concept as displayed by this list. Hence 'the noble' does not *mean* 'what would benefit others' (or: 'everyone'; or: 'the community'). Again, if an action is just or impartial, no doubt its performance is noble, especially if this does not materially benefit oneself; but its being just is not synonymous with its being noble. (Thrasymachus was not talking nonsense when he said or implied that the actions of the successful tyrant are noble.) Thus I see no warrant for Engberg-Pedersen's interpretation (see his Chapter 2) of nobility as acting 'in order to comply with the rational insight that in the sharing of natural goods one's own claim is initially no stronger than that of any other human being' (45). This Kantian interpretation clashes with passages (e.g. *Rhet.* 1389 a 30–37) which connect acting for the sake of the noble with youthful impulsiveness as distinct from reason. For a more balanced account, see Irwin [4], although he too writes as if 'for the sake of the noble' *means* 'for the sake of the common good'.

28. Since the ethical *kalon* applies (in my view, primarily) to the doing of a deed, it ought not to be rendered by 'right' (which applies to *what* is decided, *what* is done), *pace* Owens. One difference between what is right (what one ought to do) and what is noble shows up in the position of a 'despite' clause, thus: (1) it is right [to do X], despite the danger; (2) it would

be noble [to do X despite the danger]. According to (1), the danger is not a reason for deciding that some alternative to X is right; according to (2) it is a positive ground for predicating 'noble' of (the deed) X. For further discussion of the noble, see Chapter 5, Section I, and Chapter 7, Section III.

29. Aristotle's great-souled (the *Revised Oxford Translation* has 'proud') man acts from a proper sense of his own great worth (1123 b 1–2). If, e.g., he accepts or refuses an honour (1123 b 16–20), he certainly does so 'for the sake of the noble'. Here, his own excellence figures in his reason for choosing to act as he does. I would make the following points. (1) The above is typical of *great-souled* action; it is not a feature of acting-for-the-sake-of-the-noble per se. (2) It is not at all obvious that, in acting in the way that grounds our calling him 'great-souled', the agent thinks of himself as conforming to that description, or as exercising that virtue. (3) The virtue in question is said to be 'a sort of *crown* of the excellences' (1124 a 1–2), and the context shows that what it crowns are the *other* virtues. This suggests that the great-souled person's characteristic self-esteem *refers to* his other virtues, and that insofar as he *acts from* those other virtues, his actions do not express self-esteem. (4) Aristotle's doctrine that the practical virtues all hang together (see *NE* VI.13 and Chapter 4, Section XI below) may seem to imply that, because one cannot be courageous etc. without being great souled, one cannot exercise courage, temperance, justice etc. without considering that one has, and acts from, those virtues. That might follow if the *actions* typical of, e.g., courage were necessarily also typical of each of the other virtues, so that an act of courage would, as such, necessarily be an act expressing greatness of soul. But this makes nonsense of Aristotle's division of the moral virtues and in any case is not entailed by the doctrine that these virtues coexist in every virtuous agent.

30. This interpretation is inevitable if 'this' in 'this is what a good person would do' is understood as 'what I am doing'.

31. Commentators often say such things as 'Aristotle's moral agent does what is virtuous because it is virtuous (e.g., MacIntyre, 149). This is not helpful, because it ignores at least two distinctions: (1) that between *doing what a virtuous person would do* and *exercising a virtue* (which of these figures in the 'because' clause?); and (2) that between *what* one intends to achieve by the action and the *motive for* trying to achieve whatever it is (in which sense is 'because' used here?).

32. For trenchant criticism along these lines, see Hursthouse [1].

33. Cf. Urmson [2].

34. This qualification is necessary, because Aristotle holds that some types of behaviour are 'bestial' and some 'sick'. In their case there cannot be a right amount, a right time, a right place etc. See *NE* VII, 1145 a 15–33; 1148 b 15ff.; and Chapter 5, Section I below.

35. The same conclusion is drawn by Irwin; see Irwin [5], 314, ad 1107 a 9–27.

36. This is not to say that in individual cases he would take a neutral attitude to every *innate* propensity, since there can be innate 'bestial' characteristics; see note 34. (Judging these 'bad' would not be a matter of moral condemnation, for in Aristotle's view they fall below the threshold for that; cf. 1148 b 31–32).

37. Hardie [4], 104–114, clearly registers the need for an explanation (see also Hursthouse [3]). Hardie suggests that the key may lie in the physical basis (recognized by Aristotle) of psychic phenomena. But it is not clear how this answers the question. Burnyeat [1], followed by Sherman, 184, thinks that *enjoyment* is the answer: by acting in a certain way (which, presumably is in some sense in harmony with our nature) we learn to enjoy so acting, hence become more disposed so to act.

38. Not all *epithumiai* are for physical satisfaction; at 1111 a 31 Aristotle speaks of an *epithumia* for learning.

39. A rational prescription *expresses* a *boulēsis* rather than *is* one, because a rational prescription is a *prohairesis* and concerned with particular means for attaining the object of the *boulēsis*.

40. See *Rhet.* 1369 a 1–3. The appellation 'rational desire' is justified even in the face of *Pol.* 1334 b 20–24, which says that wish, along with appetite and temper, belongs in the non-rational part of the soul, and exists in children before the age of reason. Wish typifies

potentially reflective beings because reflective reason is required to make a wish effective (if it can be effective). The capacities for appetite and temper are not more basic than that for wish, if 'basic' means fundamental to human nature. They are more basic only in the sense that the satisfaction of wishes, unlike (speaking generally) the satisfaction of the other two types of desire, depends on cultivation and adventitious knowledge.

41. This is not to say that they do not involve a cognitive grasp of their objects or of the situations to which they, and the corresponding actions, are responses. It is only to say that the cognitive grasp informing the desire need not be supplemented by further thought to give rise to appropriate action. The same point holds of many emotions (see Leighton [2] on emotions such as fear as 'facilitators' of right action).

42. It is sometimes suggested that a *boulēsis* is peculiarly rational because it expresses one's idea of happiness or how to live (conceptions had only by rational agents) and that it is arrived at by some kind of deliberation. See, e.g., Anscombe, Irwin [2], Mele [5]. This does not sit happily with *Meta.* 1048 a 20–21, which refers to the possibility of finding oneself with contrary *boulēseis* at the same time. Before deciding how Aristotle understands *boulēsis,* it is necessary to make distinctions which, so far as I can see, these writers do not make: e.g., (1) between saying that a *boulēsis* has for its object the good life as the agent conceives of it, and saying that a *boulēsis* (for whatever object) expresses such a conception, e.g., in the *way* in which the agent tries to make it effective; (2) between saying that a *boulēsis* is formed through deliberation, and saying that a *boulēsis* is subject to (e.g., might be waived as a result of) deliberation; and (3) between saying that a *boulēsis* for X involves a fixed declaration, so to speak, that X is (or would be) good and saying that it depends on the provisional and defeasible assumption that X is or would be good. See Chapter 4, especially Sections IV, IX and X.

43. Cf. Hursthouse [3] on the multiplicity of things imparted in one act of training.

44. For this reason it is difficult to accept Hardie's (tentative) suggestion (Hardie [4] 110–114), that moral dispositions depend on physical traces which are the effects of repeated action. Hardie illustrates with *acquiring the ability to skate;* the hypothesis is plausible in such a case because instances of skating are physically similar. Hardie, however, himself emphasises (ibid. 104) the variety and consequently the nonmechanical nature, of, e.g., just action. See also Sherman 176 ff.

45. This is well brought out by Sorabji [1].

46. Burnyeat [1] stresses that 'learning to be good' is a matter of coming to make, of ourselves, the judgments (previously taken on trust from authority) that such and such actions are commendable; and that this making the judgments our own is achieved by our performing the actions. I depart from Burnyeat, however, in not postulating, as he does, *enjoyment of the action* as the explanatory link between doing it and coming to believe, of oneself, that this is the sort of thing it is noble to do. On this view, pleasure in performing, e.g., just actions leads to the stable disposition to act so; but Aristotle's view of the relation between pleasure in acting justly and a just disposition seems to be that the pleasure is in the exercise of the already established disposition. (This fits in with his general view about pleasure: see, e.g., 1153 a 14–15). Burnyeat must assume that there is a special pleasure in doing what one takes to be just; for the point is hardly that we learn to pay our debts spontaneously by coming to enjoy, through doing it, the handing over of banknotes, etc. But on that assumption the agent's pleasure presupposes, hence cannot be thought to explain, the love of just dealing that is characteristic of the virtue.

47. 1130 a 3–5 refers to Thrasymachus' thesis that justice is the other fellow's good (*Republic* 343 c).

48. Under these conditions the enlightened statesmen would either aim to produce a community of rational egoists, or he would inculcate the illusion that practising justice is valuable for its own sake. In the latter case he may be acting with a view to what he considers is the citizens' well-being, but hardly with a view to their happiness; i.e., *eudaimonia.* For it is not *eudaimōn* to be saddled with a systematic illusion about what virtue and happiness are. Probably we should suppose that he rightly or wrongly views the citizens as like animals, incapable of happiness: they are the flock and he is the shepherd (cf. 1161 a 12–15).

In that case perhaps he provides them, via the illusion, with a second best to happiness (whether for their own sake or so that he may exploit them [cf. *Rep.* 243 b]).

49. The present account differs from the 'defence of justice' offered by Irwin [7], Sections 211–217, according to which general altruism is a natural extension of the disinterested love of friends in the best type of friendship. Irwin's argument is Aristotelian in spirit, but I doubt whether it cuts deep enough to answer a Thrasymachus (mentioned by Irwin on p. 397). For the best type of friendship is between virtuous individuals. Hence if their virtue is assumed to include justice, the question is begged; but if not, virtuous friends are not disinterestedly concerned for each other, and in that case their friendship does not serve as a model for altruism on a wider scale.

50. Cf. Sherman, 171 ff., on the nonmanipulative nature of character training.

51. It may be complained that the argument presented here does not show that justice *is* a virtue, and the exercise of it intrinsic to human well-functioning, but, at most, that we practical beings, who depend on each other for self-development, cannot consistently deny this. But this is all that is needed for ethics, since ethics is for such beings.

# CHAPTER 3

# The Voluntary

## I. General Perspectives

Since virtue is the nucleus of happiness, by Aristotle's definition, it is not surprising that he loses no time in addressing the question of virtue: what it is and how it is attained. Yet this seems logically premature. The topic, he himself has indicated, is adverbial in nature, since the question was 'What is it for a human being to function *well?*' 'Well' he interpreted as 'in accordance with virtue or excellence'—another adverbial phrase, but one that invites detachment of the noun which then becomes a distinct object of inquiry. But now what of the verb which stands as subject to the adverb (and to contrary adverbs like 'badly' and 'indifferently')? What is it to function as a human being? Or what is that function such that to engage in it well or badly is to manifest one's human excellence or inferiority? We need an account of the activity or behaviour through which an individual's moral nature takes effect in the world, one of those effects being to reveal itself to others, if not also to its agent.

It is already clear what the broad answer will be: the functioning in question comprises emotional responses and actions. It might be unnecessary, in an inquiry on ethics, to press for more detail if it were always easy to recognise the instances. But often enough what from the outside appears as the person's own behaviour, expressing him as person or moral agent, is not really so. Not that it is necessarily anyone else's, but it is not his. To use the traditional term, it is not 'voluntary' *(hekousion)*. As Aristotle says in the *Eudemian Ethics,* the term 'voluntary' is applied only to those things of which the person *himself* is cause and origin (1223 a 15–18). And Aristotle also declares that only those things of which we ourselves are the causes are proper objects of praise and censure (ibid. 11–14). Hence the class of the voluntary includes whatever is a proper object of praise or censure.

What are the objects of praise and censure? In the first place, behaviour, or what Aristotle loosely calls 'actions', though not all behaviour and not all (in that wide sense) actions. But Aristotle also holds that the moral characteristics developed, then manifested by good and bad behaviour are themselves proper objects of praise and censure. This seems an uncontroversial position, but given Aristotle's conceptual connections, it entails the difficult doctrine that moral dispositions are voluntary, and that the person thus characterised has voluntarily characterised himself in that way. In the Eudemian passage just mentioned Aristotle infers this immediately from the proposition that virtue and vice are objects of praise and censure. The *Nicomachean Ethics* contains a similar argument (1113 b 22–30), but he there suggests a further reason for holding such qualities to be voluntary. They are voluntary because they are the inevitable and foreseeable results of voluntary behaviour. This assumes a prior understanding of 'voluntary' as applied to actions. So let us start with actions.

An action in the sense of *what* is done (or what might be done) is right, wrong, appropriate or not, for reasons grounded in the external situation. But in praising or condemning we consider not what is done but the *doing;* it is to this that 'voluntary' applies. Thus praise and censure take the action as an instance of agency good or bad, and (according to Aristotle) as a mark of good or bad character. He says, for instance, that praise and condemnation apply to virtue and vice and the *actions that issue from these characteristics* (1223 a 9–10). And his discussion of voluntary action in the *NE* likewise begins by connecting it with virtue:

> Since excellence is concerned with passions and actions, and on voluntary passions and actions praise and blame are bestowed, on those that are involuntary forgiveness, and sometimes also pity, to distinguish the voluntary and the involuntary is presumably necessary for those who are studying excellence and useful also for legislators with a view to the assigning both of honours and of punishments. (1109 b 30–35)

'Voluntary', however, is not restricted to behaviour expressing the stable, determinate, prohairetic dispositions which Aristotle calls 'virtues' and 'vices'. Such behaviour, informed as it is by a reasoned judgment of what is appropriate, is a subclass of the voluntary. Children (i.e., human beings as yet incapable of such judgment) are voluntary agents, too, and in one place Aristotle says the same of animals (1111 b 8–9). Again, the incontinent person acts voluntarily, though against his own reasoned judgment. In general, voluntary behaviour is the mark of moral agency at all levels: mature, potentially mature, and lapsed. (It is not clear how nonhuman animals fit into this picture; perhaps Aristotle views their behaviour as voluntary in an analogical sense.) But voluntary behaviour is not merely the index of the agent's moral quality, the basis on which he is judged actually good or defective as human being; it is also, and perhaps more fundamentally, the source from which such qualities develop: the *point d'appui* of moral training, which works through praising and faulting voluntary behaviour and through reward and punishment. However, reward and punishment are applied not only for the purpose of training, but also, in many cases, because they are *deserved;* and this latter sort of application is consistent with, and perhaps even implies, a character beyond need or possibility of moral training. At any rate, whatever the purpose of meting out reward and punishment, they are meted out for *voluntary* action. Thus there is a variety of angles from which we apply the concept 'voluntary', and the results reached from each do not necessarily combine in one neat system. Aristotle's discussion shows ambiguities and tensions as he tries to meet various demands which the notion 'voluntary' is meant to satisfy.

For an illustration, see his indecision in *NE* III.1 (1110 b 18–24) about the use of the term 'nonvoluntary' *(ouk hekousia)*. He is discussing the status of actions performed through ignorance. They are all, he first says, 'nonvoluntary'. But such actions then divide into those which he calls 'countervoluntary' *(akousia,* usually translated 'involuntary') and those which are not. Countervoluntary actions are those in respect of which the agent is *'un*willing' *(akōn),* and the sign of this is pain and regret, which (in the case of bad things done through ignorance) the agent experiences afterwards, on becoming aware of what he did. But learning what one did does not necessarily bring regret. The agent may not care or be pleased. But that does not make the action retrospectively voluntary. It was neither voluntary nor countervoluntary, but simply nonvoluntary. Aristotle says that *'non*willing' *(ouk hekōn)* should be our label for this agent, because he is clearly different from the *un*willing one, hence should have a 'special name'. So within the space of a few lines Aristotle uses 'nonvoluntary' for all actions done in ignorance, while also using 'nonwilling' (the cognate term which applies to agents) as a special label for agents of one subclass of ignorant actions. His problem, I think, is not merely that he needs a special term for what all ignorant actions have in common, whether later regretted or not, and also needs a term to distinguish those which are not regretted (even when regret would be called for). For the combination of these needs does not explain why Aristotle confusingly seeks to satisfy both by means of the same word. The problem is that he is caught between two points of view each of which uses 'nonvoluntary' (and 'nonwilling') in a single unambiguous sense. If we are concerned with the action as a possibly punishable offence, then all that matters is whether it was voluntarily perpetrated *or not,* and 'nonvoluntary' is correctly used as contradictory of 'voluntary'. For even if the subsequently unconcerned ignorant agent is felt to deserve a reprimand, it would not be for the action nonvoluntarily performed through ignorance, but for his subsequent attitude. If, on the other hand, we are concerned with the agent's moral quality as evinced in the entire situation, then the difference between the *'un*willing' perpetrator and the one who was ignorant and afterwards does not care may be almost as great as the difference between the former and a willing *(hekōn)* perpetrator. From this point of view, what the two kinds of ignorant agent have in common (that neither of their actions was voluntary) is comparatively unimportant. So in this context the negative term marks off one of three distinct possibilities and is in no danger of being confused with the contradictory of 'voluntary' because its moral implications rank it *alongside* 'voluntary' rather than over against it. This is not an objectionable equivocation, since it does not generate fallacies or spurious paradoxes; but the fact that Aristotle fails to register it suggests that he is not ready to draw so sharp a line as we should draw between viewing an agent's relation to his action as *a window on a character* and viewing it as the ground for holding the agent *responsible and possibly deserving of punishment.*

So it is not surprising that he fails to confront and raise the entire question of the nature and purpose of punishment, leaving us to infer which he would have endorsed of the various views that make *retribution* or *correction* or *deterrence* or *upholding the law* the central concept, or that propose some mixed account. But it is clear, I think, that Aristotle sees punishment on its various levels as an instrument of moral training and guidance. First, there is parental punishment, and the word for this *('kolasis')* literally means 'correction'. However, legal penalties *(timōriai)* are necessary to deter wrongdoers, and Aristotle implies that those who need such deterrents are beyond moral reform themselves (1179 b 10–18). Their punishment, then, is not *kolasis*. But he sees the law not, primarily, as the set of prescriptions which the state has the right or duty to enforce through sanctions threatened and executed, but rather as providing positive guidance for moral development in accordance with values of which law is the institutional expression (cf. *NE* X 9). From this point of view the punishment of lawbreakers would be intended to uphold the authority of the law as moral guide, rather than (primarily) to deter those who, not respecting that authority, can be controlled only through fear. But unfortunately Aristotle does not deliberately propose a theory of punishment, and this fact opens the way to uncritical interpretations of his remarks connecting punishment with voluntary action.

For example, if we ourselves think of punishment as primarily retributive, we are unlikely to think that the bad actions of morally undeveloped agents call for punishment to the same degree, if at all, as those of agents who 'could have been expected to know better'. So we are driven to conclude that Aristotle should either withdraw from holding voluntary misdemeanours to be in general punishable, or else should confine his concept of the *voluntary* to the actions of mature agents whom it is fair to hold 'fully responsible' for their behaviour. Either way it will seem as if his discussion sometimes recognises and sometimes ignores a distinct area of 'fully responsible' agency: on the first alternative, the latter is an unnamed subdivision of the area which he labels 'voluntary',[1] while on the second it is identical with that area, and the preresponsible behaviour of children should be given a different title which is not forthcoming. If, on the other hand, punishment is seen in its various forms as an aspect of an educational process whose termini share a single definition (since fully responsible, morally adult, agency figures in both—as initially potential and as finally actual), his failure to register the distinction demanded by the other view seems more intelligible. The boundary of 'full responsibility' may appear quite sharp when we are drawing synchronous comparisons between the misdemeanours of mature and immature agents, especially when we note how differently we feel they deserve to be treated. But if instead we consider, as Aristotle mainly does, the moral growth of the identical individual, that boundary figures only as a line to be crossed in development, not as a fence between opposed areas of merit or desert.[2]

The fully responsible agent is expected to justify his action or else take the full weight of blame and reprobation where this is applicable. The difference between him and one not thus responsible (whose actions, therefore, may in this sense be the responsibility of those in charge of him) seems stark if we focus on this one feature. But the Aristotelian connection of voluntary action with character shows what is in common. When Aristotle says that praise and censure apply to actions which issue from virtue and vice (developed conditions of character), he is not, I think, forgetting the voluntary actions of the immature. Rather, the statement is about the terms *in which* we praise and find fault. Praise and censure, all along the line, send the following message: this is what a good/bad (brave/cowardly, honest/dishonest etc.) person would do. Obviously, the message is applied to the actions of those whose characters we consider to be formed, and in that context it implies that these persons *are* good or bad. But the *undeveloped* agent, too, is meant to absorb the same lesson in connection with his own behaviour, though here it does not carry the same categorical judgment of him as he actually is. Praise encourages him to play the part of a good person by telling him that doing this or that is playing that part, and correspondingly for discouragement by reprimand.[3] The behaviour has to be voluntary, which is to say that it has to fulfil the two conditions round which, as we shall see, Aristotle mainly weaves his analysis: it must come from the agent himself, not from some external force, and he must know what he is doing. These conditions correspond to the fact that praise and its contraries are addressed to the agent himself, not to anything or anyone outside him, and are immediately effective only if, as in any communication, the addressee can apply the predicate (in this case of praise or censure) to the subject which the other intends. Here, the subject (an action) is presented as 'What you are doing/did/are about to do', and the recipient has no choice but to take this as referring to what he knows himself to be doing (have done, etc.), in the form in which he knows of it. Thus the communicator has to take care to level the communication at voluntary behaviour. Aristotle's theory of moral training assumes that under normal conditions, and with unspoilt agents, communications of this kind tend to be effective: in other words, the undeveloped agent by nature wants in general to do what a good being of his kind would do; he has a natural *formal* bent towards human excellence and happiness, but initially depends on others to supply a content. In effect, others supply him with material for his own practical assertions proclaiming more or less firmly that it is good to be someone who acts in this way.

This connection with praise and censure enables us to draw a definitional line round distinctively *human* excellence. Almost every type of being in Aristotle's universe can be said to be good of its kind, or not; but for the most part these evaluative judgments cannot be classed as praise or censure. We may rate one spruce tree better than another, and we may be judging it in its own biological terms, not merely as useful to us. But this is not praising the tree, because we do not address the judgment to *it,* and no difference would be made if we did. We do, however, praise and find fault with the actions and products of craftsmen or would-be craftsmen; yet skill and its lack are not good and bad qualities of human beings as such. Even so, the case of skill (as so often) throws light on that of virtue. Evaluative feedback might give the craftsman a motive to try for a better level of activity, but it cannot be sufficient to bring about the improvement. For as well as being told that this is the product of a bad or unskilled craftsman (which he may well be able to see for himself), he needs to be shown the technique for doing it better. And only the expert few can teach him the technique, whereas anyone who has to use his products can tell him that they are clumsily made or do not fit. But in the moral case it is not unreasonable to expect that other people's evaluation *by itself* would lead to improvement. Once the agent is aware of the evaluation, that alone could be enough. No need to work up a special technique as well. (The evaluation, when negative, may take the form of punishment.) *Human* goodness, then, is a set of desirable qualities which depend, for being developed, on nothing but the evaluation of a person's behaviour as typical of a good or (as the case may be) a bad human being; this evaluation being addressed to the agent by others speaking not as customers or consumers to a producer but as agents like him to an agent who understands that he is being so addressed.

Since human virtue is essentially communicated by being the topic, itself, of evaluative communications: and since the latter are occasioned by and focused on a voluntary action: it follows that voluntary action as such is socially accessible even though we are sometimes mistaken in supposing someone's behaviour voluntary. I do not mean by this to stress what hardly needs stating: that Aristotle here, as in all his inquiries, is indifferent to the kind of sceptical arguments which in this particular area would undermine our claims to know that anyone else is aware of what he or she is doing or that there even exist other subjects of awareness at all. While allowing that error is possible, Aristotle takes it for granted that in principle there is no more difficulty in our discovering that someone voluntarily shifted a boundary stone between his own and a neighbour's field than in our knowing that the stone is a stone, not a wax imitation or something in a dream. My point, in calling attention to the social accessiblity of voluntary action as such, is to set the notion of *voluntary* in its proper ontological perspective. If the voluntary is understood as essentially the object of praise or reproof, there is less need to resort to other accounts to bring out what is special about voluntary behaviour. For example, we are not now under pressure to conceptualise it as springing from some special kind of efficient cause called the 'will', whose mode of causation would be a topic of metaphysical or scientific interest for inquirers who lack (or set aside) any ethical interest in the person's behaviour. Now, such theoretical inquirers might assign to the will this kind of explanatory role in the context of an epistemology according to which the identification by them of acts of will in others presents no insurmountable problem. In this sense the will and its operations, like other mental phenomena such as pains, would be *publicly* accessible. But what is publicly accessible to the impersonal inquirer is not, in that context and on that account, an object of *social* concern, by which I mean an object of concern as between ethical beings.

It might of course be held that voluntary agency, while essentially an object of ethical interest, is also essentially a causal condition, empirical or metaphysical, the theoretical understanding of which would shed light on the workings of nature or reality in general. But Aristotle does not present the voluntary in this way. The voluntary agent, he says, is himself the cause and source of his voluntary actions; but this is not an attempt to explain how certain movements get caused or become events in the world. Such an attempt would offer *volition* and *voluntary agency* as solutions (however inadequate) to what gets presented as a theoretical problem; but, if I am right, Aristotle handles these concepts as if they come to life only in the context of ethical criticism and training.[4]

It follows, then, that a voluntary agent is not as such an object of empirical science, nor an object of nonempirical science, nor yet an unknowable somewhat. For of course we are acquainted with voluntary agents through our ethical dealings with them, which include our responses to their responses to ourselves as voluntary agents. But the penultimate sentence seems to carry some vague but weighty implications which I should briefly sketch and respond to. One is that *voluntary agent* and related concepts are essentially common sense notions, because essentially unscientific. Another is that voluntary agents are somehow "social constructs" (although we may also want to say that social groups themselves are constructs kept going by voluntary agents). Both remarks suggest that, metaphysically speaking, voluntary agency is a surface entity, a creature of cultural convention, not nature: collectively subjective, but subjective nonetheless, by contrast with the objectivities studied by science. Thus even though *voluntary agency* may be irreducible as a concept, its instances exist by riding on the back of something metaphysically more substantial, whether a physical system of some kind or even a "spiritual substance", to which voluntary agency stands as a sort of qualification. But now let us juxtapose a contrasting view, perhaps equally hard to pin down with precision but no less suggestive, namely that there is nothing we more fundamentally are than we are voluntary agents and possible subjects of ethical goodness, and nothing more fundamental (whether physical object, biological system, or for that matter pure intellect) to which we as ethical beings stand as accident to substance. As voluntary agents we cannot be nothing but voluntary agents, since we are necessarily physical beings and animals; but these aspects stand to our ethical nature in the metaphysically subordinate relation of matter to form. And even our purely intellectual activity represents, as God's intellectual activity could not, a practical decision to engage in what is not practical, and thereby make good use of conditions which other practical decisions made possible. We are natural substances whose essential nature is to act, feel and think as voluntary agents. Such is the view of human reality that emerges in Aristotle's *Ethics*.[5]

These considerations lead to the framing of another general perspective from which we are bound to consider Aristotle's conception of the voluntary. Is his a libertarian position, or is it consistent with some form of determinism (the view that everything happens of necessity[6])? (The third possibility, that he positively sets out to *endorse* a determinist view, can be excluded.) It is difficult to locate him in terms of this issue. His famous defence of future contingents (*De Interpretatione* 9) suggests that he takes for granted that the human agent 'could have done otherwise'. In the *Ethics* he insists that actions are voluntary only if they are in our power to perform or not, and his Eudemian discussion grounds this in the notion of the voluntary human agent as a 'contingent cause' (1222 b 29–1223 a 9). However, that, we shall see, can be interpreted so as not to entail a strict libertarian position, and much of what Aristotle says about voluntary action looks reconcilable with some version of psychological determinism. The fact is that he never satisfactorily defines his view. And this may be because his standpoint does not expose him to some of the well-known conceptual pressures leading in the direction of determinism. A glance at his general notions of causality and explanation may help to explain how this is so.

Aristotle cannot be propelled into the determinist debate by a need either to square, or else to contrast, common sense views about human agency with philosophical claims about the physical universe.[7] For example, given his metaphysics, it is natural—not contentious—to view a voluntary agent as himself the *origin* of his action. For something like this holds true of every natural substance. None, including human agents, can act in total independence of external conditions, but they are nonetheless sources themselves of the behaviour which reveals their nature.[8] Again, it is not perplexing to think of human agents as living, moving and having their being within the natural order even though they cannot as voluntary agents be subject to the physical laws governing the rest of nature. This is not a position to be dismissed as absurd or else fiercely defended, since no anomaly is implied: in Aristotle's universe there is no set of laws to which all natural things are subject. At no level, for instance, is it true that all bodies in space behave in the same way under the same conditions. The kinds of things are many and irreducibly different, in the following sense: the generic characteristics and analogical resemblances which we cannot fail to notice, and which science should not ignore, are consequential on the distinct forms of the different natural kinds. Hence the distinctive form of a substance, the source of its distinctive behaviour, is not to be explained as one of a range of possible arrangements or combinations of universal factors behaving and interacting in accordance with independently comprehensible laws. Such common features cannot explain the occurrence of distinctive kinds of behaviour, since common features occur only as properties of so to speak already subsistent distinctly natured substances.[9]

This is not to deny that the differences between the human individual and other kinds of natural substances are more remarkable than those between bird and oak tree or even between bird and stone. But from a point of view such as Aristotle's, the difficulty of accounting for human phenomena in naturalistic terms is not the extreme problem which through later developments of thought it inexorably became. And this problem is with us still, as acute as ever. So modern libertarians, who have been exposed to those developments, are in no position to take comfort from Aristotle's lack of concern about physical determinism, as if his authority could reverse the history of thought. They should find it interesting, but not particularly reassuring, to look over his shoulder at the scene as experienced from his very different perspective.

One notable difference between ourselves and nonhuman animal kinds is that the behaviour of human individuals varies significantly in the same situation, in ways which cannot be adequately represented by saying that different agents' responses are more or less perfect or well-formed instances of the same type. It is true on a level of high generality that we all seek the good in a formal sense (this, for Aristotle, does not even distinguish us from other creatures), but different people's actions proclaim different human values. Good and morally inferior human beings are not all making the same practical assertions of value, some more clearly or more successfully than others, in the way in which (as it might be held) all birds of a species are trying to live the same life, although some are weaker or more unfortunate than their fellows. Because of this we do not automatically know what another person means or meant by his practical affirmation: for example, what he does is not necessarily what I, a member of the same species, would do in the same situation. So if I see someone 'doing' (as we say) what I know *I* would never voluntarily do, I cannot assume that his behaviour is not voluntary; but since in my case it would not be voluntary, I cannot assume, either, that it is voluntary in his.

The problem arises, of course, because our voluntary agency is limited by the physical conditions in which it is necessarily played out, even when unimpeded. For how could we be practical except through physical changes arising in our bodies and extending to the environment we share with others? But the body—the instrument of the soul, as Aristotle understands it (*Parts of Animals,* 645 b 14–20)—and hence the instrument of our voluntary agency, constitutes us liable to takeover by physical forces; and even when we act from ourselves, the body cannot be the effective vehicle of voluntary agency without at the same time giving rise to movements and effects which we do not know about at the time and therefore cannot control. Hence the general conditions making possible the social interaction of voluntary agents inevitably render us opaque in this very respect to the only beings capable of the appropriate interest. Here it is well to bear in mind that Aristotle's God, metaphysically conceived, is not a personal, ethical being who sits in judgment and may therefore be supposed to read the shifting obscurities of each human heart (though see 1179 a 24–29 for a concession to a more popular view). In short, our voluntary agency is essentially subject to misinterpretation, in respect both of what we are doing and whether we are voluntarily doing anything at all. It typifies us as voluntary agents that we are subjects, too, of nonvoluntary and even countervoluntary behaviour, which (by contrast with the nonvoluntary movements of rocks and trees) occupies the logical space of voluntary action and so is confoundable with it. It is as such beings and on these terms that we succeed or fail in attaining excellence and happiness.

## II. Strains in 'the Voluntary'

I shall now examine at closer quarters certain gaps, ambiguities and oddities in Aristotle's notion of *voluntary,* some of which may be possible to explain in the light of considerations raised in the last section. I shall look at portions of *NE* III.1–2, where he expounds the two conditions under which behaviour cannot be deemed voluntary: force or compulsion and factual ignorance. It concerns him that these terms can be equivocally applied so as to exclude from counting as voluntary certain classes of actions which he wishes to include. Aristotle's efforts to guard against these misinterpretations will be the subject of my next section, but first we should face a number of curious features of his treatment of supposedly straightforward cases. I shall be concerned with undesirable restrictions which his handling of the two conditions entails on what should count as nonvoluntary; with the prominence of the concept *countervoluntary;* with a tangle of different senses of 'voluntary'; with Aristotle's neglect of the concept of *intentional action;*[10] and with his failure to consider what is common between successful and abortive voluntary actions.

The movements which occur when a person is literally subject to force (when 'the origin is outside him and he himself contributes nothing'; 1110 a 1–3; b 15–17) are classed by Aristotle as 'countervoluntary'. So, too, are actions performed through ignorance (1109 b 35 f.; 1111 a 22). But he is inconsistent on actions performed through ignorance, for at one point he says that while they are all nonvoluntary, not all are countervoluntary, but only those which the agent afterwards regrets (1110 b 19–23). It seems that Aristotle is strongly drawn towards treating 'voluntary' and 'countervoluntary' as exhausting the possibilities. Statements to this effect open and close the pair of chapters *NE* III.1–2, and the more complex division involving 'nonvoluntary' breaks through only to be lost sight of. And even so it breaks through only in connection with actions performed through ignorance. Why should this be? The countervoluntary is what is against one's will; or is what one wills, or would will, *not* to do or have happen. Being subject to force is painful, Aristotle says (1110 b 11–12); thus compelled behaviour is countervoluntary. But not everything done through ignorance is countervoluntary, since sometimes the agent (afterwards) is not pained and feels no regret at having done what he did through ignorance, and he might even be pleased. Yet surely these attitudes are possible in the case of compulsion, too. The seafarer in a boat carried out of control (1110 a 3) may be asleep, or not care, or find himself going in just the direction he had planned, or alter his plan so as welcome heading in the new direction. Yet what is happening is not by his voluntary action. Aristotle does not think that the absence of pain, frustration, and struggles to the contrary make voluntary what would otherwise be countervoluntary; for he says (1110 a 15–18) that something is voluntary if it is in our power (sc. to do or bring about, or not), and it is clear that he thinks that what is not in our power is not in our power regardless of how we happen to feel about it. So why does he not allow that while all compelled behaviour is nonvoluntary, only some is *counter*voluntary?[11] And why, having conceded this much for ignorant action, does he reverse the reasonable concession and end Chapter 2 by realigning ignorance with compulsion as a principle of the sheerly countervoluntary?

The phrases 'by force' *(biai)* and 'through ignorance' *(di'agnoian*[12]*)* are troublesome. Aristotle certainly means that each condition constitutes a sufficient ground for denying that behaviour is voluntary. This is uncontroversial if we are dealing with primary cases in which it assumed that the agent is not responsible for being at the mercy of ignorance or compulsion. Moreover, it is reasonable for the purpose of analysis to take the conditions separately, and focus on cases where (it is assumed) there exists only a single ground for denying 'voluntary'. It follows that whichever of the conditions applies is both sufficient and necessary for the denial in a given case. However, Aristotle's phrases also suggest that the behaviour to which one or other condition applies is not voluntary because it is *caused* by compulsion or by ignorance. And this in turn suggests that compulsion or ignorance makes the subject behave *otherwise* than he would have if free from the condition. For we naturally think that if A caused B, then B would not have occurred in the absence of A. It follows then that if behaviour B is rightly judged nonvoluntary on grounds of compulsion or ignorance, B would not have occurred if the agent had not been compelled or had known the situation. And from this it is easy to take the step of inferring that but for ignorance or compulsion (as the case may be) the agent would have done something different, and would have done it voluntarily. This reasoning would explain why Aristotle is so ready to assume that nonvoluntary behaviour is countervoluntary: it is countervoluntary because the agent thereby does something (or is subject of a movement) contrary to what he would have done under happier conditions. Thus the nonvoluntary behaviour necessarily represents the frustration of a voluntary project, and hence is countervoluntary.

However, the reasoning errs in assuming that a condition which, under the circumstances, is sufficient and necessary for denying 'voluntary' is also a sufficient and necessary cause of the behaviour from which this predicate is withheld. In fact, the presence of either condition renders behaviour nonvoluntary even if, absent the condition, the person would have done the same. There is therefore no ground for automatically classing nonvoluntary behaviour as countervoluntary. Aristotle may momentarily perceive this in the case of ignorance, but exactly how he interprets the point is unclear. He says that the person who acts 'through ignorance' but feels no regret afterwards is 'nonwilling', not 'counterwilling': but is this because the unperturbed agent might have done the very same thing even if he had known; or is it simply because—even if, given knowledge, he would have acted differently—he does not now regret what he did? For it is possible to know that one would not have fenced had one known that the rapier was unguarded (Aristotle's example: 1111 a 12–13) and yet not mind having fenced without it and unwittingly caused a wound.

The suggested reasoning (which is only one possible reconstruction of Aristotle's tendency to equate *nonvoluntary* with *countervoluntary*) also errs in assuming that a cause must "make a difference". For we do allow that A caused B even if B was about to happen anyway or by a different cause (although it is difficult to know what to say if we assume that B would anyway have happened at exactly the same moment). One person does kill another even if the latter was about to be killed by someone else. On the other hand, if the causation stems from an intelligent agent apprised of the facts, it operates only when it will make a difference that would not be made without it, since I do not aim to bring about what I know will happen anyway (cf. 1112 b 21–26). If one imagines a compelling force on the model of an intelligent, knowledgeable agent, then it seems that force cannot cause a nonvoluntary movement on the part of someone who would voluntarily have moved in that way. But that is a strange image (unless it is meant that an intelligent being *wields* the force), since "blind" force is usually contrasted with intelligence, and one clear mark of blindness is the use of energy to make happen what was going to happen anyway.

In assuming that what is compelled is in all cases countervoluntary, Aristotle may be influenced by these considerations: (1) we naturally resist compulsion because we hate *being compelled*—even if the compelled direction were the one that would have been voluntarily taken. Thus compelled movement is countervoluntary not because it is a movement of such and such a description, but because compelled. However, we mainly struggle (when it is useless) only if the compelling agent is seen as intelligent. Then the struggle sends a message of defiance, but otherwise it achieves nothing on any level. Second, (2) pain and struggles to the contrary are powerful evidence that the movement is indeed nonvoluntary. But the situation is not clear cut, since the person's struggles may be due to his refusal to take *voluntary* part in what will happen rather than to a first-order distaste for what will happen. Thus the prisoner on hunger-strike may not be sorry to be forcefed even though he would never voluntarily eat or let himself be fed. Now these considerations do not apply to ignorance, for the following reason: compulsion sometimes occurs, sometimes not, and it is not natural to be under compulsion; but, inevitably, whenever we act there are aspects of our behaviour of which we are ignorant. It may make sense to loathe being compelled simpliciter; but it would be absurd to loathe having acted from ignorance simpliciter, for then one would regret every action under some description, and so every action, by Aristotle's criterion of regret, would be countervoluntary under some description and a source of dissatisfaction. So regret, in the case of ignorance, must depend not the ignorance but on *what* was done through ignorance, and often this is not regretted and sometimes even welcomed.[13]

Aristotle's wavering on the countervoluntariness of actions done through ignorance may be due to a misguided desire to align the latter as closely as possible with enforced behaviour. He tends to focus on cases where what is singled out as the 'deed' was harmful, and perhaps he assumes at moments that the paradigm subject is a good person.[14] On those terms, of course, it is likely (1) that the nonvoluntary deed, whether done through compulsion or ignorance, is different from what the person would have voluntarily done instead; and (2) the agent will be distressed at the time (compulsion) or afterwards (ignorance). But in any case, the entire approach is governed by a simplistic comparison between voluntary behaviour and the natural behaviour of nonhuman Aristotelian substances (cf. *EE* 1224 a 16–24). Voluntary behaviour, after all, is precisely what is natural to human beings active as such. In the case of other substances, nonnatural movement and behaviour is by and large the result of external force, though ignorance may play a part in higher animal species. But most nonnatural behaviour will be accompanied by resistance, and is therefore *counter*natural. It is not clear, for instance, whether in Aristotle's physics it makes sense to suppose that an inanimate substance like fire or earth could be forced to move in just the way in which it would naturally move if left to itself. How should we know that force was applied if there were no resistance? Again, animals naturally struggle if interfered with, even if for their good. A fish struggles to be back in the water, but also struggles against the hand that would return it. This model, which tends to identify the nonvoluntary with the countervoluntary,[15] draws attention away from those human cases in which the agent adjusts his desires so as to welcome or accept what happens through compulsion, and ones in which (as in passive disobedience) he willingly turns himself into an object to be dragged about.

The analogy with nonhuman Aristotelian substances is restrictive for the reasons just indicated, yet some philosophers may welcome it, because on these terms there is nothing mysterious or marvellous in the fact that voluntary agency issues in physical change. To speak of the 'nature' of a natural substance is simply to speak of the substance as itself a source of certain changes. The being, by its changes, shows itself to be such as to change in these ways. Because it is *such as to,* the substance, Aristotle says, is a *cause* of the changes; but this is not a cause that logically competes with external agents of enforced change. Reference to them, their movements and positions, explains how a forced change comes about and why it has a given rate and direction; but saying that the substance is such as to change in a given way (unless prevented) does not comparably explain a natural change: it says only that it is natural. The point of referring to the substance as itself the source of its changes is not to explain or to offer (as is often complained) a pseudo-explanation, but to switch us into the mode of asking the right kind of explanation-seeking questions, which arise if and only if the behaviour is natural. These are questions referring, or expecting an answer that refers, to the subject's good or end: 'For the sake of what does it change in this way?' and 'Given that it is moving towards such and such an end, what is the concrete nature of that end that would explain why the movement is as it is?' The answers to these inquiries provide an account of the intrinsic properties and powers of the subject; and these would then be cited to explain how the thing can be affected by external force in various ways, and also how and why it can affect other things by force itself.

Physically effective voluntary agency, in this model, is a conceptual presupposition of the compelled movement of an otherwise voluntary agent. The former, therefore, is not to be treated as a puzzling case of a causal relation of which the latter is a familiar case. If the latter seems less puzzling, this is because we think of com-pulsion as an interaction of bodies, and we know what it is (or so we assume) for an external body to act as physical cause of a movement of the agent's body. But we do not in the same way know what it is for something called 'the agent's willing' to cause a movement of the agent's body. So voluntary agency becomes a mystery. But Aris-totle does not speak of an agent's willing or volition or act of will; he speaks of vol-untary agents *(hekontes)* and observable voluntary actions *(hekousia)*. And for him to say that someone's behaviour is voluntary is not (given the model of natures and natural changes) to invoke a directly explanatory factor, but to indicate what type of explanation would be appropriate to seek; for instance, it now makes sense to inquire about the agent's reasons (not, in the first instance, anyone else's) and the good which he (not anyone else) expects to achieve through the action. What kind of explanation is appropriate to seek also has implications for how to seek it; in this case, the primary and most direct method is to ask the agent himself. The fact that this "method" exists means that we are not under pressure, as we are with nonhuman substances, to assume that the subject would always behave in the same way under the same con-ditions. For how do we identify the natural behaviour of a nonhuman substance, and how do we tell whether some particular movement, in the form in which it strikes us, is natural or only an incidental accompaniment of something natural? We assume that what is natural is what occurs 'always or for the most part' *(Physics* 198 b 35), partly because the nonhuman world does exhibit great uniformity, but partly, one suspects, because we need some principle for initially distinguishing the natural from its incidentals, and it is not clear what other principle is available. But in the case of human voluntary agents, we have no reason to play down the differences at different times in a person's behaviour (and whatever the similarities, the differences are at least as ethically interesting), because we have no such heuristic motive as shapes our approach to nonhuman beings for supposing that the particular behaviour which we are concerned to explain is of a sort that always occurs in the same sort of situation. We have to suppose this in the nonhuman case, because we cannot oth-erwise be sure that we have fastened on anything that deserves to be explained by the type of explanation appropriate to natural behaviour. But with human agents, once we establish that the behaviour is voluntary, we know that we are entitled to seek (and seek *from* the agent) the appropriate kind of explanation without also being committed to holding that what we seek to explain conforms to some general pattern. We might then find by a survey of cases that it does, but this would not be because it (so to speak) has to in order to distinguish itself from its incidental trappings. That distinction has already been made, in each case singly, when we discover from listen-ing to what the agent tells us about himself whether the action is voluntary, and under what descriptions.

So, according to the analogy with other natural substances, the statement that an action was voluntary not only licenses the search for one kind of explanation, thereby excluding other kinds as inappropriate (amongst them, we shall see, the kind that appeals to innate nature, the principle of movements studied by Aristotelian science); it also assumes a perspective from which Aristotle can legitimately ignore certain problems which we might have thought central to the theory of action. These are 'What is the difference between my arm's rising and *my* raising my arm?' and

'What is in common between my raising my arm and my simply trying to?' In aiming to isolate the factor of voluntary agency, presumably with a view to identifying its nature, such questions suggest (1) that there is a kind of concrete event, consisting in my arm's rising, which in a given instance is caused by my voluntary agency, but which could in principle have had a different sort of cause; and (2) that there is a kind of concrete event consisting in my exercise of voluntary agency (or an act of will or a trying) which sometimes has, but sometimes has not, a physical result known as the rising of my arm. But according to the interpretation which emerges through comparison with the natural substances of Aristotle's metaphysics, *my arm's rising,* considered as a component of the complex *my raising my arm,* is only an abstraction from the concrete event which is the event of *my* raising my arm; and this is so even if *my arm's rising,* when considered as a component of the complex *my arm's rising through external force,* is indeed a concrete event, distinct from the *external force* component. It follows (a) that there is nothing but an abstraction culled ex post facto in common between *my arm's rising* and *my raising my arm;* (b) that what is in common (i.e., *my arm's rising*) is not something which could have been caused by the agent's volition and could equally have been caused by a force from outside the agent; (c) that what differentiates *my raising my arm* from *my arm's rising* is likewise not any concrete thing or process that could be by itself or be assembled with other items into a different complex. Hence (d) what differentiates the former is not something concrete called 'my trying to raise my arm', which might or might not have the effect of my arm's going up. My unsuccessfully trying to raise my arm is not a complete concrete whole which lacks a certain effect. Rather, it is an incomplete version of what would have been complete if I had raised my arm.

Aristotle, then, has no reason to focus on the "inner" or mental side of voluntary action as a problem for causal analysis. All the same, we might have expected him to give it some attention from the ethical point of view. If the arm is prevented from rising, the agent's trying or meaning to raise it is still of moral significance, and we can ask about his reasons and the good at which he was aiming. Aristotle says (*EE* 1228 a 11–13) that we judge a person's character by his *prohairesis* or rational choice, rather than by his action (i.e., what he is seen to do). Prohairetic action is only a subdivision of voluntary action, but perhaps Aristotle would generalise to all voluntary cases. The fact is, however, that his approach in *NE* III focuses on agency as realised, complete, out in the world for others to observe, and providing a palpable referent for their question 'Is it voluntary?' From the social point of view these cases are primary. The agent is viewed from outside, figuring not only as 'he' or 'she', but also as 'you'.

This external standpoint, as expounded by Aristotle, especially in the *Nicomachean Ethics,* is above all concerned with sorting out the conditions under which one would be mistaken in reading some movement or action as a case of voluntary agency. Perhaps this preoccupation with delineating the nonvoluntary causes him to overlook the difference between what is voluntary and what is intended. What is voluntary is whatever one does or brings about knowingly, but this divides into what one intends, and the foreseeable though not intended consequences of carrying out the intention. What falls into which category affects our judgment of character: setting out to kill someone is different (not necessarily worse) than knowingly causing death in the course of doing something else which one sets out to do. If the killing is an unjust act *(adikon),* then the voluntary doing of this deed is in both cases a commission of injustice *(adikēma),* and if it is in accordance with rationally considered choice *(prohairesis)* both cases manifest the vice of injustice *(adikia;* 1135 a 9–11; b 25; 1136 a 1–5). For the action accords with rational choice not only if it is intended, but also if it is willingly engaged in for the sake of what is intended. So in terms of Aristotle's classification of virtues and vices the two cases are the same. But morally they are different, since one killing might manifest malice, the other callousness. It is a pity that Aristotle does not muster the apparatus to represent such distinctions. This may be because no such distinction is prefigured in nonvoluntary behaviour, and his *NE* account of the voluntary is mainly an account of what, in the absence of compulsion and ignorance, we are entitled to view as *not* nonvoluntary.

Since Aristotle's treatment of voluntary action is governed by the model of natural change, he does not view my raising my arm as composed of the distinct concrete elements, an act of will and the rising of the arm; so consequently he avoids the problems of such an account. Yet this is consistent with his finding it useful to consider the bodily movement in conceptual isolation, and in fact he seems inclined to analyse voluntary action as *knowingly giving rise to a movement* (i.e., being the *ultimate* source or cause of the movement, as distinct from being a link in a physical chain which starts with an external force). Aristotle can focus on what is special about voluntary action (i.e., on *knowingly giving rise to*) without supposing that what is special is really distinct. But into this approach, in principle legitimate, he injects confusion, because he also says that we are 'causes' of our *voluntary actions* (1114 b 4; 1113 b 18–19). I am therefore a cause (by the above analysis) of *knowingly causing or originating a movement,* which at first sight hardly makes sense. But the different occurrences of 'cause' in the last sentence bear different senses. This is shown by the fact that the origination of a movement may or may not be known to the originator (and if not, it is not a voluntary action); whereas it is absurd to suggest that someone *unknowingly* gives rise to his voluntary action (qua voluntary).

Aristotle is caught in this ambiguity because the word for *cause* (i.e., origin or source giving rise to something) is *'aitia'* or *'aition',* while the cognate word *'aitios'* tends to connote the *agent answerable or responsible* (i.e., the proper locus of praise and blame, whether or not "fully" responsible as a rational mature person). Thus the strange-seeming statement above says, in fact, that I am responsible for knowingly originating M. That is, if and only if I am knowingly the cause$_1$ *(aition* = originator) of M, then I am cause$_2$ of *(aitios* of; answerable for) knowingly being the cause$_1$ of M.

The ambiguity here ties in with another, concerning the term 'voluntary' *(hekōn)* as applied to an agent. Does Aristotle mean by *'hekōn'* one who knowingly originates (voluntary$_1$), or *one who is answerable for* (voluntary$_2$)? On the second alternative, according to which *'hekōn'* is synonymous with *'aitios'* and 'cause$_2$', the statement that someone knowingly gave rise to M is only the condition for predicating *'hekōn',* and *'hekōn'* itself imports new conceptual material such as *possibly deserving praise or censure.* On the first alternative, *'hekōn'* is itself the condition for applying the further concept of moral responsibility. Aristotle, like ordinary users of the term, vacillates between these senses. This is not surprising given their connection. The semantics of 'voluntary$_2$' incorporates the pragmatics of the semantically less rich 'voluntary$_1$'; we are only interested in the correct application of the latter because we want to know whether to apply the former and make ethical judgments accordingly. Indeed, the meanings can seem virtually identical if we consider all that is meant by 'responsible' and also the way in which Aristotle probably understands the reality of *knowingly causing$_1$* or *giving rise to*. To be the knowing cause$_1$ of M is to be the one who actually or incipiently has, and so might be asked to give, reasons for causing$_1$, M, and being able to give reasons is what constitutes the cause$_1$ a possible subject of ethical judgment in respect of M and whatever else he knowingly causes$_1$ in causing$_1$ it. Furthermore, Aristotle, I suggest, would be inclined to see knowingly causing$_1$ M as itself an ethical affirmation to the effect that it is good to cause$_1$ and good to be such as to cause$_1$ M under the circumstances. Thus by being a knowing subject of causation$_1$, one is already on the ethical plane, and putting oneself forward as a cause$_2$ to be ethically judged by one's fellows. For in knowingly functioning as a cause$_1$ of M at all, I show a kind of practical confidence in the truth of the ethical claim affirmed in and by this very functioning; but I am also by the same act logically bound to concede that others (who have the right to take an interest) might or might not agree with the claim enacted by me. This is because by that same functioning I also constitute myself the one from whom others may expect, though they will not necessarily receive, what they would consider a justification for this knowing causing$_1$ of M or some consequence of M.

Do we *knowingly* become such targets of others' ethical interest, by knowingly giving rise to changes such as M and its effects? Not in the sense in which we might knowingly give rise to M etc.: a sense that allows for the alternative of giving rise to M etc. unknowingly. If I happen not to know that the button which I depress with my finger is a light switch, I am not aware of causing$_1$ the light to go on (not aware of causing$_1$ any change under this description). And I might have been in a position where I could not be aware of this however much attention I paid. But it seems that we cannot in this way fail to know ourselves to be subjects of possible praise, reproof etc., for knowingly causing$_1$ what it is in our power not to cause. This fact, unlike a fact about the external world, cannot escape us if we reflect. But it is possible, as Aristotle says in many connections, to know something yet not in such a way that knowing it makes the difference that might be expected; this he calls having the knowledge but not using it (cf. *NE* VII.3 on incontinence). Thus one can knowingly give rise to M without taking account of the fact that one thereby renders oneself liable to moral judgment; this is not a case of lacking knowledge but of failing to use what one has. The point has a bearing on Aristotle's view that we voluntarily generate our own moral qualities.

The nuances of '*hekōn*' are beautifully illustrated in the passage where he speaks of the difference between regretting and not regretting something done through ignorance. He says of the person who through ignorance *did* (aorist) whatever it was, but is not upset on finding out what he did, that 'he *has* done it [perfect] neither voluntarily or yet countervoluntarily' (*hekōn men ou peprachen . . . oud' au akōn;* 1110 b 20–21; cf. 1111 a 17). We can take this in either of two ways, both of which present the previously unknowing agent as now in a state of *having done what he did*. That presentation is effected by the use of the perfect, which implies more than that it is now true of the person that he did so and so, since it shows him as now *typified* by having done it (even unknowingly). It is like the difference (at the air terminal) between *being a passenger from Tokyo* and *being a passenger of whom it is true that he was in Tokyo at some time.* For airport purposes, the former characterises him in terms of his current passenger-status, while the latter says only what happens to be true of this passenger. On one interpretation, 'not voluntarily' and 'not countervoluntarily' in 1110 b 19–22 and 1111 a 17 attach to the deed which the unregretful person is said to be in the state of having done: he is one who has—neither voluntarily nor countervoluntarily—$\phi$-ed. On the other interpretation, 'not voluntarily' and 'not countervoluntarily' qualify his presently being in the state of having $\phi$-ed.

Similar alternative interpretations are possible for positive statements about voluntary and countervoluntary agency:

> $V_1$   He is (having voluntarily $\phi$-ed)
> $V_2$   He is voluntarily (having $\phi$-ed)
> $C_1$   He is (having countervoluntarily $\phi$-ed)
> $C_2$   He is countervoluntarily (having $\phi$-ed)

In $V_1$, the bracketed portion in parentheses can be rewritten as 'having knowingly caused$_1$ M to occur', whereas $V_2$ cannot be rewritten as 'He knowingly causes$_1$ M to have occurred'. For he cannot now originate a movement which *has* occurred. In $V_2$, therefore, 'voluntarily' must be recast in terms of 'cause$_2$', since one can now be cause$_2$ of (answerable for) what has already occurred.

What of $C_1$ and $C_2$? Aristotle is discussing the countervoluntariness of actions performed through *ignorance,* and the symptom is the agent's retrospective regret. $C_2$ is the appropriate description of this situation, whereas $C_1$ presents an agent whose countervoluntariness was contemporary with the action: this would make sense only if the case were one of *compulsion.* $C_2$ means something like this: 'It does violence (now) to his sense of who he morally is to stand forth as one who has (voluntarily) $\phi$-ed'. The person is presented as now 'counter-responsible' ('counter-cause$_2$') for what took place. This is more than the denial (which could be uttered by anyone) that he is cause$_2$, for it shows *him* actually repudiating the imputation and, so to speak, counterfactually having resisted the regrettable occurrence. He is now 'counter-responsible' for having given rise to it, for he is now ready to give the reasons he would have given against doing it had he known at the time that he was about to.

But the regret which marks the countervoluntary ignorant agent is more than a later readiness to give such counter-reasons, and also more than a sense that one would have resisted the event or declined to cause$_1$ it if only one had known so as to be able to resist or decline. And it is certainly more than a repudiation of responsibility, or of having knowingly and therefore voluntarily given rise to it; for the non-voluntary, unregretting agent can rightly repudiate responsibility, too. Countervoluntary regret is a rejection of oneself as having caused$_1$ the event at all, even unknowingly in the course of knowingly causing$_1$ something else. But this rejection is not a denial of one's own causation$_1$ of that which occasions the regret. On the contrary, it entails an admission of this (though not an admission of guilt). The rejection, I think, is best characterised as the opposite of the postpractical acceptance that is logically expected in connection with voluntary actions performed. If it now pleases me *(mihi placet)* to cause$_1$ M, I necessarily anticipate (not necessarily correctly, as it may turn out) that I shall be pleased to have caused$_1$ M. My now saying an approving 'Yes' to causing$_1$ it (a practically efficacious affirmation) prefigures my saying an approving 'Yes' to having caused$_1$ it. The latter affirmation cannot be efficacious, but it is the apotheosis of practical. For in a paradigm case where all goes well, saying 'Yes' to causing$_1$ M *turns into* saying 'Yes' to having caused$_1$ M, as doing gives way, if successful, to the satisfaction of having done. The first act of affirmation cannot, of course, necessitate the second, but the relation approximates logical necessitation enough, perhaps, to lend colour to the thought that *rejecting having caused$_1$* M (which, we are supposing, one caused$_1$ unknowingly) brings one as close as it is possible to get to *having rejected causing$_1$* it; in other words, to having knowingly and voluntarily prevented or declined to cause$_1$ it. So the person who unknowingly caused$_1$ it, and is now content to accept (because he knowingly does not reject) having caused$_1$ it, is logically as well as perhaps morally closer *now* to the paradigm voluntary agent, whose acceptance, now, of having caused$_1$ M is part and parcel of his having knowingly caused$_1$ it; even though the former at the time of the action was more like the countervoluntary agent, since he acted through ignorance and (we can even suppose) would have acted differently if he had known. For knowing that one would not have voluntarily caused$_1$ the harm is consistent with now being able to bear (or live with) having nonvoluntarily caused$_1$ it—just as knowing that one would not have wished to cause$_1$ it is consistent with the absence, now, of any wish that one had not.

Aristotle expresses these subtleties rather than keeps track of them. Keeping track would require him to clarify the difference between *voluntary$_1$* and *voluntary$_2$*, and this he does not do. The former not only provides grounds for the latter—an asymmetrical relation—but outside the human context it is capable of wider application.[16] Aristotle is reported[17] to have held that the movement of the heavens is voluntary, and, as we saw, he at one point attributes voluntary behaviour to nonhuman animals. He can mean only that these agents knowingly originate the movements in question, for the divine movement of the heavens is beyond praise[18] and nonhuman animals are not actually or even potentially answerable for what they do. But this and other reasons for prising the concepts apart are not taken up by Aristotle.

The rationale to their conflation will be further pursued in Section VI of this chapter; but meanwhile we should continue to note the verbal obstacles to clarity. Not only is there the fact that *voluntary$_1$* and *voluntary$_2$* are defined in terms of virtually the same word, *'aition', 'aitios'*. There is also the fact that Aristotle has no regular terminology for distinguishing actions from movements. Thus he fails to notice the point that what one (knowingly or not) gives rise to is a change or movement, whereas what one is answerable for is the action (if knowingly engaged in) of giving rise to it. And this issue is further confused by the fact that both movements and actions may be said to be either voluntary *(hekousia)* or not. Whether a *movement* M is voluntary depends on the fulfilment of Aristotle's *two* conditions: the person concerned must give rise to M, and he must do so knowingly. But whether an *action* is voluntary depends only on the knowledge condition, for unless the agent at least gives rise to the movement we do not have an action at all to be either voluntary or not, but an externally caused event in respect of which he is passive (cf. 1110 a 2–3). So whether an action is voluntary depends on how it is described; for the agent knows what he is doing under some descriptions and not under others.

### III. Excuses and Nonexcuses

We are still concerned with the two conditions, 'by force' and 'through ignorance', either of which defeats the claim that a subject voluntarily gives rise to a movement and its effects. Aristotle has to classify a number of cases where it is true in a way that the person was 'compelled' ('forced', 'under pressure', etc.) or 'ignorant', even though we want to treat this person as a proper subject of ethical judgment in respect of the movement or action. Either 'voluntary₁' must be dropped as a sufficient condition for 'voluntary₂', or the criteria—force and ignorance—for refusing to apply 'voluntary₁' must be refined in such a way as to exclude only those cases where we intuitively think it wrong or unreasonable to hold the person answerable.

For instance, it is not easy to classify those situations where, as we naturally say, the person was *constrained* to do something (but note that we say 'to *do*'). For example, the sea captain is constrained to jettison cargo. Such cases share salient characteristics with ones in which 'forced' clearly implies 'not voluntary' or even 'countervoluntary'. The action is painful and it goes against the grain. Furthermore, it is not thought reasonable to reproach the agent, even if what he did would normally draw condemnation. This may incline us to infer that the action was not voluntary, on the ground that otherwise the subject would deserve reproach. And since we actually describe him (and he describes himself) as 'compelled' or 'constrained' to do what he did, it is easy to conclude that the action was not voluntary because it was the result of compulsion.

Aristotle breaks this line of argument by drawing attention to a variety of reasons for not condemning behaviour that would normally draw condemnation. Thus there are other reasons than that the individual was literally not in control of what took place. For example, the action may have made good sense under the circumstances. This would be so if it was the choice of a lesser evil. In such cases the agent is 'pardoned' (i.e., initial condemnation is withdrawn once we know the full circumstances) and may even be commended for what he did (1110 a 19–20). Again, reproach and condemnation may not be in order because the alternative was 'too much for human nature to bear' (1110 a 23–26).

The main examples in *NE* III.1 are doing something disgraceful at the bidding of a tyrant who holds one's family and threatens to kill them, and jettisoning cargo in order to save the vessel and crew. In both cases the agent acts to avoid a harm or evil, but Aristotle also looks at instances where one does what would normally call for reproach, but with a noble end in view. He also includes cases where the agent not so much *acts* disgracefully as submits to disgraceful treatment so as to avoid worse evil or to achieve a greater good (1110 a 20–21). Aristotle argues that what the agent does or suffers is countervoluntary in the abstract, since no one would choose to do or suffer such things for themselves, but only for a further end which depends on the particular situation. However, he argues, they are desired *when* they are done or suffered, and the question 'Voluntary or not'? applies to the deed as embedded in the particular circumstances under which it is done. And under the circumstances in his examples the action was voluntary, because the agent himself was the source of his bodily movement. Aristotle adds that where this is so 'it depends on the agent [it is in his power] whether he acts or not' (1110 a 17–19).

I leave aside for the moment this notion of its *depending on the agent*. What is clear is that the movement was not due to external force. However, Aristotle still allows us to say that the agent was 'constrained' or acted 'under necessity' (*anankē*, 1110 a 26 ff.)—*but only provided that the alleged 'constraint' does exculpate.*[19] The agent does not count as 'constrained' if he does what would normally be condemned with the purpose of avoiding a minor evil, and in such a case he is reproached (cf. *EE* 1225 a 14–17). And there are actions, such as voluntary matricide, so wicked that no one can get away with them by pleading constraint, no matter what the alternative (1110 a 26–29). Thus if one is going to plead that one 'had to' choose so and so, one had better make sure that the choice is right; for blame to be lifted, it is not enough that one feels under pressure to make the choice. And where the choice is right (is judged so by competent judges), then exculpation takes the form of approval or even praise (1110 a 20).

But sometimes, Aristotle says, we do not praise when we exculpate; we show leniency (*sungnomē*, 1110 a 23–24). This is when the alternative would have been too much for human nature to stand. Perhaps the tyrant example is an illustration. Apparently without realising it, Aristotle has put his finger on something quite different from the choice of a lesser evil. It is not the case here that the person is exculpated because his action is found commendable after all in the light of the circumstances. He is exculpated even if it would have been better not to do what he did— given that embracing this alternative would have demanded more than human nature could bear. Aristotle's failure to notice that this is not at all like the choice of the lesser evil may be due to the fact that the name of the appropriate reaction by others is the same in each case: *'sungnomē.'* This, depending on the context, may be variously translated 'forgiveness', 'pardon', 'condoning' and 'leniency', but probably it connotes an undifferentiated concept of *letting someone morally off the hook,* on whatever grounds.

Where the alternative would have overstrained human nature, what does it mean to say that the alternative would, nonetheless, have been better? Presumably that it would represent a better choice for those capable of choosing and carrying it out without doing violence to their nature; but they would have to be superhuman. Here one is tempted to say that the normal human agent *could not* have chosen the alternative, and could not even contemplate it as an option. But if so, how can his actual action be considered voluntary?

Perhaps we should disengage the question whether the action was voluntary from the question whether the agent could have accepted the alternative. The latter would still be 'too much for human nature' even if the agent could have made himself accept it by doing something to himself which, so to say, cut a central nerve of his human nature. Perhaps simply opting for the alternative would itself be cutting that nerve. The story of the early Roman commander Manlius might be a case in point. Manlius ordered the battlefield execution, under his own eyes, of his own son for gallantly disobeying a command not to engage with the enemy. What is more, Aristotle indicates that the status of the alternative as 'overstraining human nature' is not independent of the nature of the action done. He cites Alcmaeon (in the lost play by Euripides) who killed his mother to escape his father's curse, and says that Alcmaeon's plea of 'constraint' was ridiculous. Aristotle's assumption seems to be that although to accept the paternal curse would normally count as more than human nature can bear, so that normally the agent would be exculpated for doing whatever was necessary to escape the curse, this is not the case when what he has to do is equally or even more contrary to nature—as would be matricide. Hence the contrary-to-nature alternative is not something such that one could never under any circumstances be expected to put up with it. It might be held that under the actual circumstances, the possibilities being what then they were, the agent could not accept it. But then it also might be true of Alcmaeon, given his personal makeup, that he could not choose the alternative to what he did; yet even so (Aristotle implies) he would not be exculpated. From Aristotle's brief discussion here there is no reason to think that the impossibility of taking a different course of action is either sufficient or necessary for exculpation.[20]

So, when the alternative overstrains human nature, on what ground do we exculpate? Not because the agent *could not* have embraced the alternative, for Aristotle does not claim this. So is it because the action taken by the ordinary agent was the lesser of two evils? No, because in that case we should commend instead of excusing or showing leniency. And that would leave no space for Manlius: for the hero who takes the arguably better path even when this costs him, not blood, but the renunciation of some human side of himself. The ground of exculpation is surely this: those who pass judgment, fellow human beings, take it that they in that situation *would* not (not necessarily *could* not) have done anything different. They know this even while judging the action. Thus, for all they know, the agent was of the same moral calibre as themselves and shares their moral attitudes. But they are not brought to question their own values and attitudes by the knowledge that they in his situation would do what those values ideally forbid; hence it is not logical to treat the other's action as a reliable sign of ethical inferiority. It is the action of a person placed so that his ethical character, whatever its quality, has no natural outlet. If he forced himself to act against human nature in the interest of a higher good (and who would dare to say that he should have tried?), he would not have been acting as a good human being, but (and perhaps from then on, too) as a kind of god. His virtue is above human virtue; he is not a model for us to follow (cf. 1145 a 18–30).

This takes up the theme with which Aristotle introduced his discussion of character in *NE* II: specific ethical qualities do not follow from basic psycho-physical human nature, but nonetheless they fall within limits set by that nature. Thus an action that goes against nature does not express what Aristotle would call an ethical quality; and the alternative to such an action, considered as such (i.e., simply as a nonviolation of nature) does not express an ethical quality either. This is because the kind of action that expresses some ethical quality is the same as the kind through which the quality is first acquired and strengthened by means of practice stimulated and shaped by praise, reproach, reward and punishment. But this training presupposes subjects who are persuadable with respect to the type of action: it must be possible for the action and its alternative to represent live options. And so far as the training is meant for everyone, it presupposes normal subjects. But for the normal person faced, e.g., with the tyrant's threat against his family, doing what makes the threat come true is not a possible reality whose disadvantages could be rationally compared with those of the alternative. Reproaching him and, for that matter, praising him would have no effect either on him or on others in similar situations.

Since what is voluntary is what is a fit target for praise, censure etc., one would expect Aristotle to deny the status of 'voluntary' to actions which cannot be influenced by those means, given normal human nature. Yet in *NE* III he assimilates then to choices of the lesser evil, which are plainly voluntary because commendable. This is because both kinds of case count as voluntary in accordance with the narrow conditions of force and ignorance. But Aristotle wavers on this issue; at *EE* 1225 a 22 ff. (composed earlier or later, we do not know), he classifies actions whose alternatives would be too much for human nature as countervoluntary, provided that being in the situation was not the agent's own fault (1225 a 9–11). (Aristotle seems to say here, too, that evils done to avoid a greater evil are also, with the same proviso, countervoluntary [1225 a 17–19] but the text is difficult.[21]) This wavering[22] may indicate a change of mind.[23] But it may be due to the ambiguity of 'voluntary'. So far as this word refers to a way in which movement or change arises, a way metaphysically coordinate with the modes of arising captured in the phrases 'by nature' and 'by force', the deed of a person for whom the alternative is too much for human nature may be clearly voluntary. For example, the person threatened by the tyrant writes a report that will incriminate someone else. Here, the movements are knowingly originated by him, and 'by him' distinguishes this from a case of 'by force', while 'knowingly' distinguishes it from an ordinary case of 'by nature'. If, however, we mainly think of voluntary movement not as originated otherwise than by nature or force, but as an expression of ethical quality, constituting its subject a target of praise or censure, then the case in question is not so obviously voluntary.

In terms of our earlier distinction, if 'neither by force nor through ignorance' states a condition that is sufficient as well as necessary for 'voluntary$_1$', then 'voluntary$_1$' is not (or not always) sufficient for 'voluntary$_2$'. Nowadays we might register this point by saying that 'voluntary$_1$' is a term to be studied in the theory of action, whereas 'voluntary$_2$' is a topic for the different discipline of ethics. This distinction echoes the thought raised near the end of the last section in connection with the Prime Mover and nonhuman animals: that voluntary$_1$ agents need not be, and need not as such be considered as, objects of ethical interest. But since Aristotle conflates 'voluntary$_1$' and 'voluntary$_2$', he has trouble finding a consistent line on cases where conditions sufficient for the first are insufficient for the second. Thus in *NE* III he holds that actions whose alternatives are humanly unbearable are voluntary,[24] because they stem from a voluntary$_1$ agent, while in *EE* he holds that they are not voluntary, presumably because the agent is not voluntary$_2$. This raises a question to which Aristotle, even in the *EE*, gives no clear answer: what further conditions must be satisfied for the agent to count as voluntary$_2$?

For the moment, however, we are concerned with the correct interpretation of the two main conditions which, it is agreed, must be absent if the action is to be considered voluntary at all, even in the undifferentiated sense in which Aristotle uses that term. He has insisted that movements are literally compelled only when the cause is external and the subject 'himself contributes nothing' (1110 a 1–2; b 15–17). So far, in the cases looked at, what is done is the kind of thing that would go against the grain, and perhaps does go against the grain even when done voluntarily. But now what about noble and pleasant objects (or objectives)? They are outside us, and they too 'constrain' us, we often say. But if these are cases of literal force, then everything is done under compulsion, since the noble or the pleasant is an objective in every action (1110 b 9–10). And pursuing such objects is pleasant, whereas enforced movement is distressing. Being glad to do something is a sign that the agent 'contributes'. But what if we feel driven by appetite or longing, and even that we could not have helped acting as we did? Aristotle replies that it is absurd to blame the external objects rather than oneself for being an easy prey to such passions. For we, by being thus vulnerable, 'contribute' in this way, too (1110 b 13–17).

One might object that it is not always without distress that we pursue the noble or pleasant. For the continent man is noble enough to resist his appetite but finds the resistance painful, and the incontinent person pursues physical pleasure or some noble object like honour for which he is inordinately ambitious, pursuing them against his better judgment and uneasy on account of that: thus it is as if force is used, against appetite in the one case, against better judgment in the other, to make the action come out as it did. Aristotle discusses this at length in *EE* II.8. His answer there is that although in these cases one part of the soul is prevented by something other than itself (the other part) from expressing itself in action, these are not cases of countervoluntary behaviour, because the force is not from outside the entire soul.[25] If we were to say that the continent's restrained behaviour is countervoluntary because contrary to appetite, we should also have to say that it is voluntary because it accords with his better judgment; and *vice versa* with the incontinent person. But Aristotle lays it down that the same action cannot be both voluntary and countervoluntary (1223 b 9–10), meaning that they cannot be both under the same description, which would be the case here. The phrase 'voluntary agent of M' applies to the soul as a whole even if part of the soul dissents to M; for if it applied only to one part, 'countervoluntary with regard to M' could apply to another part in respect to the same identically described behaviour. In that case, one part of the soul would be forcing M on the other; but how could anyone draw appropriate practical ethical conclusions from an account portraying one part of the soul as the voluntary agent of M, while another part is an innocent victim? For when we praise, reproach, punish etc., we address the entire *person,* not one or another part of a person's soul. The person, therefore, is the voluntary agent, if voluntary agent there is, and the force that excludes voluntary agency must be force from outside the person. 'Voluntary', then, will still be predicated even if the action "does violence" to one part of the soul, as long as this violence arises from within.

This is why, if we want to know what it is to act voluntarily—'Is it acting in accordance with desire, or in accordance with rational choice, or in accordance with thought?' (1223 a 24–26)—the correct criterion, according to the *EE,* is 'In accordance with thought (i.e., beliefs about the situation)'. For 'Did he act in accordance with thought?' is the one question that can receive an unequivocal answer. Of course someone who acts voluntarily also acts in accordance with desire or rational choice;

but since desires can conflict, with each other and with rational choice, the question posed in terms of them can be answered in contrary ways with respect to the same action or movement under one description.

So to those who complain about being 'compelled by pleasure', part of Aristotle's answer is that such actions are not compelled in any sense that would exculpate. But at *NE* at 1110 b 9–11 he makes the further reply that if actions done for the sake of pleasure or a noble object are 'compelled', then everything is compelled and nothing is voluntary. Evidently we are supposed to regard that as absurd, if only because voluntary action is typically human activity, and it is unthinkable that we should never act as the human beings we are. But Aristotle is also arguing against the doctrine of Socrates that no one voluntarily does what is bad, wicked or wrong. Socrates assumed that we do some things voluntarily, but he did not see how we can voluntarily do what we take to be wrong or bad. We only do wrong not knowing it as wrong, hence involuntarily. Aristotle rejects this position because, by his criteria, the incontinent agent voluntarily does what by his own better judgment he takes to be wrong. Moreover, if someone does what is wrong thinking it not to be wrong, he nonetheless voluntarily does *what* he thinks is not wrong. If it is argued that he does not do this (neutrally described) action voluntarily, on the ground that he is drawn by pleasure or by what he considers noble, Aristotle's answer is that *what* a right-thinking person does (neutrally described) is done from just such motives; hence by that argument good actions are no more voluntary than bad (cf. 1111 a 27–29).

The idea that we are forcibly driven by pleasure, or more generally by some nonrational impulse such as physical appetite or anger, is especially attractive when incontinent wrongdoing is the topic, since the agent would probably like to be exculpated. It had been proposed by some thinkers that only actions in accordance with reason are truly human and voluntary. Aristotle answers that reason, too, can lead one astray (so that the errors we commit through anger or appetite cannot be dismissed as nonvoluntary simply because they are errors); that appetite and anger are sometimes the right responses (so, if these emotions always render behaviour nonvoluntary, we can never take credit for the good actions they inspire); and that nonrational passions, and therefore actions expressing them, are no less human than reason (1111 a 30–b 3). The logic of the last point, according to which the status ('human' or not) of the actions follows that of the inner condition from which they spring, resembles a theme as yet to be examined: if the agent's *condition* is voluntary, actions that issue from that condition are voluntary, too. Aristotle implies this when he says that those who do wrong for the sake of pleasures (or even noble objects) should blame not the objects but themselves for being so susceptible. If the susceptibility is their fault (and he implies that it is—not everyone is thus susceptible, and resistance is not beyond human nature) then the consequent actions are their fault too.

The concept of *ignorance,* like that of *force,* can be misapplied so that what is voluntary is made to seem not voluntary. In *NE* III.2 Aristotle distinguishes what someone does *through* ignorance *(di'agnoian)* from what someone does *ignorantly* or *in* ignorance *(agnoōn).* The former are nonvoluntary or countervoluntary, the latter voluntary.[26] The ignorance of 'through ignorance' concerns factual particulars of the action; that of 'in ignorance' concerns these, too, but here it also includes the moral ignorance of the wicked who do not know what one should refrain from (1110 b 28–31). The actions of a person drunk or enraged are 'done in ignorance', Aristotle says, because they are not done through *ignorance*, but through *drunkenness* or *rage*, which confer a kind of ignorance (1110 b 24–27). This remark carries the odd suggestion that the person's behaviour is not in fact due to drunken *ignorance* (haziness, misjudgment), but only to drunkenness. But Aristotle means, I suppose, that to rectify the agent, one cannot act directly on his ignorance by giving him information, as one could if he were sober and about to act *through* ignorance; one would need to sober him first.

In action *through* ignorance, it is as if the cause of ignorance is external: it lies in the facts, which happen not to square with the agent's picture. But in drunkenness, rage, and physical passion, the source of ignorance lies in the agent. 'I acted in ignorance' seems to exculpate, but really it does not, as we see at once on substituting the name of the cause of ignorance. 'I acted from a drunken stupor, a fit of rage, in the grip of appetite' do not exculpate but incriminate. It is here assumed that the person who acts *through* ignorance is not himself responsible for its being the case that the facts lie at odds with his beliefs; and it is also assumed that drunkenness, excessive rage, etc. are the agent's business to avoid, either by shunning situations which give rise to these conditions or by disciplining his nature so as not to be so swayed. However, elsewhere Aristotle recognises cases where rage and passion stem from unnatural or pathological conditions, and says or implies that actions perpetrated in consequence are not voluntary (1148 b 30–35; *EE* 1225 a 20–23).

The two modes of ignorance are very different. '*Through* ignorance' refers to action rationally based on a false assumption regarding some particular of one's position, whereas drunkenness etc. are states of globally diminished awareness of the situation and its factual and ethical implications. Appetite sees only the object of lust, rage sees only the insulting gesture and not what else might be destroyed if one acts at once to extinguish it. This awareness of only one aspect of the situation is one of the best-known effects of passion, and would be hard to reproduce in someone who is cool and calm. Of acting *through* ignorance, Aristotle says that error can occur about what one does, about the circumstances, the results, the nature of the means employed, the degree or manner of one's action—any of which details might be crucial. But, he says, no one could be unaware of all these things unless he were insane (1111 a 3–7). It is something like global unawareness that puts the wicked person in the same class as drunken and enraged agents; for although the wicked person's picture of the facts may be clear (i.e., not hazy so far as it goes), factually true and based on reasonable evidence, it is nonetheless an ethically distorted reading through and through. The wicked person fails to notice the features of the case that would shape a good person's reaction and conversely is aware of empirical possibilities (e.g., possibilities that arise when someone's back is turned) that would not even occur to the good person.[27] As with drunkenness and rage, one cannot cure this kind of ignorance by feeding him new information, but only by getting him to care about things differently; and it may be too late for that.

## IV. 'It Depends on Him'

Focusing as he does in *NE* III on *force* (i.e., *external force*) and *ignorance,* Aristotle there neglects to consider other conditions that would render the action or movement not voluntary. He says nothing, for instance, about convulsive movements, or about actions grounded in pathological conditions of the psyche. (Some of these possibilities are briefly considered in *EE* II.8, *NE* V.8 and *NE* VII.5.) The same narrow focus also prevents him, in *NE* III, from squarely asking, 'What is it in general that must be true of the agent when he acts, if he is to be ethically answerable'? For as long as this seems neatly summed up in the formula, 'neither by external force nor through ignorance', the question appears to be taken care of. The summary is supposed to be logically equivalent to 'he himself knowingly gave rise to the movement'. But if the equivalence is accepted, 'knowingly gave rise to' is not sufficient for answerability, unless we wish to say that a person is answerable for his convulsive movements and his insane or (as we say) psychologically compulsive actions. For these are not due to external force, and he may indeed be aware of them.

We might try to deal with this by adding further conditions to the two main ones. On the other hand, perhaps their inadequacy should warn us that no list of specific conditions can be given that might not be revised and extended in the light of cases not previously considered or new conceptions of mental and physical disorder.

Yet any extension of a currently favoured list must be grounded in an abstract conception, however rough, of what it is so to act as to be answerable for the action. This suggests that a better response to the inadequacy of 'neither by external force nor through ignorance' as a formulation of this conception would be to apply further analysis to 'knowingly gives rise to' so that it now becomes clear that the phrase means more than merely that conjunction of negative conditions. The voluntary agent is more than the knowing subject of a movement whose origin cannot be traced past him to an external force; for to say this is not yet to say, in an ethically relevant sense, that *he* is its origin. But if it is possible to locate a richer meaning in 'knowingly gives rise to', then this, presumably, sets the condition which has to be satisfied if the agent is to qualify as answerable, and this will be the source of further intuitions about specific conditions of answerability.

For Aristotle, the extra meaning is carried by the theme 'It depends on the agent[28] whether or not he $\phi$'s'. In *NE* III.1 this makes a quiet first appearance in the discussion of actions which are 'countervoluntary in the abstract' but voluntary under their particular circumstances (1110 a 17–18). Here, 'it depends on him' is slid in along with 'not by force', without separate explanation. The notion takes centre-stage in III.5, when Aristotle argues that character is voluntary, but its relation to 'compulsion' and 'ignorance' is never made clear.[29] In the Eudemian account, by contrast, 'it depends on him' is carefully grounded from the start. That account opens with a classification of kinds of source or origin. Every natural substance gives rise to others like itself: man, the other animals and plants each reproducing according to its kind. Man alone of natural substances is also a source of actions *(praxeis).* Some sources, as for instance perhaps God, give rise to necessary motions, but not

everything is necessary: some things are capable of being otherwise. But it is a principle of logic that what follows from the necessary is necessary itself; hence if something is capable of being otherwise, its source must be of the same kind, i.e., capable
of being otherwise (1222 b 15–1223 a 2). Aristotle continues:

> What depends on men themselves forms a great portion of contingent matters, and
> men themselves are the sources of such contingent results. So that it is clear that all
> the acts of which man is the principle and controller may either happen or not hap-
> pen, and that their happening or not happening—those at least of whose existence
> or non-existence he has the control—depends on him. But of what it depends on
> him to do or not to do, he is himself the cause; and what he is the cause of depends
> on him. (1223 a 2–9)

This introduces the discussion of praise and blame and the voluntary. For we are
praised and reproached only for what we ourselves are the causes of, and we are
causes only of what is voluntary (1223 a 8–18).

My aim in these next few sections is to clarify 'it depends on him (or: himself)';
to examine the sense in which the human agent is a source 'capable of being otherwise'; and to locate this conception in relation to deterministic accounts of voluntary
action. For now, I shall consider it in connection with *actions* or *movements;* and in
the next section shall turn to Aristotle's thesis that an agent's *character* depends on
him.

Aristotle models the relation of a starting-point (source, cause) to its effects on
the relation of premises to conclusion in the demonstrative (i.e., explanatory) syllogism. The premises exhibit the essence via definitions, and their connection with
the conclusion shows how a derivative characteristic flows from the essence. At 1222
b 16–18 Aristotle applies this model to the relation between parents and offspring in
living species. Now in all such cases, as in the case of the human individual and his
voluntary actions (which at *NE* 1113 b 18–19 Aristotle compares to 'children'), the
real life connection between cause and effect can be frustrated: the natural substance
can be prevented from fully giving rise to its natural effect or offspring. Aristotle
ignores that possibility here. Absent prevention, the effect arises of necessity, given
the cause. However, except for God and the heavenly bodies, effects and causes themselves are all existentially contingent, since they come into being and pass away, and
might never have come into being. But if we abstract from prevention, are we entitled
to suppose even of a mortal natural substance that it might not have come into being?
For given that it is in being, supposing that it might not have arrived is equivalent to
supposing that its progenitor might have been prevented from producing it; or so it
might be argued. (The argument is more plausible if we hold, as Aristotle does, that
in all reproduction the offspring essentially derives from a single parent, with the
maternal principle acting only as matter and receptacle.) If prevention is waived, the
mortal substance necessarily exists, in the sense that its existence was necessary given
the prior existence and operation of its cause; and given its own existence and operation (both of an inherited nature), its own effects are likewise necessary.

This is to say that the effects *must* occur; but in saying that they are 'necessary'
Aristotle also means that from that cause no other effects nor kinds of effect were

possible. Not only does the cause necessitate the being of whatever effects it produces (and the same applies to the future effects of each *ad infinitum*), but it never was possible that a cause produce kinds of effects different from or opposite to those which it did. And insofar as it is the cause of its effects, they are all of one and the same stock, and so of one family or kind. So even if the cause could or did instigate an effect that turned out to be significantly different, either instead of or in addition to any of its regular effects, the difference would not be due to causation by the cause (it would not reflect the *cause*'s nature), but would have arisen by accidental inter-action of the effect with its environment.

Although the effect depends for its coming to be on its cause, and therefore its coming to be is necessary only *given* the cause, this relative necessity cannot be com-bined with contingency by saying: 'Given A, there must arise B, but since A's exis-tence is contingent, then (since A is the only cause of B) so it is only contingent that B should arise'. For it is Aristotle's view that if A's existence is now in the past, it is now necessary that it existed (1139 b 8–11). Hence if the arising of B flows by neces-sity from the existence, now past, and as past now necessary, of A, it seems that the existence of B, even if now only future, is no less necessary now than the now past existence of A (and, equally, no less necessary than the past existence of B itself in that more distant future when B, too, will be past and therefore necessary). It would take us too far to try to formulate this with precision here, but at least the logic does not obviously fail. Yet unless it fails, every natural substance that arises arises by necessity, and it was always necessary that it would arise, since the necessity of its arising was taken care of not only when its immediate cause existed and caused it, but already when the cause of that cause existed, and so on back.

All this holds only in the ideal world where nothing natural is prevented, so that the generations of species flow undisturbed as the flow of theorems on a page. We can likewise abstract from prevention when considering the human individual and his actions, and we can study the difference between this idealised case and the ideal-ised case of the natural kinds. Whatever difference appears to us on the ideal plane must surely point to a corresponding difference between the types as instanced in the real world of accident and interruption. What is more, ignoring the possibility of prevention is not just an academic fiction used in setting up a theoretical model, for the same fiction serves practise, too. We act on the assumption that by so doing we shall make *some* difference (though not necessarily as much or exactly such as we hope); hence we act on the assumption that we shall not be prevented from doing *something* towards what we aim for, even though the assumption has often been proved wrong.

It being supposed, then, that nothing will interfere between the human voluntary agent and the movements and changes which he knowingly originates as his effects, these effects are 'capable of being otherwise' in two ways. First (so Aristotle assumes), it was not always necessary that they come about; the necessitation of them goes no further back than to their agent and his originatings. And second, instead of one effect there might have been another of opposite kind: yet, even so, a genuine effect of the same cause. Speaking of natural substances, we say that if instead of the natural effect E of a natural cause C there had occurred something E′ of opposite nature to E, then E′ would not have been a *natural* effect of C, expressing C, but would have been the result of interference from outside; whereas if a human agent[30] gives rise to a voluntary effect F, then had he instead given rise to an effect F′ entailing the non-occurrence of F, F′ might equally have been his voluntary effect expressing him as its cause.

This second point rests on the assumption that whereas one and the same voluntary (and human) agent can voluntarily give rise to a certain movement and can also *voluntarily* give rise to its opposite, one and the same nonvoluntary natural substance cannot *naturally* give rise to an effect if it can also *naturally* give rise to the opposite. However, the modal terms here signify no more than that contrary effects in the one case are, in the other are not, each consistent with an identical cause. It does not follow that the voluntary agent who gives rise to F could have given rise to the opposite *under the same circumstances*. All that follows is that if, whether under the same or different circumstances, the opposite had been caused, it might have been caused by the identical voluntary agent acting voluntarily. Nor does it follow from this alone that the voluntary agent of F was the ultimate source of this or any other of his voluntary movements. Thus the second feature of contingent voluntary agency according to Aristotle's Eudemian picture does not entail the first. Nor does ultimacy alone entail the second feature, for it is possible to conceive of an absolutely ultimate ungenerated cause such that *it* cannot give rise to any effect of opposite nature to its actual effect. Indeed, Aristotle suggests that God is just such a cause (1222 b 22–23).

But if we make two further assumptions (both reasonable to attribute to Aristotle), the thesis that a voluntary agent is the possible source of either of a pair of opposite voluntary effects implies that this agent is the ultimate cause; i.e., that his actual effect cannot be traced back through him to a prior cause given which he had to give rise to the effect. The first assumption is that the relation whereby an effect can be traced back beyond its proximate cause to an ulterior cause is literally 'ancestral', applying only to hereditary properties and biological descendants. For example, an effect Y is the offspring of a parent X, its proximate cause. Or an effect Y is an instance of inherited behaviour, and the proximate cause X is the creature itself which gives rise to this behaviour. Only in these two cases, according to the first assumption, are we entitled to postulate a prior cause W, which is the cause of X and so indirectly the cause of Y. The other assumption is that inherited properties and kinds of behaviour are essential. So suppose now that F is a voluntary movement of an agent A. F, then, is not a biological offspring of A (for example, F is not another voluntary agent). And F is not an instance of inherited behaviour either, for if it were, then (by the second assumption) essentially the same agent A could not have given rise to something of opposite nature to F, and in that case F would not have been voluntary. It follows, given the first assumption, that A is the ultimate cause of F, since F cannot be traced back through A to a prior cause of A.

The voluntary agent, therefore, is 'master' *(kurios)* or 'controller' of his effects (1223 a 5–7). 'Master' is a term uniquely applied, hence appropriate to an ultimate cause. Members of series of natural kinds are sources of their own effects and indirectly of future generations', but none is *master* since none is first. The voluntary agent controls his effect, whether it shall be rather than not, and this is what is meant by saying that something 'depends on him': whether it comes about depends on him if and only if he controls whether it shall be rather than not.[31]

We are to take it that what the agent is master of is: whether F shall be *instead* of not being. Thus if he voluntarily gives rise to F, what he gives rise to is not merely F, which once in being holds its place instead of possible contraries. That is how a natural source gives rise to its effect. The being of the effect excludes that of any contrary, but this exclusion follows from the fact that the event occurs or has "taken" effect; exclusion of contraries is not written into the *doing* of what is done by a natural cause. This is because there is no need for the natural cause, operating as such, to give rise to Y-instead-of-some-contrary, or to Y-instead-of-not-Y, since the natural cause has no power but the power to give rise to such items as Y. By contrast, the voluntary agent gives rise to F as one who might have given rise to some contrary, and so the contraries must be excluded in and by the voluntary act itself, which is therefore an act of giving rise to F-instead-of-not-F.

At *NE* 1113 b 7–11, Aristotle speaks of 'it depends on him' in terms of 'Yes' and 'No', and says that if the 'Yes' depends on the agent, so does the 'No' and conversely. Aristotle assumes, I think, that the 'Yes' is 'Yes-instead-of-No', and the 'No' a 'No-instead-of-Yes'. In other words, the agent is at least implicitly aware of the options as options. Aristotle also assumes that where it is open to someone to make a difference to the coming about of F by saying 'Yes' or 'No', refusing to say 'Yes' amounts to saying 'No', and vice versa. The saying of 'Yes' or 'No' is practical, in that when F depends on the agent, if F occurs it is because the agent said 'Yes' to F, or refused to say 'No' to it, or because he said 'No' or refused to say 'Yes' to not-F. However, this formulation assumes that it is indeed open to one to say 'Yes' or 'No'. But there are conditions under which it is not open, although this is never because one is prevented in the sense that one might try to say 'Yes' (as one might try to make a movement) and be prevented from carrying out the act of affirmation. The affirmation (by contrast with the movement affirmed into being) is complete all at once and cannot be interrupted. Even so, there are disabling conditions. For example, no one can say a practical 'Yes' to what he could not envisage as a possible option for himself, either because he happens to be ignorant of it or because, although he can identify it as a physical possibility, it is not a thinkable *option.* Nor can one say 'Yes' to what one believes cannot happen; nor to what one believes must happen anyway; and correspondingly for saying 'No' and for refusing (cf. 1112 a 18 ff., 1139 b 31–1140 a 1 and 1225 b 32 ff. on deliberation). The 'Yes' is practical not simply because it gives rise to a certain effect, but is inwardly practical in that it is not possible to say the kind of 'Yes' that gives rise to its object unless one takes it that by so saying one might make the difference (or some part of the difference) between F's being and not. However, we do not say that F depends on the agent merely on the ground that he *regards* it as not ruled out that he would make this difference; for if he is mistaken in this, then the occurrence of F or its nonoccurrence is not through him and not dependent on his 'Yes' or 'No'. And the same is true if he errs in the opposite direction, i.e., is unaware that his 'Yes' or 'No' would be effective when in fact they would be. For in that case he says and refuses nothing, so that whatever happens happens without *him.* And the same is true if either F or not F is so distasteful that it could not figure to him as a possible option. For then it is as if the alternative forces itself upon him; he does not have to, and cannot, say 'Yes' to it *rather* than to the other. Thus F depends on him if and only if it is the case that (1) if F occurs it will be because he says 'Yes', and if F does not occur it will be because he says 'No'; and (2) he is aware of this and is able to envisage F and not-F as possible options for him.

By basing the *voluntary* on *what depends on the agent,* Aristotle forwards his account in two ways. First, 'it depends on him' states not a criterion but a principle in terms of which to collect a variety of factors that might justify the claim that a given action was not voluntary. Justification would require one to show either that the agent's saying 'Yes' and 'No' would have made no difference, or that one or other alternative could not present itself to him as a feasible option, whether because he was ignorant of fact (did not know that in saying 'No' to killing this man he would avoid killing his father) or because he was so constituted or in such a condition that it did not figure as an *option.* This general account allows for nonvoluntary cases to which Aristotle pays little attention; e.g., cases where saying 'Yes' or 'No' is impossible because of psychological illness, and cases where saying 'Yes' or 'No' makes no difference because of failure in the *internal* mechanisms, physical or psychophysical, that normally translate volition into action.

What counts as 'not voluntary' will depend, of course, on what we are anyway prepared to excuse. Since Aristotle is not generally prepared to excuse wrong actions done *in* ignorance, e.g. in drunkenness, rage or passion, these count as in a way depending on the agent. Such cases are conveniently dealt with in terms of the way in which the judgment-distorting condition arose. A person may be made drunk by others; in that case his drunken behaviour is not voluntary. But if he voluntarily got into the state where controlled action is impossible or severely restricted or much more likely to go wrong, then both the condition itself and what he does or what happens as a direct result of it are voluntary and to be laid at his door (1113 b 30 ff.). If it depended on him to take action to avoid being blown off course, then although his ending up in the wrong place does not now depend on him, it did so depend, hence *is now* (not merely *was before!*) voluntary and a ground for reproach. In *NE* III.5 Aristotle applies these considerations to the ethical, as distinct from physical, states from which people act and which seem to set limits on what they can do.

The second advantage of connecting the *voluntary* with what *depends on him* is that this brings to the fore the bipolar structure of the voluntary, according to which, if I do F voluntarily, then had I refrained or done something else, that would have been voluntary, too. The discussion of force, ignorance and other disabling conditions does not bring this out. For that type of discussion focuses on a nonvoluntary or countervoluntary action or movement seen as actually occurring and as thereby displacing, so to speak, a voluntary movement that would instead have occurred in the absence of the disabling condition. As we saw, in such a discussion Aristotle tends to look towards the natural movements of nonhuman natural substances to provide a model for voluntary action. From this we could not guess at the bipolarity of the voluntary; for from the bipolar perspective we view a voluntary movement as occurring instead (and *voluntarily* instead) of an equally voluntary alternative.

Bipolarity, as will become clearer in Section VI of this chapter, is what holds *voluntary*₁ and *voluntary*₂ together to form a kind of conceptual organism. In the central sort of case, which is the case of a normal human being in conditions in which human nature can operate, that someone knowingly originates M is a sufficient condition for his being held answerable for M. (The sufficient and necessary condition is that he knowingly originates either M or some condition under which it was foreseeable that something like M would happen.) But in *NE* III.1 Aristotle treats as voluntary₁ those agents who give way to pressure too great for human nature. The unbearable alternative is something which, had they done it, they would have done only because physically forced; i.e., not voluntarily. Consequently they are not held answerable for the actual deed. Here we see how, when bipolarity fails, *voluntary*₁ falls apart from *voluntary*₂. Again, a god is not an ethical agent, a voluntary₂ source of his effects; and this is because, if he has any physical effects, they are necessarily always the same, the invariant expression of his simple eternal nature. Such a being is beyond being influenced by ethical judgment, hence is not its proper target. This is not inconsistent with holding that the god knowingly originates his effects and is their voluntary₁ agent. But it is only not inconsistent because here again, in the absence of bipolarity, the normal connection is broken between *voluntary*₁ and *voluntary*₂.³²

But we must scrutinize further the bipolarity of the voluntary, and in particular must see what to make of the assumption, spelt out in the *Eudemian Ethics,* that if it depends on me whether or not I give rise to F, then with respect to F or not-F, I am a contingent cause. Does Aristotle mean by this that my voluntary action is not determined? And if so, has he grounds for the claim?

It is not at all clear, I argue below, that Aristotle takes any stand against determinism. But if he does, he lacks what we should consider adequate grounds. If necessitation by past causes is modelled on hereditary transmission of essential characteristics, then a voluntary action is not necessitated by past causes. This is because a voluntary action and its opposite are alike in being voluntary and unforced, whereas the heredity model has no room for unenforced behaviour whose opposite would also have been unforced. In the *Eudemian Ethics,* I have suggested, Aristotle may be leaning on this meagre model of determinism. In those terms, it follows without more ado that if an action was voluntary it was not necessitated, and the agent not only had the ability voluntarily to act otherwise, but could (without qualification) have acted otherwise. But on other models, the compatibility of determinism with voluntary action can be made to seem quite plausible.

If, for instance, we liken the human agent to a natural object not conceived in accordance with Aristotle's metaphysics, we can combine the view that opposite actions may be equally unforced and voluntary with the view that every action is necessitated by a cause. It is equally natural for a Newtonian particle to move this way or that, or for a substance to boil or freeze, depending on circumstances which necessitate one or the other reaction. We may use the concept of 'force' on an empirical basis, measuring the amount of force applied by the amount of difference made, but none of these reactions is 'forced' in the sense of 'contrary to the nature' of the object. The quantifiable 'force' applied is simply a kind of cause. By analogy, a voluntary action may be thought of as caused, and even causally necessitated, by circumstances, even though, being voluntary, it is not forced, and even though the alternative would have been voluntary, too, and would itself have been necessitated under different conditions.

In *De Interpretatione* 9 Aristotle declares that it cannot be that everything is necessary, on two grounds: there would be no chance events, and there would be 'no need to deliberate'—both of which he dismisses as absurd. (The argument about chance is repeated in *Metaphysics* VI.3.) These are not convincing arguments against determinism. A chance event is a set of occurrences, or something arising from a set of occurrences, whose conjunction cannot be explained by any single principle or purpose. But this is consistent with its being the case that each conjunct occurred of necessity exactly as, when and where it did, in accordance with the nature of the situation leading up to it.[33] As for deliberation, Aristotle does not explain why he thinks it would be superfluous if everything were necessary. But the easiest explanation (if this is meant as an argument against determinism) is that he understands 'X will happen of necessity' in a restricted way, as meaning 'X will inevitably happen no matter what we try to do about it'. And that entails 'X will inevitably happen, no matter how, or whether, we deliberate'.[34] However, the latter does not in fact follow from the proposition that X will happen of necessity, since one can hold that the deliberator's action of producing X was necessary given his deliberative conclusion; that his reaching that conclusion was likewise a necessary psychological event (though he could not know what the conclusion would be in advance); and that a different course of deliberation, or none at all, would have yielded a different action. Thus X was necessary, yet the deliberation not otiose.[35]

It would seem, then, that 'It depends on him' can be interpreted so as to be consistent with determinism. The theory would be that sometimes an action or movement occurs because the agent says 'Yes' to it, and it would not have occurred if and only if he said 'No'. These are the movements that depend on him. But his saying 'Yes' or 'No' (his electing to do F-instead-of-not-F, or to do not-F-instead-of-F) is an event necessitated by causes traceable back beyond him. One is not entitled to call this agent '*the* master' of his effect, so far as the phrase suggests a unique and therefore an ultimate cause, but he might still be said to 'control' the effect, given that had he said 'No' it would not have occurred. Certainly he as a voluntary agent 'contributes something' (Aristotle's words), since the actual movement would not have occurred without his (necessitated) 'Yes'. And we must add to this that the empirical conditions under which we decide that the movement depends on him (factual knowledge, absence of compulsion, ability to envisage and carry out a line of action) are arguably the same whether the voluntary agency is conceived as determined or not.

So on one showing, Aristotle's relation to the question of determinism is this: (1) he adopts an indeterminist position on voluntary agency, without producing any very compelling arguments for this stance; (2) he gives an analysis of voluntary action and its conditions which is consistent with determinism, and which perhaps could coherently figure at the centre of a determinist account of voluntary action.

It is possible, however, and I am inclined to think closer to the truth, that Aristotle no more denies universal determinism than he asserts it.[36] If that is so, then any arguments of his which fail to support such a denial are not necessarily failures. We can read them as claiming no more than what everyone must concede who accepts voluntary agency as possible at all. For instance, the Eudemian declaration of contingency may be meant to drive home the point that a voluntary agent (by contrast with an Aristotelian natural substance) is not genetically constituted so that an alternative to his actual unenforced movement would have come about only through force. This claims no more than that a contrary movement would have represented neither the frustration of his actual innate essence, nor a metaphysically unintelligible breakthrough into a different essence (as if a pear tree began to grow apricots). It is neither asserted or denied that the voluntary agent on any particular occasion, given the totality of actual circumstances outer or inner leading up to the action, could have voluntarily acted differently in the sense required by libertarianism. Of course, a philosopher who cannot entertain the idea that all our actions are necessitated from the past without automatically modelling them on the natural inherited behaviour of an Aristotelian natural substance, may easily conclude that voluntary actions cannot be thus necessitated, and that the agent is their ultimate or first cause. That is a natural position for those whose restricted metaphysics prevents them from conceiving of the kind of determinist proposal familiar to later theorists, whereby the identical agent, it is said, *would* voluntarily have done otherwise if he had willed to, but *could* not have willed to under the actual circumstances. But the restricted thinkers would not be rejecting that proposal, and they might not have wanted to reject it had they been able to consider it.

Just now I seem to be saying that if Aristotle, per impossible perhaps, had not viewed nature in terms of Aristotelian metaphysics, he might have taken seriously the idea, or at least have suspended judgment upon it, that voluntary action is determined; and have done so without compromising the connections which he so usefully draws between voluntariness and knowledge, freedom from compulsion etc. So far, then, it is Aristotle's general metaphysics that sets him at a distance from determinism; but now what about Aristotle's *ethics*? Does that play no part in the explanation of his actual and possible attitude to determinism? Indeed, it is surprising how much there is to think about here without our ever yet serving him the standard question, Is determinism compatible with moral responsibility? This question, on which he seems to express a view in *NE* III.5 in an argument to be studied presently, draws him into a living debate. For if he has a response, it should be based on his conception of moral responsibility, not on his peculiar metaphysics of substance; and whereas the metaphysics has to be considered archaic in the light of later science, Aristotle's notion of moral responsibility may be identical with whatever such notion we claim as our own.

It has been well said that if faced with a logical conflict between determinist claims and ascriptions of moral responsibility, Aristotle would have said 'So much the worse for determinism'.[37] But, as I have indicated, I do not think we should take it for granted that in the *Ethics* he has any position on determinism as we understand it. And if we seek, as we surely should, to identify what as a philosopher *of ethics* he contributes to this issue, then (here, too) we must not lose sight of the practical nature of his enterprise. Here, questions even of philosophical ethics are posed from an abstract practical standpoint, the ultimate purpose being to forward the realization of happiness by practical beings operating from concrete practical standpoints. So under this perspective let the philosopher be supposed to ask questions about what is necessary and what, if anything, contingent. The term 'necessary', in this context, takes on a connotation perhaps appreciable only by *practical* beings, implying: 'What we cannot affect by our actions but can, so far as our knowledge allows, take account of in framing our actions, so as successfully to control what we can control, partly with the aid of and partly despite the necessities and impossibilities which we cannot control'.

If *practical* knowledge, belief, and even conjecture about necessary facts (e.g., facts about the past), as well as about necessary connections and patterns of events, are concerned with the fixed elements of an agent's situation to which he should respond by intelligent adjustment of what is not thus fixed, it follows that any necessities real or alleged whereby it is necessary that he wills or decides or deliberatingly concludes as he does fall outside what counts as necessary from this practical point of view. They lie beyond the horizon of what can be considered at all. For logically we are debarred from taking account in deliberation of the laws and the disposition of particulars (whether physical or psychological events, forces or thinglike objects) which structure that very deliberation and, according to determinism, constrain it to just one outcome. To make the point, I have momentarily assumed that there are such necessary connections; but the point really is that the practical subject, on whatever level of practicality, is, in his typifying sense of 'necessary', cognitively impervious to the very possibility of such necessities, either to assert or deny them.

Hence when the philosopher declares on behalf of practical beings, speaking therefore in the language of practicality, that 'not everything is necessary', he is not contradicting determinism's absolute claim that *everything* is necessary or necessitated, because his universe of discourse does not extend beyond what confronts or could confront us potential practical deciders. He asserts only that some of what so confronts us need not be as it is or need not continue to develop as it is now developing, so that a space exists for our actions to make a difference. Dialectically the philosopher is on the firmest possible ground here, since unless this is true he cannot be speaking to and for practical agents at all, and the language of practicality would be wasted on this universe. Thus if this philosopher supports his assertion that not everything is necessary, by arguing that otherwise deliberation would be pointless and would make no difference, his argument is adequate for the conclusion. It would not be adequate if the conclusion were intended to embrace not only the situation which *confronts* that deliberating individual, but also the trains of events debouching in the deliberation itself and leading to the decision which leads to an outcome that may alter what he takes to confront him. For while alternative outcomes are possible given the state of things merely as it confronts the deliberator, it does not follow that different outcomes are possible if the state of things is taken to include factors driving his deliberation. But, I have argued, 'the state of things' in this more inclusive sense is not a concept available from the standpoint of the practical agent and whoever speaks for him. From this point of view, no fault is to be found with the argument of *De Interpretatione* 9 to the effect that not everything is necessary (though I offer no judgment about the implications which Aristotle draws concerning truth-values).

Aristotle may therefore be described as a 'proto-indeterminist' insofar as the determinist would reject a position like Aristotle's, but not as a 'libertarian' in the sense of one who knowingly takes a stand against determinism with regard to volition. To see this, consider the reasoning of *EE* 1222 b 41 ff., which is meant to establish the contingency of voluntary agency: (1) Some external events may and may not happen; (2) of these, many are in our power or depend on us for happening or not, we being their causes or starting-points; (3) if an effect is contingent, then so is its cause (i.e., the causing of it by the cause); therefore (4) the voluntary human agent is a contingently causing cause. In other words, since F may and also may not happen: and since if it does the agent's 'Yes' will have necessitated it, and if it does not his 'No' will have necessitated its nonoccurrence: it follows that the agent's 'Yes' or 'No' is contingent (because from necessary premises only necessary conclusions flow). Now the argument starts by *assuming it obvious* that some external events are contingent without qualification. In the context of a debate with a universal determinist, this cannot be assumed. All that remains obvious once the determinist spectre has been raised is that some events depend on us, since otherwise agency would be impossible. But (we have seen) this only implies that some events are not necessitated to happen or not independently of our decision. The above argument, in short, assumes that whatever is not necessary or impossible independently of our decision is contingent without qualification. This is the same as assuming that the modalities attaching without qualification to events are those which attach to them from the viewpoint of one for whom they constitute a field for choice and action.

The determinist will argue that the decision itself was necessitated by something prior, so that the external outcome was necessary, too, even in advance of the decision. Any philosopher faced with this assertion will, if he resists it, set to work to show not that the external outcome is not necessitated, since clearly it is necessitated by the agent's decision once the decision is made, but rather that the *decision* was not necessitated—either on the ground that it would not then be voluntary, or would not be a decision, or on the ground that the agent, even if in some sense acting voluntarily, could not be held morally responsible. Alternatively or perhaps concurrently, this philosopher will seek to find flaws in the arguments on which the determinist grounds his doctrine. Aristotle does none of these things. I have already indicated that some of the standard motives for determinism would not affect him; e.g., the belief that everything in the world operates in accordance with the same set of physical laws. And here in the *Eudemian Ethics,* instead of taking trouble to show that voluntary agency would not be voluntary agency or would not be morally responsible, were it not contingent, and thence deriving the conclusion that external events which depend on voluntary agency are likewise contingent (at least until the decision is made), Aristotle first takes it for granted that the external events *are* contingent and then *from this alone* concludes to the contingency of their voluntary cause. This, it seems to me, is not the reasoning of someone who sees himself as having to take up a stand against determinism.[38]

## V. Character as Voluntary (I)

In voluntary action we pursue an objective which is before us and which figures as a good to us so far as we pursue it; but on another level we enact by our action, and thereby propound into public space, a conception of the kind of practical being that it is good (or at least all right) to be: a kind typified by pursuit of this kind of goal in this sort of way under such conditions.[39] So the action expresses what may be called a vision of the human good. The vision need not be articulated otherwise than in the action and cognate actions, and it need not be reflective or even steady and consistent from one occasion to another, since voluntary action is often thoughtless, impulsive, inconsistent, and changeable in ethical direction. But it can also spring from a settled vision, and this is the same as springing from a settled moral character.

The more settled a person's character, the more it seems to be his nature, and the less the ethical difference between options open to him as voluntary agent. In choosing he will not be endorsing one way of being human over another so much as one version over another of recognisably the same way of being human. Established character, like biological nature, sets constraints on the range of what is viable to persons of that character. The individual who habitually puts himself first will find a way of doing this whichever way he acts, and genuinely self-sacrificing alternatives would not be live options to him. It may depend on him whether he does precisely this or that, and in respect of detail he may be a contingent cause, but it seems that whatever he now does, it does not depend on him whether he *behaves self-centredly.*

So, if some action of his mainly strikes us as an instance of selfish behaviour, is the action voluntary under that description, and is he to be reproached for it or blamed? It would be strange if not, since that would imply that a person of settled character is a voluntary agent only (if at all) in respect of the ethically insignificant aspects of his action; yet the concept *voluntary* is above all relevant to ethics as setting the formal condition under which an individual becomes subject to ethical judgment. The suggestion that he is not to be reproached *for his selfish behaviour* is further paradoxical because the very term 'selfish' already carries reproach. It would be strange if the person of established bad character were logically immune to having words such as 'selfish' applied to his behaviour or to him! And mutatis mutandis the same would be true for persons of established good character, except that they are not logically protected from defamation but logically debarred from praise. Or should we say that the use, now, of what once were ethical terms is only descriptive; or is evaluative but lacking in some especially moral dimension, as when we say that a smell is bad or the weather good—not passing ethical judgment but expressing some other type of preference?

But if the virtuous and vicious are not subjects of ethical judgment, who is? Virtues, vices, and the corresponding types of behaviour must therefore as such be voluntary. But how is this possible if virtue and vice are 'second nature', and if what is voluntary is what depends on the agent? This is the problem that Aristotle faces in *NE* III.5.

As he points out repeatedly in the chapter, any conclusions which hold for vice must apply to virtue, and conversely. If the involuntariness of vice proves it a mistake to condemn the wicked, it proves it an equal mistake to admire the good. However, the discussion is mainly of bad actions of bad people, since these present peculiar problems. First, an excuse is sought only for bad behaviour, and fixed character might seem to offer a kind of excuse. Second, the wicked person, according to Aristotle, is objectively wretched—he has no chance of happiness—and it seems strange to say that anyone is voluntarily wretched and voluntarily lives out and reinforces his wretchedness in action (1113 b 14–15). Third, Aristotle is aware that wicked persons at times feel trapped by their nature. This underscores the lack of freedom which leads us to question their status as voluntary agents. By behaving in the ways that characterise a certain ethical bent, one comes to *be* of that ethical bent, and a point may be reached where it is too late to change. When not caught up in moment-by-moment practical action and response, the individual may dislike what he is. Aristotle speaks of someone wishing to cease to be unjust, when by now this is impossible (1114 a 12–14 and 20–21).[40] And in discussing love and friendship he writes eloquently about the vicious person's self-hatred (1166 b 7–29; he seems to suggest here that the vicious in all cases hate themselves, but it is enough for the present that some do.)

This conflict, we should note, is similar to that which marks the incontinent person (as Aristotle notes at 1166 b 8), but it is not the same.[41] The incontinent person fails to live up to his *rational choice,* giving way to a contrary impulse. But the rational choice, even if betrayed, incorporates the assumption that one can act in the manner chosen. In this and other ways the choice is a manifestation of *practical* intelligence. But the vicious person hates himself for not being as he *wishes* to be, and wishes need not be practical. We can wish that Troy had not fallen, and for other impossibilities (1111 b 22–23). To see how this can happen in the case of character, we recall that for Aristotle a character is formed by acting as a person of such character would. In so doing, the unformed person does not go through the motions as if he were acting a part, but actually *accepts* doing what he does. The action is not only voluntary, but his, even if adopted at another's suggestion. It is as in theoretical matters. Acceptance even of a single proposition brings one closer to embracing the theory from which this and many others flow. One may end by seeing everything in terms of the theory, and by taking the theory further oneself. As rational beings we tend to stand by our assertions theoretical and practical, and we are usually expected to, even if we never first meant them all that seriously or to the exclusion of other possibilities; hence having affirmed we tend to reaffirm as occasion demands and to find reasons for rejecting opposition: reasons which perhaps would not have brought us into the position in the first place and might not have been noticed except from within it, but which once we are in it confirm us in our tenure. Now if the vicious person comes to hate himself and his modes of practical acceptance, it does not follow that he knows in a practical way *how else to be* or even how to begin to change. At the moments of choice and action he has no other moves to make, and no other ways of seeing and classifying his particular circumstances, than those which express the detested character. But being still human and therefore essentially a practical being, he must act and respond in one way or another, and so responds in the only practical language he knows, and of course all the more when he knows that others are geared to expect him to voice himself in that way. This is not at all the plight of the incontinent agent, who can in general give detailed practical content to his own idea of how he should be, but on occasion feels too much like doing something else. The incontinent's alternative to incontinent behaviour is to do *what* he knows he should; the vicious person hates what he is, but knows no practical alternative.

Does it follow that the vicious person's conduct is somehow not voluntary, or that the agent should not be blamed for it unless it can be shown that he is responsible for the character from which it springs? In *NE* III.5 Aristotle seems to accept some such inference, and indeed this seems to be a powerful motive for his attempt to show that character is voluntary. The inference, however, is problematic, to say the least; and we shall have to consider in detail how Aristotle could come to accept it or something like it. But let me begin by drawing attention to some confusions in this area: confusions which, as it seems to me, Aristotle shows no sign of noticing and from which he never gets free. To broach them, it will help to look at the *EE*'s seemingly simple argument to the effect that character is voluntary: (P) We cannot be praised and condemned for our settled qualities of character and for actions expressing them, unless the character itself was a voluntary acquisition which it depended on us to acquire or not. Now, (Q) it is evidently absurd (is it not?) to withhold praise and reproach from character and actions in character; so it follows that (R): qualities of character are voluntary acquisitions (1223 a 9–13; cf. 1228 a 9–11). That is Aristotle's conclusion. He has further arguments for R, which we shall consider in the next section, but first let us look at his grounds for Q and P.

Behind P stands the broader assumption that praise and reproach attach only to what is voluntary. Voluntary are (1) what I do knowing myself to be doing it, as e.g. the bringing about of some movement or state; (2) movements, states and situations brought about voluntarily, as in (1); (3) foreseeable upshots of states and situations that are voluntary according to (2). Under the third division come many items which but for their antecedents would count as nonvoluntary: what I do under threat or in ignorance or what I suffer through external force, when the coercion, the ignorance, or the subjection to force were foreseeable results of my voluntary action or inaction. Character is supposed to fall into the second division, and conduct expressive of character into the third. The items in these two divisions count as voluntary because of their relation to an item in the first.

It may seem strange to classify conduct expressive of character as derivatively voluntary: straightforwardly voluntary actions of the first division are surely the key to a person's character? Yes, but not only those, since what a person *neglects* tells us much about his character, and neglect does not fall neatly into the first division. But we also need to consider actions as invested with their ethical adverbs. My *selling secrets to the enemy* is clearly voluntary, and also treacherous and despicable; the question is: is *acting treacherously and despicably* likewise (under that description) voluntary on my part? Aristotle holds that it is, by relating the action under this description to something—character—which has already been established as voluntary in the second division, by means (in turn) of a presumed relation to actions in the first. Yet (one might object) he is surely confused in wanting this conclusion. We need to know that an action was voluntary before applying 'treacherous' and 'despicable' to it or to the agent on account of it; but it does not follow that the act of treachery is as such voluntary or, of course, nonvoluntary. There is no need to declare it voluntary on the ground that otherwise we could not reproach the person for treachery, because in saying 'treachery' we *already* reproach. 'It was a treacherous action' does not give a description of the action with respect to which one asks: 'Was it voluntary under that description, and therefore does it, under that description, call for censure etc.?' Similarly, 'He is brave' is said on the basis of his voluntary behaviour neutrally described, but it does not follow that his being brave should be considered either voluntary or nonvoluntary.

Several verbal traps infest this area. For example, one might reason: (1) a term of reproach such as 'dishonest' (or simply 'wicked') applies to a person only in virtue of what is voluntary, e.g., certain types of behaviour; (2) 'dishonest' etc. applies to a person in virtue of a character trait for which such behaviour is evidence; therefore (3) the trait itself is something voluntary. Here we have confusion between different senses of 'the term applies in virtue of X'. In (1) it means 'the term is predicated in the light of X as criterion or evidence' and in (2) it means 'the application of the term is made true by X'. Again, one might reason: (1) by calling a person 'dishonest' I reproach him for the vice of dishonesty; (2) by calling a person 'dishonest' I reproach him for behaving in certain ways; (3) but in the latter case, what I reproach him for must be voluntary, or the reproach is misapplied; therefore (4) what I reproach him for when I reproach him for the vice of dishonesty must be voluntary, too, since a *reproach* for dishonesty could hardly be misapplied (if 'dishonesty' is not misapplied)! This trades on the vagueness of 'reproach him *for*', and the confusion is essentially the same as above. His transfer of funds from this account to that is the kind of action in the evidential light of which I put him down as 'dishonest'. The action is also that *for* which he is reproached or punished. But I do not so much reproach him *for* being dishonest (any more than I punish him *for* being guilty), but reproach him, rather, *as* dishonest, dishonesty being not evidence for but a logical constituent of my reproachful claim.

The fact that these confusions lurk makes it not so obvious after all that Q is true. It is possible to be led to the fallacious conclusion that qualities of character such as honesty and dishonesty are voluntary like the actions which evince them, whereas the correct conclusion might be that the qualities of character are neither voluntary or not; in ascribing them we ascribe what cannot *be* voluntary because the ascription of them *presupposes* voluntariness on a different level; i.e., on the level of actions neutrally described.[42]

On the other hand, if having a dishonest character is something which I voluntarily brought upon myself, then it may make sense to reproach me for being (i.e., having become) dishonest, just as it makes sense to reproach me for knowingly encouraging dishonesty in another. That I voluntarily bring moral characteristics upon myself is, of course, exactly Aristotle's position, but he wants to establish it by means of the premiss that we praise and reproach people for their moral characteristics. What has emerged, though, is that we have to view character as a voluntary acquisition *before* it could make sense (if indeed it ever could) to praise or reproach someone *for* (as distinct from *in terms of*) honesty, dishonesty and the rest.

In *NE* III.5 Aristotle uses an analogy to argue that since we condemn character defects, these defects must be voluntary:

> But not only are the vices of the soul voluntary, but those of the body also for some men, whom we accordingly blame; while no one blames those who are ugly by nature, we blame those who are so owing to want of exercise and care. So it is, too, with respect to weakness and infirmity; no one would reproach a man blind from birth or by disease or from a blow, but rather pity him, while every one would blame a man who was blind from alcoholism or some other form of self-indulgence. Of vices of the body, then, those in our own power [i.e., that depend on us] are blamed, those not in our power are not. And if this be so, in the other cases also the vices that are blamed must be in our own power. (1114 a 21–31)

We 'blame' someone for a bodily defect or disability, and the same goes for poverty and ignorance, when and only when they come about by the person's own fault. The condemnation is because we consider that incurring these ills by one's own fault shows a bad sort of character (although the character need not be fixed and settled to give rise to the behaviour that results in irreversible physical or material damage). Aristotle wants the analogy to show that ethical defects are likewise voluntary, on the ground that we condemn ethical defects. But taken in full, the analogy should yield the result that we condemn ethical defects because the acquiring of them shows a bad sort of character on the part of the person who acquired them when he did what caused him to become thus defective. That entails that he had to have something of a bad character before he could acquire a bad character, or else the bad character acquired is not an object of censure and not voluntary—precisely the opposite of the position which Aristotle aims to uphold! For it is part of his position that we start off with no determinate character. What is more, if, as the analogy suggests, bad character is a proper object of reproach, and voluntary, only if it is the outcome of preexisting bad character, then either the latter is also voluntary or it is not. If it is, and on the same terms, we have an infinite regress and no possibility of voluntary beginnings of character at all; and if it is not, then why should we think that the later bad character is voluntary either? In fact, as this dilemma indicates, the analogy is mistaken. Illness and disablement are sometimes the sufferer's own fault and are objects of (or grounds for) reproach, but they may be due to a cause beyond his control. Consequently, we have to ascertain that they were the foreseeable consequences of his voluntary actions before we reproach him for them. If ethical ills of the soul were like that, then sometimes we should be reproached for them and sometimes not, and the ethical terms for these qualities would not always function as terms of reproach. As it is, according to the analytic distinction made above, they are necessarily terms of reproach,—i.e., terms *in* which we reproach—and as such they never, strictly speaking, stand for items *for* which we reproach people. Aristotle does not take in this point, although elsewhere he employs a distinction which is similar: between the abstract numbers of the number series *in terms of which* we count and the various numbers (i.e., groups or pluralities) of things *which* we count in terms of the former (cf. *Physics* 219 b 5–9).

It is true, and Aristotle is well aware, that some people are more prone by nature or through physical causes to become cowardly or evil tempered than others, and similarly for desirable qualities (cf. 1144 b 4–9 and 1179 b 20–23[43]). But an ethical defect (which is what he is talking about in the above passage when he speaks of 'defects of the soul') is a defect of the moral self. Its presence, therefore, is not so much the presence of the quality empirically described as 'timorousness' or 'bad temper' as the differential between what, under this description, the person has willingly himself become and what he could not help being because of illness or heredity.

## VI. Character as Voluntary (II)

So far, then, the Eudemian assumption (P) that we can be praised and reproached 'for' qualities of character only if qualities of character are voluntary gives Aristotle no good argument for the thesis (R) that qualities of character are voluntary. For that follows only given (Q) that indeed we can be praised and reproached 'for' character; and we have seen how this proposition is full of ambiguity and confusion. But in *NE* III.5 he has other arguments for R. First (1) there is this: it depends on us how we act and whether we do the noble or disgraceful things the doing of which leads to settled good or bad character; hence whether we are virtuous or vicious depends on us (1113 b 6–14; cf. 1114 a 3–21). Next (2), unless we accept that vice (and presumably, also, virtue) is voluntary, we must abandon the view that 'a human being is a moving principle or begetter of his actions as of children' (1113 b 14–19). And he also says that unless a person is 'somehow responsible [*aitios*] for the state he is in [i.e., for his character], . . . no one is responsible for his own evildoing, but everyone does evil acts through ignorance of the end, thinking that by these he will get what is best' (1114 b 1–5). Here Aristotle seems to qualify his earlier position that ignorance exculpates (renders a bad action nonvoluntary) only if it is lack of information about some fact, not if it is ignorance of how to be and how to behave. For he now apparently implies that the wicked person's moral ignorance would exculpate if the wickedness (and the ignorance that is part of it) were not voluntary. Next (3), Aristotle argues (1113 b 21 ff.) that social practices show that character is voluntary: legislators and private individuals, through sanctions and other kinds of encouragement, seek to persuade us to do what is good and refrain from what is bad—not merely so that we should perform particular actions of one kind rather than another, but so that we should become good people: 'But no one is encouraged [by others] to do the things that are neither in our power nor voluntary; it is assumed that there is no gain in being persuaded not to be hot or in pain or hungry or the like, since we shall experience these feelings nonetheless' (1132 b 26–30).

Fourth (4), he declares that only an utterly unmindful person is unaware of the fact that by pursuing certain lines of conduct we come to be *such as to* act in those ways (1114 a 3–10). That is, we all know this although we may not all make use of the knowledge, but anyone who actively cares about himself as a practical being knows it as part and parcel of his active caring. So since we know that we become unjust by doing unjust things and since nothing compels us to do those things, we have no grounds for complaining that our becoming unjust was not voluntary (1114 a 11–13).

Before commenting on the detail of any of these arguments, let us ask what Aristotle is trying to establish. He is arguing against the view that moral character, and moral values, are innate; in other words, the view that:

> the aiming at the end is not self-chosen, but one must be born with an eye, as it were, by which to judge rightly and choose what is truly good, and he is well endowed by nature who is well endowed with this. For it is what is greatest and most noble, and what we cannot get or learn from another, but must have just such as it was when given us at birth, and to be well and nobly endowed with this will be complete and true natural endowment. If this is true, then, how will excellence be more voluntary than vice? To both men alike, the good and the bad, the end appears and is fixed by nature or however it may be, and it is by referring everything to this that men do whatever they do. (1114 b 5–16)

This position is threatening in two ways. First, if it is true, then Aristotle's account of character development by habituation is false. The assumption behind that is not merely that we are not born with a fully formed character, but that we are not born with a one-way potential for development. If that were so, then presumably each individual would develop according to his innate potential as long as he was not hindered or kept back. Positive training would be unnecessary. Alternatively, positive attempts to get one to go against the natural direction would always fail. Some people could not be ruined by neglect, and some could not be got to develop the trait of, say, justice however much they were encouraged through practice to do what the just man would do. The practice would not take, and even if they did not have to be physically coerced, they could never identify with just practice or with the conception of goodness which it represents. Second, as I have indicated, Aristotle assumes (though it is not yet clear why) that if moral character is innate, an individual cannot be held answerable for the actions expressing his character. And Aristotle regards that as absurd.

Now the first threat is easily repelled. For it is not only Aristotle's theory that we are born with the potential to develop in different and even opposite moral directions: the actual practice of moral education shows that this is what everyone believes who has to do with the matter in a practical way. Argument (3) makes this point. But there is something puzzling about Aristotle's insistence that character is voluntarily acquired if his main concern is to prove it not innate. For that, he need only emphasise that if it were innate, moral education would be pointless. It would perhaps also be relevant to remind us that character develops in the young through their being encouraged voluntarily to do and refrain from certain things. So certainly character *results from* voluntary action. But why is it necessary to make the further and more dubious claim that we *voluntarily acquire our characters?*

As for the second threat, it may be absurd not to hold wicked people answerable for their wickedness and their wrongdoing, and even more absurd, as Aristotle seems to suggest (1114 b 12–13; 19–20; cf.1111a 27–30), not to hold good people responsible for their goodness and their good deeds; but not so absurd as to be prima facie unthinkable. It is not clear that every innatist would necessarily flinch from that conclusion. Hence even if the reasoning of (2) is correct, as a refutation the argument might not succeed. But perhaps (2) is intended only to spell out the cost (real, though not necessarily intolerable) of denying that character is voluntary. To prove the denial mistaken, Aristotle needs an independent argument, and this is provided by (1) with the help of (4).

The difficulty about these arguments, as has often been noted, is that their conclusion that our character *depends on us* seems to clash with the considerations brought forward in (3). Now argument (3) does make it clear that the acquisition of character has something of the structure of the voluntary and what depends on oneself; namely, bipolarity. For the practice of moral education assumes that if someone develops a certain moral character, then (a) it was not unnatural to him to develop it (so that once developed it can be like a second nature); but also (b) it would not have been unnatural to him, originally, to develop a significantly different sort of character (so that had he done so, he would have come to be of a different second nature). But this bipolarity seems to fall short of what is implied by 'it depends on him'. How can a person's character depend on *him,* given that we are started off along the right or wrong track by the persuasion of others or else by their neglect? Could anyone really have helped taking his own first steps, which then led to other steps and finally to a developed character? And if not, or if we are not able to be sure that he could, how can Aristotle be right to declare so roundly that our character depends on us? But if this is in question, it is questionable whether character is voluntary, if 'voluntary' is taken to entail 'it depends on us'.

Let us leave this for a moment and return to (2), the most ambiguous of the arguments. I repeat the passages:

> [If] wickedness [is not] voluntary . . . we shall have to dispute what has just been said, at any rate, and deny that man is a moving principle or begetter of his actions as of children. (1113 b 4–9

> [Unless] each man is somehow responsible for the state he is in [i.e., his character], . . . no one is responsible for his own evildoing. (1114 b 1–4)

Owing to the ambiguity of 'voluntary agent,' by which Aristotle sometimes means 'knowing originator' ('voluntary$_1$'), sometimes 'subject of ethical judgment ('voluntary$_2$'), and sometimes both at once, we cannot be sure whether the passages mean (a) that unless a man (or, it may be, man in general) is a voluntary source of his moral character, he is not answerable for (subject to ethical judgment on account of) his actions; or (b) that unless a man is a voluntary source of his moral character, he is not the knowing originator of those actions, and the one on whose Yes or No they depend. In my view, Aristotle not only does not distinguish these positions, but is happy to maintain both.[44]

Each can be challenged. Someone who holds that character is innate can say against (a) that people are certainly answerable for their actions; for instance, we can ask and be told their reasons for acting, and on that basis we can judge them good or bad human beings, which is surely an ethical assessment. Even more obviously, the innatist can say against (b) that the person of developed innate character would still be the knowing originator of his characteristic actions, and that they depend on him since they occur only through his assent. The innatist can also say (unless he happens also to be a total determinist) that the agent of developed character can assent to different actions, though always within the margins set by his character.

But the objection to (a) will not do, since holding someone answerable is not just being prepared to call him a good or bad human being who acts for reasons; it is, for Aristotle, treating him as an appropriate target of *praise* and *reproach.* People are appropriate targets only if these attitudes can have an ethically persuasive effect— i.e., can influence character. If in a given case the person targeted is of fixed character, there can be little effect *on him,* but praising or reproaching him is nonetheless appropriate if it can give a direction to the character-building practical affirmations of *others.* But that presupposes that immature agents can develop either way. Now their development is an obvious (so Aristotle thinks) consequence of voluntary action in response to models and countermodels targeted by praise or reproach. In their case, then, development and its result are likewise voluntary. But then it must *have been* voluntary even in the case of the now fixed models and countermodels, since these are members of the same species. Thus (a) represents the view that unless human beings voluntarily acquire fixed character, human beings are not fit targets of ethical attitudes on account of their actions. The statement divides its reference between formed and unformed agents and their actions, but nonetheless manages to refer to human beings in general, since the one class draws its membership from the other, and individuals in either may be expected to see themselves and each other as past or future members of the other class.

Now let us consider the objection to (b), and let us grant it. If character is innate, it does not follow that humans would not be knowing causes of the movements constituting the actions expressing character; nor that their actions would not depend on their Yes or No; and there might even be room for different expressions of the same character. One might wonder about the propriety of holding people responsible for those actions, if character is supposed innate; but there seems to be no reason to doubt that their actions would be *theirs* (not anyone or anything else's) and voluntary according to the criteria that refer to absence of ignorance and compulsion. Does Aristotle mean to abandon those criteria? Surely what he ought instead to do, in the light of the innatist hypothesis, is to recognise a conceptual space between *voluntary*$_1$ and *voluntary*$_2$. The innatist theory may rule it out that human agents are voluntary$_2$, without giving us any reason to cease regarding them as voluntary$_1$.

But there is a sense in which one can raise the question: in the innatist's world could it still be *true* that they are even voluntary$_1$? Truth, for Aristotle, is not a property or relation of propositions considered as abstract meanings, but of statements or utterances. Indeed truth (*alētheia,* the opposite of falsity or error) is primarily a condition of the mind rather than an attribute of the proposition minded. If it were the case that character is innate, then the conditions for stating that someone knowingly originated something, or not, would not exist, and there would be no truth of the matter or falsity either. For why should we be *concerned* to know whether someone acted voluntarily$_1$—to ascertain whether he was in ignorance of some fact or was under compulsion, and whether these conditions were results of his own earlier voluntary$_1$ actions—if not with a view to ethical judgment? If I believe that others are persuadable only in respect of what is ethically insignificant, then on what matters most they are not persuadable and, if we differ, must be left alone or else coerced. Not only can I not interact with them as voluntary$_1$ agents, except with regard to ethically trivial matters, but neither I nor they will take much practical notice of a third party's actions as voluntary$_1$ or not. For I will not be holding up someone else's behaviour as a model or countermodel of the kind of person to be, since my interlocutors (if so they can be called) are mastered by their own inbuilt model, their innate programme.

If, as Aristotle assumes, the denial that character is innate amounts to the assertion that its acquisition is voluntary; and if assuming it to be innate takes away from us the rationale of making ethical assessments and holding people responsible; and if our readiness to adopt these attitudes is the condition under which it matters whether it is true or false to say of someone that he knowingly gave rise to M: then we have Aristotle's position (b) that unless character is voluntary, it is not true that 'man is a moving principle or begetter of his actions.'

But why, in denying that character is innate must Aristotle take the, as it seems, further and unnecessary step of asserting it to be voluntary?[45] The reason is not, I think, really that he wants to be able to praise or reproach people *for* having their moral qualities. So far as that is concerned, what he should want (I have argued) is to be able to praise and reproach them *as* brave, honest, unscrupulous, dissipated etc. And in general he wishes to uphold these as ethical predicates or, as it might be better to say, uphold their distinctively ethical or practical use as terms of praise and reproach. But to achieve that he needs only to argue against innatism without incurring the problems of defending the thesis that our character is voluntary and depends (or depended) on us.

The defence consists in a combination of arguments (1) and (4), and it strikes many readers as highly implausible. Implausible it is, if according to (4) the knowledge crucial to *voluntarily* becoming brave, dishonest etc. has to be articulate, reflective, verbal. Aristotle's language does not invite us to assume that. He says that only an 'insensate' *(anaisthētos)* person lacks the knowledge that what one does makes one the sort of person one then comes to be. The word suggests that knowing this is having a feel for, rather than being able to state, the way in which our actions not only tell the story of who we are, but write it. Even an inexperienced and thoughtless person in a sense endorses what he is doing as all right to do, and takes it to be all right to be someone who acts like that. So perhaps he likewise understands that in approving of being that sort of person he comes closer to being it. Add to this that Aristotle may well have in mind the interpersonal situation in which the child is told such things as that if he persists in gobbling at meals or hiding behind his mother when an unfamiliar figure approaches, he will end up a 'glutton' or 'coward': 'and then it will be too late to change'. The message is verbal, and one would have to be insensate not to hear it or (provided one trusted the authority) not to be at all moved.

Again, it is often as if we know by instinct that others are quick to look upon us as of a certain type on the basis of even a few actions; or we should not so often say or think, even when young, on being found to have done something shameful: 'I am not really like that'; i.e., 'I did not do it from a firm and unchanging disposition.' It is as if acting thus and being such as to act thus are so linked that others are justified in reading the latter from the former unless they are expressly requested (or have some other special reason) to suppress the inference. If so, then the principle 'that's what I do, so that's the sort of person I am' seems to be something that we know from very early on and without deliberate reflection.[46]

In this way one can make a case for holding that even very young agents can know that what they do leads into what they will be, and so for Aristotle's conclusion that they voluntarily become what their actions portend, since they are not ignorant of this and do not act under compulsion. And what is true of the very young is even more plausibly true of them later, when they are to a large extent in charge of themselves but before character is completely set, if it ever is. But to say that an action was done (or a consequence brought about) knowingly and unforced is, as we saw above (Section IV), to say less than that 'it depended on the agent'. And it is the latter, or 'voluntary' as implying the latter, that sets the stumbling block to accepting Aristotle's argument. In general, perhaps, the less a young child gets ethical attention from others, the less likely he is to be aware that how he behaves is how, if he persists, he will be. For in one of the scenarios sketched above, he knows this (or is reminded of it) because others explicitly point it out to him in connection with specific behaviour. So the knowledge which supposedly renders development of character voluntary is very far from depending just on the agent, since he owes this knowledge and the entire initial direction of the process to others. And even if he knew the principle in a general way from himself, without feedback he would not necessarily become aware in crucial ways of *what* he is doing, so as to identify the type of action as one to be pursued or avoided at other times. Through criticism, and not otherwise, he becomes aware of doing what draws the criticism: talking too loudly, handling a precious object casually, taking too much time over something etc. etc. And it is often the same with praise and the actions for which we are praised.

By telling us to do or to stop doing something, others not only define for us what it is that we are not doing or doing, but they divide these off from each other as alternatives. On being told to start doing X one becomes aware of being seen as having possibly, indeed probably, willingly continued *not* doing X (where previously one was aware only of doing Y) but for the intervention. In this way, in complying, one becomes aware of doing-rather-than-not-doing-X or, in disobeying, of (now) not-doing-rather-than-doing-X. Thus we get to know of X and not-X as 'depending on us', though by no means yet as deliberate options. And the knowledge or belief that something depends on us is a necessary condition of its so depending (see Section IV). That things depend on us cannot, according to this genetic sketch, depend solely on us, and in this respect we are more dependent at first on other human beings even than we are for food and drink, since we can get the former in no other way.

It is sometimes suggested that what motivates *NE* III.5 is the following reasoning: (1) a person of formed character is *not free* to act otherwise than in accordance with it; (2) one cannot be held answerable for doing X when one is not free not to, except on condition that (3) one freely and knowingly entered into the situation in which one is not free not to do it. With this in mind, it is suggested, Aristotle makes the acquisition of character 'depend on us.' For then the fully formed agent cannot escape responsibility for his actions. He can trace them to their origin in free agency beyond his present self; but this is not like being able to blame them entirely on someone else, for their free origin was, earlier, himself (cf. 1113 b 19–21).[47]

This gives Aristotle a weak argument.[48] If the mature agent is *necessitated,* by being the sort of person he is, to act as he does, and is therefore necessitated to act in ways that further consolidate his character making it yet more inescapable, how is it not at least as likely that the young person was necessitated by his upbringing to act in the ways that generated the character? And why should we suppose that anywhere between these extremes of entrenched second nature and unformed child at the mercy of upbringing (or neglect), the agent had more free control over his character than at either end? The only change along the line of development is from necessitation from without to necessitation from within. The internal rational prescription, in the developed personality, has assumed the rôle, whatever that may be, of earlier external authority. If, therefore, the internal factor can truly be said (and this may not be even intelligible) to 'necessitate' the self to act according to it, then all the more reason to say this of the external authority, especially as the latter's influence may take the form of a felt constraint, often unwelcome and backed up by physical sanctions. Hence if adult self-necessitation calls into question responsibility for actions, so that we can save the agent's own responsibility only by grounding it in an earlier stage, the necessitation of child by parent or early circumstances raises the identical spectre, but this time in a temporal context from which there is no escape to an earlier point of freedom in the agent's lifetime.[49]

The argument at which this objection is levelled assumes a sense of 'free' that contradicts 'necessitated' and 'determined'. And according to the suggested interpretation of *NE* III.5, Aristotle is using 'it depends on him' to mean or imply 'free' in that sense. Assuming this to be so, some critics have reasonably objected that he is not justified in taking it for granted that responsibility depends on indeterminist freedom, and have complained that he does not allow for a compatibilist position. This especially seems a pity since the criteria for 'voluntary', which it was one of Aristotle's achievements to begin to classify, can obviously all be fulfilled in a deterministic universe. But I argued above (Section IV) in connection with the *Eudemian Ethics* that there is reason for thinking Aristotle unconcerned either to assert or deny that human actions and decisions are necessitated by antecedent and ultimately external factors; and that when he says or implies that not everything in the world is necessary, he means that not everything is necessary independently of what we do or decide; and that this (to us) restricted use of 'necessary' is the only use endorsed by Aristotle in this area of discussion. In this account, the human voluntary agent is argued to be a contingent cause merely on the ground that some events in the world are not pre-necessitated either to happen or not to happen, but fall in the way they do because so caused either way by a human voluntary agent; and the question whether the operation of that agency is itself necessitated (e.g., by persuasion from others) is simply not raised.

This interpretation of the Eudemian doctrine of voluntary agents as contingent causes is strongly confirmed by the fact that the argument of *NE* III.5 is inept if read (which it often has been) as an attempt to uphold ascriptions of responsibility by tracing the antecedents of action back to a point where the agent is not necessitated to operate one way rather than another by anything beyond that point. For even on the same page, as well as all over the place throughout the *Ethics,* Aristotle will not let us forget the importance of upbringing and moral persuasion.

Determinists commonly seize on the fact of persuasion as favouring their own position, since it points a way of reconciling their view with the usual beliefs about moral responsibility. Voluntary behaviour can be influenced by persuasion, yet still remain voluntary and morally responsible; so if influenced, why not caused, and if caused, why not necessitated? We need not go every step along this way to see the imbecillity of pointing to *persuasion* as evidence that voluntary action is contingent in the sense denied by determinism. The libertarian ought to focus attention on the lonely or stubbornly self-willed agent. Instead, Aristotle appeals to persuasion and persuadability to show that character-forming action is voluntary and depends on the agent. 'No one is encouraged to do the things that are neither in our power nor voluntary' (1113 b 26–27).

Persuasion presupposes a voluntary subject whose action either way depends on *him* and his acceptance. It does not bypass the voluntary subject in favour of a prior cause, since in that case it would not be treating the voluntary subject as voluntary.

And according to the *Eudemian Ethics* this subject is a contingent cause. Thus his being a contingent and ultimate cause is the presupposition of persuasion. The persuader must see him as the prime source of what he does and, the same him, as source of what he might do instead. But the persuader is not concerned to know whether, given the totality of circumstances, including the persuasion which he himself brings to bear, it will still be possible that the other acts either way. And neither believing that it will be possible, nor that it will not, will lead the persuader to treat the other any more or less as a voluntary agent and as a fit subject of praise and reproach. Here again we have contingency from the practical point of view; this time, from that of the second-order practical agent who seeks not to influence external events but to influence practice. And here, too, Aristotle takes it for granted that 'contingent from the practical point of view' is the same as simply 'contingent'.[50]

So 'the action depends on *him*' cannot mean that what the individual actually does expresses him alone and nothing beyond his control. Aristotle sets this aside when he says: 'We are ourselves somehow part-causes *(sunaitioi pōs)* of our states of character' (1114 b 22–23).[51] According to the interpretation developed here, 'it depends on him' (or, as several times in the *EE*, 'it depends on himself') says that when we address a prospective agent with advice, warnings, practical arguments etc., we direct all this to *him,* not to anyone or anything else. Is this to say that we work on him as a special kind of thing, using methods appropriate for reshaping the movements of things of this type? No, for we direct our directions to him as a *self,* capable not merely of responding with the movements we desire but (if he does so respond) of preferring this to a contrary response which he is aware he might have made, and thereby also capable of preferring to be one who responds in this way.

Aristotle's account, then, stands opposed not to any form of determinism that a modern thinker could countenance, but, on two fronts, to fatalism. On the one hand, there is the voluntary and possibly deliberating agent whose stance assumes that future events are not all so necessitated independently of him that there is no room for him to make a difference. On the other hand, there is the voluntary agent appealing to other voluntary agents, on the assumption that what they do, and their moral attitude to what they do, is not fixed independently of such appeals addressed to each by others of their kind and so understood by the individuals so addressed. Afterwards, it may seem as if things could not have gone any other way. If a person whom I hold in respect gets me to engage in some activity or practice which I was not about to sample, and afterwards I cannot imagine (although perhaps I can logically conceive) not having made it an essential part of my life, this is no proof that I was already bound to go that way. For that inability to imagine may itself be a manifestation of a moral attitude evoked, not presupposed, by my agreeing to take that different direction.

So what has Aristotle to say about (if not to) those who plead bad character and moral ignorance as a kind of excuse for their actions, or to those who would so plead on their behalf? And what has he to say about those who were neglected or abused as children, or were brought up in evil ways, and hardly had a chance? According to the present interpretation, the reply runs like this: if the reason why the bad never had a chance of being good had been that courage, cowardice, honesty and the rest are in general innate, then (if this were generally known) ethical attitudes would not operate. We would not hold the actions of the wicked against them. (But this is not because we should exonerate or excuse, for one exonerates on the basis of particular mitigating facts in the absence of which one would hold the person responsible.) In fact, it would hardly impinge on us that they, or anyone, were voluntary agents at all. But since, in general, goodness and badness depend on training, and this is known, the general situation is one in which our ethical attitudes are not only justified in operating but already do operate, since they are a major constituent of that training.

The central objects of those attitudes are voluntary$_1$ agents who fall into one of two classes. Either they are in need of training and trainable, or they were trainable but one way or another are now beyond it. Ethical predicates such as 'brave', 'dishonest', 'generous' etc. are used in connection with both classes, in either case being applied in the light of voluntary actions. In the case of the trainable, the predicates are not applied to them as subjects, but are used to indicate (and at the same time to extol and condemn) various moral directions in which those subjects might be carried by their voluntary behaviour. In the other case, the predicates are applied categorically to the agents as their subjects: subjects who are thereby presented as paradigms of what lies at the end of these good and bad paths of development. In both cases the communication is primarily addressed by trainers to the trainable. (Very often, *trainer* and *trainable* coincide in the same person.)

Aristotle recognises that some individuals suffer from congenital moral defects. (His point in *NE* III.5 is that they are not always congenital and mostly are not.) He also recognises that some are moral cripples because of illness and others because they were abused as children. We cannot, he says, straightforwardly regard these as bad *(kakoi)* human beings, where 'bad' means the opposite of what is normally meant by 'excellent' or 'virtuous' (1145 b 16–30; 1148 b 15–1149 a 1). Those who are congenitally warped or are constitutionally drawn towards monstrous activities for which normal human beings feel no inclination are classified as 'wild-beastlike' *(thēriōdēs)*. Theirs is a 'different kind of badness' (1145 b 27). This, like ordinary wickedness, and like moral weakness, is 'to be avoided' (1145 b 16–17); but, Aristotle implies, it cannot be avoided by means of ordinary moral education of the individuals concerned. It follows that the ethical use of the moral predicates and the ascription of moral responsibility has no application here. It is not clear whether Aristotle thinks that these beings are voluntary$_1$ agents of their actions, but there is no reason why they should not count as such by the criteria having to do with compulsion and factual ignorance. Since Aristotle does not distinguish *voluntary$_1$* and *voluntary$_2$*, he may assume that neither applies; but closer consideration of such abnormal cases might have led him to recognise the general distinction. How such cases are to be treated he does not say. Nor does he address the difficult problem of how we are to distinguish those who were ruined from the start, either genetically or through early abuse, from those who had a chance but threw it away. For the former do not always signal themselves by 'monstrous' or 'unnatural' desires. Their basic desires may be for the usual things, only they are unnaturally impervious to what we call 'ethical considerations'. And then there are degrees of neglect, abuse, illness, making it perhaps impossible to draw an a priori line. There is therefore room for humane discretion (*epieikeia:* see 1137 b 14–1138 a 3) in our response to such cases. But for Aristotle, I imagine, it would be of paramount importance not to respond in ways that would send those capable of human decency the message that wrong conduct is acceptable. That is a recipe for breeding more and more individuals of whom it will be true that their chances were diminished. For there is less chance for anyone to become virtuous once standards are corrupted.

The position is uncompromising but not unfeeling. Aristotle cannot have pity for those of ruined character, if pity excludes condemnation of them for what they are and what they do. And this, I think, applies to those who seem to have been lost from the start as well as to those who seem to have had a chance. But, in either case, Aristotle calls these irredeemable human beings *athlioi* ('miserable', 'wretched'), and that is a term of lamentation.

## Notes

1. This is the nucleus of the position developed on Aristotle's behalf by Irwin [2] and [7] 340–44. For apt criticism, see Nussbaum [2] 283 ff. It should be stressed (since from Irwin's treatment one would not guess it) that Aristotle does not possess a term meaning 'responsible agent' that is narrower in extension than the term 'voluntary agent'.
2. Nussbaum (see last note) rightly emphasises the continuity.
3. Cf. *Rhet.* 1368 a 7–9: 'whenever you want to praise anyone, think what you would urge people to do; and when you want to urge the doing of anything, think what you would praise a man for having done'.
4. Bonitz mentions only one scientific context in which the terms 'voluntary' etc. occur (*Movement of Animals* 703 b 3–9).
5. And in this respect Aristotle's ethics emerges from his psychology and metaphysics. For a close and comprehensive study of those connections, see Irwin [7], Chapters 10–16, especially the nodal subsections 149, 154, 183, 202.
6. Throughout, I use 'determinism' as synonymous with 'necessitarianism'. Thus it neither entails nor is entailed by the thesis that whatever happens has a cause or explanation. (A cause may not necessitate, and it is conceivable that absolutely inexplicable things should happen of necessity.) See Sorabji [3], Chapters 2, 3 and 14.
7. In *De Interpretatione* 9 he argues against what appears to be a form of determinism based on purely logical considerations. But whether this really is a determinist (as distinct from fatalist) theory is doubtful. See below, Section IV.
8. It is indicative that Aristotle regularly characterises animals as both *self*-movers and moved by the object of desire. See the discussion by Furley [2].
9. I have examined this and other aspects of Aristotle's conception of the nature of a thing as its 'inner principle of change and *stasis*' in Waterlow, esp. Chapters 1 and 2.
10. This is the most striking difference between Aristotle's and modern treatments of human action, *pace* Charles, who translates *'hekousion'* and cognates by 'intentional' etc. (Charles [1], 61–62; 256–61). That the concepts are different is clear from the facts (1) that Aristotle regards as *hekousia* acts done from culpable negligence; (2) that he regards as *hekousia* all foreseeable consequences of what we do *hekontes*. (Ackrill [5], 152, comments on the oddity of (a), but perhaps it is odd only if we expect *'hekousion'* to mean or entail 'intentional'.) See Heinaman [1] for a defence of the traditional translation, 'voluntary'. What is in common, so far as I can see, to all the items which Aristotle terms *'hekousia'*, is that in one way or another the agent says 'Yes' to their being or becoming, whether through affirmation, compliance, or failure to say 'No' (see Section IV of this chapter). Charles [1], 62, suggests that what one brings about knowingly (hence acceptingly) but not intentionally should be regarded as 'intentional in a *derived sense*' (his emphasis). This artificially coined sense of 'intentional' seems designed to encourage us to translate Aristotle's *'hek-*

*ousion'* as 'intentional' in all its occurrences and to persuade us by this usage that there are correspondingly primary and derivative senses of *'hekousion'* in Aristotle. But Aristotle seems not to differentiate. That is to say, while he does recognise that *hekousiai* actions are primary, whereas the states etc. knowingly produced by them are *hekousia* only because the actions are, he shows little sign of accepting any such proposition as that the latter are *hekousia* in a different or weaker *sense* than the former.

11. This question is also raised by Hursthouse [2].

12. *The Revised Oxford Translation* has 'by reason of ignorance'.

13. Cf. Urmson [5], 45–46.

14. Cf. Hursthouse [2].

15. A model which assimilates the voluntary and the natural not only has difficulty in keeping the nonvoluntary from collapsing into the countervoluntary; it also has difficulty in recognising that something might be countervoluntary yet natural. Thus even if we regret aging and (natural) death, it might seem out of place to call them 'countervoluntary'. At 1135 a 33–b 2 Aristotle says that they are neither voluntary nor countervoluntary.

16. And also within the human context, since Aristotle recognises the existence of human agents to whom ordinary ethical discourse does not apply. Some of these he compares to 'gods', others to 'wild beasts' (1145 a 15–33).

17. By Cicero, *De Natura Deorum* II xvi 44. The reference may be to a lost work of Aristotle's. However, if action inspired by love *(erōs)* is voluntary, the doctrine is implied in *Meta.* XII.7. Whether voluntary or not, the movement of the heaven would always for Aristotle be necessary.

18. Praise *(epainos)* implies approbation and exhortation. The highest things (which cannot be conceived as responding to either, since they are already necessarily perfect) are not praised but held in honour (cf. 1101 b 10–1102 a 4).

19. This is discussed well by Hursthouse [2]. Aristotle's way with 'constraint' (especially in *NE* III) shows him failing to draw a clear line between conditions under which it is true (or, alternatively, conditions under which one would be epistemically justified in asserting) that someone acts under constraint, and conditions under which it would be an appropriate thing to say. Since (Aristotle seems to assume) it is offered only as an excuse, the utterance is appropriate only if the excuse is reasonable. See below, Section VI, for a similar situation with 'voluntary'.

20. 1110 b 13–14 and 1114 a 13–21 strongly suggest that vicious people, once they have become so, cannot act out of character; yet their actions are certainly voluntary.

21. See Kenny [3], 41–46 and Woods [1], 142–45 for detailed discussion of 1225 a 8–19.

22. See also *NE* V.8, 1135 b 4, where actions done under threat are said to be countervoluntary.

23. This may be on whether overwhelming psychological pressure counts as compulsion. But (as Sorabji has suggested [3], 261–62) it may be on the more general questions of judicial discretion and the difficulty (for the legislator) of framing a clear and exhaustive set of conditions for exculpation. If it seems that a satisfactory set can be given in general terms, then it will seem reasonable to lay it down that acts meeting any of the conditions are nonvoluntary or countervoluntary. If no such set can be reached, it is better to legislate in such a way that difficult cases count as voluntary under the law and are then made occasions for the exercise of discretion in sentencing.

24. This interpretation is consistent with 1109 b 31–32 (linking leniency with the countervoluntary) and 1110 a 24–26 (linking leniency with 'the alternative overstrains human nature') if we take 'countervoluntary' at 1109 b 32 to include what is countervoluntary 'in the abstract' (1110 a 18–19). Both 'overstraining' cases and choices of the lesser evil are, according to *NE* III.1, countervoluntary in the abstract and voluntary under the particular circumstances. But where we commend we focus on the voluntariness, and where we are lenient on the countervoluntariness.

25. The *entire soul* here is the two ethically relevant parts of the soul.

26. At 1111 a 21–23 Aristotle implies that actions done *in* ignorance are not countervoluntary, and since this summarising passage recognises only the two categories of *voluntary* and

*countervoluntary,* he must mean that what is done *in* ignorance is voluntary. The important thing is that they are culpable. Cf. the different division of *NE* V.8, according to which actions done *in* ignorance are countervoluntary, but some are excusable, others not; and the excusable ones are said to be done *through* as well as *in* ignorance (1136 a 5–9). V.8 also differs from III.1 in implying that actions expressing morally bad choices are not done *in* ignorance (because they are voluntary).

27. The same is often true of those who are drunk or carried away by some appetite. They are not necessarily blind to or hazy about the factual nature of what they are doing and the circumstances, but the ethical significance (as it would be to a good person) is lost on them.

28. *The Revised Oxford Translation* of the *NE* has 'it is in his power'.

29. Cf. *NE* V.8. At 1135 a 24–27 it is not clear whether 'it depends on him' is equivalent to or entails 'absence of force or compulsion'; and at 31–33 it is not clear whether 'it does not depend on him' and 'under compulsion' are exclusive alternatives, or whether the second is one (but not the only) form of the first.

30. Often in speaking of this bipolarity of the voluntary I speak as if voluntary agents are necessarily human. This is because, although there may be voluntary (in a sense) agents whose voluntary action is not bipolar, such agents are never human beings functioning humanly. See notes 16, 17 and 18; and below in the text.

31. It is hard not to picture the bipolar agent as choosing between clearly envisaged alternatives. (This is because when *we* think about such an agent, we think of alternatives.) Since choice is normally governed by a reason, the bipolar agent gets construed as necessarily a rational chooser. This has surely contributed to the tendency of some (e.g., Irwin) to interpret Aristotle's account of the voluntary as an account of full-fledged adult responsibility (see above, note 1). But both *NE* and *EE* are unambiguous in making 'It depends on him' an essential feature of the (human) voluntary in general, not just of rational choice. Thus the phrase means that he has alternatives whether or not he is actually comparing them or thinking of them. See Section VI of this chapter on 'It depends on him' in connection with young children.

32. Is bipolarity a sufficient as well as necessary condition for accepting the inference from *voluntary₁* to *voluntary₂*? It would not be sufficient if we thought that some nonhuman (non-rational) animals are bipolar agents though none are *voluntary₂*. However, we might deny bipolarity to all of them on the ground that it is a property of at least potential deliberators who choose 'Yes' or 'No' *for a reason.* Alternatively, we might grant bipolarity to some of them, along with a rudimentary *voluntary₂* status, on the ground that their behaviour can be influenced by reward and punishment and that sometimes they seem to understand obedience.

33. Cf. Sorabji [3], Chapter 1.

34. Thus Aristotle is responding to fatalism, not determinism. See Sorabji [3], 227–28, on the inadequacy of the reply as a reply to determinism. In S. Broadie [1] and [3] I supplied missing links for the argument 'If determinism is true, there is no place for deliberation'. But even if those reconstructions make a convincing case for indeterminism, I now think it unreasonable to ascribe anything along these lines to Aristotle, in view of his total silence. Either, then, the remarks in *De Int.* 9 about chance and deliberation are a feeble reply to the deterministic implication of his opponents' thesis, or they are a forceful reply to the fatalistic one. (It may puzzle us how, on the fatalistic interpretation of 'Everything is necessary', it follows that nothing happens by chance. But deliberation with a view to making a practical difference to the world does presuppose that many features of the scene in and on which the agent will act are independent of his particular decision. Hence the combination of his action and these features, and any unintended results of that combination, are 'by chance' in the sense indicated in the text. Again, if deliberation and trying made no difference, no one would be lucky or unlucky, for this implies faring better or worse than might have been expected from one's own efforts; which implies that our efforts can make a difference.)

35. Cf. Edel, 394: 'He does not raise the question whether in deliberation our turnings are themselves necessary antecedently'. See also Hardie [4], 174–78 and 383—84.

36. Cf. Huby. But Hardie [2], replying to Huby, is of course quite right to say that *NE* III.5 anticipates some of the central moves in modern debates on determinism. See also Hardie [4], 380–82.

37. Cf. Sorabji [3], 245–47.

38. The impresssion is confirmed when one turns to his studies of animal desire, perception and movement, which seem to play into the hands of the determinist. The psycho-physiology of animal movement in the *Movement of Animals* allows no margin of freedom between external perceived stimulus and behavioural response (cf. Furley [1]). See also *Physics* VIII.1–2 (with the comments of Furley [2]) on the impossibility of an absolute beginning of motion by anything in the universe. These positions are, in my view, compatible with a libertarian account of human action, but they can easily be taken not to be, and Aristotle does nothing to guard against this.

39. Cf. Chapter 2, Section VIII. Given the analytic connection of *virtue* with *well-functioning,* hence with *happiness,* this conception is also a conception of happiness. Having a conception, in the sense indicated in the text, of human goodness and the human good is *not* confined to deliberators or to the ethically mature. Thus at *EE* 1214 b 29–30, Aristotle says that the sick, the insane, and children all have views about happiness. This should be emphasized against interpretations such as that of Engberg-Pedersen, 248 ff., who identifies the 'universal grasp of what should be done and the belief that acting in that way is what *eudaimonia* or *eupraxia* consists in' with practical wisdom and sees it as what distinguishes ethical adults. In fact what distinguishes the adult is a grasp that is stable and gives rise to coherent practice. This does not imply that a childish version of happiness is not, so far as it goes, *universal,* but rather that it is unstable and (inchoate as it is) falls short of being *true.*

40. These passages imply that vice *in general* is (once acquired) inescapable. But *Cat.* 13 a 23–31 shows more optimism about the possibility of reform.

41. Annas claims that 1166 b 7 ff. is not typical of Aristotle, on the ground that he normally thinks of the vicious person as a 'unity of thought and feeling'. I know no passage that says this about vicious people in general. It does not follow from the distinction between vice and incontinence, except on the assumption that incontinent conflict is the only kind of conflict. But there is no reason to think that Aristotle does not recognise other kinds, or that he sees no difference between failure to stand, on some given occasion, by one's better judgment, and pervasive self-disgust with all that one has stood for as well as done.

42. That it is a category mistake to call qualities of character 'voluntary' seems to be suggested by Ackrill [3].

43. See also 1114 b 22–23, in the light of Hardie's plausible suggestion (Hardie [4], 178–79) that *tōn hexeōn sunaitioi pōs autoi esmen* means that we *and nature* are co-causes of character.

44. For brevity, I am focusing on the ambiguity of 'voluntary' as it appears in the consequent-clauses of (a) and (b), where it relates to actions. One can of course find it also in the antecedents in relation to character: is Aristotle saying 'Unless one knowingly instigates one's character', or 'Unless one is answerable for one's character' (or both)? If the latter means 'Unless one is worthy of praise, reproach etc. *for* one's character', the formulation is a mistake, as I argued in the last section. We can salvage the statement by substituting 'as' for 'for'; then the meaning will be 'unless character-predicates are terms of praise, reproach etc.' This interpretation gives substantially the same result as I reach in the main text.

45. *ē hopōsdepote* at 1114 b 14 hints at other possibilities. A standard list is given at *EE* 1223 a 11–12: 'Either by nature, or by necessity or by chance or voluntary'; cf. *NE* 1112 a 32–33.

46. For a contrary view see Engberg-Pedersen, 248 ff., who connects this knowledge with practical widsom and with adulthood.

47. See Furley [1]; Hardie [4]; 175, Siegler [2]; M. J. White [3], 224–25; and for a different account, Sorabji [3], 227–33.

48. As those who ascribe it to him point out.

49. But substitute 'natural' for 'necessitated' and the argument works. The opponent says that people ought not to be held responsible for doing what is natural, and it is natural to the bad man to do wrong. Aristotle replies: he came to be such that this is natural, but it was not by nature that he came so to be.

50. The conflation is all the easier if biological inheritance gives Aristotle his model of a deterministic system. Given the 'one-way' nature of Aristotelian biological substances, and given the bipolarity of the voluntary, the model implies that no action can be voluntary and determined. In this context there is no need to spend time rebutting determinism interpreted in that way: its truth would make nonsense of our practical life, as would the truth of fatalism.

51. It is not clear whether the other causal factor is upbringing or, as Hardie [4], 178–79 suggests, inherited nature.

# CHAPTER 4

# Practical Wisdom

## I. The Structure of Rational Choice

I turn to Aristotle's discussion of practical wisdom *(phronēsis).* This more than most is rough terrain for commentators, being densely thicketed with controversy. Some of the difficulties spring from the obscurity of Aristotle's exposition, while some flourish through our own confusing preconceptions. Since one cannot thread a way through the layers of all this in footnotes, exegetical problems and attendent conceptual diagnoses will occupy much of this chapter.

Aristotle defines practical wisdom as the virtue by which one deliberates well: i.e., reasons well in a practical way (1140 24 ff.). What is practical reason? It has two aspects: the rational choice *(prohairesis)* on which a person acts, and the process of deliberation or reflection by which a rational choice is formed. To Aristotle these are conceptually inseparable: just as the aim of deliberation is to reach a reasoned choice, so rational choice is reached only through deliberation. The first connection goes without saying, but the second depends on what one means by 'deliberation'. In one sense the statement is plainly false. It is easy to think of deliberation and rational choice as process and product; and surely we can sometimes have what a process normally produces without the process? We have already glanced at this question in Chapter 2, Section VI, and we shall return to it later here. Meanwhile I focus on the product. This has a dual structure: a rational choice, Aristotle says at *EE* 1227 b 36, is *of* X *for the sake of* Y. It cannot be characterised without reference to both. A choice of X for the sake of Z and one of X for the sake of Y are as different (though in a different way) as the choice of X for the sake of Y and of W for the sake of Y. This complexity implies two complementary ways of evaluating rational choice. Y may or may not be an appropriate end, and X may or may not be an appropriate means.

This structure has implications for the sense in which an agent *explains* his choice of X by stating that Y is the end. For, of course, 'It is for Y' gives his *reason* for choosing X, and for doing it if he acts on the choice. But in indicating Y, the agent does not refer to a factor extraneous to his choosing of X: a factor related to that choosing in a way that would account for its coming about. Such an analysis would reduce rational choice to a two-term relation between the agent and what he chooses (namely X), and the presence of this relation would then be explained by reference to a distinct attitude whose object is Y. But on Aristotle's account choice is a three-term relation between the agent, what he chooses and what he chooses what he chooses for. Thus in saying what that is for the sake of which he chooses as he does, the agent completes an otherwise incomplete description of his choice. The choice's *direction* is a codeterminant of its identity, and *what* is chosen as leading in that direction is the other codeterminant. It is the same if, instead of saying 'for the sake of Y', we say 'because I desire Y' or 'because I intend Y'. The clause following 'because' does not invoke some factor (e.g., a desire for Y) extraneous to the choosing of X, as if the choice of X were itself a complete entity. Rather, the logical form of the whole is 'I (he), desirous of (intending) . . . , choose(s) . . .' On this view, mentioning the desire (or intention) is not explaining the choice in the modern sense in which an explanation refers to a cause that is other than what is explained. Mentioning the desire explains the choice only in the sense of making it clearer *what,* or *what sort of,* choice it is. The reason of a rational choice is structurally part of it, as distinct from being an interesting further fact *about* it.

It is hard to see how the same line of thought should not be extended to action in accordance with reasoned choice, although on this point Aristotle's guidance is less clear. That is to say, what the person did, under its full description, was X-for-the-sake-of-Y, rather than merely X, the doing of which would then be explained by reference to something outside that doing, e.g., a desire for Y. However, Aristotle did not develop a fixed terminology for the analysis of action, and he sometimes speaks as if the action is simply X. It is natural to speak in this way, and in fact it is necessary when we want someone to give us a fuller picture of what he did or is doing. We ask 'Why are you doing X?' where X is what we can see him to be doing or what we can know straight off. It is an outsider's question that identifies his doing with the doing of X. This approach is an expression of ignorance—the ignorance that asks the question—combined with the minimal knowledge needed to ask it. The case shows only that a description of the action sufficient to let the agent know which item in his behaviour one is asking about is not yet sufficient to display that item's character in full. If it were, there would be no question. Thus we can understand, even if not accept as accurate, the contrast which Aristotle draws between deeds and reasoned choice in passages like the following, where he is concerned with what we need to know so as to judge someone's moral character:

> It is from a man's choice that we judge his character—that is from the object for the sake of which he acts, not from the act itself. (1228 a 2–4)

> we praise and blame all men with regard to their choice rather than their acts (though activity is more desirable than excellence), because men may do bad acts under compulsion, but no one chooses them under compulsion . . . it is only because it is not easy to see the nature of a man's choice that we are forced to judge of his character by his acts. (1228 a 11–17; cf. *NE* 1111 b 5–6)

Now the schematic structure of *prohairesis* may be clear enough, and I have just argued that the identical structure is to be found in the corresponding action. But questions arise about Aristotle's application of the schema. What counts as X, what as Y? Must X be a so-called basic action, one that is simply done without doing something else in order to do it, or can X be anything one does for the sake of Y? If X is not basic, so that something prior is done in order to do X, is X both an end in relation to this and a means in relation to Y? But the puzzles mainly centre on the Y position. What sort of thing is to fill it? It might seem as if anything could, as long as something else is said to be done for the sake of it, but it appears from Aristotle's use of the concept of rational choice that the rationally choosing agent is one who also (in some sense) aims at *the best*. This seems strange if we mainly focus on the 'of . . . for the sake of . . .' structure. Not all practical thinking even pretends to be concerned with what is best! Nor was this lost on Aristotle. But instead of concluding that some rational choices are for the sake of ends other than the best, he holds that in these cases there is no rational choice. Even so, there is practical reflection and calculation of means. Take a person obsessed with some goal who cannot or will not consider whether it really is for the best, or who knows that it is not but does not care—in short, who behaves as if, indefensibly, the desired thing were his highest good—this agent's behaviour need not be impulsive or precipitous. His very intensity of purpose may make him all the more deliberate. He decides what to do to attain his end, and the schema 'X for the sake of Y' applies to his decision. Surely it is a reasoned choice, even if we do not approve of the reason.

Aristotle's position would be understandable if he saw human beings as either angels or brutes, or as acting like brutes whenever not acting like angels. Then every action would be done with the supreme good in view or else from the kind of impulse that looks no further than its immediate physical expression, leading to immediate satisfaction. But Aristotle is more realistic, and one of his examples of incontinence is a person who plots an occasion to satisfy the appetite to which he knows he should not pander (1149 b 13–16; cf. 1142 b 18–20). Nor does Aristotle think this a freakish phenomenon: he knows that it is typically human to apply human intelligence against one's better judgment. So when someone decides, against his principles, to encourage his wife to visit her relatives on a certain weekend, how is the devious decision not a *rational* choice? Yet Aristotle holds that incontinent actions are no more governed by rational choice than the actions of children and animals. Yet even children, he surely knows, can do things to bring about other things.

What Aristotle says in this connection about craftsmen is also puzzling. For him, as for Socrates and Plato, the craftsman is a favourite paradigm of practical rationality. But what makes the carpenter a carpenter, as distinct from someone who happens to get something right, is the former's knowledge of *what* he is doing and *why* he takes each step. And in many passages Aristotle uses examples from craft to shed light on practical thinking in general.[1] Yet Aristotle, as we saw in Chapter 2, Sections VI and VII, differentiates moral virtue from craft on the ground that the former is, the latter is not, a state that issues in rational choice (a *hexis prohairetikē*). We find him making a similar move in the *Physics* and *Metaphysics* in connection with the concepts 'form' and 'matter'. These are developed to explain the metaphysical structure of physical substances. Physical substances are relatively autonomous beings whose nature is 'an inner principle of movement and rest' (*Physics* 192 b 9 ff.). Artifacts do not count as substances, strictly speaking; they are inert (until set going or manipulated) and are not intelligibly self-sufficient, since the ends that explain their structure and operation are not theirs but men's. Yet it is from artifacts that Aristotle draws his favourite illustrations of the form-matter distinction—a distinction primarily devised to make sense of the substances which artifacts are not. So it is with rational choice and craft.

In both cases, Aristotle is attempting to formulate a concept that (1) has unique application and (2) cannot simply be read off from ordinary experience.[2] Requirement (2) dictates an approach by means of analogy, but (1) entails that the analogue cannot be an instance of the concept which it is meant to illustrate. Now in both cases, ethical and metaphysical, the ground for (1) lies in Aristotle's theory of paronymous terms; i.e., terms with a variety of related significations. The significations fall under a single principle (which is why such terms are not simply homonymous). For *one* signification, in each case, is distinguished as strict, primary or dominant, while the others depend in various ways on the first. This is not a theory about the meanings of terms as ordinarily used. Aristotle believes that there are natural or objective hierarchies of significations and that ordinary speech may not adequately reflect them. They are ascertained by philosophical reflection.

In metaphysics, for instance, substantial being is the primary signification of 'being', and the other categories are dependent. In the case of 'substance' itself, the dominant signification is *essence* (so he argues in *Metaphysics* VII), and the concrete individual is dependent. In ethics, happiness or the supreme good is the dominant signification of 'end', since it is the end of ends, without which more easily recognisable ends would have no rational force as ends. Sometimes the dominant stands to the dependent as norm to deviation, sometimes as original to copy, and other relations are possible. Thus the choice of the plotting incontinent is of a person acting now as if the pleasure he knows he wrongly desires were the only thing in life that matters. If he were not capable of being in two minds about it, then no doubt it would *be* the supreme good for him. So he acts and even *reasons* as if he were what he is not: a creature that finds complete fulfillment in such pleasures and is incapable of deliberation. His choice of means is a copy of what reasoned choice should be; it is not reasoned choice in the primary sense. For the primary signification is necessarily linked to The End, which is the primary signification of 'end'.

Regarding the carpenter in the abstract, one can say of this abstract entity that his supreme good is indeed nothing other than the production of excellent cabinet work. But a real craftsman's activity is conditioned by the human supreme good, which is the concern of the statesman (another abstraction). Considered in the light of the contrast between the craftsman's end as a craftsman and his end as a human being, a purely craftsmanly choice of materials is only a 'sort of' rational choice, or rational choice in a qualified sense; and purely craftsmanly deliberation is likewise not deliberation strictly speaking, any more than the incontinent's calculation. But it does not follow that Aristotle is wrong to hold that the logical structure of ethical choice and deliberation is the same as is found in craft. Thus when stating his doctrine that we deliberate only on means (the end being a set frame for deliberation), he quite reasonably uses craft examples:

We deliberate not about the ends but about what contributes to ends. For a doctor does not deliberate whether he shall heal, nor an orator whether he shall convince, nor a statesman whether he shall produce law and order, nor does any one else deliberate about his end. (1112 b 12–15; cf. *EE* 1227 b 25–30)

Here Aristotle considers abstractions: the doctor qua doctor etc. For it is only *that* doctor (The Doctor) who cannot be in a position to consider whether to exercise "his" craft.

So much for the metaphysical semantics by which Aristotle restricts the term *'prohairesis'* or 'rational choice' to the ethical agent acting for the best without qualification. We must now consider how this reservation is justified. Otherwise we have only the stipulation that choices made with a view to ends other than The End are rational choices in a way, but not strictly speaking.

The stipulation makes sense, because the supreme good is not just the most important end; it is the one good which there can necessarily never be a reason against pursuing. To make this clear we must extend the schematic account of a rational choice as of X for the sake of Y. I emphasized that the reference to Y explains the choice of X only in the sense of showing more clearly *what* choice the agent makes in choosing X. Mentioning Y as end is giving the reason in a sense well captured by the Greek *'logos'*, often translated 'defining formula' or 'essence'. It shows others the real nature of the project as distinct from the surface which is all that they can observe. X is thereby explained as that which (under the presumed circumstances) constitutes the effective doing of what the agent is really, though less obviously, doing: i.e., pursuing Y). So far, the explanation has the same teleological form which Aristotle applies to natural substances in general. One difference is that with human action we can find out the end by asking the agent, whereas with other creatures we can only infer it from what we observe. And this rests on the difference between articulate rationality and its absence. When a human being acts in distinctively human fashion, the action embodies an articulable claim that this is worthwhile as compared with possible alternatives.

But where there are claims, the question of justification arises. People observe that someone knowingly did or is doing X, and they understand this as the agent's practical assertion that X is a good thing to do. In this context the question 'Why is he doing it?' is prompted by more than curiosity about the factual nature of the action. It is a matter of practical interest on all sorts of levels to know whether an individual of our own kind, placed as we might be placed, has acted appropriately, and why he thinks that he has. We see the observed action as expressing a judgment of *his* in response to reasons which are reasons for both judgment and action, and so we put the question primarily to him—'Why are you doing it?'—rather than seek to answer it from our experience as observers. When the agent offers his reason for doing X—reason in the sense of a *logos* which makes clear the nature of something— he also, and mainly, offers it as a reason in another sense; i.e., as a piece of information that should justify his doing of X.

Citing the end, Y, is the first move in making a case to show that X is a good action as compared with alternatives leading to other results. Sometimes the first move is enough to settle the matter; but inherent in the situation is the possibility of a debate pitting the *logos* that backs X against *logoi* that would back alternative possible actions. 'Should you aim (have aimed) at Y via X rather than at Z via W?' Such questions arise when the rival ends Y and Z are so to speak ordinary ends. (There is also the question whether X rather than something else is the proper means to Y, but for the moment let us take it that in this regard the agent's judgment is unquestioned.) But when Y or Z is the best or the supreme good as such, there is no contest. Whichever of the two—let it be Z—is *not* the supreme good still keeps its status as reason in the sense of *'logos'*. For it is still the *logos* of the choice that would have been made if it, Z, had been the objective pursued; but in the sense of 'reason' as justification, Z neither contains nor, if pursued, would have contained any vestige of reason for preferring some choice that would hinder pursuit of Y, where Y is the supreme good.

The foregoing shows how, if we begin with the idea that rational choice is *of* something *for the sake of* something, it then makes sense to hold that choice with the supreme good in view is rational choice par excellence. This makes sense because the concept of 'reason' in the purely expository sense modulates into that of justificatory reason. Were it not for this development into the ethical dimension, the formal structure of choice would be just another example of the general form of teleological explanation. From that point of view, any choice is as 'rational' as any other, in the sense of being explicable in terms of its end. But what is special about us (in Aristotle's world) is not that such explanation applies to our behaviour, but that we apply it ourselves. We are able to explain the direction of what we are seen to be doing, because we are not merely going in that direction but know that we are. This is because knowledge in our case is necessary for the going; we would not be moving effectively in the direction which explains what we can be seen as doing had we not *chosen* what we are seen as doing with that direction in view. The fact that we, uniquely among creatures, have to know what we are doing for the sake of Y in order to *be* doing what we need to for the sake of Y is the same as the fact that we are uniquely capable of *boulēsis*—of desiring goods the means to which can be realized only through thought (v.s. Chapter 2, Section X). But the necessity of even a narrowly technical reflection on means to a bouletic end, along with the silencing of impulse which any such reflection supposes, gives breathing space for wider reflection and judgment on the comparative goodness of the project as a whole.[3] Hence my directional explanation of my visible action X becomes, without change of words, a defence of X as good, and good categorically, on the ground that by this means I pursue Y, a larger project which I take to be good and better than the alternatives. This is why a rational choice, spelt out in full, indicates the agent's character by indicating his values.

Hence rational choice, so called, is not only preeminently rational, but also unique in being unconditionally practical. For a rational agent exercising his rationality, the categorical best is the only end that elicits immediate practical response. I mean 'immediate' in the logical sense. For such an agent the pursuit of other ends would have to be mediated by the judgment that they contribute to what is best. In this way, the rational and the practical are fused in rational choice or *prohairesis.* The *prohairesis,* however, would not be unconditionally practical if it were simply a desire for the categorical best or for something conceived as the categorical best. Such a desire is practical only if what is desired is practicable. For this reason, a *prohairesis* is not a desire for a distant object O, but a desire to achieve O by means of A. And A, by the same argument, must be *immediately* practicable; i.e., without adopting a means to it.[4] Since the means to an end are revealed in deliberation, the action prohairetically chosen is chosen as or as if presented to the mind in deliberation; thus it is chosen *as* a means to an end and as the ultimate means. The choice, as Aristotle says, is deliberate desire[5] (1113 a 11): the end-point of deliberative thought and the starting-point of action.

But with human agents the action does not follow of necessity. Through ignorance the agent may propose an impracticable project, or at the moment for action he may have allowed himself to be taken over by a conflicting objective. Thus the abstract analysis of rational choice is only a beginning which has to be supplemented by inquiries into the two conditions necessary for the choice to be what rational choice by its nature is meant to be; namely, effective of the supreme good in practice. The first, which we may broadly call the 'cognitive' condition, although it breaks up into various elements, some more moral than intellectual, is a leading topic of *NE* VI, Aristotle's book on practical wisdom. The second, the strictly moral substructure of effective rational choice, has already been studied in his discussion of moral virtue, and its breakdown in incontinence will be examined in *NE* VII.

## II. The Purpose of *NE* Book VI

Amongst the multitude of difficulties besetting Aristotle's concept of rational choice, the analogy with craft is a chief source of trouble. Granted that the case demands an exemplar that is not an instance, we may still wonder how this procedure is useful and whether it will not positively mislead. For instance, it encourages us to ignore the most problematic feature of rational choice; namely, that its End (on one interpretation) is devoid of empirical content. An expert builder aims to construct a house choosing the right means because he knows what a building should be like to be the kind of house desired. Consequently, the chosen means are *these* materials, tools and methods rather than others. But how, simply by aiming at the best or supreme good (if this is what anyone really does) can we decide *how* to proceed so as to realise it? This formal goal dictates no course of action rather than another. Thus the craft analogy leaves one in the dark about the cognitive processes involved in rational choice. What can rationally bridge the gap between the undiluted abstraction of the End as such and a particular decision to do something in particular? If nothing can, the rational chooser is the least practical agent imaginable.

It seems that the craft analogy is either a gesture towards something of a nature too different to be explained by it or else works by distorting its object to a shape like its own. We shall return to this problem, noticing meanwhile that some of the analogy's limitations were not lost upon Aristotle. In a number of important passages he is firm in his use of the analogy: for example, *NE* 1112 b 14–15; *EE* 1227 a 18–21; 1227 b 25–29). But soon after the beginning of *NE* VI we find him straining to show how rational choice and decisions of craft are fundamentally different. Some scholars see this development as marking the end of his attempt to model ethical reasoning on craft.[6] According to others, the model continues to exert a confusing influence. It is difficult to weigh these alternatives, because we can only conjecture the order in which Aristotle composed the relevant texts, nor can we be certain even of the order in which he intended them to be read. Another difficulty is that it is not clear how deeply he intends the craft analogy when he does use it. For instance, when he says: 'We deliberate not about ends but about what contributes to ends. For a doctor does not deliberate whether he shall heal, nor an orator whether he shall convince, nor a statesman whether he shall produce law and order, nor does any one else deliberate about his end' (1112 b 11–15) he may mean only to drive home the point that we do not deliberate about ends, without also meaning to imply that the deliberation by which rational choice is formed is in other respects like the deliberation of specialist experts.

At any rate, a major concern of *NE* VI is to explain the difference between the activity of a craft and action governed by rational choice. The first is making or production *(poiēsis);* the second, action *(praxis)* in the strict sense. What motivates this distinction, and indeed most of Book VI, is the need to complete the account of moral excellence offered earlier. Moral excellence has been defined as having to do with a mean 'determined by the *orthos logos*'. But, as Aristotle says in the opening sentences of VI, the nature of this *orthos logos* is not yet clear. The rest of the book is his attempt to make it so.

What about it is unclear? Does Aristotle think he needs a definition of *'orthos logos'* in general? To achieve that we should have to inquire into the nature of correctness in general, and perhaps also into the nature of *logos*. But it is hard to see how to set about analysing a concept so fundamental and so abstract. For there are so many types of *orthos logos*. There are the correct conclusions of the theoretical scientist and the true opinions of the man in the street. There are also the well-conceived plans of accomplished craftsmen and right decisions by the ethically wise. An account of what they have in common would make little headway without prior examination of each of these forms. In any case, Aristotle's subsequent discussion shows him unconcerned with the question of a general definition. He explores a number of different sorts of correctness, but the main purpose is to exhibit, by comparison and contrast, the particular nature of *one* of those forms: the kind of *orthos logos* that characterises good ethical decision: i.e., good rational choice.

This is a discussion which Aristotle's readers have a right to expect whether they are following his ethics in the Eudemian or the Nicomachean version. Both treatises have to be mentioned in this connection, because *NE* VI ( = *EE* V) is one of the trio of books (*NE* V–VII) common to both. We do not know which treatise provided the original context for the book on practical wisdom. But however that may have been, it is possible and even plausible that Aristotle himself approved the inclusion of the common books in each of the two *Ethics.* If so, they fulfil various needs in each. And *NE* VI (which alone concerns us here) appears to fulfil a common need, identifiable by this question: what differentiates a virtue from other kinds of state, such as craft, which also, in their own way, 'get it right'? In *EE* II.3 Aristotle implies that what distinguishes the ethical *orthos logos* or mean are the sorts of continua in which it is found; these continua are pleasures and pains:

> Since we have assumed that excellence is that sort of state from which men have a tendency to do the best actions [*praktikoi tōn beltistōn*], and through which they are in the best disposition towards what is best; and best is what is in accordance with right reason, and this is the mean between excess and defect relative to us; it would follow that moral excellence is a mean relative to each individual himself, and is concerned with certain means in pleasures and pains, in the pleasant and the painful. The mean will sometimes be in pleasures (for there too is excess and defect), sometimes in pains, sometimes in both. (1222 a 6–14; cf. 1227 b 5–10)

This suggests that the good ethical agent is like familiar craftsmen, except that he works with pleasures and pains, actions and emotions, whereas they work with leather or stone or the hot and cold humours of the body. But that cannot be the final word. Virtue cannot be an expertise that works in a special medium, for there is no expertise of which it cannot sensibly be said that it might be used for an evil end or deliberately misused (cf. *EE* 1227 a 25 ff. and VIII.1). If virtue is expertise with regard to the mean in pleasures and pains, virtue is not necessarily a state from which people 'have a tendency to do the best actions.'

Of course, in *NE* II Aristotle has defined states of character as 'prohairetic' (1106 b 36; cf. *EE* 1227 b 8). But he did not explain what it is about *prohairesis* that makes it distinctively *ethical*. Our earlier discussion (Chapter 2, Section VI) extracted the idea that a *prohairesis* is a *categorically* practical response. But Aristotle himself never said that in *NE* II; he left it to his audience to make sense of the term 'prohairetic'. (Alternatively, he simply put the term down as an uninterpreted differentia, with the silent intention of explaining it later.) He returned to it in *NE* III.3, where he set up the connection between *prohairesis* and deliberation. This seemed to undermine his insistence in *NE* II that craft is not prohairetic (1105 a 31–b 4), for deliberation in III.3 is illustrated by the deliberations of craftsmen. So Aristotle now has to explain how a rational choice or *prohairesis,* though deliberated and in that respect like a decision of craft, is nonetheless fundamentally different from a decision of craft. This is one of his tasks in *NE* VI.

It is only one of his tasks, because the ethical *orthos logos* which informs a rational choice must also be clearly distinguished from at least one other kind of *orthos logos* besides that of a craftsman. There are, Aristotle says in VI.3 (1139 b 15–17) five states of the soul which we can characterise as states in which the soul possesses truth (or an *orthos logos*): craft, scientific understanding *(epistēmē)*, good sense *(phronēsis)*, wisdom *(sophia)* and comprehension or intelligence *(nous)*. We may well feel blank as these terms are thrown at us, and so no doubt did Aristotle's early audiences. But his discussion does not rely on vague existing connotations. The terms all have to do with successful cognition; apart from that, most of them are empty labels waiting to be assigned circumscribed senses which Aristotle is about to define by carving out distinctions between different sorts of rational cognition. However, the main distinctions, it soon turns out, are not between five types but three: theoretical wisdom (for which the term *'sophia'* is reserved); practical wisdom (to be called *'phronēsis'*) and craft or technical skill. For theoretical wisdom turns out to include both scientific understanding and intelligence *(nous)*, and intelligence is also found in practical wisdom (and presumably also in craft). Practical wisdom is the ability to arrive in a rational way at the ethical *orthos logos,* which is to say, at a good rational choice. So the business of *NE* VI is to show how practical wisdom differs from theoretical wisdom and from craft.

There is, however, a passage in the first chapter of *NE* VI which suggests a very different interpretation of the book's project. According to this, Aristotle now sees himself as bound to explain what it is that the ethical agent should aim for in his choices, if the choices are to be good. So Aristotle here undertakes to do what previously he said cannot be done: to give a single indisputable general guideline for ethically right action (cf. 1104 a 3–10). This is not only at odds with his earlier position, but also with what follows in *NE* VI itself, for the book makes no attempt to erect a single standard for right choices.[7] What it does do, as we shall see in detail, is explain in general terms (which provide no substantial guidance for the prospective agent) what sort of rightness ethical rightness is. Thus the interpretation in question entirely rests on a few lines of *NE* VI.1. To give their context, I quote the passage at length with the crucial lines italicised.

> Since we have previously said that one ought to choose that which is intermediate, not the excess nor the defect, and that the intermediate is determined by the dictates of the *orthos logos,* let us discuss this. In all the states we have mentioned, as in all other matters, there is a mark [*skopos*] to which the man who possesses the *logos* looks, and heightens or relaxes his activity accordingly, and there is a determinant [*horos*[8]] of the mean states which we say are intermediate between excess and defect, being in accordance with the *orthos.* But such a statement, though true, is by no means illuminating; for in all other pursuits which are objects of knowledge it is indeed true to say that we must not exert ourselves nor relax our efforts too much nor too little, but to an intermediate extent and as the *orthos logos* dictates; *but if a man had only this knowledge he would be none the wiser—e.g. we should not know what sort of medicines to apply to our body if someone were to say 'all those which the medical art prescribes, and which agree with the practice of one who possesses the art'.* Hence it is necessary with regard to the states of the soul also not only that this true statement should be made, but also that it should be determined what the *orthos logos* is and what its determinant [*horos*] is. (1138 b 18–34)

Here Aristotle stresses the universal scope of the notions of 'mean', 'mark' (or 'target' or 'aim': *skopos*), and 'determinant' *(horos)* of the mean states. In every kind of activity these concepts apply. When he speaks of a *mark* or *target,* Aristotle may mean (1) the goal which formally defines the activity, as *healing* defines *medical action.* Alternatively, he could mean (2) a substantial criterion, rule, standard or guideline for correct or successful action according to the type of activity. (Physicians as such aim to heal, but some are more successful than others because they have a more accurate criterion for health.) And in speaking of a *determinant* of intermediate states of the soul, Aristotle may mean (1′) that since each type of activity has its own type of intermediate states, there is in each case a way of typifying, defining or marking off by a distinctive formula, the type of intermediacy. Alternatively, he could mean (2′) that in each case there is a criterion by which we can judge what is too much, just right or too little. On interpretations (1) and (1′) Aristotle will be asking for a formal characterisation of the ethical mean as distinct from the means of the various crafts and other kinds of knowledge. On interpretations (2) and (2′) he will be asking, and seeming to promise to give, a substantial criterion for ethically right action.

'We should aim for the mean' is an unhelpful truism in ethics, as Aristotle now complains. Why? The obvious answer is that it does not tell us what to do: which things to pursue and which to avoid. But this can hardly be his point, because the reason why, as he says, the adage is unilluminating is that *the same holds good for all areas of knowledge and expertise* (26–29). This is irrelevant if what troubles him if our lack of a substantial criterion in ethics. But if, as I suggest, his current concern is to distinguish the *type* of the ethical mean and *orthos logos,* the point is utterly relevant.

What, though, of the illustration? It seems to depict the frustration of someone who is served a high-level abstraction when what he seeks is ethical *direction.* He looks for this guidance to the ethical philosopher, and the passage implies that the ethical philosopher is at fault if he fails to give specific advice. But who, in the example, is the ethical theorist's analogue? According to one way of reading it, which is probably the one which suggests itself first, the analogue is the physician whose job it is to prescribe a specific regimen for his patient. Certainly the physician would be very much at fault if he failed to do this, since he is able to do it. If the philosopher of ethics is like the physician, then he, too, Aristotle would here be implying, can and should offer a specific rule for the conduct of life. If this is the parallel, we have to suppose that the *physician* in the example, instead of giving a proper medical answer, says to the patient 'Treat the body in whatever way the medical art prescribes'. But *as coming from a medical expert,* this injunction, it seems to me, is just too inept or too perverse to constitute a possible utterance, even for the passing purpose of illustration. The line in the example giving purely formal advice is uttered, I conclude, by someone *not* a medical expert, but someone whose function it is to keep track of the generalities: someone who classifies human ends and activities. This begins to sound like the philosopher. Such a figure is not speaking stupidly, even if speaking unhelpfully, when he says that we should treat the body as the physician dictates. What *would* be helpful, and should be expected next from this answerer, would be some indication in general terms of what sort of being a 'physician' is. The answerer does not have to be medically expert himself to give a definition or description of medical expertise, so that, for instance, the sufferer would be able to recognise the right sort of person to go to with his specific problem. Just so, if anyone seeks from the ethical philosopher advice about how to make every decision, the latter is under no obligation to reply to him on this level (in this case, not because it is not his business or he is not trained, but because, as Aristotle has said, no one can give effective guidance of that sort); but he ought to be able to say something informative about the kind of person one should go to for advice—not about all decisions in the abstract, but about this or that particular problem. The kind which the philosopher shoud be able to characterise is, of course, the person of practical wisdom, who is Aristotle's subject in *NE* VI, being the embodiment of the uniquely ethical type of *orthos logos.*

But let us not take it for granted that the questioner in the example is only a private individual concerned about his own particular medical condition. If so, his analogue is an individual wanting to know what he should do, and the philosopher helps by pointing him towards the kind of person suitable to give that advice. But the questioner in the example may be someone who wants to know on everyone's behalf, and without regard for any particular circumstances, about the right balance of food and exercise for human health in general. If so, then what he wants is a *general account of* what medicine aims at, and not just to be told that what he asks about *is* what medicine aims at. The analogue, in that case, is someone who wants to know what the right balance is of feelings and impulses in the human soul, and it does not help him much to be told that it is a balance in accordance with the *orthos logos.* This is as much as to say that it is a balance which enables its possessor to form and execute the ethical *orthos logos;* in other words, a good prohairetic state. But what is still lacking is a characterisation of that type of *orthos logos.* This, again, is exactly what Aristotle seeks to deliver in *NE* VI.

If we follow this last line of interpretation, then the questioner is the present or future *politikos,* whose goal is to foster virtuous and happy citizens.[9] This questioner is asking that the earlier definition of this goal be completed. For moral virtue was defined in terms of a certain type of *orthos logos,* and now we must consider in more detail what that is. On this view, the questioner is asking about the general nature of the kind of rightness that is operative in particular wise decisions by virtuous citizens; and the achievement of this generally conceived rightness in others is the target to which he, as moral educator, looks when he seeks to create a balance of emotions and values in the young for whom he is responsible.

We have noted how the virtuous individual's dual rôle (at any rate in the *Nicomachean Ethics*) as both target for the *politikos* and as agent, himself, of actions which may include other goals, is a fertile source of confusion for Aristotle's readers; and it may even on occasion have led Aristotle to confusion himself. It is not clear to me whether in the present passage the unsatisfied inquirer whom Aristotle will now try to satisfy is a ground-level (so to speak) individual seeking clarity about the kind of person to whom to turn for particular advice, or the would-be producer (or fosterer) of that type of person. But either way, the passage can be interpreted so that its promise to state the 'determinant' of the *orthos logos* is a promise not of what Aristotle said was impossible—a rule for ground-level right action—but of a defining account of the kind of rightness in question.

### III. Probing the Craft Analogy

It is characteristic of the conceptual situation from which Aristotle launches his discussion of practical wisdom that in the opening chapter which states his purpose he cannot resist illustrating that purpose by means of an example from craft, the craft of medicine; and this though he must know very well already that he intends to show essential differences between practical wisdom and craft. By using that example he takes on board an implication (according to one line of interpretation for which I argued in the last section) which later in *NE* VI he will have to reject explicitly. According to one way of taking it, the medical example illustrates our need for a general picture of the man of practical wisdom (the *phronimos*) so that we can turn to the right sort of person for advice. The analogy with the medical consultant suggests, of course, that what we need is only the advice: to get the full benefit of medicine, we need not become medical experts ourselves (1143 b 21–33). But since practical wisdom is a human virtue (and someone who does not know this about it does not begin to know what it is), no one can get the full benefit of practical wisdom merely from someone else, since without having it himself he is humanly incomplete (cf. 1144 a 1–6). Hence, in the end, *NE* VI aims to present the *phronimos* not only so that we can consult him, but as an archetype of the sort of person to try to be[10] (and, for the educator, of the sort of person to aim at producing). Since the medical analogy is misleading on this point, the fact that Aristotle reaches for it right at the start suggests a deeply entrenched way of thinking which he has to fight to resist. The analogy of craft with virtue was the legacy of Socrates and Plato, who explored some of its problems but never to the point of official outright rejection. Aristotle, by contrast, finally saw through the analogy—in both senses. He was not deceived by it, but it nonetheless acts as a medium through which problems and their solutions appear to him. This oblique influence of the analogy upon a philosopher so alive to its flaws is one potential source of obscurity and even incoherence in Aristotle's account of practical wisdom, rational choice, and the ethical *orthos logos*. But, having said this, I must not exaggerate the depth of the shadow cast by that influence. Aristotle, in my opinion, is less misled by the craft analogy than many of his critics have thought.

In this section I shall display some of the problems generated by the analogy; but first, a general observation by way of heading to the exegesis which will extend through the rest of this chapter. The inquiry of *NE* VI proceeds within three main parameters: the nature of practical wisdom (PW) is to be explained (1) by comparison and contrast with theoretical wisdom (TW); (2) by comparison and contrast with craft (C); (3) by showing its connection with moral excellence (ME). The connection with ME is the most striking difference between PW on the one hand, and TW and C together on the other. For PW, TW and C are all alike in being intellectual, but PW alone of the three depends on moral as well as intellectual excellence. It follows from this that moral virtue contributes something to PW which intellectual excellence alone cannot contribute. Thus the contribution of ME must be different in kind from that of any intellectual component. So, for example, if one were impelled to characterise the intellectual component of PW as that which ensures correct means to the end, one would then naturally characterise the moral component in opposite fashion: i.e., as ensuring that the end itself is right.

Aristotle characterises PW, TW and C in terms of their various *ends,* the attainment of which depends on corresponding kinds of thinking. Now almost all the difficulties which we shall have to face come to a head under the question 'What, in Aristotle's view, is the end sought by the kind of thinking typical of practical wisdom?' Here I shall give three reasons, all connected with craft, why it is extremely difficult to decide this question.

First, the end towards which a craftsman deliberates is, we can easily suppose, such that he knows in advance of craftsmanly reflection what the end will look like when it is brought into being. But if the end sought through ethical deliberation is 'the best' without qualification, how can we know what this will look like *before* we start inquiring, any more than the scientist who seeks what he calls 'the truth' knows what this will look like in advance of seeking it—or even of finding it? Question: in this respect, is the end which the man of practical wisdom has in view when he deliberates like that of a craftsman or more like that of a theorist? Parameters (1) and (2) above yield no straightforward answer. The difference mentioned is immense; so unless we know on which side practical thinking falls for Aristotle, we can hardly begin to reconstruct his picture of practical thinking. Many commentators believe that he aligns practical thinking with craft in this regard. But according to the account for which I shall argue in this chapter, the parallel with theoretical thinking is much more helpfully suggestive than the parallel with craft.

Second, the analogy of craft and practical wisdom may incline Aristotle to blur the difference between the end sought in good practical deliberation and ends sought in bad practical deliberation; and also the difference between either of these and the end of practical deliberation as such.

Third, to the extent to which practical wisdom and practical deliberativeness in general are likened to craft, these concepts are infected with ambiguities that surround the notion of craft. Now *the craftsman's end* and *the craftsman's deliberation towards his end* are, it seems to me, notions on which Aristotle is not sufficiently clear. This is the source of much uncertainty when we turn to interpret his statements about practical wisdom.

I shall return to the first of these points later, and say more now about the other two. The defining end of medicine is health, and for every recognised craft the defining end is some departmental good. Now so far as they operate as physicians, the good and the inferior physician aim at the one end, health, but differ in their effectiveness. One operates well, the other badly. But the case of good and bad practical deliberation appears to be different. The good deliberator is the person of practical wisdom, but a wicked person is also a deliberator; the state of his soul is prohairetic and issues in deliberated rational choices. The difference between him and the wise is not that he is less effective in deliberation or action, but that he has a different aim, and a wrong one. According to Aristotle, whether the aim is good or bad depends on the agent's moral qualities (1144 a 8; 20–27; 1145 a 5–6; *EE* 1227 b 20–1228 a 2). But what is the aim of the wise man? Aristotle does not say what it is like in the sense of saying how the wise man's end differs intrinsically from the ends of inferior persons. He only gives an explanation of why it is good: '[moral] virtue makes the aim right'.

Now, at 1140 a 25–28 and b 9–10 Aristotle says that practical wisdom is the ability to deliberate well about what promotes good living in general (as distinct from some restricted area of life) and about what is good or bad for a human being as such. Here he contrasts practical wisdom with craft in terms of the former's unlimited subject matter. However, the contrast is really between practical deliberation as such and craft deliberation. For living well in general is the aim of every practical rational being, including even those who are morally flawed (hence cannot be regarded as 'wise'). They and wise deliberators presumably have different interpretations of 'living well'. But, again, Aristotle does not formulate the wise man's interpretation. He characterises wisdom in terms of the end of practice as such and has nothing distinctive to say about it except that it is the ability to deliberate *well* about that end.

In some places Aristotle certainly recognises differences between the aims of morally different agents. For example, at 1113 a 15–b 2 he writes as if different sorts of characters have different visions of the good. This passage is by no means atypical. But in discussing practical wisdom he writes as if everyone, virtuous and nonvirtuous alike, has the identical aim, the difference being in the quality of their deliberation about it. What we miss here is any attempt to describe the end that specially characterises goodness and wisdom. But this omission seems to spell the failure of his project in *NE* VI. For the purpose there is to define practical wisdom, and how can an Aristotelian define it except in terms of its distinctive end?

This is an astonishing lacuna in his account, if it is a lacuna at all. However, two explanations may be suggested for his allowing it to pass. They are alternatives, and neither gives Aristotle a satisfactory position. One is that he takes it for granted that his audience will understand that the distinctive end of practical wisdom is the good life as pictured in his *Ethics*. If this is so, the situation is logically defective, because central to that picture is the activity of practical wisdom. If our notion of practical wisdom is incomplete unless its distinctive end is specified, the picture of the good life given by the *Ethics* is incomplete. Aristotle must complete the picture if he is to use it to define a certain type of person; but in that case this type of person cannot appear as an element in the defining formula (namely, in this case, a formula consisting of the *Ethics*).[11] The other explanation is that when Aristotle thinks about practical wisdom (as distinct from when he thinks about good and bad qualities of character), it no longer seems to him as if good and wise agents aim for anything very different from morally inferior ones, but instead they all aim more or less competently at the same end, which he dubs 'good living in general'. Now one not unreasonable explanation for his thinking this sufficient, even though he elsewhere says that good and bad men have different visions of the good, is that he has confused the formal end of practical deliberation as such with the good man's distinctive interpretation of that end. This amounts to the conflation of two issues which the project of Book VI ought, one might think, to keep separate: (1) what is it about the ethical *orthos logos* that is distinctively *ethical* (i.e., prohairetic or practical in the narrow sense, as distinct from productive or theoretical)? (2) what is it about the ethical *orthos logos* whereby it is *orthos* or *right?* Now if this confusion occurs, the craft analogy may be to blame. For the end of any practitioner of a craft, good or bad, is indeed the same; and good and bad practitioners differ only in *how* they seek to realise it.

A related difficulty was raised at the beginning of the last section: the defining end of practice as such is the good or the best without restriction; but this is a formal concept which by itself cannot determine any particular rational choice. In deliberation, desire for the end functions as the leading premiss of an argument that issues in a practical conclusion via consideration of the particular circumstances and their causal relations to the end. *Living well* cannot, as such, figure as a starting point of deliberation in this sense; until it is specified, its causal relations are indeterminate. The craft analogy may have led Aristotle to overlook the fact that the end by which he characterises the man of practical wisdom is empty and impracticable, like Plato's Form of the Good. For the defining ends of crafts are not without empirical content: someone who aims at health as such aims at *something* rather than something else.

In discussing ways in which the craft analogy is potentially misleading, I have so far suggested no more than that Aristotle may have got stuck in these confusions. It is well to sample such possibilities; but now I will say (in advance of argument) that there are also some sound reasons, not reasons based on confusion, why Aristotle might write as if no generally statable difference exists between the ends of morally good and bad deliberators. It is possible to construct a respectable view according to which the difference, as with the craftsmen, is not in what they aim at, but in how they aim at it. Does Aristotle in fact hold such a view, as distinct from having reasons available for holding it? At the weakest, I would say that he tends to hold it. The strongest evidence for the tendency comes from his comparison of practical with theoretical thinking, which so far has received no attention in this discussion; the main apparent evidence against it (or for a countertendency) are passages where Aristotle says that virtue makes the end right, not the means. Here, however, I anticipate a conclusion whose justification depends on arguments to be given later; see especially Sections IX and X below.

For some time now I have proceeded simplistically as if the concept of a craftsman's end were clear; but problems lurk here, too. The defining end of medicine, whether well or badly practised, is health, a condition whose absence or presence ordinary people can recognise when they are aware of needing or not needing medical help and when they are satisfied or dissatisfied with their treatment. Concern for health on this level is obviously not restricted to physicians as such, since but for that ordinary concern there would be no physicians. Hence what constitutes health (or the bringing about of health) the defining end of the medical art is not the fact that the practitioner is concerned with this end as ordinarily described, but the fact that he or she qua medical practitioner is concerned with *this and no other end*. As Plato teaches in the *Republic,* it is because of this undivided focus that an ordinary agent narrows and deepens into an expert. Now, although health as ordinarily conceived is an empirically recognisable condition, we should not be too quick to assume that this ordinary conception figures directly in the premises of a medical expert's deliberation. It often figures in premises of ordinary practical deliberation, as when I wonder whether to visit the doctor or to start myself on a course of exercise. For the medical practitioner, however, the ordinary notion of health does not provide a starting point from which to deduce what medical action to take for a particular patient under particular circumstances. Such a starting point is given by expert understanding of what health consists in, both as to matter and form. This is the technical specification of health in terms of anatomy and physiology. One way of being an inferior doctor is to work from an inaccurate professional specification of the end. Hence the end which *defines* the art or science of medicine is the same for all practitioners since all ultimately aim to produce or preserve what everyone values and refers to as 'health', but the end which *figures in the premises of medical deliberation* differs with experts of different calibre or different training.

The medical expert's specification of health can be regarded as a means to health as ordinarily desired and recognised, and this in two ways. First, the physician aims to promote the latter *by* promoting the condition presented in his technical picture. Second, the picture itself—the having of the picture—is a means to restoring health in the ordinary sense. But it differs functionally from those means which the expert possessing the picture applies in a particular treatment. These vary from case to case, whereas the picture is constant by comparison. The practising expert does not choose it or choose to use it in any particular medical situation, since in the light of *it* he chooses particular treatments. So the technical picture (or what is so pictured) functions as an end (or at any rate not as a means) in the structure of particular deliberations about means. But in terms of *value* the medical picture is only a means. For example, if some people found that they could reliably effect cures without having and reasoning from a statable technical picture of health, but instead simply knowing in each case what drugs to administer, etc. (as an animal knows what to eat when it is sick), and if this ability were acquired and increased by practice, then these people would be said to have medical skill, even though it would not be a skill dependent on formal teaching. For the defining end of medical skill is health as ordinarily understood: not health only as attained via some technical picture!

These considerations suggest that there is *in general* a difference between the formal end which defines a kind of activity or practice and the end which figures in leading premisses of particular deliberations, and which may vary according to the deliberator's level of excellence. Prohairetic deliberation in its wise and inferior forms would not be exceptional in this respect; so in this respect the craft analogy would not be misleading. (But Aristotle can still be confused about craft itself even if his comparison of craft with practical wisdom shows a steadier hand than some of his critics have recognised.) The distinction just made between the defining end and the end premissed in deliberation implies a corresponding distinction between senses in which something is the starting-point (or principle) of deliberation. Health as ordinarily conceived is the starting-point of medical deliberation about how to treat a patient, in the sense of being the raison d'être of all steps taken with a view to treatment, including the deliberation; but the technical goal presented in the leading premiss is the starting-point that guides the physician to one conclusion rather than another. The former starting-point is what justifies engaging at all in the deliberation with a view to taking whatever action it will indicate; the latter explains why *this* conclusion was reached and *this* action taken.

Adverting now to the third of the difficulties earlier cited as standing between us and a clear view of the implications of the craft model for practical wisdom, I would say that Aristotle does not clearly register this difference between senses of 'starting-point'. That, presumably, is because both kinds of starting-points have this in common: neither is adopted as a result of reflection on what to do in the particular situation. Both are preconditions of such reflection, which the agent brings to bear as he faces one or another set of particulars. But there is an enormous difference. The doctor as such cannot reflect on whether to pursue the health of patients: if there is a reason or justification linking an agent to such a pursuit (so that the pursuit would be a synthetic fact about him) the agent is *eo ipso* not being considered as a doctor, but as someone deciding on grounds external to medicine whether to engage in medical activity. The doctor as such logically cannot decide anything on grounds external to medicine. By contrast, it is not the case that the doctor as such cannot reflect on his expert picture of the healthy body: how were such pictures ever formed if not by scientific medical practitioners reflecting on practical medical experience?

What lesson should we draw as philosophical interpreters from the lively possibilities of confusion inherent in Aristotle's comparison of practical wisdom with craft? Not, I think, that he is mistaken in principle (as many have claimed) in assuming a significant analogy, but rather that he fails to register ambiguities within the notion of a craft such as medicine. It is not impossible that Aristotle conflates the defining end of medicine as such with the premissed end that guides the good physician and differs in its technical content from the premissed end that guides the badly informed physician. This would have made it easier for him to conflate the formal end (living well in general) that defines practical deliberation as such (wise or not), with the distinctive end of practical wisdom—if practical wisdom has a distinctive end. And this would explain how he could hold—if hold it he does—that practical wisdom has a distinctive end not shared with morally inferior prohairetic dispositions, yet fail to tell us what that end is like, since it would seem to him that he had explained it when he explained the purely formal end.

For the purpose of expounding some of the difficulties, I have tried to drive as firm a conceptual wedge as possible between the defining end of an expertise such as medicine and the guiding end that appears in a medical premiss of deliberation about a particular treatment. This provides us with a fix on one way in which Aristotle may have been adversely influenced by the craft analogy. But other angles are also jostling for attention, and taking them into account will tend to confound that distinction between defining end and guiding end. In the first place, for instance, it is false to say without qualification that the medical expert's medical thinking is not substantially guided, but only defined as medical, by the end of health as known, desired and enjoyed by ordinary people. For when medical science works out its technical picture of health, it does so with reference to health as ordinarily understood. The technical picture presents the human body in terms of a general causal understanding not available to everyone (understanding of underlying structures and material components), but the effects of the hidden causes are healthy and unhealthy conditions that we all recognise as such. The picture is devised to account for those effects and is confirmed or disconfirmed by checking predictions based on the picture against experience of successful and unsuccessful treatments. Medical science tracks 'ordinary' physical well-being in forming its technical picture, and it forms its picture to promote ordinary physical well-being. The latter therefore figures in the premiss of medical arguments justifying the adoption of one general picture rather than some other. It guides the choice of general picture and so, indirectly, it guides the deliberations on particular treatments which the picture directly guides.

The distinction, then, between senses of 'starting-point' appears when we focus on the situation of an expert working *from* a technical picture; it disappears when we focus on his working *towards* the technical picture which constitutes a great part of his expertise. In the latter situation, the defining end *is* the guiding end. In real life the two situations are not kept entirely apart: the doctor both treats from specialist knowledge and improves on this knowledge by observing the course of particular treatments.

Second, there is the connected fact that even an inaccurate or theoretically absurd technical picture of a healthy body must stand the test of *some* experience. If a bad picture were so different from a good picture that treatment in accordance with the former predictably resulted in what everyone would recognise as diminished health, the former is not even an intended picture of a healthy body and it cannot function as a guide for medical practice even by inferior physicians. From the practical point of view, the significant difference between good and bad medical pictures is only in *degree of effectiveness,* though the theories internal to different pictures may be utterly different. Since here what is good is what is effective, a bad medical picture is *less* good than the right one (the one that is right by the standards of the best knowledge available), but it is not *contrary.* Now, the difference between the guiding end and the defining end in medicine was worked out by means of the assumption that there are divergent guiding ends, but a single defining end. However, when guiding ends are seen as differing in degree rather than kind, or when a difference of degree (e.g., of effectiveness) matters more than any difference of kind per se, we are not so well placed after all to distinguish between those notions of 'end'. From this point of view the craft analogy may make it easier for Aristotle to write about practical wisdom as if a statement of its defining end—'living well in general'—says all that has to be said about its end. But in this respect the analogy is misleading, for the wicked agent cannot be classed as a less effective version of the same kind as the good and wise agent; rather, they are contraries, as Aristotle makes clear in his classification of virtues and vices.

Third, the distinction between defining end and guiding end can be set forth reasonably clearly in connection with examples such as medicine, where a technical picture does guide particular deliberations. But there are skills the practice of which is not grounded in any sort of statable picture. Hence it could reasonably be argued that use of a technical picture developed by scientific methods and taught by verbal explanation is not an essential feature of health expertise as such. It is a feature of health expertise as this has developed in accordance with experience of methods and their results. We find from experience that those with some articulate general understanding of the body are better at curing patients than those who follow their hunches and can offer no general reason for applying a particular treatment. But we also know from experience that knowledge of anatomy and kinetic theory is not a necessary condition for successful practice of the skills of riding a bicycle, tightrope walking, or juggling. Were it not for the fact that Aristotle's favourite example of skill in the *Ethics* is his father's craft of medicine, we might find no difficulty in accepting the analogy of skill with practical wisdom. If practical wisdom is like the ability to keep one's balance, then the wise man does not have to be guided by a precise picture of what he aims at in order to succeed in achieving it. He need not be able to say more than what would also be said by nonvirtuous prohairetic agents: namely, that he is trying to strike a balance that is right from the point of view of life in general.

The investigation carried on in this section pulls one in different directions, allowing no settled view of the use which Aristotle makes of the craft analogy, or of its significance for him, or of the exact nature of any confusions to which it may have led him. Even so, we can now extract two possible models for practical wisdom and can also see how, different as they are, they may easily be confused. Somewhere between these two we should be able to locate Aristotle's conception of practical wisdom, and if not squarely on either, then closer to one than the other. According to the first, practical wisdom resembles medicine in acting and deliberating on the basis of a specific picture of the end. This ethical picture figures in the premises of all the wise man's deliberations about particular problems. In explaining and justifying his rational choices he refers to the end as pictured, showing how that end would be realised by a given action in a given situation. How the wise man arrives at his picture, and how he would justify his assumption that this is what the good substantially *is*, are difficult questions. But the content of the good man's picture will differ in statable ways from pictures governing the actions of the wicked or mediocre, and these differences reflect their differences of character and moral outlook.

The second model will take shape when we have examined the comparison with theoretical wisdom, but it is backed by the consideration that the medical expert's technical picture is only a means to the end of health and is therefore conceivably dispensable; and that where such pictures are unnecessary they do not figure at all. As Aristotle might say, in practical matters our nature is satisfied with the minimal clarity that success requires. On this model, practical wisdom is like the ability to balance. But one difficulty of applying this second model to Aristotle's account is that it seems to do away with practical *deliberation* as the essential vehicle of wisdom. For what can there be to deliberate about when there is no articulable end?

### IV.  Against the 'Grand End' View

Practical wisdom, according to one model proposed at the end of the last section, is like a craft such as medicine: it seeks to realise, not health, but the human good without restriction; and in this it takes its cue from an explicit, comprehensive, substantial vision of that good, a vision invested with a content different from what would be aimed at by morally inferior natures. This blueprint of the good guides its possessor in all his deliberations, and in terms of it his rational choices can be explained and justified. A choice shows practical wisdom only if two conditions are satisfied: (1) given the facts as seen by the agent, enacting the choice would lead to the realisation of his grand picture; (2) his grand picture is a true or acceptable account of the good.[12]

This is a neat and simple view of practical wisdom, and so are some of the reasons for believing it not Aristotle's. He himself gives us regrettably little by way of example or concrete description of practical (as distinct from technical) deliberation. Most of his discussion is concerned with the elements of deliberation taken one by one. His failure to illustrate can, of course, be interpreted as a license to fill in whatever scenario our favoured line of interpretation suggests, but it may also mean that Aristotle takes it for granted that we know pretty well in nonanalytic fashion what practical deliberation is like, from our experience. This tells against the Grand End[13] theory, as I shall call it, since few of us would claim to know either at first or second hand what it is like to deliberate with a view to realising a Grand End. We can hardly imagine this except schematically, whereas we can easily reproduce in our heads quite passable versions or imitations of deliberations pertaining to various crafts, as well as nonspecialist deliberations concerning familiar describable ends such as buying a house, helping a friend out of difficulties, or obtaining a diploma. One of Aristotle's few portrayals run like this:

Having set the end they consider how and by what means it is to be attained; and if it seems to be produced by several means they consider by which it is most easily and best produced, while if it is achieved by one only they consider how it will be achieved by this and by what means *this* will be achieved, till they come to the first cause, which in order of discovery is last. For the person who deliberates seems to inquire and analyse in the way described as though he were analysing a geometrical construction (not all inquiry appears to be deliberation—for instance mathematical inquiries—but all deliberation is inquiry), and what is last in the order of analysis seems to be first in the order of becoming. And if we come on an impossibility, we give up the search, e.g. if we need money and this cannot be got; but if a thing appears possible we try to do it. By 'possible things' I mean things that might be brought about by our own efforts; and these in a sense include things that can be brought about by the efforts of our friends, since the moving principle is in ourselves. The subject of investigation is sometimes the instruments, sometimes the use of them; and similarly in the other cases—sometimes the means, sometimes the mode of using it or the means of bringing it about. (1112 b 15–31)

Aristotle envisages the situation in which only one means presents itself: he writes as if this were just as common as the situation in which we have options. He also envisages the situation in which we encounter an impracticable step: then we give up. What do we give up? If what turned out impossible was what had appeared as the only means, then we give up the entire project. He writes as if this is familiar, and of course it is. But if the project were that of realising a Grand End, it is hardly credible that one would give it up and turn to something else. For the Grand End is living well in general, and if one cannot do something to forward this in one way, one can always do something to forward it in another, so comprehensive is that end. Aristotle, it would seem, is writing here about deliberation on ends such as buying a house or getting a diploma.

Aristotle is famous for saying:

Matters concerned with conduct and questions of what is good for us have no fixity, any more than matters of health. The general account being of this nature, the account of particular cases is yet more lacking in exactness; for they do not fall under any art or set of precepts, but the agents themselves must in each case consider what is appropriate to the occasion, as happens also in the art of medicine or of navigation. (1104 a 3–10)

Aristotle cannot want living well and doing right to be more difficult than it has to be. If he believed in a single constant end that justifies every rational choice, he would surely hold this up as one 'fixed answer', even though it were a high-level answer not easy to apply to particulars. According to one way of interpreting *NE* VI.1, this is just what he promises to do when embarking on the discussion of practical wisdom, having become presumably less pessimistic about the possibility of fixed answers. But, as I argued, there is no good reason to adopt that interpretation of *NE* VI.1; thus Aristotle's stated intention there provides no evidence whatsoever for ascribing to him a Grand End theory of practical wisdom.

The person of practical wisdom would have (on such a theory) to be a philosopher or to have absorbed the teachings of philosophers. How else would he or she come by that comprehensive vision? Aristotle sees the activities of philosophy and theoretical science as perfecting the life of practical virtue so as to render it a life of complete (or perfect) human happiness (1177 b 24; cf. 1178 b 7–8). But in *NE* VI he shows no sign of holding that practical virtue itself, which includes practical wisdom, necessarily presupposes a command of philosophical ethics.

If Aristotle believes in a Grand End for practical wisdom, he with his practical concern should try to state what that end is like. He does not try, and what could he say if he did? He cannot ascribe to what he calls 'wisdom' a vision of the human good much different from that which he develops in the *Ethics* or he would call into doubt the *Ethics* and its account of practical wisdom. But he cannot, we saw, ascribe without circularity the picture of the good which he himself is developing, since this picture includes a portrait of practical wisdom. If the portrait (and hence the *Ethics* as a whole) is complete only when the wise men's Grand End has been painted in, the portrait is necessarily incomplete not as an outline which may be filled in, but as something in principle defective. That is only not true of Aristotle's *Ethics* if the Grand End theory is false.

Aristotle says that moral excellence contributes to wisdom by making the end right and that wickedness corrupts and distorts our vision of the end. Perhaps we can understand how wickedness cuts someone off from a clear vision of the good, since even if he grasped the description of its nature, he would not value it as good. But can we understand how being courageous, just, temperate, liberal, friendly, self-respecting and the rest, should generate a full, true and articulate picture such as it would be the business of philosophical ethics to provide? Perhaps Aristotle means that these qualities are only necessary conditions for being in possession of such a picture. Then what further condition must be met? No one is born able from himself to muster a true explicit picture. Philosophy might provide it, and so might divine illumination. The problem is not that we cannot conceive ways in which such a picture might arrive. It is that its having arrived in some such way must be considered essential to practical wisdom, if practical wisdom thinks in terms of a Grand End. But the ground-level practical wisdom that keeps us decently going as human beings precedes philosophical ethics (which comes on the scene at leisure), hence cannot depend upon it. Nor can ground-level wisdom depend on divine illumination, if this means miracles or uncontrollable favours by beings beyond us; for in that case human virtue, and happiness as Aristotle understands it, would not be *humanly* practicable.

Ground-level practical wisdom of course involves practical intelligence *(nous)*. Some interpreters have striven to see in practical *nous,* as Aristotle presents it, the source of a grand ethical vision. Thus the Grand End notion can influence our understanding of Aristotle's conception of practical *nous,* just as it influences our understanding of the project proposed in *NE* VI.1. The influence is distorting in both cases. We shall have more to say later about Aristotle's conception of *nous.* For now it is enough that Aristotelian practical *nous* is above all an ability to grasp particular situations and draw particular conclusions. This ability would work to forward a Grand End if such an end were already operative, but how, itself, can it generate the vision of that end?

But surely, it may be asked, we can develop such an explicit comprehensive vision by reflection on our moral experience? Yes; and Aristotle would be the last to deny that philosophical ethics must be rooted in such reflection. But if we take account of experience, we must recognise that in so doing we recall particular practical responses, our own and others', which seem and have seemed to us right; and we bring to mind the kinds of personalities which those responses represent. Some of them seem to exemplify what, speaking unguardedly, we should be happy to term 'practical wisdom'. Are we now to withhold, any more than before, the predicate 'wise' until we have made sure that the subjects possessed an explicitly pictured Grand End? And if we do now withhold it for the sake of a theory, does not our same moral experience show that practical wisdom defined now according to the theory is not a necessary condition for good decisions and virtuous actions? But if that is so, practical wisdom as defined is not to be considered an essentially *practical* virtue (and if not practical, why a virtue at all?), since it would appear that we can function well in practice without it.

Furthermore, Aristotle holds that one cannot be considered in the full sense morally excellent unless one has practical wisdom too. This does not imply that whenever the situation especially calls for courage, it also especially calls for an exercise of practical wisdom, since often it takes mere character to know what to do, and not any special intelligence or power of reflection. Aristotle's position implies, rather, that courage is not truly courage unless it is consistently at the service of the *orthos logos*—a consistency which depends on the agent's general ability to come up with the right prescription even when not immediately obvious to a well-brought-up person. This general ability is practical wisdom, and in defining moral virtue as a 'prohairetic' disposition for hitting the mean, Aristotle has so defined it that, in a person lacking practical wisdom, the qualities which would otherwise be moral virtues are not virtues strictly speaking, but potentials or prefigurations of virtues. We shall return in more detail to this connection of the virtues, a connection that sets rather stringent conditions on the predication of terms such as 'courageous person', 'temperate person' and so on (see Section XI below). But the conditions for assigning these predicates become utterly unrealistic if, in addition to moral virtue's entailing practical wisdom, practical wisdom entails possession of a true, comprehensive articulate picture of the human good.

Those two entailments result in some very Socratic conceptions of the moral virtues: conceptions which the members of Aristotle's audience would lack the authority to apply, since calling a person 'temperate', 'brave' etc. now carries the judgment that that person has a vision of the good which is full, articulate, justified and true. Those who come to the lectures on ethics probably do not regard themselves as possessing such a vision, let alone as competent to recognise it in others. On the other hand, they do have a prereflective grasp of what the human excellences are; and, as we have seen (Chapter 1, Section VI), Aristotle depends on this understanding to give content to his otherwise purely formal definition of the good.

In arguing against the Grand End interpretation of Aristotle's theory of practical wisdom, I shall seem to have belaboured an exaggerated model which goes beyond what anyone would squarely ascribe to Aristotle. But I am really concerned with the tendency towards this model: a tendency to see Aristotle's account as approximating that starkly implausible view. I have focused on the stark view so as to make clear the nature, less noticeably mistaken, of the tendency, the effect of which is that we scan Aristotle's account for elements which have no reason to be present and look less closely at what is there. Thus we strain to extract from his conception of practical *nous* a rôle that was never conceived for it, and we fail to make the most of his comparison of practical with theoretical wisdom.

The Grand End picture is a confusion sprung from between the two levels on which Aristotle operates in the *Nicomachean Ethics*.[14] The picture models Aristotelian practical wisdom on a certain kind of craft, allowing only these differences: practical wisdom aims at the unrestricted good and is categorically oriented towards action. Hence just as its end is the End of ends, so practical wisdom is the Craft of crafts. Now, the statesman in *NE* I is indeed presented as a sort of supreme craftsman of the good. For at the beginning Aristotle is more concerned, as we saw, to establish the reality of the statesman's supreme end than to combat any misleading impressions arising in the course of that argument. But in *NE* VI, as I understand it, Aristotle decisively corrects any tendency to extend this craftman model to the "product" of the statesman: i.e., to individual moral virtue informed by practical wisdom. Whatever view we might now have to take of the statesman as a philosophically enlightened builder of human virtue, *what* such a one purports to build is not to be defined as a capability for even the noblest species of building. That much is made clear in *NE* VI.4 and 5, where Aristotle draws his famous contrast, now to be examined, between making and acting.

## V. Practice and Production

Taking it for granted that art or craft and practical wisdom are in some ways fundamentally similar, Aristotle explains their differences in *NE* VI.4 and 5. He says:

> Now it is thought to be a mark of a man of practical wisdom to be able to (a) deliberate well about what is good and expedient (b) for himself, (c) not in some particular respect, e.g. about what sorts of things conduce to health or to strength, but about what sorts of thing conduce to the good life in general. This is shown by the fact that we credit men with practical wisdom in some particular respect when they have calculated well with a view to some good end which is one of those that are not the object of any art. Thus in general the man who is capable of deliberating has practical wisdom. . . . [It cannot be] art because action and making are different kinds of thing. It remains, then, that it is a true and reasoned state of capacity to act with regard to the things that are good or bad for man. For (d) while making has an end other than itself, action cannot; for good action itself is its end. It is for this reason that we think Pericles and men like him have practical wisdom, viz. because they can see what is good for themselves and what is good for men in general; we consider that those can do this who are good at managing households or states. That is why (e) we call temperance by this name [*sōphrosunē*], we imply that it preserves one's practical wisdom [*hōs sōzousa tēn phronēsin*]. Now what it preserves is a belief of the kind we have described. For it is not any and every belief that pleasant and painful objects destroy and pervert, e.g. the belief that the triangle has or has not its angles equal to two right angles, but only beliefs about what is to be done. (1140 a 25–b 16)

But further (f), while there is such a thing as excellence in art, there is no such thing as excellence in practical wisdom; and (g) in art he who errs willingly is preferable, but in practical wisdom, as in the excellences, he is the reverse. Plainly, then, practical wisdom is an excellence and not an art. (1140 b 21–25)

Practical wisdom is essentially (a) the capacity to deliberate well. Ordinary usage sanctions this statement, Aristotle says, because in a broad sense we call people 'wise' when they are good at working out answers to practical problems of a restricted kind that fall outside the scope of any craft. Thus deliberation is necessary when there are no rules; for the arts and crafts, as Aristotle thinks of them here, have rules which can be stated and taught.

But all the time new craft techniques are developed, and problems that once required deliberation come to be soluble by rule. Rules, though, could not supersede deliberation in the sphere of practical wisdom. Practical wisdom is essentially deliberative in a sense not captured by the ordinary wide usage of 'wise'; for that is applied to cases where deliberation and practical ingenuity can be rendered redundant through the establishing of rules, whereas practical wisdom cannot hope to be replaced in this way.

Why is this? Perhaps the reason lies in the already familiar point (c), that the wise man is concerned with what is good without restriction. But even if we grant that there cannot be rules of practical wisdom, is Aristotle right to make this a fundamental difference between practical wisdom and craft? For even if crafts have rules, in general they also involve much more than rules, as he himself often recognises. Some crafts and skills are virtually mechanical once acquired (e.g., spelling; see 1112 a 34 ff.), but others demand ingenuity and intelligence for the effective application of their rules. And some skills, we noted earlier, seem to depend on no rules at all. What is more, rules of a craft are developed without recourse to preestablished rules; yet surely it belongs to the craft itself, not to any other kind of ability, to develop its own rules. And in this the craftsman shows himself more artful and more admirable than if he merely follows rules. The question is: In what respect is craft most typically craft? It is because craft involves deliberation that craft resembles practical wisdom enough to have to be distinguished from it. Thus in focusing on the resemblance, Aristotle thinks of the *master* craftsman as paradigm. But in saying that they differ because craft follows rules, Aristotle shifts to another aspect of craft: craft as mechanical, instead of inventive. This is equivocation on different senses of 'craft'.

Not the least of our problems in assessing his comparison between craft and practical wisdom lies in the fact, already hinted at in Section III above, that Aristotle is not decided on what constitutes the core of craft. For example, in *NE* II he is equally ready to compare *moral* excellence and craft. (This taken in conjunction with his present concern suggests that if 'craft' bears the same sense in both comparisons, then practical wisdom is a moral virtue, or the moral virtues are forms of practical wisdom. But while Aristotle certainly recognises a close relation between wisdom and the moral virtues, he is clear that the relation is not identity nor that of species to genus in either direction [cf. 1144 b 16–21].) It is not, of course, craft in its deliberate aspect, but as involving habitual skills automatically applied, that permits the parallel with moral virtue. Moral virtue is 'second nature': for those who possess it, virtuous actions are as natural as the actions of that primary nature which in Aristotle's science and metaphysics is constantly likened to craft. The natures of natural substances are principles of purposeful activity that need no monitoring; and in this context craft appears as another such principle. For craft, he says in *Physics* 199 b 26–28, 'does not deliberate'.

However, the ambiguity of 'craft' is perhaps not an objection if Aristotle takes the different senses as essentially connected: on the ground, for instance, that it belongs to deliberative craft to discover rules to be followed by the more mechanical exercise of craft. He might then maintain the contrast with practical wisdom by arguing that practical wisdom cannot, like craft, bring any part of its concerns under the scope of rules devised by itself. But would this be true? People do come to articulate substantial conceptions of the good of man, and such a conception, once developed, might indeed serve as a standard to guide behaviour, even if not a rule to be applied mechanically. This is what Aristotle himself hopes to achieve by his own inquiry. It is true (so I argued in the last section) that such grand conceptions are not developed prior to the making of wise rational choices; but this does not prove a fundamental difference from craft. For craft, too, hauls itself up by its bootstraps to create rules for itself.

A true, articulate, substantial conception of the human good, such as he means to present in the *Ethics,* is in Aristotle's view an instrument to aid the statesman in his work of maintaining and developing a flourishing human community (1094 a 22–24). Because of his grasp of this substantial conception, the statesman is something of a professional—a craftsman. But even if practical wisdom, in the first instance, is not guided by the philosophical statesman's Grand End, it does not follow that practical wisdom is not a craft or craftlike. On the contrary, it could be held that nothing is more craftlike than an ability to work without rules and, from practice and reflection, to develop a rule or rulelike standard for oneself. In just such a way, it seems, practical wisdom can develop into political wisdom. So is practical wisdom a craft: the same craft, potentially, as political science?

Charting the relations of practical and political wisdom is a topic in itself,[15] which Aristotle grazes at 1141 b 23–24, where he says that they are the same disposition but different in their definitions. Presumably he means that the same upbringing fosters both, but they differ in their spheres of operation. In any case, *politikē* is not monolithic. It is most obviously *practical* in its executive aspect, but it is legislative and judicial as well as executive (1141 b 25–33).

Yet at moments in Aristotle's exposition the ordinary wise person does seem to merge with the statesman: witness the mention of Pericles as an example of practical wisdom (1140 b 7–10). But Aristotle immediately corrects the impression when he says that 'this quality belongs to those who understand the management of *households* and states' (ibid., 10–11). The man of practical wisdom is concerned with his *own* good (point [b] in the quoted passage). This means not that he has no regard for the interests of others, but that he sets his sights on his own responsibilities as one citizen amongst his fellows. Politicians are not necessarily superior individuals because they operate on a larger canvas; at 1142 a 1–6 Aristotle endorses the commonplace that real life politicians are often ambitious busybodies.

Yet practical wisdom does not merely 'know its own business' (cf. 1141 b 33–34) in the way prescribed by Plato for the commoners and other classes in the *Republic*. The commoners there are craft professionals whose 'own business' (and autonomy) is confined to the exercise of their specialities. The ideal of the *Republic* is a good and flourishing *city,* and this conception, as Plato develops it, leaves no room for *general* excellence in the common citizens—apart from the virtue of obedience. Strictly speaking, it is not the business of anyone but the professional rulers to exercise practical wisdom, since, as Aristotle says, practical wisdom is 'prescriptive' (1143 a 8; 1143 b 35; 1145 a 9). But Aristotle's primary ideal is not a flourishing city considered as a kind of organic substance, but a society of actively excellent *human individuals.* Practical wisdom is a part of human excellence, hence its exercise should not be confined to any one class in society or to those most politically active. Aristotle upholds this by pointing out what Plato missed: that many nonspecialist areas of ordinary life are best managed by the persons immediately concerned. These constitute the primary sphere of Aristotelian practical wisdom.

The needs of the community and the values for which it collectively stands play their part in shaping the wise individual's rational choice. Thus his personal interest is not an absolute consideration in making the choice, but the choice once made is an absolute demand on *him* to carry it out. And that he make the right choice, whatever it turns out to be, is also an absolute demand. Hence the peculiar dependence of practical wisdom on moral virtue. And here is one vital difference of practical wisdom from craft. Without temperance one cannot be wise ([e] in the quoted passage), for too much concern with pleasure and pain destroys one's focus on the good. If (point [g]) a craftsman voluntarily goes against the dictates of the craft, this does not undermine his title to be considered that sort of craftsman. Like the doctor who poisons, he exercises his craft knowledge in deciding precisely what technical rule to break. But if a person voluntarily acts against the dictate of practical wisdom, this is not an exercise of practical wisdom; it is incontinence. Nor (point [f]) is there any room for distinguishing good from bad exercises of practical wisdom in the ways in which we distinguish good from bad exercises of a craft.

I have left point (d) until last. In the chapter preceding our quoted passage, Aristotle has defined craft as a rational capacity for *making* or *producing* (1140 a 9–10) and stated that acting *(praxis)* and making *(poiēsis)* are different types, neither of which includes or embraces the other (1140 a 2–17). This is because: 'While making has an end other than itself, action cannot; for good action *(eupraxia)* is itself its end' (1140 b 6–7). The point evidently is that craft aims at an independent product; but we must consider the meaning of 'end' here, and of 'independent'. In one sense, the craftsman's end is the product, but in another it is his own successful making (or having made) it. For here he touches the peak of *being* the sort of craftsman he is. Thus when in III.5 Aristotle wants to illustrate the point that we do not deliberate about ends but only means, he speaks not of intended results, but of productive actions: 'For a doctor does not deliberate whether *he shall heal,* nor an orator whether he *shall convince,* nor a statesman whether he shall *produce law and order*'. (1112 b 12–14; emphasis mine)

We know from the beginning of the *Ethics* that happiness, also called *'eupraxia'* (= doing well), is an activity, not a thing or a state producible by activity; that the activity of happiness is not subordinate to a higher good or end; and that happiness is exercise of virtue, including practical wisdom. Now could this exercise itself be some kind of productive activity or making? Indeed it could, if we could identify for it a product such that enjoyment or use of that product is not a higher and better activity than the producing. Now, when a product is a restricted good relevant to one department of life, we can say for sure that an activity in which it is used is higher than the producing of it. For a restricted good is ultimately used with a view to 'the whole of life', whereas the producing craft has only that narrow good in view. And in general, wherever the activity that uses is different in kind from that which produces, the latter is subordinate. But perhaps there could be a productive activity which, though productive, is highest because it aims at producing the conditions of its own continuing and continuingly productive exercise, whether by the agent himself or by others of his kind later.

Such a self-sustaining, self-reproducing structure seems a fitting attribute for the supreme activity of happiness, especially as happiness is the highest expression of human *vitality*. And if happiness is essentially productive in this way, so is the virtue of practical wisdom. There is a certain beauty in the notion of practical wisdom as a craft producing a product which is then the basis of further such production; but in *NE* VI Aristotle will not allow that practical wisdom is any kind of productive capacity or craft. So in effect he refuses to equate it even with the super-craft of producing virtue and the conditions for happiness, whether this super-craft is carried on, as it mostly always has been, through bringing up children and maintaining social institutions in accordance with untheorised perceptions of what is worthwhile and what sorts of qualities are virtues, or whether it is illuminated by a philosophical account that articulates the spirit of those perceptions in terms of explicit principles. The first can develop into the second, but in neither case is it the self-reproductive structure as such that answers to the definition of practical wisdom. For practical wisdom and the other virtues are the intended product of education, and if the product were no more than the capacity to reproduce itself, the nature of the product could logically never be stated. It belongs to every living species to reproduce itself in new vehicles of reproduced capacity for further reproduction; so if the nature of a being and its vital activity were spelt out solely in terms of self-reproduction, all species would fall under one definition and would be the same. So the reproducible natural powers of a species include the power of self-maintenance and reproduction, but must also include differentiating characteristics whereby *what* is reproduced is specific. Just so, human virtue and wisdom, second nature for their possessors, are inevitably expressed in active concern for the transmission of those same qualities, but *what* is transmitted must be explained otherwise than as the capacity for its own transmission, and otherwise, too, than as the exercise of that capacity.

Given that craft is essentially productive, the above considerations show a powerful reason for Aristotle's insistence that practical wisdom is not any sort of craft. (The way in which wisdom positively differs from craft has not yet been fully explained.) Summarised, the reason is this: if practical wisdom is a craft, then either it is defined in terms of a product to be used in some higher activity, or its definition is self-referential. The second alternative is logically repugnant, and so, it would seem, is the first, given that agents of lower activities follow the prescriptions of agents of higher. For nothing prescribes *to* practical wisdom, since practical wisdom is nothing if not prescrip*tive* (1143 a 8). Moreover, happiness, we have been given to understand, is the exercise of practical virtue, and nothing is higher than happiness.

The argument is strong, but it contains one chink which might never be spotted except in hindsight by those who have followed Aristotle to the end of his inquiry, although he does drop a hint or two in Book VI (1141 a 20–22; 34–b 2; 1145 a 6–11). Suppose there is an activity A higher or nobler than any activity formed and monitored by practical wisdom and the other practical virtues; and suppose, too, that A, though higher, is not of a nature to generate practical prescriptions. In that case we might be justified in regarding practical wisdom as productive—productive of the conditions for A—without its following that it takes orders from something else or is self-referential. But not much can be made of this proposal at the present stage, when we are still struggling to determine the nature of practical wisdom. We know from elsewhere that Aristotle recognises *theōria* as noblest of all activities and that he scrupulously denies it any practical interest or practical power. But more conceptual analysis of our current notion, vague as it is, of practical wisdom is not going to reveal that practical wisdom stands in the suggested relation to *theōria* (or, for that matter, to any other activity) in the way in which, for example, an analysis of *bridle-making* instantly finds an upwards connection with *riding*. In the absence of any such immediately obvious connection, we need to look further into the nature and conditions of practical wisdom and into the nature and conditions of various non-practical manifestations of the human spirit, before being in a position to declare the subservience of the former to any one of the latter.

Let us return to the stage we have reached. Practical wisdom is being distinguished from craft on the ground that action is different from making. Now a contrast based on the notion of craft as essentially an ability for *making* is more effective than other contrasts which have come to the fore. That craft is rule-governed whereas practical wisdom is not, is a questionable distinction, because not all crafts are rule-governed; few rule-governed crafts are entirely rule-governed; and activities that are not rule-governed can become so. That the familiar crafts seek only restricted goods is superficial: if the ability to achieve the unrestricted good were in other respects craftlike, of course it would count as a craft. And if it did, another notable contrast would disappear: that between conditional and categorical practical attitudes. An ordinary craft is conditionally practical not because it is craftlike, but because it aims at a restricted good.

Let us resume examining Aristotle's statement (*d*): 'While making has an end other than itself, action cannot; for good action *(eupraxia)* itself is its end' (1140 b 6–7). We saw that the craftsman's good productive activity is, in one sense, his end: the perfection of him as craftsman. The product, which is other than the activity, is his end in a different sense: it is that by which one judges his success, hence judges him to have achieved his end in the first sense. We assess the excellence of the making, hence of the maker, by the quality of what is made. This is because what is made is not merely a product: it is a thing or a state of a certain kind—a pair of shoes, a condition of health, a thoroughly convinced audience. What is made is 'other than' the process of making because it is judged not primarily as something *made,* but as a good or bad whatever it was that was meant to be made, e.g., a pair of shoes. Thus it is first judged in terms independent of its being a product, since if shoes grew on trees the criteria for good and bad shoes would still be the same. So the product, as *what* it is, is an independent standard by which to judge producing and the producer.

This interpretation of the 'otherness' of the product in terms of independently determined excellence avoids difficulties which arise on other interpretations. On some, for instance, Aristotle is taken as saying that the product is a physical object which exists independently. But many of his favourite examples are crafts concerned with producing states or conditions of substances. Again, it may be thought that the product is called 'other' on the ground that whether it is a thing or a state of a thing, it can survive the process of production. But this is too narrow, since there are crafts, as dancing and singing, that create something which physically depends on the movements by which it is made. On the present interpretation these cases fall into line; for although a concrete dance is not ontologically independent of someone's act of dancing it, it can be contemplated and judged as if it were simply a beautiful *event,* and on this basis we may then assess the dancing and the dancer.[16]

With action *(praxis)* or, as we might more perspicuously say, conduct, there is nothing by which to judge the case as an instance of doing well *(eupraxia)* apart from the action itself. If the action is good it is a case of acting well, and on this basis (and others like it) we judge the agent good as a practical (as distinct from productive) agent, or as having achieved the perfection of good agency. This has to do with criteria for judging excellent performance; it is not a point about an agent's motives. It is sometimes suggested that when Aristotle says that good action itself is the end of practical activity, he means that the agent does what is good or right from no ulterior motive, or because it is good or right, or 'for its own sake'. In a sense this is true of the practical agent, although even that depends on how you describe the action: as 'helping a neighbour' or as 'carrying a heavy basket upstairs'. Practical wisdom does not do the latter for its own sake. And moral decency (a sine qua non of wisdom) might be thought to help someone in order that the person be better off: an ulterior result. But in any case how could action for its own sake enable Aristotle to distinguish practical wisdom from craft? For the physician as such heals because he is a physician; he cannot as such pursue a further interest in bringing about his patients' recovery.

The difficulty may be raised that in saying that good action itself is the end of action, Aristotle seems to say that we must assess the excellence of an action by the excellence of the action itself. This is nonsensical, since nothing can be judged by reference to itself. (It is not yet clear *how* Aristotle thinks we judge actions as such to be good, but that should not lead one to suppose that he thinks we do it in an impossible way!) Even so, the passage implies that in action, as in making, something is judged by reference to something (thus 'end' in the context has the second of the senses above). The meaning is that the practical *agent* is judged good as such on the basis of his good action (which is something sufficiently not himself for it to make sense to judge him by it). We judge the producer by his producing, and this in turn by his product, so therefore the producer (indirectly) by something other than his activity. But we judge the practical agent simply by his doing and not in turn by anything external by which the doing is judged.

*How* particular doings are judged as such will be clearer when we have examined Aristotle's conception of deliberation. The *type* of such judgments can be illustrated at once, and above all by cases where the doing happens to be an act of production. Once the production is assessed as a production, there is still the question 'But is (was) this a good thing to do?' The *this* is a particular act of producing (actual or prospective). It is particularised by the circumstances as these appear to be agent. By contrast, the production of just such a product is a universal instantiable under different circumstances, and as a case of production it is equally good under all of them. Thus actions, in the strict sense, are in a special way particulars. For although any given production must as a matter of fact *be* particular if it occurs at all, its particularising conditions are external and accidental to its *nature* as a that-sort-of-production. But the particulars of an action belong to its essence as action, since these are features of *what* it is that is judged good or not. The verdict depends on the when, the where, the agent's relations with those affected, the foreseeable consequences, the cost, the alternatives sacrificed etc. Thus Aristotle rightly declared that acting and making do not 'include' each other (1140 a 5). For if the action that is making is a good or a bad action, it does not follow that the making is correspondingly good or bad; and so conversely. It may be right on occasion to do a botched job (whether or not deliberately) and a fine job may be a foolish or wicked action.[17]

Is this so in all possible cases? Might there not be a product of such overriding importance that it makes no difference how it is produced, as long as it is produced effectively? In that case an effective act of production is automatically a good action, and the most effective such act is the best action. No doubt the most plausible candidate for such a product would be the good of the citizens according to an ideal statesman's substantial conception of that good. But Aristotle makes no exception even for this case. No matter what the clearly understood benefits of a proposed policy, and no matter what degree of skill available for its execution, even Pericles—especially Pericles—finds himself considering the pros and cons of putting it into operation under the given circumstances. So do his fellows in the assembly. Considering these pros and cons is practical wisdom and also good statesmanship. Thus even if the statesman's ability to conceive and execute the policy is a kind of practical wisdom akin to craft, the operations of this craft, like those of humbler crafts, are always subject to his own higher authority as one who takes responsibility for the *circumstances* of operation. This higher authority is practical wisdom and statesmanship of a logically different order: that which secures good *action* even perhaps at the expense of good *production*. Practical activity, unlike theoretical, certainly seeks to make changes and is concerned about the effects of its responses; in that sense of course it is interested in production (cf. Chapter 1, Section VI). But *praxis* aligns itself with *theōria* in not being assessed as a productive capacity is assessed. Practical wisdom is as radically different from craft as it is in other respects from its theoretic counterpart.

With regard to any more or less determinate product and any set of particular circumstances, there is a real question for sane human beings whether it would be good to produce the product under just these circumstances. This fact shows that we find ourselves unable, on the practical level, to identify the supreme good with anything determinate that we might produce, or with the producing of anything determinate. If we did so identify the supreme good, it would be absurd ever to hesitate over bringing about the product in question. The possibility of hesitation with regard to every suggested product reads like a kind of practical rejection of the naturalistic fallacy. There is no P whose nature guarantees that producing P is always a good thing to do. For Aristotle, however, the futility of looking for that sort of guarantee shows not that 'It is good (now) to produce P' predicates a nonnatural property, nor (the historical next step) that the sentence makes no objective claim but only expresses an attitude; it shows, rather, that the goodness, objective as it is whenever it obtains, of the action of producing P (as distinct from the goodness of the P) varies with circumstances in accordance with no rule. How, then, are we to achieve the supreme good if it is not to be achieved simply by producing P (for some specified value of 'P') and, more generally, if there is no rule? The beginning of Aristotle's reply has emerged: we might achieve it by considering, for any P that seems desirable, whether it is good here and now to produce it, and then acting in accordance with whatever answer we find through deliberation. (I shall show before long how this reply is not inconsistent with his doctrine that we deliberate only on *means* to the end; see Section IX below.)

Aristotle's account of practical wisdom as concerned with good action rather than products has sometimes been equated with the view that acting well consists in performing certain kinds of action no matter what the results. This lands Aristotle in a rigid deontology quite alien to his ethics. He certainly holds that some kinds of actions have a strong claim on us: actions which are fine or whose contraries are usually shameful.[18] But it contradicts some of his best-known positions to hold that any neutrally described kind of action (let alone all the members of some set of kinds) is always right to perform.[19] That rigid deontological interpretation misses the point of his distinction between production and practice. For the distinction can be generalised so as to cover all kinds of action (however kinds are demarcated), not only productive kinds. A process of production, after all, is simply a well-defined type of action—defined in terms of the object. But action-kinds can be specified in all sorts of other ways: thus walking and running are kinds; so is ridiculing someone, greeting someone, paying a debt. The generalised point is that for any kind of action, productive or other, we can distinguish between an effective performance of it, and its being a good thing to do under given circumstances. This follows directly from Aristotle's doctrine of the mean, and it is why practical rationality is essentially deliberate. *Deliberation* decides whether to do a certain thing; the decision is never taken care of by the description of what might be done.[20]

Therefore the Grand End theory of practical wisdom can be written in two forms, in both of which it is mistaken as applied to Aristotle. Aristotle's practical wisdom is not characterised by the aim of realising a substantial conception of the unrestricted good, whether by striving on every occasion for a special kind of product (however far-reaching the product might be, as for instance the greatest happiness of the greatest number) or by always seeking to enact a certain kind of action. For however comprehensively good the kind may seem as a kind, it is not necessarily good to produce or perform it under these or those particular circumstances. In short, Aristotle's conception of ground-level practical wisdom *leaves no room* for the idea of a grand substantial vision of the good which remains constant from one situation to another and thereby acts as the deliberator's lodestar.

Hence when Aristotle says that practical wisdom, and all practical deliberation, is concerned with 'living well in general', he has to be thinking of this unrestricted good in terms of an unrestricted openness to any kind of consideration when deciding what to do. The physician's deliberations admit only medical pros and cons, the professional runner's only those concerned with running. As we noted earlier, what makes them professionals is not their focus on a special restricted good, but the restrictedness of their focus. Hence the practical agent differs not by being focused on another special sort of good that is special because unrestricted and categorically demanding, but by being focused on a restricted good (not always the same one, either) with a focus that sets no limit on the considerations that could affect which way he goes with regard to that good or to the points of view that might make a difference. It is not that he carries round a divine checklist of points of view, but, rather, in response to whatever occurs, he either adjusts his deliberation to that or he himself rules it irrelevant. This is in contrast with the craftsman, for whom some considerations are rendered automatically relevant by his very terms of reference and others automatically irrelevant. The limitless nature of prohairetic choice consists in openness to possible revision bit by bit from any quarter, not in mythical adherence to an exhaustive plan that encodes the grounds of every pro and con simultaneously and in advance.

I have just written as if the choice is necessarily formed in a temporal process of deliberation. For there is no getting round the fact that Aristotle presents the matter in this way: he says that deliberation is a 'seeking' (1142 a 32 ff.; 1112 b 20) and defines rational choice as the conclusion of deliberation (1113 a 2–5; cf. 1139 a 21 ff.). This is awkward, for reasons touched on earlier in this book (see Chapter 2, Section VI). Any sort of prohairetic response, even if only a feeling, is the work of practical intelligence, and practical intelligence often has no need to deliberate. For instance, it is a matter of intelligence to know when it is necessary or worthwhile to deliberate at all. In studying practical wisdom, Aristotle ought to be studying practical intelligence working well. Good deliberation is only one of its manifestations and should not be made the central issue. Yet he virtually defines practical wisdom as the ability to deliberate well (1142 a 32 ff.; cf. 1140 a 25 ff.).

Considerations raised earlier in this chapter help explain this bias. It is of the utmost importance to Aristotle to be able to say something about the nature of practical wisdom and the prohairetic *orthos logos*. He can characterise the moral virtues in terms of the empirical continua of kinds of action and feeling in which the mean is found. Thus courage hits the ethical mean on the fear-confidence scale. But there is no single empirical field, whether action, object, type of situation or feeling, in terms of which he can characterise the *orthos logos* which is that by reference to which the ethical responses are excessive, deficient, just right. And so Aristotle fastens on to the one conspicuous occurrence in which practical reflectiveness is sometimes shown: the temporal process of deliberation. (When there is no such process, the thought in the concrete prohairetic response is hardly to be distinguished from the response itself. So there seems to be no form in common between different responses, even by the same agent, since a practical agent's reactions are visibly different from one situation to another; unlike the craftsman he is not always, when active, engaged in the same easily identifiable kind of project.) In other words, the process of deliberation functions, I suggest, as a quasi-empirical surrogate for the form of the practical *logos*, or what all such *logoi* have in common. And perhaps in this Aristotle is not far out, because a prohairetic response, even if actually undeliberated, is always (until a dead letter) poised for possible revision; and even if not formed by actual choosing from envisaged alternatives, it expresses a kind of suspended choosing or readiness to divide, discard, regroup at the touch of new input.

In the light of the foregoing let us look briefly again at Aristotle's ambivalence about craft deliberation. It is important for him, especially in *NE* III, that craft deliberates, because there he illustrates practical deliberation with examples from craft. But it also important that deliberation is not central and perhaps not even necessary to our general conception of a craft. Such and such a kind of craftsman is one who is good at producing so and so's, whether deliberation enters into it or not. When there is a recognisable product constantly and more or less successfully aimed at, the craft-activity can be characterised just by reference to that. This highlights the fact that for practical reason there is no such characterisation. That very lack is what characterises practical reason. But it cannot be characterised *just* in terms of a lack. In insisting that practical wisdom deliberates, Aristotle is trying to give it a distinctive face which he hopes that we can recognise.[21]

The lengthy and often, no doubt, frustrating discussion carried on in the last few sections has brought us to a view of Aristotle's grounds for breaking with the Socratic and Platonic tradition whereby practical wisdom is conceived as a kind of craft. We have also seen how the power of that tradition lives on in his refusal at several crucial points to abandon the analogy with craft, even while preparing to expound fundamental differences. But the discussion has left largely unsettled some difficult questions engendered by the analogy and raised above at the beginning of Section II and in Section III of this chapter. What is the relation between practical wisdom's formal end and the substantial end that guides particular deliberation? And given that bad as well as good individuals are practical deliberators, and often effective ones, what distinguishes their deliberations? The Grand End theory answers both questions neatly. It says that the guiding end is, so to speak, a definition of the formal good— i.e., a substantial comprehensive universally relevant account of what it consists in— and that morally good and bad deliberators are guided by different such definitions. But these answers fail if, as I argued in Section IV, the Grand End theory fails. I shall be able to confront the unsolved questions from a better position after exploring Aristotle's comparison of practical with theoretic wisdom and his views on deliberative thought and practical intelligence. These topics will take up most of the rest of this chapter. We turn first to the relation of thought and desire in rational choice.

## VI.  Thought and Desire in Rational Choice

We divided the excellences of the soul and said that some are excellences of character and others of intellect. Now we have discussed the moral excellences; with regard to the others let us express our view as follows, beginning with some remarks about the soul. We said before that there are two parts of the soul—that which possesses reason and that which is irrational; let us now draw a similar distinction within the part which possesses reason. And let it be assumed that there are two parts which possess reason—one by which we contemplate the kind of things whose principles cannot be otherwise, and one by which we contemplate variable things; for where objects differ in kind that part of the soul answering to each of the two is different in kind, since it is in virtue of a certain likeness and kinship with their objects that they have the knowledge they have. Let one of these parts be called the scientific and the other the calculative; for to deliberate and to calculate are the same thing, but no one deliberates about what cannot be otherwise. Therefore the calculative is one part of the faculty which possesses reason. We must, then, learn what is the best state of each of these two parts; for this is the excellence of each. (1138 b 35–1139 a 17)

Here for the first time Aristotle departs from his division of the distinctively human soul into rational and reason-responsive elements, and offers a new subdivision of the rational into practical and theoretic. This raises a question. What notice should the student of ethics take of the theoretic part? Should he leave it on one side much as he leaves on one side the nonrational powers of sense perception in which we resemble other animals, and the capacity for nutrition which is universal to living things? The inquiry up to this point has proceeded largely on the assumption that *practical* activity is what is characteristically human. Aristotle now reminds us that the rational capacity to contemplate and think theoretically is just as fundamental to human nature as its practical counterpart. So, since ethics is concerned with the distinctively human good, ethics may have to set its sights beyond mere excellence in practice. And since the soul, however complex, is a unity, not a concatenation of independently describable parts, we should perhaps be prepared eventually to find that just as practical wisdom cannot be understood without reference to the emotional part that is conditioned into character, and just as the virtues of the latter cannot be understood without reference to the *orthos logos* of practical wisdom, so practical wisdom in the end makes sense only in terms of some relation to theoretic activity.

For the present, however, these themes are strictly in the background. Aristotle's chief concern in the passage before us is to show in what ways the ethical *orthos logos* differs from its theoretic counterpart and at the same time to take advantage for ethics of the very resemblance that necessitates this distinction. Plato had held, for instance in the *Phaedo,* that reason or intellect is concerned with the eternal Forms and with sensible particulars only so far as these present themselves to the reminiscent eye as reminders of those archetypes. Thus practical life in the world of change is part of the dream from which, to the philosopher of the *Phaedo,* death is the longed-for awakening. To the possible objection that it cannot then matter how we live in this world, Socrates replies, in effect, that the soul which mostly dreams in this life is nonetheless itself eternal, and so even in this life can prepare itself for complete repossession of its eternal inheritance by withdrawing into rational contemplation—which is nothing but practising death in advance. In the *Republic,* however, Plato came to hold that under ideal political conditions philosophers would govern the affairs of cities from knowledge of the Forms and their relation to the supreme Form of the Good. This admission of philosophy into the realm of practice may be an advance over the earlier position, but it is less coherent theoretically. The *Republic* poses a famous practical problem: how, except under utopian conditions, can the philosopher's knowledge of the Good take practical effect; and how can those utopian conditions be created except from conditions already ideal? But this is nothing by comparison with the problem of how, if reason's proper concern is with eternal verities, reason can be conceived as bearing on changeable things at all. How can reason take account of them except peripherally, as imperfect adumbrations of the objects of rational contemplation? And what room is there here for practical knowledge, if knowledge is the privilege of reason and reason's objects are eternal? The Platonic Form of the Good, even though in some sense supremely good, is not a practicable end. It already necessarily exists and cannot be increased or diminished.

On such an account, no practicable good can be an object of *reason,* and practice even at its best is no true expression of our rational nature. This last conclusion is inescapable unless we recognise a function of reason distinct from that concerned with the eternal and necessary. Hence that practice is ever an activity of reason is a proposition which it would be more logical of Plato to deny than to affirm. The *Phaedo* verges towards denial, while the *Republic* opts for a resounding, though confused, affirmation: confused, because inseparable from Plato's insistence that the ideal city is governed by the only kind of reason that Plato at this stage was able clearly to contrast with sense perception and floating opinion. Yet that very mistake of Plato's speaks for the kinship, at some level, of theoretical reason with the faculty that governs practical life, despite the fact that the latter's domain falls within the field of Platonic *opinion.*

A related mistake is to think that because the objects of practical reason are contingent, they are simply a subdivision of the objects of Platonic opinion; and that 'practical reason', therefore, is a name for a kind of opinion. Objects of Platonic opinion are perhaps best characterised in terms of their failure to be suitable objects of scientific knowledge. As Aristotle says, 'when they have passed out of our view, we are unable to tell whether they exist or not' (1139 b 21–22). How can science build itself, in the systematic way that makes it *science,* unless it can take for granted that what on any one occasion it has found to be true remains true when the mind passes on to that truth's roots or ramifications? The objects of Aristotelian practical reason, however, are human actions, and their contingency is the contingency of what depends on the agent *to do or not to do.* When the soul affirms as real the objects of Platonic opinion, this affirmation, for Plato, manifests not the soul's excellence and power, but its enslavement to illusion. But when affirmation is of some action at the soul's command *to perform or not to perform*—the affirmation here being the decision to make real by *doing*—then the soul exhibits not its weakness but its strength to realise values worthy of itself even under the shifting conditions of sensory existence. To dignify such an act by the title 'rational' is not to degrade the title, but to recognise its true scope as applying to what is neither the contemplation of eternal objects nor a degenerate version of this on the level of sense experience. In recognising the distinct nature of practical reason, Aristotle corrects but also preserves Plato's conviction that the conduct of human affairs is a proper task for the highest human faculty.

But the recognition is hard won, and it requires strenuous explanation. Aristotle must show how Platonic epistemology overlooks a *tertium quid* that is neither sense perception (along with judgments about sensory objects as such) nor knowledge of the eternal. He begins by observing that 'there are three things in the soul which control action *(praxis)* and [the attainment of] truth—sensation, thought *(nous)*, desire *(orexis)'* (1139 a 17–18). But the role of sensation is subordinate, since, as he goes on, 'of these, sensation originates no action *(praxis);* this is plain from the fact that beasts have sensation, but no share in action' (18–20). Consideration of brutes also shows, as Aristotle's general psychology makes clear, that sensation and animal desire are intrinsically connected (see, e.g., *On the Soul* 414 b 1–15; 431 a 12–14; *Movement of Animals* 700 b 16–25). Thus the three divisions of the passage just quoted are not mutually exclusive. Just as sensation entails animal desire (whose contribution, if any, to human action would also be subordinate), so we should expect that thought and intellect, too, are involved with a kind of desire, i.e., a kind of desiderative tendency that works itself out through physical change.[22] Aristotle now brings thought and desire together:

> What affirmation and negation are in thinking, pursuit and avoidance are in desire; so that since moral excellence is a state concerned with choice, and choice [*prohairesis*] is deliberate desire, therefore both the *logos* must be true and the desire right, if the choice is to be good, and the latter must pursue just what the former asserts. Now this kind of intellect and [kind of] truth is practical; of the intellect which is contemplative, not practical nor productive, the good and the bad state are truth and falsity (for this is the function of everything intellectual); while of the part which is practical and intellectual the good state is truth in agreement with right desire. (1139 a 21–31; cf. *On the Soul* 431 a 8–11)

Is Aristotle identifying rational choice as a compound or synthesis of two psychological elements, one belonging to the sphere of thought, the other to that of desire; or as a single act that may be viewed either as a thought (or judgment) or as a desire? Coming to this passage from modern ethics, we may be tempted to see the *logos* or judgment as an assertion of fact (e.g., that this action would have this result) and the evaluative aspect of choice as the function of a separate noncognitive faculty of desire or feeling.[23] This is the division that a philosopher such as Hume would approve, and we may be further reminded of Hume by Aristotle's statement a few lines on: 'Thought by itself moves nothing; it is a source of movement only when it is for the sake of something and practical' (1139 a 35–36). But the resemblance is only skin deep. Aristotle means that thought is not in general the source of an actual change, since a craftsman's thought (not to speak of that of a theoretical thinker) is not, as such, an unconditional spring of action (see Chapter 2, Section VII). Thus Aristotle goes on: 'For *practical* thought rules craft too' (1139 b 1). Hume's is quite a different point: that it is not in the nature of any kind of thought to be practical at all.

On a Humean view of the psychology of action, choice is the product of two faculties which can be defined independently of each other and each other's objects. Choice of a means A to an end R is a desire for A grounded in a desire (or "passion") for R and mediated by the purely cognitive judgment that A will lead to R. Desire is for what is useful or agreeable (or for avoidance of their opposites), while reason is concerned only with judgments of fact and relations between ideas. Reason's deliverances are, in themselves, 'disengaged' (*Second Enquiry,* Appendix I, §246); they are the 'cool and indolent judgments of the understanding' (*Treatise,* III. I. 1). Thus motives and evaluative attitudes have their source in some faculty external to reason. Reason, according to this view, provides knowledge useful for practice, but it is not on that account *practical reason.* For although it so happens that reason's products—knowledge and true beliefs—are sometimes useful for directing action so as to realise desires, it is not the *nature* of reason to supply its products for this purpose, any more than to withhold them; its concern with them is only as *truths* whether factual or a priori.

The nearest evidence for its not being this position which Aristotle endorses lies in his statements (1) that desire's pursuit of its object is equivalent to affirmation in the sphere of thought, and (2) that in rational choice what is affirmed and what is pursued are *the same.* Whatever exactly his meaning, it cannot be accommodated to a theory that parcels out thought and motivation between separate faculties. If thought can only affirm such things as that A will lead to R, then the pursuit of either R or A as desirable is not an affirmation by desire of *what* is affirmed by thought. Nor (conversely) can thought affirm the *same* as what desire affirms in pursuing its object as desirable. It belongs, moreover, to the Humean view to insist that even if the term 'desirable' can be brought within the scope of thought and indeed of reason, something logically external would still be needed to supply motivation. This is not meant to apply merely to weak-willed agents: it is a universal claim based on the Humean analysis of agency as such. The point is that even if there are "value-facts" for thought to grasp in one or another of the cognitive ways in which it grasps ordinary facts or abstract relations, this would still have no intrinsic bearing on practice. The evaluative terms that figure in such a thought cannot in that context represent what Aristotle calls the *'prakton agathon':* the good not merely as realizable, but as *to be* realised through action. On the Humean view, 'good' or 'desirable' in such a context stands only for an observed or contemplated quality of something. It does not make the thought in which it appears any more practical than a thought cast in purely descriptive terms.

In a sense it is true, on the view which originates with Hume, that desire and thought have the same object when they come together in action. For desire desires to perform some action or to bring about some result, and thought makes an intrinsically nonpractical affirmation about the very same action or result: e.g., that it will cause or be caused by so and so. But this analysis does not fit Aristotle's account. The analysis allows that thought and desire refer to the same object—this object being the logical subject of the thought; but Aristotle says more than this. He speaks of desiderative pursuit of an object not as a kind of yearning *reference* to that object, but as analogous to *affirmation.* However (as Aristotle knows very well) one cannot affirm the logical subject of a thought. For example, a declarative judgment does not affirm its subject; it affirms its subject to be so and so (it predicates something *of* it). Hence if pursuit of an object is an affirmation, pursuit must affirm the object to be so and so. Presumably it is an affirmation to the effect that the object is desirable or ought to be pursued. But then, if thought makes a purely factual affirmation about the object, it is not the case that thought, as Aristotle claims, affirms *the same* as what desire affirms by pursuit. Desire's pursuit will be a different affirmation, since although its subject is the same, what is affirmed will be different.

Taken strictly, therefore, Aristotle must mean that thought, like desire, affirms of the chosen action that it is good or desirable in a practical way, or in short that it is to be done. And when he says that in a good choice the thought-affirmation (the *logos*) must be true *(alethēs)* and the desire-affirmation right *(orthē)*, it is clear that he has none of the qualms that we might feel about applying the notion of 'truth' to what does not purport to be a purely factual assertion. But it would be a mistake to think him a simpleton in this area. True, he does not have the legacy of Hume to contend with; but he cannot ignore the legacy of Platonism. This is the Platonism of the *Republic,* where the only real truth is truth about entities factually "there" in the strongest possible sense—namely, eternal entities. To a Platonist, the affirmation that a particular contingent action is right or good cannot count as *true:* not because (as for Hume) this is an evaluation, but because its subject is a transient thing.

This exposition suggests that in rational choice the thought that A is to be done is identical with the impulse to pursue A as desirable. For how are we to discriminate the 'Yes' of practical thought and the 'Yes' of desire when what is affirmed is the same? So is Aristotle's statement that thought must affirm the same as what desire pursues simply a way of saying that these are the same act? This does not quite fit his remark 'They must agree' (1139 a 29–31), which implies harmony, hence not identity. But really there is no contradiction. We are bound to think of rational choice as a composite product of thought and desire when we view it in terms of its roots in different parts of the soul; but the concrete product itself is a natural unity of complementary aspects. The prohairetic agent confronts his situation in a state of general orectic readiness to do whatever he intellectually sees to be appropriate, and practical thinking provides the determinate *logos* that converts this into a definite *orexis.* His choice to do A is a good *prohairesis* if and only if two conditions are satisfied: (1) the *logos* or thought that A is right or good to do is *true;* (2) the general orectic readiness is *right (orthē),* i.e., ready to accept (and so be determined by) the correct *logos,* whatever it might be.

On this theory, the motivation (or drive) *to do* what thought or reason specifies is presupposed in advance of the specification.[24] Thus the motivation to do the chosen action A does not spring, as the Humean view would have it, from an independent desire for some remote but definite object O, which desire is then channelled towards an action which reason presents as causally conducive to O. Thought or reason, on that view, contributes nothing to motivation; its only function is to show a way to bridge the causal gap between agent and object. On the Aristotelian account, reason contributes to the motivation itself; not by providing the *drive* (impossible for Aristotle as for Hume), but by giving the drive direction. For without a definite direction, it cannot motivate anything. The drive, or general orectic readiness, is reflected in the question 'What am I to do?' as asked by a person who wants the answer so as to act on it. This question holds out a prescription-shaped variable, so to speak; the answer is a value offered by reason in reply. This presentation of a determinate prescription is not initiated on the side that gives the answer, but on the side that poses that form of question. Thus reason prescribes, but only in the sense that it fills a blank prescription form held out to it by the nonrational part of the ethical soul. But at this point Aristotle's division of the soul no longer makes sense except as a reminder that the same thing can be viewed from different perspectives. Insofar as the nonrational part's indeterminate readiness is expressed by the question 'What am I to do?' the readiness is that of a rational being qua rational. For it is the task of reason (conceived according to the standard division) to find an answer to the question; and the capacity to answer is not separate from the capacity for asking.

We can understand the unity of the soul in rational choice in terms of the formal fit of answer to question. This angle, however, takes in the prescription but not its grounds. If we now consider the grounds, and especially the factual judgments, particular and general, on which the prescriptive answer is founded, we find here, too, a community of parts of the soul. In the first place, the factual judgments and the determinate prescription grounded on them are both works of thought or reason: both have articulate conceptual content. Second, Aristotle's metaphysics and general psychology point to an underlying generic continuity between the kinds of affirmation involved: some factual and one prescriptive. According to Aristotle's natural teleology, the perceptual capacities of an animal are geared to its needs. Hence particular exercises of these capacities must in general be so geared; which means that the creature sees, hears, or takes sensory notice, in ways naturally suited to generate just those particular directed impulses that ensure its well-being under the circumstances. Aristotle surely sees human desire and cognition in similar teleological terms.

Particular practical prescriptions, and the factual judgments on which they are based, vary with the situation, but on all occasions the same interlocking capacities are at work to form a structure of practical argument with premises and conclusion: 'Since these are the circumstances, I should do this'. Particulars are observed; observations interpreted; experience and knowledge of general patterns invoked; aspects of particulars are found relevant or irrelevant in the light of these general patterns. Such operations are necessary in theoretical contexts too; for instance, if one wishes to understand a particular phenomenon in terms of its causes and to see it as instantiating a universal pattern which those causes express. But for now we are concerned with these mental operations only so far as they occur in response to the need to *decide what to do.* In this context they themselves are practical in nature, even though the finished products which represent them are factual assertions. As I have already had occasion to point out (Chapter 2, Section III), it is not as if the agent's agenthood is expressed only in his prescriptive affirmation, whereas in affirming the factual premises he functions as a nonpractical, purely cognitive, subject. In the light of his desiderative interests and general beliefs, an agent scans his circumstances for factual particulars suggesting a line of action. In the light, again, of his interests, general beliefs are activated that might have a practical bearing on observed particulars. He may check his facts, particular or general, but not from the wish for knowledge as such; what is checked, and how far, depends on his particular practical concerns, and on their general nature *as* practical. Thus he attends to those aspects of things and events whereby they are most quickly recognised or effectively controlled and adjusted to: these aspects are the practical essences, so to speak, and would coincide only by chance with those philosophically celebrated theoretical essences in terms of which nature becomes intelligible to the scientist. Thunder for the practical agent is not the 'quenching of fire in the clouds', but the sign to run for shelter.

Theoretical and practical reason are alike for Aristotle in fundamental ways, as we shall see. The capacities may even be the same for both. But the modes of employment are not the same, and there is no single set of fact-gathering activities whose harvest can be used indifferently for theoretical and practical purposes. Fact-gathering in the context of practice is adjusted to the general demands of practice even *before* the agent has decided exactly what to do. Hence the nonprescriptive components of practical arguments must be considered results of *practical* thinking. In this, they are closer kin to the prescriptive conclusions of those same arguments than they are to theoretical affirmations of fact.

'There is thunder' is not in itself specifically action-guiding, since one may respond with different actions to the same facts; but it is not on that account, as Hume would have it, 'indolent' and 'disengaged'. To be not yet engaged in any particular line of action in response to fact F is not to be disengaged from action; especially when the grasping of F takes place for the sake of the agent's doing whatever would be appropriate (it is not yet determined what) in the light of it. We easily overlook this teleological unity of nonprescriptive with prescriptive practical affirmations, because of the modern obsession with justification. Factual assertions, even in the practical context, remain subject to well-canvassed types of verification appropriate to the type of fact: particular or general, empirical or a priori. But a prescription founded on them embodies an evaluation, hence cannot be fully and squarely founded on them. For a prescription cannot be verified, and it cannot be upheld purely by those procedures. If types are distinguished by method of justification, the prescription is a creature of alien type.

How moral evaluations can be rationally justified at all is the leading problem of classical modern ethics. In this regard, Aristotle's moral philosophy is remote and offers no answers, for he does not confront that radical question. This may seem a severe limitation, and there is a temptation to seek to explain it by the assumption that Aristotle speaks in and for a morally homogeneous circle unriven by the dissensions that lend credibility to moral scepticism and moral relativism. How far this cosy picture fits the historical facts would be a question for treatment elsewhere. We can, however, point out that moral scepticism is backed by a variety of inspirations, one of which is a tendency to apply to the field of practice an epistemology developed in connection with the sciences. Aristotle, though, does not start from the dogma that the only respectable sorts of cognition are those which feed the sciences. Consequently he is able to ignore what for us is the glaring disparity between prescriptive conclusion and factual premises in a practical argument. Thus in *NE* VI he is happy to call even the conclusion 'true' (or 'false', as the case may be). Being not much interested in a difference which is fundamental, perhaps, for our epistemology but not so important for his, Aristotle freely deploys a functionally grounded conception of *practical truth* (1139 a 25–31). As 'truth', it applies even to prescriptions; and as 'practical', even to their factual premises.

## VII. 'Practical Truth'

We are concerned with rational choice or *prohairesis* as the point in which deliberation culminates and from which action should begin.

> For every one ceases to inquire how he is to act when he has brought the moving principle back to himself and to the ruling part of himself; for this is what chooses. (1113 a 5–7; cf. 1112 b 23–24, 1226 b 13–14; and 1227 a 16–18)

> The end aimed at is, then, the starting-point of our thought, the end of our thought the starting-point of action. (1227 b 32–33)

Rational choice is the prescriptive conclusion of a practical argument some of whose premisses are factual. (The nonfactual premiss, which presents the end-for-the-sake-of-which, we shall consider later, having already dismissed one conception of it when dealing with the Grand End theory.) The connection of rational choice with deliberation and argument prompts the ever tempting comparison with craft; but, more important now, it upholds the claim of practice to be considered a genuine sphere of reason alongside the theoretical. Happiness was defined as the exercise of reason in accordance with excellence, and excellence has all along so far been understood as practical. In *NE* VI Aristotle has the task of showing how these notions—*reason* and *practice*—knit together to form the core of a coherent notion of happiness.

In rational choice, thought converges with desire, and rational choice must be understood under both aspects. Thus Aristotle calls choice 'either desiderative thought or intellectual desire' (1139 b 4–5). He has to work to secure the identity of this concept. Rational choice is not simply thought, since not all thought is a source of movement (1139 a 35–36). It is not straightforwardly any kind of desire, because the forms of desire are appetite *(epithumia)*, temper *(thumos)* and wish *(boulēsis)*, and rational choice is none of these (1225 b 18–1226 a 19; 1111 b 10–29). It is neither of the first two, because they have a different origin, being essentially expressions of the nonrational part of the soul unmoderated by reason. It is not wish, although it is closely related to wish, because we wish for things at a practical distance and even for what is impossible. But the object of rational choice is the action finally specified by deliberation: between us and the doing of it there is no distance requiring further deliberation to overcome. Choice is not opinion *(doxa)* either, since the objects of opinion can be anything you like, but the possible objects of rational choice are only those over which it make sense for us to deliberate: matters which we see as contingent and in our power (1112 a 18 ff.; 1226 a 26–30). The connection with deliberation is borne out by the word: a choice is a *prohairesis,* the preference of something over something else, which implies weighing up alternatives (1112 a 16–17; 1226 b 7–9). Rational choice is a 'deliberative desire' (1113 a 10–11; 1139 a 23).

In the last section I argued that the combination of thought and desire in rational choice is not the combination of a desire for some objective with the factual judgment that such and such an action would lead to it. Instead, I argued, thought specifies a particular action as what is to be done, and the desiderative element is a willing acceptance to do whatever is specified. Thus thought and desire together affirm a prescription: thought affirms it in response to the need for guidance on the part of the desiderative side, and desire affirms it by way of acceptance. And Aristotle says that when the prescription is a good one, the soul is in possession of 'practical truth' (1139 a 24–31).

What are we to make of this notion of truth? We can understand how 'truth', even with the addition of 'practical', applies to the factual premises of a practical argument; but how can we understand it as applying to the prescriptive conclusion? Truth, surely, is the value which a statement has if and only if things are as they are stated to be;[25] but a prescription does not state. Aristotle cannot mean that the prescription is semantically true. So does he mean no more than that it is good, right or appropriate? And does he lack the vocabulary to say this without falling back on the word 'true'? For instance, why is it not enough to say that the good rational choice is right (*orthē;* cf. 1144 a 20)?

He has chosen the term 'true' precisely to make the point that practice like theory is an exercise of reason, its success a success of reason. He says that truth is the business of 'everything intellectual' (1139 a 29) and that truth is the business of both intellectual parts of the soul; so their respective virtues are the states that will best enable them to arrive at the truth (1139 b 12–13). Since the business of practical reason evidently is to reach good practical conclusions (i.e., rational choices), there can be no doubt that Aristotle thinks that the truth sought by practical reason is the truth of such conclusions, as well as of the factual premisses in practical arguments.

Since his use of 'true' in these passages is anything but casual, let us probe it a bit. Again, we are reminded (by contrast) of Hume, who also held that truth is the concern of reason and reason alone. But Hume had in mind factual and mathematical truths, and he made this the basis of his famous argument that value-judgments cannot be true because if they could they would not be practical or action-guiding. For him, then, 'practical truth' is a contradiction in terms. So, for that matter, is 'rational prescription'; for, if reason is concerned only with 'the knowledge of truth and falsehood' and 'true' and 'false' do not apply to prescriptions, then no prescription can be *rationally* preferred to any other. None is better *grounded* than any other, since the notion of rational grounding does not apply. For Hume then (anyway by implication), a prescription or choice cannot be the conclusion of any kind of argument. It may be the upshot of a process which we call 'practical deliberation'; but practical deliberation, on this view, is not a kind of reasoning.

So does Aristotle think, as Hume appears to, that *being rationally grounded* applies only to truths and their negations; and does he therefore try to save the rationality of practical decisions by speaking of them here as 'true'? But is he not aware (as apparently Hume is not) that reason is concerned with rational connections in general, not only with connections between true/false propositions: so that if a premiss set contains a prescriptive element, a prescriptive conclusion may follow or be grounded, even though it is neither true nor false? And if Aristotle believes that rational connections are possible only between bearers of truth-value, is he not committed to the view—absurd, surely—that the truth of a practical conclusion is truth in some single sense of 'truth' that presumably applies to all the premisses, including those which are factual statements? But how can prescriptions be not only *true,* in some sense of that word that deserves to be taken seriously, but true in the same sense as factual statements? For factual statements are true if and only if they state what is the case, and statements of what is the case are not, as such, prescriptive.[26]

It may be thought unreasonable and ungrateful to expect Aristotle's moves in this area to be as subtle and precise as these highly academic questions suggest they should be. Thanks to Aristotle, the foundations of a theory of practical reason were laid, even if his terminology leaves something to be desired. This kindly attitude assumes, however, that his use of 'true' in the present context is careless, woolly, arbitrary or somehow deviant. But, as I shall now seek to show by standards internal to the argument, his use of 'true' falls short in none of these ways.

It arouses suspicion in the modern philosophical reader, probably because this reader endorses the semantic conception, which restricts 'true' to statements. That endorsement probably springs from the belief that this is the only precise conception of truth available to philosophers. This belief not only draws strength from the fact that the conception in question can be captured in formally precise terms, but is further bolstered by our concern about justification: a concern which leads us to equate *truth* with *truth verifiable by the methods of science and mathematics.* The suspicious modern reader will either find fault with Aristotle in *NE* VI for endorsing a different and sloppier notion of truth, or else will assume that he, too, works from the semantic conception but tries to force it beyond the point where he should have let it go and stopped talking about truth altogether.

The following lines may foster the impression that Aristotle means 'true' here semantically:

> Both the *logos* [sc. in choice] must be true and the desire right, if the choice is to be good, and the latter must pursue just what the former asserts. Now this kind of intellect [*dianoia*] and [kind] of truth is practical. Of the intellect which is contemplative [*theoretikēs*], not practical nor productive, the good and bad state are truth and falsity (for this is the function of everything intellectual); while of the part that is practical and intellectual the good state is truth in agreement with right desire. (1139 a 23–31)

This seems to imply that theoretic reason aims at the truth in the strict or most proper sense of that word. For the passage says that the objective of *theōria* is truth, without qualification, whereas it calls the practical analogue of this not 'truth' but 'a *kind of* truth [that is] practical', or 'practical truth'. So it is as if he says that theoretic truth is not one sort of truth, distinguished as theoretical, but is simply *truth.* If so, then the qualifying term 'practical' in the phrase 'truth [that is] practical' does not mark off a genuine species of generic truth, but says that so-called practical truth is truth in some sense logically deviant or secondary. Thus when in the last sentence Aristotle says 'truth is the function of everything intellectual' he seems to imply that practical intellect has a share in truth not because it is concerned with generically the same attribute, but because its object imperfectly resembles or is in some other way related to the single genuine truth that concerns the theoretic intellect alone.

This interpretation is tempting for those who assume that truth proper is semantic truth, because their assumption primes them to read into the text a distinction between this and a deviant sense of 'true'. However, the interpretation also depends on another assumption: that Aristotle takes knowledge of semantic truths to be the goal of theoretic activity. That this is an assumption may go unnoticed, since prejudice combined with the principle of charity makes this very passage tell in its favour. The presumption that truth is really semantic leads one to view practical truth as deviant and to suppose that Aristotle views it with like suspicion; so when we find him apparently equating theoretic truth with the norm, we read this as evidence that *theōria,* for him, is concerned with semantic truth.

But the text warrants none of this. There is no compelling reason to see in it an Aristotelian distinction between strict and deviant senses of 'truth'. The fact that Aristotle designates the object of theoretic activity 'truth' without qualification does not entail that he regards it as 'truth without qualification' (which phrase would demarcate a strict as compared with a deviant sense). The reason, I believe, why he adds no qualification is that he sees no need to explain or prove to his audience that theoretic reason seeks truth. This is a platitude. But, as with other platitudes, those who take it for granted do not necessarily have a definite view about the meanings and extensions of the terms. They are not, for example, obliged to hold that 'seeking truth' means something that will turn out to be strictly applicable only to theorising. Aristotle here takes theorising as the most obvious kind of truth-seeking, but he is free to develop the idea that there is another kind, less obvious but no less genuine. In marking this off as 'practical', he merely indicates its difference from the more familiar species of the genus.

What, then, is the genus of which theoretic truth is one species and practical another? The answer must be based on Aristotle's conception of the case most obvious to his audience, and for this we turn to the *Posterior Analytics,* which Aristotle expects to be familiar to readers of his *Ethics* (cf. 1139 b 26–33). Here he explains what the goal is of theoretic activity and how it is achieved. The aim is scientific knowledge *(epistēmē),* and scientific knowledge is understanding and being able to explain general facts in terms of their causes.[27] We start by taking ourselves to know that something is the case, and we then seek to understand and explain it by reference to first principles from which it follows syllogistically. One who has an adequate syllogism at his command is said to be able to 'demonstrate' the fact to be explained, and this demonstrative grasp *(epistēmē)* is grasp of truth. Having the truth about a fact is having the explanation; it is not having grounds or evidence *that* the fact obtains.[28]

Since the goal of reason in its paradigm form is not to grasp semantically true propositions nor even to be assured that they are thus true, but to understand and explain, there is no basis for imagining that Aristotle downgrades practical truth because it is not semantic or that he struggles to make practical truth respectable by extending the semantic notion to prescriptions. His conception of truth as the objective of theoretical science provides no ground for supposing that in *NE* VI he sees *practical* truth as truth of a kind less thoroughbred than the truth sought by a scientist.

But we still have to identify what is in common. Narrow adherence to the theoretical model would yield the ludicrous picture of practical reason (deliberation) as starting with an ungrounded impulse to behave in a certain way, for which one then seeks explanatory reasons. An agent would exercise intelligence only in attempting to understand his own behaviour as a spectator might and not at all in the forming of that behaviour. Nor could he seek to understand his own behaviour in the way in which he might seek to understand someone else's intelligent action. For it would not *be* intelligent action, if *his* intelligence is at work only in the effort to understand it as a given. Instead of assuming that truth in general has to do with explanation and understanding or any other obvious feature of the theoretical case, we should take it that 'truth' here means nothing other than *whatever* is the business of reason to seek, according to the kind of reasoning. For the theorist, truth is a scientific explanation; for the ethical deliberator, it is a good rational choice; for the craftsman (covered by Aristotle's statement at 1139 b 15–17), it is the right technical decision.

To say that a good rational choice is practical truth is not to explain the nature of rational choice or of the relevant type of reasoning, since 'practical truth' simply means 'what practical reason aims at'. But this is disappointing only if we expect 'practical truth' to mean something that would justify the claim of practical reason to count as a genuine kind of reason. Aristotle, however, is not defensive on this score. He writes as if he need only call attention to practical reason for us to accept it as what it is. And it is important for him to speak of *truth* in this connection, not merely of *the good, right* or *appropriate,* because these terms also apply to the non-rational infrastructure of rational choice. The *truth* of a choice is its distinctive excellence as an articulate product of *thought,* whereas 'right' simply rates it as excellent without differentiation, or else, more narrowly (as at 1144 a 20), points to its *moral* goodness.

The foregoing interpretation of 'practical truth' stresses what is common to theoretic and practical reason at the expense of treating semantic truth as irrelevant for the interpretation. But I now call attention to another account which exploits a notion akin to the semantic. While rational choices (and the enacted choices of craftsmen) cannot *be* semantically true, it is of their nature to bring about the semantic truth of a statement to the effect that the envisaged change took place. For such a statement to be made true, external circumstances must not interfere with the action or give grounds for reconsidering the choice; and the agent must be nonrationally disposed to *do* what his thought dictates. So far, the 'truth', in this quasi-semantic sense, of an effective choice owes nothing to thought or reason. Hence the concept fails to explain why Aristotle aligns the rational choice, in respect of its truth, with the truth sought by theoretic *reason.* So far as enactment of the choice depends on the agent, its quasi-semantic truth (when enacted) is not a quality of the choice as a rational conclusion, but results from his standing by it instead of abandoning it incontinently. Truth in this sense is a function of character rather than reason or intellect. But in the passages under discussion Aristotle is not concerned with incontinence or its absence, but with practical *reason*'s contribution to a good choice.

Nevertheless, we can shape this quasi-semantic account to the present context by adding the thought that the clarity and coherence of a choice—intellectual achievements both—do contribute to the agent's success in getting done what he intends. These qualities of choice involve a clear grasp of the factual truths (in the straightforward semantic sense) of his situation. A similar point also holds for the theoretical thinker, since the premises by which he explains the phenomenon must at least be true in that sense. On the other hand, the semantic truth of the theoretic conclusion (which qua conclusion presents the explanation as now explained) is not a function of its status as conclusion: what is now a conclusion began life as an isolated proposition whose semantic truth was assumed. By contrast, the quasi-semantic truth (the effectedness) of a clear rational choice made under the right external and moral conditions certainly owes something to its being the conclusion of a practical argument with true premises giving features of the situation. For the choice was effective largely because it was formed in view of the circumstances.

It follows (embarrassingly for our earlier preconceptions) that the semantic conception of truth sheds less light on the nature of the goal of theoretic activity than its quasi-semantic cousin sheds on the goal of practical reason! This is because the theoretical product (the conclusion seen as following from the premises) is not made semantically true by the explanatory process that yields it. In short, if we explain 'practical truth' in terms of the quasi-semantic truth of effective rational choice, we make *theoretical* truth anomalous—it being neither quasi-semantic nor semantic! Such an account cannot do justice to the generic resemblance claimed by Aristotle for the different branches of reason. Another and conclusive objection is this: for a rational choice to be quasi-semantically true, it need only be fortunate, resolute and clear; it need not also be virtuous. But Aristotle is explicit that practical truth is the attribute of a *good* choice[29] (1139 a 25; 30–31). Practical truth is the intellectually particularised response of the *virtuous* agent;[30] and, for this, 'clarity is not enough'.

The quasi-semantic account of 'practical truth' all the same draws attention to something important. Although the objective of practical reason is good rational choice, its ultimate objective is good action. This is logically inevitable, since the choice is a choice to act, and one works out what is the right choice so as to act on it, thereby acting rightly. Hence although, as I have argued, 'practical truth' simply means good rational choice and does not mean the quasi-semantic truth of any choice, good or bad, these two concepts of truth are closely connected. An agent is not virtuous in a practical way unless he wills the good; thus the excellence of a good rational choice depends in part on its author's concern that it be effective. Thus practical truth as I have expounded it entails the corresponding quasi-semantic truth, except when the agent is weak or finds reason to change his mind, or when unforeseen circumstances nullify the action.

## VIII. The Works of Reason

Just as theoretic reason works to convert an initially brute fact into a fact intelligible to a mind seeking understanding, so it is the work of practical reason to convert the agent's particular situation into elements of a realised good action. The scientific inquirer is confronted by the fact that all S is P; being a theoriser, he looks for a middle term, M, such that once he knows that all S is M and all M is P, he understands why S is P. The practical inquirer tries to identify a possible determinate action, the doing of which would render his circumstances, C, circumstances under which the practicable good or best is achieved. The chosen action (call it 'A') is like the theoretical middle term because it is selected as mediating in practical fashion between the agent's situation and his objective. The precise sense in which this is so will become clear in this section. Meanwhile, we can say in a general way what A has in common with M, the theoretical middle term: in either case, the success of the rational project depends on intelligent selection of the middle term. To select the theoretical middle, M, is to perceive M as the term common to a suitable pair of propositions entailing that all S is P; and to select A, the practical middle, is to accept the prescription to do A as grounded in relevant features of the situation. These grounding features will be the agent's reasons for choosing and doing A. Thus in each case the act of selection in which the search culminates is also the act of formulating an argument from premises to conclusion. But the direction of interest runs in opposite ways. For the theoretic search begins from what, when it ends, will figure as *conclusion* of the scientifically explanatory argument; whereas deliberative seeking starts from propositions (descriptions of the circumstances, for example) some of which will appear in the completed practical argument as *premises*. In both cases an argument (i.e., something having the *form* of an argument) is *sought* by reason. In the case of theory, we call this argument an explanation. But it is not so clear what name we should give to the practical argument sought by deliberation. It is not an explanation or justification of something which the agent was already going to do, in the way in which the scientific argument explains an already recognized fact. The practical argument, rather, is an explanation or justification of the prescription formed as conclusion *of that argument;* and the prescription points to an action which the agent would probably *not* have performed if he had not come to be in possession of the argument that gives him reason to perform it.

There is much more to be said about parallels and differences between the two kinds of reason, but first I must counter a misconception. I have leant on the analogy with theory in order to stress that the practical argument associated with a rational choice is as much a *product* of deliberation as is the choice itself. In fact, this argument *is* the choice displayed in terms of its reasons, and the generic name of such an argument is 'rational choice' or *'prohairesis'*. Now, it used to be imagined that Aristotle's demonstrative syllogisms are maps of processes by which it is soundly established that the syllogistic conclusions are true. Similarly, the practical argument is now sometimes thought to represent the *process* of deliberative search for a right rational choice. But what deliberation seeks to find is a satisfactory conclusion-from-premises: it does not seek, from premises, to find a conclusion. Deliberation is sometimes pictured as a process of sliding down a ladder of argument whose top rung is a set of assembled premises. Thus what it reaches is not an argument, but a conclusion reached by means of an argumentative process. This picture, however, not only destroys the parallel with theoretical inquiry, where an argument is undoubtedly the product; it also, as I now explain, makes nonsense of Aristotle's repeated assertion that practical wisdom is excellence in deliberation. And third, the picture is utterly unrealistic.

Although Aristotle insists that there is no excellence in deliberation where the starting points (*archai;* cf. 1144 a 31–36) of deliberation are not as they should be (whether good, right or true), it would be absurd if such excellence did not also include a superior ability to find one's way *to* a practical conclusion. Even if, in a given case, the starting points have themselves been settled by deliberation from a prior set of starting points, it is evident that some starting points must be undeliberated if the starting points are premises of a practical argument and if deliberation is a process of reaching a conclusion from premises. So, especially on the picture we are considering, the wise person's excellence in deliberation cannot be exhausted by his command of good starting points, since command of good starting points is not, as such, a deliberative achievement. Then is excellence in deliberation the ability to see what follows from the starting point? If this is a set of already assembled premises, then in logically simple cases only an imbecile could fail to draw the conclusion.

If I hold that O is good or desirable and that I am in situation T and that in T the only way to obtain O is by W, I already know that I should do or pursue W. Yet even this academically simple argument might in fact be the fruit of deliberation which only a few could manage. It is *I* who assemble what in the event will figure as the reasons for my final choice, and my doing this is deliberation.[31] It may take time or special discernment, whereas drawing the conclusion from the collected premisses needs neither. I do not, absurdly, start by assuming that *p*, *q*, and *r* will be my reasons for whatever choice I shall make, and then infer from them what the choice is for which they constitute reasons. Real life deliberation consists in focusing on some initially salient consideration, as that my situation is S or that O is desirable, and then finding relevant considerations which, together with the first, point to an action within my power that would convert S into a situation from which I achieve O.[32]

My situation presents me with hosts of features, and I come to it full of interests and apprehensions; but it is not usually written on the faces of any of these which are relevant to which and under what aspect. The knowledge I have of general connections that backs the insight that O in S can be achieved only by W may have to be translated out of the form in which I initially held it before it connects with the circumstances and my desires. If somebody is anxious to help a friend who is ailing and heavily overdrawn at the bank (considerations which may not occur at once or simultaneously), his general knowledge about the beneficial effects of a certain foreign climate and his general knowledge about bank accounts should, if he is practical, translate themselves into the consideration that helping the other in such a case means putting the travel ticket into that person's hand, not writing him a cheque. One draws on experience or general knowledge of this or that feature of the present case for what will later be seen as reasons for the preferred choice, whatever that turns out to be. As a rule, the process involves trying out alternative practical arguments: i.e., considering alternative possible actions each of which presents itself as loaded with its own set of reasons. Often enough, the features of the case which lead to rejection of one of these (and which therefore help ground whichever conclusion is finally accepted) would never have occurred if one had not momentarily considered the rejected project as worthwhile or at least feasible. Thus only when the agent thinks of writing a cheque does he realise that the bank, not his friend, would benefit.

In *NE* III 3, Aristotle gives this sketch of deliberation, which we have already had occasion to quote:

> We deliberate not about ends but about what contributes to ends. For a doctor does not deliberate whether he shall heal, nor an orator whether he shall convince, nor a statesman whether he shall produce law and order, nor does anyone else deliberate about his end. Having set the end they consider how and by what means it is to be attained; and if it seems to be produced by several means they consider by which it is most easily and best produced, while if it is achieved by one only they consider how it will be achieved by this and by what means *this* will be achieved, till they come to the first cause, which in the order of discovery is last. For the person who deliberates seems to inquire and analyse in the way described as though he were analysing a geometrical construction (not all inquiry appears to be deliberation—for instance mathematical inquiries—but all deliberation is inquiry), and what is last in the order of analysis seems to be first in the order of becoming. And if we come on

an impossibility, we give up the search, e.g. if we need money and this cannot be got; but if a thing appears possible we try to do it. By 'possible things' I mean things that might be brought about by our own efforts; and these in a sense include things that can be brought about by the efforts of our friends, since the principle is in ourselves. The subject of investigation is sometimes the instruments, sometimes the use of them; and similarly in the other cases—sometimes the means, sometimes the mode of using it or the means of bringing it about. (1112 b 11–31)

It is obvious from this that general causal knowledge about ways in which things can be made to happen is brought to bear *in the course of,* and *by,* deliberation. Yet such knowledge will logically figure as *premisses* of the argument showing the final choice in terms of its reasons.

The scientific inquirer starts from an unexplained fact or description of an unanalysed object. He proceeds by replacing the original statement or description with equivalents suggested by various definitions and assumptions. The replacements bring him closer to seeing the original in terms of its underlying cause or the elements from which it may be regarded as constructed.[33] When he has analysed sufficiently, he sees without further ado why what he started from had to be as it was in the initial presentation. Having a sufficient analysis simply *is* seeing why. There are no surefire rules for conducting a fruitful analysis: as in the practical case, it is a matter of mental (perhaps also physical) experimentation. The transition from not seeing why to seeing why may seem a mystery when we think about it. But making that transition (a sceptic may say: seeming to oneself to make the transition) from not understanding to understanding is as natural to us as our capacity to breathe, since we are by nature beings who seek and enjoy knowledge of why things are as they are. This is the sort of knowledge which Aristotle has in mind when he says, in the first sentence of the *Metaphysics,* 'all men by nature reach out towards knowledge' (980 a 21).

Having arrived at the causes or elements, the scientific inquirer turns round, so to speak, and makes these the premisses (or terms in premisses) of a chain of explanatory syllogisms whose final conclusion corresponds to the original presentation.[34] Ideally, this is not a chronological sequence of events: arriving at the causes as causes just *is* seeing them as the first premisses of a complete explanatory argument. The explanatory argument, unlike the the process of feeling one's way towards it, is or ought to be logically valid at every step. (It should also satisfy other statable criteria.) This is because, scientific explanation being what it is, the explanatory premisses do not count as explanatory unless they entail what was to be explained.

In similar fashion, the practical inquirer starts with a set of circumstances, C, and a desire for some objective O. They define his problem. For it is as if he assumes[35] that he will realize O in C; the question is, How? He proceeds to analyse the complex starting point replacing description by description (not that these steps need all be formulated) in the light of current observations and background experience and interests. Thus C is recast as D, then as E; O as P, then as Q, etc. This is deliberation. With ingenuity and perhaps some luck, he finally sees the original situation in terms such that it is now apparent what he is to do, without further consideration. He is now in possession of the prescriptive conclusion of deliberation, and possessing it is in effect to have made the rational choice which it represents. The theoretic inquiry concludes when the cause is grasped as a first premiss (or a term in first premisses) of an explanatory argument. In the practical case, likewise, seeing a choice (say, of action A) as emerging from the redefined practical problem is a seeing that concludes the deliberation by installing that action (the concept of it) into position in the first premiss of a causal argument whose conclusion represents the once problematic starting point. For the practical inquirer is now in possession of this: 'Since (because) I will do A (or: by doing A), I shall realise Q in E, and therefore P in D, and therefore O in C'. The theoretic argument premisses a cause in the sense of the 'Why?' of a phenomenon already existing; the practical argument premisses a cause in the sense of the 'How?' of a state of affairs not yet in existence.

So the purpose of deliberation is to invest the inquirer with knowledge of the answer to 'How?' so that, by enacting this answer, he becomes, himself, the efficient cause of O in C. The content of the rational choice—i.e., the *what* (we could call it the 'essence') finally specified in answer to 'How?'—is efficiently causal, but only by having been sought *as an answer to a practical question,* hence only by the questioner's grasping it. He, having that answer, has all he needs that reason can provide for his being a reflectively rational source of definite change. As Aristotle says: 'and such an origin is a human being' (1139 b 5).

The scientist is able to assemble grounds for his claim that such and such is the cause of a certain phenomenon. In this justificatory argument, the claim that such and such is the cause appears as conclusion, since this is the claim being justified. So the scientist's inquiry puts him in possession of two arguments, in which the contents of first premisses and final conclusion are opposite ways round. One is explanatory, the other justificatory. Or rather: one purports to explain the phenomenon, the other explains (in the sense of 'justifies') the scientist's belief that he has explained the phenomenon correctly (or more successfully than others).

In the *Analytics* Aristotle does not directly address the questions about method that arise when one focuses on scientific explanations as needing to be justified. What he does do there, however, is spell out very clearly the general form of what we should aim at in seeking an explanation. 'Are we not more likely to achieve our aim if we have a target?' (1094 a 23–24). To that extent the *Analytics* gives guidance for theoretic inquiry, saying in effect: reflect on the data in whatever ways are necessary for attaining an argument having the formal properties of a demonstration.[36] Since this is Aristotle's approach, the kind of theoretical argument that gets the limelight is explanatory, not justificatory. The former, in any case, is what the scientific inquirer primarily seeks and what others expect from the scientific inquirer. It matters that his explanation is justified, but only because what he wants, and what others want from him, is not that he be justified, but the true explanation of an interesting fact. For the deliberator, too, the primary objective is not to have good reasons for deciding whatever he will decide, but to know what best to decide so as to do it, thereby himself causally solving his practical problem.

The deliberator's primary objective (the primary work of practical reason) is therefore to form a practical argument in which the *premiss* presents the rational choice or the 'How?' In this respect, the objectives of theory and practice are matched: both look for arguments whose premisses give the cause. But there is a fundamental difference in the way in which the possessors of these arguments are related to other people, and this makes a difference in the way in which their arguments figure for others. The original scientist shares his explanation (that he can do so proves him master of it) with others who, it is assumed, desire to understand the same thing. If they absorb the explanation presented, they are now able themselves to explain the phenomenon. The argument which passes from mind to mind in this way is primarily the explanatory one, in which the cause figures in the premises. The inversely formed justifying argument may be a necessary accompaniment, but is not the main object of interest. Practice, however, is different, because the primarily practical argument cannot be generally shared. For grasping *how* to realise O in C is primarily a matter of being ready to become, oneself, the vehicle of a causal first premiss displaying the answer to that practical question. The argument exists in this form for the one whose practical problem it is to realise O in C and who is in a position to enact the solution. The argument is a *logos,* a communicable structure; but to whom can it be communicated in this primary form? Only to someone in the same position as the agent. Then communicating it is giving advice. But in practical life, arguments are not communicated only in order to bring others into the same practical position as oneself. Nor are others interested only with that in view.

The scientist's followers are chiefly interested in external nature, and the mathematician's in the objects of mathematics; but the practical agent's fellows are interested in *him* as a moral agent and in his action as issuing from one who is expected to take responsibility. This is not the deliberator's immediate interest; as such he is more concerned with solving the practical problem than with what the solution says about *him.* But he is also an essentially moral and social being, dependent for his development and well-functioning on the interest in him as such by others of his kind; thus it is natural even to the deliberator himself to see his choice not merely as the yet-to-be determined answer to his own practical question (or else as a determinate answer being now enacted) but also as externalised into a public phenomenon (an observable action) which he needs others to understand and which they cannot understand unless they know his reasons for it, reasons which explain more fully its direction and justify what can be publicly seen. Therefore the practical argument forged in deliberation naturally assumes the reverse form: the choice appears as conclusion, being for others an explanandum, and the practical problem (to realise O in C) figures in explanatory premises. The deliberator deliberates as one who knows (or should know) that the to him as yet unknown cause of an obvious (to him) desired effect will for others—outsiders—stand as the obvious effect of a cause unknown to them—namely, the practical problem as he saw it.[37] This connection between rational practice and accountability to others explains why it is natural to present the practical argument in a form in which rational choice, the product of reason, is a conclusion-from-premises, even though the primary product of theoretical reason is premises-for-a-conclusion. Aristotle's examples of practical and craft arguments generally follow the first of these forms.[38]

It is sometimes complained that his examples of practical arguments are unrealistically simple and linear. And so they would be if they were meant as descriptions of the course of deliberation; but this is not how they are meant. The examples need not be complicated to make the general point that practice is rational. And in actual cases, the practical purpose of explanation and justification has a simplifying effect. It may be reasonable for scientific inquirers to want to know exactly why some general phenomenon or pattern is as it is. But when we take a human or moral interest in someone's particular action, we do not wish to hear exactly why the agent chose as he did (i.e., all that he took account of in arriving at that choice). We might want to be told why this rather than some more expected alternative, or why this way rather than the way *we* should have taken. Often it is enough for the agent to say only what he was aiming at. Sometimes it is necessary to point out some of what he saw in the circumstances, but if it were necessary to explain all that was relevant for just this choice, one might well wonder whether those to whom the explanation is offered could understand it at all.

There is another reason, though, for the oversimplicity (even on a schematic level) of Aristotle's examples of practical argument. He sees animal behaviour as having the same general form of explanation as human behaviour.[39] Because the animal desires O and perceives some circumstance C (for example, the presence of an O) it moves toward O. It is as if the behaviour were informed by a practical argument in which what is desired and what is seen figure as premises, and the action is the conclusion (see especially *Movement of Animals* 701 a 6–b 1). Our own purely animal or impulsive behaviour is like this, too. Here there is no deliberation: no controlled process of analysing the circumstances and replacing the descriptions under which they were first perceived with other, more practically relevant, descriptions. This is because there is no need for deliberation. The creature is constituted by nature so that, generally, when it desires O, it acts appropriately merely on perceiving C; or else so that on perceiving C it is immediately subject to an occurrent desire for O, and moves towards that object. The animal may do what we call 'scan' its situation before moving, but this is as if it instinctively waits for the right button to be pressed: the scanning is not, as with human agents, informed by the sense that *it matters to be right*. Thus the animal's *nature* forms the practical argument for it under circumstances in which immediate effective action is possible. Indeed the "argument" is nothing but the visible behaviour itself understood by observers as the enactment of a desire triggering or triggered by perceptions geared with desire to produce just such behaviour. Deliberation tries to reproduce this situation, since otherwise thought cannot issue in action. We confront, initially, a state of affairs which we are not already geared by instinct or habit to perceive and respond to in some definite way; and deliberation translates the initial terms into terms to which we can finally respond by action which no further thought is needed to execute. Having deliberated conclusively, we move into action (if the occasion offers) as naturally, and indeed automatically, as a thirsty animal moves towards water in front of it. For what makes the final terms *final* is precisely the fact of their being such that, to respond, we need only perceive them as obtaining—although perception here is not just sensory, but invested with recognition, as when we see a knife or can smell that the bread is baked (cf. 1142 a 26–30 and 1112 b 34–1113 a 2).

Practical arguments representing the structure of animal behaviour lack the complexity of arguments formed through deliberation or practical analysis, for their conclusions are not mediated by the conscious replacement of terms with other terms or by the reasoned rejection of options considered but found inferior. All this must already be over in the human case by the moment at which the parallel with animals takes hold. What then remains should really be thought of as the act of *applying* a decision reached through deliberation. In other words, it does not correspond to a step *within* the deliberative process, since that can go on only for as long as we do not know what immediately to do. However, since the application of the decision can itself be analysed into 'premisses' standing for perceptual and desiderative components of the action, it is easy to slip into the error of confusing the process of deliberation with the decision in which it results. For deliberation itself starts from a statement of a practical problem, and it is natural and convenient to treat this statement as a set of premisses. Aristotle, it must be admitted, says nothing to warn us against conflating the starting points of deliberation with the components of the final choice of action, and even he may have been confused on this score. The fact that in the case of nonhuman animals there is an action analysable into its components may delude one into thinking that a similar set of components adequately sums up the human case. Whoever thinks this in general will either, in effect, eliminate deliberation from the human scene or will be identifying the components of a final choice with deliberative starting-points. Either way, the assimilation of reflective human conduct to animal behaviour makes the work of practical reason seem much simpler than it is.[40]

## IX. End and Means in Deliberation

Animal movement, as Aristotle understands it, is structured by desire and perception. The object of desire is general or universal: drink, safety, protecting the young; of perception, a particular circumstance. The desire is a tendency unsatisfiable by itself, since it could be satisfied only by a determinate movement—towards or away from *this*, at *this* place, at *this* moment; but by itself the desire cannot issue in anything determinate. So perception of particulars is needed to make it a definite tendency and an actual movement.

Aristotle's model for intelligent human action is superficially the same. But here the desire is a 'wish' *(boulēsis)* and not, as in animals, an appetite *(epithumia)*. The wish is converted into a determinate practicable action by a kind of perception of particulars, but the conversion, as we have seen, is not immediate; it is effected by deliberative intelligence, which scans the particular situation as a field out of which will emerge an answer to the question, 'How to achieve the objective?' The topics of the present section are the nature of wish or (bouletic desire) from which deliberation starts, and the meaning of the question 'How is the objective to be realised?' The two following sections will be about the faculty of intelligence *(nous)* by which such questions are answered, and the way in which the answer depends on qualities of character.

Let us ask first: 'What is the object of wish?' Aristotle says that practical reason is concerned with living well in general (1140 a 25–28); with what is good and bad for human beings as such (1140 b 5–6; 20–21); with the end *simpliciter* (1142 b 30); with what is good and useful to oneself (1140 a 26; b 9). These I take to be all equivalent and to mean that the objective is the good or the best so far as it concerns the agent as a practical being; i.e., so far it is in his power, and without restriction to any compartment or segment of life. Is this the object of deliberated wish? If so, it cannot be the whole story, because Aristotle holds that the object wished for (which naturally he calls the 'end') is the starting point of deliberation. We deliberate with a view to attaining what we wish, and this objective sets a direction for working out what to do. Aristotle says that the end is 'posited' or 'assumed', comparing it with a mathematician's assumption (1151 a 16–17; 1227 a 7–10). But the mathematician assumes something specific: he does not assume 'the true' as such. The object of wish is therefore not the mere unrestricted good, the formal end of practical deliberation. I suggested in Section III above that we might be able to make sense of the idea of 'aiming' at this formal end as such, and of its making a practical difference to aim at it. The model would be keeping one's balance by focusing on what one cannot specify except as 'keeping my balance'. But the balancer works by feel, not by what Aristotle would call 'deliberation'. (He need not maintain that there is always a clean line between 'feel' and deliberation in particular cases, in order to be justified in drawing the boundaries of the latter concept so as to exclude mere 'feel'.) So deliberation as Aristotle depicts it must start from something more specific than desire for the good as such. It must start from a desire which contributes to the *content* of the practical conclusion.

This picture is too narrow if intended to describe practical thoughtfulness in general. Often we face a situation with no very definite occurrent desire. The natural first question is not 'How to attain O in C?' but 'What am I to do about *this?*' where 'this' refers to some circumstance. Thus on receiving an unexpected legacy one may wonder what to do with the money, and this question evokes a specific desiderative interest. It may evoke several interests, and then there is the problem of deciding between projects. Each is not merely possible at first sight, but also desirable, or one would not consider it. The next step is to focus on one of them, and set oneself to consider what would be involved in accomplishing it. Aristotle calls this 'considering the *means (ta pros to telos)*', and deliberation, for him, starts here. Strictly speaking, therefore, the beginning of Aristotelian deliberation is not necessarily the beginning of that inspection of the circumstances which gives him his parallel with mathematical analysis, for in some cases the inspection starts first and opens the way to deliberation by providing a focal wish.

Since the initial inspection is practical and reflective, and deliberation is practical thinking, what point is made by withholding the term 'deliberation' from the reflection that evokes a focal wish and confining it to debate about means to a wished for objective? Before pursuing this, let me return to the question 'What, for Aristotle, is the wished for object, given that it cannot be the good or best merely as such?' The answer that fits his account better than any other and possesses the additional merit of realism is that the object can be anything that a person finds desirable without having to think about it. We have just noted that reflection may precede the self-presentation of a desirable object; the point, then, is that although the *presentation* may depend on reflection, no reflection is needed to affirm the *desirability* of its object.

The object need not be an ultimate end. For example, Aristotle says, the end might be pleasure or *wealth* (1227 a 14–15). There are many things which we desire immediately, as soon as it occurs to us that they might be possible, because nature or upbringing disposes us to seek them, even though reflection shows them to be valuable mainly as signs of or means to other things.[41] Examples of such ends are gaining a college degree, making a fortune, establishing useful contacts, moving to a place with good opportunities, getting one's affairs into good order, successfully defending one's reputation against libellous attack, winning a war. These objects (or the successful pursuit of these objects) count as ends in the context of ground-level practical thinking because they *begin* by presenting themselves as worth pursuing, and also because there is no need to explain or justify one's desire for them to others of similar background. They are, so to speak, superficially self-explanatory. By contrast, the means to them are actions or arrangements which (even on a superficial view) would not have seemed worth troubling over if one had not seen them as necessary for something else.

We confront a particular situation already desiring or disposed to desire various things, but we are not already disposed to take exactly the steps that are necessary. Pre-established dispositions for adopting specific means are possible only where rules and techniques can be fixed and learnt in advance, but even here the rational agent must recognize the relevance of the rule. *Intelligence* applied to the particular case provides what general knowledge cannot provide: the grasp of how to pursue one's end in and from *this* situation. Again, an initial pause for reflection may be necessary to activate a relevant general concern or interest, which takes the form of a wish; but the shape of this wish when it first appears is not the special work of practical intelligence, which is essentially applied ad hoc to the particulars; and for that reason Aristotle does not consider such a wish the product of *deliberation.*

This account is plainly very different from that which attributes to Aristotle what I earlier termed the 'Grand End' view of practical reason, whereby the wished for end on which deliberation focuses is a comprehensive panorama of the good in which the agent's values and priorities are all subsumed or represented, either in terms of some interminably complex state of affairs to be brought about or in terms of some action to be done providentially designed to take care of all of them. The present account implies that the focal end is different on different occasions for the same agent, not because his sense of values has developed, but simply because he is differently situated so that different dispositional desires are activated to supply the bouletic focus of deliberation.

Aristotle, I suppose, would have thought it too obvious to need stating that the initially activated desire is one of many rather narrow concerns and interests contributing to the actual course of deliberation. When the focal objective is narrow enough to be the sort of thing that we all know what it is like to set our sights on in some particular situation, only an obsessed person would pursue it disregarding all other desiderata. And only a lunatic would have no other desiderata. From the examples above it is clear, as it would be from any other set of realistic examples, that no such objective would be of any value if gained at the expense of everything else.

Does that mean that what the deliberating agent really aims at is some harmonious combination of desiderata, or of those compossible under the circumstances? Yes, if by 'what he aims at' we mean the totality of what he takes steps to promote or secure in an entire course of deliberation and consequent action; but No, if the phrase means the objective from which deliberation starts and concerning which the deliberator asks 'How am I to achieve it?' The fact is that we do not begin with all (or even all relevant) dispositional desires activated. Some are in abeyance until we consider ways of satisfying one of them and then notice how these might affect lateral concerns.[42] Thus the initial narrow objective has the special status of being the only end that colours deliberation all the way through from the beginning.[43] It is therefore not unreasonable that a given course of deliberation, and the choice in which (if concluded) it results, should be logically identified in terms of this end rather than any or all of those interests that made a difference along the way. This logical pre-eminence does not imply superiority in value or importance. For example, in almost every project, large or small, we think and act in such a way as to avoid being killed, but do not on that account describe ourselves as 'trying to stay alive'.

Even so, from an analytical point of view is it not arbitrary to attach such significance to the occurrent desire that presents itself first chronologically? For it would seem that materially the same rational choice might be made taking account of the same set of interests in view of the same circumstances, except that the order of activating the interests is different. Hence which occurs first is accidental. This may be true if we consider the formed choice, but our present concern is with the forming of it. What impresses Aristotle, I suppose, is not the chronological difference between first and subsequent occurrent desires influencing deliberation, but the difference between occurrents which do and which do not owe something to the work of *intelligence*. A desire which, it so happens, is activated as a result of intelligent scanning for means here and now to realise another, already activated, desire is functionally different from the one which first sets the scene for this activity of intelligence, even if either might have played the part of the other. But in any case the reversal of rôles fails to make a difference only when we think of the choice as already forged, and attend to what the choice is of and not to the fact that reaching it is something of a moral achievement. As such, any particular choice stands forth in contrast with one or another humanly possible moral failure, and the contrasts depend on the deliberative history of the choice. Thus an agent who chooses A, having begun deliberating with a view to O and having subsequently modified his interest in O so as to accommodate some other desideratum, P, is to be contrasted with one who obsessively pursues O; whereas one who also chooses A, but was struck by O and P in the reverse order stands over against those who would have thrown away everything for P. From this perspective, the two A-choosers are as different from each other as O is different from P or as an obsession with O is different from an obsession with P.

Since Aristotle is more interested in deliberation as an activity of character and intelligence, and we in modern ethics are more interested in (or at any rate are more accustomed to worry about) the grounding and justification of deliberated choice, it is not surprising that we fail to see, and he to explain, the point of his special attention to the initially presented objective. The order of presentation of various interests in the course of deliberation need not affect their status as grounds for the agent's choosing as he does. They are all equally starting-points in the sense of logical premises. This fact encourages the analyst to view them as essentially premissed all together, as indeed they are in the completed practical argument. (But the completed argument, I have stressed, is not the activity but its upshot.) So our analytical sense of their purely logical togetherness as jointly grounding the conclusion leads us astray if we apply it descriptively to the account in Aristotle's pages, which plainly show a bouletic desire *preceding and leading* deliberation. For then it seems to us as if the only way to accommodate this feature of his account is by supposing him to hold that all the desires which help form the choice are together in place *in advance* of deliberation. And now we see them as aspects of a single antecedent desire for a Grand End or Grand Harmony of Ends.

Caught in this trap, one may begin to lose faith in Aristotle's ability to convey his meaning, since he ought to have said something about the Grand End on which (we assume) ground-level practical reasoning focuses; yet we find him silent about it. We recall, however, that he is full of common sense, and our own common sense reminds us that real practical debates, whether public or private, start up without benefit of a grand picture. The notion of an *implicit* premiss now comes to the rescue: most of those desiderative premisses are implicitly held, and this explains why the Grand End never appears as an object to ground-level practical consciousness and why Aristotle never writes as if it does so appear. What appears at the start of deliberation is only ever a tip of this Grand End iceberg.[44]

Aristotle would happily endorse the general observation that some practical premisses are implicit and that the resulting practical conclusions are none the worse for that. For example, he says that we should respect the undemonstrated findings of people with wisdom and experience no less than those which they can demonstrate (i.e., explain and justify in words) (1143 b 11–14).[45] But it sheds a false light to introduce the notion of implicit premisses in the way in which it was introduced above, i.e., as an attempt to save the Grand End theory as a theory about the objective from which Aristotelian deliberation takes its start. Aristotle says that we posit the end and deliberate about how to attain it. At *EE* 1226 b 25–26 he says that the deliberating part of the soul has the power to *consider* or *reflect on* what it aims for. His comparison with mathematical assumption overwhelmingly suggests an explicit positing of a stateable object. And how do we (as he says) 'calculate' (1139 a 12–13; 1140 a 30; cf. 1141 b 14) the means if the end is defined by a set of desiderative premisses many or most of which are not articulately present to consciousness?

No doubt anything we aim for is more than the aspect we grasp while aiming for it; but if our aiming is controlled by the reflective quest for means, then the end as object of aim is what we know of the thing to the extent that we know it, and this knowledge is articulate in a manner that matches the articulacy of the question. It may be wise to acknowledge that our identified target is no more than the tip of some iceberg, but it does not follow that the entire iceberg is our target, or that we can approach a submerged whole otherwise than by setting our sights on what we can see of it. If the 'How?' question is articulate and expects an articulate answer, then so is its object articulate; and this holds true even if the grounds of our answer are not altogether apparent to us. An animal's movement in response to its surroundings can be seen as its answer to the problem of survival posed by those surroundings. But we do not think of the animal as *itself* posing that question in articulate form. So although the movement which is the answer is the animal's answer simply because it is *its* movement, this answer is not *its* in the sense in which an answer would be if it had taken shape in response to the animal's own questioning. The creature does not make the question his own just by answering it with his body, which is the same as saying that his body "answers" without *his* ever putting the question.

Aristotle's explanation of animal movement invites us to compare it with rationally chosen action. But his psychology draws a sharp distinction between human intelligence and the cunning of nature. In *On the Soul,* intellect *(nous)* stands in radical contrast with all other functions of the soul, being said to be 'not blended with the body' (429 a 18 ff.). It is often assumed that this doctrine refers only to the theoretic intellect, and perhaps the assumption is correct. But whatever Aristotle may have thought about the metaphysics of practical intellect when composing *On the Soul,*[46] in his *Ethics* he clearly places practical and theoretic intellect on one side of a line.[47] He would never, for example, have said that a nonrational animal 'posits' its end as a mathematician makes an assumption. Nonhuman animals do not deliberate any more than plants deliberate,[48] because in their case the only being whose business it is to know articulately what they do and why they do it is the scientific observer. But the scientist belongs to a species whose members must themselves formulate what they do and what they aim for in doing it, because it belongs to their nature to seek objectives which cannot be attained unless formulated by them individually. This is so whether the objectives are theoretical or practical. But on a different level the parallel between humans and other animals holds, since it is not the case that everything that could properly be termed a human end is attainable only if formulated by whoever attains it. Metaphysically speaking, it is an end of every human individual to realise his potential as a rational practical being, and this can surely be done, and done well, without being formulated. It could also be said that deliberation (about one or another narrow objective) is our *nature's* means of realising the end just stated; but it is not a means which the rational agent as an individual *self* (not merely a metaphysically individual substance) rationally chooses as a result of deliberation!

A rational choice is the intelligently reached answer to a question about how to attain an objective, and I have argued that the answer cannot be articulate unless the question is, too. I have also indicated that an answer can be articulate even if the subject is unable to articulate all his grounds for it. In the absence of an articulable project, e.g. a definite action which the agent could explain or defend, it is not clear whether one can speak of grounds at all. In that absence, what we have is (arguably) not something *meant* (meant as right or appropriate and backed by a readiness to justify), but a reaction for which there are no grounds to uncover, although there may be an explanation in terms of desires and perceptions. On the other hand, unless *grounds* are allowed to be to some extent inarticulate without its following that what is grounded is infected with inarticulacy, it is doubtful whether a grounded affirmation would ever be possible to human beings, at any rate in the practical mode. Hence this combination of articulate question and answer with unarticulated grounds is an inevitable feature of rational choice on any realistic view. But it is easy to overlook this fact if we consider the choice ex post facto, as something to be explained or as something to be justified.

This is because the latter perspective tends to equate the chosen action with what is open to public view. The end which figured in the agent's initial deliberative question is now looked upon as one of many not immediately apparent desiderative factors on which one could fasten in explaining or criticising the observed action, A, and which the agent might cite in defending it. It is therefore easy for the analyst to lump all these together as jointly representing what the agent was seeking and what A was chosen for; and since some of them would not have been explicit at the time, the analyst thinks of this joint objective as inexplicit over all. But this restructuring of the situation, whereby the end aimed for in the action becomes indifferently one of the action's grounds or the grounds all part of a complex end, takes off from a necessarily truncated, because external, view of the choice which represents it as the choice of A *tout court* and connects it synthetically with the end. But on Aristotle's conception of choice (examined in the first section of this chapter), it is not accurate to think of A as the action chosen, the choice of it being partially grounded in desire for O; rather, *A-for-the-sake-of-O* is chosen, and the choice of this whole is what is grounded. The end of choice, and of action in accordance with choice, is functionally different from the grounds. Hence there is no good reason for transferring, so to speak, the inexplicit quality of some of the grounds of choice to its end; an end which in any case (I have argued) it makes no sense to suppose inexplicit when it is an end of deliberation.

I have stressed the articulacy of the deliberative end in order to settle accounts with the Grand End interpretation. Whatever the confusions that draw us towards this picture, we can hardly feel comfortable with it as long as the End is presumed explicit, whereas the contrary presumption lends a semblance of respectability.

The deliberative end, then, is a narrow objective. Why does this matter? Because on it depends the correct interpretation of the deliberator's question 'How is O to be attained?' and also the correct interpretation of the ways in which intelligence and character contribute to the deliberative process.

It is often assumed that the 'How?' question is purely causal. But that assumption makes sense only in the context of a Grand End representing the entire range of the agent's interests in order of priority. Such an End may be envisaged as an ideal state of affairs to be brought about or as an ideal action to be enacted, but either way there is no room for the agent to prefer one means of realising it on the ground that he thereby takes care of some interest not represented in the End. For from his point of view no such extra interest exists, granted that he trusts his own Grand image of the good. Hence when he considers that it would be better to do A than B, 'better' can only mean 'more certain to be effective in promoting or securing one and the same comprehensive value'. 'Effectiveness' here covers two ways in which something can be a means: external and constitutive. If the End is thought of as a resulting state of affairs, the means is an action separable in time and place. If the End is to perform a Grand action, the means will be some more narrowly conceived action the performance of which, under the circumstances, constitutes performance of the Grand one, just as pressing a switch under given circumstances constitutes lighting the room. Either way, the agent has only to consider the factual question whether, by doing A under the circumstances, he will realise E; and if there is a choice of viable means, he only has to consider which would be most effective.

The Grand End theory does not entail that one can only ever consider means and not reconsider one's picture of the end. The Grand End agent can be conceived as possibly coming to suspect that his picture does not represent the right values and priorities, and he may become aware of being insufficiently clear about the empirical nature of his end. But as long as his values remain the same or unquestioned, he subscribes to the value-judgment that the end is worth pursuing. And if he changes his view of it, then from his new perspective the reconsidered end is and would have been worthwhile under any circumstances. Hence he cannot ever ask himself whether it is worth pursuing in *this* situation while acknowledging that for him, even as he is, it would certainly have been worth it in some other situation. Again, as long as he takes himself to have a clear view of the end and does not question his values, he cannot ask himself whether attaining it is the best thing he could do, or whether, in attaining it, he would attain the unrestricted good and the best.

All these questions are possible and very much alive for the real life rational agent whose deliberative end is narrow and easily stated, and who, I contend, is fairly accurately portrayed by Aristotle. Deliberating on the means to O may show that pursuing O under the actual circumstances would cost something one values more or something without which O would be useless or unsatisfying. Hence giving up the pursuit of O on this occasion is no sign of changed or wavering values, but, if anything, proof of their constancy. The 'How?' of this agent's deliberation is not purely causal; it means 'What way is there for me to pursue and attain O in this situation so that the pursuit and attainment would be acceptable in terms of all else that matters?' Deciding this question requires him to make comparative evaluations to the effect that O is or is not worthwhile given this amount of trouble, these undesirable consequences etc., as well to make factual judgments about the causal possibilities.

The question can also be framed as 'How am I to pursue O so that in so doing I pursue what is best under these circumstances?'[49] It is in this way that the practical agent's formal end—the unrestricted good or best as such—combines with an empirical end that gives determinate content to deliberation. The formal good is not the object which he has in view when deliberating, but shows up, rather, in the way in which he decides to pursue that object. He decides to pursue it only on condition that in so doing he is pursuing what is here and now best to pursue. Now this *best* which is the formal end of practice implies, as we saw, an unconditionally practical attitude. It therefore implies an unconditionally practical attitude to whatever it is that is taken to *be* best. But this unconditional attitude is not on that account universal in the sense of affirming that the object in question is always to be pursued. For the practicable best is whatever is best to achieve under *these* particular circumstances, since it is only under particular circumstances that anything can be put into practice, and 'these' has a different referent each time. The identification, under these circumstances, of the best with X amounts to a categorical imperative with regard to X, but not one that transfers to other occasions. The mythical Grand End agent is one whose object is seen by him as best under all circumstances, and the particularity of any new situation in which he finds himself only sets the stage for repeated pursuit of the same. The Aristotelian agent, by contrast, always deliberates with a view to the best; but what that best is, with a view to which he deliberates, is different in different particular situations. Just so, the medical practitioner always deliberates with a view to healing, but what healing is (i.e., what it is, considered as an end, even before the means are apparent) differs with individual patients; thus with one it is getting him walking again, with another getting rid of his headaches, and so on.

Just as what it makes sense to pursue as best differs from one to another occasion, so it differs from stage to stage of deliberation as the same situation reveals itself differently to practical scrutiny. We begin by assuming O as the end; the assumption is not arbitrary, since O presents itself as initially desirable, and perhaps more so than anything else, but we are not committed to pursuing O no matter what as long as it is causally possible. O remains our focus of deliberation only so long as our view of the situation is such that we judge it best to pursue O in that situation. The judgment may change as we become clearer about the conditions of pursuit and its consequences under those conditions. Practical wisdom is not the ability to select effective means to a goal which is rightly seen to be good no matter what. It is the ability to pursue a goal initially worth pursuing in such a way that it continues to *be* worth pursuing, when this might easily not have been the case; and it is also, therefore, the ability to tell when something is not worth the necessary means and to drop it as an end accordingly.

This parallels the work of the scientific researcher, who begins by assuming not without evidence the reality of some fact which he hopes to explain, and looks for an explanation that will also do justice to other known or assumed facts and their explanations. The original fact may be cited as a ground of the explanation finally offered, but obviously there are additional grounds for preferring this to alternative theories. We are clear enough about the methodology of science not to be tempted into lumping all the grounding facts together and drawing the conclusion that together they compose his single original grand explanandum. Yet in ethics one of the unconscious moves by which the Grand End theory is made to seem plausible is the precise equivalent of that.

If the scientist concludes that, given his assumptions, no satisfactory explanation is possible for whatever interests him, he may question the reality of this appearance or the truth of one of his other assumptions. It may be decided that the original appearance was not of any*thing* to *be* explained. However, the scientist can suspend judgment about whether an explanation is possible. He can afford to wait, because his ideal desideratum is an explanation (a work of reason) in the light of which anyone, however, wherever and whenever situated would find the matter intelligible; hence the explanation would never go out of date. But the practical reasoner has a limited time in which to reach a practical conclusion about O under *these* circumstances; and if he finds no acceptable means of pursuing it, he must abandon that particular project, thereby abandoning it for good. He cannot keep it on hold indefinitely, because it was only ever the project of *his* pursuing O under *these* circumstances, and they will be gone. Hence abandoning the search for an acceptable choice (the work of practical reason) amounts to a judgment that no such choice is available, and that O is not an appropriate goal in this case.

So now for the question that has soaked up more than its share of ink: 'Can Aristotle escape the charge of irrationalism with regard to the ends of deliberation?' Practical reasoning is deliberation, and he holds that we deliberate not about the ends, which we posit, but only about the means *(ta pros ta telē)*.[50] It has seemed to follow that practical reasoning in the form of Aristotelian deliberation cannot yield an answer to the question 'Should I pursue the end O?'

In saying that the practical agent does not deliberate about the end (just as the physician does not deliberate whether to heal, or the public speaker whether to persuade; cf. 1112 b 13), Aristotle means (1) that the practical agent does not ask whether he should pursue his formal end, i.e., doing what is best under the circumstances. Aristotle may also mean (2) that the specific end O from which deliberation starts presents itself as worth pursuing without one's having had to find this out by deliberation or by any special exercise of practical intelligence. But neither separately nor together do these points entail that the deliberator cannot ask himself whether O is in fact now worth pursuing, or that he cannot *deliberate* his way to a reasoned answer. Asking *how* to pursue O, I have argued, is asking how to pursue it so that pursuing it is best in the situation. And one who asks this assumes, until he is forced to accept the contrary, that there *is* a How that meets that condition. The deliberative discovery that there is such a How, or that there is not, is the same as discovering that O is or is not to *be* pursued in this situation. In this way, deliberation yields an answer to the question 'Should I pursue O?'[51] But the point is lost if we confuse formal with substantial ends or if we fall into the connected error of the Grand End view. For in either case the substantial best is identical through all change of circumstance, so that pursuit is ethically obligatory except when causally impossible. The analogy of medicine feeds these confusions if we think of it as introducing one and the same substantial conception of health into every case that the doctor handles.

Then why does Aristotle insist that the question for deliberation is how to, not whether to, pursue O, when both questions are decided by the same rational process? The 'How to?' question is prior, because settling it settles 'Whether to?' not vice versa. That is one answer. Here is another: he is not finally concerned with deliberation in general, but with *wise* deliberation. Now the deliberator can be truly described as reflecting on 'How?' and also as reflecting on 'Whether?' but the second description points in a false direction. A person who asks 'Should I pursue O?' could be one who weighs O against other possibilities without considering it as a thing *that has yet to be realised:* he attends only to the nature of O and its consequences as they would be were it an already established reality. He of course knows it not to be a reality, or he would not be talking about 'pursuit' at all; but aside from that, his thinking about O is strangely like thinking about a Platonic Form and its formal relations. He considers O and alternatives in abstraction from the particularities of any situation from which one or another might be brought to be. It is like a child thinking about whether to become a football star or a world-famous brain surgeon, by thinking what each would be like if one already were it. There is perhaps a universal tendency to think in this way when one is supposed to be thinking practically. But it does not take *wisdom* or even acumen to compare one dream with another and know that each is good, or that one is better, in a world that contains nothing else of determinate nature. Whoever deliberates about O in this way will be satisfied if O in the abstract implies no conflict with anything else he values, and will overlook the possibility that closing the gap between wanting and having would generate just such a conflict. So this kind of deliberation is not only not wise, but foolish. Having opted for O, such an agent pursues it in thought and action as if the personal environment within which he has to operate contains nothing of significance or will simply have dropped away on the dawning of the era marked by attainment of O. Naturally, therefore, if he takes practical steps at all, they are steps taken as if nothing matters but effectiveness. Aristotle's doctrine that deliberation is of 'How?' can be construed as a warning against practical fantasizing and its brutal, self-stultifying consequences. He is recommending *how* we should deliberate, and, as in other cases, recommendation passes over into definition.

So it is with his stress elsewhere that the theoretical inquirer seeks the 'Why?' As long as this cannot be taken for granted, it is as much a recommendation of what theorising should be as a definition of what it is. Some may think it the aim of theoretical inquiry to attain a vision of universal forms or essences. If so, they are as mistaken as if they equated that aim with aesthetic contemplation of surface phenomena. The real scientist seeks the Why, and if he grasps it he grasps the essences in the only way that should concern him: i.e., as explaining something *else*.[52] Just so, we should deliberate first and foremost on the 'How?' and then the question of *whether* to pursue O resolves itself in the only way in which it can be rightly resolved: by being conjoined in thought with something *other* than O—namely, the situation from which one would seek it. If this interpretation is correct, it is almost unbearably ironic that when Aristotle insists upon 'How?' rather than 'Whether?' as *the* question of deliberation, he is so commonly heard as saying that deliberation considers only causal possibilities.

## X. Character and Intelligence in Deliberation (I)

If we take the view that the practical deliberative end is the *best* seen as consisting here and now in some narrow specific objective, the adoption of an end by an agent is not a puzzling phenomenon. As practical rational beings we have the innate capacity to think of something as best under the circumstances, and the specific object of this thought on any occasion depends on nonmysterious desiderative and cognitive factors which can be explained by reference to ordinary experience, upbringing, and human nature. If, on the other hand, we suppose the specific end to be something Grand and also accept that it has to be explicit, we shall expect from Aristotle an explanation of how such an end is formed and endorsed, and shall consequently be forced towards distorted interpretations of his account of the various dispositions and abilities at work in practical reasoning. Now the last section was concerned with the end and the 'How?' of deliberation in general; but since Aristotle's primary topic is *excellence* in deliberation *(euboulia)*, which he equates with practical wisdom (1140 a 25–26), I shall begin to concentrate as he does on the qualities that issue in good practical thinking. On the side of character there is moral excellence; and on the intellectual side, astuteness *(deinotēs)*, which when allied with moral excellence takes on the more honorific title of *'nous'*, here usually rendered 'intelligence'.[53]

Aristotle divides the contributions of moral excellence and intelligence between end and means, saying that the first makes the end or the target *(skopos)* right, while the second makes right the means (1144 a 7–9; 1227 b 19 ff.). Because practical wisdom combines these two kinds of qualities, he tends in making his point about either to use the term 'practical wisdom' to refer to the other contrastingly. Thus when the focus is on ability to find means, 'practical wisdom' is his label for the right grasp of the end (e.g., 1142 b 33); and where the topic is correctness about ends, 'practical wisdom' refers to intelligence about means (e.g., 1144 b 15 ff.). For moral excellence *is* practical wisdom, when allied to astuteness or intelligence; and intelligence *is* practical wisdom, when backed by moral excellence.[54] Here I only sketch these connections and shall take them up again after a general discussion of the rôles of character and intelligence.

If the deliberative end is the good according to a Grand substantial conception, then when Aristotle says that moral excellence makes the end right, he lays on moral excellence a burden which it cannot intelligibly sustain according to his own account of it earlier. How can a disposition to light upon the mean in feeling and action, developed, as he says, through practice of right actions, contain in itself or generate a general, correct, substantial, comprehensive, *explicit* picture of the end of man? And why should it need to?

Setting aside this second question, presumably on the dogmatic ground that wise deliberation must start from such a picture, some interpreters concede, in effect, the unanswerability of the first one by invoking on Aristotle's behalf the aid of reason or intellect. Thus it has often been suggested that the wise person enjoys an intellectual intuition of the right Grand End, or that he has forged a conception of it by some kind of dialectical or inductive procedure, or by some kind of synthesis from narrower objectives or values. Enough has been said in Section IV of this chapter about what this does to Aristotle's conception of the ground-level wise human being, whose necessary equipment must now include a good chunk of ethical theory. Here I am concerned with what it does to Aristotle's account of the rôle of practical intellect or intelligence. Quite simply, it ignores the boundaries which he draws round this concept, and it assigns to practical intelligence a spurious function which then has to be cobbled together with the one presented in the text.

The end O (the object of bouletic desire) figures first to the agent as a universal, and the same is true of the corresponding project, *pursuit of O*. As such, it is not practicable: the practicable project is pursuit of O under (hence particularised by) *these* conditions. In the practical argument, the conditions are represented by what Aristotle calls 'the second proposition (or: premiss)',[55] and he states emphatically that practical intelligence is to do with particulars *(ta kath'hekasta)* and 'the second proposition (1143 a 28–b5). In this respect, as I understand him, he consciously contrasts practical with theoretical *nous,* whose objects are universals. In effect, therefore, he denies that practical *nous* has universals as its objects.

Scholars debate how particular Aristotle's 'particulars' are. In some occurrences (possibly including some in *NE* VI) the term means species of a genus. Sometimes it means the elements of a thing (which may be a logical universal) considered severally rather than as undifferentiated parts of a whole (e.g., *Physics* 184 a 21 ff). It seems that he uses 'particulars' in the informal sense that applies when, e.g., we ask someone to 'particularise'; i.e, to present a thing in its peculiar detail rather than in wider terms covering other things too. Now, when the end O is considered without reference to the nature of the circumstances, being first desired before one even sees just what they are, so that O is initially seen as worth pursuing under a variety of indeterminate scenarios, the pursuit of O is certainly a universal by comparison with one or another determinate set of circumstances; and they are particulars by comparison with it, even if they can be adequately described, themselves, in general terms.[56] Hence doubt about the precise sense and reference of 'particulars' in Aristotle's usage is not a reason for not concluding that when he says that practical intelligence is concerned with particulars, he implies that the *end* of deliberation is not its object. And this is anyway just what we should expect if the end is narrow and (so to speak) ordinary, since it takes no special acumen actually to wish for most of the things which we wish for. (This is not to deny that wishing presupposes intellect, in the sense that it would be meaningless to ascribe wishing to beings incapable of deliberation.)

The idea (1) that (textual evidence notwithstanding) the deliberative end, on Aristotle's view, cannot be grasped except in a special exercise of intelligence is an offshoot of (2) the Grand End theory, which demands this position just as it demands (3) the causal interpretation of 'How?' This unholy triad of exegetical assumptions gains strength as a group from confusions examined earlier that directly feed the Grand End notion; but all three, I now further suggest, have also been sustained (the first directly, the others through their logical association with it) by an old fashioned misconception of the rôle of theoretical intellect.

Aristotle contrasts theoretic and practical intelligence, but he also observes a similarity: both are concerned with 'ultimates' *(eschata),* but in each of two opposite directions (1143 a 35–b3; cf. 1142 a 23–27). Since theoretic intelligence grasps the explanatory first principles of a science (1140 b31–1141a8), he probably has it in mind that what practical intelligence grasps lies furthest *from those principles.*[57] These objects, presumably, are particular phenomena given in advance of scientific reflection, hence not seen as informed by their causes nor as instancing universal types whose regular conjunctions betoken some principle present though not yet identified.[58] This material is what Plato called the 'indeterminate', which falls below the level of classification into species and genera (*Philebus* 16 c–e). But in saying that this is the domain of practical intelligence, Aristotle should not be taken to mean that the objects grasped by practical intelligence are raw data absolutely. They or their descriptions are *theoretically* raw because untransformed by scientific activity into logical consequences of an explanatory theory. But they are not (we shall see in more detail presently) raw from the standpoint of practical reason, which does its own work of intellectual transformation quite different from the theoretical. Hence the objects grasped by practical intelligence, remote as they are by scientific standards from the first principles of science, nonetheless occupy in the practical field a position analogous to the principles of theory, since they (we shall see) make up an answer to the practical 'How?' which mirrors the theorist's 'Why?' (questions not directed at the *same* set of givens, since the given of science is an unanalysed fact, that of practice, an unanalysed project).

According to the old-fashioned misconception, Aristotelian scientific demonstration is a movement of *inquiry* from more evident starting points to less evident conclusions. Thus the demonstrative first principles are certainties or comparative certainties from which the scientific process is supposed to *begin.* So Aristotle's statement that theoretic *nous* grasps the first principles was taken to mean that it grasps propositions whose function in the context is to provide grounds for believing less obvious propositions. On this basis it was natural to equate practical intellection with a grasp of the starting points of practical inquiry; i.e., of deliberation.[59] These are the problem-setting factors: on the one hand the object bouletically desired, on the other the agent's particular circumstances. To the prospective agent these are plain and they provide the basis for his rational transition to something not yet plain to him; namely, a decision on what to do. However, the misconception about the noetic grasp of theoretical first principles implies (by analogy) that we owe it to practical *nous* that the deliberative starting points are plain.

This interpretation seems to be supported by 1143 b 3, where Aristotle relates practical *nous* to 'the second (or other) proposition'. This is usually taken to refer to that premiss in a practical argument that states the circumstances from which deliberation starts. Thus prima facie he seems to suggest that intelligence apprehends these circumstances as they present themselves in *advance of deliberation.* But it is odd, to say the least, to dignify this initial cognition by the word 'intelligence' in a situation where the heavy demands on intelligence are still to be made.[60] Still, this oddity may seem a small price to pay for an interpretation that gives to practical *nous* the custody of a deliberative starting-point; for if it is responsible for such starting-points at all, then presumably it is responsible for the other main starting-point, namely the end— which, if Grand, stands sorely in need of this patronage. But on one plausible reading of 1143 b 3 Aristotle never says that practical intelligence grasps the second premiss: he says that it grasps what '*belongs to* (or *under*) the second premiss'.[61] This implies that these objects of intelligence do not constitute a deliberative *starting*-point at all; rather, they are the results of *analysing* the material presented by the second of the two main premisses from which deliberation starts. So the fact that Aristotle connects intelligence with the second deliberative premiss is no evidence that he connects it with deliberative starting points as such. Consequently, the theory that practical intelligence provides the other starting-point, the end, is based on nothing but a parallel with theoretical *nous* understood as providing the start of scientific inquiry. But that is upside down. Theoretical *nous* grasps what is first in order of explanation, reached last in order of inquiry. Hence practical *nous* should grasp what is first in the order of action, last in the order of deliberation.[62]

The discussion so far of practical intelligence has been intended to establish the unsurprising point (were it not overlaid by the self-compounding errors of the Grand End view) that Aristotle means it when he says that moral goodness—i.e., *not* intelligence—makes right the aim of deliberation. Let us now go back to moral goodness and return to practical intelligence further on.

Aristotelian deliberation, as I understand it, does not proceed on an inertial assumption of the end as worthwhile, but entails continual re-evaluation in the light of means, means to means, and their consequences. So when he says that moral virtue makes the end, or the target, right, he is not saying that virtue reveals to the agent which of various possible ends is the right one to aim for, but that virtue ensures that whatever is aimed for is aimed for rightly at any stage and pursued only in terms on which pursuit is best.[63] As reflection brings out new relevant considerations, the value of O under the circumstances (its worthiness to *be* an end) is judged and rejudged, and the rightness of these judgments depends on character. Moral virtue is active throughout wise deliberation, not only in the form of a general thrust or readiness to discern and do the best whatever it might be, but as a plexus of specific evaluative dispositions expressed in a series of differently focused but mutually cognisant responses.

Since the contribution of moral goodness (and of character in general) is serial in this way, virtue is involved in selecting *means* to O.[64] For the steps of deliberation constitute a chain of choices of means. The business of virtue is not just to set up an end and then sit back while intelligence sifts means. But does this not contradict Aristotle's division of the functions, whereby moral virtue makes the end right and intellectual capacities take care of the means? No, unless we make the unnecessary assumption that they do not operate *simultaneously.* According to the present account, the selection or rejection of means at each stage represents both sides of that division, integrating (1) a factual picture (due to intelligence) of a possible course of action M and its conditions and consequences under the envisaged circumstances, with (2) an evaluation (due to moral character) of O as an end worth or not worth pursuing under the conditions and with the results implied by pursuing it through M.[65] Since 'worth pursuing' here means 'worth pursuing given the cost', (2) is a comparative judgment. This judgment could go one way or the other, and which way it goes is a matter of character. In these stage by stage preferences character is shaped as well as revealed; whereas it is neither shaped nor especially revealed through pre-deliberative wishing.

Thus moral differences between agents do not necessarily surface in differences between the kinds of end pursued, for many narrow ends such as health, security, pleasure, are common if not universal concerns. Difference of character shows up in the ways and occasions of particular pursuit, or, we might say, in the pursuit of ends particularised by our occasions and ways of pursuing them. So, for example, when Aristotle says:

> Arguments which deal with acts to be done are things which involve a starting-point, viz. 'since the end, i.e. what is best, is such and such a thing', whatever this may be (let it for the sake of discussion be what we please); and this is not evident except to the good man; for wickedness perverts us and causes us to be deceived about the starting-points of action (1144 a 31–36)[66]

we must (according to the interpretation advanced above) think of the arguments referred to here not as processes of deliberation but as their (timeless) products. Consequently, that element in a finished practical argument which presents the end presents it in a context in which all else that is relevant is ideally held in view. If an end thus framed is 'evident' to (i.e., is still an end to) a good person (and consequently explains his doing something for it), then not it, but something which conflicts with it, would probably be held as end by a bad person in the same situation. The perversion which Aristotle speaks of here can be of two kinds: in one (which may be rare) the end is such that (in the good man's view) only a wicked person would ever pursue it at all; in the other, the sentence 'the end (or the best) is O' is acted upon as if it were a practical truth (which *sometimes* it is) on occasions when the good man sees that it is not.

Although Aristotle more often says that moral virtue makes the end 'right' *(orthon),* in one place he speaks of the grasp of the end as *'true' (alethēs):* 'Excellence in deliberation will be correctness with regard to what conduces to the end of which practical wisdom is the true apprehension' (1142 b 32–33). This is a simultaneous definition of *practical wisdom* and *excellence in deliberation,* terms which are virtually interchangeable. Excellence in deliberation is the ability to be factually correct about means, in the context of a true grasp of the end; practical wisdom is a true grasp of the end in the context of factual correctness about means. In other words, 'he is excellent in deliberation' is truly said only of one who is right in such comparative value-judgments as that O, on these conditions, is worth pursuing; but what it says about him is that he is factually canny about means; while 'he has practical wisdom' is true only of the canny person, but (practical wisdom being here equated with the moral contribution) it says about him that his evaluation of O is right. Why, though, does Aristotle speak of this evaluative rightness as '*true* apprehension of the end'? (This is not just elegant variation.) Because, I think, he is here considering the final selection of means; i.e., the concluding rational choice. Every previous step in deliberation has depended on a combination of factual and evaluative judgments, but as long as there was need to continue deliberating, the evaluation of O as worth pursuing fell short of being categorically practical. For as long as we need to ask how some means might be realised, we have not yet taken account of all the conditions and consequences attending possible means to the means. Thus the situation in which O would be pursued is still deliberatively indeterminate, and the judgment that O is worthwhile in the terms dictated by the circumstances remains provisional. The intermediate evaluations are *right,* i.e. on the right track; but only the ultimate one is *true,* expressing as it does an outright practical and factually fully informed commitment to O as end. The agent's view of the facts is sufficiently determinate (and the rational choice is made) as soon as he perceives a means immediately within his power and at the same time morally knows that how precisely he handles it is of no negative evaluative significance. Then and only then is he in possession of *truth,* the final achievement of reason. The scientist grasps the truth about a fact of the universe only when he has come to understand it in terms of its ultimate cause. Similarly, the person of practical wisdom apprehends the truth about a desired object O when and only when he knows what is best to do about O, for him here and now and all things considered.

On the account as we have it so far, there are two elements in Aristotelian practical deliberation: a wish for O (which is a provisional affirmation of O as end) and an intelligent grasp of particulars. We must take it that the latter includes a grasp of particulars as instancing relevant causal relations. This factual awareness converts the wish into rational choice according to the formal requirement of the best. But are there not also specific ethical principles, including principles of value priority, guiding the conversion? These, it seems, have no essential place. Generalities or universals appear in the form of unparticularised objectives and commitments; one of which, in any given case, is the focal material for the choice, while the others act as constraints on what counts as acceptable conversion. But Aristotle does not tell us anything about general principles of priority mediating the move from factual picture to practical decision. If no such principles operate here, what bridges the surely obvious logical gap? The move is made by a deliberator informed by a gamut of concerns; but the conclusion of his practical argument will not be logically justified unless he employs general principles which generate a particular weighting when applied to the factual premisses.

These would be principles of ethical inference from end-cum-facts-cum-other-concerns to means. Their presence would raise obvious questions about how they are acquired and justified. Since Aristotle is silent on these points, it appears that such principles play no essential part in his scheme. This fact has, of course, contributed to the Grand End theory, whereby the End comprises within itself all values in due order, and the only nonlogical principle of inference is the causal dictate 'Do whatever most certainly and directly conduces to this End.' That reshuffling of the picture transfers problems of acquisition and justification to the End-giving premiss, but at least it provides a logically intelligible grounding of the practical conclusion. From this point of view (leaving aside the other pressures which contribute to the Grand End theory) the reshuffling has but one purpose: to meet the demand for a logically intelligible argument.

Why should we suppose that it has to be logically intelligible, whether by means of a Grand End premiss or through independent principles of value? Presumably because it is hard to see how, in the absence of such logical grounding, the conclusion can rightly be thought of as *rationally* generated. If, as Aristotle's account suggests, the agent loaded with his various interests simply responds to his view of the particulars by selecting one or another means, what is the difference really between supposedly rational deliberated action and any animal's desire-structured response to its circumstances? Except in number of desires and degree of their sophistication, as well as complexity of the factual findings, is there any fundamental difference? For the animal manages without knowing the general principles whereby it is proper for a creature with its desires or needs to do this under these circumstances; and so, it seems, can the human deliberator.

It is admitted, of course, that human beings are unique in their ability and desire to explain and justify their actions by giving reasons. The deliberator explains his choice of A by saying, e.g., 'I wanted O, and this was the situation, but at the same time it was important not to jeopardise P'. But it does not follow that he can or should be expected to justify the priorities implied in wanting O on these terms. Aristotle says that no reason or argument can be given for this aiming at O: i.e. (as I understand it), for aiming at O in this situation with an aim informed by concern for P and whatever other values are expressed by adopting A (*EE* 1227 b 24–25). These values have already been taken on board without argument, and nothing is said about general principles of priority and combination.

But without such principles, the choice of A is not logically grounded in what the agent states as his reasons. How, then, is the choice rational? And how are the proffered reasons really reasons at all? We can say that the choice was formed *as if* in the light of one or another general principle; but similar 'as if' statements can be made about the behaviour of animals and teleological systems in general.

For Aristotle, the difference between a deliberated response and an animal's response lies in the fact that the former is mediated by intelligence. This for him is the fundamental contrast: between the presence and absence of the play of intelligence on the particulars, not between the presence and absence of general ethical or practical principles. In the context of this attempt to expound the position of Aristotle, I would say that having such principles is a surrogate for Aristotelian practical intelligence.[67] If we could understand clearly the rôle he assigns to intelligence, we should no longer feel it a lack that practical principles do not appear in his account of the formation of rational choice. This sense of lack, I here suggest, is a measure of our deference to a theory of knowledge which sees a cognitive gap between the agent's knowledge of his position and his practical conclusion. The theory implies that a rational agent (with his various desires and concerns) might *know the facts of his position, yet still not know what to do.* For example, I might have many true justified beliefs about my circumstances (which I have *because* they are true and justified), yet not know what to do. Equally, different agents with desires and concerns for similar objects might have the factual knowledge, yet reach different practical conclusions. Hence the presumed need for one or another mediating principle if the conclusion is to be rational.

Aristotle, I suspect, would be baffled by the claim that one can '*know* the facts of the position' yet not know what to do. He might think that we were talking about some very difficult case of conflict of values or interests where even the wise man's wisdom fails. But these are rare, whereas the point was meant universally. Or Aristotle might think that we were using strange language to make an obvious point about theoretical knowledge: one might have theoretical knowledge of something, yet 'not know what to do' in the sense that neither the knowledge nor what is known calls for any practical response, so of course we have none in the face of it, and this is not a lack. This is because, according to his doctrine, theoretical knowledge is about the eternal and necessary, so nothing thus known is in our power to affect. What he would not have understood without explanations drawn from later philosophical theories is the general claim that we can have *knowledge* of our contingent circumstances, yet be wondering what to do in response. For where we are called upon to respond to the circumstances somehow (in a practical way), knowledge of those circumstances would be knowledge for the sake of practice; and not yet knowing how to respond implies that, so far as knowledge for the sake of practice is concerned, we do *not* yet know the circumstances. In the same way, the scientist has not adequately grasped his material if he still wonders how to explain it. There is therefore no cognitive interval between knowledge of the particular position and knowing what to do about it, and no cognitive gap[68] for a general principle to bridge.

Aristotle's view does not presuppose a mysterious faculty of cognition; rather, it presupposes a different view from the one until recently prevailing of what counts as successful cognition. Successful cognition, according to the latter, is the ability to make a correct *justified* assertion. Knowledge is the ability to prove that one is right. But for Aristotle, successful cognition with respect to whatever material is the ability to make the kind of response appropriate for anyone taking an interest in that material. Thus in a hardheaded sense (from his point of view) we are not sufficiently knowledgeable about a work of art unless we respond with sensitivity to its aesthetic and technical qualities, and we are not sufficiently aware of the facts of a practical situation until we know what to do in it.

I can now begin bringing together practical intelligence and the moral dispositions. A moral disposition is a disposition to respond in certain ways to certain situations: the kind person responds to trouble with help, the friendly person greets when he is greeted, respect for parents issues in deference to their wishes, etc. Intelligence or astuteness is the ability to read an initially opaque situation (i.e., one which at first sight is not the object of any determinate ethical response) in such a way that the moral dispositions come to be faced with what they naturally respond to. But this is oversimplified, because a specific moral disposition, even if desirable in general, is not a virtue if the agent is inclined to express it on inappropriate occasions or in ways that fail to accommodate his other concerns. The astuteness of wisdom is therefore the ability to read the facts in such a way that a general disposition to do what is best, all things considered, will issue in a response that does justice to *all* that one cares about. But more is needed for wisdom than sensible concern for all that one happens to hold dear, since one might hold dear what is worthless. The specific values, pursuit of which is constrained by the general disposition just mentioned, must be sound. With this provision, astuteness is called 'intelligence', because for Aristotle the term 'intelligence' implies a grasp that is *true* (1139 b 15–17; 1141 a 3–5). One has not read the situation correctly or truly until one knows what to do in it; and knowing what to do in it is not just knowing by one's own lights what to do in it, but knowing what is really right to do in it, which is the same as knowing what the virtuous person would know.

This takes us back to a question raised in Chapter 1, Section VI, of this book, where we saw Aristotle locating the essence of happiness in our well-functioning as the rational beings we are and rewriting this as 'rational activity in accordance with excellence'. The question was 'Granted that the rational activity is *good* when grounded in the various qualities acknowledged as virtues, by what right can Aristotle regard this goodness as a goodness of reason as such?' For, it seemed clear, a villain may be as rational and intelligent as a morally admirable agent. In the light of our detailed study of deliberation and cognate matters, the question loses its force. Such force as it had depended on the assumption that excellence in reasoning and cognition is judged by standards wholly internal to reasoning and cognition. Thus, e.g., good reasoning is logically or inductively sound reasoning, and good cognition is justified true belief. The intellectual elements of vicious deliberation may have these properties to the full. But from the Aristotelian point of view, it is still, even so, bad deliberation, i.e. bad as a specimen of deliberation, because the vicious deliberator fails to attain the practical *truth* which is the end of practical reason. Rational activity is not a game played equally well in any kind of moral arena. It is not played well at all if, from the start, there is no hope of gaining the *knowledge* which our rational equipment is meant by nature to achieve. Since knowledge in the practical sphere is knowledge of what to do, and this depends on goodness of character, reason in the practical sphere is hostage to the nonrational: its excellence, even as *reason,* depends on quality of character.

## XI. Character and Intelligence in Deliberation (II)

Before pursuing further the interlocking functions of character and intelligence, let me not get too far ahead of questions which arise from the way in which the concept of intelligence was introduced in the last section. Pausing over these will also help to clarify the phrase used in its penultimate paragraph: 'a general disposition to do what is best, all things considered'.

I suggested that Aristotle's conception of practical intelligence takes care of a theoretical concern which, on a different model of knowledge, is met by supposing that general ethical principles play a major rôle in the forming of a rational choice. I do not wish to imply that general maxims never enter into Aristotelian deliberations, but only that they are not required parts of the machinery as they are on that other model. In that context, ethical principles are postulated to cover a cognitive gap between the agent's knowledge of his position and his practical conclusion, but I pointed out that no such gap can appear in an Aristotelian framework. However, it was also suggested at a slightly earlier stage that the operation of such principles might have to be postulated so as to maintain the classic distinction between animal response and deliberated choice. Now according to the account just delivered of intelligence, the validity of that distinction (if supposed fundamental) is still open to question. For intelligence has emerged as the ability to read a particular situation in such a way that the agent's character responds according to its kind. But this 'reading' ability is surely present in animals, whether or not we call it 'intelligence', though linked in this case to innate dispositions. This smell spells danger, that one food, this chill in the air is the message to starting moving in the direction which men call 'south'. Thus the appeal to intelligence as so far explained does not preserve the contrast which Aristotle rightly or wrongly claims between distinctively human and animal behaviour.[69] And what can save it (if it should be saved) except those general principles which seem to have no necessary place in Aristotle's account of deliberation?

I shall sketch what I take to be the answer representing Aristotle, while admitting that he does not make it altogether clear. Let us look more closely at the connection between desiderative disposition (innate or culturally acquired), reading ability, and response. The first needs the second in order to issue in the third. But we should not think of the desiderative disposition as a potentiality or capacity stimulated to actualisation by a read situational particular. The desiderative disposition is an already incipiently active interest in a certain type of object, and it falls short of expression in determinate action not because it is a bare potentiality, but because by itself it is general and indeterminate. *It* carries with it a general cognitive alertness regarding the type of object in question; in other words, a readiness to read situations in ways that present them as containing or not containing that object or its possibility. Similarly, a desiderative disposition implies focus away from aspects of the situation insignificant for its expression. Thus the desiderative disposition *is* a cognitive disposition to read in the relevant ways.

This much is clearly part of the Aristotle's picture. What he does not say clearly, although his account implies it, is that the human ability to 'read' goes far beyond what is part and parcel of a set of inbuilt specific desiderative dispositions. The moral dispositions are concerned with different types of situation and object, and are inculcated in a variety of kinds of practice. The reading ability that goes with each is the ability to recognise a particular as an instance of a universal already present in the subject's desiderative vocabulary. Here we are speaking of appropriate response to a situation perceived as instantiating one such universal or another. But what about situations in which more than one is instantiated? The apparatus outlined does not in general include a pre-established disposition for right reading and right response in such a case. This is because the combination is accidental and rare. The agent's experience prepares him à la Hume to read a C as a D, an I as a J, an L as an M, but not to make the most in a practical way of a C-I-L combination. Where combinations are predictable, dispositions for ranking responses may have been inculcated, just as in animals there exist mechanisms whereby a major concern automatically dominates another when the situation presents objects of both. Good moral training builds in certain general rankings. Thus in situations that present an occasion for 'noble' action along with an alternative opportunity for physical pleasure, Aristotle's well-brought-up person presumably grasps the former. But no humanly acquirable set of evaluative habits could ensure appropriate responses in all cases of accidental combination, and there are few, if any, really firm rules for choice or adjustment of claims. However, this is not to be lamented, because the multiplicity of pre-existing interests, as well as being a source of doubt and potential conflict, also provides opportunity for the identification of new values and new kinds of worthwhile projects suggested by the accidental conjunctions. As Aristotle says at *Politics* 1332 b 7–8, 'men do many things against habit and nature if reason persuades them that they ought'.

So 'practical intelligence' (that honorific title) is, I suggest, Aristotle's name for the quality that takes us human agents beyond the several deliverances of whatever special sensitivities (grounded in our standing or pre-existent concerns) we bring to a situation. It is the ability not merely to grasp the practical significance of "words" one by one or in familiar combinations, but to recognise and read them well when they occur in unfamiliar patterns thrown at us by chance.[70] As with real words, the significance of a combination may not be the sum of the significances of the elements combined. This intellectual disposition is activated by the general moral disposition which it in turn makes effective in a determinate way: the disposition, namely, of desiring the formal *best,* which in any given case receives a specified content, but different contents from case to case. Where the moral disposition is inferior, the intellectual disposition is *cunning* or *astuteness*; where what is aimed at is a limited good (e.g., health) as such, the intellectual disposition is *craft.* Aristotle notes: 'In a sense chance and art are concerned with the same objects; as Agathon says, "art loves chance [i.e., luck] and chance loves art"' (1140 a 17–20).

Deliberation is needed when the right response depends on intelligence as interpreted above, and this operation of intelligence could even be taken as definitive of deliberation. If so, deliberation is not necessarily a time-consuming process. An instantaneous response counts as deliberated when not prepackaged by existing dispositions, and thus we avoid the artificial position that practical wisdom is shown only in decisions made after a period of indecision. And in saying that intelligence illuminates unfamiliar combinations, we do not imply that it has work to do only on rare occasions or that the intelligent response is always unusual. Every situation has chance components and connections, and intelligence makes the most of whatever comes its way. It may issue in a response that coincides externally with someone else's more mechanical reaction, but the intelligent agent is the one who was morally and cognitively prepared to come out with something original had it been called for.

But of course a person's intelligence draws particular attention to itself in connection with actions whose point we fail to see straightaway, but which make sense when the agent mentions a feature which we overlooked or did not realise was relevant.

Aristotle speaks of a disposition called 'understanding' or 'excellence in understanding' (*sunesis, eusunesia;* 1142 b 34–1143 a 18). This is not the same as scientific understanding *(epistēmē);* it has the same kind of objects as practical wisdom, but is not immediately practical since its manifestation is the assessment of another's rational choice. Aristotle's brief remarks can be construed as covering two grades of understanding, though he does not distinguish. Let us take the case where the choice is judged to be right. There is comprehension by a person who has only to hear an outline of the agent's situation to see that the choice was good; and there is comprehension by a person who sees that it was good when the relevant details are brought to his attention, but would not himself have taken account of them all in the situation as originally presented to him. The former is a sort of bystander's version of practical wisdom; the latter is only the potential for that virtue. It is more than a set of one-track moral dispositions, because the subject can put things together in a morally significant way when the elements are pointed out as concurrent, but he needs them pointed out.

From this condition and in this way, presumably, we acquire practical wisdom.[71] Aristotle does not say much about how this consummate virtue is developed. At 1142 a 14–15 he mentions that it depends on experience and at 1103 a 15 that the intellectual excellences (of which it is one) are acquired through 'teaching'. In the case of practical wisdom, this does not mean through formal instruction[72] but through explaining: having it explained to you why another's choice was a good one or not, and being shown how one's own failed to take account of something relevant. From this the learner learns more about what relevances to look out for, and also the general habit of looking out for more relevances.

So in Aristotle's account, the radical distinction between deliberated response and animal behaviour is sustained by the concept of practical intelligence, without resort to the notion of ethical principles. If we wonder how a reason for a practical conclusion can properly be considered a reason when the conclusion falls short of being logically grounded in it along with the rest of the reasons, the answer surely is that in the only known species of reason-giving animals, reason-giving works despite this academic defect. For giving reasons (as distinct from acting from reasons which one could give) is not an end in itself: one gives them to instruct another or to justify or explain oneself. On the practical level, as on the aesthetic when beauty or harmony are explained, those purposes can be accomplished without its being shown (supposing this even possible) that given the various interests involved, together with the picture of the circumstances, it would be *formally* illogical not to accept the conclusion.[73] It is enough if, by stating the considerations which weighed with us, we get others to see our choice as right: to see it as the choice that they would have made, or would have made had they been sufficiently alive to the circumstances. We also give reasons in order to expose our choice to criticism, so that in that way we can learn something. And by giving a reason we knowingly license others to consider us irrational if we alter or abandon the choice without having a new reason that is felt to make sense of the change. A choice thus imposes a rational limit on action in similar situations, since divergence has to be justified by appeal to some factor not present in the previous case. In this way, a particular choice grounded on particulars assumes the status of a defeasible (and no doubt reinterpretable) norm, the gist of which may come to be formulated in general terms. Practical wisdom shows its power by generating choices that deserve to become norms in this way, more than by forming its choices in accordance with the already available standards.

I have argued (focusing on *wise* deliberation) that within the context of Aristotelian deliberation, no Grand End is grasped, either by intelligence or by moral virtue. The Grand End is something to be explored in abstract ethical inquiry; but although such thinking is ultimately for the sake of practice, it is not what Aristotle means by 'deliberation'.[74] Deliberation on any occasion aims at solving a particular practical problem. I have also argued that within deliberation there is no essential rôle for general ethical principles. Such principles, like the Grand End picture, can make an appearance *after* wise deliberation, as a general by-product of particular rational choices. This account, moreover, permits the Aristotelian deliberator to do what it is often denied that he can, namely decide through deliberation, which assumes an end, whether or not to pursue that end. The account also fits those passages where Aristotle says that moral virtue makes the end or the aim right; I have argued that this does not mean that virtue sets up a special kind of virtuous end which cannot attract nonvirtuous persons, but that virtue ensures that one is right to pursue in the particular situation the end which one does pursue. In itself, that end may be the kind of thing that most people find desirable, whether they are morally good or bad or mediocre.

But a debt of attention still remains to the notoriously difficult and far from casual passage where Aristotle says that intelligence is 'of the *archai* (starting-points, origins, principles, dominant factors)'. I discussed this up to a point in the last section, but now it should be possible to give a fuller exegesis, which will summarize the main conclusions of this entire exposition of Aristotle's notion of practical intelligence. He writes:

> Intelligence [*nous*] is concerned with the ultimates in both directions; for both the primary definitions and the ultimates are objects of intelligence and not of argument, and in demonstrations intelligence grasps the unchangeable and primary definitions, while in practical reasonings it grasps what is ultimate and contingent and belonging to the second proposition. For these are the *archai* of that for the sake of which, since the universals are reached from the particulars; of these therefore we must have perception, and this is intelligence. (1143 a 35–b 5; cf. 1141 a 7–8)[75]

The interpreter must explain (1) what those ultimates are which relate to practical intelligence; (2) the assimilation of intelligence to perception; (3) the meaning of 'these ultimates are the *archai* of that for the sake of which'; (4) the meaning of 'universals are from particulars'.[76]

(1) I have already indicated (*a*) that practical ultimates are entities which from the point of view of science are furthest removed from the primary objects of science (i.e., the explanatory primitives). In the present passage, the ultimates grasped by practical intelligence are, I think, meant as ultimate in the above sense; but this is

not the only sense meant here and not the most important. Something is also ultimate if (*b*) it is reached last in the order of inquiry,[77] and (*c*) no account, argument or explanation can be given for it. The objects of practical intelligence are said here to be ultimate in these ways, too.

What is reached last in practical inquiry is the rational choice of A, the initial move, which strictly speaking is the choice of A-in-light-of-its-reasons: the reasons being the end and the circumstances as they display themselves to intelligence. Thus what is ultimate in this sense (*b*) is also the completed practical argument. The rational choice considered in this way has (*c*) no rational account *(logos),* since the agent can have no reason why the argument which completes itself to his satisfaction is a satisfactory argument—which is the same as to say that he can have no reason why the factors which figure as his reasons for the action chosen *are* reasons for it. For another agent they might not be, but the difference is due to a difference in moral perspective (cf. 1227 b 22–25).

(2) Moreover, no action A′ stands to A as A to some means B intermediate between A and the end O. For deliberation shows that by doing B one would, under the circumstances, be acting for the best in pursuing O—but only provided one does B by doing A. Doing A is one way of doing B, which has to be done in one way or another if it is to be a concrete act. Thus where B is done by doing A, doing A is what it is about this concrete doing of B that renders that a doing-of-the-best with regard O. Doing B, and for that matter doing or pursuing C, D, E etc. on the ladder of means to O, is, in this concrete case, an instance of *eupraxia* (good action); and doing A is like the formal cause *(logos)* of the goodness of this *praxis.* Now if someone thought it right to pursue O by B, and merely happened to do B by means of A, his judgment would not be incorrect, but it would not be practical wisdom, since practical wisdom would know that *this* doing of B is right because and only because it is a doing of A. For practical wisdom, the rightness of this doing of B (and C, D, etc. up to and including the action described merely as 'pursuit of O') is grounded on the fact that it consists in the doing of A; thus practical wisdom, in grasping what is right to do, grasps B not as just B, but as B in the special form of A. But if we are ever to finish deliberating (and should this be supposed not possible, there would be no deliberation, since deliberation is with a view to action and *having* deliberated), we must reach an A such that there is no special way of doing it that renders this the doing of what is best under the circumstances. There must be an A such that in grasping what is right to do, wisdom grasps it simply as *A,* and not as the right thing to do *provided one does it, A, in the right way.* A, qua the right thing to do, is indivisible *(atomon)* into right and wrong ways of doing A. Consequently there is no halfway house between knowing that A is the right thing and being ignorant that it is, in the way in which holding that B without restriction is the right means to O stands between the mistake of holding that something quite else is the right means and the knowledge that B is right (in this situation) if and only if done by doing A. One's grasp of the (mediated) rightness of B (which is more or less accurate depending on whether it registers the mediating factor) is a sort of assertion, whereas the all or nothing grasp of the rightness of A is comparable to perception (cf. 1142 a 25–30; *Metaphysics* 1051 b 17–28).

Now, if rational choice is ultimate, the passage just quoted implies that rational choice is the object of (grasped by) practical intelligence. In that case, how are we to interpret the statement that the objects of intelligence belong to the second proposition; i.e., the premiss which states the particular facts? For making the rational choice does not depend on the particular facts alone, but also on evaluations—the evaluations that go into the selection of means at each stage of deliberation. Now a selection of means, though evaluative, is an exercise of the agent's factual intelligence or astuteness. Indeed, it is virtually the same act as that by which he grasps the totality of factual elements so far seen as relevant (i.e., relevant to its remaining true at this stage that pursuit of O is pursuit of the best). For given that the astute agent is endowed with moral dispositions or desiderative concerns, his cognitive grasp of the set of relevants is not for him an experience distinct from his practical response. The latter could even be called his act of practical attention to them all as relevant. The final stage occurs when the set of relevants-seen-so-far becomes the set of relevants unprovisionally, and the grasp of this as no longer provisional is the categorical choice. This choice, therefore, prescriptive as it is, is a compendious reflection of all the facts seen as relevant by the agent. But the chosen action thus textured by the relevants (which thereby help to constitute the identity of the particular action chosen) is nothing but a *way* of pursuing the end, which was to realise O while maintaining that project's coincidence with the best. Hence that-for-the-sake-of-which draws its substance as a realised end from the relevants grasped as relevant, and in this way they are its *archai* or collective origin. This answers to (3) above.[78]

Since, moreover the act of grasping the relevants as relevant is identical with forming the choice of A, the initial move, in response to them: and since in choosing A one takes oneself to be choosing a move in terms of which it is true that pursuing O is best in this situation: it follows that grasping the relevants is grasping how that is true, or what makes it true. Before the choice was concluded we only *assumed* it true that 'O is the end and the best' without yet knowing what makes it so (*as* making it so). Here we have a precise analogy with the object of theoretical intelligence. That object is the cause of the fact initially focused on; and here, too, the assumption of truth (that it is a fact), though perhaps less easily abandoned, is confirmed when we grasp the principles in virtue of which it is true. Practical wisdom mirrors scientific understanding: both conclude by *affirming* true what was so far *assumed* as true, in the light of what makes it true. In this sense, too (see [3] again), the ultimates grasped by practical intelligence are the 'sources of that-for-the-sake-of which': the sources, this time, not of O's being *made real,* but of its being true that O *should be made real*—a truth which qualifies it to *be* an end actually sought for.

Finally, the end O is a universal realisable differently in different situations and is not brought to reality at all unless through some particular choice substantialising it in terms of circumstantial particulars. And it is good and best (more universals) only when rightly particularised. In this way 'the universal is *from* the particulars', which answers to (4).

Nearing the end of this discussion of practical wisdom, I turn to a question which Aristotle raises not far from the close of *NE* VI and a few lines after the passage just expounded. What is the use of either practical or theoretic wisdom, hence (by implication) why should we value them (1143 b 18 ff.)? Aristotle's rather complex answer continues the parallel between these forms of rationality, and at the same time completes his investigation of practical excellence by bringing practical wisdom into relation with moral virtue. It also, as his audience would have seen at once, defines his position in relation to Plato.

Aristotle is as certain as Plato ever was that some ethical responses are right, some wrong, and that right and good are not matters of opinion on which anyone judges correctly who judges as he happens to feel. But Aristotle has rejected any attempt to underpin the difference between practical truth and falsehood by appeal to Forms or eternal paradigms. The only models we have are the wise among us, and their wisdom is shot through with the metaphysical imperfection of what is and is not and comes to be only through chancy development. Further, these models in any case are to be taken only in the light of one's *own* intelligent grasp of the situation. The same must be true of wise advice and recommendations. Once a person is sufficiently master of his nonrational soul to be able to use his practical intelligence, he should use it to the full, because this is the source of what no one else can take care of: his own good rational functioning. Thus the purpose of practical wisdom is not, as Plato depicts it in the *Republic,* to pilot the lives of others: making and keeping them good as a physician cares for his patients. If that were so, the unambitious might reasonably opt for the easier life of a passenger: not necessarily out of a sense of their own intellectual inadequacy, but (it might be) because they know of a higher and more beautiful employment for the mind, one that does not look beyond itself to any ulterior good. If theoretic activity makes for human happiness, (and Aristotle quietly assumes this here without argument), it can only be because it is the sort of activity *in which* our happiness consists. But, we are to understand, the same is true of the activity of practical wisom (1144 a 3–6). Practical wisdom is not a craft which it makes sense to engage in only for the sake of some product at which it aims. (This is not to deny that the person of practical wisdom, as we have seen, pursues this, that and the other quite definite end). Therefore practical wisdom is good for reasons having nothing to do with usefulness even if it is also useful. If that were not so, how could we defend the value of *theoretic* wisdom, supposing it necessary to defend it? Perhaps we could, but not so easily as when we see clearly that practical wisdom is not a craft, so that even *practical* activity is to be prized as an end in itself.

Aristotle's ethical defence of theoretic wisdom comes in *NE* X, and will be the topic of my final chapter. Meanwhile, if practical wisdom were a craft like medicine, then although the *community* would need it, no single individual would need it himself in the way in which he needs the health it brings. The view that makes practical wisdom a craft is the theory of the *Republic,* where practical wisdom is the virtue of those specialists whose function is to govern the community and to develop and maintain the various moral virtues suitable in the other classes. The specialist rulers must themselves have moral excellence (this is a presupposition of their practical wisdom), but the purity of the distinct moral virtues in the lower orders depends on the rulers' monopoly of wisdom. The one consummate virtue which everyone ideally has is that of attending only to one's proper concerns, called by Plato 'justice'. Aristotle, however, reinterprets this notion of attending to one's own concerns by arguing that the activity of one or another of the moral virtues without practical wisdom cannot be the whole of anyone's proper concern, since such an activity is impossible.

This position is grounded on his earlier definition of moral excellence as a pro-hairetic disposition (cf. 1144 a 13–20). But only here in *NE* VI does it become clear what this entails: that no one can be morally virtuous, strictly speaking, unless he is also practically wise (1144 b1–32). This is because only the agent's own astuteness can issue in *his* brave or temperate or just actions. Without intelligence, good moral dispositions are only amenabilities to external direction. That kind of excellence may be good enough for members of Plato's Utopia, but followers of Aristotle's (and of Plato's) argument could hardly admire it in themselves or in those they respect, and they could not consider the activity of it to be *their* happiness. Their happiness must be *their* activity, but a virtue which is nothing but obedience has to be activated from outside, by rulers, parents or laws.

For the most part, though (anyway outside Utopia), these good dispositions would not be properly directed. And without directive intelligence they are blind, Aristotle says (1144 b 8–13).[79] If the right response is made, it is mechanical, and its rightness is due in part to accident. Thus even if the undirected *response* were to express the individual, its *rightness* would not be his. If the morally virtuous action is right, and the agent of the morally virtuous action is the agent of it qua right, so that *he* lights on the ethical mean in each case, then this is due to *his* intelligence, and the capacity for morally virtuous action must include practical wisdom. Other-wise a human being is like a nonrational animal, of which we can say that *it* pounces or darts away at the first sign of danger, but not that the accuracy of response is *its* achievement. Plato's doctrine is dangerous (at least if interpreted as a political theory, not, as he also intended it, as a model of the individual psyche); for if we or some of us came to believe ourselves limited to responses whose rightness is accidental or due to others or to an underlying mechanism of habit or biological nature—all causes of rightness beyond us individuals—then should we still care about what, on this hypothesis, we could not attain: being right *ourselves?* But for us to lose this active general concern for the *orthos logos* would be to lose the substance of moral virtue.

So moral virtue depends on the astuteness of practical wisdom, and practical wisdom in turn (as Plato saw) on moral virtue. Without virtue, astuteness is no more than ingenious alertness to what only *appears* relevant, appearing so from a morally corrupt perspective (1144 a 20–b 1; 1140 b 11–20). Aristotle concludes that none of the moral virtues, strictly speaking, is possible for an individual without the others, since each requires and is required by practical wisdom (1144 b 30–1145 a 2).[80] This paradoxical result shows him now a long way ahead of those ordinary notions of human goodness on which he had to rely at the start. The divergence is the price of a theory in which, as for Plato, practical wisdom depends on the substructure of moral virtue, but in which, *contra* Plato, it is every citizen's business to aspire to and exercise practical wisdom. Aristotle's egalitarian conception of practical wis-dom carries with it a tightening of the philosophical standard for predicating moral virtues.[81]

But does that follow in fact? If practical wisdom is a single indivisible quality, then it seems true that practical wisdom is marred in the absence of any of the various moral virtues. For if there is any area of life—money, personal safety, honour, pleasure, parents or children—where the agent is disposed to care too much or too little, this limits his ability to take the right sort of practical notice, since we see situations in terms on which we are morally disposed to respond. But should we suppose from this that none of the moral virtues is possible without the others? Cannot one be morally well disposed and intelligent, and therefore effectively virtuous, in one but not another area of life? Why should a given kind of virtuous action require the unrestricted practical wisdom that would be wise on every front?

Presumably it is because the situation faced by, say, the courageously disposed agent has dimensions to which courage is irrelevant. The courageous response that failed to take account of these in the right way might be wrong or wrongly executed. It might be unjust or unnecessarily brutal. Now if we insist, as Aristotle would, on the connection between *virtue* and *acting well,* we cannot say that courage is a virtue and suppose it separable from the other virtues without in effect postulating a different type of *acting well*—which is to say a different type of *orthos logos*—for each moral excellence. There is then a practical wisdom of courage, another of temperance, and so on. This is not absurd *ex vi terminorum;* indeed Aristotle reports (1144 b 17–18) that some people thought that the virtues are 'practical wisdoms' *(phronēseis).* But it does make the virtues more like crafts. We can say that the courageous action was good and noble as judged in terms of fear and confidence, but we cannot on that account suppose it noble and admirable without qualification. Again, the inference is blocked from 'Callias is courageous' to 'Callias is a good human being', unless we give up the contrariety of 'good' and 'bad' so as to allow for the legitimacy of simultaneous inference from 'Callias (the one who is courageous) is dissolute' to 'Callias is a bad human being'.[82]

Does this matter? The ordinary notions of say, *courage* and *profligacy, courage* and *arrogance,* do not fall apart if we use them compatibly. Nor should they, as long as our interest in character is mainly anecdotal: the interest that generates novels and biography. Someone is temperate and unscrupulous about money. Someone else is imaginatively generous but hates anything toilsome. Asked whether he or she is a good or bad *person* all told, we shrug and say 'Both' or 'Neither' or 'Why do we have to decide?' These are instances of what is already the case, and what (given the nature of our interest) we are not called upon to do anything about. The morally mixed character need not be an incoherent personality, and the mixed ethical description is only too often true. But in Aristotle, the various characters and their kinds of action are models of what ought or ought not to be. Telling a child to be brave is telling him how he ought to be, and initially we say these things in simple situations where (as we give him to understand) he will do the all-round right thing if and only if he acts bravely. 'Honest', 'courageous', 'generous', etc. connote models (whether persons or actions), and the contraries countermodels. A mixed pair of ethical terms can hold of the same subject, but then this subject is not an appropriate model, since a model should not send mixed messages. It makes sense in a work of practical ethics to shape the logic of the terms in such a way that they cannot send mixed messages. Thus the action will not be treated as brave if it is also unjust, or if it is done for a wager of beer, or if we know that the person who risked his life for his country on the battlefield was one month later selling secrets to a foreign power. From the verdictive or anecdotal point of view it is absurd to insist that we cannot apply 'honest', 'generous', etc. in any instance without first ascertaining that the subject is free of every vice. But where the terms are to be used of models (i.e., of what are assumed to be apt models), this demand is not so unreasonable.[83]

## Notes

1. Craft gives Aristotle a handle on practical *thinking*. But in a few places where he wants to bring out the *moral* relation in which an agent stands to the actions which are his and which stand for him in the world, Aristotle likens them to offspring: 1113 b 18–19; 1222 b 15–20; cf. *Magna Moralia* 1187 b 4–9.
2. Another example is unformed matter introduced in *Phys.* I.7 by analogy with the substantial subject of change.
3. Once we see ourselves as able to bring about a desired result by some means, we can hardly not also see ourselves as able, by the same deed, to bring about unintended consequences. This is where comparative judgment enters the picture.
4. A is immediate in the required sense even if it is not practicable now, if all that the agent has to do before doing A is to wait for the occasion when A is practicable.
5. What is the object of this desire? It is usually taken to be what is chosen (the *prohaireton*); i.e., A (or better, A for the sake of O). But the *prohairesis* can also be construed as a desire whose object is O; namely, a desire for O by means of A.
6. Notably D. J. Allan [2].
7. Cf. Rowe [1], 109–13. Numerous commentators (e.g., Greenwood, 44; Ross [1], 217; Gauthier and Jolif ad 1138 b 23 and 34) think that Aristotle (anyway at times in the *Ethics*) regards promotion of *theōria* (or of one's own *theōria*) as the one standard of right action, and they take this doctrine to be implied if not stated in *NE* VI. It is true that at 1145 a 6–11 Aristotle says that practical wisdom sees to it that there should be *theōria*. But this does not imply that there is no other ground for judging an action right.
8. The *Revised Oxford Translation* has 'standard'.
9. Cf. 1094 a 23–24, where the same archery simile is used as at 1138 b 22–23.
10. How, if we lack practical wisdom ourselves, do we know what to aim at? Answer: if we are brought up in the right values (which is assumed), we only need to be able to identify someone in our community who shares our values and is shrewder, more imaginative and more perceptive than we are in putting them into practice. That, by comparison with ourselves, is a person of practical wisdom. Of course, if we assume that practical wisdom is a special craft or science, as in Plato's *Republic,* we shall not be able to recognise any instances of what we take practical wisdom to be; and we shall miss the otherwise easily recognisable examples of what it really is.
11. In Chapter 1, Section VI, I argued that Aristotle's *NE* I definition of happiness is necessarily incomplete, but that this does not matter. Why then should it matter now if his definition of the good man is incomplete? Because in the former case the missing element could readily be supplied by common sense, but in the present case, where the missing element is an account of the 'Grand End' (see the next section), this is not so.
12. Many interpreters ascribe this view of practical wisdom to Aristotle or write at times as if they do, but the clearest statements I have encountered are in Cooper [1], 96–98; Kenny [3], 150–51; MacIntyre [2], 131–33.
13. For the phrase, cf. Cooper [1], 59.
14. Cf. Hardie [4], 251–52.
15. See e.g. Gauthier and Jolif, vol. II, part 1, 167–68 and 193; Cashdollar; Irwin [7], 399–410.
16. At 1103 a 32–34 playing the harp is classified as a skill.
17. On this interpretation the *praxis/poiēsis* distinction of *NE* VI is not the same as the *energeia/kinēsis* distinction of *Meta.* IX.6. For a very different interpretation which identifies the distinctions, see Charles [2].

18. Actions which are wrong though generically noble are mentioned at 1110 b 9–13 and 1148 a 28 ff.

19. Aristotle may carelessly contradict himself on this at 1110 a 26–29, which suggests that it is always wrong knowingly to kill your mother. We should not on that account ascribe to him an *official* doctrine inconsistent with another of his official doctrines.

20. Consequently, it is difficult for Aristotle to given an example of a good *doing* (in the sense in which this is contrasted with a *making*). Cf. Ando, 51.

21. Cf. M. J. White [1].

22. There is also much to be said about the part played in all this by the emotions. See Fortenbaugh [2] and, for a detailed study of portions of this field, Leighton [1].

23. Such a view clashes with the statement at 1226 a 4–6 that a sentence such as 'I ought to do so and so' is true or false and represents a *doxa* (judgment), not a choice.

24. Cf. Greenwood, 50–51.

25. The semantic conception of truth appears in Aristotle, e.g., *Meta.* 1011 b 27, but a glance at Bonitz s.vv. *alētheia* and *alēthēs* shows 'truth' by and large lining up with 'knowledge', 'understanding' and 'reality' ( = 'reality as it is to the discerning mind or fundamentally').

26. Cf. Kenny [3], 94. At moments Aristotle himself denies that truth can apply to rational choice: 1112 a 5–7; 1226 a 4. (Presumably here he does mean 'semantic truth').

27. See Barnes [1], Burnyeat [3], Kosman [1].

28. More accurately: demonstrative premisses do not present first-order grounds for believing what is stated in the conclusion. But that this already believed-in fact can be demonstratively explained gives further justification for holding it to be a fact; see p. 256 and cf. Irwin [7], 530–31, note 24. (Being able to justify one's belief that *p* by being able to explain the fact that *p* must not be confused with being able to justify one's claim to be able to explain *p*).

29. *Pace* Kenny [3], 94.

30. On practical truth as the effectiveness of moral virtue, cf. Anscombe and Milo, 64–65.

31. *Movement of Animals* 701 a 25–b1 suggests that, when there is deliberation, it provides *premisses* for the practical conclusion. Thus to deliberate is to produce a practical argument, rather than to use one. See also Aubenque, 139–40.

32. Does Aristotle think that one who holds a practical conclusion ipso facto acts accordingly unless prevented? In my view, No. But defence of this interpretation belongs in the discussion of his notion of incontinence. See Chapter 5, Section VI.

33. The comparison at 1112 b 20–24 of the last step of deliberation with the last step of geometrical analysis recurs, obscurely expressed, at 1142 a 26–29 (with *en tois mathēmatikois* retained). One would never guess this from the *Revised Oxford Translations*'s version of the latter passage. Cf. Cooper [1], 33–41 and 183–86, who mainly agrees with Burnet, 271–74 and xxxiv–xxxvii.

34. Since there are these opposite stages, it is unhelpful to say (as, e.g., Joachim, 4) such things as 'the zoologist begins by defining *animal*'. A nominal definition might be the beginning of *inquiry*, a real definition is the ideal first principle of *explanation*.

35. For the parallel with theoretical assumption, see Burnet on *hupothesis,* xxxiv–xxxvi and 324–25 (*pace* Joachim ad 1151 a 16–170).

36. In this respect, scientific research is like craft-activity: the scientist seeks to form an explanatory account according to general canons knowable beforehand. Aristotle does not think it possible to give a general description of a good *prohairesis* that would guide deliberation. This is why, when trying to characterise practical wisdom in the *Ethics,* he spends much more time examining the *activity* of practical inquiry (deliberation) than he does on examining the activity of research when trying to characterise excellent science in the *Posterior Analytics.* Not being able, in the practical case, to get or give general insight by holding up a model of the product (a good *prohairesis* or a good action), he tries to compensate by looking at the activity.

37. There is plenty here to confuse analysts of action and interpreters of Aristotle. In play are different points of view, agent's and spectator's, and different sense of 'cause' and 'because'; and these are being juggled in nontechnical language which does not signal the difference

between human action and the physical movements constituting it, nor the difference between act and content in connection with systematically ambiguous terms like 'starting-point', 'premiss', 'conclusion', *'prohairesis'.* (1) For the agent, the practical elements of his problem, i.e. the situation C and the unavailability of the desired O, are like the material cause of what he prohairetically proposes to do about it (cf. A Broadie; see also Fortenbaugh [1], who identifies the middle term or cause with the objective O). (2) If the agent enacts the *prohairesis,* the elements of his problem constitute, for others (and now in the third person) the formal cause of his observed behaviour, while his physical movements are its material cause. (3) If he enacts the *prohairesis,* his *holding* it, where *what* he holds is resoluble into elements according to (1), is the efficient cause of the necessary physical movements. For discussion of some of the ambiguities, see Santas.

38. On the intrinsically social dimensions of the practical argument, see Nussbaum [1], 103 ff.

39. Cf. Nussbaum [1], Interpretive Essay 4, esp. 193–94, 201–10.

40. These considerations help to explain the evidence which led Allan [2] and Cooper [1], Chapter 1, to question (in different ways) the traditional connection between deliberation and the practical argument (syllogism). See also Hardie [4], 249—57.

41. Nonetheless, at 1147 b 29 wealth is said to be 'desirable for itself'; see also 1248 b 18 ff. On the interpretation of this, see below, Chapter 7, Section III.

42. Cf. Wiggins.

43. Aristotle's remark at 1227 b 32–33 that the end ( = goal) is the *archē* (principle, starting point) of deliberation, while the end ( = conclusion) of deliberation is the *archē* of action is often understood in a temporal sense. But he is more likely to mean that the goal gives to deliberation a typifying form and the *prohairesis* gives another such form to the action.

44. This may be what McDowell [2] has in mind when he ascribes to Aristotle the ideas (1) that the orectic premiss of a virtuous person's practical argument incorporates that person's conception of the sort of life a human being should lead; and (2) that such a conception is incapable of being 'definitively written down'. Certainly Aristotle accepts (2), but it is not at all clear that he holds (1). Whether he does so depends on whether he thinks that the premiss in question presents the end in the light of which the agent deliberated. Aristotle's failure clearly to signal the difference between deliberative starting-points and components of a finally chosen action makes it difficult to decide the last question. If, however, the premiss to which McDowell refers does present the deliberative end *as it figures at the start of deliberation,* then (for reasons for which I argue in the text) I regard (1) as non-Aristotelian. It would be truer to Aristotle to treat the 'life-conception' not as a premiss but as what it is in the agent that converts his deliberative starting-points into his *prohairesis.*

45. See also *Movement of Animals* 701 a 25–29.

46. Practical intellect is discussed in III.9–10.

47. This leaves it open whether human *nous* in the *Ethics* (or in different portions of the *Ethics*) is ultimately a single faculty with two modes of functioning or a pair of faculties, practical and theoretical. The language of *NE* VI 1139 a 3–15 suggests the latter view, whereas the former (so I argue; see Chapter 7, Section IX) is operative in *NE* X.

48. On teleonomy without mind in Aristotle, see S. Broadie [2].

49. This question surfaces at 1112 b 16–17: 'if [the end] seems to be produced by several means they consider by which it is most easily and best *(kallista)* produced'. *Kallista* means 'most admirably', not 'most effectively'. Cf. Hardie [4], 166–68; Dahl, 32 and 252 (note 14); Sherman, 83 ff; Irwin [7], 335–36.

50. This is clearly the position of *NE* III.2–3, but in *NE* VI it is not so clearly put forward. However, I see no reason not to regard this as the doctrine of VI, too.

51. The present account supersedes that proposed in S. Broadie [4]. It differs, too, from a popular line of interpretation according to which the question 'Should I pursue O?' can be decided by Aristotelian deliberation, even though Aristotle's language suggests that he confines deliberation to 'How?' questions. The interpretation is based on Greenwood's suggestion that *ta pros to telos* (i.e., means) covers constituents or components of an end by

means of which that end is realised, as well as external means (see Greenwood, 46–47; 53–54). The idea is that what you or I would call deliberating on whether to pursue O is what Aristotle would call deliberating on whether O is a (constituent) means to the ultimate end, which is happiness; thus it is deliberating on *how* to achieve happiness. In my view this misrepresents what *Aristotle* understands by 'deliberation' (although it may be a plausible way of talking about actual deliberation). I do not deny that *'ta pros to telos'* might cover components of an end. But whether means to an end are components of it or external measures, in saying that we identify them through deliberation in the light of the posited end, Aristotle implies, as I understand him, that the agent reasons *from* a substantial, articulable conception of the end. Consequently, on the view in question Aristotle is committed to holding that no one can do what you or I would call deliberate on whether to pursue some narrow end O unless he or she has the above sort of conception of happiness. This is the Grand End theory of Aristotelian deliberation, against which I have argued. However, some interpreters take the 'component means to happiness' idea in a different way; i.e., deliberating whether O is a component means to happiness is considering whether (or to what extent, or with what degree of dominance etc.) O in general figures in the best life for man. But this is not what Aristotle means by 'deliberation'; deliberation for him is a process of deciding what to do in a particular situation. Having thought about general ethical questions might help one deliberate better (by making one aware of more kinds of considerations), just as it helps to know regularities of nature. But ethical pondering is not part of deliberation any more than scientific research is. The Aristotelian *phronimos* must, himself, be good in deliberation; hence if good deliberation involves making progress, oneself, in moral or political philosophy, no one has practical wisdom who is not an actual philosopher. The only way to avoid the absurdities inherent in the 'component means' idea (i.e., in the use made of it along the lines sketched above) is to declare inexplicit the ethical insights involved. Thus, *phronimoi* have a potentially articulable Grand End or are potential ethical theorists. This is surely true, and *because* it is true, Aristotelian deliberation does not include ethical theorising. For Aristotelian *phronimoi* are not merely *potentially* good deliberators.

52. Cf. *Phys.* 185 a 5: 'a principle must be a principle *of* some thing or things'.

53. The *Revised Oxford Translation* renders *nous* in *NE* VI by 'comprehension'; in *NE* X by 'intellect'.

54. See Natali [1] for an account of the evolution of Aristotle's treatment of this Janus-like concept.

55. This is the usual interpretation. But other possibilities have their supporters: Kenny [2], 170–73, argues that the second proposition here is the premiss that presents the end; Dahl, 44 and 231, that it is the conclusion of deliberation.

56. Cf. Joachim ad 1094 b 1; Cooper [1], 28 ff; Devereux [2].

57. This need not exhaust the meaning of *eschata* here. See next section, pp. 254–55.

58. This seems to be the meaning of *eschata* (contrasted with 'universals') at *Meta.* 1059 b 26.

59. There is widespread agreement that in Aristotelian practical wisdom, *nous* apprehends the end-setting starting-point of deliberations (although there is disagreement on the origin or foundation of this practical cognition, some saying 'induction', some 'intuition', some 'moral training', some 'dialectic', and some a combination); e.g., Greenwood, 51; Lee; Ross [1], 219; Hardie [4], 226–28; Sorabji [1]; Cooper [1], 65–66; Kenny [2], 151–52; Dahl, 48–60 and 227–36; Irwin [7], 135 and 531, note 2; MacIntyre [2], 91–93. Several of these writers stress the (supposed) parallel between grasp of the starting-points of deliberation and theoretic grasp of demonstrative starting-points.

60. What gives this point force is the fact that here and often elsewhere in *NE* VI Aristotle uses the term *nous* to name not an intellectual faculty (or 'part of the soul'), but an intellectual virtue. See Greenwood, 69–73, 150–51, 153, 179–80; Kenny [2], 172.

61. The second *kai* in 1143 b 3 is more naturally taken as conjunctive than as epexegetic (as in the *Revised Oxford Translation*). In that case, either (1) *tēs heteras protaseōs* is one of two or possibly three objective genitives governed by *ho de* in 2, or (2) it is one of three

qualifications on a single objective genitive introduced by *tou*. If (1), we should expect either *te* before *eschatou* or *tou* before *endechomenou*. If (2), the meaning is 'Practical *nous* is of what is ultimate and contingent and belonging to the second remiss'. Cf. Engberg-Pedersen, 214 f. (with footnotes 10 and 11).

62. Of course, it might require *nous* on the part of an observer to grasp what set the agent his deliberative problem, but this does not prove the *agent* intelligent in that respect!

63. Thus when Aristotle says at 1151 a 16 that virtue preserves *(sōzei)* the first principle, which is that for the sake of which (cf. 1140 b 12), he means, I take it, not (1) 'Virtue keeps the agent in a condition in which he endorses and strives to realise the right values or a true vision of the human good, but (2) 'Virtue ensures, as our view of the circumstances changes, that we continue to be right in judging some given narrow end worthy to be our end (under the circumstances)'.

64. Aristotle says this (by clear implication) at 1113 b 3–6, a passage which Gauthier and Jolif (vol. II, part 1 ad loc.) see as directly contradicting the doctrine of *NE* VI. See also 1114 b 16–21, which suggests that moral differences are shown in different ways (acquired through moral training or the lack of it) of pursuing the ends implanted in us by nature.

65. Lesher has argued convincingly that in demonstration the contribution of theoretic *nous* is represented by middle terms at every stage in a chain of demonstrative syllogisms. This parallels the way in which practical *nous* is operative at every stage of deliberation.

66. This translation departs slightly from the *Revised Oxford*.

67. It is probably also a surrogate for the Aristotelian moral virtues. Otherwise it is inexplicable that so many contemporary interpreters, with no encouragement from examples in the texts, depict the good Aristotelian agent as aiming to do something called 'acting courageously', 'acting generously' etc., and also as telling himself things like 'courage (or generosity or honesty etc.) requires that I do this'. It is as if having virtues consists in adhering to rules such as 'Be honest', 'Be courageous' etc.—which rules function as *reasons* for one's choices and actions. See e.g. Sorabji [1]; Cooper [1], 84 ff; Kenny [3], 153; Charles [2]. Question: does the defective character adhere to rules such as 'Be dishonest', 'Be lazy'? If not yet he can have those vices, why is following the rule 'Be courageous' necessary for being courageous? Aristotle says that we are voluntarily virtuous or vicious, but this seems different from saying that we are one or the other though following rules like the above.

68. There is still a logical gap; see p. 253.

69. At *Phys.* 199 a 21–23 Aristotle comments on the end-directed behaviour of animals: 'People wonder whether it is by intelligence or some other faculty that these creatures work—spiders, ants, and the like'.

70. This nondepartmental character of *nous* is emphasized by Aristotle in *On the Soul*, 429 a 18.

71. I am not suggesting that to exercise understanding *is* to acquire practical wisdom (Aristotle denies that it is, at 1143 a 11–12), but that the exercise of understanding puts us in the way of acquiring wisdom.

72. At 1143 b 6–9 he says that practical wisdom, by contrast with accomplishment in theoretical matters *(sophia),* gives the impression of being a 'natural growth'.

73. The parallel with theoretical demonstration fosters the illusion that the practical conclusion must be logically implied by the premisses if the latter are to count as proper reasons for it. But this is because the parallel has been falsely drawn. The practical conclusion is analogous, not to the conclusion of the demonstrative syllogism, but to its set of first premisses. The agent's reasons for his practical conclusion are analogous to the scientist's reasons for settling on one, rather than another, set of explanatory premisses (see above, Section VIII). We do not insist that the scientist's grounds for his preferred explanation be such that it would be logically inconsistent to accept them and not it, even though (in Aristotelian science, anyway) we do insist that the *explanans*, whatever it be, logically imply the *explanandum*.

74. See note 51 above.

75. The translation departs slightly from the *Revised Oxford*.

76. As I understand it, this passage is entirely concerned with the operating of intelligence

*within* a particular wise deliberative inquiry. But many commentators see here an allusion to a supposed way in which the intellect extracts universal principles and values from particular ethical insights; these then become ends of wise deliberation. The fullest argument for an interpretation of this type is that of Dahl, 42 ff. and 227–36, who sees a sort of induction at work. Cf. Greenwood, 51 and 70–71; Ross [1], 219; Sorabji [1], Engberg-Pedersen, 212. See also Burnet, 281 (he sees the process as dialectical); Joachim, ad loc; Gauthier and Jolif, vol. I, part 2 (translation), 178; Dirlmeier [2], 135–36; Kenny [1], 172, and [2], 152. For opposing views, see Cooper [1], 42 (note 52), and Woods [2].

77.  For this interpretation of 'ultimate' see Cooper [1], 33–41 and 183–86.

78.  Cf. Cooper [1], 42, note 52.

79.  It is puzzling that at 1144 b 1 ff. Aristotle refers to the good disposition unenlightened by intelligence as 'natural'. Why no allusion to culture and habituation as a source of potentially good dispositions which go astray without intelligence? Possibly because the exercise of acquired dispositions is assumed to be always under the direction of someone's intelligence, even if only that of external authority. Thus we cannot subtract intelligence without undercutting the level of culture.

80.  The interdependence is also definitional, since moral virtue is defined by reference to the ethical *orthos logos,* and the latter is distinguished from, e.g., theoretical correctness by its dependence on moral virtue (cf. 1140 b 11–20). The circle is not vicious if Aristotle is attempting an exposition of the concepts; it would be if 'acting in accordance with moral virtue' and 'acting in accordance with the *orthos logos*', were either of them meant to denote a criterion for detecting the applicability of the other.

81.  This may be awkward for Aristotle's own conception of continence, if continence requires practical wisdom, since the continent person lacks the moral virtue of temperance. This problem is raised by Woods [2]. However, it is not clear that Aristotle thinks that continence involves practical wisdom. It involves the ability to make the right decision (anyway, at times), but the same is true of incontinence, and Aristotle is clear that the incontinent person lacks practical wisdom (1152 a 6–9). See below, Chapter 5, note 11.

82.  The doctrine of the interdependence of the virtues is sometimes thought to entail that there can be no ultimate conflict of particular obligations. (See, e.g., Irwin [4], corrected in Irwin [8]). But there can be a conflict even under the single heading of the virtue of justice. Aristotle's brief discussion of difficult choices (1110 a 4–b 1) does not lay it down that some situations present insoluble dilemmas even to the wise man, but neither does it rule this out.

83.  Cf. Ackrill [5], 137.

# CHAPTER 5

# Incontinence

## I. The Field of Incontinence

Sometimes an agent reaches a rational choice—a judgment of what it is best to do given his situation—and fails to act on it, not for any good reason nor because of external interference, but because he does not want to do it or wants to do something else more. This is the phenomenon of moral weakness or incontinence *(akrasia)*. We all know that this often happens; thus we know that it can happen. We are also naturally drawn to describe it in terms like those just used. Yet some philosophers have declined to accept the phenomenon at face value, or have refused to accept at face value the coherence of the description. Some, headed by Socrates, have argued that incontinence is impossible, so that what we call 'incontinence' must be something else if it is anything. Others, Aristotle among them, not surprisingly have found it necessary to respond to this challenge by arguing that 'incontinence' does make sense after all.

Aristotle's treatment (*NE* VII.1–10) of this troubled topic presents peculiar difficulties.[1] In the first place, it would be a mistake to think that there is such a thing as *the* problem of incontinence.[2] Whether a problem exists in this connection depends on what model we adopt of the human mind so far as it relates to action; different models set different problems. The difficulty addressed by Aristotle differs from some of the difficulties appearing to other philosophers; thus his solution may be misunderstood unless these differences are identified. Part of our task therefore is to distinguish what is from what is not his problem. At the same time, however, we cannot avoid considering why and with what right Aristotle passes over these other problems, and whether their failure to touch him shows strength on his part or narrowness. And even when his problem has been identified and his solution assessed, there remains the question of the interest to us of his discussion and its relevance to our own thinking. Thus his problem about incontinence may seem generated by culturally based assumptions or local linguistic usages which carry no interesting philosophical lesson. Alternatively, our own insensibility to some of the influences influencing Aristotle may reflect prejudice on our side.

266

As these remarks may suggest, Aristotle's treatment of incontinence, as I under-stand it, is less interesting as a piece of first-order philosophical analysis than as a stimulus for reflection on ways in which we may fail to grasp what Aristotle's analysis is about. *His* solution to *his* problem I shall argue to be, for the most part, straight-forward and obvious, almost anticlimactically so, and if it seems otherwise this is because for historical reasons our understanding of his problem has been 'dragged about' and distorted.

But first let us see how he locates incontinence in his division of moral qualities. Its opposite number is continence, which is not the same as virtue, for the continent person enacts his choice but not without a struggle against bad impulses, whereas the truly good person is free from these. Similarly, incontinence, though certainly a moral defect, is not vice, for the vicious person acts according to vicious choice (1146 b 22–23; 1148 a 16 ff.; 1151 a 5 ff.). Some bright spirits had argued that incontinence may even be a virtue, when the agent chooses badly, fails to live up to his choice, and consequently behaves well. Aristotle dismisses this paradox (1146 a 27–31), without saying why. But the reason is obvious: for him, virtue is not just any char-acteristic resulting in good or acceptable behaviour. Good behaviour manifests virtue only if it manifests a complex excellence of soul, which is to say a harmony between rational and nonrational parts each functioning with its own kind of virtue. More-over, no rational being could be considered a good one on account of those episodes in which, having made a rational choice, he acts as if he were not a rational chooser at all, but an animal or child incapable of rational choice. That is what the inconti-nent person does: so far as his choice fails to affect his behaviour, he might as well never have made it. Virtue, moreover, is achieved through the right training and discipline: it is the end which training is meant to produce. But no one, whether by himself or his guardians, could be coherently trained both to choose in accordance with whatever values are recognised *and* to renege on those choices. Thus inconti-nence, even where its results are harmless or beneficial, is never a virtue, since virtue develops through training.

Not every failure to stand by rational choice counts as a case of incontinence in Aristotle's book. If only a person of heroic or superhuman virtue would have stood fast, giving way is not incontinence. Otherwise hardly anyone would count as vir-tuous in an ordinary way, since incontinence entails absence of virtue. Virtue, Aris-totle assumes, must be attainable through ordinary decent upbringing. 'Incontinence' can apply only where the concept of ordinary goodness might have applied, and the same is true of 'continence'. Again, a person is not to be considered continent or incontinent properly speaking if the desires which he contains or gives way to are 'bestial' or inhuman or pathological in their nature or their intensity. Aristotle's examples range from cannibalism to nail biting (1148 b 15–1149 a 1).

The point is not that persons subject to such desires cannot help giving in to them. Aristotle makes it clear that in some cases of disease the agent could not have controlled himself, but he does not assume that unnatural desires are necessarily uncontrollable (1149 a 12–15). Nor does he assume that persons properly called 'incontinent' would necessarily have been able to act differently at the moment when they acted. Aristotle's exclusion of unnatural desires from the area of true inconti-nence is probably to be explained in the same terms as his exclusion of cases requiring heroic virtue. An unnatural desire is always excessive, so to speak: there is never a right amount of it, or a right amount of corresponding activity. Thus in respect of these there is no mean possible, and no virtue, hence no incontinence. It might also be argued that ordinary decent upbringing cannot be expected to prepare its charges to cope with desires that spring from disease or deformity, since upbringing in general is geared to those who are normal. Thus having and giving way to such impulses (even when controllable) is not, strictly speaking a defect of the person's *moral* nature, insofar as 'moral' refers to the side deliberately developed by habituation in society.

But this last consideration is unconvincing, especially if we apply it to Aristotle's examples. People can certainly be trained not to bite their nails, and any ordinary decent upbringing should aim, one might say, at general self-discipline in the face of desires of whatever sort. It could also be objected that Aristotle's conception of incontinence rests on a distinction impossible to draw objectively: that between natural and unnatural desires. What is unnatural in one culture is natural in another, and different healthy constitutions may naturally desire different things. Or so one can argue. Does it matter, though, that Aristotle does not offer us a criterion for what is unnatural, or that if he did we should almost certainly dispute one or another of its results? I think not, if what concerns us is his fundamental point which is surely this: some desires, as for physical satisfactions and reliefs, are grounded in the needs of our biological nature; others, as for power, honour and many kinds of pleasures, are concerned with specifically human enhancements of the animal substructure; still others are such that their satisfaction is neither a human enhancement nor needed for the physical well-being which provides the conditions of life in accordance with 'second nature' and reflective reason. Thus desires of the third sort, even when not particularly damaging or repulsive, are so much lumber, and the human individual would be better off as such if they were excised completely. This is an important distinction even if its application is sometimes difficult and controversial.

Incontinence, then, as Aristotle understands it, has for its field desires which we should not be humanly better off without. Thus the practical problem of potential incontinence cannot be solved by simply eradicating the desires in question, even if this were possible. The incontinent person occupies the same logical space as would have been occupied by the virtuous person he ought to be but is not. The space is defined in terms of desires where a mean is possible, hence also a deficiency. So eradication would destroy the possibility of human virtue along with the possibility of incontinence. In general, therefore, the conditions for virtue are necessarily conditions where incontinence might reign instead.

But for Aristotle, the field of incontinence strictly speaking is much narrower than these remarks imply. It is the field constituted by normal physical pleasures and pains (1147 b 20–1148 a 14). Thus the corresponding virtue is temperance, the main corresponding vice intemperance. (There is also the rare vice of deficiency; i.e., an unwarranted insensibility or exaggerated asceticism with regard to physical comforts and enjoyments. But this hardly figures in the present context, for Aristotle is concerned to distinguish incontinence from the vice which it most resembles: namely, excessive devotion to physical comforts and pleasure.)[3] Incontinence is giving in to physical appetite against one's better judgment. (Where the giving in to appetite is a wrongful shrinking from physical pain, the condition is called 'softness'.) Giving in to excessive anger, or to excessive desire for honour or wealth, is incontinence only in a derivative and qualified sense.

Perhaps Greek usage supports this distinction, sustaining an inference from 'incontinent' said without qualification to 'incontinent with respect to bodily desires'. But is there any good reason for carrying it over into a philosophical classification? Perhaps not if we are mainly interested, as most contemporary analysts are, in the logical (or illogical) structure of practical irrationality. From this point of view it is immaterial what sort of wrong impulse is yielded to. But Aristotle's distinction makes sense if we consider moral characteristics as the products, more or less perfect, of moral training. The educator's first task must be, literally, to 'raise' the child: to raise him from the condition of 'first nature,' in which, left alone, he would function as a young animal. The first lessons must be in not giving way to every physical impulse, for otherwise the capacities for distinctively human ends, innate though they must be, get no chance to be regularly actualised. Of course, healthy nature sets limits to the amount of physical satisfaction of whatever sort pursued on any occasion; but even healthy first nature cannot take account of the right time, the right place etc., as prudence and decency demand. Thus for Aristotle, the paradigm of incontinence is the condition in which an agent, actively rational as a rule, sinks back to the original condition. The point is not merely that this person behaves irrationally because he acts against his better judgment, but that in so acting he pursues objects that he would have pursued had he never been touched by reason (cf. 1118 a 23–25). So his condition deserves to be distinguished from that of an agent who gives way to excessive anger or to temptations concerning wealth or honour. Caring about wealth and honour at all, let alone too much, already implies attainment to a truly human level of activity, and this achievement is expressed in the wrong action itself and is not, as in paradigmatic incontinence, blotted out altogether. As for anger, Aristotle ranks incontinence in this respect alongside those other forms because, like Plato, he sees anger as a distinctively human function: it is our emotional response to what we take to be unwarranted assault (1149 a 32–34). Anger, unlike the physical passions, depends on a more than merely sensory assessment of the situation, since it expresses self-respect and a sense of justice.

In one sense, then, there is a well-grounded moral distinction between incontinence in the strict sense and the qualified forms. From this it would not follow that strictly incontinent behaviour is more reprehensible than its analogues. Aristotle, however, does regard the *disposition* as worse: it is not merely a fault, but in a way a moral deformity (*kakia pōs*, 1149 b 20; cf. 1151 a 6). He is concerned, of course, with the kind of difference that incontinence makes to the soul; thus he does not measure the flaw by the magnitude of damage or even of injustice that corresponding action might cause. By that standard, incontinence with regard to physical pleasure and pain is arguably less grave than yielding to the temptation to give or accept bribes through excessive desire for wealth or office. We, however, may be inclined to judge the latter more despicable, independently of its consequences. A state of mind that abuses the system which it understands seems worse than one that has temporarily sloughed off the system altogether. Perhaps Aristotle fails to consider this type of example when he speaks somewhat tolerantly of the qualified forms. Or perhaps he is harsher towards the unqualified form because it is more to be expected that every-one should learn to deal with normal physical impulses. Proneness to incontinence in the strict sense is a direct consequence of our biological nature; the moral problems set by this nature are therefore much the same for everyone and have been with us all from the start. Most people mostly take them in their stride. But (it might be argued) excessive ambition and the like depend on individual temperament and cir-cumstances which do not confront everybody. Qualified incontinence is like a failure to spell certain words correctly (where it is something even to attempt to spell those words), but the unqualified form shows failure to master the A-B-C of moral life.

Aristotle may also be influenced here by his taxonomic doctrine that the field of incontinence is shared with continence and also with a corresponding virtue and vice. If the field is physical pleasure and comfort, the virtue is temperance. But how does temperance differ from continence? Aristotle says that the temperate person *finds nothing pleasant* that conflicts with reason, whereas the continent one finds conflicting things pleasant but does not give way to them (1151 b 34–1152 a 3). This is a stringent condition for temperance, for it is possible to be aware that something would be pleasant, and also to mind foregoing it, without for a moment being actually *tempted* to prefer it.[4] A person in this state with regard to some physical pleasure would not be responding temperately by Aristotle's standard. He might for instance be sorry that the rational course entails foregoing the pleasure, even though he unswervingly sets the pleasure to one side. He might even for the moment regret his general commitment to rational decency without being inclined to break out of it. For Aristotle, these conditions count as 'continence', every bit as much as the condition of the agent who experiences and resists actual temptation. Aristotle makes no distinction, even though being tempted is (one would think) worse than merely regretting having to give up what reason says we should.

But it is understandable that Aristotle should lump these states together when what is foregone is a physical enjoyment. For, not implausibly, there is something base and hence not virtuous in caring at all about a physical pleasure when it conflicts with the right action. A might-have-been pleasure, in such a case, simply does not deserve regret by a decent person, though there is something wrong with a person who does not take pleasure in such things when it is proper. But a difficulty arises if this principle is extended to cases where the object of continence or incontinence is respect, honour or even money. It is not at all clearly the mark of a virtuous person to be wholly indifferent when reason requires him to forego some honour—well-earned, perhaps—even if he is not in the slightest tempted to err against his better judgment and accept it. Nor is it clearly the mark of virtue not to mind at all fore-going revenge in some cases, even though the agent is not actually tempted to take the law into his own hands. He does not have to drag himself back from doing this, or even to remind himself that it would be wrong, yet he is strongly aware that revenge would have been sweet. Would he be a better human being for not caring? Many would not say so, and I believe that Aristotle would sympathise with them.[5]

The fact is that minding the sacrifice, but without being tempted, is good, not base, when what is sacrificed is something that has its own nobility. For it retains its nobility even when it would be better not pursued. The good man loves what is noble, and he cannot turn his love off and on when something more important is or is not at stake. Thus although Aristotle recognises a kind of continence and incontinence where the object is honour or revenge, this lets him in for difficulties which would have been obvious if he had probed the meaning of 'continence' further than he does. If continence in general entails *being tempted,* then a person could be considered virtuous and temperate even if, without being tempted, he ignobly regrets some physical pleasure foregone, If, on the other hand, mere *regret* proves continence even in the absence of temptation, there will be cases in which the continent person is nobler than the person of corresponding virtue! For the latter does not care enough about honour etc. to mind when he has to set it aside.[6]

This embarrassing dilemma emerges if we assume a single interpretation of 'continence' and generalise the doctrine that continence, incontinence and virtue (along with vice) are distinct competitors for the same logical space. One way of evading it is to refuse, as Aristotle does, to generalise the space of continence and incontinence, by restricting them to an area in which the difference between regretting the sacrifice and being tempted is least ethically significant since both attitudes show lack of nobility. This is the area of physical pleasures and comforts. The restriction enables Aristotle to assert consistently that virtue is always nobler and better than continence. Hence he can say that, if this requirement fails to hold or suddenly seems to be dubious, this is because 'continent' and 'incontinent' are being applied beyond their proper sphere, so it is hardly surprising if the results are paradoxical.

To the modern theorist, Aristotle's restriction of incontinence proper may seem arbitrary or a sign of ascetic prejudice. After all, the modern most interesting problem—'How is it possible at all to act against one's better judgment?—has the same formal structure whatever the desire to which the agent surrenders. But if the above analysis is correct, Aristotle's restriction is not arbitrary: it depends on the far from formal assumption that it is *base* to care about a physical pleasure foregone in the line of duty. For if he allowed that it is permissible or even reasonable to care, he would have been forced to acknowledge the difference between caring and being tempted, and would have equated continence with refusal to yield to temptation, and virtue with not being tempted, whether one cared or not. And in that case he would have had no reason (apart from current linguistic usage) for not extending the strict notions of continence and incontinence to cases where honour or position or some mental pleasure must be sacrificed.

As it is, Aristotle's restriction is grounded in his views about physical pleasures and comforts. In general these are, as he says, 'necessary' (1150 a 16–17), because we are (also) animals; but indulging in them is never noble although sometimes it is proper up to a point. That they are not noble is something of a tautology, given that we first learn to give practical content to the idea of 'the noble' by being taught that it is what you pursue even if you do not feel like it—at an age when (it is assumed) the distracting feelings are physical impulses. Though it is sometimes right to give in to them, it can never be right to give in to them (merely because it would be pleasant) when something noble is at stake. In any such clash they necessarily deserve to lose. By contrast, even though it is sometimes wrong to pursue a given kind of noble object, there may be situations in which just this sort of object rightly takes precedence over something else deemed noble. We respond (or should respond) to such conflicts by valuing the object sacrificed *even when* we sacrifice it willingly. What is more, by the time we are disciplined enough to be capable at all of valuing such noble things in a practical way, we are also capable of valuing things without automatically being drawn to pursue them on any given occasion. A young child is not necessarily able to make that practical distinction. Thus the way to teach him not to be *tempted* by what would be wrong to have is to get him to feel that he should not even *mind* not having it; and the effects of that lesson persist in adult temperance.

It is easy to dismiss as cultural prejudice Aristotle's categorisation of some kinds of goods as 'noble'. Someone might say that there are all kinds of good things, and some better than others—perhaps even better than others in most situations—but the term 'noble' simply expesses a subjective opinion. There has been some discussion already of the 'noble' (see Chapter 2, Section VII) and there will be more later (Chapter 7, Section III), but meanwhile I have in mind the sort of modern theorist who would feel impatient with Aristotle's restriction of incontinence proper to the sphere of physical pleasure, on the ground that this is irrelevant to the philosophically important problem. For the important problem is how someone can act or be tempted to act against his better judgment; and (or so it may well be assumed) in considering this, it is of no philosophical interest to consider whether what is desired despite better judgment is the sort of thing that a good person would or would not have minded having to forego. But this, I think, shows a narrow view.

We are not talking about a conflict between abstractable psychic items—one a rational practical judgment to do X, the other a desire to do something else—but about a rational being who makes or has made the judgment, and who experiences the contrary desire. And his rationality, even as it relates to just this situation, is not exhausted by his making or having made the judgment as it might be stated in words. To clarify this, let us take the case of a virtuous person who finds that the course of action judged right entails setting aside some honour important and deserved. This is not a matter of indifference to him even though he is not tempted. It may be quite clear to him and others that a world in which he accepts the honour under those circumstances was never for him a possible world. But what does his caring about it amount to? We should expect it to be manifested in various past and future responses, as well as in his present feeling. We should expect him to have made efforts to avoid, in general, situations like the one which now faces him, so far as they could be foreseen. One can arrange things so as to avoid unhappy choices. We might not respect him for caring about the honour foregone if he had been insouciant about avoiding such conflicts. We might doubt whether he really cared all that much (as distinct from experiencing a gush of regret just at the moment of choice). Again, in the situation itself, we should expect him to act in a way that not merely conforms to his judgment of what it would be better, now, to have done (as if this were his last day), but leaves open future opportunities for pursuing or accepting what he now, though he values it, has to reject. The calculation that takes account of this is part of his calculation on how he should act for now. The prescription to allow for future opportunities is written into his present judgment no less than the prescription that entails present rejection, even if only as a background theme. Thus even now he takes practical trouble over the value foregone, and its value to him is reflected in the judgment on which he now acts, though not necessarily in what he can easily say or in the visible action. If I now have to break a promise in order to do what I judge best, I seek a way of acting that allows me to make amends to the injured party.

If, as I am suggesting, the valuing of something which one sets aside in some instance entails taking this kind of trouble, it follows that when the situation is such that the conditions for taking this sort of trouble do not obtain, the object foregone is not an appropriate object for valuing. For example, if the agent is too immature to be able to plan or look beyond the present, he cannot, on the above account, act or be expected to act as one who values what he foregoes even while foregoing it. If that is the case, then if he minds losing it now, this minding is just a feeling, not the surface ripple of an underlying practical concern that joins the present to the future; and as a feeling it is nothing but a potential source of distraction from the right course. How then is the agent not better off without it? So for such an agent its sheer absence is better than its presence. The application to children and physical impulses is obvious. But the inability to plan (which inability, this argument assumes, does not exclude a sense of moral commitment) is not the only condition under which the object foregone lacks the status of 'valuable'. Some goods require no planning for their claims to be eventually satisfied. This is true of the pleasures attendant on normal physical functioning. Normally speaking, if I have to miss a meal now, I can leave it to forces outside my control to ensure that I will enjoy a meal in good time. (If there is a question of my getting a meal at all later, then the issue is not between right action and physical enjoyment, but between right action and health or survival.) It is damaging to desensitise oneself to the pain or frustration of foregoing something good if the good thing can in general be had only by taking trouble or holding it dear in a practical way. Unless we hold it dear we shall not get it, since it is not the kind of thing that comes up automatically. If one switches off to the appeal of such a thing, one effects a possibly irreversible change, and if the thing is indeed a good for the agent concerned, the result is self-mutilation. But where the object foregone is a standard bodily pleasure, there is normally no such need to *plan* to have it another time. The healthy body itself takes care of that. Thus there is no call and hence no space for those planned accommodations that constitute the practical valuing of something even when one foregoes it. One may hanker after the physical pleasure and feel that in losing it now one is losing, now, something good, but, as with the young, this feeling can make no practical difference that is not obstructive. The pleasure would have been good, so far as it went, and other instances will be so in the future, but the fact that it would have been is of no present significance to the well-conditioned agent. That is reflected in his lack of interest in the pleasure passed over by him.[7] He does not turn aside from it or even desire it, but is dead to it even as a might-have-been. He can afford to hold it cheap (and, if he moralises, to think it cheap not to hold it cheap) just because it is the kind of thing that comes so cheaply.

In this way perhaps we can make sense of Aristotle's restriction of incontinence proper to the sphere of physical pleasures—pleasures which he considers 'necessary' but not 'noble'—without relying on an unexamined notion of the noble. Some such restriction is needed, given his assumption that the continent man is inferior to the virtuous merely through *caring about* the forbidden object. For the upshot is that it is better to lack than to have that sort of desiderative interest (even when having it does not involve being tempted) in just those cases where the forbidden thing is of such a kind that it is not appropriate to value such things in the sense of holding them dear in a practical way, by planning for them. Basic bodily pleasures and comforts may not be the only examples of goods that do not demand to be valued in the above sense, but they are universally familiar examples. According to the analysis just given, it is better (whether or not we choose to say 'noble') to feel nothing about foregoing some physical pleasure, because regret and minding have no positive functional rôle in the forward-looking practical activity of a healthy embodied agent. Such feelings may therefore be said to be irrational and, however slight, excessive.

These considerations suggest a way of understanding 'the noble' that avoids the charge that this is an élitist category. To regard something as noble is to regard it as in general requiring distinctively human activity to bring it about, it being, in general, worth human effort and unlikely to come our way unless by our achievement. So whether some good thing counts as noble depends partly on empirical facts about human and environmental possibilities, both natural and social, and partly on one's judgment that the object is or is not worth going out of our way for. Pleasures of the flesh, from Aristotle's standpoint, fall short of being noble for a complex reason: the ones attendant on normal biological functioning take care of themselves; and recherché versions, extensions or elaborations of the former, in Aristotle's austere judgment, are not worth a good person's trouble.

## II. How Incontinence Is Possible (I)

If, like Hume, we think that valuing something or taking it to be right, or best, entails desiring to do, have or promote it, we shall not be able to account for incontinence except by explaining it as really something else. For it seems clear that the incontinent person knows or believes (it makes no difference which; cf. 1146 b 24–30) that he should do A or should pursue O by means of A, and yet he does not want to do this or he wants to do something else more. How then is it true to say that he desires to do A? Initially the answer seems to be that he does desire to do A, but not enough to do it given the contrary desire. For his attitude to A is not sheer indifference, even though he fails to do it. He *would* do it if doing it did not require him to accept pain or miss some pleasure. And until he became aware of this implication, he did mean and want to do A, and perhaps sought out the opportunity and will do so again in the future. In the light of these facts or reasonable inferences we judge him incontinent because we take them as showing that even when he fails to do A he nonetheless in some sense does have A (or O through A) as his practical objective and still thinks A best to do. Thus we draw a stronger conclusion than that he *would* think A best if he were not subject to that other desire or that he *would* desire to do A were it not for that. He *does* think A best; but if he does, and if this nonhypothetical practical attitude towards A entails a correspondingly nonhypothetical desire, what and where is this desire in the case where he fails to act upon it? The answer has to be that the desire is certainly there, but is weak enough to be overridden by a contrary desire.

It seems, then, that judging A best need involve nothing more than a comparatively weak desire to do it. If incontinence looks unproblematic on these terms, it is because there is nothing mysterious about a weak desire's being overridden by a stronger one. (In fact we may reasonably think that 'stronger' in one very obvious sense just means 'overriding'.) But now it is difficult to avoid concluding that the agent's desire to do A was always comparatively weak, even before he is assailed by the contrary desire, although only then was its weakness shown up. For in some sense his practical attitude towards A is the same both before and in that moment. So now it looks as if the difference between him and the virtuous agent lies in the strength of their continuing desires to do the right action A. The latter desires it so strongly that contrary desires are automatically overridden or suppressed or never arise. And the difference between the virtuous and the continent is again in degree of desire: the continent person desires to do A less strongly than if he were virtuous, but still strongly enough for the contrary desire to be overridden as weaker. But then, as Aristotle points out, if the continent person's contrary desire is weak or comparatively weak, there is nothing particularly admirable about continence (1146 a 15–16); yet continence *is* admirable, even if not as good as temperance.

Perhaps we can shuffle the relative strengths in a way that preserves superficial distinctions between continence, incontinence and virtue, but the underlying difficulty remains. The point of Hume's doctrine that a value-judgment expresses a desire was that otherwise the judgment would not be practical. Its practicality depends not merely on its content, but on the nature of the judgmental act, which on this view, incorporates an active tendency towards the object. Otherwise it would be only a 'cool and inert judgment of the understanding'—a faculty which Hume, in this context, takes to be entirely concerned with factual and a priori truths and causal or logical relations. Thus even if evaluative terms can appear in the content of such a judgment—e.g., if there were an intellectual intuition or demonstration that parents should be honoured (and even if there are "value-facts" or quasi-mathematical "value-relations" making such judgments objectively true or false)—without desire for the object, no such judgment would be practical.

If desire is to carry the burden of explaining practicality, we should expect the degree of the agent's *practical* endorsement to be reflected in the desire: in its degree. If I think something well worth going out of my way for and that something else merits little effort or none, surely I feel *more* strongly about the first and desire it *more?* To deny this is to incur the obligation of explaining what, besides degree of desire, makes the difference between levels of practical commitment. Such an explanation would show that the practicality of a practical judgment does not depend on strength of desire but on something else. If, however, one accepts the inference from 'greater practical endorsement' to 'stronger desire', then one must accept the conclusion that the incontinent agent does not have much of a practical commitment to the action A or its objective O. Thus he does not set high value on A or O. But this is hardly a paradigm case of incontinence. In fact, is it incontinence at all? And if practicality is desire, why should we not take the next step, which is to equate desire in general with practical evaluative endorsement? In that case, even if the supposed incontinent agent sets some value on the right action A, we are bound to conclude that he values it less at the time than he values the conflicting action. So he, by his own lights then, would have done wrong in doing A; whereas if we believe him incontinent, we believe that by his own lights he does wrong in not doing A. So is it that usually he thinks it wrong not to do A, but sometimes thinks the opposite? Then perhaps the difference between so-called incontinent persons and those not so called is that the former's practical value-judgments change and change back—a difference, as before, in degree not kind; here it is degree of stability. It is not that the incontinent fails to live up to his judgment, for it is simply replaced by another. There is little to be gained by insisting, as one might, that the agent *dispositionally* judges it best to do A, and that this disposition remains and is not replaced by another disposition in the moment of incontinence. For how can he truly be said to have the disposition unless it issues in an appropriate occurrence? And if the latter would be an occurrent judgment that A is best, how, on the kind of theory in question, can it not embody an occurrent desire to do A that is stronger than any other and hence is enacted?

No doubt I have represented what I am calling the Humean approach more crudely than would be justified if we were discussing it on its own merits. A refined version may be possible or may have been developed which accommodates the difficulties roughly outlined above. But it would be an important fact about such a position that it evolved in this way. To appreciate the point of later sophistications, one would need to understand that they represent an improved version of *that* earlier draft. (It might be debatable whether some finally approved account retained enough of the spirit of the original to be properly considered a version of it at all. But it would still be characteristic of the new position that it had developed from that starting point.) Thus it is not within my brief to claim that no refined descendant of the Humean view would provide an adequate account of incontinence. The point is, rather, that it would be a very different account from Aristotle's. Aristotle does regard incontinence as problematic, but, for reasons to be detailed presently, he is not vulnerable to the problem generated by the Humean approach to desire and valuation. Consequently, we should not be in a hurry to construe his own treatment as an effort to come to terms with that.[8]

The nature of *Aristotle's* problem will be our question in the next section. Here I wish to bring to the fore those elements in his position that protect him against Humean objections to the notion of incontinence. First, there is the obvious point that Hume was forced to interpret practicality in terms of something nonrational called 'desire', because for him a rational judgment cannot as such be practical. If reason is concerned only with factual and abstract truth and inference, practicality has its source outside reason, in passion or sentiment. The findings of reason are, of course, applied in practice, but it is not within the competence of reason itself so to apply them or to discover or register them so as to apply them in this way. Thus the informational input of reason is sought, welcomed and applied by the agent solely qua subject of desires. On this view, the work of reason is already complete and perfect when we have obtained clear knowledge or justified true beliefs and have made sound inferences. Thus it is not a defect of *reason* or *intelligence* (unless intelligence is to be classed as a nonrational capacity) if, for example, the informational input is of no practical relevance to the agent's project, or if the saliences noted by reason contribute nothing to right action. Thus if I see a fatal accident in my neighbourhood mainly as exemplifying Newton's laws, the fault is with my heart, not my head.

Aristotle holds that rational choice is desire—desire which has been subjected to deliberation. The choice is properly called 'rational' because it is a genuine function of reason to form a choice, as distinct from merely providing information which, it so happens, a different psychic agency uses in reaching *its* choice. But if what practical reason generates is a kind of desire (or it would not be practical), how can we think of this in a way that does not breed the Humean problem for incontinence?

That problem, we recall, is that judging it better to do A than B seems to imply a stronger desire to do A than to do B: how then can we be tempted to do and finally *do* (unless by mistake) something that conflicts with what we judge better? A satisfactory answer would be an answer enabling one to see rational choice *both* as a source of action, and in that respect akin to the incontinent desire which opposes it, *and* as sufficiently different to preclude direct comparison in terms of strength and weakness. Aristotle's conception satisfies these desiderata. Let us first consider points of difference. A rational choice is not merely a deliberated desire, but is essentially deliberated in a way in which the desire to have a drink or even to obtain some honour is not. For rational choice is the desire, made determinate by deliberation on the How, to realise *the best* in realising some specific goal O. Because of the formal emptiness of its ultimate object, desire for the *best* (even though now focused specifically on O) could not give rise to a determinate tendency to act before reason determines the details. In this, it is fundamentally different from desires for objects more or less empirically determinate. If I desire a drink, a drink satisfies this; if I desire a fruit drink, I should be satisfied by any drink of that sort. But not just anything answering to the description 'O' will fulfil the desire to *realise the best in realising O.* The ethical agent cannot ever pursue O as best without knowingly electing to pursue it some*how,* however near at hand O might be. By contrast, I might just see a drink and take it, without ever considering *how.* A desired honour comes my way, and I simply accept it, paying no attention to what *else* is involved in my accepting it as I do. Of course the desired thing may be at a causal distance. Then I calculate, and do, what I must to obtain it. But unless I seek it as that which is *best* to seek, what I obtain is something that might have been obtained without deliberation. The metaphor of distance implies this. I may be far from some object in space or be almost where it is. The object itself allows for both possibilities. If I move towards it, I exchange a position from which I had to move towards it to be where it is for a position from which I do not have to do anything to be where it is. And I might have been in this latter position in the first place.

When a rational choice of A is formed, there must then be a desire and indeed a tendency to do A if possible. But, as we saw in Section VI of the last chapter, the desire to do A, is not, qua desire, the *product* of the deliberation which formed the choice. The agent who chooses to do A desires to do it because he already desired to do whatever he must in order to pursue O as best. Deliberation simply shows what this is. Practical reasoning produces not a desire, but the answer to a question. Thus even if he ceases to desire to do A (which ceteris paribus entails that he ceases to desire to realise O as best), it does not follow that he ceases to possess the result of the work of reason. He still knows the answer to the question, even though he may not now be interested or care about what he sought it for.

Thus a rational choice is practical and is a source of action no less than a non-deliberated desire, because the formation of choice is inspired by desire to do whatever would be specified in the choice. Yet the desire can evaporate, and the choice, in a sense, can be left. What is left is not, of course, the act or process of forming the choice. The desire for the best was the substance of such an act, but even where that desire continues as lively as before, the very same choice, once made, is not continu-ally refashioned and re-formed by repeated thrusts of deliberation. Once the choice is reached, the agent is in the cognitive state of *having* formed it and need not re-form it unless he has reason to modify it. And even in that case he needs to re-form it not because the cognitive state lapses without constant re-creation, but because under new or newly noticed circumstances the content of that state is not longer appropriate. Perhaps it is the nature of cognitive activity to leave the subject in a state whose continuance does not depend on the continuing of the conditions that generated it. We remember what we perceived when we can no longer perceive it, and we continue to possess the results of theoretical investigations even when we are no longer capable of that kind of investigation or have lost the interest that led to it. At the moment of temptation the incontinent agent lacks the will and perhaps even the capacity to deliberate about what is best. Or, if he did deliberate now, he would reach the wrong answer. It may well be the same for the continent person under stress of temptation. And the virtuous person, too, may, at the moment for action, be in a position where he cannot deliberate. But nonetheless they all know what to do because they *have* deliberated.

Thus rational choice as form*ed,* not form*ing,* is consistent with the absence of any desire to act on it. The agent *is* in that cognitive state of knowing what to do, and he *has* reason to do whatever it is: yet he may now lack even a weak desiderative interest in doing it. Thus if he is tempted to act otherwise, the opposition is not between stronger and weaker desire. The state of having formed the choice is prop-erly called 'practical' not because of entailing a concurrent desire, but because of its genesis in past deliberation and in the desire, presupposed by that deliberation and present *then,* to enact the deliberated answer.

So is the conflict experienced by an incontinent (or continent) agent a conflict between one desire which he *had* (and no doubt will have again) and another which he has now? This seems the wrong way to put it, for how can there be conflict unless the antagonists coexist? The conflict is between what the agent at the moment of acting *wants* rather to do and what at that moment he *has reason* to do rather than anything else. First he deliberates to discover what it is he has most reason to do. But he cannot at $t_1$, when he forms the choice, have most reason to be going to do A and not also have it at $t_2$—unless the situation at $t_2$ presents grounds for modifying the choice. In the absence of a modifier, he cannot at $t_2$ lack reason to do A rather than anything else, even if at $t_2$ he does not desire to do it. The clash, then, is between what at $t_2$ he has most reason to do and what at $t_2$ he most desires to do.

This account not only assumes that having most reason to do A is compatible with having no desire to do it; it also assumes that (for the agent who has most reason to do A) wanting something that entails not-A provides no good reason against doing A. In general, this must be assumed. Simply wanting to do something different, no matter what and no matter what the circumstances of wanting it, cannot constitute a reason for preferring this to the original choice. The point is not just that at $t_2$ the agent may not be in a good state of mind for deciding what would count as a valid reason. Rather, it is that we deliberate in the first place because we do not trust impulse to lead us to the best course. It is the same whether we deliberate on action to be executed now or later. There is no point in engaging in such thinking if we allow that feeling like doing something when the moment for action arises will automatically be a good reason for preferring to do it. On that assumption, the rational course would always be to wait and see how we feel like acting. So the capacity for deliberation would be useless: a position which Aristotle could no more accept than a theoretical thinker could accept that the truest verdict on some subject is always the one conveyed by the first unreflective impression. Although the correct practical verdict, unlike its theoretical counterpart, will be different under different circumstances, it cannot be supposed to change with every shift in our feelings. The art of deliberating well lies in being able to decide which changes in ourselves and our circumstances do count as good reasons for modifying or abandoning a choice, and to ignore those which do not.

The fact that some changes may so count means that a rational agent must remain cognitively and affectively open to unforeseen aspects of the unfolding situation. He even has to be ready to change course completely (cf. 1151 b 4–22). Just this necessary flexibility renders us, as a species, vulnerable to temptation. We cannot in advance turn away from precisely the new factors that would constitute irrelevant distractions, because we cannot anticipate exactly what they will be and how they will affect us. Beings endowed with that sort of omniscience would likely not need to deliberate in the first place. Thus the general possibility of incontinence lies at the heart of human practical rationality.

Granted Aristotle's conception of practical reason, the phenomenon of incontinence is only to be expected. It may seem now that continence is the greater mystery. Since in the nature of the case the rational agent is liable to temptation, how is it possible *not* to give way? The general Aristotelian answer would be, I think, that nature has endowed us with the general capacities needed for realising our good. Thus we have the intelligence to deliberate well, recognising some things as relevant, others not; and we have the capacity to discern the occasions for acting on our deliberation. Similarly, we have the ability in general to stand by a choice even when it is difficult or unwelcome.

Basic moral training presupposes this, since it often involves getting young children to do what goes against the grain (v.s. Chapter 2, Section X). Their early doing of it is not, of course, an instance of continent behaviour, for they have made no rational choice to which to adhere, and continence is sticking to one's choice. But they become capable of their own rational choices only through having learnt to act against inclination. If the power to act against inclination is presupposed by the very ability to make a rational choice, it should not surprise us if that power is sometimes exercised in the adult execution of rational choice.

From the fact that we possess the general capacity to act even against inclination, it does not follow that the incontinent person, at the moment of surrender, could have helped his behaviour. Aristotle is clear that sometimes he cannot because the body takes over (1147 a 15–16; 35; b 6–9). But it is still the agent himself who has come to be in a state such that his giving way is inevitable, perhaps through physical causes. It was up to him to anticipate the possibility and avoid it. Here we should remember that people are considered incontinent only in respect of temptations which a normal person can reasonably expected to be in a state to ignore. Moreover, good deliberation presupposes realism about the possibilities of executing a choice, including one's own capacities to carry it out and prepare for carrying it out; and the paradigmatic incontinent is supposed to act badly though he has deliberated well. He assumed when he deliberated that he would be able to do what he decided. He cannot, then, both take credit for having deliberated well and always afterwards plead the excuse that his condition made it impossible for him to carry out the choice.

### III. How Incontinence Is Possible (II)

The modern problematic of incontinence starts from the assumption that the incontinent agent is subject to conflicting desires. The question then is how to reconcile this with the fact that he voluntarily does, because he desires it *more,* something which (given the assumption) he also in a sense desires *less* (since he values it less, and valuing is a kind of desire). The paradox is the ascription of apparently contradictory desires. The problem which Aristotle mainly addresses is quite different: it is that describing someone as incontinent seems to entail contradictory ascriptions of knowledge and ignorance.

What is it, according to Aristotle, that the incontinent agent both knows and does not know? The simple answer is: that his situation calls for a response other than the one which he voluntarily makes. Thus if he has rationally chosen to go on a dry-food diet (cf. 1147 a 5–6), but rejects a serving of the recommended food in favour of something more appetising, he both knows and does not know that he ought to accept the dry food and reject what is oily or moist. That is Aristotle's view. But Aristotle complicates this simple answer by analysing the action which the incontinent agent should, but does not, perform into different components, one of which, Aristotle maintains, is more properly to be considered the locus of incontinent ignorance. Before pursuing these important details (see Section VI) we should ask why Aristotle is impelled at all to say that the incontinent person both knows and does not know what action is called for. And in order to take hold of this question from the right end, we must identify the point which Aristotle sees himself as needing to uphold. He sees himself as needing to show that the agent's knowledge is compatible with his ignorance. But is this because Aristotle thinks that we must otherwise view the agent as simply ignorant and altogether lacking in knowledge; or is it because we must otherwise view him as simply knowing and not at all ignorant? In other words, is Aristotle taking it for granted that the incontinent knows and arguing that he is also ignorant; or is he taking it for granted that the incontinent person is ignorant, and arguing that he also knows?

To many modern readers it seems obvious that in some cases the incontinent person knows (or believes, which is subjectively the same) perfectly well that he is doing what he should not: both what he is doing and that he should not do it. Indeed, we tend to regard this as the paradigm of incontinence, at least so far as incontinence presents a problem for analysis. Thus, for instance, we do not think it so remarkable that a person who resolved to do A should simply lose his head at the moment of action, perhaps through panic, so that the resolution is driven clean out of his mind. At that moment the subject would not even be able to say what he was supposed to do, so how can he be said to know it? We can easily understand that people are thrown off balance by shock or excitement, so that they then act without even being aware of what they resolved or that they resolved anything at all. The possibility of this is a practical problem and an effect which should interest psychologists, but what is the philosophical difficulty? I think we are inclined to say that there isn't one, and that this, therefore, is not strictly speaking a case of incontinence since incontinence is traditionally a philosophical problem, even if it shares some of the ingredients of the panic example. But as for what we take to be paradigmatic incontinence, where the agent is well aware of the wrongness of what he does: we wonder, first, how it can be true to say, with Aristotle, that this agent is also ignorant of the same thing; and, second, what this ascription of ignorance can be meant to explain.

Since we find it problematic that Aristotle should wish to ascribe ignorance in every case of incontinence, we naturally assume that he has some special reason for the ascription and that what he is trying to prove or defend is that the incontinent is *ignorant*. So from the outset we are inclined to view Aristotle as going out of his way to establish a necessary place for *ignorance* in the incontinent situation, because for *us* to accept this would require a more than powerful argument! We then try to find an explanation for his engaging in this, as it seems to us, misguided enterprise. One kind of explanation goes like this: Aristotle thinks that the incontinent agent must act in ignorance, because to Aristotle it seems impossible that a person should voluntarily do what conflicts with an earlier resolve while remaining aware of that resolve, of what he is doing, and of the clash, in just the sense in which, it seems clear to us, the paradigm incontinent *does* remain aware of all these things. Having started along this path, we probably conclude that although Aristotle undertakes to find a way of conceptualising incontinence that 'saves the phenomena' (1145 b 3; 27–28), this is just what he fails to do so far as he addresses incontinence in what we take to be its paradigm form. Alternatively, we might draw the equally disappointing conclusion that Aristotle's concern was never in fact with what we consider incontinence par excellence, but with a different phenomenon and one that strikes us as not particularly paradoxical.

The approach which results in these conclusions seems confirmed by Aristotle's comparing incontinent agents to people who are drunk, asleep or in fits of madness (1147 a 12 ff.). And on incontinence of anger he writes:

> Anger seems to listen to reason to some extent, but to mishear it, as do hasty servants who run out before they have heard the whole of what one says, and then muddle the order, or as dogs bark if there is but a knock at the door, before looking to see if it is a friend; so anger by reason of the warmth and hastiness of its nature, though it hears, does not hear an order, and springs to take revenge. (1149 a 25–32)

Here incontinent rage is represented as a kind of heedlessness. All this suggests that if Aristotle recognises the existence at all of so-called clearheaded incontinence, he tries to explain it by assimilation to the sort of case of which it is natural to say that the agent does not know that he is acting wrongly and perhaps is not even aware of what he is doing.

In general, however, Aristotle's texts fail to support the conclusion that he assimilates all incontinence to the kind of case illustrated by blind rage. Nor do they support the conclusion that he regards that sort of blindness as uniquely paradigmatic. For in *NE* VII he notes the difference between the kind of incontinent person who gives way through weakness and the kind who is caught off guard by passion before he can collect himself enough to identify what he should and should not do (1150 b 19–28). And he also recognises instances of what we should call 'clearheaded' incontinence. He speaks, for example, of the incontinent who 'plots' access to a forbidden pleasure (1149 b 14–18; cf. 1142 b 16–20). If this agent is right minded enough to plot effectively, he is collected enough to be aware that his course is wrong. His trouble is not that he has temporarily lost his ethical bearings, but that he does not now care about the wrongness of the deed; or, if he does care, he means to go ahead anyway, even perhaps knowing that he will repent later. Aristotle also often speaks of the incontinent person as at odds with himself (e.g. 1102 b 14–25; 1111 b 13–16; 1166 b 6–8; *EE* II.8; *On the Soul* 433 b 5–8; 434 a 12–15), and we are surely to understand that the agent himself is frequently aware of the conflict. But (as many have commented) awareness of conflict entails awareness of each side.[9]

The gamut of Aristotle's examples suggests, in fact, that for him the blindness of passion, panic or extreme rage is not a necessary feature of incontinence in general; and that the plotting incontinent's awareness of behaving shamefully is not necessary either. It follows that the ignorance which in *NE* VII.3 Aristotle regards as essential to incontinence is not the unawareness just illustrated; also that the knowledge essential to incontinence is not the agent's clearheaded awareness that what he is doing is wrong, since this, too, is not present in all cases.

This last point is reinforced by the consideration that the knowledge of right and wrong which Aristotle ascribes to the incontinent agent as such *is the knowledge from which the agent would act if, instead of being incontinent in character, he were either continent or temperate.* Now there is no reason to think that the temperate agent necessarily acts with clearheaded awareness of refraining from what would be wrong. In very many cases the temperate person scarcely notices the pleasure which he foregoes nor, therefore, notices himself foregoing it. He may attend to what he is doing, but not necessarily to the rightness of what he is doing so far as this would be spelt out by a comparison between his mode of behaviour and that of an intemperate or incontinent person. He need not summon the thought of himself as committed to a mode of conduct requiring temperance in just the respect in which he is now showing it, or take note of his present behaviour as falling under that universal. If this kind of self-consciousness is only incidental to temperate behaviour, then it is incidental to incontinent behaviour, too, and its absence does not ground a description of the agent as 'ignorant'. If it did, then often enough it must be said of the temperate agent, too, that he fails to know how he is (voluntarily) behaving or that he fails to know that how he is behaving is how he should be behaving.

It may be suggested that even if the Aristotelian incontinent need not be acting blindly as in a fit or a stupor, he nonetheless does not act clearheadedly because, at the very least, his behaviour manifests self-deception. Somehow he has convinced himself, or has allowed himself to believe, that his diet does not really forbid this food or that, if it does, this breach does not count. Some of Aristotle's remarks seem to take in such cases, but he does not say that the agent *must* be self-deceived or otherwise blind. The concept of 'self-deception' has its own problems, and anyone who runs to it in order to account for incontinence, on the ground that clearheaded incontinence is too paradoxical to be possible, must defend that solution against the objection that it exchanges one paradox for another. For it can be argued that self-deception presupposes a kind of underlying clearheadedness with regard to those aspects of the situation which the agent in some sense deliberately shuts out. Since it is not accidental that he represents his action to himself in just the ways necessary for judging it harmless, justified or excusable, we have to say that he *knows* what aspects not to be aware of when awareness would stand in the way of the desired action, and hence that he somehow knows what it is that he manages not to know. Aristotle takes no notice of this problem, but, if I am right, he is under no particular obligation to do so, for he does not insist upon self-deception as a necessary feature of incontinence nor on the disjunction 'self-deception or blindness of passion'.

In any case, 'self-deception' of one or another kind may enter into virtuous action, except that here we might not call it that pejorative name. A good practical attitude often requires that we not look at certain things too closely to draw those conclusions from facts and principles which an uninvolved observer might be entitled to draw. The temperate person's state of mind as he passes by some chance of pleasure may be likened to a practical pretence that what he foregoes is in general worthless, even though he happily enjoys it when appropriate. These intermittent practical pretences may demand no effort of will, but the same is true of corrupt self-deception. We call it 'corrupt' not because the practical vision falls short of perfect objectivity, whatever that might mean, but because that vision is tailored to subserve wrong action.

The temptation to suppose that the ignorance distinguishing Aristotelian incontinence is a sort of blindness, like the blindness of rage, or a sort of self-deception, stems from a certain reading of the Socratic legacy in relation to Aristotle. Socrates had argued that 'incontinence' is the name of what is impossible, on the ground that someone who really knows that B is the worse course of action cannot voluntarily follow B rather than the better. Hence if he voluntarily follows B, this must be because he does not know it to be inferior. It is often assumed that Socrates reached this view because he held that real practical knowledge of what to do is a kind of power necessarily giving rise to right action: a power that seals the agent off from the possibility of voluntary deviation. It is further assumed that Aristotle accepts this view in essentials—i.e., the view that practical knowledge necessarily gives rise to action in accordance with it—although he introduces an important qualification ⁀f his own. The qualification is that whereas Socrates had simply said that the so-called incontinent acts from ignorance, thus denying to him any relevant knowledge at all, Aristotle holds that as well as being ignorant of his wrongdoing, the incontinent agent also in a sense does know what he should do.

On this interpretation, Aristotle ascribes ignorance to the incontinent on the ground that the corresponding knowledge would produce right action as its necessary effect. Such knowledge, therefore, belongs only to those who act rightly, and of these perhaps only to the virtuous, not to the continent. For if the knowledge is a watertight shield against wrong action, surely this could only be because it is a watertight shield against the *temptation* so to act? However reasonable this seems, we must beware of going too far in regarding the Aristotelian incontinent as lacking knowledge with which the virtuous person is blest. For Aristotle wants to establish, *contra* Socrates, that in a certain sense or on a certain level, continent, incontinent and virtuous agents are cognitively on equal terms. They share what we might call the same cognitive apparatus, which has logical, psychological and physical components. The logical component is a formed rational choice to do A; the psychological comprises the faculties of sense perception, memory, imagination etc. necessary for the agent to identify his situation as one to which the choice applies; and the physical component consists in those external and bodily conditions necessary for the unimpeded functioning in general of those faculties, as for instance adequate light by which to see. It is because the incontinent person has all this that Aristotle insists that he is knowing though also ignorant.

Now, on the 'Socratic' interpretation which we are presently considering, the incontinent is said to be ignorant because the corresponding knowledge, of which this ignorance is the absence, necessarily gives rise to right action. The ignorance, therefore, is a sine qua non of the incontinent's bad action, and helps to explain how it got to be performed. On this view we naturally identify the ignorance with some condition of the agent which is not the actual action; for the ignorance is supposed to *explain* how the action was possible. Consequently, it is natural to identify the ignorance with a condition of blindness or of self-deception, since these are not actions but they certainly affect and to that extent explain behaviour.

But this account is dubious, for two reasons. First, as we remarked, Aristotle does indicate that he recognises the possibility of cool, and so to speak internally controlled, incontinent behaviour. This rules out blindness in such cases, though it does not rule out the kind of self-deception in which the agent convinces himself that what he is doing is all right. But if Aristotle relies on the assumption that the incontinent always acts without a clear sense of the wrongness of his action, then he, Aristotle, ought to explain in what this absence of clarity consists when the behaviour is cool and controlled. An obvious candidate would be what we call 'self-deception', but Aristotle says nothing about it. What he does suggest in one place is that the incontinent person knows that he is doing wrong but does not care and does not identify himself with this knowledge; he is like an actor speaking his lines (1147 a 18–24). The self-deceiving agent, by contrast, feels bad about doing what he knows is wrong; hence the self-deception by which he turns a blind eye to what it is that he does or to its wrongness.

Second, as we shall see, Aristotle maintains that the difference between the incontinent person and the other types of agent who share (as we noted) the same cognitive apparatus is that the former, like them, *has* the knowledge he needs to act rightly but, unlike them, does not *use* this knowledge (1146 b 31 ff.). Aristotle writes as if having but not using that cognitive apparatus is distinctive of incontinence. But in that case, the continent agent who acts correctly although he is tempted otherwise, *uses* his knowledge of what he should do no less than the virtuous agent. Now the knowledge which the incontinent person lacks, according to the proposed account, is knowledge whose presence would necessarily give rise to action in accordance with it. And it seemed reasonable to assume that the power of this knowledge to give rise to right action is a power that seals the agent off from even being tempted in an opposite direction. In that case, this knowledge should be exclusive to the virtuous agent; the continent lacks it no less than the incontinent.[10] From this it would seem that there are three cognitive items in play in this theory: (1) possession of the cognitive apparatus (common to all three types of agent); (2) a condition of knowledge which shields its owner from acting contrarily and from even being so inclined (unique to the virtuous agent); and (3) use of the cognitive apparatus (shared by the virtuous and the continent). But Aristotle writes as if just two levels or modes of cognition are sufficient for a coherent picture, namely (1) and (3).

A further difficulty concerns the possibility of *continence*. If the continent person lacks (2) and if lack of (2) is what explains the incontinent's bad action, how is it that the continent agent manages not to do what is wrong; in other words, to maintain the distinction between himself and the incontinent? But any account which threatens to obliterate continence from moral life, or to make it hopelessly paradoxical, is surely as unacceptable to Aristotle as a theory that implies these things for *in*continence. For just as adult incontinence harks back to the natural unruly childish state that creates the need for moral education at all, so adult continence harks back to the possibility presupposed by that education: the possibility of doing what one is told even when one does not feel like it.

I think it clear that these problems all arise because it is assumed that item (2) plays a part. Item (2) is what gets interpreted as that legendary clearheadedness which Aristotle (on the proposed account) ought to say, but never does say, is absent in all cases of incontinence. Item (2) is what is supposed to explain the difference between virtuous and incontinent behaviour, but can do so only in a way that puts continence in conceptual jeopardy. It has to be concluded that, whatever Socrates may have thought, Aristotle does not think that any sort of condition of practical knowledge necessarily gives rise to the right action. In other words, there is no cognitive condition which, if added to (1), brings it about that (1) will issue in (3). There are only (1) and (3); and, given (1), the occurrence of (3) is contingent.

This gives rise to the question: 'If the ignorance that typifies Aristotelian incontinence is not the absence or contrary of (2), of what is it the absence or contrary?' The answer can only be (3); but before coming to this in the next section, it is worth dwelling on the claim just made, that for Aristotle there is *no* sort of practical knowledge that necessarily gives rise to the corresponding action. Unless we are convinced of this, we shall continue to suppose that the incontinent agent's ignorance is not, as I have just now implied and shall argue further, his sheer failure to use his shared cognitive apparatus in appropriate action, but is, rather, a defective mental condition which *explains* his failure to use it.

In several passages outside his special discussion of incontinence, Aristotle affirms it as a commonplace that practical knowledge or the right evaluative attitude is no guarantee of good behaviour (e.g. 1095 a 8–9 and 1110 a 29–31; cf. 1179 b 4–7).[11] This is obvious, given his own doctrine and Plato's earlier (but post-Socratic) doctrine of the different parts of the soul. Being different and developed by different procedures, hence not necessarily evenly developed, they may or may not be in harmony.[12] The plain fact of incontinence was, of course, Plato's most striking argument for the soul's complexity. Contrast this with the Socratic position, which may be summed up as follows: the notion of incontinence is incoherent because it implies that a rational agent is not a rational agent. If someone fails to act according to his own rational prescription, he is a rational agent (since capable of a rational prescription); but to act against the rational prescription is not to be a rational agent. The argument assumes that rational agency is monolithic and, so to speak, indivisible over time. Aristotle's theory of the soul affords an adequate answer: one may be actively rational enough to form a rational choice and then be properly described as in the state of having formed it; but more is required for being actively rational in the sense of enacting one's choice. The 'more' depends on continued co-operation of that side of the soul not directly expressed in the determinate detail of a rational choice elaborated in deliberation. Deliberation presupposes a nondeliberative interest in the summum bonum, which interest provides the ethical atmosphere, one might call it, for deliberation to occur. If the atmosphere is sustained, the conclusion of deliberation naturally translates into overt action. But there is nothing in the act of deliberation itself, nor in its cognitive result, that necessarily sustains that atmosphere through whatever perceptual and emotional changes may occur between deliberation and the moment of action, this being supposed not immediate.

The agent's knowledge—his rational choice—may be considered as simply "there", a possession achieved by him; and once he has it, he is inescapably different from before. There are ways of divesting oneself of such states, but these are rational procedures of the same nature as that which generated the state. The state may, of course, lapse, if the agent suffers some general impairment or if what the choice refers to ceases to be practicable. But lapsing aside, only redeliberation to a different conclusion can negate the original condition. Thus change on this level would be from one such cognitive state to another. Such a change would require a continuance or reawakening of the same ethical interest that buoyed up the agent's deliberative passage to the first state. That first state (of having made a certain rational choice) may function as a logical starting point for redeliberation (it harbours the plan that is up for reconsideration) but it cannot by itself be the source of that activity any more than it was the source of the activity by which it came to be, *or of any other action.*

It may be helpful to compare the cognitive state (the rational choice having been made) with the physical structure of a living creature; i.e., the empirically knowable shape and organisation of parts. The form in this sense is realised in matter through vital functioning on the level of growth and nutrition. The form as shape or pattern is intrinsic to the physical apparatus necessary for these and further vital functions. Locomotion, for instance, depends on parts of such and such build, proportion and arrangement. Sense perception depends on the structure of the organs and a balance of their materials. But the perceivable realised shape is not itself the active source of movement and perception, nor of the growth that transforms it into new shapes in orderly development. Similarly, the cognitive state which we designate when we say that the agent *has* made the rational choice of A is both a product of rational functioning and a piece of necessary equipment for further rational functioning (whether in action or in further deliberation), but is not its soul or vitalising source.

Such states are preconditions for the peculiarly irrational behaviour of those who 'know better', and it is no miracle that given such states such behaviour sometimes occurs. The cause, according to Aristotle, is appetite or impulse and the agent's disposition to be taken over by these. (Aristotle appears not to recognise the possibility that the ethical interest prompting the original deliberation should simply flag and die, so that the agent would just not do what he was supposed to, as distinct from positively doing something else.) The deviant impulse can sometimes rattle the agent so that he hardly knows what he is doing. Sometimes it warps his assessment of the situation so that the rational choice seems not to relate to it. Sometimes he struggles to stick to the choice, but gives in. Sometimes, under the influence, he simply finds himself not caring about what he has chosen or about having chosen it. Sometimes, we might say, he has made the choice but no longer feels that it has to do with him. Phenomenologically these effects are different. And their causal rôles are not necessarily the same. Thus warping of judgment might sometimes pave the way for the wrong action by making it seem all right; but sometimes the corruption of judgment seems more like the by-product of an impulse which (even if judgment had not been affected) would have been sufficient to issue in the action. The differences suggest different points of susceptibility or different thresholds of disturbance answering to variations in physical and psychic constitution.[13] People who easily lose their heads are not necessarily prone to self-deceptive incontinence or the temporary brazenness of the person who knowingly flings his principles aside. Aristotle indicates that there is plenty of room for closer studies of an empirical kind. He, however, groups this heterogeneous set of cases together, because it is what they have in common— namely, *failure to use the practical knowledge possessed*—that sends the moral educator the crucial message: no amount of good deliberation is enough in the absence of a moral nature prepared and able, when the time comes to act, to grasp *by actually doing it* what there is most reason to do.

## IV. Incontinent Ignorance

For Socrates, the question 'How is it possible to know what one should do, yet voluntarily not do it?' poses a problem which can be laid to rest only by denying the possibility. For analysts in the Humean tradition, it likewise poses a possibly insoluble problem, though surely one different from the problem found by Socrates. But for Aristotle, I have argued, the question hardly arises, in that when it does it has already been virtually answered by his anatomy of the soul. No new theory is needed, by the time we reach *NE* VII, to explain 'how incontinence is possible', in the sense of 'how incontinent behaviour can possibly come about'.

What, then, *is* the Aristotelian problem of incontinence? It is a strictly logical problem and, we may think, gratuitous. The incontinent agent, in Aristotle's conception, acts in ignorance; and in this Socrates was right. But the incontinent agent also knows to do better than he does; and such knowledge had no place in Socrates' account. What Aristotle must do is establish senses of 'knowledge' and 'ignorance' that are predicable together without contradiction. This is one of his principal aims in the famous third chapter of *NE* VII. What I would stress is that Aristotle's notion of incontinent ignorance plays no part in his *explanation* of how incontinence is psychologically and metaphysically possible for embodied rational agents whose nature is such that there is bound to be a difference between how they anticipate the circumstances of their deeds and those same circumstances lived through at the time. Incontinent ignorance *sets* Aristotle his problem; it is no part of the solution. And the question of *how* that ignorance is metaphysically and psychologically possible is exactly the same as the question how incontinent action itself is possible.[14] Thus the answer is straightforward (given Aristotle's theory of the soul), since the answer, too, is the same.[15]

The only difficulty, then, from Aristotle's point of view is that the correct description of an eminently possible situation seems to break the rules of logic. This difficulty deserves the special discussion he gives it, because the psychology that explains the possibility of incontinence does not automatically generate a logically exact way of describing what it explains. However, Aristotle easily produces a logical distinction to help him out: that between 'knows' in the sense of having knowledge and 'knows' in the sense of using it. This logical distinction, like the psychological theory of the parts of the soul, is an already familiar item in Aristotle's repertoire (see, e.g., *On the Soul* 417 a 24–b 1).

Aristotle's solution to the problem of incontinence, I therefore suggest, would have struck both him and his immediate audience as quite obvious, though not as insignificant. The real possibility of incontinence is so important from the point of view of moral education that we cannot afford to let our focus on this possibility waver, even if only under pressure of sophistical arguments trading on verbal ambiguity. But the move (the distinction of senses of 'know') which sets matters straight in a way that will silence the sophist provides no deep new insights into the nature of human agency. Those who find Aristotle's solution exciting, as well as those who imagine that they have missed his meaning because what they find him saying seems unexciting, are, I venture to say, on a wrong track.

Aristotle's problem, I have claimed, is easily solved by Aristotle. The puzzle that remains is ours. Why is he impelled to assume that the incontinent agent acts in ignorance? It is an assumption which Aristotle seems to see no need to prove, defend or explain. I have argued it a mistake to think that he reaches for it in order to *account for* incontinent action. Yet such an awkward position would surely not be adopted without compelling reason. Not only does it give Aristotle nothing that he needs in order to explain how incontinence is possible, but without it he is free from the embarrassment of a seemingly inconsistent description. He can still talk about incontinence in the ways in which we talk about it today. He can say that the incontinent person voluntarily does what he knows he should not, and there is no appearance of logical error in that. Aristotle can also employ his own distinction and say that the incontinent person has knowledge but does not use it. There would be no semblance of self-contradiction in that. It is not logically problematic that people have things which they do not use. But Aristotle does have a problem, because he takes what seems the entirely unnecessary extra step of equating *failure to use the knowledge* with *ignorance concerning the objects of the knowledge unused.* He thereby lumbers himself with a sense of 'ignorance' which does no work that we can see, and which puts him to the trouble of distinguishing it from another sense on pain of inconsistency.

The explanation must be that 'the incontinent acts in ignorance' is not adopted by Aristotle as a formal thesis. Rather, for him it is wholly natural to speak and think of incontinent behaviour as ignorance. And it must have seemed no less natural to those to whom his lectures were addressed.[16] This would be why Aristotle never questions Socrates' claim that the incontinent acts in ignorance but seeks only to rebut the Socratic implication that knowledge is wholly lacking. Without lucubration he applies the term 'ignorance' to the wrong action itself or to the drive manifested in that action.

But 'ignorant' here, like the term 'incontinent' which implies it, is applied on the assumption that the agent does know what he should do and fails to act accordingly. Since the possibility of this is no problem, the possibility of the ignorance is no problem either; but we still have to be careful to define the sense in which the agent is thus ignorant, since it is a sense that entails the prior application of 'knows' said with respect to the same objects. So this sort of ignorance necessarily breeds the appearance of self-contradiction[17]—which suggests that where incontinent behaviour is attended or even facilitated by a type of ignorance that might have occurred outside the context of incontinence, this is not the ignorance in which incontinent action essentially consists. An example would be the blindness of panic, which of course might occur when the agent could not be expected to be armed with a relevant rational choice. Again, the incontinent's self-wrought illusion that really this oily food is harmless is not, qua false belief, the ignorance of incontinence, for this false belief might occur in someone who had never undertaken the dry-food diet.

Let us consider how it makes sense to equate incontinent action with ignorant action. It is natural to speak of the incontinent action as 'unwise' and also 'irrational'. This is not just a trick of Greek idiom. The agent was rational and 'wise' enough, let us suppose, to form a good rational choice. But, if he then fails to live up to it, he shows himself lacking in practical wisdom (cf. 1152 a 6–9), however excellent the deliberation that put him in possession of the choice. There is a special kind of unwisdom and stupidity in failing to act it out when one can. This is the foolishness of wasteful behaviour. It is as if the agent no longer understands what the rational choice which he went to the trouble of pondering over is *for*—to be acted on. But this is worse than ordinary wastefulness. The indiscriminate spender may never have 'known the value' of money. Not having had to work for it, he lacks the sense that it is to be used for ends worth the labour of production. But one cannot pick up and use as one's own a rational choice handed over by someone else,[18] and no one can form his own choice except from his own serious intent of acting on it; thus the incontinent agent will throw away what he himself has constructed.[19]

Calling the incontinent 'unwise' and 'foolish' are ways of talking, but what does this show except that language can lag behind philosophy? The words denote cognitive failure which is somehow moral failure, too.[20] Should we not sweep such uses aside as belonging to an age which, for all Aristotle's efforts, was very far from understanding the diversity of the soul and its attributes? One can allow that intellectual errors may arise from character (consider impatience) without identifying those errors *as* failures of character. Conversely, cognitive error can give rise to undesirable action, but how does that justify equating the action itself—not an intellectual move but the bringing about of results in the world—with cognitive error? Certainly there is something wrong in having but failing to use a valuable resource for its proper purpose, if it has one; but if we speak accurately, should we not describe the failure as moral tastelessness rather than as irrationality? Aristotle makes it clear that incontinence is a defect of the nonrational part of the soul (this follows from its having the same field as temperance). The other part, by which we reason and think, cannot be either continent, incontinent or morally virtuous. So it seems that in falling in with the tendency, however natural, to call incontinent action 'ignorance', he fails to make proper use of his own ethical psychology, equating reason with nonreason.

From the opposite angle it might be argued that Aristotle's mistake is not that he abandons his division of the soul, but that he takes it too seriously, laying excessive weight on the metaphor of command and obedience. One can fail to obey an order through failing to take it in, and this sort of heedlessness is a kind of ignorance or ignoring. But that is not a good reason for calling incontinence 'ignorance'. A literal servant is heedless because he fails or refuses to use his *intelligence* to listen and obey. Applying this model to the parts of the soul only unlocks the possibilities of regress inherent in such an account. The nonrational part which ought to heed reason must be subdivided into a cognitive part that may or may not understand the orders of reason and transmit those orders to another, supposedly executive, part, which in turn has to be able to understand; and so on. In fact, however, Aristotle does not think that it is the nonrational part of the soul that acts or fails to act in the world, but the agent as a whole. The agent as a whole is incontinent, but in virtue of one kind of inner failure, not another. It is *his* failure, and *he* is rational and cognitive. But the failure of a rational cognitive being is not on that account the failure of that being qua rational and cognitive.

So why is incontinence *ignorance,* when incontinence is a malfunction of the nonrational part of the soul—a defect of will, not reason? It is a voluntary lapse from that general pre- and subdeliberative interest in pursuing the best. This interest is nonrational, in that it is nurtured by training through habituation and cannot be aroused (though its focus might be altered) by argument and analysis. But it asks to be made determinate on particular occasions through deliberation, and only so does its objective become practicable. Such a nonrational interest is peculiar to rational beings and is itself as distinctive a mark of rationality as any process of argument. If we refuse to call it 'rational' because of not itself being the rational inquiry that bears it out, how can we regard as 'rational' that longing for theoretical understanding of which Aristotle speaks at the opening of the *Metaphysics?* For that, too, is an interest that powers, hence cannot be the same as, rational investigation. The incontinent agent lacks something genuinely rational and on that ground is called 'ignorant', although nothing is wrong with the cognitive state from which he acts.

Let us consider this cognitive apparatus which the agent brings to the situation when overt action should start. We suppose it nondefective, even in the incontinent. But even when nondefective, it can be no more than what it is: a resource for appropriate action. As a resource, it is in a technical sense 'imperfect', being brought to fulfilment only through use. Failure to use it as its nature prescribes is a failure of the agent qua possessor of this equipment, hence a failure of him qua cognitive. The one who primarily suffers from this is the subject himself, whose weakness costs him the blessing of his own excellent practical activity. But his possessed knowledge is unchanged in cognitive content: so if it was knowledge before he was tempted astray, surely it is knowledge still? This inference assumes that knowledge is nothing but a type of cognitive relation to some object, fact, prescription or whatever: one that differs from other types of cognitive relation (such as belief) in ways which we need not pursue, but which have to do with reasons and justification. But is it absurd to ask concerning someone's cognitive relation to something—it being allowed the title 'knowledge' on epistemic grounds—'Yes, but is it *knowledge?*' Surely not, if the word 'knowledge' is used to stand for something we rightly value (as is sometimes held to be the case with the word 'freedom'). But the incontinent's cognitive state, acquired as a resource from which to act, is rendered useless, and by none other than its owner. He does not treat it as precious knowledge, one might say, and so it ceases to *be* knowledge, since the state that is his cannot be used by anyone else.

Since knowledge possessed is essentially knowledge-for-use (whether of the axioms of a science to use in demonstration, or knowledge of how to respond when offered a third Martini), a proper account of what it is to have knowledge makes reference to something beyond, which is the use. Since the use is also the final actuality of what is possessed, it is virtually inevitable, for reasons of logic and metaphysics, that Aristotle will equate the activity of using knowledge with *knowledge* in the strict and primary sense of the term. For the primary significate of a term is its referent in full actuality. (So much for the twentieth-century linguistic stricture that knowledge is a state, not an activity of knowing.) Thus doing what one should do, from the state of knowledge that one should do it, is more properly to be considered knowing what one should do than the state itself. It follows that failure (under that condition) to do what one should is not just practical ignorance, but practical ignorance in the primary sense.

Thus practical life provides its own proof of the opening words of the *Metaphysics:* 'All men by nature reach out for knowledge'. As agents we also desire to *do,* but this is not fundamentally different from desiring to think and perceive; for doing, too, is a mode of knowing, an exercise of knowledge. If this seems far fetched to Aristotle's modern readers, it is because we think about knowledge in terms forged in the modern dialogue with scepticism. In this framework, what is most precious about knowledge is being justified. We treasure most the goods that seem most precarious, and those who are threatened with total dispossession desire nothing more than rightful ownership. To them, the most significant cognitive work consists in gathering stores of knowledge and devising methods to prevent the admission of anything rotten that could infect the surrounding possessions. Reason, on this view, is divorced from practice, because even if value-judgments could be rationally justified, the justification of an action is nothing but the justification of the laid-up choice so to act. Thus the actual *doing* of the action is not an enhancement of our rational nature, since enacting the choice cannot render the choice more justified than if we failed to act. And the person who enacts his justified choice, a choice which he can explain and defend, certainly need not be acting on the similarly by him justified assumption that one is justified in acting on a justified choice! That is a question for philosophers, whereas well-conditioned agents, as Aristotle knows, enact their choices regardless of what general view philosophy takes of the matter. Thus by acting, one is not more justified than if one did not act, hence not better off or more fulfilled as a rational and cognitive being.

The assumption that our rational good terminates with being justified is not in conflict with the perceived facts of moral life. But it forces us to interpret those facts along one of two lines. Either there is no kind of perfection to be gained or enjoyed by the *doing* of what one has rationally chosen because one has rationally chosen it; or there is, but it is not a perfection of us as rational beings. Setting aside the first alternative, we are bound by the second to see acting (as distinct from being justified) not as the flowering of our rational nature, but as representing some separate domain of, say, will or sensibility, depending on one's theory.

## V.  Essential Features and Contingent Manifestations

We shall presently examine Aristotle's detailed account of the incontinent's failure to act on the knowledge he has of what he should do. Our discussion so far of this cognitive apparatus, as I have called it, has focused mainly on the rational choice. But the apparatus includes more. It comprises all that a well-conditioned agent would need for right action. Thus it includes the perceptual and recognitional capacities by which one identifies the situation as calling for action in accordance with the choice. And it must also comprise the conditions needed for those capacities to function adequately. With all this, the agent is cognitively *in a position* to act as he should.

But, it may be said, if he is in the grip of a contrary appetite, he is not in a position to do so; and, in general, if he were in such a position, he would act accordingly. Moreover, as Aristotle recognises, powerful emotion can impede the functioning of the faculties just mentioned; thus in at least some cases of incontinence they do not function adequately. It seems to follow, first, that no incontinent agent is 'in a position' to do what he should; and, from this, that he lacks the knowledge presupposed by calling him 'incontinent', given that being in a position is having this knowledge. And granted that emotion sometimes impedes perception and recognition, it seems to follow, second, for this more specific reason, that the incontinent agent sometimes lacks the full complement of cognitive apparatus. In short, the thesis that in general he has it unimpaired seems convincing only as long as we identify the entire apparatus with one element in it, which is the state of having made a rational choice.

This difficulty can be surmounted if we assume that Aristotle implicitly distinguishes those malfunctionings that arise because of the specific natures of the capacities concerned from those characteristic of incontinence. If a panicking person fails to see a relevant signal, the chances are that he would have failed to hear it had it been audible rather than visible. If, being tempted, one fails to take in the waiter's murmur of the name of a dish whose name is on the forbidden list, one would probably have failed to take it in when reading the menu. Such failure to see or hear, or to connect what is seen or heard with what one knows, cannot be corrected by treatment for deafness or short sight, or by general memory training, or by developing reading skills. Just as in self-deception precisely those beliefs are adopted or accented that portray the forbidden action as permissible, so with these blocks of perceptual attention. The attention, whatever its sensory mode, gives way at just the points necessary for the free play of impulse or appetite. The perceptual and recognitional faculties are not malfunctioning in the sense in which this would be true of a medically disabled person; their functioning, rather, is organised to the end to which appetite points. Thus the agent is *cognitively in a position* to do what is right in the following sense: there is nothing wrong with him that could be cured by treatment for problems germane to the intrinsic natures of the faculties concerned.

In this sense, then, he knows what he should do (let this be A). And by virtue of this knowledge he also, in the same sense, knows that what he actually does, namely B, is wrong. For a virtuous agent similarly placed knows in this sense that B excludes A, hence that B (for him a counterfactual action) *would be* wrong. The difference between incontinence and temperance is not in what they know, but in the relative positions of 'actual' and 'counterfactual' with respect to A and B. Now the virtuous agent's knowledge that B would be wrong does not entail that he summons up the thought of this. Sometimes, as we have seen, the virtuous response pays no attention to B and is all the more virtuous for that. This suggests two conclusions concerning any parallel failure on the part of the incontinent agent to pay attention to the rightness of A and the wrongness of his doing B. First, such inattention is consistent with his knowing what he has to know (in the way in which he has to know it) to merit the charge of incontinence in this situation. (Otherwise we should have to hold that the temperate person who takes no notice—out of temperance—of the possibility of some pleasure is literally not apprised of the fact, and similarly for the courage that ignores danger. But then the actions represent no moral achievement.) Second, if the incontinent agent does not have on his mind, so to speak, the wrongness of his doing B, this does not explain his incontinent lapse or his failure to use his practical knowledge. For the virtuous agent, too, may not have that on his mind, yet the phrase 'uses his knowledge' applies par excellence to him. But if not having the wrongness of B on one's mind is not responsible for the incontinent lapse, there is no reason to think that having it on one's mind would protect one from such a lapse. Certainly it is not what protects those virtuous agents who pay no attention to B. Consequently, it is possible for someone to do B incontinently and yet be even acutely aware that he ought not to be doing B.

What is essential to incontinent behaviour, then, is that the incontinent has all that he cognitively needs for the voluntary execution of his choice, yet, because of passion or appetite, he fails to execute it. The presence or absence of a clear awareness of wrongdoing is, I have just argued, contingent. Since the cognitive apparatus is or embodies the knowledge which the incontinent as such must *have* and the use in action which he fails to make of it would be that knowledge *used,* it follows that the presence of clear awareness of wrongdoing is compatible with the truth of the statement 'He has but does not use the relevant practical knowledge'. But although the awareness of wrongdoing is contingent, we need not conclude that it is accidental, if by that is meant that, when it occurs, it is irrelevant to the agent's incontinence. On the contrary, it is typical of one kind of incontinence—or a set of kinds, since there are a number of very different conditions which we call 'not being clearly aware'; but these are by no means the only kinds.

Aristotle's distinction between knowledge had and the use of it is logically clear, but it does not follow from this that the same experiential material always falls on the same side of that logical line. The distinction is meant to remove the appearance of self-contradiction from ascriptions of incontinence; it is not meant to offer a general empirical picture of the incontinent's state of mind. In my view, there is no way in which Aristotle's discussion can be given a consistent interpretation if one comes to it expecting to be given such a picture.

For consider the fact that in a morally disciplined agent the connection between perceiving the situation and recognising it as the occasion for enacting his choice, and the connection between this and the acting, is so close that we cannot, when we view the agent in action, draw a line between what counts as knowledge that he has and what counts as his use of it. Recognition is already incipient action; so, since action is use, recognition is use. But perception is recognition. It seems that the only cognitive items which this agent definitely has in advance of his using what he has (and therefore definitely distinguishable from the use) are the rational choice itself and the capacities of perception and recognition. Should we then say that this in general is all that the incontinent agent has, and that everything else falls on the side of use or failure to use? No, for if the incontinent is clearheaded about his misdemeanour, this condition is certainly not in itself a *failure to use* knowledge. It is knowledge, not absence of knowledge. But nor can it be a *using* of his practical knowledge. For, though clearheaded, he fails to act accordingly, and this failure to act is his failure to use his knowledge. Clearheadedness, then, belongs with what this incontinent agent has but fails to use.

Now it would seem that the agent who loses his head through fear or desire—who does not perceive his situation as having those properties which, it so happens, make it an occasion for enacting the choice, or does perceive it as having those properties but fails to relate it to his choice, so that it is as if he has forgotten the choice—he, it would seem, *has* so much less than the clearheaded incontinent that one hesitates to say that the former has what he needs to be considered incontinent at all. Aristotle registers this difficulty by distinguishing in effect between different grades of *having* knowledge; some, by comparison with others, seem almost like not *having* (1147 a 7 ff.; b 9–12).[21] After all, the blindness of panic is the privation of clearheadedness (though not a privation of anything of practical value, if the clearheadedness were only to be had and not used in right action). But Aristotle, in my view, does not distinguish correlative grades of *using* practical knowledge. Right action alone is the use. (It follows that the distinction *having/using* does not exactly correspond to the distinction *potential/actual*. For it is reasonable to say that the basic cognitive apparatus possessed by all incontinent agents, including those who lose their heads in the situation, is the potential for a clearheaded grasp of what should be done, and that this accordingly is the correlative actuality. In the next section I shall argue that the text of VII.3 supports my rejection of the common assumption that if X stands to Y as *actual knowledge* to the corresponding *potential,* then X stands to Y as *use* to *possession.*)

Hence there is one main division, between use and various grades of having. In particular cases the main line is drawn at the point (varying with the agent's personality and circumstances) where feeling or appetite breaks the proper connection between rational choice and action. With some personalities, if there were perception of the situation, it would automatically carry recognition, and recognition would automatically move into action according to the choice. When that is so, appetite or emotion can only spoil the show by attacking perception. In some cases, the agent is not of a nature to do what at the time he feels bad about doing. When that is so, appetite can have its way only by making him not care. On the opposite side (there are intermediates) is the person who is clearly aware of it all and even feels shame. *His* clarity and shame belong with what he has but fails to use; in the other cases, the lack of clarity or the lack of shame is part and parcel of the failure to use what he has.[22]

The fact that clearheadedness about what one should and should not do is an actuality of the cognitive apparatus (but not the same actuality as the correct behaviour itself), together with the assumption that what is actualized is thereby *used,* has done much to create the common impressions (1) that Aristotle distinguishes incontinent failure to use one's knowledge from incontinent failure to act on it; (2) that therefore he can, and accordingly does, explain the latter by the former; (3) that therefore he blames incontinent behaviour on lack of clearheadedness; and (4) that (in sum) he regards clearheaded incontinent behaviour as impossible. These linked impressions are reinforced by the statement with which he introduces his account in *NE* VII.3:

> But we speak of knowing in two ways, and ascribe it both to someone who has it without using it and to someone who is using it. Hence it will matter whether some-one has the knowledge that his action is wrong, without attending to [*theōrōn*] his knowledge, or both has and attends to it. For this second case seems extraordinary, but wrong action when he does not attend to [*theōrei*] his knowledge does not seem extraordinary. (1146 b 31–35)[23]

This seems to be intended to apply to incontinence in general. It says that it would be unduly paradoxical to describe someone as 'incontinent' if this implies that he disobeys his own prescription while currently *'attending to'* it. But whether this rules out clearheaded incontinence depends entirely on how we interpret 'attends to' *('theōrei').* The word is often translated 'contemplates', 'reflects on' or 'thinks about'. Ordinarily, it connotes active observation or scrutiny—focusing on something rather than merely 'bearing it in mind'. Aristotle also uses it to mark the active theoretical deployment of theoretical knowledge. Now it is with examples of theoretical knowledge that he standardly illustrates the distinction between having knowledge and using it (see *On the Soul* 417 a 21 ff.; *Generation of Animals* 735 a 11; *Metaphysics* 1048 a 34; 1050 a 12–14).[24] Thus it is not surprising if, in these contexts, the verb *'theōrein'* functions as a virtual synonym for 'use one's knowledge'. I conjecture that here in the *Ethics* he falls into the same form of words, even though the knowledge here is for *practical* use. In that case, the passage just quoted lends no support to the view that Aristotle denies that you can do what at that very moment you are consciously thinking you should not. It simply invites us to think of the incontinent agent as failing to use his knowledge; i.e., as failing to do the practical equivalent of what the philosopher or scientist does when he applies what he knows in active theorising.[25]

In considering what to conclude from this concerning the relation of using knowledge to knowing something clearheadedly, it is worth noting that what the theoretical thinker engages in when he uses his theoretical knowledge is not aesthetic contemplation of facts and principles, but an endeavour to explore or understand further by means of them or to uncover underlying principles. Looking at them is not yet employing them in the required sense, for (it is not too much to say) they are not there just to be looked at.[26] It would not be easy to characterise in general the mental condition of a thinker who is using his knowledge in the required sense; i.e., as a scientist or philosopher. Having it all clearly in front of him is arguably not (perhaps cannot be) a necessary condition of appropriate use, and it certainly is not sufficient if, as is possible, someone may have everything clearly tabulated in consciousness yet be unwilling or unable to do anything scientific or philosophical with it. It looks as if 'theōrein', in Aristotle's discourse about theoretical knowledge, connotes whatever would count as an appropriately scientific or philosophical engagement and does not stand for any particular independently describable psychological condition.[27] If that is so, then at 1146 b 34–35 'theōrei' applied in the practical dimension cannot literally mean what it means in the theoretical: i.e., 'actively engages as a scientist or philosopher should'. This is a resounding contradiction in terms, given that practice has to do with the contingent and particular, science with the necessary and universal. It is therefore likely that in this practical application the verb is, as I suggested above, used loosely to mean, in effect, 'actively engages in the practical equivalent of *theōrein*'. But the practical equivalent of the scientist's appropriate use of scientific knowledge is appropriate use of practical knowledge; and this is not holding it clearly in mind, but acting in accordance with it.[28]

As we move on from Aristotle's reminder of the two senses of 'knows', it soon becomes clear that the sort of incontinent who loses his head and cannot now say what he is supposed to be doing or even, perhaps, what it is that he does, is not, in Aristotle's account, the only sort. Aristotle recognises him first, comparing his state to sleep, madness and drunkenness (1147 a 10–16) and then notes other possibilities.[29] What we have been calling 'clearheadedness', Aristotle sees in terms of being able to *say* what one is supposed to do: 'The fact that men use the language that flows from knowledge proves nothing [i.e., does not prove that they are not ignorant]' (1147 a 18–19). He is not claiming that the agent can utter the words as meaningless noises (what would be the point of that claim?) but that the saying does not express what it should, i.e., the actively serious purpose which is the grasp of practical truth. This incontinent is like the student who can tell you that Plato's theory of Forms leads to an infinite regress, but without being able to explain why. It is not that the incontinent does not understand what he knows, but that he and the philosophy student alike fall short of the goals of reason, practical and theoretical respectively. Aristotle also makes a comparison with actors speaking their lines. He may have in mind the sort of case where what the incontinent person knows he should do seems to have no connection with *him*. But we should not forget that actors *feel* their lines; so the illustration is apt even for the case where the incontinent feels shame and guilt at the moment of action. At 1147 b 12 Aristotle combines his illustrations: the drunk person too may be *compos mentis* enough to come out with the right statement, but its meaning is not alive for him as it should be, as is shown in other things which he says or does.

The incontinent's knowledge of what he should do, and of what he does instead, is sufficient ground, Aristotle holds, for classing the behaviour as voluntary (1152 a 15–16[30]). Thus we are right to condemn the agent for it. He knows that he is taking a sweet dish and that the choice ruled out sweets. So he voluntarily takes what is sweet and voluntarily takes what his choice forbade. This is true in all cases, whether or not the action is also intentional. If 'doing B intentionally' entails 'being articulately aware that one does B', then taking the sweet dish may not be intentional (as when one conveniently fails to take in the waiter's description). Nor need the incontinent agent be articulately aware that in doing B he is doing what is wrong or betraying his rational choice. Thus he can act incontinently yet his action not be intentional either under the description 'B' or under the description 'incontinent action'. Like clearheadedness and its absence, intentionality in the sense indicated is not an essential feature of incontinent action.

## VI. Aristotle's Analysis

The thrust of Aristotle's argument in *NE* VII.3, as I understand it, is to show how it is true that the incontinent agent acts *in knowledge.* He is addressing an audience for whom it is a datum that incontinent behaviour is a kind of ignorance, although they may not yet give this a precise meaning. This point about ignorance is not introduced by Aristotle as the explanation of anything or as having to be defended, partly because it would have been natural for his audience to speak of incontinence as ignorance and partly because the position has the famous support of Socrates. What does have to be established, in response to the way in which Socrates developed this idea, is the coherence of the thought that the incontinent agent is also in some way knowing. Aristotle sees this as his first task. 'We must consider first, then, whether incontinent people act knowingly or not, and in what sense knowingly' (1146 b 8–9; cf. 1145 b 21–22) For Socrates had dismissed incontinent knowledge out of hand, and thereby denied that incontinence is even possible. Here he flew in the face of the obvious, since it is another datum for common sense, as well as an implication of Aristotle's ethical psychology, that incontinence is all too possible. Aristotle solves the logical problem regarding the 'possibility of incontinence', which, I have argued, is his only problem, by appealing to a distinction by which one may be said, with reference to the same object, to know (have knowledge) and not know (not use the knowledge) at the same time. And Aristotle's purpose is to show, not (what is already taken for granted) that the incontinent can rightly be called 'ignorant' on the ground that he does not use his knowledge, but rather that the incontinent can rightly be called 'knowing', on the ground that his much-proclaimed ignorance is nothing but the failure to use *knowledge* that he has.

Having introduced the distinction between possession and use of knowledge, Aristotle brings it to bear on actions analysed as conclusions from universal and particular premisses. This way of analysing actions is not restricted to those involving rational choice. Aristotle applies it to animal locomotion in general, or to any behaviour governed by perception and desire (*Movement of Animals* 701 a 7 ff.; *On the Soul* 434 a 16–21). Take the action of (as it might be described) *eating this.* It is (we may suppose) the conclusion from 'Anything sweet is delicious; this is sweet.' These premises are known by the agent in that they are given by his cognitive apparatus. From the agent's point of view the action is the application to this situation of a universal (or complex of universals). Thus *eating this* is *eating-what-is-delicious-(because sweet)* as applied to *this* situation. The premises display what *eating this* is (i.e., *what* action would be taken if it were taken) by displaying its why (why it would be taken): *eating this* would be engaged in because it is *eating something delicious (since sweet)*. The eating is end-directed, because focused on what is sweet and the associated pleasure, but it is not on that account necessarily intentional in the sense employed at the end of the last section. The action could be the incontinent one of somebody who conveniently failed to hear the waiter's description or to remember the number of calories. His actual taking of the dish is focused on the pleasure of sweetness, whether the agent himself could tell you so or not. We might even say that far from end-directedness implying intentionality (in the above sense), the more intense and exclusive the focus and (these facts tend not to be independent) the more purely somatic the appeal of its object, the less need there is to intend anything or to engage in intentional action in order to obtain the end, especially when the object is immediately available.

The enacted action concludes (in a way) what is called a 'practical' argument. However, this is a genuinely *practical* argument only for the agent or potential agent, and from the latter's standpoint what is concluded is presented gerundively, as something to be done. This gerundivity presupposes that the agent not only knows (believes) the premises (in no stronger sense of 'know' than is necessary for displaying the action as structured by these premises) but also has (to follow the example) a positive attitude towards enjoying delicious things. The universal premiss indicates a good or apparent good (for something to present iteself as pleasant is a way of its appearing good), and it is a practical premiss only for an agent who wants or has some interest in that good. Again, we can interpret 'want' minimally; it may be no more than a tendency to seek.

Is the conclusion (in Aristotle's view) an actual action, or is it a gerundive formula: i.e., a prescription to act (which, in the case of rational agents, may be implicitly hedged by 'unless it is better not to')? The question is ambiguous and much debated.[31] In some passages Aristotle seems to write as if grasping the conclusion is actually taking action (or attempting to act) (e.g., 1147 a 28; *Movement of Animals* 701 a 21–22). But this interpretation is not mandatory; it is arguable that he is talking about grasping a prescription to act. Unfortunately his language does not register the difference between 'conclusion' in the sense of 'act of concluding' and in the sense of 'what is concluded', nor the difference between 'action' in the sense of 'doing' and in the sense of 'what is done'. Nor does he say anything clear about 'unless it is better not to'.[32] No doubt he often writes taking it for granted that this condition is fulfilled, though without meaning to imply that it always must be. When it is, grasping the conclusion is indeed the beginning of actual action—unless the agent is incontinent and tempted to do something else. And even when one does not act on it (perhaps because it seems better not), grasping the conclusion is like a potential performance of the action. Some potentialities never make it to actuality, but (like all potentialities) they can be designated by the name of the actuality, as when we say that the acorn is an oak (not a hazel), whether or not it will succeed in becoming one.

So we can understand Aristotle's saying that the practical conclusion 'is an action' without taking him to mean that grasping it is an actual action or effort to act. He has often been taken to mean this, but it would be a pity if that view were correct, as it commits him to denying that we can ever wonder which of two attractive competing options to choose. For each has a universal and a particular aspect, so can be represented as a conclusion from corresponding premisses. But if grasping a conclusion must be, in each case, an actual incipient action, one could not consider, because one could not enact, more than one so-called option at a time.

Since the textual evidence is inconclusive, there must be an additional motive driving the many interpreters who ascribe to Aristotle a position entailing this absurdity. A misunderstanding of the rôle of ignorance in incontinence provides that motive. The thought is that Aristotle postulates 'ignorance' in order to explain incontinent behaviour (rather than, as I have argued, using 'ignorance' as a label for the same thing). That thought is tied to the assumption that he believes in a kind of practical cognition that necessarily gives rise to the proper action. But why should Aristotle believe in such a strange thing? A neat explanation is available if we hold that he sees the agent's grasp of the combined premisses of a practical argument as generating the actual action (or at least an attempt to act). In that case Aristotle's agent cannot fail to be moved to act except as a result of failure to grasp a premiss or failure to put them together.

In support of this view (which I am calling into question) it may be argued that the agent's grasp of the practical premisses is what we refer to when we want to explain his action or attempt to act. And he, too, if articulate, would explain it by saying what the premisses were. But (so goes the argument) such explanations succeed in explaining why someone acted as he did only if the *explanans* (the grasp of the combined premisses) is a sufficient (or necessitating) condition for the action (or effort to act). Thus it makes sense for Aristotle to hold that incontinent failure to do what one should is due to ignorance of premisses (either or both). For then he is explaining the failure to act by reference to the absence of what, if present, would give rise to the action, and this is an acceptable type of explanation. And in that case his account of the incontinent's aberration does not depend on a belief in anything 'strange', as I said a moment ago, but, rather, is bound up with a sensible view of what is involved in the explanation of action. To this I reply that we can explain a person's action by displaying what are here being called the 'premisses' without assuming that his grasp of them was (under the circumstances) a sufficient condition for the action. When we explain an action, we start, of course, from it, enacted as it actually was. If we are explaining it, then, necessarily, it was performed. But that it 'must' have been performed is grounded in the fact that we are trying to explain it (for we explain only what we take to be real), not in the explanatory factors themselves! At any rate, it is dogmatic to hold that they necessitate because they explain.[33] Perhaps some sorts of cause cause only by necessitating, but this is not to be assumed in every sort of case, especially when we deal with Aristotle. It is plausible to say that in providing an account of premisses grasped by the agent, one provides an explanation of *what* he did rather than why it came about that he did it. And it fits in with this to hold that the agent himself, in grasping a set of practical premisses, is simply grasping what it is that he would be doing *if* he were to do it.[34]

As I understand it, then, the practical conclusion, in the sense of conclud*ing,* is the grasping of a gerundive (or action prescription), whether or not to enact it.[35] The gerundive is practical even if set on one side, for if it is not enacted (when nothing prevents) the explanation may be not that the subject lacks practical interest in it, but that there is a better or seemingly better way for him to act just now. But now what exactly is the concluding, and how is this act related to the holding of the premisses? The answer will influence our understanding of the way in which Aristotle uses the notion of the practical argument to explicate incontinence. Does he see the gerundive as inferred from the premisses: a conclusion extracted from them? Is grasping the conclusion a *consequence* (even if instantaneous) of holding the premisses, so that holding them explains that grasp? This interpretation is possible, but not, in my view, correct. Aristotle is not really concerned in *NE* VII.3 to explain how the agent comes to grasp the gerundive, but with what is grasped. His point is that we can view it as a synthesis of universal and particular premisses. Combining the premisses does not give rise to grasping the gerundive, but *is* that grasping, since what is grasped is a complex of those components.

We must now consider how this conception of action relates to the concept of rational choice and how it bears on the distinction between knowledge had and knowledge used. The action that would constitute the execution of the incontinent agent's rational choice is analysed into universal and particular premisses. Is the rational choice itself one of the premisses (in which case it would have to be the universal, since the particular premisses are judgments of fact), or is it the conclusion? I take it that the rational choice (the product of deliberation) has already been formed when the agent confronts the facts given by the particular premisses. The conclusion, then, is not the rational choice per se, but the result of applying it to a perceived opportunity. Thus (to take another of Aristotle's examples) in 'Eat this, because dry food is healthy and this is dry food', the universal premiss represents a rational choice to follow a dry diet for the sake of health. (*What* is chosen [dry food] is particular or narrow as compared with its goal [health] but universal so far as it implies a directive covering many occasions.)[36]

Aristotle applies the language of 'has' and 'uses' to the premisses of the action which the incontinent person ought, by his choice, to perform. Do the distinctions *having/using* and *having/failing to use* apply to the premisses of any action, or only to those involving rational choice? Here I simply raise the question. It is usually assumed that *having/using* applies to *any* set of practical premisses, but the text does not demand this interpretation. However that may be, Aristotle says that what the incontinent fails to use is the knowledge represented by the particular premiss of the argument (call it the A-argument) whose universal premiss represents a rational choice (1147 a 1–4; b 9–17).[37] Now some troublesome questions present themselves. First, why is it that here in *NE* VII.3, while discussing incontinence, Aristotle resorts to his analysis of action into two premisses? Presumably it is so that he can pinpoint the incontinent's failure as precisely as possible. But why is this necessary, if, as I have suggested, his principal task in this chapter is to show that it is not self-contradictory to say that the incontinent both knows and does not know? For this, it would have been enough to explain senses in which the incontinent knows and does not know what he should here and now do. Why dissolve this into a universal and a particular premiss so as to locate the ignorance at one premiss only? Second, how can it make sense to say that the particular A-premiss alone is not used, especially if, as I have contended, the failure to use (which is incontinent ignorance) is identical with failure to *act?* The incontinent's failure to act is a failure to use the conclusion of the A-argument. Hence his failure to act is surely a failure to use what constitutes the conclusion; but (I have claimed) the premisses—both—are what constitute the conclusion. Third, Aristotle implies that the incontinent has *and uses* the universal A-premiss; but how can he be said to use it, given that he does not act on it (does not act in accordance with rational choice)?

The last two questions naturally suggest that failure to use—incontinent ignorance—is not after all a failure to act on one's knowledge; for one cannot either act or fail to act on either premiss apart from the other. And this returns us to the thought that what Aristotle identifies as incontinent ignorance is causally prior to the failure to act and explanatory of it. For, it is often argued, failure to use one A-premiss results in a failure to draw the A-conclusion—how can one be expected to draw a conclusion if one is not aware of what is given in one premiss?—and therefore the incontinent is not even in possession of the A-conclusion, which is why he does not enact it. As my wording has just betrayed, the temptation now becomes overwhelming to interpret nonuse of one premiss as failure of clearheaded awareness with respect to it. For 'use' and 'nonuse' are applied to the premisses individually; and, whereas it is not possible to act and fail to act on one premiss on its own, it is possible to be or fail to be clearheaded about one premiss on its own (not that one would think of it on its own as a 'premiss').

It follows from such an interpretation that the incontinent person cannot be clearheaded about what it is that he ought to but does not do. For this is an argument-conclusion which (so goes the interpretation) the incontinent does not even know by way of having, let alone by way of using the knowledge of it. Apparently, though, he is clearheadedly aware of having made the rational choice, since this is represented by the universal premiss which, Aristotle says, he does not fail to use. But is it not extraordinary that someone with the normal perceptual and mental apparatus should be clearly conscious at a given moment of having made a certain rational choice, yet not be equally clearly aware of his current situation as an occasion calling for action in accordance with the choice? We make so many choices, are committed to so many projects, and for the most part one or another of them comes consciously to mind only when and because the particular situation appears relevant. Hence it hardly seems possible to be using the universal premiss and not also using the particular, if 'using' means being clearly conscious.

Aristotle's words do not all fit the interpretation according to which the incontinent does not even have the A-conclusion because he has not drawn it. For at 1147 a 31–34, Aristotle gives this example: it is the rational agent's rational policy not to eat things of a certain kind; here is such a thing; reason tells him 'avoid this'. Here the A-conclusion is shown as drawn. If that depends on clearheadedness about both premisses, and if incontinent ignorance is what Aristotle says that it is, namely a failure to use the particular A-premiss, then failure to use that premiss is not failure to be clear about it. What is more, if the agent is clear about both premises *and* draws the conclusion, how is he not also clear about the conclusion? In that case he is clear about everything and still acts incontinently.

The points just made are damaging for interpretations which (1) identify use with clarity and (2) assume that a conclusion cannot be drawn (hence is not available for use in action) unless both premises are clear. But according to the line of interpretation for which I have argued in Sections III-V of this chapter, the incontinent agent has the A-conclusion (has knowledge of what he should do) if he has all the knowledge that a well-conditioned agent would need for enacting that prescription; and, if use in general were a matter of clarity, then even virtuous agents half the time would not be using their practical knowledge (although they act in accordance with it); hence if use is clarity, failure to use does not distinguish the incontinent agent from very many good agents, and it neither explains nor even sums up the fact that he behaves badly while they behave well.

But if failure to use the particular A-premiss is not failure to be clear about it, what can it be but failure to act on or in response to it? Yet a failure to act on the A-particular must be a failure to act on the A-universal as well. How can Aristotle charge the incontinent agent with the first failure while refusing to charge him with the second? Two explanations suggest themselves. One is speculative, since Aristotle says nothing that would either confirm or disconfirm it; namely, that the universal A-premiss can occur in other practical arguments whose conclusions the agent uses by acting on them even while he fails to use the A-conclusion. Here we have to suppose that the A-argument is, e.g., 'Moist food is unhealthy; this food ($F_1$) is moist; do not eat this' and that the incontinent eats $F_1$ not because it is moist, but because, though moist, it is sweet. In this situation he may be actively rejecting other moist foods which are not sweet, on the ground that they are unhealthy. Thus he is acting on the universal in respect of other particulars and other actions, though not in respect of eating $F_1$. By contrast, he cannot in this context use or act on the particular '$F_1$ is moist' otherwise than by refraining from eating $F_1$; therefore in eating it he absolutely does not use that premiss.

The other explanation is that by confining incontinent ignorance to the particular premiss, Aristotle means to locate the cause of the trouble. The trouble is really a failure to use the entire set of A-premisses; but it is a failure of the agent considered as *subject of the particular action-situation,* rather than subject of earlier deliberation or possessor of its results. Incontinence occurs at the point of contact between rational choice and the moment for applying it, and the agent is *in* that moment only so far as he has knowledge of the particular premiss. Failure to use the set of premisses is a failure by him as owner of them all; but the failure occurs because he has the particular. For he owes his possession of the particular to the same perceptual and physical mechanisms that render him subject to appetite.

What Aristotle ought to have said, I think, is that appetite knocks out the entire system of premisses (renders it as a whole inoperative), but does so *from the side of the particular.* Instead, he says that appetite paralyses the particular but leaves the universal untouched—so that the universal is *not* unused. Hence the famous remark:

And because the last term is not universal nor equally an object of knowledge with the universal term, the position that Socrates sought to establish actually seems to result; for it is not what is thought to be knowledge proper that the passion [*pathos*] overcomes[38] (nor is it this that is dragged about as a result of the passion), but perceptual knowledge. (1147 b 13–17)

Aristotle puts his point misleadingly because he is not on guard against the ambiguities of the term *'pathos'* and of the familiar but deceptive 'slave-dragging' metaphor (which originated with Socrates himself; cf. 1145 b 24 and Plato, *Protagoras* 352 b). When a captured runaway is dragged home, there is, it might seem, no difference between *what* is dragged and *that in virtue* of which he is dragged; for what is dragged is the slave's body, and he is dragged because his body is. In a sense, of course, the person is what is dragged, since 'is dragged' is true of him; and the dragged person is not the same as his own dragged body in virtue of which *he* (and not just his body) is said to be dragged. But unless one observes this distinction between the person and the person's body, it would be easy to conflate what is dragged (the person) with that in virtue of which (the body) what is dragged is dragged. And that distinction, we have to recall, is one which Aristotle might have refused to apply to those whom he labels 'natural slaves' (living instruments which wholly belong to the master, not at all to themselves, being essentially bodies without selves of their own to belong to; see *Politics* 1254 a 11–17). Add to all this the fact that *'pathos'* ('affection' or 'passion') is Aristotle's word for feeling, emotion or appetite, but is also used more abstractly by him to mean any sort of being affected (especially if for the worse). In incontinence, an affection in the narrow sense affects (in the broader sense) the whole system of A-premisses, because it renders the system inactive. That is to say, so far as the agent fails to use the premisses, appetite affects him (in the wide sense) as owner of the *set* of premisses. But it is only as owner of the particular premiss that he is affected by (i.e., *feels*) the appetitive longing. The particular premiss represents that sentient side of the ethical soul through which appetitive affections (in the narrow sense) can attack (i.e., affect in the broad sense) the whole set of A-premisses so as to render it null and void in incontinence. The part that has to do with particulars is uniquely the part through which the whole is subverted, and so it might easily come to be talked about as if it, uniquely, is subverted.

If I am right, lining up ignorance (failure to use) with the particular A-premiss is not a way of explaining how, at the moment of action, incontinent behaviour occurs, for 'ignorance of the particular' is simply a way of describing that behaviour. But it is not even an accurate description, since the ignorance is of action A itself, which is *both* premisses combined. So we are bound to ask why Aristotle distinguishes the premisses at all in this context, since the distinction sheds no explanatory or descriptive light. He surely does not mean to parade this interesting analysis of action simply for its own sake here. His point, rather, is educational, referring to a distinction that is real and observable only when we consider the possibility of incontinent behaviour in advance. This is the distinction between the different kinds of training and practising necessary for the development of virtue. By highlighting the particular premiss, Aristotle is saying that incontinence can be avoided or cured only by disciplining our appetitive nature (not by training our moral sensibilities, or by exposing us to plenty of experience, or by encouraging us to deliberate and to criticise and appreciate other people's reasons for doing what they do). This discipline must focus on one part of the soul, but incontinent behaviour itself is a malfunction of the whole.

To test, as well as to spell out further, the interpretation developed in this chapter, I turn to perhaps the most controversial passage of *NE* VII.3, the passage about the conflicting practical arguments (1147 a 24–b 3). Up to this point Aristotle has focused on incontinent *failure* to use the A-argument (the argument incorporating rational choice) through failure to use, as he says, its particular premiss. Now he turns to the *cause* of this, which is appetite working away in a contrary direction. A is the action which the person ought to do; B is what he actually does. Thus there are two practical arguments. From Aristotle's rather obscure example they appear to be as follows:

A. (U) Anything sweet is unhealthy
and to be avoided in one's diet

(P) This is sweet

(C) Refrain from eating this

B. (U) Anything sweet is pleasant

(P) This is sweet

(C) Eat this

The conclusions and the particular premisses refer to the same *this*. Now there is a practical conflict only if both conclusions are absolute prescriptions. In general, this need not be so. In many cases an action is viewed as absolutely to-be-done only granted the extra condition 'it would not be better not to'. But when the action embodies a rational choice, that condition is already granted, given that the choice is considered final, not subject to rational revision. Thus here the A-conclusion is an absolute prescription, not because of the logical form of what it or its premisses say, but because it expresses a rational choice. Similarly, the B-conclusion is not in itself an absolute prescription. For instance, the B-argument could coexist with the A-argument in a temperate person. He would hold the B-conclusion as hedged by 'Only if it is not better not to', and the rational choice expressed in A implies that this condition is not fulfilled.[39] Thus A keeps B suspended, so to speak, when the agent is temperate. The possession of B suspended, as distinct from the sheer absence of the B-argument altogether, corresponds to the fact that Aristotle's temperate individual is not someone who takes no interest in physical pleasures, but who takes it to the right extent, in the right way etc. and who therefore *would* have enjoyed eating what he can tell is this sweet dish had his choice not ruled it out, even though now, with that pleasure ruled out, foregoing it costs him nothing.

The appetites and impulses, however, know nothing about holding a conclusion conditionally. Their objects are just what they are: *drink, food, sweet things*—not, *drink* (or *food etc.*) *only if* (for reasons having nothing to do with these objects as they figure for the appetites) *it is not better not*. Thus when appetite is present, the conclusion is unconditional to that extent.[40] The appetites function in a way that by right should belong only to rational choice, since the dictates of rational choice are the only deservedly unconditional conclusions. There can be no conflict between some particular prescription of reason and any other option (however desirable in general) unless appetite is present to brutalise the latter into unconditionality. This is the necessary condition for both incontinence and continence.

If, as I have indicated, the presence of potentially conflicting arguments is a feature of most if not all human action and is certainly not restricted to continent and incontinent behaviour, why does Aristotle at 1147 a 24 ff. particularly mention the B-argument? His main concern up to this point has been to show how we can speak of incontinent ignorance and knowledge without self-contradiction. Now he turns to those natural facts, psychological and also physical (cf. 1147 a 24–25; b 7–9), from which that logically unexceptionable phenomenon arises. The cause is appetite, he says, although this is not exactly news. At any rate the B-argument as such is not the cause. So why does Aristotle draw attention to the B-argument? I think for two reasons. First, it is important that what appetite prompts is no less an action (and voluntary) than the one which the incontinent fails to perform. It is not a mere physical event, although the fact that paradigm incontinence is concerned with physical pleasures, hence with states of the body, might lead one to suppose that it is. As he says at 1147 a 34–35, 'Appetite has the power to move each of the [relevant] bodily parts'. But in so doing, appetite moves one to *act,* i.e., to carry out the conclusion of a practical argument. And since the agent has the premisses of that argument, he not only knows what he is *not* doing (A), but what he does instead. Thus from both points of view his behaviour is voluntary. Second, Aristotle is responding to the point that since B is the conclusion of an argument, the incontinent person in a way does act 'from reason', this reason being given by the universal B-premiss. Some clever person might draw the paradoxical lesson that incontinent behaviour is rational since it is through reason (1147 a 35–b 3) that the person does B, thereby acting incontinently. Aristotle's reply is that although, of course, the B-premisses give the reason or *logos* of B, the agent is incontinent only so far as doing B conflicts with doing what he ought to do. But B and its premisses do not create the conflict, for that is due to appetite. So in a weak sense ('incidentally', 1147 b 2), the person is incontinent because of the reason for B, but this reason only explains (i.e., spells out) his doing B *if* he does it. It cannot explain his actually *being* the agent of B under the circumstances, since this is due to appetite and an undisciplined character. But it is only because he *is* the agent of B that he acts incontinently.

From the text it seems that the A-argument and the B-argument have the same proposition as particular premiss, and I have set them out accordingly. Now Aristotle's language suggests that the incontinent is very alert to this proposition ('This is sweet') *as a premiss of the B-argument.* And in doing B he acts on that premiss. It appears that he definitely *uses* 'This is sweet'. The premiss is not just potentially there; as Aristotle says, it (or the B-argument which it is part of) is *active* (*energei;* 1147 a 33; cf. 7). Given that the particular B-premiss is the same as the particular A-premiss, must we not conclude that in 1147 a 24–b 3 the incontinent both has and uses both premisses of the A-argument (which Aristotle says is impossible), or else that he has both but the one which he fails to use is the universal (which Aristotle also denies)? In view of this difficulty, some commentators conclude that the A-argument has no premiss in common with the B-argument. They envisage a situation like this:

A'. (U) Moist food is unhealthy    B'. (U) Anything sweet is pleasant

(P) This food is moist           (P) This is sweet
_____          _____
(C) Refrain from eating this      (C) Eat this

It so happens that both particular premisses refer to the same food; the agent, then, does not use or respond to the fact that it is moist, but only to the fact that it is sweet.

Such an interpretation commits Aristotle to the unrealistic assumption that the feature which makes an object desirable to appetite must *always* differ from the feature in virtue of which it is prohibited by rational choice. There is also the fact that he does not make it clear that the conflicting arguments have no common premiss. That they do not is important, on this interpretation; thus the interpretation ought to explain why Aristotle does not state more fully what (on this view) he must have considered important.

However, the assumption of a common particular premiss presents an insuperable problem for anyone who thinks that using a premiss means having it clearly in mind, and who assumes that the incontinent agent, in doing B, uses both premisses of the B-argument. For given that the incontinent fails to use the particular A-premiss, it follows that he is both clear and not clear about 'This is sweet'. There is less of a problem for those who accept that using a premiss means acting on it. For one cannot act on either of a pair of premisses except in the context of the other; thus although 'This is sweet' is both acted on and not acted on, there is no contradiction, since as a B-premiss it is acted on and as an A-premiss it is not. But there is only the semblance of a problem here because we all assume that Aristotle holds that the incontinent agent *uses* the common premiss at all and therefore both uses and fails to use it in his incontinent action. He acts on it, yes, in doing B and may well be clearly aware of what the premiss represents. And, as Aristotle says (1147 a 33), the pair of B-premisses is active: they are what make an impact on the world through the person's actual behaviour. Yet nothing in the text entitles us to infer with confidence that the common premiss would therefore be said by Aristotle to be *used*. I suggest, on the contrary, that he means 'used' and 'not used' to apply only to premisses of the argument representing rational choice. To use a thing is not simply to do something with it, but to use it *as it should be used*. The right use of the A-premisses is to act on them; of the B-premisses, to act on them only when it is not better not to. Since in our case this last condition is not fulfilled, the question of using or failing to use either of the B-premisses cannot arise except insofar as one of them happens to be an A-premiss. When the incontinent acts, he acts on and actualises one set of premisses (the wrong set), but he *uses* (i.e., makes good use of) neither this set nor any other.

It is easy to think that 'active' means or entails 'used' if one assumes that the incontinent's failure to use the particular A-premiss is an ignorance postulated to *explain* his incontinent behaviour, rather than *being* that behaviour viewed through the terms of a technical ethical analysis. For if the failure to use explains, then it must be other than what it explains; and it is easier to exhibit it as other if we think of that failure to use in neutral terms, by contrast with the ethically slanted term, namely 'incontinent behaviour', by which we refer to the explanandum. 'Active', of course, is a neutral term (applying to both use and misuse); thus it comes to seem obvious that 'used' and 'not used' may be substituted for 'active' and its negation in any context.

We might have expected that Aristotle would complete his close analysis of incontinence (in terms of the two arguments and the presence of appetite) with a similar analysis of continence. In fact by comparison he says rather little about continence, and does not face the puzzles which arise when we consider how it resembles incontinence in logical structure and in other respects. In the case of continence, too, the B-argument and its conclusion must be held unconditionally, to the extent that appetite is present creating an actual conflict. No doubt there is the same gamut of possible forms: sometimes appetite distorts or hampers perception; sometimes it gives rise to self-deceptive misinterpretation; sometimes it takes away the sense of the shamefulness of doing B. And any physical changes set going by appetite (1147 a 15–16) can be the same as occur in incontinence. The difference is that the continent agent (called so on the basis of what he does) pulls himself together in time to respect his rational choice.[41] By what mechanism does he resist temptation, when the other does not? Aristotle does not trouble about this question, let alone about the next round of questions, such as whether the incontinent has the same mechanism and whether, if so, he lacks a further mechanism for activating the first. Perhaps there are metaphysical reasons why Aristotle does not try to hunt down the source of the difference between continence and incontinence, but there is also a reason based on practical ethics. From the point of view of the moral educator the two conditions present more or less the same problem, since it is the purpose of training to minimize both, and the same sorts of methods are called for.

## Notes

1. *NE* VII.3 in particular has surely generated more commentary than any similar sized portion of Aristotle's text, apart from *De Interpretatione* 9 and *On the Soul* III.4–5. But the conceptual log jam has recently started to break up. Of recent discussions, the two most helpful known to me are those by Mele [2], and Dahl. Dahl's main conclusions on Aristotle's theory of incontinence are similar to mine, although the detail of our arguments differs considerably.
2. For a vigorous demonstration, see Matthews.
3. At 1151 b 23–32 he describes a condition, analogous to incontinence, in which the agent goes against his rational choice in refusing a legitimate pleasure. Aristotle's own excessive love of triads of moral qualities leads him to say that continence stands to this condition as mean to deficiency, with incontinence being the excessive member of the threesome. But since Aristotle sees continence as entailing excessive appetite *for* pleasure, he ought to define a fourth condition, analogous to continence, in which reason prevails against excessive aversion *from* pleasure.
4. By 'being actually tempted' I mean, for instance, that if there were time for consideration, one would seriously consider taking what is tempting.
5. It is often remarked that Aristotle's virtue of courage, which involves pain at the thought of death (1117 b 7–16), resembles continence more closely than it resembles a virtue such as temperance. See, e.g., Joachim, 118; Ross [1], 203 and 206; Pears; Leighton [2]; for a different angle see Hardie [3], Appendix, and [4], 401–4.
6. Cf. 1110 a 4 ff. on 'hard choices'. But we should not assume that whenever what is set

aside is rightly regretted, the choice was 'agonising'. There may have been no moral dilemma; i.e., it may have been clear what the right course was. In that case, the well-conditioned agent would not have had to struggle, either intellectually or morally, to reach the right decision.

7. Some readers may be reminded of McDowell's notion of 'silencing'. According to this (see McDowell [1] and [2]), once the virtuous person sees that he should do X, the reason why (as he sees it) he should do X is apprehended by him not as outweighing but as annihilating the force of any reasons the situation might suggest for doing something else. But McDowell does not make it clear whether silencing entails only that (1) once the agent sees that he should now do X, he finds himself *without reason*, at all, now to follow an alternative; or, in addition to (1), that (2) he finds himself *uninclined* (or free from all *temptation*) now to follow an alternative; or, in addition to (1) and (2), that (3) he has no *positive interest* at all in any of the alternatives, where 'having a positive interest' includes wishing that it had not been morally necessary to forego it.

8. However, his review of standard difficulties at 1145 b 31 ff. suggests that he may have been acquainted with objections of the sort associated with the Humean position. But the language of 'strength' and 'intensity' is much more prominent in the posing of some of the difficulties (e.g., 1145 b 36–1146 a 1; 4–5) than in Aristotle's replies (1146 b 24–31; 1152 a 6–9). It seems that he does not take seriously problems constructed on the assumption that *judging it better* to do X than Y entails a *stronger tendency towards* actually doing X.

9. See Dahl, 205–11 for a close discussion of the evidence for Aristotle's recognition of clear-headed incontinent action.

10. This conclusion is actually drawn by McDowell [2], who takes it to be Aristotle's position. But why in that case does the discussion of ignorance in *NE* VII.3 never connect *continence* with ignorance? McDowell argues as if the fact that the continent agent is tempted to do B (when the right course is A) shows that he sees the situation as providing *some reason* to do B; whereas the virtuous person, in seeing that A is right, sees the situation as providing no reason to do B (when doing it entails not doing A). If that is so, then no doubt the virtuous and the continent view the situation differently; in which case the perception of one of them must be at fault, and it cannot be that of the virtuous person. But this argument collapses when one withdraws the questionable assumption that it is not possible to be tempted to do that which one regards oneself as having, under the circumstances, no reason or justification for doing.

11. It is essential not to confuse reasoned knowledge of what to do (i.e., a correct rational choice) with the quality of practical wisdom. Aristotle says that the person of practical wisdom is (as such) a *doer* of what wisdom dictates (1152 a 8–9). Furthermore, of course the wise and the incontinent may arrive at an identical rational choice, but it does not follow that the difference between them shows up only at the level of action and not at the level of deliberation. The incontinent may deliberate well on one or another occasion, but he cannot be relied on, as the wise person can, to deliberate well. If the temptation which deflects him from acting had occurred instead when he was deliberating, he would have been distracted from deliberating well.

12. The point is stressed by Burnyeat [1].

13. Cf. A. Rorty's question (and paper title): 'Where Does the Akratic Break Take Place?' (Rorty [3]).

14. Cf. Burnyeat [1]: '[Aristotle's] treatment of knowledge [sc. in *NE* VII.3] pinpoints what is to be explained. It is not itself the explanation'. Walsh, 158 ff., canvasses the thought (in my view, correct) that incontinent ignorance in *NE* VII is nothing but the incontinent's failure to act as (he knows) he should. According to Kenny [1], this interpretation goes back to Albertus Magnus (whereas the interpretation that makes the ignorance an explanatory factor goes back to the Greek commentators). Both Walsh and Kenny reject the former, on the ground that 'the incontinent person acts ignorantly' would in that case fail to explain incontinent action (Kenny) or would be tautologous (Walsh). But its being a tautology matters only if it is meant either as an explanation or to tell Aristotle's audience something startling. I argue that neither of these is Aristotle's intention.

15. The view that Aristotle (1) puzzles about the very possibility of incontinent action, and (2) invokes ignorance to *explain* it, is not based on strong textual evidence. For (1), see 1145 b 21–22 *(Aporēseie . . . akratēuētai tis)*. This may be taken as asking either (1a): 'How can a person judge correctly, yet still be subject to incontinence?' or (1b): 'In what sense (or mode) of *judge correctly* does the incontinent agent judge correctly?' For (1a), which seems to have gained most ground, see, e.g., Dirlmeier [2], 142; Ostwald, 176; R. Robinson; Gauthier and Jolif vol. I, pt. 2, 186; Kenny [1]; Matthews. For (1b) (which I take to be the correct interpretation), see Hardie [4], 266–67, *Revised Oxford Translation* (Urmson), 1809; Irwin [5], 174; Dahl, 163–64. For (2) there are two passages: (2a) 1145 b 29 *(ei di'agnoian* etc.) and (2b) 1147 a 24–25 *(eti . . . aitian)*. (2a) puts forward the thought that incontinence is *due to* ignorance. But this is only hypothesized here by Aristotle, not asserted. And it echoes the immediately preceding summary of Socrates' view, according to which the incontinent does wrong 'through ignorance' *(di'agnoian,* 25–27; cf. *Protagoras* 358 d–e, which has datives, *amathiai* etc.). (2b) is another ambiguous sentence. It can mean either: (2bi) 'Again, we can also study the cause in the way in which a student of nature would—as follows', or: (2bii) 'Furthermore, we can also, like students of nature, take a look at the cause—as follows'. (The cause in question is the cause of incontinent behaviour, and the main discussion of knowledge and ignorance precedes this point.) On (2bi), the sentence introduces a new ('scientific' as opposed to 'logical') way of looking at the cause. This sounds like a new kind of *explanation;* but, if it is, the preceding passage must have offered another explanation. Most of the writers whom I have consulted take 1147 a 24–25 in this way. (Many detect at least three "solutions" having to do with knowledge and ignorance in 1146 b 31–1147 a 24; see, e.g., Thomson, 231–33). On (2bii), the sentence implies that no effort has so far been made to understand the cause of incontinent action. For this interpretation, which I favour, cf. Burnyeat [1], especially note 23.

16. I say this *pace* Barnes [4], who describes as 'bizarre' Aristotle's adherence to the Socratic thought that incontinence is in some sense ignorance and gives it as an example of Aristotle's occasional lapsing from his own 'Method of *Endoxa*'. However, though (as I assume) it is natural for Aristotle to think in this way, it does not follow that he must always have this aspect to the fore. It comes to the fore when he remembers Socrates on incontinence; and in a full discussion, as in *NE* VII, Socrates is bound to surface. Elsewhere when speaking (usually very briefly) of incontinence, Aristotle does not connect it with ignorance. See especially *NE* V.9, 1136 a 32–b 4, where the incontinent, being a voluntary agent, is said to *know.* Sorabji [3], 275–78, finds a contradiction here with *NE* VII.3, but I see no conflict of doctrine, although plainly no attempt has been made to coordinate the terminology or the perspectives of V.9 and VII.3. See below, note 30.

17. In the *Theaetetus,* where the *has/uses* distinction is forged to provide a coherent account of mistakes, much is made of the paradox that one must know something about a thing if one is to fall into the 'ignorance' of making a mistake about it. See especially 199 d 1–5.

18. Recall that the rational choice is not merely of the (initially observable) action, but of the action in the light of all relevant concerns and circumstances.

19. He nullifies not merely the work *(ergon)* of his mind but what is virtually his 'offspring'; for references, see Chapter 4, note 1.

20. Cf. Plato, *Laws* 689 a–b: 'dissonance between pleasure and pain and reasoned judgment . . . I call the worst folly *(amathia)* . . . when the soul sets itself at variance with knowledge, judgment, reason, its natural rulers, you have what I describe as unwisdom *(anoia)*'.

21. For further interpretation, see note 29 below.

22. Several writers have pointed out that blurred perception of the situation (where the agent is cognitively well-placed) would need to be explained no less than incontinent behaviour needs to be explained and is even a part of the same phenomenon. See, e.g., Milo, 107–8; Burnyeat [1]; Charles [1], 161–64; Mele [6], 6–7.

23. Irwin's translation. Irwin's 'attends to' does justice, as the *Revised Oxford Translation*'s 'exercises' does not, to the intellectual flavour of *theōrein.* To suppress this is to suppress one of the few pieces of evidence in favour of the view that Aristotle rules out clearheaded incontinent action.

24. Cf. Plato, *Theaetetus* 197–98, where the example is theoretical.
25. In ordinary use, *'theōrein'* is transitive and takes as grammatical objects terms for items watched, inspected etc. It is often intransitive when it figures in Aristotle's statements of the distinction between having and using knowledge. This detachment from an ordinary grammatical object, plus the fact that in that context it is virtually synonymous with the contrary of 'have' (sc. some type of knowledge), nudges (I think) Aristotle and his readers towards hearing between the lines (and accepting) a technical use in which *'theōrein'* again takes a grammatical object, but one that names the type of knowledge (say, *grammatikē* or *arithmetikē*) that is being put to work as distinct from merely possessed. The object is now an internal accusative, and *'theōrein tēn arithmetikēn'* means 'to operate as an arithmetician'. In this sense, Aristotle can deny that Socrates *theōrei tēn arithmetikēn* without implying that Socrates is not thinking about numbers. (For example, he might be thinking that numbers are more orderly than human beings.) And on the practical front, too, we need not hold Aristotle bound by a supposed equivalence between 'think about' and *'theōrein'*. In particular, he is free to assert that the incontinent may even be thinking about what he should do while not *theōrōn* what he should do (thinking about his duty, but not operating dutifully). See Mele [2] for a good discussion of the textual evidence for not interpreting 'theōrein' as 'be conscious of' or 'have an occurrent belief about'.
26. That theoretic activity is not a movement or process, according to the distinction made in *Meta.* IX.6, does not entail that it is a static gazing. It is contrasted with process insofar as process, on Aristotle's conception, has its raison d'être beyond itself.
27. The engagement might sometimes be a matter of scrutinizing an item, sometimes a matter of using one. For the slide in meaning of *theōrein* (see note 25) permits the following linguistic situation: the geometer (e.g.) *theōrei* (= examines, scrutinizes) the diagonal of the square in order to determine how to express its ratio to the side. He discovers that, although the lines are incommensurable, the squares on them are not (thus rationality is restored by the shift to the second dimension; cf. *Theaetetus* 147 d–148 b). He discovers this by employing (= *theōrein* in the more technical sense), not scrutinizing, various principles and prior results.
28. Aristotle several times illustrates the difference between having and using theoretical knowledge by pointing to the difference between having the skill to build a house and *building* one (*On the Soul,* 417 b 8–10; *Meta.* 1048 b 1; 1050 a 11–12). If 'using' means 'doing' (not merely 'thinking about') in *poiēsis,* it ought to mean the same in *praxis.*
29. Cf. Charles [1], 117–32, for the view that *NE* VII.3 recognises two types of incontinent, one who is, and one who is not, clear about what he should do. But it must be admitted that the chapter offers no definite evidence for this. If the distinction is not made in VII.3, it does not follow that according to that chapter incontinents are never clearheaded, any more than that they always are; but only that the difference is not considered important. If this is the right interpretation, the comparison at 1147 a 13–14 with drunks, sleepers and madmen must be meant to apply to all cases of incontinent behaviour (cf. b 6–8) and attention is being called to two similarities: the incontinent condition is one in which the agent fails to respond appropriately even when the occasion offers; and however it comes about, its existence has a physical basis and it does not disappear without changes in the body. These comparisons do not imply that the incontinent agent is foggy, half-blind or somnambulistic. Again, on this interpretation the disjunction 'does not have or does not exercise' (1147 a 7; b 11–12; cf. a 10–13) also applies to all cases of incontinence, and indicates not an exclusive division into kinds but vacillation on how to classify (in general) the incontinent's relation to his knowledge. That is: Aristotle hesitates to say outright 'he has but doesn't use it' because the straightforward notion of having-but-not-using knowledge was first framed for cases of skill and theoretical knowledge where the subject lacks the opportunity for exercise, but (it is implied) would exercise it given a suitable opportunity. See especially *Physics* 255 a 30–b 11, where the transition from mere possession to exercise of knowledge is compared with the natural motions (to their 'proper' places) of the unobstructed simple bodies. In *that*-sense, the incontinent agent, clearheaded or not, does not 'have' knowledge of what he should do, but in a different sense (the truth con-

ditions of which are that he has formed a rational choice, his faculties are medically unimpaired etc.) he does, and it is the latter that is presupposed by incontinence. This is what Aristotle would be getting at when he says 'having in a way, and not having' (1147 a 12). This interpretation is compatible with either of the main MSS readings of 1147 a 7.

30. Cf. 1136 a 31 ff. and 1138 a 9–10. It is noticeable that Aristotle does not attempt to incorporate the notion of *incontinent ignorance* when discussing the voluntary in *NE* III, *NE* V, and *EE* II. At *EE* 1225 b 10–14 he recognises the distinction between having and using practical knowledge, but instead of classing failure to use as 'ignorance' in the style of *NE* VII.3, he says that, when the failure is due to carelessness, the agent cannot properly be called 'ignorant'. 'Ignorant' here is a term of exculpation, not condemnation. (*Pace* Kenny [3], 56, the only relation between this passage and Aristotle's employment of the *has knowledge/uses knowledge* distinction in *NE* VII appears to be that of mutual nonrecognition.)

31. For a survey of the textual evidence, see Charles [1], 90–94.

32. This proviso probably makes an appearance at 1147 a 30–31, *mē kōluomenon*. Some commentators take it to refer only to external prevention, but (as *kōluousa* at 32 shows) *kōkuein* does not mean only that. '*Ti kōluei* . . . ?' is quite a common way of saying 'What reason is there against . . . ?' (cf. 1101 a 14).

33. For detailed criticism of this view, and references to relevant literature, see Sorabji [3], Chapter 2 and 227–33.

34. One potent source of confusion in this area is the fact that Aristotle applies the practical argument schema to the explanation of nonrational animals' behaviour. In their case, since they are incapable of choice or entertaining options, 'grasping premisses' may be automatically expressed in action (if nothing else prevents). This is not because of what it is to 'grasp premisses', but because the 'graspers' are not reflective.

35. This interpretation fits Aristotle's treatment of the B-argument ('Everything sweet is to be tasted, this is sweet, etc.') at 1147 a 29–34. That reason forbids tasting, and that appetite for tasting is at work, are presented as facts *extraneous to the argument itself* (like the absence of physical incapacity mentioned at 30, *ton dunamenon*). In itself the argument does not motivate (despite the presence of terms such as 'should' or 'pleasant' in the universal premiss), if by 'motivate' one means 'give rise to a tendency to act'. To be practical, it does not have to incorporate motivation: it is practical because *if* acted on it gives an account of the action, and because the object mentioned in the universal premiss is the kind of thing in which we are disposed to take a practical interest from time to time.

36. Thus this practical argument does not represent a piece of deliberation; cf. Cooper [1], 22–32 and 46–58. (But I do not go so far as to claim, as Cooper seems to, that Aristotle never treats a practical argument [syllogism] as the correlate of deliberation or some portion of deliberation. For the present purpose it is enough if Cooper's view holds for the practical arguments appearing in *NE* VII.3.)

37. Thus I take 'the last proposition' at 1147 b 9 to refer to the particular premiss. Some interpreters fear a contradiction between the doctrine of *NE* VII.3 and that of *NE* III.1, 1110 b 31–1111 a 1, according to which ignorance of the particulars renders the action nonvoluntary and the agent nonculpable, whereas ignorance of the universal implies the opposite. 'Ignorance of the universal' means ignorance about values, but the point is badly put, because someone might err out of nonculpable ignorance of a causal law, say, in which case his action (under the relevant description) would not be voluntary. More to the point is the classification of drunken and enraged agents as culpable, at 1110 b 25–27. Presumably Aristotle would group the incontinent with these.

38. The *Revised Oxford Translation* incorporates Stewart's conjecture at 1147 b 16 (*periginetai* instead of the MSS' *parousēs ginetai;* see Stewart, vol. II, 161 ff.). Anyone who feels it necessary to emend might also consider the following (which gives, like Stewart's, the desired sense but supposes less disturbance to the text): *ou gar tēs kuriōs epistēmēs einai dokousēs* [*pathousēs*] *ginetai to pathos* etc. That is, 'The *pathos* that comes about is not a pathos, of—i.e., does not affect—what is held to be knowledge proper'. (*Pathos* at this occurrence can refer either to incontinent ignorance itself or to the rush of appetite, but

the latter gives the better sense.) *Pathousēs* entered from a gloss and a subsequent copyist mistook one letter.

39. When Aristotle introduces the B-argument at 1147 a 29–31, he allows for the possibility of its not being acted on because reason forbids, since he says that the agent must act unless he is forbidden *(mē kōluomenon)* or unable. (I take it that *kōluomenon* at 31 denotes rational prohibition, like *kōluousa* at 32. See above, note 32.)

40. I do not mean that there are degrees of unconditionality, but that the agent may be closer to or further from unconditional acceptance of ( = action upon, if possible) the B-conclusion. (On the unconditionality of appetite, see above, pp. 81–82.)

41. In terms of *having, using* and different levels of *activity,* we can say this: the continent resembles the temperate in that both use the A-premisses. He resembles the incontinent in that appetite for B is present, and consequently the B-premisses are active ( = the agent is drawn towards B), whereas the temperate, by comparison, only *has* the B-premisses. However, the continent only has them by comparison with the incontinent's fully fledged B-activity, which is the doing of B.

# CHAPTER 6

# Pleasure

## I. Why the Investigation of Pleasure?

Following Aristotle's order of inquiry in *NE* VII, I turn to his general theory of plea-sure and its place in the good life. This topic is investigated twice in the *Nicomachean Ethics,* in the form in which we have the treatise. There is one discussion in VII, a book which also belongs to the *Eudemian Ethics;* here Aristotle moves to the general question of pleasure after examining incontinence. The other account occurs at the beginning of Book X—not a common book—where it succeeds the lengthy discus-sion of friendship in VIII and IX. In what follows I consider both accounts and shall be mainly concerned with the lessons they hold in common. There are interesting differences, but the most significant lines of thought are the same in both, though more developed in X.[1]

Whether this verdict is shared depends, of course, on what one considers 'most significant.' If we assume that Aristotle's primary task is to explain what pleasure is, we may make out important divergences between VII and X. Book X seems to sug-gest a different answer to the question 'What is pleasure?' from the answer given in VII; and it has even been argued[2] that VII is not concerned with this question at all, but with the different problem of characterising pleasures, or the things that please. The difference, roughly, is that between asking 'What is it to enjoy something?' and asking 'What is common to everything enjoyed or enjoyable?' But in neither book does Aristotle study pleasure because he wants above all to know what pleasure is. He seeks to understand pleasure to determine its ethical significance.[3] From this point of view differences between the accounts are not fundamental unless they indi-cate divergent doctrines about the rôle of pleasure in the good life for man and, in particular, about the relation of pleasure to human excellence and excellent activity.

On this score, however, his positive conclusions in both books are substantially the same. The detail of the arguments differs considerably, but this is perhaps because they respond to different concerns. In both, Aristotle maintains that the highest good is necessarily pleasant; but in X he is more concerned to locate his position in relation to the less discriminating hedonism of Eudoxus, whereas in VII his main adversaries are philosophers who deny that any pleasure is good or that any is an end. This difference in emphasis may reflect different states of contemporary discussion at the time of composition in each case. But it may also owe something to the position of each treatment of pleasure in the larger inquiry to which it belongs. The analysis of incontinence in the first part of *NE* VII might be seen as encouraging an unduly negative attitude to pleasure, since in that context pleasure has appeared as linked with temptation and excessive appetites. Thus the rest of VII represents a corrective move in the direction of what, by comparison, might be classed as a kind of hedonism. The discussion of pleasure in Book X, by contrast, shows clear affinities with an argument in IX to the effect that virtuous friendship is pleasant, and for that reason (amongst others) is an ingredient of the ideal life (1170 a 13 ff.). Here in IX it is taken for granted that the ideal life is pleasant. So when, in Book X, Aristotle moves into the discussion of pleasure from this direction—as already a spokesman for pleasure and to that extent an ally of the hedonists—it is incumbent on him not only to uphold what is true in their position but to make clear where he diverges.[4]

But now we must consider more closely why Aristotle thinks that his ethical inquiry should include a general study of pleasure. He gives reasons at the start of the discussion in VII and in a similar passage at the beginning of X.

> The study of pleasure and pain[5] belongs to the province of the political philosopher; for he is the architect of the end, with a view to which we call one thing bad and another good without qualification. Further, it is one of our necessary tasks to consider them; for not only did we lay it down that moral excellence and vice are concerned with pains and pleasures, but most people say that happiness involves pleasure; this is why the blessed man [*makarios*] is called by a name derived from a word meaning enjoyment [*chairein*]. (VII, 1152 b 1–8)

The passage combines two lines of thought, both suggested in the first sentence. One is that the supreme good, which it is the aim of political craft to promote, may or may not turn out to be or involve pleasure (or some kind of pleasure); thus pleasure is a relevant topic for whoever is concerned with this end. This reflection is closely connected with the observation that happiness (the supreme good) is held by most people to involve pleasure. Such a prevalent view must be looked at carefully, especially since (we soon see) it is subject to much dispute (cf. X, 1172 a 27). But the view itself has stronger and weaker forms. Some of its adherents may mean no more than that some kind of pleasure is an ingredient of the supreme good, while others hold that pleasure *is* the good. And the latter may mean either that whatever is pleasant is good and vice versa or that pleasure is the highest good even if there are other goods that are not pleasure and perhaps not even pleasant. However, all these positions are threatened by those who hold, as some do, that no pleasure is good or even that all pleasure is base (cf. X, 1172 a 28 ff.) For if no pleasure is good, then nothing is lacking to the supreme good even if pleasure or everything pleasant were lacking; hence even on the weakest interpretation, it would be false that happiness 'involves' pleasure.

The second line of thought is prompted by the description of the *politikos* as 'ruling craftsman' *(architectōn)* of the supreme good. This good is crafted by moral training; and pleasure and pain, on different levels, are this craft's raw materials, its instruments, and its product. The objective is to develop individuals in whom the pleasant and painful demands of their 'first' (i.e., animal) nature are subordinate to the requirements of good conduct. And this is done by encouraging them to delight in what is fine and worthy of human beings and to hate and be pained by what is base: not merely so that they will act well, but so that they will be such as to take pleasure in so acting. For acting well grimly and against the grain is not virtue but (at best) continence. People can do what is painful to them and can refuse to do what is pleasant, but at all stages of development they tend to do what pleases and to avoid the opposite. As Aristotle says in the parallel passage in X:

We ought perhaps next to discuss pleasure. For it is thought to be most intimately connected with our human nature, which is the reason why in educating the young we steer them by the rudders of pleasure and pain; it is thought, too, that to enjoy the things we ought and to hate the things we ought has the greatest bearing on excellence of character. For these things extend right through life, with a weight and power of their own in respect both to excellence and to the happy life, since men choose what is pleasant and avoid what is painful; and such things, it will be thought, we should least of all omit to discuss. (1172 a 16–26)

And here he explicitly adds that pleasure should be examined because people hold conflicting views about it: 'For some say pleasure is the good, while others, on the contrary, say it is thoroughly bad' (1172 a 27–28).

Now these preambles may leave us still wondering what Aristotle means to achieve by a general discussion of pleasure and pain. His discussions of moral virtue, moral education and incontinence have already made it clear that what is pleasant is not necessarily virtuous. And since virtuous activity is the life and soul of happiness, it is equally clear that happiness entails foregoing such pleasures as the virtuous man would forego, whether in general or because the circumstances forbid them. Thus even though some hold that pleasure is the good, for Aristotle this is not an open question. Or should we suppose that he now genuinely opens it, even at this late stage, thus rendering provisional all the preceding results? This is hardly likely. Should we then think that he pursues an account of pleasure because the concept of pleasure has figured in those earlier analyses, and Aristotle with academic thoroughness seeks to define the constituents of his definitions down to the last? This is possible—it is the method which he pursues in the *Physics*[6] with regard to the terms entailed by the concept 'nature'—but there is no indication that it is his programme here. Again, knowing what pleasure is in general will not help us to know which pleasures to avoid and when, for the same definition will apply to all pleasures, desirable or not; and in any case if we are well brought up and are willing to think in a practical way, we know what to pursue and avoid without knowing abstract definitions.

It seems, then, that the study of pleasure in general is not intended to confirm, add to, or qualify what we may call the antihedonic strain in Aristotle's theory of virtue and the best life. For it is obvious to common sense that the good life requires some curbing of the impulse to pleasure. This is clear because, initially at any rate,

the paradigm instances of pleasure are the pleasures associated with obvious biological functions. These, for very good reason, are compulsively pleasant and therefore,
at the basic level, intensely so, even if inspection and analysis reveal in them the
presence of concomitant pain or discomfort. And because of the compulsive intensity, it is of the very nature of these pleasures that they can be taken to excess. Led
by these paradigms, we start off by thinking of pleasure as an agreeable physical sensation, and we also equate the pleasant with whatever is the object of a strong predeliberative inclination. This second vague conception is wider than the first, which
centres on agreeable sensation, but initially they are hardly distinguished. However,
the second, though wider, provides at least as strong a ground for antihedonic caution, since it is obvious that the right objective is often very different from the object
of predeliberative inclination, and that even where they coincide, the right one is not
in general preferable to others *because* it happens to be what the agent is inclined to
pursue. So much for plain common sense; but the same general suspicion of pleasure
follows immediately from the philosophical doctrines that the human good is activity
in accordance with reason and that ethical virtue is, and aims at, a mean.

But now we must consider the contrasting hedonic strain which is also present
in those doctrines, for here Aristotle's ground is less obviously secure. He asserted
vigorously in *NE* I that the virtuous individual takes pleasure in virtuous activity:

> To each man that which he is said to be a lover of is pleasant; e.g., not only is a horse
> pleasant to the lover of horses, and a spectacle to the lover of sights, but also in the
> same way just acts are pleasant to the lover of justice and in general excellent acts to
> the lover of excellence. Now for most men their pleasures are in conflict with one
> another because these are not by nature pleasant, but the lovers of what is noble find
> pleasant the things that are by nature pleasant; and excellent actions are such, so that
> these are pleasant for such men as well as in their own nature. Their life, therefore,
> has no further need of pleasure as a sort of adventitious charm, but has its pleasure
> in itself. For, besides what we have said, the man who does not rejoice in noble
> actions is not even good; since no one would call a man just who did not enjoy acting
> justly, nor any man liberal who did not enjoy liberal actions; and similarly in all
> other cases. If this is so, excellent actions must be in themselves pleasant. (1099 a 7–
> 21)

This position plays an important rôle in clarifying the aim and process of moral training and in pointing up the difference between virtuous action and right action that
fails to manifest virtue, whether because motivated by fear of sanctions etc. or
because done in the teeth of base temptation. But outside this context the assertion
is dubious. Aristotle is justified in taking it for granted so long as he means that the
virtuous person takes the right course because it is right, and takes it willingly and
ungrudgingly, being identified with his action. The action must reflect not only practical judgment and rational commitment, but the depth of the individual's ethical
personality. He is eager and glad to act well, because all of him is behind it. But this
does not entail that what he does is pleasant in the sense in which, say, physical
enjoyments are paradigmatically pleasures. A good person will do gladly many things
which he finds thoroughly unpleasant,[7] and, as we pointed out when discussing
incontinence (Chapter 5, Section I), not to be pained would not necessarily be to his

credit, since it might show a less than virtuous insensibility if he did not mind the cost.

It is true that moral training works by encouraging the young, through practice, to enjoy civilized activities. Hedonic energy, Aristotle might have said, is directed into higher channels, and many discomforts and frustrations arising from our animal nature cease to matter and perhaps finally cease to be felt by those caught up in distinctively human pursuits. Thus the virtuous person may often be found doing what through culture and training he has learnt to enjoy doing, and here he does take pleasure in his action in a sense that goes beyond that of the statement that he acts gladly and without holding back. However, in learning to enjoy higher things, we learn to love and value them, and this entails a willingness to undergo pains and privations for their sake. Just as the moral educator cannot be expected to train us so that we have no need of our own deliberation, he cannot be expected to tailor our dispositions so that we always enjoy doing (as distinct from being thoroughly willing to do) what is necessary when we act rightly.

Thus the virtuous agent, if he is not too unlucky, does many things which are virtuous and also pleasant in a sense which above we associated with paradigmatic cases of physical pleasure. For although what we have in mind are not the pleasures of eating, drinking and sex, but, say, of debate and conversation, of friendship, of sport, of rule-governed play in general, of the arts, of designing things well and crafting them, these can be and should be objects to which we are drawn by prereflective inclination, having, through culture, an affinity with them like a hungry animal's affinity with its food. But then precisely this predeliberative quality implies that these pleasures, too, can be taken to excess; for our love of them, in every case, is not limited to just those times and places where we can pursue them without detriment to a more important end.

So although the virtuous life is graced with such fine or noble pleasures (and certainly the happy life is), and although virtuous action may often consist in engagement in such a pursuit, is that a basis for characterising the virtuous agent as 'taking pleasure in his virtuous action'? Surely not. It is true that developing the ability to appreciate these cultured pleasures is part and parcel of the development of moral virtue, since without that ability the agent has nothing of specially human significance to which to direct his efforts, whether on his own behalf or others'. But one need not be established in virtue to enjoy those pleasures, and they can also be enjoyed by individuals of morally flawed character. And the virtuous agent's enjoyment is not as such different in kind from enjoyment by those of inferior character. It would be misleading, therefore, to say on this ground that the virtuous person takes pleasure in his virtuous actions; and Aristotle's words to this effect do not even lend themselves to the above interpretation. For Aristotle says, e.g., that the temperate person delights in acting *temperately* and the just person in acting *justly* (1104 b 5–8; 1099 a 18–20). Such remarks suggest that the ground of the pleasure is the virtuous action as such and that the pleasure is an essential expression of virtue, not merely of what we might term the cultural matter of virtue which even the nonvirtuous share. Pleasure in virtuous action, if there is such a pleasure, could never be out of place or excessive, any more than the action. But just this fact about it calls into question Aristotle's right to speak here of pleasure at all, if he means to invoke the concept for which physical pleasure provides the most obvious paradigm, not (in this context) because of its agreeable sensations, but because the inclination towards it is prereflective. The virtuous action, by contrast, is deliberately chosen, so that although the agent's positive involvement may, of course, be called an 'inclination' (Aristotle analyses the choice itself as a 'deliberated desire'), it is not a predeliberative inclination. It resembles the obvious pleasures in being unforced and unconstrained, but that cannot be a good reason for calling it a pleasure in the same sense. For the obvious pleasures flow free by contrast with restrictions on them which order sometimes requires; but the rationally chosen action is an ordering, not a something possibly needing to be ordered.

So it seems that when in the earlier books Aristotle talks of the virtuous agent as taking pleasure in virtuous action, this should mean no more than that the agent acts wholeheartedly, which is compatible with his not enjoying what he does. We can characterise the difference between (1) wholehearted engagement and (2) the enjoyment which may or may not be present, as the difference between (1') being moved to do A and (2') what it is about doing A that explains (or partly explains) being moved to do it. The fact that one enjoys doing A may explain the doing or continuing to do it, and it may be the agent's reason. Here it is a question of why he does A rather than something else, and enjoyment is one possible reason. But his identifying himself with what he has reason to do is not a reason for doing it, but a mode of the doing itself or even its very substance.

Is Aristotle aware that doing A with full willingness does not entail enjoying doing it? And if he confusedly assumes the entailment, would this be his reason for asserting that virtuous action is pleasant? If the statement of his view were confined to the *NE* I passage quoted earlier and to similar smaller passages (e.g., 1104 b 5–8), the question would not greatly affect our assessment of the *Ethics*. The mistake, if he makes it, does not undermine his reasons for holding that whatever the highest good is, it is an *activity* of the soul. And we would surely agree that if it is an activity, then it is truly best only when engaged in positively and fully, since that is the perfection of activity. The grounds for denying that the highest good is a state of potentiality or mere disposition like virtue itself are equally grounds for denying it to be an activity less than fully actual. We can further agree with his declaration that those who live the life of this highest activity do not need the addition of pleasure 'as some kind of adventitious charm' (1099 a 15–16). Since it is their second nature to engage in that activity, they find in it the satisfaction of their nature. Extrinsic pleasure could not motivate them more than they are already motivated, and they would not miss it if absent. When Aristotle says that the activity is intrinsically pleasant, on the ground that it does not depend on extrinsic pleasure, this might be a harmless locution by which he means to say only that extrinsic pleasure is not necessary, not that intrinsic pleasure is. And the concept of willing engagement is sufficient to establish his account of morally virtuous behaviour and to ground the necessary distinction between this and nonvirtuous correct behaviour. It appears that talk of pleasure in the sense of enjoyment adds nothing to these results that could not have been said without it, and we may think that Aristotle would readily concede the point. He need not, for instance, fear lest the concession commit him to a picture of the best and happiest life as a life without enjoyment. For certainly that life will contain all sorts of civilised enjoyments, and physical pleasures, too, in moderation. To satisfy com-mon-sense qualms about calling a life 'happy' that is completely lacking in enjoy-ment, Aristotle need not assert that the metaphysically central activity of that life is necessarily enjoyed. According to what he has said in *NE* I, that activity is the activity of ourselves simply qua practical beings. So defined, the activity is all-pervasive and might take any empirical form. In itself it is neither enjoyed nor not enjoyed, we might say, but provides the frame for whatever else is excellent, including excellent enjoyments. Nor should it worry Aristotle that what he considers the best activity might seem less attractive to the uninitiated if presented as not necessarily pleasant. For it is the essence of his view that this activity could not *be* a draw except to those already disposed to it.

If we had only the earlier discussions of happiness, moral virtue, practical wis-dom and incontinence, we could dismiss as verbal, a *façon de parler,* what I called the hedonic strain. But in *NE* VII, and especially in X, Aristotle goes out of his way to prove that the best activity is enjoyed. Some of his arguments are against those who hold that the highest good cannot be a pleasure. Others are meant to show that pleasure or enjoyment is unimpeded activity or a dimension of unimpeded activity. Every such activity is necessarily pleasant. Thus Aristotle can conclude that the high-est and best human activity is a pleasure in exactly the same *sense* of 'pleasure' (though not with the same kind of *pleasure*) as eating, drinking, and listening to music are pleasures when one enjoys them. The intensity of his argument puts it beyond doubt that in his view the conclusion is substantial. He would not concede that it rests on a turn of phrase. It is therefore not open to us not to take the doctrine seriously. If it is founded on conceptual confusion, then something important in the *Ethics* is founded on conceptual confusion.

Then does Aristotle mistakenly infer enjoyment from involvement (so that whoever does the nastiest chores with full willingness automatically enjoys doing them); and does his doctrine that the best activity is pleasant depend on this? It is true that he never explicitly registers the difference between gladly doing the chores and enjoying doing them. His not attending to the difference may have made it easier to arrive at the doctrine, but in my view does not explain it. Neglecting the distinc-tion is a symptom rather than a factor of his approach, for he is already disposed on other grounds to look in a direction where the important lines will be drawn without its help. But in any case Aristotle apparently recognises that virtuous action some-times requires the agent to do what is painful or extremely unpleasant. For instance, he says of the courageous man in battle:

> the more he is possessed of excellence in its entirety and the happier he is, the more he will be pained at the thought of death; for life is best worth living for such a man, and he is knowingly losing the greatest goods, and this is painful. But he is none the less brave, and perhaps all the more so, because he chooses noble deeds of war at that cost. It is not the case, then, with all the excellences that the exercise of them is pleasant, except in so far as it reaches its end. (1117 b 9–16)

Aristotle does not imply that the war hero submits to wounds and death otherwise than gladly, without hanging back. Nor does he revoke his view that the active exercise of virtue is pleasant, although the last sentence may give this impression. In fact, the sentence does not deny but asserts that the exercise of virtue is pleasant. It is not pleasant insofar as the particular action in which it consists is painful, but it *is* pleasant so far as the agent attains his end; i.e., manages to do and get himself to do what he knows is noble. So it is with athletic contests:

>  The end which courage sets before it would seem to be pleasant, but to be concealed by the attending circumstances, as happens also in athletic contests; for the end at which boxers aim is pleasant—the crown and the honours—but the blows they take are distressing to flesh and blood, and painful, and so is their whole exertion; and because the blows and the exertions are many the end, which is but small, appears to have nothing pleasant in it. (1117 a 35–b 6)

Here Aristotle says that the circumstances of the brave enterprise, the punches and hard training involved, make it appear unpleasant in the eyes of those (the spectators) to whom all that looms large. The fighter himself thinks more of the punches he gives than the pain he receives, and to *him* the 'end is pleasant'. Aristotle's brevity should not lead us to suppose that he thinks that for boxers the end is literally the crown and the honours.[8] What is pleasant for the boxer would not then be the exercise of his prowess, but something to be had in the future, the having of which is not an exercise of virtue at all. But Aristotle need not spell out what everyone knows: that the boxer's end is *attaining* the crown, and until he gives up or is defeated he sees himself in process of attaining it. This is what is pleasant and what he is here for.

In Aristotle's view, then, (1) the virtuous agent enjoys or takes pleasure in the exercise of his rational and moral nature, and this is consistent with (2) his not taking pleasure in doing what he might have to do in the course of exercising it, even though, as a virtuous agent, he is thoroughly *willing* to do whatever is necessary. Thus the boxer enjoys boxing, but not taking the punches; yet he takes the punches without the slightest reluctance, since it is the nature of a boxer to be ready to do whatever his boxing requires.

Is this a plausible view about pleasure and about virtue? It is, of course, a good deal less implausible than the view sometimes ascribed to Aristotle that the virtuous person takes pleasure in whatever he gladly does in the course of acting virtuously. Even so, one is left wondering why he finds it necessary to assert (1). I argued above this his conception of virtue does not depend on the substantial claim that virtuous activity is pleasant and that he would not need to rely on such a claim in order to show that the best life is far from empty of pleasure. Nevertheless he makes the substantial claim. Possibly this is because he confuses willing action with enjoyed or pleasant action, but, as I have just now pointed out, there is reason to think that he was not trapped by that fallacy. What then are the grounds of his position?

## II. Pleasure and Natural Inclination

The principal elements in Aristotle's theory of pleasure are the metaphysical concepts of *nature* and *activity*. Every living creature is a substance of a given nature, and in the *Physics* Aristotle defines the nature of a thing as its 'inner principle of movement and rest' (192 b 11–33). What here concerns us in that definition is that nature is expressed in unforced behaviour which the substance initiates itself. Artifacts lack natures in this sense; they are inert things that move only when manipulated. It is the nature of a live substance to act so as to attain its natural end or perfection. For those endowed with awareness, which is to say animals in general, there is pleasure in the perfect functioning distinctive of their natures. The kind of pleasure depends on the kind of functioning, and this in turn depends on the nature, for the functioning is nothing other than the nature in action. Thus there are pleasures of seeing and hearing and other perceptual activities, and of eating, hunting and copulation. For human beings there are also pleasures distinctive of human nature, such as those of friendship, music and intellectual pursuits. Within the human race individuals fall into different 'pleasure species' according to their particular loves and enthusiasms: thus some love sailing, some writing, some athletic sports, some mathematics. Each such activity has its pleasure, since each betokens something analogous to a nature in the individual concerned; namely, the bent or disposition expressed in his enjoying the activity in question and being inclined to pursue it. Given that established moral character is, as Aristotle says, a 'second nature' it must, presumably, be a pleasure to exercise one's moral character; and the pleasure of this would also be pleasure in practical rational activity, since character shows itself in this.

I have been using the term 'activity' indiscriminately, as roughly equivalent to 'functioning', but Aristotle's theory of pleasure depends on a more technical conception of activity, whereby it is contrasted with *process*. Not just anything that we might regard as a functioning would count as pleasant according to the theory; for pleasure is not grounded in natural *processes*, but in natural *activity* in a strict sense. An activity seeks no end beyond itself, whereas a process is towards an external end in which it terminates.

Aristotle's distinction between activity and process,[9] and his reasons for associating pleasure with activity, continue to fascinate philosophers. Here the interest is logical and metaphysical, while on the ethical side his theory of pleasure is admired as the source of a fatally effective argument against any form of hedonism that relies on the idea of pleasure as a single quantifiable commodity. Where pleasure is so grounded in activity that it takes its character as the pleasure it is from the nature of the activity, it is nonsense to assert or deny that *pleasure* is better than anything else, for there is no such thing as pleasure to which a single comparative value can be assigned. There are specific pleasures, and the worth of each depends on the worth of its activity. Thus the pleasure of this and the pleasure of that cannot in general be compared in respect of intensity, frequency and duration so as to yield the result that one is better than the other, for unless they happen to be of the same species that method of decision is useless.

Here, however, what I first consider is neither of these celebrated angles, but the connection between what is *pleasant* and what is *natural*. We may well suppose it predictable that Aristotle would locate pleasure in natural activity and that his theory takes this for granted. On that interpretation, his real work begins *from* this point and consists in elaborating the distinction between activity and process and in spelling out the consequences for ethics. For it is a tautology that a creature will be *inclined* to do, when the occasion arises, what it is its nature to do; and where the creature is capable of feeling, it is a short step from speaking of inclination to speaking of pleasure. We may be critical of this second step, since for a variety of reasons we may suspect that the concept of pleasure cannot be tied down as easily as it would imply, but my point is that we probably take it as obvious that the move is obvious to Aristotle, and that he would regard it as no less tautological than the first. On this view, his theory rests on a proposition which purports to be an analytic truth of ordinary language. This is similar to the hypothesis that the theory rests on a false inference from *doing something gladly* (in the sense of *willingly*) to *enjoying doing it*. Both in Greek and in English, language makes the latter seem a plausible move. So, perhaps, with the inference from 'is naturally inclined to $\phi$' to 'takes pleasure in/enjoys $\phi$-ing'. Indeed it may be said that the main difference between this and the *gladly* inference is that the former avoids the obvious absurdities of the latter. It is clear that we sometimes gladly (willingly) do things which are odious. Thus the move from *gladly* to *enjoyingly* is often paradoxical. But it is not at all so clear that we are *naturally inclined* to do what is odious to us. Thus in this case the move to *enjoyingly* will not suggest the strange conclusion that we can enjoy what we loathe or what gives us pain.

So Aristotle's theory of pleasure may be thought to be founded on an inference (by no means obviously fallacious) not unlike the fallacious inference from 'gladly' to 'pleasure' which in the last section we considered as a possible basis for the theory and rejected on the ground that his examples show him not taken in by the fallacy. The two are similar in that both would be justified, if at all, by appeal to a straightforward analytic connection between premiss and conclusion.

In fact, however, Aristotle was not in a position to assume it uncontroversially true that functioning in accordance with nature is pleasant. For in the *Ethics* he confronts a school of thought whose theory depends on a refusal to accept the connection. There were those in the Academy[10] who argued on various grounds that no pleasure is good in itself and even that all pleasures are base (1152 b 8–9; 1172 a 28). Common to those different shades of opinion was the view that the best condition is one of freedom from pain and pleasure. There may have been disagreement on whether this neutral condition is a 'best' that human beings can hope to attain or whether it is merely the best conceivable. Socrates in the *Philebus* hints that God's life would be pleasureless as well as painless (22 c), but concedes that a realistically desirable human life would have to contain certain genuine pleasures, though of severely restricted kinds (63 d–e). And these admissible pleasures, which are 'pure' and 'true' by contrast with the mixed and largely illusory coarse pleasures of the body, are ranked as least worthy among the ingredients of the ideal human life (66 a ff.). The message is clear that the ideal human life would be better still if, per impossible, it were liveable without pleasure; and that the pleasure in it is not the mark of its perfection, but a concession to human imperfection. Now we can see from the *Philebus,* if not from Aristotle's discussion in the *Ethics,* why the neutral condition was considered superior to pleasure: not at all because this vacuity is to be prized as such (an unthinkable position for all concerned) but because the neutral condition permits or follows from (it is not clear which) total absorption in rational activity. A being, whether human or divine, who is so taken up in his exercise of intelligence that there is no space for pleasure any more than for pain, cannot be described as enjoying his thinking; yet he cannot not be also described as utterly involved and bent on it. And although one might hesitate to speak here of 'natural *inclination*', this is only because 'inclination' is eclipsed by 'absorption' as weaker by stronger term. The subject of this activity must surely be considered to engage in it from natural inclination and yet to engage without enjoyment—not because he lacks pleasure but because he is beyond it.

Aristotle may have been familiar with this position from within, because there is some evidence that at one stage he accepted the closely associated theory that pleasure is not an end in itself but a process towards a further end (see next section). If Aristotle ever held this,[11] it is virtually certain that he would have held it in conjunction with the view that the highest human good is in the exercise of our rational nature. Thus he would in effect have endorsed the conception of a kind of functioning in accordance with natural inclination that does not entail pleasure. But whether or not he ever sided with the neutralists, Aristotle was intimately acquainted with their view, and in the *Ethics* he argues hard against it and the arguments on which it rests. If at some stage he came to believe it an analytic truth (as we should say) of ordinary language that activity in accordance with natural inclination is pleasant, he would not have hesitated to point out that the neutralists are committed to the absurd view that those who by nature are capable of the highest activity not only do not enjoy it but are not even inclined towards it, so that it becomes questionable whether they would ever freely engage in it at all! Yet he never comes near to charging them with this. For instance, he has the neutralists in mind when he mentions that some people attack pleasure on the ground that the wise man seeks not pleasure but freedom from pain (1152 b 15–16). If he saw this as entailing the to him absurd conclusion that wisdom aims at an end of inactivity in the total absence of inclination, he would certainly not have let them get away with it. Instead, he immediately goes on to retail another stock objection to pleasure: that pleasures interfere with the *activity* of intelligence (1152 b 16–18).

I do not mean by these reflections to qualify the opening statement of this section: that Aristotle's conception of pleasure must be understood in the light of his concept of nature. So much is obvious from a cursory reading of either of his accounts of pleasure. My purpose, rather, was to clear the deck by pointing out that his theory cannot depend on naive acceptance of some supposedly analytic connection between *pleasure* and *inclination* (not in the narrow Kantian sense, which opposes inclination to reason, but as meaning any kind of tendency to action or activity). This matters, because such a connection lends itself to being elaborated into one or another theory of pleasure that can easily be confused with Aristotle's. Accepting the connection leads some philosophers to explain pleasure as resulting from the coincidence of actual behaviour with inclination to behave in that way, while pain results from divergence. It is to be observed that on such an account the relation, if any, between *pleasure* and *nature* is indirect, being mediated by *inclination,* with *nature* perhaps regarded as in some sense the basis of inclination or even as the sum total of inclinations themselves. On such a view, a pleasureless painless state would be one where no inclination is followed and none is thwarted; hence there would be no inclination to act, and so, presumably, no action. Alternatively, the supposed connection can be developed into a theory according to which explanation goes the opposite way: inclination to act is explained as the effect of pleasure and pain (including the pleasure and pain of anticipation). On this view, too, there is no action without pleasure or pain.

The first sort of theory shows its not particularly Aristotelian character by the fact that the rôle of *pleasure* would be the same no matter how we interpret the concept of *nature* and even if we discarded it altogether. Yet the second sort of theory, in certain classic presentations, is still more un-Aristotelian, since pleasure and pain are there seen as mechanical pressures analogous to those external forces that alone account for changes in the state of motion of naturally inert bodies. The purpose of conceptualising pleasure in this way was to bring the science of human nature into line with an already established post-Galilean mechanics. But in Aristotle's physics, even inanimate objects are endowed with their own inner principles of movement, so that under appropriate conditions a body springs into motion simply because it is released. Aristotle knows no conceivable motive to treat (of all things) sentient subjects as entities whose intrinsic inertia keeps them at rest until they are pushed by logically external psychological impulses. Such entities, physical or spiritual, would literally be *natureless* in the Aristotelian sense of 'nature'. Aristotle, therefore, could not have viewed inclination to act as having, in general, to be explained by pain or pleasure or painful or pleasurable anticipation; for to regard action, activity, movement and tendency to move as 'natural' in his sense is precisely to regard them as requiring no explanation by extrinsic causes. Nor, to return to the first type of theory, can he view pleasure in $\phi$-ing as an *effect* of $\phi$-ing in accordance with the inclination to $\phi$. For, we shall see, he understands pleasure as a dimension of or even identical with the subject's activity as source or uncaused *cause* of what it does.

## III. The Challenge of Neutralism

The principal target of Aristotle's arguments supporting pleasure as an attribute of the highest activity is the doctrine which I call 'neutralism'[12] and which for the moment I characterise by two propositions: (1) the highest good is rational activity at its best, and (2) such activity is neither pleasant nor painful. Now it is not clear whether neutralists in the Academy recognised rational activity in a practical as well as a theoretical form. Nor, if they did acknowledge practical reason, can we be sure that they regarded this as reason at its best. Here, too, there are different possibilities. For instance, if God exercises reason in some practical way, this might be considered a flawless rational activity, but it would not follow that *human* practical reason is human reason at its best. It might be held that human practical rational activity is not only less perfect than a divine version of the same thing, but also than human theoretical activity. The latter was probably Plato's position even as late as the *Philebus,* and by the end of the *Nicomachean Ethics* we know it to be Aristotle's. The problems of reconciling this with his earlier indications that for human beings there is no higher end than a life centred on the exercise of moral virtue and practical wisdom will be a major concern of the next chapter. Here, however, I take it that the neutralist conception of the human summum bonum, so far as this conception is caught by the two propositions above, can be interpreted so as to apply to practical reason, whether or not the historical neutralists would all have accepted this application. And I shall assume, in short, that the essential point in neutralism is that for human beings the highest good is some form of rational activity, which, whatever its form, is without pleasure and pain.

The assumption is justified because Aristotle's opposing arguments do not logically depend on any premiss concerning the particular nature of the highest human exercise of human reason. They are rooted in general considerations about pleasure and its relation to the good and in a metaphysical analysis of what it means to say that a being exercises its nature. On the other hand, we must be prepared to weigh the implications of the various possible interpretations of 'highest rational activity', not forgetting the additional possibility that Aristotle and the neutralists do not agree on the reference of this phrase. For example, in either of his discussions of pleasure, or in both, he may have it in mind that the highest activity is what the earlier books (in both *Ethics*) suggest, namely practical, and at the same time he may be aware that the neutralists see it as purely theoretical. Now if they were able to convince him that the highest activity, even if theoretical, carries no pleasure, Aristotle would surely concede that the conclusion holds good even if the highest activity is, or is also, practical. It is an a fortiori argument: if theoretical activity is not pleasant, then certainly no other sort of rational activity is pleasant as such. Why he would think this need not be spelt out here.[13] If, on the other hand, he can show that the highest activity is pleasant even when he is thinking of it as practical, then it has all the more reason to be considered pleasant by those who regard it as purely theoretical.

Alternatively, however, Aristotle may not be attending at all to any views which he or the others may hold about the precise form of the activity. As I said, the logic of his arguments leaves this open, and in constructing the arguments his idea of the subject may just be 'the highest activity, whatever it is.' Again, this may be the situation in one of his accounts of pleasure and not the other. Then there is another possibility: that in either or both accounts Aristotle has it in mind that the highest activity is purely theoretical. If he does, this has a bearing on the motivation of his arguments about pleasure, though not on their internal logic. For it suggests the hypothesis that he hopes by means of a theory of pleasure to pave the way to an ethical finale in which the highest human good is found to centre on pure theoretical activity. He might think that if he can show that the highest activity, whatever it may be, is necessarily pleasant, it will be easier later to represent that activity as theoretic, there being (as we said) reasons why he would be inclined to hold that theoretic activity is more evidently pleasant than practical, or evidently more pleasant. This would explain why he wants to maintain that the highest activity is pleasant, even though the thesis adds nothing to his earlier analysis of virtuous action.

I have tried to state this hypothesis in a way that does not beg questions about the relation between Aristotle's seemingly ambivalent views about the happy life: such questions as whether the final picture is the same in both ethical treatises; whether theoretic is combined with practical activity in a single ideal or stands alone at the summit; whether either of these possibilities is consistent with the earlier arguments about happiness; and whether, if not, this is because Aristotle changes his mind. All this will be faced in the next chapter. Here I only point out that if there is a change of mind, the above hypothesis does not explain it, since the hope which the hypothesis attributes to Aristotle would be an *effect* of that change. Hence, if we believe that he changed from a practical to a theoretical ideal of happiness, we can explain this better on the assumption that in discussing pleasure Aristotle does not have in mind any particular kind of highest activity. For then we can suppose that his discovery that, whatever it is, it is pleasant, provides a new criterion for deciding what it is: a criterion which, it may turn out, practical activity satisfies less well than theoretic.

I mention these possibilities so that they should come to mind where it might make a difference; but as I have said they concern Aristotle's motive, not his grounds, for arguing that the highest human activity is pleasant. And other motives—if any are needed beyond the intrinsic interest of the subject—may suggest themselves as we continue to consider the grounds.

Neutralism as defined by propositions (1) and (2) draws strength from the uncritical assumption that the only pleasures are the gross and often violent physical ones. Aristotle rejects the assumption, but he has something of the neutralists' negative attitude to those pleasures. Their objects or occasions are not noble or ennobling, being necessary somatic processes (1147 b 24–28). So there is nothing distinguished about such pleasures, and we need not go out of our way for them. On the contrary, they are dangerous because a person engrossed in them is often even physically incapable of determining the right moment to disengage, as the study of incontinence shows. It is fortunate therefore that inbuilt animal nature, anyway for healthy individuals, sets its own bounds to these necessary pleasures by the mechanism of the underlying processes, which cannot be prolonged beyond the point where their end is accomplished. In this area reflective reason has no control from close quarters and must deal with these pleasures very much at arm's length. Aristotle himself has said earlier that for the purpose of discipline it is better to lean too far in the opposite direction and regard all pleasures with suspicion, and all the more so when the case concerns a pleasure that springs from our basic (i.e., precultured) nature. In that way we may realize the mean, since (he assumes) there is no danger that the underlying nature will not reassert itself (1109 a 12–17).

This is a pragmatic approach, to be applied piecemeal in particular training situations. But in *NE* X he issues a warning: it is a mistake, he says, to elevate this into the doctrine that all pleasure (or even all these pleasures) should be avoided. Those who preach this will not be able to live by it, and this discrepancy between actions and words will discredit even the part-truth of what they say, since it takes discernment to see that part-truth, and most people are not discerning (1172 a 27–b 7). So the doctrine plays into the hands of those who regard physical pleasure as an unconditional good, perhaps even viewing it as a divine power that proves its sovereignty less by rewarding its adherents than by vanquishing its critics.

However, the philosophical neutralists are no more committed than Aristotle himself to a universal prohibition against physical pleasure. Their mistake, rather, is in assuming these gross pleasures to be the only pleasures or the most typical. Aristotle can explain the mistake. The fleshly ones have appropriated the name of 'pleasure' because they are universal and are pursued even at great risk, and because they are the only ones that many people take account of (1153 b 33–36). The pleasures best known 'to us' (i.e., in advance of reflection) may not be the most essentially pleasant. But even in the ordinary way of things they are not the only pleasures. We enjoy seeing and hearing, Aristotle points out (1173 b 17–18), reminiscing and looking forward to good things (1166 a 24–26), and less universal pleasures such as music (1175 b 3–5), the theatre (1175 b 12), dice, hunting, athletics and philosophising (1172 a 3–5). So long as he holds that pleasure has a constructive rôle in moral training, Aristotle must insist that there are genuine higher pleasures. Pleasures and pains of the flesh might be effective for conditioning the young like animals, but a conditioning that relied on them alone could never bring about the transition to human values and human sensibility. Here, then, neutralism's equation of pleasures with gross pleasures does contradict an important tenet about moral virtue. But once it is clear that the equation is a mistake, Aristotle can accept proposition (1) while rejecting (2), for there is no reason why the highest activity should not be a pleasure.

However, the rôle of higher pleasures in moral education cuts two ways. For it associates these pleasures with lack of development; and whereas Aristotle can see them as pointing forward to adult excellence, the neutralists can claim that once this is gained, the time for pleasures is over. The good activities previously enjoyed will now be pursued from a stable character, but pleasure is no longer necessary, and if it remains it remains as a trace of childishness.

The neutralists, then, are not so easily driven back. What is more, they can draw on a theory, one which they may have developed themselves to give their position an intellectual foundation. This is not a claim about what kinds of pleasures there are (as for instance that they are all physical), but a metaphysical analysis of pleasure as a process of coming-to-be in a natural or healthy condition (1152 b 12–15; 1173 a 29–31). A pleasure, on this view, is an entity essentially directed towards an ulterior end, which in this way of thinking is necessarily better than its coming-to-be. Aristotle defines process as 'imperfect' (or 'incomplete') actuality (*Physics* 201 a 10 ff.), because the subject qua actually in process necessarily lacks the perfect actuality of the end, and because the process itself is never complete while going on. This account of pleasure leans, of course, on the somatic paradigm cases, where what takes place is a physiological filling up (*anaplērōsis;* cf. 1173 b 8 ff.) or overflowing.

This theory of pleasure assumes an observer's perspective, which may be appropriate for a scientific investigation but jars in the context of ethics. It ignores a fundamental point which, according to Aristotle, was brought to the fore by his Academic associate, Eudoxus: that all pleasure is endlike. 'That is most an object of choice which we choose not because or for the sake of something else, and pleasure is admittedly of this nature; for no one asks to what end he is pleased, thus implying that pleasure is in itself an object of choice' (1172 b 20–23). To the one who enjoys it, what he enjoys is itself an end, since the enjoyment necessarily focuses on it, not through it on to something else. And the enjoyment, too, is had for itself: one cannot enjoy oneself as a means to anything. Thus if pleasure were really a process to something ulterior, we should only know pleasure for what it is when we are disengaged from pleasure, since the face which pleasure shows us while we are actually involved in it utterly misleads us as to its nature. This is an extraordinary view. Everyone agrees that one cannot know what some given pleasure is unless one has experienced it: how strange, then, to hold that what experience tells us about the general practical structure of pleasure should be the opposite of the truth about it.

Now if one wished only to defeat this theory it would be enough to point to examples of enjoyed activities that are not processes to anything further. The highest good could not be a pleasure if all pleasures were processes, but the examples show that there is no reason why that good should not be a pleasure, since some familiar pleasures are activities with no ulterior end. Aristotle, however, goes much further: he maintains not only that the highest activity is necessarily pleasant, but (in *NE* X) that *every* kind of activity has its own pleasure (1175 a 20 ff.). And he maintains, against the process theory, that all pleasures (including gross ones) are activities *rather* than processes, and that this is so even when the pleasurable activity happens also to be a process.

All this is difficult. What is the difference between an *activity* and a *process?* How can an activity also be a process? Why must pleasure be activity, not process, and why is activity necessarily pleasant? And when Aristotle speaks of pleasure, does he mean *what* is enjoyed or the *enjoying* of what is enjoyed, or does he shift? We must begin to move in on his theory of pleasure as activity. To start with, let us stay with some of the points already raised. And for the moment we shall have to live with the interpretational uncertainties which arise as soon as one notes the ambiguity of 'pleasure', meaning both the enjoying and that which is enjoyed.

Let us return to Aristotle's observation that those who sincerely preach total austerity pursue physical pleasures in some degree, and so bring even a duly limited austerity into disrepute in the eyes of people unable or unwilling to distinguish exaggeration from falsehood. He says: 'True assertions [*logoi*] seem, then, most useful, not only with a view to knowledge, but with a view to life also; for since they harmonise with the deeds [*erga*] they are believed, and so they stimulate those who understand them to live according to them' (1172 b3–7). Does he mean that we disbelieve the truth of the assertions if we see that the speaker fails to live up to what he says? Perhaps, but this disbelief in the truth rests on prior disbelief in the preachers' sincerity. Their actions are taken to show that they do not mean all that they say, and perhaps not any of it. And if someone is seen not to mean what he says, his saying it is no evidence that he has reason to think it true, and so is no evidence that it might be true. For in general the fact that someone believes something is a ground for others to think that he has what he considers reasons for believing it, and his reasons may be good ones which we should find cogent if we knew them; so even when we do not know why he is right, if he is, the fact that he believes gives us, too, some reason to believe. So when actions do not measure up to words, we first doubt the sincerity of his claim and then, as a result, its truth. We know he makes the claim because he wants us to believe it true, but unless we have independent ground for accepting it (and if he thought we had, he might not be trying to present it to us) our only ground for acceptance stands and falls with our ground for believing him sincere, since only then will we think that he wants us to believe it true because (in his view) it is, and he has reason to think so.

This logic, whereby the assumption of sincerity helps constitute authority, instinctively structures all our relations with others. So does the assumption that a person's actions show his real attitude. We read the actions as his judgments. And so does Aristotle. For instance, Aristotle thinks that the behaviour of those who applaud the pleasureless-painless condition is an argument against their doctrine. They accept that pain is bad, but deny the implication that pleasure is good, claiming that the best state is the mean between the two and that extremes on both sides are bad. Aristotle agrees that if they are right, pleasure and pain are of equal value: both bad if pain is bad and both indifferent if (as some hold) pleasure is indifferent. So both should be shunned or be neither shunned nor pursued. But, he says, we actually see these people shunning pain as an evil and preferring pleasure as a good (1173 a 7–13). Their actions show that their real values are not what they claim.

He ignores the possible reply that the actions show only that we cannot always live up to our values. To say this would be to confess constitutional incontinence, which would do nothing for one's authority on matters of ethics. Aristotle, I take it, assumes that these people live and see themselves as living decent lives, no more torn by temptation than other good people. They are not ashamed to pursue pleasure sometimes in a decent way, any more than the sceptic is ashamed to fall back into the ordinary way of 'knowing' that the world beyond his room existed all the time he sought to doubt it. Aristotle would question whether the sceptic really did doubt it. The natural belief, not the theoretical doubt, is the real attitude, since it is lived by.[14] Just so, we vote with our feet for pleasure sometimes, and that vote represents our real judgment.

This argument affects those who hold the highest good to be neither painful nor pleasant. Considered in the abstract, their thesis does not entail that no pleasures are good, but nonetheless it has this consequence. The best condition is pleasureless and painless because pleasure and pain interfere with the activity of reason. And although this is especially true of physical pleasures, it is also true of all others (given that there is no pleasure in the activity of reason itself), for it is of the nature of pleasure to be engrossing even when not gross (cf. 1175 b 1–13). So they all threaten what is best and should be shunned as bad. They may be bad only in their effect, not in themselves, but in practice this makes no difference: what is always damaging must be always avoided every bit as much as if it were intrinsically evil. The neutralists might say that some pleasures, sometimes, are necessary for health. Thus if pleasures are good at all, it is only as painful surgery is good or throwing the cargo overboard in a storm. They are what in themselves no enlightened person would choose, but sometimes one has to. Yet that 'having to' ought to show itself in the felt quality of the necessary choice. But pleasure, when taken, is not grimly undergone with a view to something else more valuable. Enjoying something, which is enjoying it for what *it* is, is a kind of affirmation that it is good in itself, much as pursuing something is an affirmation that it is good in one way or another. And even the neutralists, by their actions, sometimes embrace as an end in itself what they tell us is worthless except possibly as a means to something else.

Aristotle speaks of pleasure as 'the apparent good' (*EE* 1235 b 26–28; *On the Soul* 431 a 8–11).[15] He means that something's being pleasant is a prereflective way of its seeming to be good. By being pleasant it recommends itself as good even if reflection were to show that it is not (or not on this occasion). Thus responding to Z as pleasant—e.g., pursuing it as pleasant—is one way (the most primitive) of taking Z to be good.[16]

Logically, the pleasantness is not a quality of the object, but a mode of the subject's pursuit of that object as good. The point is not merely that what is pleasant is so *to* a subject, by contrast with the physical properties which we take the thing to possess independently of observation. And in saying that pleasure is the apparent good, Aristotle does not mean that something seems to me good because I find it pleasant; i.e., I judge it good and worth pursuing on the ground that it is pleasant to me. That some object is pleasant to me might be my ground for pursuing it, but my ground for pursuit is not a mode of pursuit. In exactly the same sense of 'pleasant to —', that something is pleasant *to you* might be my reason for judging it good and pursuing it, with exactly the same kind of pursuit as if my reason were its pleasantness *to me*. The subject to whom, in this sense, the thing would be pleasant is only per accidens the same as the subject who pursues and judges it worth pursuing. But pleasure as Aristotle's 'apparent good' is necessarily pleasure *to the subject pursuing* what thus appears to him good. For the pleasantness of Z is Z 's seeming or being found good in what we might call the hedonic mode of seeming good; thus it is essentially pleasantness to the being to whom Z thus appears good. Now, on the prereflective level, Z's appearing to me good is indistinguishable from my affirming Z to be good and a proper object of pursuit; hence on this level my finding Z pleasant, and my pursuing it as pleasant, is my affirming it to be good.[17] And in this sense it figures as pleasant even when I am only pursuing it but am not yet enjoying it, since an objective figures as good when pursued, not only when attained (otherwise it would not be pursued). If, on the other hand, Z's pleasantness to me is my *reason* for pursuing it (just as its pleasantness to you might be my reason) what figures as the reason is not strictly that Z is now pleasant to me, but that it will be when I get it.

Aristotle mentions a stock objection to the claim that pleasure is the good: there is no craft for producing pleasure (1152 b 18–19), whereas (it is assumed) every kind of good is the product of a corresponding kind of craft. Aristotle replies that, by that argument, no activity can be good because there can be no crafting of an activity. For an activity cannot be a product; only the conditions for it can. That is why there is no craft of pleasure, since pleasure is an activity. He also replies, somewhat inconsequentially, that there *are* crafts of pleasures, such as the craft of confectionery (1153 a 23–27). The replies illustrate the two senses in which something is pleasant to someone. The confectioner's craft, or the entertainer's, produces what would be pleasant to any consumer, and the confectioner himself is a consumer only per accidens. But pleasure in Z considered as a mode of active pursuit of Z is necessarily pleasure to the pursuer only, and can be generated only by him.

Pleasure as a prereflective mode of pursuit, or of affirming something as good, is logically analogous to Aristotle's conception of the nature of a natural substance. But let us look more closely at his notion of nature as an *inner* principle of movement and rest. For the craftsman's craft is such a principle, too. It determines changes in the material which is to be worked up into the product, and it is a principle internal to the craftsman. But the changes due to craft are brought about in something external. Or if they are in the craftsman himself, this is only per accidens. Thus a doctor himself might be the patient whom he restores to health, but in that capacity he no more figures as doctor than does the bricklayer who is also his patient. So far as he is a patient he might as well be someone else and not the doctor that he is; hence he might as well be some other doctor's patient. Nature, Aristotle says, is not this sort of principle of change (see *Physics* 192 b 24–33). The nature of a substance is essentially the principle of that thing's natural change and no other's. Thus if, as can happen, one substance by its nature acts on another so as to make it change, this change is not of a kind that could have come about from the thing itself; and any change that does come about from itself is not of a kind that could just as well have been administered by an external agent. Just so, pleasure considered as a prereflective affirmation that something is good is necessarily a source of movement *by the affirmer,* who as affirmer is the efficient cause of that good's being realised, since his affirmation is in the practical language of pursuit. It begins to look as if pleasure and the active nature of a substance are intimately connected, if not the same.

There are, we should note, two interpretations of ethical hedonism, corresponding to Aristotle's two answers to the objection that there is no craft of pleasure. On one, we are enjoined always to act so as to produce pleasure, which is to say: produce the conditions or possibilities for pleasure. It is logically open *whose* pleasure is concerned, so that the injunction has to be qualified to yield egoistic hedonism or universalistic hedonism or any other comparable version. In any version, it will be reasonable to take it as prescribing the maximisation of pleasure-possibilities for the given field of subjects, and thus interpreted the doctrine lays down a plan for living and a principle of deliberation that generates reasons why its adherents would choose as they do. On the other interpretation, we are told to reach out for things as good only so far as our reaching out is our finding them pleasant. If we add a corresponding injunction concerning pain, the hedonistic principle tells us, in effect, to do and avoid what we prereflectively feel like. This makes deliberation redundant, since deliberation determines whether what 'appears' good via an hedonically charged impression or impulse is the 'real' good: i.e., would be judged good by reflective reason. The assumption of deliberation is that impulse and the findings of reason do not necessarily coincide. But the hedonistic principle, on the second interpretation, forbids any questioning of appearances and tells us to equate what is best with what we most happen to feel like. Unlike the other sort of hedonism, this is not a recipe for a possible human life at all.

## IV. Pleasure as Value-Judgment

We were seeking earlier for a compelling answer to the question why Aristotle sees pleasure as a major topic for ethics. We find such an answer in the notion of pleasure as a mode of pursuit. Pleasure and pain (understood in a corresponding way) are woven into the fabric of human and animal behaviour, and any special connections with the human end and with moral development must be grounded in that fundamental fact. Nor can we understand rational choice except in relation to pleasure. For if pleasure and pain are undeliberated inclination and aversion, then pleasure and pain are the matter from which the formation of rational choice takes its start.

It is worth developing the implications of this conception of pleasure, not only for its own interest, but because fuller exposition throws light on some of the peculiarities of Aristotle's stated positions. Pursuing Z as pleasant is a way of affirming Z as good. And enjoying Z (the actual taking pleasure in Z) when one has it is a sort of continuation of the pursuit: it is pursuit turned into adherence. Thus the actual enjoyment of Z is likewise a way of affirming it to be good. But one does not enjoy just having a thing, but doing something with it or in relation to it; thus even if Z, a thing or condition, seemed the object of pursuit, what was really pursued was the Z-ward activity: eating Z, playing with it and so on. The subject, then, may not know with clarity *what* is pursued, enjoyed or affirmed as good: that Z is the focus does not mean that it is the true object. (Aristotle never challenges the theory that what is enjoyed is a restoration of the body's natural condition on the ground that animals do not necessarily know that what they are enjoying is this.) In rational choice, by contrast, the agent knows what, by his doing, he affirms to be the good action, since it is his deliberated answer to his own practical question. And what he knows is complex as well as articulated, since it is not just A, the action lifted out of context, but A-under-these-conditions; and the conditions must be kept track of in case a change invalidates doing A. Even if the agent has a natural disposition to do A, he does not have a special natural disposition to do A under just these conditions, which is why he needs deliberation to inform him what to do.

Pursuit-for-pleasure and enjoyment do not depend on an achieved knowledge of what it is that is enjoyed, although they need not lack such knowledge. Rational choice presupposes analysis, but enjoyment gives rise to it. Since the enjoyment is nothing but a kind of focusing, one comes to know *through* enjoyment more about what it is that one enjoys. The activity itself generates a discriminating awareness of the activity and its foci, and with this comes greater control: not the control that adjusts our doing to an antecedently determinate form or intention, but control that is really a dimension of our discriminating awareness itself. Here, we are feeling our way *to* the form. For beings such as ourselves, whose nature on every level reaches out for more knowledge than we have, it is metaphysically inevitable that gross physical pleasures modulate into gourmet pleasures. The idea that an enjoyed activity makes itself knowable in and through the enjoyment may seem mystifying; but there is a symmetry too neat to be ignored between this and a point which stood up to hammering in an earlier chapter. Rational choice, it was argued there (Chapter 4; see especially Section VIII) is knowledge (of what to do) essentially directed to enacting itself; whereas pleasure, on the present showing, is self-discovering action.

These implications become more compelling when we consider the logically reflexive nature of affirmation. In affirming something to be the case we implicitly affirm that same affirmation to be true and right. We also thereby affirm it to be good (since a true affirmation is good), and ourselves (artificial though the words make it seem) to be affirming well. So, too, in practical affirmation, whether rational choice or pleasure. We have to distinguish between the two senses of 'action': as meaning *what* is affirmed to be good and as meaning the *doing* or engaging in this; i.e., the affirming it to be good to do. In affirming$_1$ good (to do) *what* one would be described as doing, one implicitly affirms$_2$ the excellence of affirmation$_1$ and also one's own excellence as affirmer$_1$ (i.e., doer). Making and enacting a rational choice to $\phi$ is affirming₁ the goodness of *φ-ing rather than any alternative, in this situation,* and the implicit affirmation₂ is of the rightness of this choice. In the case of pleasure, on the other hand, the ground-level affirmation issues from a natural or quasi-natural disposition simply to $\phi$, i.e., to engage in $\phi$-ing; thus one is naturally disposed to affirm₁ the goodness of *φ-ing simpliciter.* So the implicit affirmation₂ of the goodness of affirmation₁ declares the goodness of engaging in $\phi$-ing as such, not rather than something else or as called for by these circumstances. This second-level affirmation is pleasure in engaging in $\phi$-ing. And the same logic points to an implicit affirmation₃ of the goodness of affirmation₂ and the affirmer₂'s excellence as such. Pleasure, then, is not only an affirmation of the goodness of doing, but carries an implicit affirmation of its own goodness as pleasure, and of the self's well-ness in *enjoying* (not only *doing*) what is enjoyed.

The higher level affirmations are affirmations of goodness per se. What is affirmed₁ good (what is engaged in or done) may or may not be affirmed₁ good for its own sake. But the doing of it (affirming₁) is affirmed₂ to be a good doing; and this doing must figure to the creature concerned as a good per se for itself, since to claim something as a good doing is to claim it as an instance of good activity or functioning, or (in short) of being alive in a way that is good for a being such as oneself. So, too, for the goodness predicated in affirmation₃. Enjoyment, then, declares the value per se of *doing* what, by one's very doing of it, one claims to be good to do; and enjoyment necessarily announces its own goodness per se.

This explains why pleasure is endlike, but without implying that pleasure in $\phi$-ing is the goal sought when one $\phi$-s. Just so, in factual affirmation one does not affirm₁ that *p in order to* affirm₂ affirmation₁ to be correct; and similarly in the evaluative case. A person might take steps to acquire a set of beliefs simply so as to have something to assert as true. One might feel a need to be equipped with *opinions,* just as a man may marry someone because he wants *a wife,* rather than marrying that person because he wants *her* as wife. In the case of belief this shows a perverted emphasis, and so with pleasure: one might take steps to acquire the disposition to do something simply so as to have something one enjoys doing; but given the analogy with belief, this goes against the nature of pleasure. In neither case does affirmation on a given level necessarily presuppose affirmation on the next level up; this would mean a vicious infinite regress. Rather, each higher affirmation is a development *from* the immediately lower; we could say, its self-development.

The assumption that Aristotle conceives of pleasure in terms of this model of logically reflexive affirmation helps to make sense of his arguments. Let us turn to the texts with this assumption in mind.

It seems as if *NE* VII and X deal with different sides of the topic of pleasure. The treatment in VII is concerned with the question '*What* is it that we enjoy?' Is it a coming to be in a natural state or is it an activity, which as such is *not* a coming to be? Book X, by contrast, tries to answer the question 'What is it to *enjoy* something?' Here, too, Aristotle contends that pleasure is not a coming to be; but now he is referring to enjoyment, not to what is enjoyed. Another very noticeable difference between the two discussions is that in VII he offers little support for the thesis that pleasure is an activity, not a coming to be, whereas the position of X is carefully argued. In VII he merely points out that some pleasures are not processes to a further end satisfying a prior need; for instance, theoretical activity. We theorise, but not because it leads to something else for which we hungered. From this example Aristotle concludes that even when what is enjoyed is a lack-driven process like eating, it is not a pleasure on account of being a process, but on account of being an activity—which it also is:

> One kind of good being activity and another being state, the processes that restore us to our natural state are only incidentally pleasant; for that matter, the activity at work in the appetites[18] for them is the activity of so much of our state and nature as has remained unimpaired; for there are actually pleasures that involve *no* pain or appetite (e.g., those of *theōria*), the nature in such a case not being defective at all. (1152 b 33–a 2)

And he also says:

> It is not necessary that there should be something else better than pleasure, as some say the end is better than the process; for pleasures are not processes nor do they all involve process—they are activities and ends; nor do they arise when we are becoming something, but when we are exercising some faculty; and not all pleasures have an end different from themselves, but only the pleasures of persons who are being led to the completing of their nature. (1153 a 7–12)

For the moment I keep on one side the question how we are to understand the difference between activity and process, and how an activity can nonetheless be a process. The present point is that in VII Aristotle gives no good reason why pleasures are none of them processes. The fact, shown by examples, that some are not proves nothing about the rest. Indeed, if we were to go by examples, we could object that some pleasures *are* processes, even if not all. But the above passages show that Aristotle would respond with the claim that pleasures such as eating and drinking, which are processes, are pleasures only because the processes are *also* activities: a pleasure that is a process is a process only incidentally to its being a pleasure; qua pleasure, it is an activity.[19] Underlying this claim is the assumption that all pleasures belong to one metaphysical category:[20] since some are evidently not processes towards an ulterior end, none is. But no evidence drawn from examples could justify this last claim, nor therefore the implied claim that apparent evidence for process-pleasures is only apparent (since all it shows is that some pleasures happen to be processes, not that those pleasures are not really, as such, activities).

At first sight, the arguments in Book X that pleasure is not a process compensate the lack of argument in Book VII. It seems as if we might justify the dogmatism of VII by assuming that VII uses results obtained in a previously composed X; or we might see X as a later attempt to make more secure the position put forward in VII. But on a second look, the argumentative extra in X and the argumentative lacuna in VII simply do not fit: the former concerns pleasure as *enjoying* something, the latter pleasure as *that which is enjoyed*. For example, it is argued in X that pleasure is not a process, because processes can be quick or slow, but it makes no sense to say this of pleasure (1173 a 31–b 4). It seems that the process-theorists of VII could accept that argument and still maintain that *what* is enjoyed is in every case a process. (They would have to reject the example—theoretical activity—which Aristotle in VII takes for granted would be accepted by everyone as showing the possibility of a pleasure that is not even accidentally a process. But the process-theorists, some of them, would regard theoretical activity as a prime example of something neither painful nor pleasant.)

In X Aristotle compares enjoying to seeing, which he also insists is not a process. Hence it would seem that using the argument of X to compensate for the weakness of VII is no better than arguing that since seeing is not a process, what is seen is not. (Aristotle holds that we perceive movement [*On the Soul,* 418 a 17–20]; he does not think that really we only string together successive perceptions of the moving object at different stages.) But the objection just raised assumes that what is enjoyed stands to enjoying as what is seen to seeing. For Aristotle, as for common sense, what is perceived is external to the perceiving, not generated by it nor necessarily generative of it, since it might exist unperceived (cf. *Metaphysics* 1010 b 30–1011 a 1). But on the affirmation model, the relation of enjoyment to what is enjoyed is not like this. It is more like the relation of awareness of one's seeing to the seeing itself. Awareness of perceiving, Aristotle holds, is an essential aspect of perceiving (*On the Soul,* 425 b 12 ff). He may even mean that, for the percipient, his perceiving O *is* awareness of his perceiving O. And at one place Aristotle almost says that our awareness of our own activity, such as seeing, *is* the enjoying of it (1174 b 14 ff.). Now it is understandable that he should virtually say this, if, as I suggested earlier, he regards enjoying as a mode of engagement which by its very nature renders the subject more determinately aware of his activity with an awareness that is also a controlling. Thus the subject is aware of the doing as his, not as something that might be "there" for anyone (in the way in which even objects imagined are "there", since one imagines them as they would be, one assumes, for anyone). In short, enjoying doing something explains not only one's awareness of doing, but one's awareness of the doing as one's own, and as such accessible only to one's own awareness.

If the doing—that which is enjoyed—essentially goes over into the enjoying of itself (though not by temporal succession), just as the enjoying in turn becomes a glorying in that enjoyment, an argument showing that one is not a process shows this for the other. For even if we hesitate to assert identity of enjoyment with activity enjoyed—and in X Aristotle does stop short of this—the affirmation model, while justifying that hesitation, implies that the enjoyment and the doing which is enjoyed are items of the same type: both are acts of affirmation. Hence whichever can be proved to be not a process proves this for the other. We do not know whether Aristotle was aware that between VII and X (in whichever order) he shifts from the question of what is enjoyed to the question of enjoyment; but, on the interpretation which I am suggesting, even if he was aware of the difference of topic he would have had no compelling reason to alter his position in either book from the position we find.

The affirmation model also sheds light within the discussion in X. Reasons for denying that enjoying is a process are reasons for holding it to be an activity. But is the activity of enjoying the same as the activity enjoyed or is it something else? At 1175 b 30–35 Aristotle says:

> But the pleasures involved in activities [e.g., activities of thought and perception] are more proper to them than the desires [for the activities]; for the latter are separated both in time and in nature, while the former are close to the activities, and so hard to distinguish from them that it admits of dispute whether the activity is not the same as the pleasure. (Still, pleasure does not seem to *be* thought or perception—that would be strange; but because they are not found apart they appear to some people the same.)

This is what we should expect if enjoying an activity is the activity itself in reflexive mode. His fullest attempt to depict the relation comes a bit earlier:

> Since every sense [*aisthēsis*] is active in relation to its object, and a sense which is in good condition acts completely in relation to the most beautiful of its objects (for complete activity seems to be especially of this nature; whether we say that *it* is active, or the organ in which it resides, may be assumed to be immaterial), it follows that in the case of each sense the best activity is that of the best-conditioned organ in relation to the finest of its objects. And this activity will be the most complete and pleasant. For, while there is pleasure in respect of any sense, and in respect of thought and contemplation no less, the most complete is pleasantest, and that of a well-conditioned organ in relation to the worthiest of its objects is the most complete [or: perfect]; and the pleasure completes [or: perfects] the activity. But the pleasure does not complete it in the same way as the object perceived and the faculty of perception, if they are good, do—just as health and the doctor are not in the same way the cause of a man's being healthy. (That pleasure is produced in respect to each sense is plain; for we speak of sights and sounds as pleasant. It is also plain that it arises most of all when both the sense is at its best and it is active in reference to an object which corresponds; when both object and perceiver are of the best there will always be pleasure, since the requisite agent and patient are both present.) Pleasure completes the activity not as the inherent state does, but as an end which supervenes as the bloom of youth does on those in the flower of their age. So long, then, as both the intelligible or sensible object and the discriminating or contemplative faculty are as they should be, the pleasure will be involved in the activity; for when both the passive and the active factor are unchanged and are related to each other in the same way, the same result naturally follows. (1174 b 14–1175 a 3)

For much of this passage it is not clear whether Aristotle is saying that enjoying is something beyond the perfect activity enjoyed or simply is that perfect activity. For when he says that pleasure perfects the activity, he may mean only that the pleasure *consists in* its being perfect. On this interpretation, what *makes* it perfect in a substantial sense of 'makes' is the excellent condition of the subject and the fineness or suitability of the objects to which the activity is directed: the objects of perception and thought, which are Aristotle's main examples in Book X. These are responsible for its being a perfect activity when it is engaged in, and its being engaged in under these perfecting conditions simply is its being enjoyed. Thus enjoyment only 'makes' it perfect in the sense in which health 'makes' a person healthy: there is no perfection that enjoying either is or imports beyond the perfection already guaranteed by the good conditions of subject and object.[21] But the metaphor in the final sentence strongly suggests to most interpreters that enjoying is more than this, even if inseparable. The contrast drawn there between pleasure and the underlying state of the subject seems to be a contrast between a distinct consequence of perfect activity and a precondition of it.[22]

Enjoyment, moreover, is not merely a perfection grounded in the perfect activity: it is also a cause of the latter's perfection, and in more than one way:

> An activity is intensified by its proper pleasure, since each class of things is better judged of and brought to precision by those who engage in the activity with pleasure; e.g. it is those who enjoy geometrical thinking that become geometers and grasp the various propositions better, and, similarly, those who are fond of music or of building, and so on, make progress in their proper function by enjoying it; and the pleasures intensify the activities, and what intensifies a thing is proper to it, but things different in kind have properties different in kind. This will be even more apparent from the fact that activities are hindered by pleasures arising from other sources. For people who are fond of playing the flute are incapable of attending to arguments if they overhear some one playing the flute, since they enjoy flute-playing more than the activity in hand; so the pleasure connected with flute-playing destroys the activity concerned with argument. (1175 a 30–b 6)

Also 'Now since activities are made precise and more enduring and better by their proper pleasure, and injured by alien pleasures, evidently the two kinds of pleasure [sc. proper and alien] are far apart' (1175 b 13–16).

Through enjoyment the activity enjoyed becomes itself more perfect—clearer, more discriminating, more fully what an activity of this kind should be. This increase in perfection cannot be explained merely by pointing to the suitability of the object and the excellence of the subject's pre-existing cognitive or sensory equipment. Those factors give rise to an activity perfect enough to be enjoyable, and that gives rise to enjoyment, which again builds itself on itself by perfecting the activity more. And through enjoyment the activity becomes more perfect not only in its quality but in its being. It is more self-assertive, less easy to break by distraction. For pleasure in one activity is death at the time to other activities, hence excludes any other pleasure that might otherwise undermine the activity and hence the enjoying of it.

We now see that the compresence of excellent subject and object is not quite sufficient for perfect activity. For it is also necessary that the subject not already be enjoying something else intensely. By perfecting the activity in the sense of making it *finer,* enjoyment also perfects it in the sense of *strengthening* it against competition. And this dual development is rooted in the subject's perfect, in the sense of *full,* absorption, which maintains and increases its own fullness by making the activity more interesting to a subject ever more keenly attuned to respond with the appropriate interest. There is a two-way dependence between determinacy as a property of the activity—its degree of form and refinement—and the subject's determinacy as undivided subject of just that activity, rather than host of an indiscriminate mass of inclinations. His concentration on what he is doing is not a deliberate carving of the activity into shape; rather, it creates an atmosphere in which the activity takes shape from itself. At any rate, that is what it is like in thinking and perceiving. This is analogous to practical thinking, where the sustained aim to pursue the summum bonum in pursuing an objective O sets up a kind of field in which the relevant aspects of the situation spring to attention and sort themselves out. This sorting out is the play of practical intelligence, and the analogy shows that something like intelligence permeates hedonic involvement.

Aristotle argues that for each specific activity there is a correspondingly specific pleasure (1175 a 21–30). Otherwise it would be a mystery that pleasure in one activity tends to kill other activities. For if every pleasure were the same in kind, the pleasure in one activity could extend itself to activities of other kinds, so that they could all be engaged in concurrently; and since the pleasure would be one, perhaps they would merge into one activity. As it is, pleasure not only keeps its activity going, but keeps it individual and distinctive. Pleasure is the source of form in the sense of *characteristic type* or *species* as well as of form in the sense of *shape* or *structure*. It is to the activity enjoyed (enjoyed into being, we might say) as soul to the living organism.

But now if enjoyment is something more than the activity enjoyed (although perhaps all we can say on Aristotle's showing is that it is neither something more nor nothing more), perhaps one is not entitled to hold that different sorts of activities imply different sorts of pleasures? For if pleasure in activity of type A is something other than A, why should it not be generically the same as pleasure in activity of type B?[23] We can avoid this if pleasures are nothing beyond the perfect activities themselves, but can we avoid it otherwise? If not, we lack grounds for accepting one of Aristotle's most important ethical conclusions: that pleasure in an inferior activity is an inferior pleasure, and pleasure in a good one is good (1175 b 24–29). It may also be suspected that if enjoyment of A is not just the activity A, this is because enjoyment of A is an effect of A. (This thought is readily combined with the thought that all pleasure is generically the same. In classical utilitarianism, the effect-status of pleasure is closely linked to the assumption that it is one homogeneous commodity.) But if Aristotle is moving in this direction, he may not be entitled to the claim that pleasure is itself an activity. For it is hard to categorise an activity as an effect.

Again the affirmation model helps. According to it, enjoying is an activity distinguishable by analysis from the activity enjoyed, as affirmation$_2$ from affirmation$_1$. The affirmations at every level have the same source: the subject's nature or nature-like disposition, manifested first in natural activity different for different natures, and logically next in that nature's welcoming and knowing the activity for its own. The common link with nature ensures the correspondence of kind of activity with kind of pleasure. Whoever understands enjoyment as a sort of knowing, and knowledge as a kind of mingling with or conforming to what is known, must regard it as reckless nonsense to claim that the knower runs no risk of acquiring a worth like the worth of his objects, or to claim that enjoyment may be good although what is enjoyed is not. So, too, in the model: if one affirms$_1$ that *p,* and *p* is false, affirmation$_1$ is faulty along with every higher-level affirmation that the next one down is sound. It is the same if one affirms$_1$ good (engages in) an activity that is not good: affirming$_2$ good (enjoying) affirmation$_1$ is worthless because the latter is, and so on up.

In the first two sections of this chapter I pressed the question why pleasure for Aristotle is so important a topic as to demand the penetrating discussions of *NE* VII and X. For it seemed as if all that he needed to say about pleasure for the purpose of ethics had already been said further back. At the start of the present section, I suggested an answer: that the clue to his involvement lies in the idea of pleasure as a form of pursuit and value-affirmation. But in this connection it is worth recalling that Aristotle is not more concerned that we value what deserves to be valued than that we value it in the right way. This consideration may be of some assistance when we start to address the difficult turns of his final arguments about happiness (see Chapter 7 below). But it also carries implications worth extracting now. First, *taking pleasure in* some good and noble activity is the quintessentially right way of valuing something valuable for its own sake. Since only through enjoyment are we undividedly engaged with it, our enjoyment is the most decisive possible acknowledgement of intrinsic worth. Second, if, as we are about to see detailed reasons for holding, enjoyment—and therefore what is enjoyed—can only be an activity, not a thing or a state or a product of action, nor the satisfaction of the need for some product or state or thing, then we have from this quarter further proof of the doctrine that happiness (the central good of the life rightly deemed happy) is an *activity*. For whatever it is that deserves the title of 'happiness' thereby counts as the ultimate good; hence it must be of a category such that it can be valued as the ultimate good should be; i.e., entirely for its own sake and with total practical commitment. It must therefore be logically capable of being enjoyed and hence must be an activity. And since happiness is the perfection of life, the activity which is happiness must actually *be* enjoyed when engaged in by those whose happiness it is. Simply being host to the activity is a lesser perfection than actively valuing it in the way it deserves.

## V. Against the Process Theory

The question whether pleasure, in either sense, is a process or activity matters to Aristotle because process, according to his technical concept, essentially arises from its subject's lack.[24] The subject moves or is moved into a new condition because the latter is better than its previous state, and when the new state is achieved the process must end, because mission accomplished there is nowhere else to go. Since process is grounded on lack of the end, i.e. lack of perfection, the seeming affiliations of *pleasure* with *knowledge, control, final good* and *nature* are all called into question if pleasure is process. Those other four concepts hang together, because first a being's final good is active functioning in accordance with its nature, the inner principle of its behaviour and definable form, and second the natures of all living things, including the insensate, are understood by Aristotle on the model of craft or skill (see, e.g., *Physics* II.3, and 199 a 9 ff.). Although a creature in the natural course of its existence is subject to privations, and so to restorative processes, its nature, strictly speaking, is not the source of these imperfections. Nature is active essence, definable only in positive terms. A restored healthy physical condition is not a state of inertia but a basis for healthy activity. Such activity is the most obvious manifestation of living nature, but it should also be seen as the logical continuation of the restoration process, since the goal of restoration is not simply a healthy state, but a state for further exercise. Since the exercise of health is nature at work, so, too, must the restoration process be. Thus the restoration too expresses the positive nature; the lack which it also expresses is not the *nature's* lack (for nature as such is not characterised by lack) but its occasion for restorative functioning.

Aristotle compares a natural living substance to a doctor treating himself (*Physics* 199 b 30–31); the difference is that the nature's 'patient' is *necessarily* the substance itself under its own nature's charge. Restoration, then, is both a restoring and a being restored: not easy to distinguish when agent and patient are necessarily the same individual. Restoration considered as a change in the patient is technically termed a 'process' or 'coming-to-be'; considered as the causing of that change, and as logically continuous with the exercise of the state restored, restoration is an 'activity'. In fact, restorative activity is already an exercise *of* (not merely *for*) health, since recovery assumes that the diseased creature is *healthy* enough to recover. Health, like pleasure, is self-reinforcing. Thus Aristotle says: 'Further, one kind of good being activity and another being state, the processes that restore us to our natural state are only incidentally pleasant; for that matter, the activity at work in the appetites for them is the activity of so much of our state and nature as has remained unimpaired' (1152 b 33–36; cf. 1153 a 14–15).

There are arguments in two places in *NE* X that pleasure is not a process. ('Pleasure' here means enjoying, but the affirmation model entails that the arguments also apply to pleasure in the sense of what is enjoyed.) Aristotle assumes the metaphysical triad: *process, state, activity*. Pleasure in either sense must be one of these. To reach his ultimate conclusion that it is an activity, he must show it to be neither a state nor a process. The first argument (1173 a 31–b 4) only proves it not a process: processes are fast or slow but enjoying is neither fast nor slow, although it may take more or less time to start enjoying oneself. But a state, too, is neither fast nor slow, though it may take more or less time to get into.

The second stretch of argument (1174 a 14–b 14) shows that enjoying is neither a process nor a state produced through a process. At moments Aristotle distinguishes these conclusions, but for most of the passage he seems to treat them as aspects of a single position. The point to which he wants to draw attention is that when someone goes on enjoying something, this is not because there is still more enjoying to do before full enjoyment is achieved. If that were so, we should stop enjoying something as soon as we were thoroughly enjoying it. But, if anything, the more we enjoy something, the more we go on doing and enjoying it; there is no intrinsic cutoff point as there is with a process. Enjoyment ceases because of external factors. (Here, 'external' covers physical impediments, distractions, fatigue, reasons for stopping based on other interests, and any other factors that undermine the conditions for excellent performance. For the moment let us leave to one side the classification of cases where enjoyment ceases because what is enjoyed is intrinsically limited or offers limited scope for enjoyment.) Aristotle begins by observing that enjoying is like seeing:

> Seeing seems to be at any moment complete [or: perfect], for it does not lack anything which coming into being later will complete its form; and pleasure also seems to be of this nature. For it is a whole, and at no time can one find a pleasure whose form will be completed if the pleasure lasts longer. (1174 a 14–19)

Aristotle does not mean that enjoyment cannot *increase,* though the words seem to imply this empirically false claim. What is his contrast? At this stage, not of enjoyment with process nor with the end-state of process, but, I think, with living creatures and artifacts considered as developing-then-developed. It takes time for the growing dog—the building under construction—completely to reach its form. And what the fully developed thing is, is what it could not completely be except through having developed. It essentially has a history, because its completeness is the completeness of something previously incomplete. The finished thing is an end, no doubt, but an end for which there had to have been a 'means'—its earlier developing self. Yet in the developing stages the creatures was just as truly a dog rather than a cat or a rat, the building as truly a warehouse rather than a temple or hospital, as when it is complete. For these are species whose members as such are developing-then-developed, since they cannot be fully actual otherwise. Thus the term 'dog' applies at every stage, but always with backward or forward reference to incomplete or complete development, and at mid-stages both forward and back. (The completed thing must be understood as a matter-form compound, and the reference to matter, from the 'complete' point of view, tells us that it grew or was made *from* something. Conversely, the 'incomplete' point of view refers to the form which is the limit of the development.) Now, Aristotle is saying that enjoyment is not a developing thing in this sense; which is not the same as to say that it cannot increase, for he surely knows that it can.

One can see something in a flash, and enjoy something in a flash, yet see or enjoy it fully (1174 b 5–9). Complete enjoyment does not require to be led up to by enjoyment previously incomplete. But Aristotle also means a stronger point: no enjoyment is incomplete through having its raison d'être in another, complete, version of itself. A thing that is underdeveloped exists at this stage only for the sake of being (having later become) developed. The building under construction is not merely an unfinished house: it is not a finished anything. Perhaps the walls and foundations are completely in place, but does it follow that nothing needs to be added to complete the form even of walls and foundations? They cannot actually function as what they are meant to be until they support a roof. The unfinished structure is of no significance as being anything now, and indeed there is nothing that it now *is*. It is significant now, of course: as now *becoming* the finished thing—hence now significant only as *that* (which it isn't) unfinished.

One can do something with mounting enjoyment, but the lesser enjoyment makes a point by itself, not merely as part of the greater. One learns that it was lesser by retrospective comparison. One did not miss anything of its essence, so to speak, if at the time one did not know it to be on the increase. (By contrast, we may not learn that the roofless walls were a temple under construction until we see the later stages of the work. In such cases we cannot learn until afterwards *what* it was that we saw before.) And when enjoyment increases, the less is not just a step towards the more (even if the more presupposes it), since one cannot enjoy in order to obtain greater enjoyment or for the sake of anything whatever ulterior.

Reasons for holding that enjoyment is not like an organism or artifact, essentially either developing into or developed from its finished or unfinished self, are also reasons for denying it to be either a pleasure-wards process or the end-state achieved by such a process. 'It is a dog' means 'It is becoming or has become an adult dog'. 'He is enjoying himself' does not mean 'He is coming to be, or he already is, in a state of fully developed pleasure'. In fact, on Aristotelian terms the first disjunct is absurd, since on those terms it implies that enjoyment is for the sake of something; and the second disjunct is false insofar as it implies that enjoyment is something that can be at the full only by having developed gradually.[25]

However, these considerations do not all quite show that enjoyment is no sort of process, only that it is not a coming-to-be of 'full grown' enjoyment. Now the process theorists made their mark by claiming that pleasure is a coming-to-be of the healthy or natural condition, whether they meant that what is enjoyed is such a process or that to enjoy something is to be subject of such a process. They did not consider the healthy condition to be a state of complete pleasure, but saw it, rather, as pleasureless and painless, and on this basis they held that pleasure is never an end but only the means to some good beyond the pleasure. On this view, it might seem consistent to hold that though all pleasure is process, sometimes ongoing pleasure is as full as it can be; for the process which pleasure is, on this theory, has an end other than fullness of pleasure.

Against this Aristotle points out that every process takes time—for instance, building a temple—and is complete only when the end is achieved (1174 a 20–21). His argument now (1174 a 21–b 6) becomes obscure, but I think it is this: suppose that there is a single process (e.g., a process of recovery) defined by its terminal states (or points), since these determine the form or kind of the process. And it is complete when it reaches its end. Now when is there any single pleasure that is fully enough pleasure to deserve the name? Is it when the process is complete, or is there pleasure throughout the process? Aristotle takes for granted that the first alternative is absurd. If there is no pleasure full enough to count as such except when the process reaches its end, then if pleasure is a process, there is no pleasure that is not wholly in the past, since the process is over upon reaching its end. Pleasure, then, must be an ongoing process, if there is any hope for the process theory of pleasure. But an ongoing process consists of many subprocesses, each with a different pair of termini, and therefore different in kind from each other and the whole. This is clear from his temple example, since temple building has different stages requiring workers with different skills, such as fitting stones together and fluting the columns (1174 a 21–24). We may not realise this, though, if we consider more homogeneous processes such as walking from here to there; but this, too, subdivides into smaller processes of distinct kinds, since every stage has its own pair of termini. He does not mention here that mathematical continuity ensures an infinity of stages within each stage, but probably means us to recall this. But if pleasure is the whole process while it lasts, there is no one pleasure throughout the time. For during each part of the time there is a subprocess that is not the whole. Perhaps these subprocesses are parts of something called 'pleasure' which is identified with the whole, but none of them *is* that pleasure. That is to say, we cannot think of the whole process as consisting of successive parts each the same in kind as it, hence each the same sort of pleasure as it, but shorter. For the parts differ from the whole not only in duration but form. Thus if any part is a pleasure, it is a distinct kind of pleasure from that consisting in the whole, as well as distinct from that consisting in any other part. Another point: it is even more dubious to identify subprocesses with pleasures than it is to identify the whole process with pleasure as a stretched out whole. For whereas a whole process is complete when it reaches its end, since then the purpose is achieved, each part is incomplete even when its own terminus *ad quem* is reached, because this terminus is not the end for the sake of which that part occurred. Nobody flutes a column for the sake of having done just that: this part of the process, even if carried through, is pointless in itself. But that cannot be true of any pleasure, however short. So if there is any single pleasure that is the process, this pleasure must be that process at its moment of completion, and we have not escaped the first alternative.

In fact, pleasure is more like the completion itself on which a process terminates. For the completion is 'endlike and whole' (whole in the sense of unitary and indivisible) (1174 b 7). This difference between pleasure and process should be clear from the fact that process requires divisible time, whereas pleasure is possible in a flash (1174 b 7–9). But if pleasure is completion, this explains why it is not itself brought to completion by a process. The temple is brought to completion, but the *completion* of the temple cannot be brought to completion. One cannot achieve the achieving of an end. Things that are brought into being by processes are divisible (which is why they have to develop bit by bit), but pleasure is like seeing, like a unit, like a geometrical point: these are all indivisible, like completion (1174 b 9–14).

What does Aristotle mean? Is it simply that pleasure can be instantaneous? But it can also last for a time, so is not much like a geometrical point which can *never* extend. And how can we make sense of pleasure's being *spatially* indivisible or without dimension? The literal suggestion is as meaningless as that pleasure is square or one inch long. But Aristotle invokes the geometrical point to illustrate something more fundamental which has nonspatial applications. A point is not first and foremost dimensionless, as if the question of size, finite or zero, were the main concern. 'Point' is a functional concept; geometrical points are what terminate and define lines. Because of this function they cannot have measure, for then they would not be determinants but parts of what is determined. A mid-point in a line has a further function in addition to its being one end of each of the subdivisions: it is the reference point whereby opposite directions away from it are determined. In this sense the present in time is a point determining past and future (*Physics* 223 a 4–8). It also unites past and future (222 a 10–20), since the reference point is necessarily shared by the opposite fields that converge on it. A point is what functions as a centre, and a percipient may be likened to a point (cf. *On the Soul,* 427 a 3–14). We perceive white things and black things at the same time, not to speak of things of different sense modalities, thus holding together in cognitive unity items which exclude each other from the same place or are too alien even to exclude each other. It is natural, too, to schematise unified growth as growth from a point: growth must, we think, be from somewhere "within" the body that grows, and where it is from must be one and without quantity (since otherwise *it* would have first to have grown). And growth and every development is to an end that limits it definingly as a point limits a line. Plato had consigned pleasure to the category of the indeterminate but determinable *(Philebus);* Aristotle's arguments make pleasure, like a point, a principle of determination (cf. 1173 a 15–17).[26]

Enjoyment, then, is not a *process,* nor a *product* or *state* built up bit by bit through process. But it seems that this argument for its being an *activity* proves too much. For when activity is distinguished from process and state, the most obvious example of activity is the exercise of the good state reached or the employment of a product (e.g., *playing* the flute). These exercises are not comings-to-be of anything; thus they are not intrinsically limited. Because of this they can go on indefinitely unless impeded, and the stages are of value in themselves, not only as means to what follows. These exercises are pleasures in the sense of *what is enjoyed,* and the affirmation model shows how the status of the enjoying follows that of what is enjoyed. Thus enjoying is an activity because what is enjoyed is. But now for the difficulty.

The process theory of pleasure was inspired by examples of physical pleasures in which the organism reverts to a stable or healthy condition. And Aristotle does not dispute that these are genuine pleasures. But the enjoyed recovery and the enjoyment of it are necessarily over when the lack has been repaired. How can these fail to count as pleasures, but how, if they count, can pleasure be activity? Aristotle's discussion in *NE* X seems to skirt this problem, since there his constant examples are perception and thought, where nothing is brought into being through development. But even these examples, when one considers them more concretely, present a difficulty. The intellectual or perceptual activity enjoyed may focus on a temporally limited object, as when one plays a sonata or listens to it being played. How is the playing or listening not intrinsically limited and so also the enjoyment of it; and how does this not endanger the conclusion that pleasure is an activity? For it seems that at least some *things that are enjoyed* are more like processes, with a beginning, middle and end; and if that is admitted it is not clear why one would be justified in maintaining that at any rate *the enjoying* is not a process, however odd it may seem to say that it is. The only alternative would be to insist that the only things enjoyed are activities that can continue indefinitely without running out of themselves. But this goes too far, because much, if not most, of what we enjoy is not like that. Some enjoyments are essentially transient, and one cannot shuffle out of the difficulty by claiming that this is true only of low-grade pleasures attendant on physiological processes without discounting one's own experience—or else betraying an inability to enjoy such "higher" pleasures as sonatas provide. And if the music is at all understood, it is not the case that each phase is enjoyed in self-sufficient isolation from the rest, any more than it was composed in isolation.

To the last point, however, we should add that although a passage is executed, heard and enjoyed in the light of *what* follows and *what* precedes, this is not at all only in order that what follows should actually *follow* and be enjoyed. In fact, if the work is familiar one could be said to be enjoying what follows before it physically arrives, and this is not made false if it fails to. Hence one may find it worth while to play or listen to something even knowing that one will have to stop before the end. But the earlier stages of a *process,* according to Aristotle's teleological conception, might as well never have occurred if they are not carried through to the end.

Despite his emphasis on thinking and perceiving, at 1175 a 34 Aristotle mentions house-building on a list of enjoyed activities—building being also a favourite example of process. What is enjoyed, of course, is not the growing of the structure— a series of changes in shape and placement of materials. The pleasure is not theirs but the builder's in exercising his skill and observing the successful outcome that confirms his powers. Even where a process is involved, pleasure is not an attribute of that process, which is nothing but the filling of a space in its passive subject; for pleasure is the manifestation of agency and positive nature. But to see clearly how this case falls into line with those paradigms of activity where no intrinsic terminus applies, we must go beyond the distinction between active and passive sides of building and other such cases which aim for an external product or state. Leaving aside, then, the patiency of the changed materials, let us look at the agent's action in two ways. We can think of him either as building these materials up into a house or as engaging in house-building, the occasion for which is provided by these materials. (In a real life case it may be a bit of both.) On the first description he cannot continue what he is doing when this unfinished house is finished. On the second, the rôle of the materials is less that of patient affected by what he does than of means by which he does what he does; namely, exercise his craft. And this can continue even when those particular means are played out. He enjoys himself as a builder of houses, not of *this* house. Enjoyment relates to the logical universal in a way in which process does not. For although the process is from these materials to *a* finished house, not to any one in particular (since a particular house would be one that exists already), the process is so that there should *be* a house which will be pointed to as 'this particular house'. The objective of process, then, is expressed by a universal representing a future instance of the type in question, and destined to be superseded by an actual particular of the type. The moment of superseding is the completion of the process; thus the logical universality of the end proclaims the process incomplete. By contrast, enjoyment of house building focuses on the universal 'house' for the sake of that very focusing. It, too, is concerned with a future *this house,* but the future particular will get built only because concern with such a thing while as yet unbuilt is a vehicle to support the principal concern, namely the agent's interest in building *a house* or *houses.* Since the house-building, here, is not engaged in primarily so that there should *be* a future particular, the fact that as yet no particular house has resulted is not a ground for saying that the end of house-building is unattained and the activity incomplete. Similarly, when a particular house does result, this is no ground for saying that the activity called 'building a house' is now (as not before) complete and cannot continue. For if it was not incomplete before and still continued from then until now, it may also continue on from now, even though now complete. Perhaps in this way we can understand how Aristotle sees *enjoyed* house-building as an activity whose end is possessed and present even as it still goes on.

I indicated a distinction between ways in which universals function as objects, respectively, of an enjoyed activity and a process. In the latter context the universal holds the ring for a future particular, in the former it does not. This difference corresponds to, and indeed might also be analysed as, a distinction of grammatical aspects. The objective of process is to *have reached* the end: of an activity such as the exercise of a productive skill, the objective is to *be reaching*—not any particular *it,* but something of this kind. This is why the difference between activity and process cannot be adequately characterised as the difference between active and passive sides of, for example, building. For an agent, qua agent, may be concerned only to get done (or made) what he is doing (or making). He may be doing it so as to have done it, whatever the benefit of this may be. When his end is to have done, he proceeds only because it is not yet the case that he has done. This agency counts as process since it stems from a negative condition. But enjoyment centres on doing, not on having done, where having done is a result that supersedes doing. It would therefore be reasonable to say that enjoyment is not at all concerned with having done (except incidentally). This assumes that *having done* lies beyond *doing,* as in the developmental examples. Certainly it is these examples that teach us the aspectual distinction. Aristotle, however, prefers to think of *having done* as not necessarily the remote and external product of doing. This is because he equates *having done* with perfection and full actuality. The equation is not self-evidently necessary, and it may even be a mistake. There seems no incoherence in holding that one type of perfection is in doing, another in having done. Thus metaphysical perfection need not be restricted to the perfect tense. But Aristotle in effect does so restrict it; hence he is obliged to hold that if what is enjoyed is perfect and enjoyed as perfect, then what is enjoyed is a doing that is, at each moment, a having done. Thus the best examples of enjoyed activities are ones such as seeing and intellectual grasping, of which one can say: 'To see is to have seen, to grasp is to have grasped' (*Metaphysics* 1048 b 22–34). This does not imply what it may seem to, that to see is immediately to put the seeing behind one as over and done with, but rather the opposite: that the perfection of seeing is *not* in its being over and done with, since *present* seeing is perfect.


### VI. Nature, Pleasure and Reason

Eudoxus, Aristotle tells us, held that pleasure is the good:

> because he saw all things, both rational and irrational, aiming at it, and because in all things that which is the object of choice is what is excellent, and that which is most the object of choice the greatest good; thus the fact that all things moved towards the same object indicated that this was for all things the chief good (for each thing, he argued, finds its own good, as it finds its own nourishment); and that which is good for all things and at which all aim was *the* good. His arguments were credited more because of the excellence of his character than for their own sake; he was thought to be remarkably temperate, and therefore it was thought that he was not saying what he did say as a friend of pleasure, but that the facts really were so. (1172 b 9–18)

These are surprising remarks about the credibility of Eudoxus' position, because this passage comes on the heels of the one where Aristotle takes certain moralists to task for preaching a rule which they cannot keep—that all pleasure is to be avoided—with the consequence that they bring discredit to the limited truth behind what they say. But in Eudoxus' case, the difference between doctrine and practice makes the doctrine more compelling. If Eudoxus had adopted the way of life which perhaps he prescribes—that of following every impulse towards pleasure—no one could take him seriously enough even to consider whether his position is consistent, either internally or with his behaviour. Someone who lives like that, a slave to every passing inclination, cannot be expected to represent a position at all. Philebus, in Plato's dialogue, is the devotee of pleasure who lives his devotion; and Philebus, as Plato shows, is incapable of putting forward a rational case for pleasure or listening to anyone else's arguments. The work has to be done for him by Protarchus, who is very soon induced by Socrates to qualify his position on rational grounds—whether or not he 'feels like it'.

But it is not only easy but wasteful to dismiss this sort of hedonism on the ground than in its unadulterated form it cannot offer a rational case for itself. The dismissal is strictly fair, and it may entitle us to assert a contrary view, but this victory sheds no light on the truth, if any, in that form of hedonism. The enemies of all pleasure can be led easily enough to see that their stated position exaggerates; they can, and should, modify it themselves. The slaves of pleasure are led solely by impulse; thus we cannot leave it to them, since this is the same as leaving it to chance, to carve out what is true in their claim. Whoever does this for them must be one who does not live their claim to the full; and the same is true of whoever (like Protarchus and Eudoxus) proposes the claim for serious consideration.

In reporting that Eudoxus' arguments were found plausible because of their author's character rather than on account of their own merits, Aristotle may mean to indicate his own disagreement with some of the arguments, or he may be saying that even if the arguments were intellectually sound, this was not why they succeeded with Eudoxus' followers. In any event, Aristotle himself endorses the argument retailed above. The grounds and extent of his endorsement are our main questions in this section and the next, though we can surmise in advance that Eudoxus' position in the form in which Aristotle accepts it has none of the sting that made it initially remarkable that a person of outstanding temperance should hold such a view. At any rate, the position is that pleasure is the good, on the ground that (1) all animals, rational and nonrational, seek pleasure, and (2) what is sought by all is the good, although what is pleasant and good for each kind depends on the kind, just as what is nutritious.

On the second premiss Aristotle says: 'Those who object that that at which all things aim is not necessarily good are talking nonsense. For we say that that which everyone thinks really is so; and the man who attacks this belief will hardly have anything more credible to maintain instead' (1172 b 35–1173 a 2). Given his own starting point in the *Nicomachean Ethics,* we can hardly expect Aristotle (who perhaps borrowed it from Eudoxus) to question the principle 'That at which all things aim is the good'. Here, moreover, the principle rests on an argument: what all aim for is what seems good to all, and what seems good to all is good, since what seems so to all is so—or at any rate we have to proceed as if it is, since if we reject universal intuition, we shall get no firmer a starting point.

Certainly, *if* the first premiss is true and all creatures seek pleasure, so that there is a universal behavioural judgment that pleasure is good (and, if nothing else is sought, that only pleasure is good), this universal intuition cannot be taken less seriously than various unargued shared assumptions by which Aristotle himself got started earlier, as for instance that justice and temperance are virtues. But the premiss is weak. This version of hedonism needs the support of the rest of the animal kingdom, for if one consulted men alone they would say that often enough they shun pleasure or ought to shun it. But do animals experience pleasure? We know that they do many things that we consider pleasant. Only do they notice pleasant sensations, or experience an enhanced sense of vitality, or do they simply do whatever they have to in order to survive? Do they, any more than we, enjoy all those things, such as the struggle to reach the breeding grounds on time, the labour of feeding and defending their young? Does 'pursuing pleasure' perhaps mean no more than pursuing whatever one is unreflectingly driven to? In that case, premiss (1) fails for much human behaviour. Or does it mean doing whatever one does that is not done under compulsion? In that case it holds tautologically for animals and men alike.

These remarks are not so much intended in criticism as to show the utterly unempirical nature of premiss (1).[27] So far as it applies to nonrational animals, it appears to have been accepted on all sides of the early Academic debate about hedonism. One suspects that 'pleasure' here means little more than 'what all nonrational sentient beings pursue'. From Aristotle's last quoted remarks, it seems that opposition centred on premiss (2), that what is sought by all is the good. It also centred on the application of both premisses to human beings; thus at the end of the *Philebus* Plato says:

> And not even if every cow and horse and the whole animal kingdom spoke for it by their pursuit of enjoyment should it [sc. pleasure] be given first place; although most people put in animals the trust prophets put in birds, and so think pleasures are the most powerful factors in making a good life for us. They consider the loves of animals the decisive criterion rather than the loves of arguments which have constantly prophesied under the inspiration of the philosophic muse. (67 b)[28]

Reason in us, Plato asserts, plays or should play the guiding role of pleasure in animals. And if we, too, must make concessions to the pleasure principle, this is because of the nature we share with animals, not because of what is distinctively ours. No doubt there are pure pleasures of perception and reasoning, as Plato himself points out, but might not these belong to us only because we are embodied intelligences, and not because we are intelligences? And the demotion of pleasure, as well as its restriction to the physical sphere, is further reinforced by the uncritical dogma (not shared by Plato) that pleasure is only process.

This view or collection of views threatens Aristotle's position, but not because he thinks for a moment that human beings should follow the lead of other animals in the kinds of pleasures they seek. The threat stems from his connection of *pleasure* with *nature*. Aristotle accepts that every kind of creature has pleasures proper to its kind (1176 a 3–8), and he wants to extend this principle to human beings. For if the pleasure of animals is the expression of their nature, anyone who contends that rational functioning is or should be intrinsically without pleasure opens the way to doubts about rational human nature. We may be uniquely rational, but is rationality our *nature* if it is pleasureless? And if reason is beyond nature, including any nature of ours, how can *our* good be our good as *rational* beings, since the good of each kind is marked out by its nature? We have a share in rationality, but if it is not our nature, perhaps we have no special nature, and no distinctively human good. Or (which is almost the same for ethics) rationality is something additional to our nature: it is only incidental or at most instrumental to our real, natural, nonrational good. And on what model can we understand that good if not by the example of healthily functioning animals?

Such a conclusion need not commit us to denying significant distinctions between the human good and the various goods of nonhuman species. The human good, like that of no other species, is realised through acquired culture: by a second nature built up and maintained through habituation. But it is by a kind of instinct that the elders of each generation pass on their cultural ways, and as if by instinct the young assimilate these lessons. Culture is as truly a form of life as life on the biological level, since culture is naturally self-transmitting. What place is there here, if all goes as it should, for the tinkerings of reflective reason? Reflective reason takes on a distinct identity only when it stands over against the forces of cultural inclination. Its relation to these when it undertakes to steer and shape them, either day to day or on a grander scale, is logically the same as its relation to the lower animal impulses. Now even if there is room for improvement by reflective reason, does it follow that reflective reason is the truest expression of human nature? Does it not rather follow that true human nature, the prereflective spontaneity of culture, is not always as healthy and coherent as it should be? Sometimes we need skilled medical attention, but that was never a ground for arguing that we ought each to develop medical skills ourselves in order to be well (cf. 1143 b 32–33). It is better, because more self-sufficient, when the organism finds its own untutored way back to health. And there could *be* no recovery, even with a physician's aid, unless health 'underlies' the sickness to reassert itself in spontaneous response.

Those who elevate reflective reason to a sphere beyond pleasure and pain may think that they are setting the highest human activity on the pedestal which it deserves. In fact they invite the antirationalist response that reason is not integral to our nature, since nature on every level speaks the language of pleasure and pain. Practical wisdom is an external subsidiary, called in to help correct the occasional deficiencies of our nature. It cannot then be that nature's *own* peak and flowering. But practical wisdom has this much in common with the non-rational nature which it serves: both are concerned to realise a good necessarily dependent on one or another set of material and social conditions. Hence if practical wisdom is adventitious, what are we to say of reason in its theoretical mode, whose objects are 'forms without matter' and whose operation is not limited by dependence on a physical organ nor (ideally) coloured by cultural perspectives? How can this activity of reason be ours by *our* nature, even if we sometimes 'participate' in it or think we do? There are difficulties enough in understanding this even for those whose own experience testifies to the delights of pure theoretic activity. But theirs is not a common experience. Most people feel left out of the conversation when intellectuals enthuse about intellectual activity. So if in addition certain experts lay it down that intellectual activity is really neither painful nor pleasant, others have all the more reason for taking no interest and dismissing the whole thing as eccentric vapouring. Philosophers who declare the pleasures of the intellect nonexistent or incidental risk unravelling the one thread binding such activity to our nature as human beings. On what ground, then, can they claim a place for it in society?

Reason is divine; what else is God but the free play of intelligence undistracted and undiluted by physical and historical embodiment? So (it may be thought), although we may hope to benefit from reason sometimes, and even to glimpse its nature, we cannot regard it as ours. Aristotle will argue against this humility when he turns explicitly to the place of theoretic activity in human life:

> We must not follow those who advise us, being men, to think of human beings, and being mortal, of mortal things, but must, so far as we can, make ourselves immortal, and strain every nerve to live in accordance with the best things in us; for even if it be small in bulk, much more does it in power and worth surpass everything. (1177 b 31–1178 a 2)

This makes sense only if the human essence, like the divine, is rational. We shall see in Chapter 7 how considerations about pleasure help to uphold the claim of *theōria* to be reckoned the perfection of genuinely *human* happiness. But in the debate on pleasure more is at issue than the simple suggestion that in fancying our nature rational, we set ourselves up as more divine than we are. So far as this implies that we may be offending a deity, Aristotle could answer that taking ourselves to be less than we are would be no less offensive to what we are than taking ourselves to be more; and no less an offence against the divine when the divine is a principle *in us*. But warnings not to offend in this direction carry no single message when different kinds of divinity are possibly involved. Divinity is immortal and eternally self-regenerating, and Aristotle's audience is under no religious or theological constraint to reserve the title of 'god' to a unique being. Human divination interprets the flight of birds, but that flight itself, by comparison with the calculated steps of human beings, is a kind of inspired behaviour more regular in its workings than human prophecy. Nonrational animals divine their way to their good of which they have not the slightest inkling except to follow the dictates of pleasure and pain. In short, the advocates of nonrational pleasure can invoke divinity on their side, too, whether they speak of Aphrodite, the universal power of union and propagation or whether they suppose for each species a special unquenchable spark that sustains it in being to eternity. For example:

> And indeed the fact that all things, both brutes and men, pursue pleasure is an indication of its being somehow the chief good:
>
> > No voice is wholly lost that many peoples. . . .
>
> But since no one nature or state either is or is thought the best for all, neither do all pursue the same pleasure; yet all pursue pleasure. And perhaps they actually pursue not the pleasure they think they pursue nor that which they would say they pursue, but the same pleasure; for all things have by nature something divine in them. (1153 b 25–32)

Those who warn that we transgress our boundaries if we claim reflective reason as our own nature need not be implying that reason is divine and we dross, but rather that *our* divinity is different: a force as immortal as the force of reason, but one that works through impulse and pleasure, not argument. To this one can return the following reply (and the passage above from Aristotle prepares the way for it): if even in animals (and in humans as animals) there is something divine that intimates itself through pleasure, how can divine *reason* be without its pleasures?

The debate carried on in these schematic terms might swing indefinitely from side to side: closer analysis is needed to force the issue. Aristotle's analysis (which is also something of a construction) is conveyed in his theory of pleasure as self-enhancing activity. This is sufficient to answer the neutralists and any who twist the neutralist thesis into a ground for advocating animal hedonism or cultural inclinationism. Let us see how the answer is effective.

The standard observation that intellectual activity is enjoyable cannot carry much weight in this context, even if one adds that the pleasure in question does not presuppose noticeable pain or defect. As an empirical claim this is easily discounted in a debate where all parties agree in treating 'pleasure' as a metaphysical symbol from which each seeks to derive a different universal lesson. (If the neutralists find themselves having to concede that human intellectuals enjoy intellectual activity, they can always insist that intellectualising *at its best* carries no enjoyment.) Instead, what is needed is an account that grounds pleasure in the ruling principle of each species. That will secure the connection of reason with pleasure and hence the connection of reason with human nature. Now these connections do not have to be argued from scratch: it is enough to dispel the negative appearances that bring them into doubt. Aristotle does this by means of his conception of pleasure as activity, which is founded partly on arguments special to the topic and partly on his general metaphysics.

'Pleasure is activity' owes its significance, as well as its cogency, to more than one metaphysical assumption: as, for example, (1) that *process, state* and *activity* exhaust the possible categories, (2) that process and the development of a state are grounded in privation. The second in particular, declaring as it does the metaphysical inferiority of process, gives Aristotle his motive for arguing that pleasure is not process. And his argument, it must be admitted, rests partly on considerations that have no independent force; for instance, the endlikeness of pleasure, self-evident from everyone's experience. That says nothing about whether pleasure is process unless we assume that process is essentially a means to an ulterior end the lack of which provides the raison d'être of the process. But other considerations carry weight of their own. Whether or not one accepts the teleological interpretation of process, it is a fact that processes take time, are comparable as faster and slower, are characterised as *from* something *to* something. Analogous facts hold for the states and products developed through processes: they take time to build up, they grow quickly or slowly, they are built up from something given or from a starting point. As for pleasure: whatever one's theory of pleasure, it is a fact that one can enjoy something in a flash; that it is meaningless to speak of enjoying fast or slowly; and that it is meaningless, too, to apply 'from A to B' to enjoying.

For these independent reasons pleasure does not fit into the category of process. Aristotle can explain the failure of fit by invoking the standard metaphysical assumption that process is meanslike and privational, and simultaneously stressing the positive, endlike character of pleasure. But that by itself does not establish the conception of pleasure as activity, even if we were to grant in an abstract way that what is not a process or a state developed through process must be an activity. So far, all that we know about the third member of this trio is that it does not presuppose privation; but the notion of activity is a good deal richer than that. The arguments against pleasure as process or state really serve only to confirm the starting point of Aristotle's theory. For the positive, endlike quality of pleasure would normally be considered a datum for any account; but the theory that pleasure is process (under a teleological interpretation of 'process') challenged our right to take this datum at face value. Aristotle's attack on the process theory (and its affiliate that pleasure is a state) merely reaffirms that right.

The route to the activity theory goes through Aristotle's metaphysics of living substances. For he means by 'activity' not merely an actual thing definable in positive terms, but a living source of actuality. Animals and all organic beings are clearly substances, according to this metaphysics, because they have within themselves the principle of their organised being. Artifacts are dubious substances, because they cannot 'come alive' in action (fulfil the end which explains their design) except through external agency. Aristotle castigates various opponents for making animal pleasures the paradigms; but he, too, takes them as paradigmatic though not in the sense of providing the definitive empirical examples of pleasure. Animals are paradigm subjects of pleasure, since it is a "fact" accepted on all sides that animals live by and for pleasure; and animals for Aristotle are paradigm metaphysical substances. These two "facts" cannot be unrelated, and the relation, as Aristotle discerns it, is that pleasure marks the activity of the self-substantiating essence which, according to him, is what an animal is.

The paradigm concept of *animal pleasure* has utterly different ethical implications under different metaphysical theories of natural entities. A contrast will clarify Aristotle's position. One may hold that the natural world, individual animals included, is the product of divine craft. This was the vision of the *Timaeus,* which in this connection can be ranked with theologies where 'creator' replaces 'craftsman', since natural living things, on either view, are products, whether *ex nihilo* or from unformed matter. So, if animals feel pleasure, that is their nature as the *products* that they are. Even the soul is a made thing, in the *Timaeus.* The nature (so-called) of a living thing, including its soul, is not metaphysically self-explanatory nor explicable as the presently instanced principle of self-propagation already instanced by earlier members of the species. The ultimate explanation lies in an external divine maker, a being of altogether different type. The pleasures of animals are amongst his effects, and the functional rôle of those pleasures is just what we should expect, given divine external design. Those pleasures, and anything analogous, are his only as a product is his and not as an activity. For if animals are the paradigm subjects of pleasure and animals are products, it is certain that paradigm pleasure does not belong with the originative principle. So any philosopher disposed to assimilate reason in us to divine reason is bound to conclude that reason, the sole originative principle, is beyond pleasure and beyond human nature so far as human nature is part of the natural world. Modern idealist theories give a similar result: if the paradigm subjects of pleasure belong (as nonrational animals are supposed to) squarely within the order of nature, they and all their dispositions, the psychological included, are nothing but ideas or phenomena. Whatever in us is or is like the power which constitutes the world of experience must stand beyond pleasure and inclination.

But Aristotle's God is not the craftsman of nature, because nature is full of living things; and life, as Aristotle understands it, is a source and cannot be an effect, product or infusion. The animal paradigm of pleasure no longer implies that pleasure is metaphysically deficient or dependent. For this reason, the concept of pleasure can now be dissociated from that of a body perceived by the senses. Pleasure belongs with the forming principle, not with the matter under formation, nor even with the empirical formed result except so far as this is viewed as the living animal itself, hence as the *source* of continuing self-formation. Pleasure and life are 'yoked together':

> One might think that all men desire pleasure because they all aim at life; life [*zoē*] is an activity, and each man is active about those things and with those faculties that he loves most; e.g. the musician is active with his hearing in reference to tunes, the student with his mind in reference to theoretical questions, and so on in each case; now pleasure completes the activities, and therefore life, which they desire. It is with good reason, then, that they aim at pleasure too, since for everyone it completes life, which is desirable. But whether we choose life for the sake of pleasure or pleasure for the sake of life is a question we may dismiss for the present. For they seem to be bound up together and not to admit of separation, since without activity pleasure does not arise, and every activity is completed by pleasure. (1175 a 10–21)

It is perhaps common ground that pleasure is a dimension of life as lived by the particular being that lives it. What is distinctive about Aristotle's view is the underlying metaphysics which ensures that the living being is its life's own source, and *as such* is the subject of pleasure. The individual lives by engaging in its natural activities; these are *its* natural activities only because by engaging in them it constitutes itself a living *it;* by engaging it appropriates them as its own, and this appropriation is pleasure: the agent's celebration and also its sign to itself of successful self-constitution.

There are different spheres of life and self-realisation. Once we understand that pleasure is a dimension of vital activity as such, we draw the correct lesson from the animal paradigm: that animal pleasure is physical because the life of an animal is defined in terms of functions played out through exercise of bodily organs. The governing principle here has a physical sphere to govern; this fact determines the kinds of pleasures possible on this level. Just so, human practical reason operates in and through the nonrational cultural material of second nature; and theoretical reason, again, has its own objects and objectives. Bodily pleasure is bodily not qua pleasure, but because the body and bodily sensations are central to certain pleasurable activities. But these represent just one level, the commonest, of keen vitality, and the rational and spiritual levels necessarily generate pleasures of their own.

## VII. The Limits of Hedonism

In Aristotle's opinion, the respect accorded to Eudoxus' hedonism owed more to Eudoxus' exceptional morality than to the intellectual quality of his arguments. Aristotle himself, it would seem, has repaired any theoretical inadequacy in Eudoxus by advancing the metaphysical analysis of pleasure as grounded in activity. But now we may wonder whether Aristotle's assistance has not cost him the independent position carved out earlier in the *Ethics,* in terms of which the pleasant is often opposed to the noble and the good. For the deep connections, on the one hand of pleasure with nature (or naturelike disposition), on the other of nature with the good of the indi-

vidual thus natured, suggest that whatever activity is pleasant is also good, at any rate
for the individual concerned. Is Aristotle now committed to this conclusion?

One could express this as a question about the extent of Aristotle's commitment
to hedonism. But it is important to be clear about the form of hedonism at issue. It
is not the theory that 'good' means 'pleasant' or vice versa. Nor is it the theory that
the pleasantness of something is necessarily a 'good-making' characteristic, so that
what is pleasant is good because pleasant (as distinct from, e.g., known to be good
because known to be pleasant). We cannot be sure that Eudoxus did not mean or
partly mean to propose either or both of these positions. But neither would have
attracted Aristotle in the slightest, I suspect. What Aristotle does take seriously is the
assumption that animals, *in* pursuing pleasure, pursue their good. 'Good' here refers
to healthy survival and propagation. These are the proper ends or goods of the species
independently of its being pleasant to pursue or attain them. For nonsentient creatures, too, survival and propagation is the end and good. In lacking pleasure, as they
lack perception, plants do not lack some extraordinary kind of good; rather, they lack
(not needing it) a hedonic guidance system. Whatever Eudoxus may have meant,
whether clear or confused, the force of his position from Aristotle's point of view can
only lie in this generalisation about nonrational animals: in them their good speaks
in the language of pleasure, because they are constituted by nature to enjoy and be
attracted to what conduces to their good. If pleasure as a rule led animals to sickness
and premature death (an impossible hypothesis, if one holds, like Aristotle, that the
species are eternal and that animals act for pleasure), no one would take seriously
the proposal that pleasure is the good even in their case; and philosophers on all sides
would not be faced with the question 'Should that proposal be extended to take in
man?' The neutralists answer 'No' to this, not on the modern ground that the 'pleasant' means one thing and 'good' another, but on the ground that reason in us takes
the place of pleasure in animals. As Descartes might have said, animals have only
the *teachings* of nature, whereas we have the *light* of nature (although he himself
would not have applied this concept to anything in the sphere of ethics and practice).
The process theory, a pillar of neutralism, should be read as an attempt to accommodate the near-necessary connection in animals between pleasure and well-being
in such a way as to block any inference to unrestricted hedonism for man.

Animals are like Eudoxus. They "believe" (in action) that pleasure is the good
(or that whatever is pleasant is good). Possessing no independent concept (let alone
independent knowledge) of their good, they "believe" that what is good (what is to
be pursued) is good because it is pleasant, and for them it is by no naturalistic fallacy
that 'good' and 'pleasant' mean the same. They cannot make a theory out of this,
and we who can—who can raise all sorts of questions about truth and meaning—are
well placed to see that such a theory is false, even though if we were mere animals
we should be unable to conceive of any other truth. Whoever by argument seeks to
elevate the animal viewpoint into an ethical theory has to be arguing poorly. Yet the
viewpoint in its own sphere should command respect. For most animals resemble
Eudoxus in the goodness and moderation of their lives, though he in this is exceptional amongst members of his own kind. Animals' pleasures, however intense, are
seldom ill-timed or inordinate, because their nature generally ensures that the con-

ditions under which a hedonic interest is beneficial are just the conditions under which it is aroused.

Human individuals can survive even habitual indulgence in excessive and untimely pleasures, because society has the resources (family support, medical skill etc.) to counteract the damage. Often the individual himself organises his life so as to reduce the risks. Aristotle regards it as a vicious abuse of reason to plan one's life around lowly or trivial pleasures when other goals are possible. But the enjoyed activities may be good in themselves because healthy, and harmless when not taken to excess. On the other hand, some enjoyments by their very nature show a stunted or perverted character. Pleasure perfects the activity, which is to say that it locks the agent in still further, developing even in the act his propensity for acting so. If, for example, the activity is childish, unchecked indulgence keeps the subject on the same childish level. It may be that immature nonrational animals enjoy things to which their elders are indifferent, but the same plexus of instincts that switches hedonic interest on and off for the appropriate occasions also takes care of the normal passage to maturity; thus animals become adult without having to go out of their way to learn new pleasures or give up old ones. In us there is necessarily a gap between our first nature, childish and animal, and human life at its best, since otherwise there would be no scope for second nature and reason. The gap is a space in which misplaced or deforming pleasures can flourish, often with the aid of culture and reason themselves. Such pleasures conflict with the human good; but the conditions which make them possible are necessary for that good.

Aristotle's metaphysical account of pleasure may not be hard to reconcile with the ethical commonplace that some of our pleasures are bad, so long as the commonplace is confined to circumstantially bad pleasures, indulged in at the wrong time of life, on the wrong occasions, to an immoderate degree etc.; and so long as we do not consider too closely the standing dispositions of the individuals concerned. For the pleasures are not bad in principle. But what if the person is constituted (whether or not by his own fault) so that he cannot engage without engaging immoderately, or can never fulfill the normal human potential for 'higher pleasures'? What is more (though we may disagree about examples), many would wish to say, and among them Aristotle, that some people take pleasure in things which it is never all right or good to enjoy: which are always disgusting, despicable or even wicked. Some natural or naturelike dispositions are mutilations or perversions of the human norm. And if it is true that the temperate and just take pleasure in their temperate and just actions, how is it not also true that the greedy and arrogant enjoy their greed and arrogance?

There is a dilemma.[29] Aristotle can stress the deviance of these dispositions from the sane and decent norm, while identifying that norm with human nature. In that case he can retain the connection between nature and the good: good human activity is in accordance with human nature. It follows, however, that constitutional deviants do not, qua deviant, exercise any sort of nature: they are not properly human beings nor properly anything else. That would not matter (for the purpose of the present discussion) were it not for the fact that they get genuine pleasure from the activities in question, and Aristotle grounds pleasure in the exercise of what is positive, not what is defective. But the alternative leads towards a disturbing relativism: those individuals have positive natures different from what we parochially take as the human norm or ideal. The proof is that they do enjoy acting accordingly. So must we not admit that each such disposition is a distinct species, only generically human? In that case, each has its own characteristic pleasures, the good man his and the corrupt man his, just as dogs and men have different pleasures. The point is that the corrupt man's pleasures are not corrupt by the standard of his nature: they are merely different from the pleasures of those who judge him corrupt. As Aristotle says:

> Each animal is thought to have a proper pleasure, as it has a proper function, viz, that which corresponds to its activity. If we survey them species by species, too, this will be evident; horse, dog, and man have different pleasures, as Heraclitus says 'asses would prefer sweepings to gold'; for food is pleasanter than gold to asses. (1176 a 5–8)

If we go this way, we should no more condemn or sorrow over the corrupt man (as we term him) for his peculiar pleasures than we condemn the donkey for preferring oats. And the corrupt man has equal right to regard us as corrupt or as donkeys. The fact that some enjoyed activities are undesirable under what we may regard as normal social conditions shows only that that is not where their subjects belong (any more than a wolf belongs among sheep); not that they have no legitimate place of their own in the scheme of things, perhaps in some other culture. Thus all undesirable pleasures in the end are 'intrinsically good but misplaced'. This preserves the connection of pleasure with positive nature, but by sacrificing a unitary notion of human nature.

For Aristotle the second alternative is out. He cannot accept a position which entails that a bad human being is really a good or passable human being, even if in some different sense of 'human being' from that which we thought we were committed to in the *Ethics*. He adopts a version of the first alternative, making a move similar to a move which he made over rational choice. Rational choice, in the strict, unqualified, primary sense is taken with a view to the unrestricted best; thus the choices of craftsmen as such, and of incontinent agents, are rational choices in a secondary sense, since they are directed towards a restricted good or what is good only under circumstances different from those that obtain (see Chapter 4, Section I). He says this about pleasure in *NE* X:

> They [sc. pleasures] vary to no small extent, in the case of men at least; the same things delight some people and pain others, and are painful and odious to some, and pleasant to and liked by others. This happens, too, in the case of sweet things; the same things do not seem sweet to a man in a fever and a healthy man—nor hot to a weak man and one in good condition. The same happens in other cases. But in all such matters that which appears to the good man is thought to be really so. If this is correct, as it seems to be, and excellence and the good man as such are the measure of each thing, those also will be pleasures which appear so to him, and those things pleasant which he enjoys. If the things he finds tiresome seem pleasant to some one, that is nothing surprising; for men may be ruined and spoilt in many ways; but the things are not pleasant, but only pleasant to these people and to people in this condition. (1176 a 10–22)

At first sight this passage says that morally degenerate pleasures are not real: they are only illusions of enjoyment, and nonillusory pleasures are the prerogative of the virtuous. But other passages show that the contrast is not between really enjoying oneself and being under the mistaken impression that one is enjoying oneself. That is, the difference is not between someone who does and someone who does not correctly recognise his state of mind as one of enjoyment.[30] It would be strange indeed if shameful likings were never really likings at all but only felt as if they were. And it would be almost equally strange for Aristotle to preach this improbable doctrine. In fact, however, the contrast is between something's being pleasant *absolutely* or *without qualification* (or, as he sometimes says, *by nature*), and something's being pleasant *only to* or *for someone*. For example:

> When their nature is in its settled [i.e. healthy] state . . . they enjoy the things that are pleasant without qualification, [otherwise they enjoy] the contraries of these as well; for then they enjoy sharp and bitter things, none of which is pleasant either by nature or without qualification. Nor, then, are the pleasures; for as pleasant things differ, so do the pleasures arising from them. (1153 a 3–7)

And

> Things absolutely pleasant to a body are those pleasant to a healthy and unaffected body, e.g. seeing in light, not darkness, though the opposite is the case to one with ophthalmia. And the pleasanter wine is not that which is pleasant to one whose tongue has been spoilt by inebriety (for they add vinegar to it), but that which is pleasant to sensation unspoiled. So with the soul; what is pleasant not to children or brutes, but to the adult, is really pleasant; at least, when we remember both we choose the latter. And as the child or brute is to the adult man, so are the bad and foolish to the good and sensible. To these, that which suits their state is pleasant, and that is the good and noble. (*EE* 1235 b 35–1236 a 6)

Pleasures grounded in defective dispositions are not pleasures in the unqualified, primary, sense: they are pleasures merely *for* (or *to*) the person concerned. Thus shameful pleasures, Aristotle says, should not be called pleasures at all except in relation to corrupted people (1176 a 22–23). Of course, the corrupted people themselves regard them as pleasures without qualification. That is the mistake: not to imagine that they are enjoying themselves when they are not, but to suppose that when they do enjoy (and know that they do) something shameful, they are entitled to regard the thing as simply 'pleasant', without qualification, rather than as pleasant merely to *them*. Only the good person's pleasures are pleasant without qualification, 'since what is really so is what appears so to the good person'.[31]

What does this distinction amount to? The comparisons with *sweet, hot, bitter,* and *sharp* suggest two interpretations. (1) Aristotle regards 'pleasant' and the other terms as names of objective or mind-independent properties of things which, in the normal or healthy case, cause the subject to experience the thing as *pleasant* or *sweet* etc. The subject need never be wrong about whether he is finding the object pleasant or sweet etc., but unless he is well-conditioned he will be wrong in inferring that the object is, in itself, sweet or pleasant. For in a defective subject the genuine experience of sweetness or pleasantness will be caused by something other than the objective properties denoted by those terms. Thus someone who claims, on the basis of his own taste experience, that the juice of aloes is sweet and pleasant makes two false claims about the external object as it is in itself.[32] (2) *Pleasant* and the others are subjective properties, so that 'pleasant' always means 'pleasant to so and so' (or 'pleasant to a being in such and such a state'); but for some reason it is convenient or appropriate to drop the subjective reference when the subject is sound or good. Thus only the good subject has the right to say 'It is pleasant' of what he enjoys; others should say 'It is pleasant to me'.

It is difficult to decide between the interpretations, but the second is more plausible. Whatever Aristotle may have thought about *sweet, bitter* and *sharp,* he does treat *hot* as an objective property (see his theory of the transmutation of the simple bodies, which is at the basis of his meteorology). But I do not think that he considers that anything is pleasant in the absence of a subject-to-whom, in the way in which fire, a primal material of the universe, is hot per se. Thus when he treats *hot* on a par with *pleasant* (as at 1176 a 14) he probably means 'suitably hot' or 'uncomfortably hot', which would suit the medical context. In that case, *hot* here is subjective and so is *pleasant.*

So, turning to the second interpretation, we ask straightaway for the rationale of dropping the subjective reference when the subject is sound or good. It may seem that this is simply a device for holding together those concepts which otherwise threaten to fly apart: *nature* (or *naturelike disposition*), *pleasure,* and *the good.* Aristotle can say that the connection obtains, as his theory requires, when 'pleasant' is taken without qualification by subjective reference, since he rules that this is how it is to be taken when and only when the subject or disposition is good. And in saying, as at 1153 a 5–6, that sharp and bitter things are not pleasant *by nature* he also implies that a disposition which enjoys them is not a *nature* in an unqualified sense. Presumably it is only a *nature* from the point of view of its possessor. So the apparent counterexamples are not examples of *pleasure* and *nature* but only of *pleasure to someone* and *someone's nature.* But is this not a stipulation ad hoc, designed to protect an otherwise inadequate theory?

No, because Aristotle sees enjoyment and pursuit of something as an affirmation, maybe inarticulate, that the object is *to be pursued*—i.e., that *it is good.* Pleasure is the apparent good, and the appearance may be true or false, though either way the pleasure—a species of evaluation—is real. Aristotle links the unqualified *pleasant* to the unqualified *good.* In *NE* VII he says:

> Since that which is good may be so in either of two senses (one thing good simply and another good for a particular person), natural constitutions and states, and therefore also movements and processes [and also pleasures, Aristotle implies, since so far in VII he has not disentangled *pleasure* from *process*] will be correspondingly divisible. Of those which are thought to be bad, some will be bad without qualification but not bad for a particular person, but worthy of his choice, and some will not be worthy of choice even for a particular person, but only at a particular time and for a short period, though not without qualification. (1152 b 26–31; cf. 1235 b 30–32)

What is without qualification pleasant is the object of a *correct* hedonic affirmation of value, and only a well-constituted being can affirm in this way correctly. The correct affirmation (the enjoyment) is good as an affirmation because it is true and also because, as enjoyment, it reinforces the pursuit of what is good. Now if pleasure is a kind of value-judgment, it is not ad hoc to treat as primary those cases of pleasure that represent true value-judgments. We cannot in general understand falsity in judgment except as a defect in what purports to be true; truth is primary.

Aristotle's notion of unqualified pleasure is baffling if we assume that he treats pleasure mainly as a psychological phenomenon: an event in the soul, like a feeling. An act of affirmation, too, can be treated as a psychological event, and from this point of view its truth or falsity is incidental. As an event in the soul, a true affirmation is experientially indistinguishable from what it would have been like had it been false. Hence from this point of view the notion of *true affirmation* sheds no light on the notion of affirmation or judgment in general; it is not prior in the order of explanation, but in fact is irrelevant. Thus we fail to understand Aristotle if we psychologise pleasure. We also fail if we moralise it, by which I mean: if we take the full significance of pleasure to be revealed through such questions as 'Should we—moral agents—pursue pleasure?' or 'Is pleasure the highest good?' The issue raised by these questions is whether to choose pleasure or, perhaps more realistically, whether to choose other things solely for the sake of pleasure; thus pleasure figures as a possible principle in terms of which value-judgments and moral decisions are made, and it also figures as the subject matter of some or all of these decisions. This point of view blocks the realisation that pleasure itself can be treated as a kind of right-or-wrong value-judgment, and that it is so treated by Aristotle[33].

What I have just termed the 'moralising' approach also disconnects pleasure from the natural teleology which in nonrational animals grounds a general link between pleasure and their nonhedonic good. Though no creature enjoys for the sake of something else (in the sense in which one might choose to do X for the sake of Y) they are naturally constituted so as to achieve their nonhedonic good *by* enjoying (for its own sake) whatever they naturally enjoy. This view, I am assuming, is shared by Aristotle and his hedonist opponents, as well as by Plato. The disagreement is over extrapolating to *human* animals. Plato is inclined to block extrapolation altogether; Aristotle accepts it but interprets 'nature' in the human case as 'rational nature'. All sides also agree that the value-judgments of pleasure can be correct or not. The hedonists are struck by the fact that nonhuman animals mainly get these judgments right; Plato and Aristotle by the fact that human ones very easily get them wrong. Of course, if we think that there is no right or wrong here, we shall conclude that an object's seeming good to a subject (because of being pleasant to him) is the same as its *being* good, and we shall add 'to him' in every case. In other words, we continue to hold that finding something pleasant (being pleased by it) entails finding it good, but there will be no such thing as O's being good independent of someone's finding it so. Thus the phenomenon of finding O good, like that of finding O pleasant, is nothing but a psychological state of a person, which it may or may not be convenient for him to be in, but which no more involves a right-or-wrong *claim* than the state of having a headache. (Unlike the latter, the state of finding something good is in an obvious way motivational; but motivation now—as in Hume—is something quite other than judgment.)

But if pleasure in general is nature's device for realising what on quite other grounds is good, it is not unreasonable to construct an account of pleasure in which good pleasure (i.e., pleasure in what is independently good) figures as conceptually primary. For if pleasure is functional, the paradigm case is pleasure functioning well. Thus we can explain why, for Aristotle, the good man's pleasure in good activity must be pleasure in the primary sense. But what exactly is the logic by which that primary sense has shed its subjective reference? We can understand how a theory which takes account of the natural teleology of pleasure in the animal kingdom would put its emphasis on what is pleasant to the well-constituted subject; but why not leave it at that? Why say further, as Aristotle does, that what the good man enjoys is not merely *pleasant to him* (he being the sort of enjoyer it is good for a human being to be) but simply *pleasant,* as if pleasantness were an objective property? This is confusing enough, but Aristotle plays with more confusion when (as in the passage last quoted) he applies the 'without qualification'/'to him' distinction to *good* as well as to *pleasant.* The applications seem to follow pari passu from his principle 'what is really so is what appears so to the excellent person . . . virtue is the measure of each thing' (1176 a 15–19; cf. 1113 a 31–33). But the results do not correspond.[34] What the bad man takes to be good is good only *for* or *to* him (these are not distinguished in the Greek); i.e., it is not really good at all, but good only *in his opinion.* But what the bad man finds to be pleasant is pleasant for or to him in a different sense. For he really does enjoy it; thus it is not true that he is only under the illusion that it is pleasant. Thus 'pleasant for him' entails 'really pleasant' even though it does not entail 'pleasant for everyone' or 'pleasant for the good man'. If we try to align the case of *good* with this, we get the result that what the bad man takes to be good *is indeed really* good, though only *for* someone like him. And this opens the door to the relativism which Aristotle cannot countenance, according to which the good for each individual is just what that individual takes to be good.[35]

The value-judgmental character of pleasure gives a passage through these difficulties. In the first place, the judging is by the enjoyer, and it is in, not about, his enjoyment. It is about *what* he enjoys: a declaration in feeling and action that this is good to pursue and enjoy. His actual enjoyment of Z *is* his finding that Z is pleasant, and the finding pleasant is the value-judgment. But my enjoying Z is not my finding that Z is pleasant *to* (or *for*) *me,* any more than my statement that S is P is the statement that *I take* S to be P. One might, in finding something pleasant, be aware that others do not or would not, or that one finds it pleasant only here and now. But a judgment contrasting self with others, or here and now with other occasions, is not the judgment voiced by an enjoyer qua enjoyer; it is, rather, a reflection on that. For enjoyment is an undivided focus on what is enjoyed; and as such it knows nothing of the relation of this to the subject, nor of the subject's possible difference in this respect from others or from himself at other times. Thus 'Z is pleasant', as expressing enjoyment, is complete without the addition of 'to me'.

Second, a differently constituted person can accept that the enjoyer of Z really does enjoy it, yet not accept the implied evaluative claim. Here we must distinguish two situations: (1) the other person knows that he would not, himself, enjoy Z (which he finds detestable), hence would not, himself, make the claim which the other makes by enjoying Z and enjoyingly announcing 'Z is pleasant'; (2) the other person's attitude implies *rejection* of the first one's announcement 'Z is pleasant' and the implied evaluative claim. If we stay with (1) without advancing to (2), we have a situation in which one subject says 'Z is pleasant' and the other 'Z is not pleasant', but there is no conflict, because each declaration simply expresses its utterer's own attitude (though without referring to the utterer). There is no logical conflict between the one's pursuit and the other's avoidance of Z, and hence no conflict between the statements, which, we might say, are respectively nothing but the pursuit itself and the avoidance itself each seen from its inside, so to speak. Now this is not the situation which Aristotle has in mind, for he believes that there are objective differences between good people and bad people, and he holds that the good man's judgment (in whatever field) is the standard or measure of how things are. In (1) without (2), neither subject's pleasure or displeasure functions as a standard against which the other's attitude shows up as generally unacceptable. For, as we have described the case, in (1) without (2) neither subject sees his own attitude as a standard by which to condemn the other's; hence neither sees his own as a standard by which to advise some third person to reject the other's. In short, neither subject functions or takes himself to be functioning as a 'good man'—a proper model for others.

Just as my enjoyment of Z is not, qua enjoyment, the announcement that Z is pleasant to me now, whether or not also to others or to me later, so (presumably) my enjoyment does not, simply qua enjoyment, carry the implication that Z would be good for everyone to pursue and enjoy, nor the implication that there is something wrong with anyone who does not follow suit. Enjoyment as such does not look beyond its object: it does not lay down the law to other selves nor even refrain from laying it down. But amongst social rational beings, as we have seen, one individual's pursuit and enjoyment is already a kind of prescription to others in general. The young are of unformed character, always tending to completion in some form or other. That makes possible deliberate training, but it also means that they tend to see rules and models in every adult action. Perhaps other animal species learn through imitating their elders, but there one would have to say that the elders' activity triggers in the young a universal potential for one style of behaviour. Perhaps they learn through copying it, but a particular model does not teach them to copy this when they might have copied something quite different, a model of bad or unhealthy ways. Just as nature generally takes care that physically defective creatures fail to transmit their defects by reproduction, so one would expect nature to ensure that undesirable characteristics come to other kinds of dead end; thus the young, if healthy, would be constitutionally insensitive to bad models. But with human animals, *any* adult way of being is apt to be grasped as a standard of how to be, by those who by nature are looking to develop into *something,* but are not by nature determined as to *what.* And responsible members of the community know this. They know, without needing to spell it out, that human pursuit and enjoyment carry in effect a prescriptive message—addressed to no one in particular, hence as if addressed to everyone.

Under conditions of human community, then, hedonic pursuit and aversion function as action-guiding value-judgments. When hedonic responses diverge with respect to the same object, they do not pass each other by, but stand opposed. And when they converge, they agree. A and B might initially agree in enjoying Z. Alternatively, A might accept B's enjoyment as a ground for accepting, himself, that 'Z is pleasant', and its evaluative implication. In this case A treats B as an authority, one who (in this regard) enjoys what is good to enjoy, even if A does not yet enjoy it himself. A's acceptance of B's authority is shown by the fact that A takes over B's attitude *in the primitive unqualified form in which B holds it.* This is what is meant by Aristotle's claim that what is pleasant and good to the good man, who is the standard, is so absolutely.

On the other hand, A may initially find Z detestable himself; or, without yet having his own reaction, he may distrust B's taste on other grounds. In either case he sees B's enjoyment of Z as ground for no more than the qualified judgment 'Z is pleasant to (or for) B'. Hence A may also hold 'Z is good to (or for) B'. What do these qualified statements convey? I am not sure, and we need not assume that Aristotle has decided. The important point is that both statements can be treated in the same way, and however they are treated, the practical implication is the same. A may indeed use both to convey that B makes or implies an unqualified evaluation, but that this is *only B's opinion.* Such a message would normally be taken to imply that the opinion is not to be trusted as correct. Or A may mean that B has a good (in the shape of Z) which *is* a good, but only for B and those like him; and that B's hedonic evaluation of Z is correct for B and others like him, but correct *only for them.* Either way, A admits the fact that B does enjoy Z, does find Z proper to enjoy, and does regard it as good without qualification. And either way, A proclaims that this fact about B is not a ground for sharing B's attitude to Z. On either reading, the effect of the 'to (for) B' qualification is to block logical transference of B's attitude. It is an academic question whether A thinks or ought to think that there is an "objective" value which B is wrong about, or that there is a "subjective" value which exists only for B and which he cannot be wrong about: for either way, A proclaims that B, or B's hedonic attitude, is not to be treated as a model for the community in general.

Thus Aristotle can maintain the metaphysical connections traced above between *pleasure, nature* and *the good* without falling into the unmitigated hedonism that claims that whatever is pleasant to a person is good because natural. The coherence of Aristotle's position, I have argued, depends on his viewing pleasure and the pursuit of it as an implicit judgment of value. The primary judgment is unqualified by reference to its subject; when others regard that subject as a fit authority on the good, they inherit his judgment in the form in which it was his: i.e., still unqualified by reference to him. They in turn, invested with such judgment, are to that extent authorities themselves in their own eyes; thus they retain it and pass it on without adding any reference to themselves either, and in that way they and others participate in the original person's attitude in its original unrestricted form. Refusal to participate is registered by automatic introduction of a reference to the subject. In this way, Aristotle can hold both that what is pleasant *simpliciter* is good *simpliciter,* while denying that everything found pleasant is good.

The *NE* X discussion of pleasure concludes with this passage:

> Those [pleasures] which are admittedly disgraceful plainly should not be said to be pleasures, except to a perverted taste; but of those that are thought to be good, what kind of pleasure or what pleasure should be said to be that proper to man? Is it not plain from the corresponding activities? The pleasures follow these. Whether, then, the complete and blessed man has one or more activities, the pleasures that complete these will be said in the strict sense to be pleasures proper to man, and the rest will be so in a secondary and fractional way, as are the activities. (1176 a 22–29)

To identify the pleasure or pleasures that are par excellence human, we have only to identify the best human activity or activities. This, one might think, should be easy, since did not Aristotle say at the beginning that the best activity is the exercise of reason in accordance with virtue, thus deliberately directing our attention to the moral virtues and practical wisdom? But does that formula refer to one kind of activity or more than one? And if to more, are they equally expressive of our nature at its best? This is Aristotle's topic for the rest of *NE* X and ours in the next chapter. There may have been one or two hints earlier in the *Ethics* that these questions could arise, but Aristotle begins to face them only now. Perhaps the discussion of pleasure is what finally provokes the questions, and perhaps this is because that discussion shapes answers which could not have emerged before. If, for example, there is reason to doubt whether one kind of human rational activity, even at its finest, is as pleasant as one other, the connections just forged between *pleasure* and *nature* would prompt the conclusion that the former should not be awarded the title of 'highest human activity'.

## Notes

1. But note Gosling and Taylor's arguments (Chapter 15) against the traditional view that the treatment in X is later.
2. By Owen.
3. Cf. Gosling and Taylor, 264–65.
4. Every one of the issues touched on in this paragraph is studied with immense thoroughness by Gosling and Taylor, Chapters 11–15.
5. Aristotle, like Plato and almost every other philosopher, does not question that pleasure and pain are contraries. But see Ryle.
6. 200 b 12–24.
7. Cf. Gosling and Taylor, 277–81.
8. As Gosling and Taylor assume, 280.
9. See Waterlow, 183–91, for discussion and references. See also M. J. White [2].
10. Speusippus, for one. See Gosling and Taylor, 294–96, for speculations about antihedonist opponents outside the Academy.
11. For discussion of the evidence (*Phys.* 247 a 15–19; *Rhet.* 1369 b 33–35; 1371 a 31–34), see Gosling and Taylor, 194–99.
12. This was probably not a single theory but a theme common to several positions.
13. See below, Chapter 7, Section X.
14. Cf. *Meta.* 1008 b 12–27, against those who claim to hold that the same thing is both P and not P.
15. See also *Movement of Animals* 700 b 28–29; *Meta.* 1072 a 27–28.

16. Cf. Milo, 13–22; Charlton, 54–58; Irwin [7], 332–33; Urmson [5], 38–39.
17. These equations break down in the reflective context, where one may find Z pleasant yet not affirm it to be good or pursue it (this is either temperance or continence, depending on whether Z is desired); or one may find Z pleasant, pursue it, yet not affirm it to be good (incontinence). This distinction is made at 1235 b 26 ff.
18. 'In the appetites' means 'in the case of the appetites'; see Bostock.
19. Owen notes as a curiosity of this argument the implication that we can be mistaken about what we enjoy: the thirsty man takes himself to enjoy the process of filling up with liquid, but really what he enjoys is the exercise of his physical powers in so doing. But this is not, as Owen implies, a failure of self-awareness (as when people think they are enjoying the food in a restaurant when really they enjoy being waited on). The thirsty man is not mistaken in supposing that he enjoys having the drink, but only (perhaps) in the metaphysical category to which he assigns (if he does) *having a drink* considered as something enjoyed.
20. Cf. the complaint of Urmson [1] and [5] 104–8, that Aristotle fails to distinguish enjoyment of activity involving the body from having pleasant physical feelings of the kinds that constitute the sphere of temperance. But Aristotle might reply that having the sensations associated with eating, drinking or sex is in each case an activity (the exercise of a capacity) and is enjoyed as such.
21. The textual evidence for this interpretation is the comparison at 1174 b 25–26 with different kinds of causes of health. The interpretation leans heavily on the assumption that a precise comparison is intended: just as health is the formal cause of being healthy and is not anything distinct, so pleasure is the nondistinct formal cause of the enjoyed activity (thus Gosling and Taylor, 249–53). But Aristotle may only be making the point that just as there are different ways of being a cause, so there are different ways of perfecting something, and pleasure perfects in one way, the underlying state in another. This tells us only that the relation of pleasure to the activity is not that of the underlying state; which is consistent both with its *following from* the activity and with their being *identical.*
22. This interpretation is inevitable if we take line 32 as saying that pleasure supervenes *on the activity.* (Aristotle has already spoken of pleasure and pain in this way at 1104 b 4–5.) However (1) 32 can be read as saying that the end or perfection which is pleasure supervenes *on the underlying state;* in which case it would *be* the activity. And (2) 'supervenient' may be intended to stress not so much the distinctness of pleasure from that on which it supervenes, as the fact that pleasure (on this theory) is not (or should not be) a goal aimed at, but is essentially consequential on the achievement of something else. Cf. Irwin [5] ad 1174 b 33.
23. Cf. Gosling and Taylor, 213.
24. For a detailed exposition see Waterlow, Chapter 3, Part I.
25. Some things (e.g., points, acts of perception, pleasure) are not, then are, without process of coming-to-be. See *Phys.* 258 b 16–20; *Meta.* 1060 b 18; *Sense and Sensibilia* 446 b 4.
26. Cf. Gosling and Taylor, 259.
27. Cf. Gosling and Taylor, 283.
28. Tr. Gosling.
29. The general form of the dilemma and Aristotle's response to it is very clearly set out by Evans, 53–73.
30. However, Aristotle does allow that illusions of enjoying oneself are possible. See 1152 b 31–33.
31. Gosling and Taylor, 330–44, assume that this is meant to give a criterion of what is really pleasant (and similarly for what is really good). That is, first we are to identify the good man, and by seeing what he likes we can tell what is really pleasant. The authors then complain that the criterion is useless because we cannot identify anyone as good without prior commitment on what should be classed as really pleasant. However, I know of no passage where Aristotle clearly intends to propose the good man as an independent criterion of 'what is really so'. And in the present context he obviously assumes that we already know that some things are really good and others really bad. For his problem is to find a

way of keeping what to him is valuable in hedonism while at the same time being able to say that some enjoyments are bad.

32. Cf. Gosling and Taylor, 338–41.
33. And by Plato; see especially *Philebus* 37–40.
34. As Allan [3] notes.
35. Cf. Ackrill [1], ad 1113 a 22 ff.; Irwin [5], ad 1113 a 27, 1173 b 20–25, 1177 a 10–24; Evans, 53 ff.; Gosling and Taylor, 340–41.

# CHAPTER 7

# Aristotle's Values

## I. New Directions from Old

In the last few pages of the *Nicomachean Ethics* Aristotle returns to the original question 'What is human happiness?' One expects the end of a long inquiry to glance back towards its starting-point. The moment of ending is also of course the occasion for glancing forward to what might be built on what has been done. And it is the opportunity for final selective emphasis on some theme, perhaps implicit but hardly stated, which the philosopher especially desires to leave fresh in his listeners' minds—fresh in the sense of alive, but not in the sense of philosophically unmotivated by what goes before, at any rate if we are to take the work as a more or less unified development. And it is only reasonable in the first instance to take the *Nicomachean Ethics* as that.

As for what sort of inquiry is next in order, Aristotle reflects on this in the final sentences of X.9, in which he closes the *NE* with a call for work in political science.

> Now our predecessors have left the subject of legislation to us unexamined; it is perhaps best, therefore, that we should ourselves study it, and in general study the question of the constitution, in order to complete to the best of our ability that philosophy of human nature. First, then, if anything has been said well in detail by earlier thinkers, let us try to review it; then in the light of the constitutions we have collected let us study what sorts of influence preserve and destroy states, and what sorts preserve or destroy the particular kinds of constitution, and to what causes it is due that some are well and others ill administered. When these have been studied we shall perhaps be more likely to see which constitution is best, and how each must be ordered, and what laws and customs it must use. Let us make a beginning of our discussion (1181 b 12–23)

In fact, the transition indicated by the last sentence has already begun. Aristotle has just been spelling out some proposals for moral education which cannot be effective except by public action through legislation. For this reason he will now undertake a thorough study of legislation and political institutions in general. Is it then arbitrary to treat the *Ethics* as a separate inquiry, when by the time that treatise closes it seems that the work on political science has already taken its start? No; there is this difference: the conclusions of political science cannot evoke a practical response except through state or community action, even if under the leadership of a few enlightened individuals. By contrast, the practical lessons of the *Ethics* are mostly such that, to begin to make a direct difference, they need only be brought to the reflective attention of the persons in Aristotle's audience.

As this chapter goes on, it will become clearer than it has been so far just what practical effect Aristotle hopes the *Ethics* to have on his listeners. We know him not to expect that his lectures will make anyone morally good or more disposed to do what is noble and refrain from what is shameful. For he said at the start that lectures of this sort are intended only for persons who can benefit from them, and that no one stands to benefit who is not already brought up in good ways of feeling and acting. Moreover, such students can also be assumed committed (in advance of argument) to taking seriously their own responsibilities for any young in their charge, and so for imparting these same values. The importance of good upbringing and its general nature are not matters on which Aristotle needs to get his audience to change their minds. On this front, then, so far as basic attitudes are concerned, there is no room for improving individuals through philosophy, since those who lack the basic attitudes would not acquire them by such means.

On the other hand, there is, Aristotle thinks, room for improvement in the conditions under which moral goodness is developed. The task is too important to be left entirely to individual heads of families. What is at stake is nothing less than the human excellence of the members of society. Hence what is at stake is their chance of realising their highest good or happiness, according to Aristotle's definition of happiness as an activity in accordance with such excellence. Thus it should be the duty of the state to legislate guidelines for good upbringing and to throw the weight of its authority behind good practices in general.

> But it is difficult to get from youth up a right training for excellence if one has not been brought up under right laws; for to live temperately and hardily is not pleasant to most people, especially when they are young. For this reason their nurture and occupations should be fixed by law; for they will not be painful when they have become customary. But it is surely not enough that when they are young they should get the right nurture and attention; since they must, even when they are grown up, practise and be habituated to them, we shall need laws for this as well, and generally speaking to cover the whole of life. (1179 b 31–1180 a 4)

Morality, this passage indicates, is not a children's diet to be left behind when one reaches independence. So discipline instilled in childhood is less the mark of current immaturity than of future maturity under development. And while one vital purpose of law is to curb wrongdoing through fear of punishment (1180 a 4–5), this cannot be its primary purpose, which is to hold out standards for those who already aim at what is 'noble', encouraged in that aim by parents and legislators alike. Law, like family discipline, should first and foremost address itself to fostering the potential good in us and deal as necessary with the bad by the way.

> This is why some think that legislators ought to stimulate men to excellence and urge them forward by the motive of the noble, on the assumption that those who have been well advanced by the formation of habits will attend to such influences; and that punishments and penalties should be imposed on those who disobey and are of inferior nature, while the incurably bad should be completely banished. A good man (they think), since he lives with his mind fixed on what is noble, will submit to argument, while a bad man, whose desire is for pleasure, is corrected by pain like a beast of burden. (1180 a 5–12)

Law cannot supplant parental training, but should supplement it, because

> the paternal command indeed has not the required force or compulsive power (nor in general has the command of one man, unless he be a king or something similar), but the law *has* compulsive power, while it is at the same time an account proceeding from a sort of practical wisdom and intellect. And while people hate *men* who oppose their impulses, even if they oppose them rightly, the law in its ordaining of what is good is not burdensome. (1180 a 18–24)

Thus law is not an extension of parental authority, since then it would arouse the natural resentment felt against individuals who control us, even when the control is just. Nor is it a set of prereflective attitudes given institutional form. Rather, law should be, and be regarded as, the embodiment of divine reason and general ethical wisdom (cf. *Politics* 1287 a 2–30); and as such it should reflect our best knowledge in this area. So legislators ought to heed the findings of systematic inquirers into ethics and politics. And Aristotle lays great emphasis, too, on empirical knowledge of the laws and institutions of other societies, implying that we need to be historically aware of how real systems work.

Such is the programme for educating legislators, and much of the work of gathering and analysing its material is still to be done by Aristotle himself and his colleagues. Meanwhile, the very idea that legislation at all should play a major rôle in moral education remains, for the most part, no more than a hope. For

> In the Spartan state alone, or almost alone, the legislator seems to have paid attention to questions of nurture and occupations; in most states such matters have been neglected, and each man lives as he pleases, Cyclops-fashion, 'to his own wife and children dealing law'. Now it is best that there should be a public and proper care for such matters; but if they are neglected by the community it would seem right for each man to help his children and friends towards excellence, and that they should be able or at least choose, to do this. It would seem from what has been said that he can do this better if he makes himself better at legislating. For public care is plainly effected by laws, and good care by good laws; whether written or unwritten would seem to make no difference. (1180 a 24–b 1)

Aristotle anticipates controversy on two fronts. First, it may be objected that upbringing, like medicine, cannot be summed up in a set of rules or laws, since it ought to be adapted to the individual case. He willingly concedes that point, but also stresses that: 'individuals can be best cared for by a doctor or gymnastic instructor or any one else who has the universal knowledge of what is good for every one or for people of a certain kind' (1180 b 13–15).

Second, there is the question 'Who are the proper exponents of the generalities of ethics?' Is it the practising politicians? They may be good effective leaders, and they have experience, but they seem unable to articulate their principles. Is it the sophists, who advertise themselves as teachers of politics, but are so far from knowing what political science is that they confuse it with rhetoric or some yet inferior craft (1181 a 12–15)? Aristotle does not need to give a name to those most fit to delve into the fundamental principles of legislation, and perhaps any name he might have given, such as 'philosophers', would have carried unwanted Platonic associations. The model he presents is his own procedure, both up to and from these final pages of the *Ethics*, where dispassionate methodical analysis of the central ethical concepts gives way to the more empirically based approach followed in much of the *Politics*.

My main topic in this chapter, however, is not Aristotle's view of the need for political science, or of its contribution to the life of the community. Rather, it is the status he envisages for theoretic activity in the good life. But among the reasons for dwelling for a short space on the rôle of political science there are some which bear more or less directly on the question of *theōria*. The point to which I now draw attention is a general pattern of thought for which the discussion of legislating for moral virtue stands as a good illustration. We find Aristotle still taking for granted, as he has done so far throughout the *Ethics*, a shared commitment to good upbringing in qualities standardly accepted as fundamental human excellences, but at the same time now implying that this attitude is not by itself sufficiently knowledgeable or reflective to do itself full justice in a practical way. Thus from a basis in received opinion he moves in a direction that is novel and controversial, so as to require rational defence. At the same time, the accepted basis itself has been to some extent illuminated by his own philosophical account of moral character and practical wisdom. On this score, common sense notions and common sense ways have found themselves passing the test of Aristotle's philosophical scrutiny; thus they constitute suitable potential for adopting the more institutional attitude towards moral education which he is now recommending. To the eye of one who has observed and studied many political systems, the emergence of this attitude is by no means a historical necessity, since in most societies upbringing is left to private families. Such a step forward therefore depends on a new, more reflective vision for justification and guidance.

Aristotle evidently expects those who share the basic attitude to be rationally led by his arguments into recognising not only the wisdom of the particular reform which he advocates, but the general potential which exists for progress in excellence, even at a fundamental level. Thus he can expect his mention of 'sophists' to trigger certain responses in his audience. Whoever he may have particularly in mind, his audience knows that sophists entered this fray long ago with claims to be specialist teachers of virtue and civic excellence. And however convincing the by now classic refutations of those claims by Socrates and Plato, no refutation could cancel the one unquestionable legacy of the sophistic movement: an awakening, namely, to self-awareness of immense human possibilities waiting to be tapped for good or ill through systematic education. Nothing could remove the sense once created of a gap at the centre of human life which unreflective values and practice, even at their best, would never fill from their own resources; though the shape of the gap and the expertise that should meet it were as differently diagnosed as by Callicles in the *Gorgias* and Plato in the *Republic*.

But the ethical innovator ought to recommend what is practicable, not only in terms of its external implementation but of its inner normative implications as well. Hence a viable programme must take account, as Plato in the *Republic* did not, of actual human nature under actual conditions; and it must not violate, as did some of the earlier sophistic theories, the moral intuitions of ordinary decent citizens. It is significant in this connection that those whom Aristotle refers to as 'sophists' in *NE* X.9 appear here only as possible candidates for the task of drawing up laws intended to carry forward the work of familial upbringing. It is not, in other words, a live option in this context that sophists might now figure as proposing the kind of radical revision of established values for which some of their predecessors were historically notorious. Aristotle, it is true, does here represent the sophists as confusing political science with rhetoric, a theme which connects them with some of the most disturbing implications of earlier sophistic views; but that remark need not be construed as a hit at, say, the sweeping subjectivism represented by Protagoras in Plato's *Theaetetus,* and in the present context any such construal seems exaggerated. That sort of relativism is by now a dead issue thanks to Plato, and what presently concerns Aristotle, I would suppose, is the difference between those whose governing idea, were they to be assigned the task of new legislation, is that law is nothing but an instrument for nonrational persuasion, and those for whom law is the social voice of reason addressing rational individuals.

I have tried to indicate how Aristotle's argument about moral virtue and legislation in *NE* X.9 assumes in his audience a solid prereflective acceptance of traditional values; an acceptance meshed, however, with incipient awareness of its own inadequacy to make those values tell to the full unless guided in new practical directions by a more philosophical vision. I have stressed this because it seems to me that we cannot make sense of Aristotle's ethical stance towards theoretic activity except in terms of just such a pattern of thought.

## II. The Problem

If the *Nicomachean Ethics* had come down to us minus Chapters 7 and 8 of Book X, our overwhelming impression from the work would be that Aristotle means to define the essence of happiness in terms of morally virtuous activity informed by practical wisdom. The opening argument of Book I purported to show that the supreme human good, whatever it may be, is the end at which the statesman aims. Indeed, we saw how Aristotle at that stage would have been entirely without grounds for presuming a single supreme end if he could not point to the existence, however imperfect, of some sovereign activity the end of which it must be; this is the activity which he calls *'politikē'*. From here it was only a short step to identifying the supreme good of the human individual with a life of moral excellence; for, as common sense has it, the proper concern of the practitioner of *politikē* is to make 'the citizens be of a certain character, *viz.*, good and capable of noble acts' (1099 b 31–32; cf. 1102 a 7–10). It would be unnatural to suppose that when Aristotle speaks of the citizens as 'good' he could expect his audience to understand that goodness as anything but moral and social excellence, or their 'noble' actions as noble in any terms other than these.

This mode of characterising the supreme good would also lead us to expect the *Nicomachean Ethics* to end exactly as in fact it does: with a renewed consideration of the ethical rôle of political institutions and the qualifications desirable in those who will shape them. True, *NE* X.9 might still be relevant and coherent even if by this point Aristotle had dropped or radically altered his initial position on the nature of happiness. But nothing is more obvious than that this chapter shares with Book I the assumption (nowhere else questioned, either) that the statesman's concern is for the *moral quality* of his citizens. Consequently, it would be more than a little disingenuous of Aristotle to refrain from openly declaring any departure from the (in I) associated view that identifies *happiness* with that statesmanly objective (1102 a 5–9). At least, it would be disingenuous unless a change of mind had taken place unawares.

This would have to be not only unawares but deeply buried for Aristotle to apply, as he does in X.9, the unqualified term 'excellence' to what are evidently the familiar *moral* excellences (see, e.g., 1179 b 33). For we must assume that he still stands by the celebrated argument in I.7 that equates happiness with human well-functioning, and still takes it as an analytic truth that excellences or virtues are just those qualities whose exercise distinguishes good functioning. It is not open to Aristotle to hold, as it might be to us under some different abstract conception of virtue, that a person can be actively virtuous (in conditions favouring the activity), yet not to that extent be happy. Soon after he mounts the function argument in I, we find him granting the title of 'virtue', unquestioned, to just those sorts of quality that his well-brought-up audience would naturally rank as such. Happiness, therefore, in Book I is essentially the exercise of these; and since these still count as 'virtues' by the end of X, one would suppose that happiness at the close of the *Ethics* is still what it was at the start.

The problem for this otherwise inevitable interpretation stems from Aristotle's discussion of theoretic activity in X.7 and 8. Now some discussion of this topic has all along been due, for quite early in Book I Aristotle spoke of three competing standard conceptions of the good life: as centred on pleasure, on 'political' activity and on *theōria* (1095 b 17–19). He implied that he would settle the contest. We need not see this as committing him to finding grounds for preferring one of the three without qualification.[1] It would be enough if, by the end, he gave an account of the best life which saves what is true in each of the competing claims and fits those truths together. This is exactly what he does with the first two. The 'life of pleasure' gets summary treatment in Book I, where its supporters are described as extolling a bovine existence (1095 b 19–20). But it soon becomes clear that the best life cannot exclude pleasures proper to the best, most human, activities. Again, the 'political life' is faulted at once on the ground that its supporters conceive of the good as honour, which Aristotle argues is a confusion: really they value the excellence which honour recognizes (1095 b 26–30). But inactive excellence cannot be the good, because excellent *activity* is better (1095 b 31 ff.; cf. 1098 b 31–1099 a 7). Now the ideal that results when these mistakes are corrected is that which appears to win the day in the bulk of the *Ethics:* it is the happy life defined as an active life of moral excellence informed by practical wisdom.

In Book I Aristotle reserves his position on the 'theoretic life', and he keeps almost silent about it until Book X. It is noteworthy that he never says anything negative about this third contender even by way of preliminary skirmish. However, if the best life is 'political' according to the corrected conception, the theoretic life, as some kind of competing option, cannot be rated the best. Even so, it might still be reasonable to argue that theoretic activity should play some part in whatever life is best; and it might be possible to reconcile this claim with the claim that the best life is essentially practical and political.

In X.6–8 Aristotle returns to the three lives, and from this and abundant other evidence it is clear that these chapters consciously draw on themes and arguments developed in Book I. Forgetfulness of what he had said in I is therefore not a viable explanation of anything in X, even though in X.7 and 8 we suddenly seem to be in a different ethical world. It is a world in which, for example, without any sense of awkwardness, Aristotle declares:

> If happiness is activity in accordance with excellence, it is reasonable that it should be in accordance with the highest excellence; and this will be that of the best thing in us. Whether it be intellect [*nous*] or something else that is this element which is thought to be our natural ruler and guide and to take thought of things noble and divine, whether it be itself also divine or only the most divine element in us, the activity of this in accordance with its proper excellence will be complete happiness. That this activity is theoretic we have already said. (1177 a 11–18)

> That which is proper to each thing is by nature best and most pleasant for each thing; for man, therefore, the life according to *nous* is best and pleasantest, since *nous* more than anything else *is* man. This life therefore is also the happiest. But in a secondary way[2] the life in accordance with the other kind of excellence is happy; for the activities in accordance with this befit our human estate. Just and brave acts, and other excellent acts, we do in relation to each other, observing what is proper to each with regard to contracts and services and all manner of actions and with regard to passions; and all of these seem to be human. (1178 a 8–14)

> Happiness extends, then, just so far as *theōria* does, and those to whom *theōria* more fully belongs are more truly happy, not accidentally, but in virtue of the *theōria;* for this is in itself precious. Happiness, therefore, must be some form of *theōria*. (1178 b 28–32)

A virtual nonentity before in Aristotle's scheme of the worthwhile life, *theōria* now towers at the center. By what passage was this possible?

Questions which occur are these. (1) Does the *Nicomachean Ethics* harbour a radical contradiction concerning the nature of happiness? (2) Is the evaluation of *theōria* in X.7–8 a new turn or was it prefigured further back in the work? (3) Does X introduce an *additional* conception of happiness or does it *replace* the one expounded earlier? (4) How, if there are different forms of it, can any form of happiness be ethically secondary to anything else, even some other form of happiness? For Aristotle maintained in Book I that happiness is whatever is highest. (5) Is the life of practical excellence, according to the passages above, inferior to that of theoretic wisdom? (6) Are what Aristotle calls the 'life' of practical excellence and the 'life' of theoretical wisdom aspects of a single coherent existence; or are they mutually exclusive in the sense that both cannot be lived to the full in a single career? (7) Does the theoretic life have a practical component, and the practical a theoretic, or is either supposed to be purely what its label suggests? (8) How are the lives (on whatever interpretation) connected with each other, both in the individual case and in society? (9) For example, is the activity of practical wisdom and moral virtue in some sense a means to *theōria?* (10) Is it then not good in itself? (11) If practical wisdom does, or should, aim at promoting theoretic activity, is this its only aim? (12) If it has other aims, too, are they to be sacrificed when they conflict with that? In general, are there any limits to the claim of *theōria,* if it is the supreme activity, and on what principle would the limits be drawn?

These questions arise as we ponder the ethical and systematic implications of Aristotle's seemingly sudden elevation of *theōria* in *NE* X.[3] Another set of questions has to do with his reasons for that elevation, which we have not begun to consider. I shall attempt in this chapter to shape an account doing justice to these issues, but should say in advance that I do not regard this last lap of the *Nicomachean Ethics* as a home straight. It is not 'straight', because Aristotle's view is a response to a multitude of pressures, and he is perhaps more concerned to respond to them forcibly as they arise than to negotiate an explicit settlement between these and previous conclusions; and not 'home' because a vista is opened in *NE* X.7 and 8 which Aristotle knows may seem alien ground to many who are glad to accept the equation previously proposed (austere, to be sure, but in tune with much in ordinary moral consciousness) of the happy and worthwhile life with a well-lived practical life.[4] But before addressing this Nicomachean material, we should see what light is shed by the *Eudemian Ethics.*

### III. Goods and Ends in the *Eudemian Ethics*

Which of three commonly favoured lives is best is a prominent question in *EE* I:

> We thus see that there are three lives which all those choose who have power, viz. the lives of the political man, the philosopher, the voluptuary; for of these the philosopher intends to occupy himself with wisdom and contemplation of truth, the political man with noble acts (i.e. those springing from excellence), the voluptuary with bodily pleasures. (1215 a 35–b 5; cf. 1216 a 28–29)

This division is associated with a logically more fundamental division of three desirable things—virtue or excellence, wisdom *(phronēsis)* and pleasure—of which people take different views on the one most vital for happiness:

> Now to be happy, to live blissfully and beautifully, must consist mainly in three things, which seem most desirable; for some say wisdom is the greatest good, some

excellence, and some pleasure. Some also dispute about the magnitude of the contribution made by each of these elements to happiness, some declaring the contribution of one to be greater, some that of another—these regarding wisdom as a
greater good than excellence, those the opposite, while others regard pleasure as a
greater good than either; and some consider the happy life to be compounded of all
or of two of these, while others hold it to consist in one alone. (1214 a 30–b 4; cf.
1215 a 32–35)

This last passage suggests that Aristotle does not see himself bound to settle for
preferring any one of the three models of existence considered as exclusive options,
since happy living could turn out to involve a combination of two or more of the
desirable things.[5] And the remarks about combination leave it open whether, if a
combined life is found to be best, a verdict will be in order that ranks one component
above the others.

Now 'wisdom' ('phronēsis') in the above passages of *EE* I has its usual sense[6]
which does not differentiate between practical and theoretical wisdom, whereas in
*NE* VI ( = *EE* V) Aristotle reserves this term for practical wisdom (and 'sophia' for
theoretic). Whoever, then, says that wisdom is best, or a component in the best life,
is making an ambiguous claim according to the usage of *EE* I (though not all claim-
ants are necessarily aware of the ambiguity). They may mean (1) philosophical or
theoretic wisdom; (2) practical wisdom; (3) both, whether distinguished or not. Now
since practical wisdom entails moral virtue, as Aristotle will show, and since such
total practical excellence is (or should be) the keynote of the 'political' life, it follows
that the life of 'wisdom' would be either (a) philosophical or (b) political or (c) a
combination. But Aristotle himself, even in *EE* I, is clear, I take it, about the difference between theoretic and practical thinking masked by the term 'wisdom' as there
used; thus he is clear from the start that options (a)–(c) are different.[7]

He dismisses the life of pleasure (pleasure here being supposed only bodily) on
much the same grounds as in *NE* I. Happiness, he says, is good activity of the distinctively human soul, a complex of rational and reason-heeding emotional parts.
Each has its own type of virtue, and the virtue of the whole is the combination of the
virtues of the parts (1219 b 26–1220 a 12).

He emphasises that the virtue of which happiness is the activity must be *complete;* i.e., it requires the virtues of all the parts (1220 a 2–4; 1248 a 11–16). Thus
when in *EE* V ( = *NE* VI) he subdivides the rational part into theoretic and practical
reason (1139 a 5–17), we must conclude that he sees both types of wisdom as essential to happiness. The happy life, then, turns out to be a combination of what in *EE*
I were distinguished as the political versus the philosophical life; for wisdom in both
senses must be present, and in one of those senses it entails moral virtue (cf. *NE* VI,
1144 a 1–6).

This is confirmed by Aristotle's closing remarks in the *Eudemian Ethics.* Their
subject is the person of complete virtue (1248 b 8 ff.). Aristotle explains that such a
one is not merely good but 'noble-and-good', a difference which we shall consider
presently; and that without 'noble-goodness', the virtues earlier discussed—i.e., the
moral excellences and practical wisdom—are not complete. Having declared this
additional angle on those practical virtues, Aristotle makes another new move, this
time in connection with choice:

But since the doctor has a limit[8] [*horos*] by reference to which he distinguishes what is healthy for the body from what is not, and with reference to which each thing up to a certain point ought to be done and is healthy, while if less or more is done health is the result no longer, so in regard to actions and choice of what is naturally good but not praiseworthy, the good man should have a limit both of disposition and of choice and avoidance with regard to excess or deficiency of wealth and good fortune, the limit being—as above said—as reason [the *orthos logos*] directs; this corresponds to saying in regard to diet that the standard should be as medical science and its reason direct. But this, though true, is not illuminating. (1249 a 21–b 6)

These remarks recall the opening of the book on practical wisdom. In connection with that, I argued[9] that Aristotle is not there concerned to lay down a standard by reference to which all particular wise choices are to be made, but to expound the general nature of the ethical *orthos logos* in a way that will contrast it with the *orthoi logoi* of theoretic wisdom and craft. This is the best that the philosopher can do by way of guidance, for there *is* no single goal at which we should aim in our choices except for the formal goal of doing what is right or appropriate. Now despite its verbal similarity,[10] the present passage, I believe, is crucially different in its reference to 'things naturally good but not praiseworthy' (1249 a 25).[11] Aristotle is about to offer, not a limit by which to decide the mean in all cases of action and feeling, but one by which to decide it in a narrower set of cases having to do with possession and pursuit of material goods and other kinds of things that can come about by good fortune (*eutuchēmata;* 1249 b 2–3).[12] Those are the goods which he categorises as 'natural but not praiseworthy'. The philosopher can, and should, pronounce on the limit for these, as we see from the way in which Aristotle continues:

One must, then, here as elsewhere, live with reference to the ruling principle and with reference to the formed habit and the activity of the ruling principle, as the slave must live with reference to that of the master, and each of us by the rule proper to him. But since man is by nature composed of a ruling and a subject part, each of us should live according to the governing element within himself—but this is ambiguous, for medical science governs in one sense, health in another, the former existing for the latter. And so it is with the theoretic faculty; for god is not an imperative ruler, but is that for the sake of which practical wisdom issues its commands ('that for the sake of which' is ambiguous, and has been distinguished elsewhere [sc. as the objective of the action and as the beneficiary of the action], for *god* needs nothing.) What choice, then, or possession of the natural goods—whether bodily goods, wealth, friends, or other things—will most produce *theōria* of god, that choice or possession is best; this is the noblest limit [*horos*], but any that through deficiency or excess hinders one from *theōria* and service of god is bad; . . . this is the best limit for the soul—to perceive the non-rational part of the soul, as such, as little as possible. So much, then, for the limit[13] [*horos*] of nobility and the goal [*skopos*] of things good without qualification. (1249 b 6–25)[14]

So ends the *Eudemian Ethics.* Leaving aside for a moment the obscure connection between theoretic activity and God, let us make out the passage's main drift. It is that the divine, whether as object or subject of *theōria,* should dominate the best human life. This dominion is not of the kind that exerts influence by means of imperatives on the part of that which dominates, for God and *theōria* are not practical: they issue no commands; their dominion, rather, is to consist in the fact that practical wisdom at its best is at their service, prescribing with a view to '*theōria* of the god' (cf. *NE* VI, 1145 a 6–11). In this sense, what is valued 'governs' or 'rules' both the valuer and that which the valuer governs by means of prescriptions.

But this sovereignty of divine *theōria* does not extend to the whole sphere for which practical wisdom prescribes. It relates to choices of things 'good by nature but not praiseworthy'. The contrast is with things not merely good but 'noble', which echoes the contrast between the merely good person and the person of *noble* goodness. Now this distinction of goods is a subdivision in a comprehensive classification of goods laid out at 1248 b 18–25. This passage, as I understand it,[15] first divides goods in general into those (G1) which are *ends,* being suitably pursued for their own sake, and (by implication) those (G2) which are not ends. (We shall examine this distinction later.) Then *ends* are divided into those (E1) which are *noble,* being *praiseworthy,* and those (E2) which are not thus praiseworthy and noble but are nonetheless ends and good. Examples of E2 are honour, wealth, bodily excellences, prosperity, fortune, capacities or abilities (1248 b 28–29). These are 'naturally' good or desirable or, as Aristotle also says, 'good without qualification' (1249 b 25).[16]

We rather tend to think of natural goods, like health and prosperity, as definitely good things to have whoever has them, even though they can lead to material and moral harm. In effect, then, we disconnect the sense in which these things are good from the sense in which the morally good person is good. Aristotle, by contrast, sees the natural goods as good only provisionally, so to speak, with a goodness that derives from their being used *by a good person.* That they are *in fact* beneficial to him depends on his own prior goodness.[17] For they cannot truly benefit the bad man, i.e. enable him to fare well and do well as a human being, since for him they are not opportunities for virtuous action (1248 b 27–34). (It does not follow, and Aristotle does not say, that it would therefore be *just* to deprive him of them.)

The good man, then, is one for whom the natural goods *are* goods (1248 b 26–27); i.e., who uses them in virtuous activities. But he is not on that account *noble-and-good.* For as well as the natural goods there are goods that are 'praiseworthy' (1248 b 19–20). What are these noble things? They are virtues and actions expressing virtues (1248 b 36–37). Moreover, the natural goods, Aristotle says, when associated with the noble-and-good person, are not merely good but are themselves ennobled by his use of them for noble ends. It is fit that he have them (e.g., wealth, high birth, power), since when they are his they are noble (1249 a 4–14). So their nobility derives from their relation to the noble person, while his nobility in turn derives from his valuing as noble the intrinsically noble objects; namely, virtues and virtuous actions.

Thus although it is sometimes appropriate to apply the word 'noble' to something naturally good (but not praiseworthy), this nobility is not such as to make noble the pursuit, possession or use of that object, any more than the object's natural goodness automatically makes the pursuit, possession or use actually beneficial. For the object itself is not noble at all except so far as it figures in the already noble aims of an already noble person. Similarly, it is the agent's goodness that makes an object and the pursuit and use of it good. But there is this difference: the good man's goodness does not derive from the goodness of any merely good objects, whereas the noble person's nobility derives from that of certain noble objects: the actions and personal qualities that are intrinsically noble. Yet it is also clear from Aristotle's statements that even *their* nobility is not alone sufficient to ennoble the person who values them, for it is also necessary that he value them *as* noble and commendable in themselves.

Assuming for a moment that we understand Aristotle's distinction between the noble person and the one who is merely good, we can apply the nobility-relations outlined above so as to frame a question about the ethical status of *theōria*. Does Aristotle see this activity as, or as like, a natural good ennobled through being pursued by an anyway noble person, or is it one of the goods noble-in-themselves which ennoble their pursuers? For there is no doubt that *theōria* is noble: Aristotle calls it the 'noblest limit' for measuring excess and deficiency of natural goods (1249 b 19).

He does not expound a straightforward answer, and we shall presently see a reason why his attitude is veiled. But the first option is clearly out. The examples given of natural goods are all useful things, and the distinction between their being and not being truly beneficial is explained in terms of their use. It is *because* they are useful that one can make the mistake which that distinction is meant to correct: of thinking that the final pronouncement of them as good depends on their mere usefulness, not on the ethical quality of the user. But *theōria* in general is not useful at all, and one could hardly make that mistake in connection with it. Again, there is no suggestion in the passages under consideration that the noble person (who is the person of complete excellence) lacks anything important if he lacks some merely natural good, provided that its absence does not undermine his noble activities. But Aristotle certainly thinks even here in the *EE* (where his treatment of *theōria* is low key and laconic to a degree compared with the lengthy fervour of *NE* X.7–8) that a life untouched by *theōria* is defective in a way that matters, however good in other ways. So *theōria* is intrinsically noble, like the recognized virtues and virtuous actions, and ennobles those who value it in the appropriate way.[18]

Hence just as ordinary moral goodness and practical wisdom fall short of complete excellence unless perfected by nobility, nobility itself is incomplete without devotion to *theōria* as a noble end in itself. But before pursuing that thought, we should consolidate Aristotle's distinction between goodness and nobility. This, in itself a fascinating ethical contrast, has a particular bearing on the question of *theōria*. If usefulness is the hallmark of the merely natural goods, and if the good person is the one for whom these goods *are* good, there is no ground for including theoretic activity and theoretic excellence among the elements of the ideal life unless the ideal life surpasses the merely good life by recognising a distinct category of the noble *in which goods of no practical use can find a home*. Without such a category, we have no more reason to treat *theōria* as a topic of ethics than any other activity in which people engage for pleasure rather than to get something done, such as fishing on holiday, playing dice or gossiping. These are all human activities, and not necessarily not respectable, but they are not important except to those to whom they happen to be important. Each is ethically optional. If someone takes no interest in making a living, or in parents or children, or in his standing in the eyes of his peers, something is wrong even if it may also be wrong to let one's life be dominated by one of these values. But there is nothing wrong with someone who cares not at all about the sport of fishing. Hence there has to be a distinct category of the noble suitable to receive important items which fail to get into the list of obvious natural goods, and it has to be clear that *theōria* belongs in that category—or Aristotle the philosopher's special concern for *theōria* will carry no more ethical weight than any other personal bias. But need we be anxious on this score, given that he has already said in *EE* V ( = *NE* VI) that one part of the soul is theoretic, and has also said in *EE* I that happiness involves the virtues of all the parts? For this puts theoretic wisdom firmly in the picture. So it does, but only on the assumption that the theoretic part of the soul is significant enough to deserve to be noticed alongside the parts which get most of Aristotle's attention in the *Ethics*. And this is the same as assuming that *theōria* is an activity which everyone should care about; i.e., which is not ethically optional.

But now is the difference between Aristotle's noble-and-good person and his merely good (hence incomplete) person that the latter lacks the category of the noble? I do not think so, as I shall now explain. The good man is not made good by natural goods which he has, uses or pursues; the dependence goes the other way. This is reminiscent of practical wisdom, according to the interpretation which I offered in Chapter 4. Good deliberation, the activity of practical wisdom, does not merely begin from an end conceived as good, but continually works, through successive consideration of the How, to uphold the claim of that end to be a good and worthy end. Thus the good rational choice that is formed is a guarantee (so far as it is up to the agent) against its turning out that the end was better not realised: in which case this supposed good would have been no better than many things known as 'bad'. So it is not by some mystical osmosis of goodness, nor by an abstract logical transmission, that the good man *makes to be actually good* the otherwise only provisionally good natural goods, but by practical intelligence in the service of moral decency. In that case, however, he is exercising the virtues[19] and is above all concerned to act well from the right choice; so in what way does his nature and attitude differ from the *noble* person's focus on virtue and virtuous action?

Aristotle states the difference in this way:

> There is also the civic disposition, such as the Laconians [i.e., the Spartans] have, and others like them might have; its nature would be something like this—there are some who think one should have excellence but only for the sake of the natural goods, and so such men are good (for the natural goods are good for them), but they have not nobility and goodness. For it is not true of them that they acquire the noble for itself. (1248 b 37–1249 a 3)

This appears to be a comparison between *general attitudes* to virtue and virtuous actions. The point is not that the merely good man acts on the principle that nothing is more important than the natural goods. If that were so, the good man would sometimes act in a shameful way, for instance choosing slavery (whether for himself or others) over risk in battle; but that is not consistent with goodness. Nor can Aristotle mean that the merely good man does not have such terms as 'noble' and 'fine' in his ethical vocabulary. He has surely been brought up to regard some actions as shameful (whether harmful or not) and to refrain from them accordingly; but 'shameful' belongs in the same category as 'fine' and 'noble', being the contrary. In any case, Aristotle has said in *EE* III.1: 'all goodness involves rational choice; it has been said before what we mean by this—goodness makes a man choose everything for the sake of some object, and that object is what is fine [or noble]' (1230 a 26–29; cf. 1229 a 2–4).

Rather, the point concerns different *reflective* attitudes to virtue and virtuous actions *in general*. The noble person prizes these because they are noble in themselves. The merely good man certainly cares about virtue: he seeks to inculcate it in his children; he deplores its absence in others; in each situation he wants to know what is right to do so as to act upon it; and he may put even his life on the line in doing what he sees himself called upon to do. He behaves as if good conduct matters most, and his behaviour itself is a judgment to this effect. But when asked why virtue matters, the answer he gives, if he makes anything at all of the question, is that it is for the sake of the natural goods. We should note that for a person to count as good and as living a life of virtue, it is not necessary that he have any general view about why virtue is important. Nor is it necessary that he think about his own virtues or about his actions as exercises of virtue. He may simply make and stand by good decisions, each as it comes along.[20]

The merely good man, then, is one who either has no views about the value of virtue or who, when he has to give an opinion, can find nothing better to say—and think—than that it is for the sake of the natural goods, even though, he being genuinely good, his practice shows him on any particular occasion wholeheartedly setting rightdoing above anything else. Thus the theory contradicts the practical evaluation, but there is nothing impossible in that. It follows, however, that one with this view misconceives the nature of human well-being or happiness. So far as happiness is virtuous activity, he attains to what it is that happiness is; but intellectually he does not believe this, since he reflectively opines that virtue and virtuous activity are for the sake of a different sort of good, whereas happiness is not for anything beyond itself.[21] On the other hand, his practical as distinct from reflective priorities set virtuous action above everything else; hence on the practical level he does identify that with the essence of happiness. If one must hold views, it is obviously better that they not be at odds with realities: better in itself and also because false opinions end by corrupting practice. Nobility is goodness reflectively valuing itself and its actions as they should be valued: not as natural goods which can be used and misused, still less as means to such goods, but as admirable in themselves.[22] Nobility in reflective beings must be superior to mere goodness, and the line between these qualities should be firmly drawn by the ethical philosopher. The need for that line arises because virtue and practical wisdom, *pace* Socrates, do not depend on or carry in their train an articulate knowledge of the good. This means that those who *are* good can be mistaken in the stated value they put on goodness. Hence we run the risk that the very persons otherwise most qualified by character and action to function as walking models of happiness, and of how to live and to be, will become, by their words and stated views, potential sources of corruption.

In sum, we should understand Aristotle's delineation of the distinct category of the noble as providing an ethically necessary qualification on his frequent statement that the best is what the good man or the man of practical wisdom finds to be best. This is true so long as the 'finding' is embodied in particular actions and decisions (for were it not true on this level, we should not be dealing with practical wisdom at all, but with poor judgment or inferior character); but it may not be true when the reference is to the ordinary wise man's general talk. But if Aristotle rejects the wholesale Socratic view, he also, I think, understands it as containing a limited truth; namely, that although (as Socrates did not see) there would be no topic to discuss when people discuss virtue were it not that virtue is *first* made real in action—action which "knows" virtue only by exercising it in response to contingent particulars—it is nevertheless a fact that once this virtue, real independently of self-reflection, begins to be 'examined', the conclusions drawn from the examination can crucially affect (and, it may be, infect) the character of their object.

This however, assumes that while practice can make its way without reflection, reflection once started can alter practical values. But is Aristotle right to assume this? Speculation aside as to how he would have received certain modern suggestions to the contrary—as, for instance, that we can solidly act as if moral values were objective even though rational reflection sees this to be meaningless[23]—does not Aristotle himself say in the *Nicomachean Ethics* (in connection with pleasure) that a man's deeds, not words, are the real measure of his values (1172 a 34–35)? If that is so, why should what the person *says* injure him or anyone else? Or if anything is injured, is it not only our trust in his words (not our trust in his lived values), as Aristotle suggests in that place?

Here we should note, first, that it is not always so easy to tell when practice diverges from words and, second, that much depends on the extent to which the practice itself is carried on by means of verbal generalities. Take the sort of person whom Aristotle's audience would identify as fine and noble. He is a gentleman and lives a gentleman's life of honourable pursuits. On the other hand, he is continuingly prosperous enough to support all this, and he may even be opulent. He takes care or makes sure that others under him take care of his material interests; he may well be ambitious; his deeds may be grand, but so are his possessions; his worth is measured by the power and influence which so obviously mark his career. Even if he himself in the inwardness of his practice respects nothing in others so much as virtue and virtuous activities, however humble their circumstances, he cannot be said to present to ordinary observation an easily intelligible message to this effect. His own life-style is conspicuous for so much else. How, in such a case, can others be expected to separate the individual from a life-style which perhaps only intimates know to be a reflection less of him than of his inherited position? And for every such case, how many more would there be of persons regarding themselves as noble, and not being questioned in this by others, on account of just those visible pursuits and external goods which make the rare pure-hearted case a difficult one to recognise? Thus the very practice of those who are commonly thought noble would reinforce anyone's belief that the natural goods, or some of them, matter more than who one morally is. For this reason, I suggest, it is important to Aristotle to emphasise that such goods are not ennobling but themselves come to be ennobled by something else to which they are peripheral and subordinate.

When a person's sphere of influence and responsibility is narrow, it may not be hard to discount utterances by comparison with nonverbal deeds. But those who play a significant part in public life operate principally through speech. They shape policy and institutions by persuasion and argument, bringing generalities into play. As the scope of a person's practical concern expands, it becomes less feasible for those affected to check declarations of principle against the author's practical responses to the particular situations as they affect *him*. Leaders often do not have to execute their own decisions or live with the results, and legislation is meant to survive the legislator.[24] Even if people are trusted with such positions only because of their personal probity, their prescriptions are then trusted as issuing from an impersonal seat of authority. Under these conditions, not necessarily separated by a hard and fast line from the condition of ordinary members of the community, the enunciation of general principles is a major component of practice, and faulty enunciations of principle can spell the ruin of what is best in the mores of a society even though their authors in person exemplify the best. Mere goodness eventually degenerates unless safeguarded by noble natures who knowingly and articulately prize fine deeds for their own sake.

If virtue and virtuous deeds are held to be valuable for the sake of natural goods, this can only be because possession of the natural goods is assumed to be the supreme end. Aristotle implies that it is easy to slip into this mistake, for he classes the natural goods as *ends* and *to be pursued for themselves* (1248 b 18–25). The difference, as he states it, between them and the intrinsically noble goods is not, as we might expect, that the former are only means or instruments of the latter, hence *not* truly desirable in themselves; but that *amongst* ends desirable in themselves the noble goods are laudable, the natural goods are not. But can Aristotle in propria persona really mean that, e.g., wealth and power are ends desirable in themselves, when without use of them possession can make no difference? At *NE* 1096 a 6–7 he says that wealth cannot be the ultimate good, because it is 'useful and for the sake of something else'. Should we take his contrary suggestion in the *Eudemian Ethics* to be scouting a vulgar view which he does not share? We hardly can, because the distinction of goods in which it occurs heads the analysis of nobility, which cannot but represent Aristotle's own position.

The most obvious examples of natural goods are general resources which can be employed for any number of quite different projects; e.g., health, wealth and power. Aristotle also mentions friends and honour (1249 b 18; 1248 b 28). He may be thinking of these less in terms of particular occasions of acclaim or amicable intercourse, than as constituents of social position, which is another general resource. Now, it is logical for human beings to seek these goods without having any definite idea of how they will use them, because these goods are of a nature to be useful for almost anything. But if *usefulness* is their salient attribute, how can they be considered *ends* at all unless by someone who totally misunderstands their nature? Yet, as I have said, Aristotle speaks for himself in calling them 'ends'; not for someone so ignorant, say, of the nature of money as not to understand that money is something you spend, or hoard only so as to spend it (even if on further money-making activities) at a more advantageous moment. Does Aristotle then mean that anything is an end to the extent that it is sought, even if, like many things sought, it is also a means to something else? No, for in that case anything good or considered good would count as an end; but this is ruled out by his classification of goods at 1248 b 18 ff., which contrasts goods (G1) that are ends because desirable in themselves with goods (G2) that are not thus desirable, hence are not ends, but which are (presumably) sought for the sake of ends. And he places the natural goods firmly in the class (G1) of 'desirable *in themselves*'.[25]

The reason, I take it, is that a process of building up wealth, health or political power is not logically structured by any specific further purpose for which these results will be employed. The practical thinking and skill necessary for money-making is the same whether one plans to use money for war, education or pleasure. There is no one kind of medical science serving farmers and another serving fisherman, since one and the same kind of healthy physique is everyone's basic resource. The fact that a doctor should adjust his treatment to the needs of the patient's life-style does not entail that 'surgery', say, is the name of a genus of skills of which surgery-for-farmers and surgery-for-teachers are species. Contrast the case of 'tool making', which names a genuine genus of specifically different skills. Learning how to make fishing nets does not at all equip one for knowing how to make beehives or saws. The purpose for which a fishing net is to be used determines the design of tools, preparation of materials, and choice of methods employed in making the product. The good production of such nets will depend on knowing what they are for, hence on knowing what would be a proper or improper use. 'Proper or improper use' has here a technical sense analytically connected with the concept of that which is used. But phrases such as 'proper/improper use of funds or political influence' would normally be taken to express *ethical* assessment of the use.

'How wealth should be used' (in the sense which most readily comes to mind; namely, the ethical sense) is not part of our concept of wealth. Thus people can be very effective in acquiring wealth or the other general resources without knowing how to use them well. And yet it does not make sense not to care about using them well, given Aristotle's connections between practical wisdom and good action, and between good action and happiness; whereas one might deliberately misuse, in the technical sense, a fishing net, and be right to do so (cf. *EE* VIII.1; *NE* 1140 b 22–24). It is an ironic fact of the human condition that the things whose use it matters most to get right are those general resources which do not come to us with their correct use stamped on their conceptual faces. All this is as much as to say that practical wisdom is not a craft; which is why practical wisdom is necessary as well as the crafts, and also why an ethical inquiry such as Aristotle's is necessary.

At any rate, the above considerations explain why Aristotle classifies the natural goods as ends and as things desirable in (or *as*) themselves. This refers not to the psychological motive with which they are sought (which may be for some quite specific ulterior purpose), but to the logical form of effective practical seeking, which is geared to the nature of each of these resources as the kind of general resource that it is. Seeking wealth is valuing wealth in a practical way; thus if the activity of seeking wealth logically terminates in *wealth* (whatever the agent's special motive for engaging in it, and even if he has none), and does not logically terminate in some special use of wealth, since there is no such single use, then wealth is something which, in the very form of our seeking, we value *as itself* and not as a means to something else. It makes sense to say that wealth and the other resources are *ends,* and not stress equally that they are means even while admitting that they are nothing if not useful. This is because their difference from each other, hence the identity of each, belongs to them as *objectives to be secured* rather than as *presupposed possessions for use.*

For each affords entry to many of the same possible further advantages, whereas the process of building economic wealth is quite different from that of building physical strength or creating a political following.

Since natural goods such as health, security and livelihood are in some measure preconditions for everything else and usually depend on ceaseless work and attention, and since those goods figure in that work mainly as ends, not means, it is not surprising if essentially *practical* beings, even the virtuous, look no further when formulating their views about the chief end of life. The noble character, by contrast, consciously values good agency above its material products, and this opens up a new range of objectives. Whereas the good man pursues objectives which everyone has, but pursues them well by choosing good means, the noble person has the objective of *pursuing the original objectives well.* It fits in with this that he will seek out occasions for acting which challenge his qualities of character and intelligence, whereas the merely good person responds well to each occasion as it arises and would be neither sorry nor glad to have further opportunities to test and strengthen his virtues. But nothing in this difference suggests that the good agent is any less motivated than the noble agent to seek and do what is right or best in the particular situation.

## IV. *Theōria* in the *Eudemian Ethics*

To the noble person, whose practical focus is on excellent human agency as such, the most desirable actions and activities, the ones he would most encourage in others, are those which in one way or another express fine agency to the maximum. This is so whether we consider the action as *what* the agent does, or as his *doing* of what he does. An action may be noble in the doing or in what is done, or both. Aristotle does not raise this distinction, but it helps us understand how he connects nobility with *theōria.* Acts of meeting basic material needs are not noble in *what* is done. Since we all have those needs, the action so far as it expresses such a need expresses nothing outstanding. But the doing of it may, if the circumstances are difficult and provide a test of virtue. In such a case, the occurrence of the intended change owes most to the agent's will and intelligence, least to natural conditions or chance. However, material goods can in general come about through natural causes or chance as well as through human agency (human agency getting in where chance, too, could get in, and making up for the absence of a natural cause). Since it is not of the essence of material goods to exist only through *our* interest or concern that they should, they as the *kinds* of products they are represent no distinctively human investment, although the particular producing of them very often does. Again, some of Aristotle's 'natural goods' do represent a human or cultural investment, as, e.g., inherited social position, but not an investment by the individual possessor. *What* is most noble to do or bring about is what only oneself can: what can exist only through us as individuals operating in the specifically human mode. Thus among actions prized by the noble, not only are there those where the intended effect depends on the individual's exceptional *will,* but also, and by the same principle, those where what is done or made, even if easily done in the particular case, is an achievement uniquely ours, as, for example, a work of art or creative intellect.

By the criterion relating to *what* is done, *theōria* certainly counts as a noble activity, and it is ranked as such in the *Politics* (see, e.g., VII.3). However, here in the *Eudemian Ethics* Aristotle says only that it, or the promotion of it, is the '*noblest* limit' (1249 b 19) by which to decide how far to go in having, pursuing and using the natural goods.

There is no reason to suppose that he has in mind only the pursuit of these goods for oneself and only one's own theoretic activity. The noble person, who is surely the subject of this recommendation, is an aficionado of the noble wherever found. We should also, I think, take 'noblest limit' as implying that *theōria* is not the *only* end by which to measure the pursuit of natural goods. Other kinds of noble activity are ends for the noble person; hence wealth in excess of what is needed for leisure spent in *theōria* would not necessarily be in excess of the ethical mean, since it could well be needed for other noble practices. This would not arise, of course, if nothing is noble except the pursuing and engaging in *theōria* or if no rational choice were wise unless made with this end in view. But there is no ground in the *Eudemian Ethics* for such a monolithic interpretation, and much to suggest that Aristotle recognises a plurality of noble ends: the best kind of friendship is one example, and his sketches of the virtues of courage and magnificence suggest a variety of other noble possibilities.

Other noble activities have in common with *theōria* that they all satisfy Aristotle's closing dictum: 'This is the best limit for the soul: to perceive the nonrational part of the soul *as such* as little as possible' (1249 b 21–23; my emphasis). He is referring, I think, both to the purely biological stratum of psychic activity and to the appetitive side when it makes itself felt in opposition to reason, so figures *as* nonrational. Thus he does not mean that the best person is a practical or theoretical intellect purified of all feelings fostered and shaped by prerational training, but that these feelings in the best soul are in tune with reason. Hence they can be very much in evidence at times: the noble person is delighted, shocked, grieved when appropriate, and he sets a value on noble emotions as well as actions (cf. *NE* X.1179 b 24–26).

On the other hand, with regard to the biological part of the soul and purely somatic feelings, Aristotle probably does mean that in the best life these make as little noise as possible. Not merely in *theōria,* but in noble actions and even in ordinary decent conduct, one lives beyond the biological and animal self. Even if the theoretic intellect is separable from the body (which elsewhere Aristotle may give reason to believe; see *On the Soul* 429 a 18–b 5[26]), the ethically important contrast here is not between bodiless and embodied activity, but between sheerly biological activities and those distinctively human.

The statement that the nonrational part of the soul as such should be as little as possible in evidence points to a reason why *theōria* should be made a goal by which to limit the natural goods. The argument would be that since noble *praxis,* which imposes such a limit, is focused away from the body, *theōria,* too, should impose a limit, since it involves the body even less, hence is more noble still. But if *theōria* is one noble activity among others, even if the noblest, why does Aristotle single it out for special attention? The emphasis is such that he has sometimes been taken to insist upon *theōria* as the sole end by which to limit the natural goods. Yet it is clear that noble *practical* deeds need natural goods; so the requirements of noble practical deeds imply their own determinants of the measure of natural goods. There would be no problem if promotion of *theōria* were held to be the sole type of noble deed, but it is not credible that Aristotle's audience or that Aristotle held this view. There is, then, a range of noble activities, of which *theōria* is one and the others are practical. So why does Aristotle not simply say that *theōria* has a high place in the best life, as one (even the noblest) of a range of different noble activities, any one of which could on occasion be cited as ground for pursuing more or less of some natural good? Alternatively, he could have said (and this, too, would have been simple) that there is one general limit for the natural goods, namely noble activity in general, perhaps citing *theōria* as a leading example among others.

But Aristotle, strangely, does not take this line. Instead, he first (1248 b 8–1249 a 16) presents a picture of nobility as if that picture were *complete without reference to theōria* and only then (1249 a 21 ff.) turns to the latter. This order is responsible for the impression that in the end he proposes *theōria* as the only limit for natural goods. It is clear in the initial picture that, in the context of nobility, natural goods are for the sake of noble practical deeds, which therefore function as a limit. But it then becomes apparent in the next step that in this picture of nobility there was room for superfluity. For Aristotle now implies that his ideal character has or possibly has *more* natural goods than noble practical deeds require. The audience would surely have expected Aristotle to say that the noble person would eschew such redundancy. For otherwise he will be pursuing or holding on to some natural goods for their own sake and so would be less than noble. Yet Aristotle positively wants us to see that noble individual as having something to spare. And at this point we realise that this picture of the noble person, who is presented first as noble because of noble practical deeds and then as disposing of more natural goods than he needs for such deeds, is incoherent *unless* there is some *new* limit—something else for which the extra goods might be too much or too little.

So Aristotle first invokes a notion of nobility in which his audience would see noble practical deeds as the only kind of limit; and then implies that pursuit and use of natural goods are not adequately limited by it alone. Perhaps this is not just the clumsiness that sets up a position and then corrects it, for the net result of the manoeuvre is that Aristotle has insinuated the thought that nobility, which is said to be complete virtue, is not complete unless endowed with more than is required for noble practical deeds: it needs more by way of natural goods to use and more, too, by way of a further goal in the light of which to use them. And along with this he has also insinuated the thought that without that goal, but with the extra goods, nobility is not stably noble. *Theōria* is not only glorious in itself, but is a moral safeguard: it preserves practical nobility in superfluity much as practical nobility preserves sheer basic goodness.

The only explanation I can find for this oblique and confusing approach (as compared with a simple statement that *theōria* is one, or even the best, of various noble activities) is that Aristotle *cannot take it for granted* that his audience would acknowledge *theōria* as a noble activity amongst others. This is simply not one of the things which he can expect them automatically to have in mind when he first presents the general conception of nobility. On the other hand, he has to present this general conception (which he needs only to put into words for the audience to know it as one they share) in order to get *theōria* admitted into the best life. Since *theōria* generates no natural goods, its only hope of entry is via the category of the noble; but Aristotle cannot invoke this familiar category without also invoking its commonly accepted extension. So he then has to struggle to extend that extension to include *theōria,* too.

He writes, however, as if the barrier to recognising *theōria* as noble were less philistinic prejudice than logical perplexity about its status. By now it is firmly entrenched in the argument that the noble side of human nature *rules* the side immediately concerned with natural goods. But ruling seems to be practical: one rules by giving orders to another. Nothing higher than practical nobility gives orders to practical nobility, for any higher level of command would itself be practical nobility. So it seems as if nobility is essentially only practical and that there is nothing higher than this practicality. And since, if *theōria* is an option, practical wisdom naturally determines when it makes sense to pursue it or not, it is easy to suppose practical intelligence higher than the theoretic side of the soul (cf. *NE* 1143 b 34–35). Aristotle responds by distinguishing meanings of 'rule' and connected meanings of 'that for the sake of which' (1249 b 9–16).

In one sense (1) a person is 'ruled' by a valued objective, in another (2) by the practical wisdom that sets about obtaining it. And in one sense (a), *that for the sake of which* is the good which one aims to achieve, and in another (b) it is the beneficiary of that good. That which *rules* in sense (2) rules by issuing instructions (one part of the soul to the other, for instance, or a doctor to a patient), and *what* is ruled (i.e., managed) in this way is that for the sake of which in sense (b). The good which is aimed for is also *that for the sake of which,* but not in the sense that implies that it is ruled. It is not ruled by anything, but this is not straightforwardly because it is a ruler—as if everything in this area of discourse is either ruler or ruled—for it does not rule in sense (2). Yet even so it conforms to the principle (if such it is) that everything either rules or is ruled; for it does rule in sense (1).[27]

*Theōria,* then, can be said to 'rule' supreme even though practical wisdom is in charge of arrangements for it. Its being under the charge of practical wisdom does not imply that practical wisdom rules *it,* for this would follow only if *theōria* were an instrument of practical wisdom or its beneficiary. But, as Aristotle says of practical wisdom at the end of *NE* VI ( = *EE* V),

> . . . again it is not *supreme* over [theoretic] wisdom, i.e. over the superior part of us, any more than the art of medicine is over health; for it does not use it but provides for its coming into being; it issues orders, then, for its sake, but not to it. Further, to maintain its supremacy would be like saying that the art of politics rules the gods because it issues orders about all the affairs of the state. (1145 a 6–11)

Rule in the sense in which *theōria* can rule is the rule of the good simply as good; for the good as such can cause only as final cause (cf. *Metaphysics* 988 b 6–15). An efficient cause causes through having the power and not immediately because it is good. Hence whatever can affect our lives through final causality alone is closer to a kind of perfection of goodness than things which cause by efficiency. For if something has being to the extent that it makes a difference, then what makes a difference *as and only as a final cause* has being identical with the goodness attributed to it. This would be a reason for ranking *theōria* higher than practice, and also for holding, as Aristotle does (*Metaphysics,* 1072 b 1 ff.) that God, who is best, causes only as object of love.

I shall not pause here over the connection, obscure in the *Eudemian Ethics,* between God and *theōria.* Whatever the sense in which *theōria* here is 'of' God (1249 b 17), the *theōria* is ours, and an end for us. Its divine relevance (which need not be precisely expounded to make the point) gives it a right to a preeminent place in human life. With this conclusion Aristotle has carried out the main task of the *EE,* which was to show, first, that happiness is activity in accordance with complete excellence[28] (1219 a 38–39), and then, by attending to its various aspects, what complete excellence is. He has also in effect answered the initial question about the three lives: if they are exclusive alternatives, the best is none of the three; otherwise, the best is 'political' *and* theoretical. It is a life of practical wisdom enlightened by nobility and looking towards *theōria.* This, I think, is more accurate than saying that the best is a *conjunction* of practice and *theōria,* for in the ethics Aristotle's focus never ceases to be practical. He views *theōria* not internally, so to speak, but as a practical objective: an objective within the educator's general objective, which is the best kind of person leading and shaping for himself, through his practical choices, the best life.

It would be absurd, though, if the best life included only provision for *theōria* and not also the enjoyment of it. Vain provision cannot be part of the perfect (even if only humanly perfect) life; and in the best, complete virtue must be exercised, i.e., the excellence of every part of the soul including the theoretic part. However, when we consider actual human engagement in *theōria* as an element of the best life, we should, I think, consider it not merely as engagement in *that,* but as an activity made possible by practical wisdom and the love of human noble things in general. Thus the concepts *practical wisdom* and *virtue of character* will figure in the ethical account of each of the parts of the soul. An explanation of each of these levels of practical virtue makes reference (we have seen) to the other, while the ethical account of the rôle of the theoretic part makes reference to practical wisdom and to nobility, a virtue of character. Thus in the *Eudemian Ethics,* the best life has a definitional unity grounded on concepts of *practical* virtue.

Nobility is not a species of practical wisdom, since practical wisdom is deliberative, whereas a sense of the noble shapes the ends in terms of which we deliberate. It belongs, therefore, with the virtues of the nonrational but rationally amenable part of the soul; but while the others relate more directly to the soul's nonrationality as such (being qualities which make the difference between its listening and not listening to reason), nobility is the self-celebration of those qualities and of their having *made* that difference. This logical reflexivity does not entail that nobility cannot be developed, like the other moral virtues, through prerational training; and of course it mostly is (cf. *NE* 1179 b 8–9). But nobility has an intellectual affinity which the others lack. It is not possible to become courageous or temperate through argument, but perhaps it is possible to come to love excellent action for its own sake through being brought to see, by an inquiry such as Aristotle's, that excellent human activity is what in essence the supreme human good must be. This noble seeing, which is brought to a head by arguments, involves an intellectual grasp of principles previously grasped only in practice, and these principles once abstracted can be rationally extended to bring to light new ethical possibilities, as, for example, those which concern *theōria*. In this respect, the Eudemian position on *theōria*, according to the interpretation which I have offered, resembles the argument in *NE* X.9 about legislating for morals, where accepted views are made the foundation of a far-reaching departure from common practice. It remains to be seen whether the Nicomachean approach to *theōria* follows similar lines.

### V. A Sketch of the Nicomachean Position

The Eudemian treatment leaves important questions untouched or virtually so. For instance, (1) why should it be accepted that *theōria* is a noble activity, let alone the 'noblest limit' for natural goods? We have seen hints of reasons: a connection with God, and the irrelevance to *theōria* of the nonrational part of the soul. But these points are so abstract, and the first so ambiguous, that there is no telling whether on closer consideration they would lead to the same conclusion without pitfall. (2) Apart from the one remark about its being noblest limit, Aristotle does not say whether the activity of *theōria* is in any sense better than all other activities. (3) There is no guidance on whether *theōria* and its promotion should ever, never or sometimes take precedence over other noble activities.

The answer to the second question might determine the answer to the third, and both might depend on the answer to the first. However, so far as (3) is concerned, Aristotle is under no obligation to produce a general principle of priority. He may well think none is possible. There are different noble activities, and they can conflict on occasion; but it is up to on-the-spot practical wisdom to decide. The conflict could be between an activity connected with *theōria* and one that is not, or between two that are not, or, for that matter, between noble action and some humdrum action related to the necessities of life and requiring no special virtue to accomplish. This would be in keeping with Aristotle's general approach in both ethical treatises, as well as with common sense.

On the other hand, the shape of the Eudemian argument as I have interpreted it does leave the impression that natural goods are to be employed in the service of *theōria* only when the claims of practical nobility have been satisfied. That suggests that *theōria* never takes precedence. It is difficult to know whether Aristotle means to communicate this, or whether it is only an appearance due to his having to present nobility and *theōria* in, as we saw, two separate stages—and in that order. The assertion that *theōria* is 'the noblest limit' does not sit comfortably with an account in which it seems to be served with leftovers. Again, it is difficult to know what to make of the sentence with which the *EE,* as we have it, ends: 'So much, then, for the limit [or: definition] of nobility, and the goal of the things good without qualification [sc. the natural goods]' (1249 b 24–25). This may refer to *theōria* as setting a *limit* to the claims of noble practical activity, in which case it entails that the latter should not always automatically have priority. But the remark can also equally well be translated as referring to the *definitive account* he has given of nobility in general. In that case it is consistent with the view that the noble person takes care of noble practical deeds first. And giving priority to the practical (either sometimes or even always) may or may not be incompatible with holding *theōria* nobler. For 'nobler' need not imply 'better' in a sense that would justify granting it general practical priority.

In the *Eudemian Ethics,* Aristotle builds a case for *theōria* by showing that a life of 'complete excellence', which has so far been understood in practical terms, must include it as an objective. Turning now to the Nicomachean account, we are struck by the differences, the most drastic of which are Aristotle's assertions (1) that *theōria* is complete or perfect happiness (1177 a 16–18; 1178 b 7–8); and (2) that the life of practical excellence is 'happiest' only 'in a secondary way' (1178 a 8–9). The argument for these conclusions, by its length and complexity, shows up the Eudemian approach as abrupt and dogmatic in comparison. The conceptual content of the *NE* is also very different. The notion of noble-goodness plays no explicit part, and the special term for it used in *EE* appears only once (1179 b 10); the divine character of *theōria* is expounded at length; certain formal features of happiness set out in *NE* I (with no corresponding treatment in *EE*) play a pivotal role; and so does the idea of pleasure in the sense of amusement or diversion (1176 b 9–1177 a 11).

These differences notwithstanding, Aristotle's intention in the *NE,* so I would argue, is fundamentally the same as in the *EE.* Just as the latter tries to show that the life of practical excellence at its best naturally reaches out to *theōria,* so the former tries to show *theōria* as the culmination of the same life: the life of practical excellence at its best. Both works give the same answer to the question 'What is human happiness?'—that it is the happiness of essentially practical beings, hence of beings whose essential virtues are practical. But, according to the interpretation which I offer, the analysis of what is entailed by the fullest exercise of practical virtue shows that a life of this stamp must do active honour to a sort of value which in itself lacks practical justification and by its nature gives rise to no practical concern even for its own instantiation. It is therefore wholly dependent, under human conditions, on the good will of practical virtue for being realised otherwise than haphazardly or with no more security than would be shared by anything trivial enough to be rightly left to chance or individual taste. But the good will vital in order that *theōria* should flourish is not an act of quixotic grace on the part of practical virtue. A virtue that does not fundamentally enhance its possessors is not a true virtue in Aristotle's sense. No doubt we as potential subjects of theoretical activity benefit from the support we as *practical* beings can give it, but this is of ethical significance only if it is also true that we *as* practical beings are better off through giving that support. For if we are essentially practical, to support *theōria* will not enhance us if supporting *theōria* is an ornamental appendage to practice at its best, but only if supporting *theōria* is squarely required for our *practical* best to be realised.

In maintaining that the basic intention in both treatises is the same, I do not mean to imply that the differences are not profound, but that they relate, rather, to the execution of the intention and the concrete results. In the *NE* the final emphasis is such as to make it appear that *theōria* is not merely vital but of *supreme* importance—a question on which the *EE,* so far as it suggests anything at all, sends a more ambiguous message.[29] The *NE* conclusion owes its extreme character to that part of the argument which relates *theōria* to God, a matter on which the *EE* remains enigmatic. Now while I do not suggest that Aristotle is not happy with his conclusion in the *NE,* it is worth raising the question whether he in his position could call upon any considerations in support of *theōria* that would not have been either too weak or too strong. It is possible to be in a situation in which, in order to argue effectively that something, whatever it might be, deserves a substantial place in the good life, one is conceptually compelled to go over the top, since the only reason for taking it seriously at all requires that one take it so seriously that everything else seems to pass into insignificance. Although we have no evidence that he would have desired the shelter of such an apology, it is a reasonable guess that, faced with the choice of overstatement or understatement on this matter, Aristotle at any stage would have incurred the dialectical costs of the former, perhaps in the spirit of his attitude on moral training and pleasure:

> For of the extremes one is more erroneous, the other less so; therefore since to hit the mean is hard in the extreme, we must, as a second best, as people say, take the least of the evils. . . . But we must consider the things towards which we ourselves also are easily carried away; for some of us tend to one thing, some to another; and this will be recognizable from the pleasure and pain we feel. We must drag ourselves away to the contrary extreme; for we shall get into the intermediate state by drawing well away from error, as people do in straightening sticks that are bent. (1109 a 33–b 7)

Not at the beginning, and perhaps also not at the end of the *NE,* does Aristotle suppose his own word final.[30] We recall how, when rounding off his discussion in Book I of happiness as excellent functioning in accordance with human nature, he wrote:

> Let this serve as an outline of the good; for we must presumably first sketch it roughly, and then later fill in the details. But it would seem that anyone is capable of carrying on and articulating what has once been well outlined, and that time is a good discoverer or partner in such a work; to which facts the advances of the arts are due; for anyone can add what is lacking. (1098 a 20–26)

This is rooted in the fact that, as he has said all along, a philosophical system of ethical values should be practical. Thus he continued:

> And we must also remember what has been said before, and not look for precision in all things alike, but in each class of things such precision as accords with the subject-matter, and so much as is appropriate to the inquiry. For a carpenter and a geometer look for right angles in different ways; the former does so in so far as the right angle is useful for his work, while the latter inquires what it is or what sort of thing it is; for he is a spectator of the truth. We must act in the same way, then, in all other matters as well, that our main task may not be subordinated to minor questions. (1098 a 26–33)

This contrast between carpenter and geometer does not relate to a particular exercise of carpentry skill. The context shows that Aristotle is comparing craft and science in terms of their *development* as kinds of knowledge. The demonstration of new theorems depends on rigorously defined starting points from which theorems have already been deduced by the same methods; but the progress of a craft is not like this, nor is the progress of ethics. Crafts advance with discoveries of new materials and physical processes, as well as in the light of new understanding of the purpose to be served. The development is rational, but there is no reason to suppose that the same new possibilities would have come to our attention if we had not already been engaging in the craft or had been engaging in it under different physical circumstances. So with ethics: only by entering into and following a general investigation of the good, using the conceptual materials available at any stage, do we come to perceive the relevance of considerations not entailed by the starting-points and so come to perceive new dimensions of value.

So even supposing we grant some degree of exaggeration in Aristotle's *NE* doctrine of *theōria,* it is not easy to know how this should affect our judgment of him as a philosopher (which here means a practical philosopher), if we also suppose him principally concerned to establish for *theōria* a firm basis of practical commitment, the scope of which he willingly leaves it to others to refine once the general spirit has taken hold. That would be a practical approach if, as I shall elaborate further, he has reason to think that some such unqualified initial push is necessary to overcome the 'natural' tendency: a tendency which, if left to itself, would accord *theōria* too little importance in human affairs. But in any case, the charge of exaggeration, if applicable at all, is applicable only within bounds set by a conceptual scenario in which considerations grounded in the intrinsic splendours of *theōria* are framed by other considerations more down to earth but no less crucial. I shall now attempt in slightly more detail to sketch the form, as I see it, of the whole position, stressing its contrast with a different form which may easily be confused with it.

Aristotle contends that *theōria* is our best activity and complete or perfect happiness. Stamped into his later readers' minds is the schema of a type of ethical theory according to which something—Z—is said to be what is best, and all other goods are then said to be good so far as they lead to Z or are its constituents. (Such theories characteristically ignore different senses in which something 'leads to' another: as child to adult; as rain and sun to the growth of crops; as the dentist's drilling to dental health?) Reading *'theōria'* for 'Z' in the modern schema, it would follow either that the best decision in every situation is that which most conduces to *theōria* (whether one's own or everyone's remains to be determined); or that the general exercise of practical virtue would be good only as a means to *theōria* (since obviously the latter activity does not include the former as a constituent). But nothing in the *Ethics* before X.7–8 prepares us for such conclusions.

In this shape of argument, the worth of the practical is made to depend on an alleged relation to *theōria,* whose supreme value is presupposed. By contrast, Aristotle's argument, as I view it, grounds the supreme importance of *theōria* in the value, already assigned, of excellent practice. His reasoning is two pronged. He shows (1) that if the life of practical virtue is to maintain its claim to be the best, it must include something higher than the exercise of practical virtue. And the antecedent of this hypothetical is not in question. Aristotle, I have indicated, speaks as one to others of a group for whom that proposition states the values by which they already live. Then he shows (2) that *theōria,* by its intrinsic nature, is an activity superbly qualified above others to fill that requirement in the life of practical virtue. His display of those qualifications may be overzealous, given the purpose of this argument. But more important is the purpose itself, which is to endow the life of essentially *practical* beings with a content required for it to approach the ideal of *such* a life at its best. The endowment does not logically convert it into a kind of life not essentially practical, but from good to best of the same type.

Aristotle's argument for the first prong is grounded in considerations about leisure, pleasure, and the need for serious goals; for the second, in attributes of *theōria* itself. This present sketch does not explain how the position will fit his statements that *theōria* is 'perfect happiness' (implying that practical activity is not perfect happiness) and that the life of practical virtue is 'happiest only in a secondary way'. These are questions for later sections. Meanwhile, though, we can already see that Aristotle has a difficult path to tread, and one that will lend itself to misinterpretation. For the more powerful the considerations supporting the second prong, the harder it is to suppress the inference that the best life is not really practical at all or is so only incidentally.

## VI. The Need to Justify *Theōria*

Human *theōria* is utterly dependent on practical wisdom for securing it regular conditions. This is because *theōria* can make no practical contribution to anything at all, not even its *own* maintenance. This impracticality is, in a way, *theōria's* own worst enemy in the context of human existence. *Theōria,* we could even say, would have a better chance of flourishing if it were not so truly itself and theoretic. That being its nature, how does it merit serious *practical* concern: concern on the part of essentially practical beings? What proper business can it be of theirs? Yet unless *theōria* is made their business, it has little chance to develop.

The two-pronged argument outlined in the last section is meant to show *theōria* to be indeed our practical concern. And in showing this, the argument shows something by no means obvious about the nature of practical life at its best. I have so far emphasised this aspect, since I think it the area of greatest misunderstanding. But the two-pronged argument is also a justification of *theōria.* For essentially practical beings, who want to live well according to their nature, there could hardly be a more powerful justification, if the argument is sound. The situation is the reverse of what is implied by a schema of the classic utilitarian type referred to in the last section. According to that, practical decisions are correct if and only if they aim at *theōria,* or practical virtues and virtuous practices are worthwhile because they promote it. These suggestions are inapplicable to Aristotle, so far as they imply that a practical decision or a practice, in particular or in general, is justified only by its relation to *theōria*—where 'justified' means that we need to know that relation before we can rationally make or endorse any particular practical decision, or before we can rationally commit ourselves to good practice and practical virtue at all. This last notion is arguably incoherent; for if we were not already by nature committed to practice, and to looking for our good within that sphere, we could take no interest in anything at all as a *practical* objective. So however glorious *theōria* seemed, the idea of our taking steps (let alone being rationally committed) to close some practical gap between ourselves and it (or the conditions for it) would never occur. In that case, it follows, I think, that *theōria* would not figure to us as a good at all within a wider scheme of things, some of them subordinate to it and deriving value from their relation to it. For (on the supposed condition that we perceive nothing as a practical objective) *theōria* could not command our interest at all except by already filling our horizon as when we are actually in the midst of it and absorbed. We should have to be "grabbed by" *theōria* if we were ever to move from indifference to absorption, just as an animal is grabbed by fear or appetite on suddenly perceiving some object; but in the case of *theōria* there seems to be no physical or sensory mechanism that could make that happen, and *theōria* cannot *itself*, of course, grab anything!

On the contrasting view which I shall argue in detail is Aristotle's, we can come to realize philosophically that practical life is the human potential for *theōria;* hence that practical life (to the truly educated eye) is not the end of ends, since its metaphysical nature (like that of any potential) is to lead to something else. But for rational beings such as we, i.e. beings already at source committed to practice but neither born nor brought up knowing all that we need to know about it and its value to us, this discovery about the relation of practice to *theōria* cannot motivate us towards practical goodness as such, since we are already motivated.[31] The discovery can only give a new form to existing practical aspirations. To this it might be objected that if practice without *theōria* is the potential for *theōria,* then *theōria* should develop naturally out of practice. This is false if it means that we mechanically progress into *theōria,* but true if 'natural development' is allowed to include the reflective realisation that *theōria* is justified in terms of the self-same practical excellence which we already see to be our human good. Thus the full potential for *theōria* is self-reflective practice under conditions that allow for this kind of reflection. Broken down, that potential consists in (1) the thing—good conduct—which Aristotle's *Ethics* is mainly about and which is already there in individuals and communities before he starts to study it; together with (2) the reflective mind that engages in this sort of study; under (3) conditions permitting the study to occur.

Under one aspect, then, the two-pronged argument provides a full statement of the nature of practical life at its best, and under another it defends and justifies *theōria.* Aristotle, I think, it more concerned with this second, apologetic, side. This stress of his has helped foster confusion because it distracts attention from the first aspect. It has even made Aristotle seem to be addressing a problem not his but ours. For reasons of culture and temperament, Aristotle's modern readers, as their studying shows, are at home with the thought of happiness as bound up with intellectual and spiritual activity; and, for reasons arising from later philosophical developments, they are not so at home with the idea that happiness is in virtuous conduct, since this seems sometimes to require the sacrifice of happiness. Thus we read Aristotle's discussion as amorally declaring that good conduct matters less than the happiness of theoretic activity or is worthwhile only when it leads to that end. And the difficulty of making such a position plausible by sober argument may seem to explain his paean to *theōria* in *NE* X.7–8. But, in my view, the balance (or imbalance) of Aristotle's approach betrays quite a different, and even an opposite, attitude; an attitude in which it is clear and firmly established that the best and happiest life is one of practical virtue; and is not at all clear or firmly established that *theōria* can be justified as a serious pursuit.

This is confirmed by the oddity (as it would be otherwise) of his failing to say straight out in the *Eudemian Ethics* that *theōria* is of course one of those activities which a noble person would value (see Section III above). It is further confirmed by general considerations. Why should Aristotle find it necessary to glorify *theōria?* We can rule out any suggestion that he personally needs a justification before being willing to give himself to theoretic activity. We should also respect the practical intention of the *Ethics* enough to dismiss any suggestion that he engages in this defence simply because it would be interesting to see what it looks like. The remaining hypothesis is that it is needed for or by his audience, among whom there are possible future leaders of cities.

From our own point of view, the practical question that arises about *theōria,* as about many other valuable activities, is not whether it is worthwhile at all, but how much time and effort to devote to it compared with other goals, some of which are possibly more urgent on practical or moral grounds. Hence it puzzles us that such questions of priority and the distribution of resources are hardly touched on by Aristotle. This is because we approach the matter committed, not only as individuals but as members of societies institutionally committed, to supporting such activities as astrophysics, pure mathematics, and the study of ancient philosophy. If we have a theory by which to justify this commitment to *theōria,* its foundation is probably to be found in Aristotle's *Ethics.* But we peer in on Aristotle and his audience from a world that is ours, not theirs, and we have no reason to assume that he, along with us, enjoys the security of any such general commitment.[32]

Addressing his audience on ethical matters, Aristotle can rely on their common-sense intuitions, along with well-known findings of philosophers. But so far as safeguarding *theōria* is concerned, the findings to date are unpromising. Aristotle himself bears heavy responsibility for this, as we can see if we go back, for contrast, to Socrates. Socrates, Aristotle points out near the beginning of the *Eudemian Ethics,* held 'knowledge of excellence to be the end [of life], and used to inquire what is justice, what bravery and each of the parts of virtue; and his conduct was reasonable, for he thought all the excellences to be kinds of knowledge, so that to know justice and to be just came simultaneously' (1216 b 3–8). Socrates, in other words, did not distinguish rational and nonrational parts of the ethical soul, so could not see how knowing what to do would not necessarily result in doing it or how an intellectual grasp of the definitions of the virtues might leave someone morally unenhanced. Socrates, of course, was interested in defining the virtues not because these definitions held *knowledge*—knowledge such as one might also have of other sorts of things—but because, in his view, this knowledge would be *virtue.* It was for this reason that 'Socrates . . . busied himself about ethical matters and neglected the world of nature as a whole, but sought the universal in these ethical matters, and fixed thought for the first time on definitions' (*Metaphysics,* 987 b 1–4).

Thus Socrates' pursuit of his vocation proceeds as if on these assumptions: there are no worthwhile abstract investigations that are not abstract ethical investigations, and there are no abstract ethical investigations that are not processes of moral improvement in respect of the virtue investigated. Plato unravelled the second of these connections. He constructed his political ideal in the recognition that moral development (even when ideal) must begin with prerational training of the emotions in and through appropriate exposure to particular situations; also that virtues such as courage and temperance not only do not start but need not end in the intellectual grasp of their own definitions. However, Platonic practical wisdom, at any rate in the *Republic,* is the wisdom of *philosophers* who govern in the light of rigorous knowledge of the Forms: eternal natures which express the Form of the Good, the ground, Plato says, of their being and being knowable. It would seem that the domain of theoretical knowledge is nothing other than a cosmic system of values. However we understand this, the vision allows no possibility of a split between the study of the Good in all its forms and the study, in all its forms, of Being; nor, consequently, of a split between the kinds of questions and methods appropriate when human good is at issue and the kinds appropriate to the abstract sciences.[33]

If Plato's single most important contribution to ethics was the recognition of the nonrational part of the soul as posing its own problems of education, Aristotle's, we must surely say, was to recognise the fundamental difference between pursuit of truth for the sake of intellectual understanding and pursuit of truth for the sake of better doing and living (which latter pursuit is not homogeneous either, since practical wisdom's deliberation about particulars is one thing and the ethical inquiry of Aristotle himself another, and there may be yet other forms).

It seems clear at first that the separation of practical and theoretical reason[34] can only benefit both sides, each receiving the philosopher's blessing to operate according to its own nature unburdened by alien principles and alien subject matter. But under these enlightened conditions, what becomes of *theōria?* With Socrates and Plato, theoretical methods and standards of rigour, and (in Plato's case) propaideutic studies in such subjects as arithmetic, geometry and pure kinematics, rode in on the back of profound ethical concern. This influence is apparent even in such hard-headed dialogues as *Theaetetus* and *Sophist,* where Plato makes war on cognitive relativism and sophistic paradoxes about falsity and nonbeing.

Socrates and Plato saved logic and argumentative method from being mauled to pieces almost at birth by abusers who, wilful or ignorant, confounded thoughts with words and rational argument with rhetorical pressure. Socrates' contribution was his own first-order practice of philosophy; Plato's was the exploration of what that practice implied or presupposed on the level of metaphysics and epistemology. But there can be no winnowing of logic from fallacy unless truth matters, so that standards are set for reason; and taking truth seriously needs no apology when 'grasping the truth' is held virtually synonymous with 'knowing how we should live', or even (for Socrates) with 'courage', 'temperance', 'justice'. So true philosophy began to sort itself out from foolish or pernicious rival pretenders to the name of 'cultivation'; but philosophy did this under the aegis of a high ethical purpose. Once that ethical connection is broken and theoretic activity allowed out entirely on its own recognisance, what entitles it to more consideration than any eccentric hobby?

This last note had been raucously sounded almost three generations earlier, by Aristophanes in the *Clouds,* and would not be hard to stir up again without necessarily reviving the by now less relevant features of Aristophanes' attack. What he parodied in the conceptual rough and tumble of his *'phrontisterion'* was not just *theō-*

*ria,* but an unholy amalgam of *theōria,* eristic and rhetoric blended under the name of 'sophistry', as the audience of his time perceived them. Since then, each of these strands of 'sophistry' has been cut down to the size of its true identity; but while that may help the image of *theōria* as an innocent or socially harmless pursuit, it does nothing to make it important.

Hence Aristotle faces in the *Ethics*[35] the falling apart of Socrates' creed that intellectual activity at its finest should be the business of every right-minded citizen. Plato in his writings tried to preserve the essence of this conviction by narrowing its application to the rulers of his ideal state.[36] De facto, however, under the far from ideal conditions in which Plato lived and influenced the lives of others, that noblest activity was, even in our sense of the word, 'academic'. It was at home in a school, and there it flourished, becoming ever more potent in scope and subtlety to generate its own world (indeed, worlds) of theoretical problems and interests, and its own self-authenticated methods. What has this to do with being a good citizen in a real society?[37] If nothing, how can that activity be noblest?[38] Or does its noblesse entail that it ought to be suspended until such time as the ideal state comes about on earth, and only then allowed to enter the lives of already ideal citizens? If this is absurd, it may not be much more absurd than the alternative, which is to insist even now that we sponsor this cultivation, on grounds of its utmost dignity, without even trying to pretend it anything but useless!

If *theōria* really is the fine thing that its devotees affirm, then of course it is not useless in the sense of being a waste of time. The problem is not one of crude verbal confusion between 'useless' in that sense and in some sense contrasted with 'effective'. Aristotle has already said when discussing practical wisdom that even if practical wisdom produced no external results it would be worth having simply because it is a human excellence, so that the mere possession and exercise of it is happiness already (1144 a 1–6). On the other hand, practical wisdom and the moral virtues are exercised only in making and trying to carry out decisions that relate to contingent particulars. That is the nature of these virtues: to be in essence and intention practical, even where the corresponding efforts fail to be practical in the sense of accomplishing what was intended. The problem is to see how, if the summit of human excellence is located in such qualities, any privileged position can be justified for an activity essentially impractical. That is why we cannot take for granted that theoretical activity is 'noble', once it is freed from its historical association with practical virtue. It is noble and good to (in the eyes of) those who happen to love it, just as it is pleasant to them. But Aristotle is concerned in the *Ethics* with what is noble and good without qualification (cf. 1152 b 26–30), not with tastes and subjective predilections.

This is Aristotle's problem, and no one has done more to create it than he. Not only does he show how human practical cognition has its own sphere and standards, being neither a genus nor a species of theoretical knowledge. He has also insisted that practical thinking is a genuine exercise of reason (1139 a 5–15). A philosopher who holds that what we call practical 'thinking' is nothing but a kind of nonrational habituated response could then go on to elevate *theōria* as the unique fulfilment of our rational nature and could reserve for it special privileges not dependent on its exploded pretensions to generate practical virtues. But Aristotle has knocked that support away too. For him the virtue of practical wisdom is practical *reason* at its best, and so it would seem, since we are practical, to be reason *in us* at its best.

The plight of theoretical wisdom vis à vis practical virtue in Aristotle's *Ethics* recalls that of justice vis à vis external goods in Book II of the *Republic*. The brothers Glaucon and Adimantus challenge Socrates to come to the rescue of justice, and part of the challenge is expressed as follows (Adimantus speaking):

> Parents and tutors are always telling their sons and wards that they are to be just; but why? not for the sake of justice, but for the sake of reputation; in the hope of obtaining for him who is reputed just some of those offices, marriages and the like which Glaucon has enumerated among the advantages accruing to the unjust from the reputation of justice . . . they throw in the good opinion of the gods, and will tell you of a shower of benefits which the heavens, as they say, rain on the pious. (362 e 8–363 a 4)

> And now when the young hear all this said about virtue and vice, and the way in which gods and men regard them, how are their minds likely to be affected, my dear Socrates—those of them, I mean, who are quickwitted, and, like bees on the wing, light on every flower, and from all that they hear are prone to draw conclusions as to what manner of persons they should be, and in what way they are to walk if they are to make the best of life? (365 a 5–b 2)

> No one has ever blamed injustice or praised justice except with a view to the glories, honours and benefits which flow from them. (366 e 2–5)

> Let others praise justice and censure injustice, magnifying the rewards and honours of the one and abusing the other; that is a manner of arguing which, coming from them, I am ready to tolerate, but from you [sc. Socrates] who have spent your whole life in consideration of this question, unless I hear the contrary from your own lips, I expect something better. (367 d 5–e 1)[39]

That Socrates spent his whole life in considering the question of justice and the other moral virtues is exactly what we should expect of one who saw the path to such virtues as lying through intellectual inquiry about the nature of those very virtues. If it seemed to Socrates that the inquiry itself and the human goodness which is its topic are both supremely worthwhile, this common feature can only have confirmed his conviction that virtue and abstract knowledge of virtue are one. If, on the other hand, he separates them enough to prize such knowledge only as a means to virtue, then he makes the abstract intellectual enterprise vulnerable to some of the same objections to which justice is exposed by those who laud it for bringing in its train what Aristotle terms the 'natural goods'. Those already committed to justice for its own sake may not be affected by this vulgar attitude, even if they are at a loss to give any better rationale of justice; but 'the young' will be affected. People quickly realise, as Adimantus stresses in the nearby passage, that material goods arise from the appearance or reputation of justice. But if justice matters because of external goods, then what matters is the appearance, and justice itself matters only as a means (often unnecessary) to the appearance.

From Aristotle's point of view the issue is reversed in the case of Socratic intellectual inquiry, since inquiries about virtue result, not in virtue, but in its conceptual representation—a kind of appearance to the mind. 'Taking on the form' of virtue in this way is as different from virtue as the external semblance of virtue. If virtue itself is what matters for the good life, the intellectual activity of taking on the form is surely as beside the point as an empty reputation for virtue. And as for inquiry into matters unrelated to ethics and practice, this must be still more irrelevant. Now given how he himself lives, Aristotle is as personally bound as Socrates to defend his protegé against friends who open the gate to its enemies by valuing it for the wrong reasons. But when the protegé is theoretic wisdom, its proper apologist is precisely one who does *not* spend all his life over this and other ethical problems, but one who, like Aristotle, lives and is known to live away from them much of the time in the areas of science and metaphysics.

Aristotle's Nicomachean audience is surely sympathetic to *theōria,* since an audience of philistines would neither need nor comprehend his earlier warnings not to expect from ethics the rigour of exact science. But they have the right to know why their enthusiasm for clarity and rigour is *worth* the care of being channelled in proper directions, rather than simply being brushed aside—especially as Aristotle means to reach out through his hearers to the wider social environment. For his new proposals at the very end of the *Nicomachean Ethics* surely have to do not only with the form of character training, but with its content, too. Law should provide the framework for rearing good and happy citizens; and high among the qualities demanded should be love and respect for *theōria.* Such a disposition needs no recommendation to those who possess it already, but Aristotle is concerned for its precarious future.

I have tried in this section to provide a perspective on the almost desperate intensity of Aristotle's Nicomachean arguments for *theōria.* If he protests too much, this may call to mind the spirit in which Socrates accepted the challenge of Glaucon and Adimantus:

> On the one hand I feel I am unequal to the task . . . and yet I cannot refuse to help, while breath and speech remain to me; I am afraid that there would be an impiety in being present when justice is evil spoken of, and not lifting up a hand in her defence. And therefore I had best give such help as I can. (368 b 4–c 3)[39]

## VII. Divine Activity versus Human Happiness

In the last section I set out the dialectical context in which it comes about that Aristotle must provide an ethical justification for *theōria.* Accepting this context commits us, I think, to accepting certain limits on what, from Aristotle's point of view, can count as a viable justification. Aristotle, I have suggested, is responding to the new perception, largely the result of his own analysis of the practical virtues, that *theōria,* once seen for what it is, fails to support the ethical weight placed upon it by Socrates and Plato. Hence it must either be shown to bear a different weight or lose out on special privileges.

Those philosophers had integrated *theōria* into the good life by directly relating it to the development of moral virtue and practical wisdom. We can say that in their accounts theoretic wisdom subserves the practical virtues, but it would be going too far to ascribe to either thinker a position consciously framed in such terms: terms which recognise (by rejecting) the contrasted view that *theōria* is not a way to practical virtue, but is nonetheless valuable in its own right for reasons having to do with its own unique nature and with that unique side of ourselves that comes alive in it. For example, no one sets greater distance than Plato in the *Theaetetus* between the activity of the pure philosopher and the mundanities of law court and marketplace; but instead of drawing the implication that the same distance divides the philosopher from justice, temperance and practical wisdom (as well as from the opposite vices), Plato lifts *those practical virtues* up out of the sphere of daily doings in order to preserve their connection with pure philosophy. Thus day-to-day practical intelligence and civic involvement go hand in hand with meanness of spirit, dishonesty and the perversion of reason through rhetoric, while all true goodness belongs only to the godlike philosopher, who is laughed at by ordinary mortals for his 'helpless ignorance in matters of daily life' (*Theaetetus* 172 d 4–177 b 7).[40]

Since Plato never wrote his projected dialogue *The Philosopher,* we do not know his full thinking on this question,[41] but it would be unrealistic to suppose him to have broken through to an unperplexing separation of the powers in which practical and theoretical are allotted their distinct and noncompeting ends and excellences. To surrender the vision that these excellences spring from a common root would make nonsense of the life of Socrates. And any thinker soaked in this atmosphere would view the justification of *theōria* as an *ethical* task in a narrower, and to us more controversial, sense than that in which anyone's decision to support any goal, policy or life-style is 'ethical' because it reflects a value-judgment. The argument for *theōria* must be 'ethical' in the sense of relating that activity to topics at the heart of ethics, such as *virtue, good conduct* and *practical wisdom.* Aristotle sees that practical goodness and theoretic wisdom cannot be integrated in the ways which Socrates and Plato assumed possible, but his own divergence on the nature of the relation should not mask his acceptance, in new form, of the shared assumption that *theōria* is to be valued as enhancing the very same rational human nature that reaches its more easily recognised peaks in the *practical* virtues.

I am suggesting in effect that the two-pronged argument is not just *a* way to make a case for *theōria,* but for Aristotle under the conditions of his thinking would be the natural and even the only way. However, as I also indicated, the materials from which such an argument is built must include at least one premiss concerning the nature of that activity considered on its own. This premiss or group of premisses is now our topic.

At the beginning of *NE* X.7, Aristotle asserts that *theōria* is the expression of the supreme excellence, it being the activity of 'that which is best'. What is best is theoretic *nous* or understanding, whose objects are the best of all knowable objects (1177 a 12–21). Now insofar as this statement amounts to a 'serious call' to *theōria,* it is ineffectual by itself, for anyone who questions the claims on us of *theōria* will refuse to accept that this activity is best in any sense that entails its fitness to be *our* supreme end. The sceptic need not adopt the cheapening tactics of an Aristophanes. He can make his point while sincerely conceding to *theōria* the glories for which philosophers extol it. Aristotle himself adverted in *NE* I to a good conceived of by some which is beyond any good that we can either win or lose (1096 b 32–35). The case in point was Plato's Form of the Good. But might this not also be true of a living activity such as *theōria?* Something might be counted a glorious good and be also to some extent practicable by us; but that does not make it *our* good, and a *human* end, unless it is also good when engaged in by us. The goodness of the natural goods depends, we saw, on who has and uses them. And the goodness of *theōria* must surely likewise depend on who—or what—engages in it.

The reason why *theōria* counts as best, or why that element counts as best of which *theōria* is the activity, should have a bearing on this question. It is best because 'divine'.

> Whether it be intellect [*nous*] or something else that is this element which is thought to be our natural ruler and guide and to take thought of things noble and divine, whether it be itself also divine or only the most divine element in us, the activity of this in accordance with its proper excellence will be complete [or: perfect] happiness. (1177 a 12–17)

Here Aristotle separates and connects the two sides of the ambiguity left unresolved in the *Eudemian Ethics.* The activity's subject, *nous*, is divine or of a divine nature; and its objects are also things 'noble and divine'. What are these objects? We need not assume them restricted to God and God's attributes considered as the field of a special subject, theology.[42] For Aristotle, the divine objects of *theōria* surely include the eternal patterns of the universe, as for instance the celestial motions and the ever-recurring cycles of perishable natural kinds. They would also include abstract mathematical relations and nonmathematisable forms of order and beauty found in plants and animals. Aristotle's statement that the objects of *theōria* are 'divine' is a formal characterisation of those objects which sets no limit on their possible range. The word draws attention to these features: the object, whatever it may be, is in some sense timeless; it is not at the mercy of chance or at the disposal of another's will; it is what it is, whether simple or complex, entirely from itself and not by external constraint. Such, too, are the attributes of the intellect *(nous)* itself, which is therefore at home with those objects.

This is not the place for more than a passing allusion to such questions as whether for Aristotle the objects of intellect exist only in or for the intellect; and whether their timelessness and unity are preconditions of the intellect's grasp or the results, rather, of the activity by which the intellect disengages its objects from time and accident and assimilates them to itself. In Plato's case one might doubt whether his ethics could survive a reinterpretation of Platonic Forms as conceptual structures created and sustained by the mind's own abstractive activity. For on such an assumption he could not so easily argue to the eternity of the soul from the already premissed eternity of the Forms on the ground that 'like knows like'; and without that metaphysical basis, the ethics of the *Phaedo* and the *Republic* would be decidedly less compelling. But Aristotle, typically, allows more space between ethics and metaphysics even at this juncture. His statement in the *Ethics* that the intellect and its objects are of divine nature is literal in the sense of being wholly serious—not rhetorical hyperbole and not a heuristic metaphor of passing usefulness. But at the same time we should not consider that statement a piece of finished doctrine. It is more like an intuitive starting point for any theory of God or the intellect, and hence is open to a variety of metaphysical and epistemological interpretations. The *Ethics* does not depend on one or another technical theory of God or intellect, but only on the principle to which any such theory would conform: that God, intellect and the objects of intellect, whatever they are and however related, are of the same nature. No more than that is needed for Aristotelian ethics.

Before we turn to the ethical implications themselves of this, something must be said about the meaning of *'theōria'*. We should not reduce it by the translations 'study' or 'speculation' though these may be suitable in some contexts. The first suggests laboriousness, the second the posing of questions and hazarding of hypotheses. These are features of much of what passes as *theōria* on the human level, but they do not easily transfer to a god's activity or capture the measure of what Aristotle means by 'the divine element in us'. *'Theōria'* covers any sort of detached, intelligent, attentive pondering, especially when not directed to a practical goal. Thus it can denote the intellectual or aesthetic exploration of some object, or the absorbed following of structures as they unfold when we look and stay looking more deeply, whether by means of sensory presentations or abstract concepts. The traditional word 'contemplation' would still be preferable if we could overcome its suggestion of a locked gaze. This contemplative activity (which may be equally described as the mind's penetration of its object and as the object's opening itself to the mind) can be triggered or focused by a statable question or problem, but it is not necessary that this be so. It may be necessary only when *theōria* is carried on through dialogue between persons. *Theōria* cannot be equated with the search for solutions to problems or the quest for scientific or metaphysical explanations, since the same mobile receptiveness underlies the dawning of interesting problems no less than of their answers. Proposing a definite problem calls the mind to disciplined attention, but often (as in much aesthetic experience) the object takes us along with it without our having imposed a preconceived structure on our receptivity. It tells us about itself, and even suggests the illuminating questions, in accordance (so to say) with its own priorities. If we find ourselves chasing after something with a question, this may be because we are not yet (or no longer) being guided by the structure of the object. Aristotle says that it is pleasanter, because more perfect, to know than to be seeking knowledge (1177 a 25–27). He is sometimes misunderstood as meaning that the state of having discovered a truth is pleasanter and more perfect than the activity of inquiry about it. This is absurd, since pleasure attaches not to states but activities. In fact he is comparing one activity with another: the activity in which we are at one with the developing object, and the less fulfilling activity in which we cast about trying to locate it.

Aristotle is not in a position to argue that *theōria* is a divine activity on the ground that it is the best,[43] for the latter proposition, so far as it has any practical bearing for us, is what has to be established. Instead he argues the other way round. Suspending the question of the value for us of *theōria*, we can see that this is the only kind of activity we know of that it makes sense to ascribe to a god. God is eternal and absolutely autonomous; therefore whether the divine has or has not a corporeal dimension, this would not be of perishable nature. Not without body, in some sense,

God may be; but, even so, not with a body requiring care and protection. Psychic development is also ruled out. For whatever develops, develops from a beginning, but the imperishable is without beginning, so is not subject to growth on any level. The divine is necessarily perfect and fully actual, hence has no need for sensory activities whose primary function, in beings that have them, is self-preservation. There is no place for fear, hope and the pains and pleasures of physical lack and recovery. God has no family or community, since these are networks of interdependence. Social emotions such as affection, anger, envy and pride are as absurd to ascribe to God as feelings of physical satiety or emptiness. Subject to no passions and to no external contingencies, the divine life provides no point of purchase for the moral virtues or practical wisdom:

> But that complete [or: perfect] happiness is a theoretic activity will appear from the following consideration as well. We assume the gods to be above all other beings blessed and happy; but what sort of actions must we assign to them? Acts of justice? Will not the gods seem absurd if they make contracts and return deposits, and so on? Acts of a brave man, then, confronting dangers and running risks because it is noble to do so? Or liberal acts? To whom will they give?[44] It will be strange if they are really to have money or anything of the kind. And what would their temperate acts be? Is not such praise tasteless, since they have no bad appetites? If we were to run through them all, the circumstances of *praxis* would be found trivial and unworthy of gods. Still, every one supposes that they *live* and therefore that they are active; we cannot suppose them to sleep like Endymion. Now if you take away from a living being *praxis*, and still more production, what is left but contemplation? Therefore the activity of God, which surpasses all others in blessedness, must be theoretic; and of human activities, therefore, that which is most akin to this must be most of the nature of happiness. (1178 b 7–24)

But how can this follow, if happiness is a genuine *human* goal? Aristotle has already raised against himself a profound objection. Having reached the conclusion that theoretic activity is complete and perfect human happiness, which (provided a full span of life be granted) lacks nothing that it needs for the title of 'happiness' (1177 b 24–26), Aristotle then writes:

> But such a life would be too high for man; for it is not in so far as he is man that he will live so, but in so far as something divine is present in him; and by so much as this is superior to our composite nature is its activity superior to that which is the exercise of the other kind of excellence. If *nous* is divine, then, in comparison with man, the life according to it is divine in comparison with human life. (1177 b 26–31)

The implication is that a life centred on *theōria* would not be a human life at all. Thus a human being who lived so would be living as god, not man. As man he is a compound of body and soul: a soul whose characteristic activities irretrievably refer to the body for their occasions and expressions. But the theoretic mind is not thus dependent on the body. Whether it is literally separable so that it—the same it—could exist apart from this or any body is not a question which Aristotle for present purposes need have decided. The unique independence of *theōria* amounts to this: all other human activities are made manifest through physical behaviour and in response to external circumstances, and this is written into the nature of those activities as intended by the agent. Thus whatever the person is observed to do or not do (and he may be mistaken about what actual external changes he makes and may even be dreaming that he makes any), he takes himself to act as an embodied agent. Just as Cartesian doubt cannot affect that point, materialist scruples cannot affect the point on the other side; namely, that so far as the theorising subject is concerned, engaged as he is he might just as well not have a body. Even if his mental activity does involve a physical mechanism, the kind of activity which that mechanism makes possible is such that the subject can, without contradiction, know himself to be engaging in it while supposing himself to be bodiless.[45]

If natural human activity is activity that intends effects on the physical or social environment, the theorising subject might as well be asleep or a vegetable (or, as Socrates elaborates in the *Phaedo*, dead) for all the human difference he makes. How then can *theōria* be the perfection of *human* existence? Instead it should be rated insignificant. Time spent on it is wasted humanly speaking, unless we suppose it a necessary withdrawal like sleep or occasional bouts of "doing nothing." Even so, its occurrence spells human vacancy and serves only as one more embarrassing reminder of our incapacity to be always at full stretch what we are. Asleep, one is no one, because no one in particular, since there is no distinction among sleepers as such. They are 'burdens on the earth' or 'strengthless heads', and each in his ano-nymity could be anyone else. From this perspective, to pursue *theōria* is indeed to pursue a kind of self-extinction.

But this is to concentrate on the negative side, presenting *theōria* merely as absence of human life and action. Yet the ethical result is much the same when *theō-ria* is held out as positive perfection. For it is only a *divine* perfection, and to offer God as model for us is impious or absurd.[46] How can we even approximate to the divine activity, which is such as to be necessarily eternal and to fill God's entire exis-tence? The theoretic element in us seems neither distinctively human nor divine; for if in us it were divine, its activity would not be weak and intermittent as even great thinkers find from their own experience. If, however, we refuse to measure this by experience, dismissing the interruptions as breaks not in *it* but perhaps in our aware-ness of it, in order to go on claiming the activity eternal and divine, we set it beyond the scope of our practical decisions (cf. *On the Soul* 430 a 23–25). It is not at the mercy of our care or neglect; and how we humanly live can no more affect its perfect reality than it can affect how we humanly live. This is not to suggest that we should not reverence the divine activity, extolling it as an attribute of God; but it does mean that we cannot take steps to make such activity our own, any more than if it were the action of turning the heavens or ensuring that spring follows winter. It may be said that at least that intermittent awareness of it is truly ours and worth pursuing. But this awareness is not of an external object, but of an activity as if from the inside (so that, of course, it feels like our own activity); and it may well be asked what business we have impersonating, as it were, an activity to which our nature in itself is not adapted. Further, those who are convinced that through this they nonetheless make contact with the eternal should consider whether we are not already, like other animals, sufficiently endowed with divine eternity simply by being and propagating what we are through the endless relay of generations (cf. *On the Soul,* 415 a 27–b 8).

Such are some of the objections brought to mind by the passage most recently quoted. What is strange is not that Aristotle, speaking from his cultural background, should invoke such doubts against himself, but that straightaway he turns his back on them, with no more argument than this:

> But we must not follow those who advise us, being men, to think of human things, and being mortal, of mortal things, but must, so far as we can, make ourselves immortal,[47] and strain every nerve to live in accordance with the best thing in us; for even if it be small in bulk, much more does it in power and worth surpass everything. (1177 b 31–1178 a 2)

This is followed by the assertion

> This [i.e., *nous*] would seem, too, to be each man himself, since it is the authoritative and better part of him. It would be strange, then, if he were to choose not the life of himself but that of something else. And what we said before will apply now; that which is proper to each thing is by nature best and most pleasant for each thing; for man, therefore, the life according to *nous* is best and pleasantest, since *nous* more than anything else *is* man. (1178 a 2–7)

In other words, if the theoretic part is supreme in the human soul and is 'authoritative' or 'controlling', then the individual should identify him*self* with it above all, since we identify ourselves with what we consider the best in us.[48] In that case, in *theōria, we* are not extinguished or quiescent, but are most alive and actual. This will not satisfy someone who questions the human value of *theōria,* because whether the theoretic part *is* humanly supreme is the point at issue. As in the *Eudemian Ethics,* its activity can 'rule' only by being the final cause or raison d'être of all else. But that will be so only if we make *theōria* an end for ourselves; hence we cannot be persuaded to make it an end on the supposedly independent ground that it is what rules.

However, the last passage advances the argument in subtle ways. First, and more obviously, it tells us that *if* there were (what we have not yet been shown) independent reason for making *theōria* an end above others, this should disarm fears that we then should be opting for our own nonexistence through nonidentity. Underlying this point is the metaphysical assumption that an agent acts out his *own* good as grasped by him in the action; thus if a practical being takes steps towards *theōria,* it follows from the fact that the theorising part of the soul is the beneficiary that taking those steps is an affirmation of his, the practical agent's, identity with that part. It is difficult to see how this kind of affirmation could be true or false in accordance with some preexisting fact of the matter; thus the question is not whether the glutton or the philosopher already really *is,* above all, that part of the soul which he most seeks to serve, but which it is better to become through practical self-identification.

The idea just raised is that we as individuals make who we are by identifying ourselves with whatever side of our nature is activated and enhanced by some preferred activity. We have already seen this play a part in Aristotle's discussion of our responsibility for character, our own and that of others. In the present context it carries the interesting implication that *if* (and this has yet to be defended) our supreme happiness is an activity in some way divine, then divinity or godlikeness can belong in some way to us as particular individuals. In this we human beings would be exceptional, for our share in the divine would be more than is found in creatures of every species, who partake in eternity *because their species is eternal.* As individuals they have nothing resembling eternity. But happiness belongs to us as individuals, being a function of our personal ethical achievement. It follows (granted the undefended assumption) that we can resemble God or the gods in the individuality of godlikeness. For God is a divine individual, and we as individuals can somehow partake of something divine. Our happiness, therefore, is more than merely the human good (just as, in the *Eudemian Ethics,* our supreme excellence is not mere goodness but nobility). Every kind of living thing has its corresponding kind of good or flourishing, attainable by individuals of the species. But in other species the good, even when perfect in its way, is never *happiness.* In them, the individual relates directly to its good (*its* because it individually seeks it), but only indirectly to divine eternity by its membership in a species always instantiated. The individual, of course, by living and propagating, contributes to this always-instantiation (which is not taken care of otherwise than by individuals following individuals in the chain of heredity).[49] In this way the species is eternal, hence *it* in a way is divine (though with a curious divinity dependent on what is not eternal). But the *species* is not a subject of happiness. For happiness is the good (at least) of those capable of it, and although a species may be good or goodly, a species is not a subject of good in the sense which concerns us here. This is the sense in which the good (1) is final cause of movement and behaviour and (2) is realised in the one for whom it thus functions as cause. A species does not move or behave; hence "its" good means only the good of typical individual members. By a reverse dependence, the individual's part in divine eternity (except in our case) is via the eternity of the species. So only in us (aside from God) do the godlike and the good meet on the level of individuals so as to be united as *eudaimonia.*

Thus Aristotle observes that none of the other animals is happy, as we can be and as God is, and in *NE* X he connects this with the fact that other animals are incapable of the activity of *theōria.* Hence he concludes in good scientific fashion that since happiness and *theōria* are present together or absent together, the first is grounded on the second and the extent of the second determines that of the first:

> This is indicated, too, by the fact that the other animals have no share in happiness, being completely deprived of such activity. For while the whole life of the gods is blessed, and that of men too in so far as some likeness of such activity belongs to them, none of the other animals is happy, since they in no way share in *theōria.* Happiness extends, then, just so far as *theōria* does, and those to whom *theōria* more fully belongs are more truly happy, not accidentally, but in virtue of the *theōria;* for this is in itself precious. Happiness, therefore, must be some form of *theōria.* (1178 b 24–32)

Let me now take stock of this discussion and draw out some of the difficulties in Aristotle's position. We began by observing him argue that since (1) *theōria* is the only activity which it makes sense to ascribe to God, it follows that (2) *theōria* is the best human activity. We then faced the question how (2) can be derived from (1) if (2) is to be taken in a sense that has any practical implications for human life. From the fact that a certain activity is divine, it does not follow that it is especially suitable to us rational animals, any more than the equivalent conclusion follows from the premiss that a certain activity is characteristic of pigs. We may sometimes be drawn to wallow like swine and sometimes to theorise like gods, but since we are neither gods nor swine neither of those tendencies can ground the claim that its object should have the status of a major human end. The fact that divine activity is more noble than swinish behaviour should not distract attention from the deeper thought that each of these as a way of life is alien to *human* perfection. We can dismiss swinish behaviour on the ground that it is morally objectionable, but we still need an argument to show that *theōria* should command some special moral respect. Whether it is even harmless is questionable, given the supposed divine affinity. Subtract the latter, and *theōria* appears trivial, pointless and, so to say, contingently eccentric. Add it, and the call to *theōria* seems to voice a deathly contempt for human values, telling us to centre *our* ethical universe in a place where we secular beings are not to be found. Doubts about the logic of this dizzying message have little weight against its seductive power to corrode our sense of the worth of human ways. Perhaps it was not narrow prejudice, but a healthy instinct in the old comedian that turned his barrage of ridicule even against the unworldly stargazer, the latest enemy in our midst.[50]

Now, however, initial doubts about Aristotle's right to move from (1) to (2) are beginning to merge with anxieties which might have to be faced even if, (1) being granted, the move to (2) is found cogent. Let us focus again on that step. It fails if taken as immediate. But we have also seen that Aristotle makes (1) the ground for (2′): *theōria* is happiness. And 'happiness' *('eudaimonia')*, we find, is not just a name he gives to the good of human beings comparable with names which might be coined for the good of spiders or hawthorns. For such kinds of goods as other creatures enjoy are not only different from that called 'happiness', but less. 'Happiness' implies a further dimension of good, and this is shown by the fact that the term, along with 'blessedness' *('makariotēs')*, is traditionally applied above all to the gods (cf. 1178 b 8–9). In other words, happiness, whatever it is, is what the gods unbrokenly enjoy; and this should be our clue to the nature of happiness. For we now need only consider what the gods might be said to enjoy, and that will be happiness.

But will it be *our* happiness, we not being gods? The answer is 'Yes', as long as it is assumed that we are capable of happiness. If happiness is what-the-gods-enjoy, then wherever it occurs it must be an activity describable in much the same terms as the divine activity. This should give pause to anybody reaching for the argument that says: gods are one kind of being, we are another, hence the good which God enjoys is not one at which we should aim. This latter position can still be asserted, but now only at the expense of openly denying that *happiness* is the human goal. As long as the latter is accepted, Aristotle can reasonably say that we ought to assimilate ourselves to God as much as possible, and he can reasonably pass from (1) '*theōria* is the divine activity' to (2) '*theōria* is the best human activity' via (2′) '*theōria* is happiness'. For given that happiness is what the gods enjoy and that the human best is happiness, (2′) follows from (1) and entails (2).

Aristotle constructs another similar argument which does not rely on the gods. The conclusion is the same, and again the concept of happiness plays a mediating role, this time by means of features many of which were exhibited in *NE* I.7–10. The premiss now is that *theōria* more than any other human activity is self-sufficient, pursued only for its own sake, capable of being engaged in continuously, a source of pure and lasting pleasure.

> It is the most continuous [activity], since we can [engage in *theōria*] more continuously than we can *do (prattein)* anything. And we think happiness has pleasure mingled with it, but the activity of [theoretic] wisdom is admittedly the pleasantest of excellent activities. . . . And the self-sufficiency that is spoken of must belong most to *theōria*. . . . And this activity alone would seem to be loved for its own sake; for nothing arises from it apart from [the actual] engaging in it. (1177 a 21–b 4)

Later we shall look at Aristotle's reasons for these claims about *theōria*. For the moment we need only have to see them as answering more or less to the attributes of happiness agreed upon in Book I: finality (1097 a 34–b 6), self-sufficiency (1097 b 6–15), permanence or stability (1100 b 2 ff.), intrinsic pleasantness (1099 a 7 ff.). Assuming that these are the features of happiness, and granting the premiss that *theōria* has these features more than any other activity, we can infer as before that *theōria* is happiness, and hence (assuming happiness to be the human best) we can proceed to the conclusion desired by Aristotle: namely, that *theōria* is the best human activity.

But there seems to be a trick in this argument, because one can accept the premiss and the assumptions and still find the conclusion to be saying a lot more than one had bargained for. The trick lies in the assumption that lists those attributes of happiness. Are we to equate our happiness with any activity of which we are capable that has those characteristics more than any other; or with only some suitably *human* activity that has those characteristics to the highest degree? The unbargained for conclusion follows only if the assumption is taken in the first, unrestricted, sense. It is this sense that permits Aristotle to identify our supreme end with an activity whose human suitability is far from obvious. We can retreat to safety by confining the assumption so that it picks out some activity already agreed to be thoroughly human. Thus we avoid having to consider every conceivable form of happiness, as, for instance, that of a god; so Aristotle's conclusion about *theōria* cannot now be drawn without an independent argument to show that *theōria* is suitably human.

But Aristotle would certainly oppose an attempt to restrict the assumption. He would remind us of the deeply entrenched intuition that *happiness* (eudaimonia) *is what the gods enjoy.* Thus there is no such thing as a special kind of human happiness. Granting him this, we are bound to concede that *theōria* is not only happiness but *our* happiness—on one condition: that we do not question his identification of happiness with the *human* end. But why allow him that assumption? The denial, to be sure, is verbally paradoxical, but what harm will that do (what harm to ethics) as long as it is allowed that there *is* a best life and a supreme goal for human beings, just as there is for every other kind of being, and that this human summum bonum is humanly practicable: by which is meant not only 'feasible' but that we can give it our total practical loyalty without betraying our human nature?

It seems that for most of the *Ethics* Aristotle has been investigating this human summum bonum, and that its essence or core is excellent practical activity. Nor is there anything objectionable in his terming it 'happiness' or even 'blessedness' until at the end he begins to exploit the received opinion that happiness is what the gods enjoy, treating this as criterial for what, specifically, is to count as happiness, and thus apparently displacing the practical human ideal. But why such deference to that opinion? Is it because the word *'eudaimonia'* points to a divine (or at least super-human) connection? Traditional views leave their conceptual deposits on terms, but it is a matter of philosophical judgment whether or how to use these deposits in con-structing a systematic account. The theme that happiness is divine was not invented by Aristotle, but it is Aristotle who lets it dominate his final arguments. Is he obliged on general grounds to take that theme so seriously, or does he wield it ad hoc, in the personal hope of securing an ethical conclusion in favour of *theōria?* Such a man-oeuvre, especially if inspired by such a hope, should rationally be set aside, since the harder one argues that *theōria* ought to be prized as uniquely divine, the weaker one's ground for insisting upon it as a life-shaping human objective.[51] Before deciding that Aristotle is stuck in this predicament, it is worth looking about for another approach.

## VIII.  Living like the Gods

According to the discussion of the last few pages, the strength of Aristotle's conclu-sion about *theōria* depends on the strength of those two assumptions: (1) happiness is the supreme human good; (2) happiness, whatever it is, is what the gods enjoy. We from our point of view may find it easy to dispense with either assumption. Giving up the first need involve no more than a verbal sacrifice, and the second can be exchanged either for humanistic silence or for a revised position whereby divine hap-piness is one thing and human happiness something else. Aristotle, however, has emerged as surprisingly unhumanistic, as well as rigid in his adherence to traditional connotations.) On the above point I would say that his ethics has, unquestionably, a religious dimension, though it lacks the characteristics which humanism most likely finds objectionable. There is no vestige of 'divine-command ethics' which grounds moral obligations on the imperatives of a transcendental personal God. And there is no suggestion that our achievement of our own true good depends on divine grace, or on special revelation, or on sacramental performances, or on a theologically defined reversal (atonement) of a theologically defined condition (sin). We achieve happiness, according to Aristotle, through our own efforts, cultural and individual; and these efforts are describable in familiar ethical terms such as 'character', 'voli-tion', 'choice'. But ought we to expect him to have set aside either assumption? I think not, for a two-sided reason: to do so would have gone against a strong tradi-tional current (as yet to be described); and the observable facts of human life would have seemed to him to bear out that current's direction.

Let me begin by suggesting that we not consider assumptions (1) and (2) as inde-pendent propositions in the present dialectical context. They amount between them to the assertion that (3) the supreme human good is godlike existence. The assumptions are the logically distinguishable factors in (3), their syllogistic conclusion. But the matter of interest is (3) itself, which expresses a unitary thought.

It was *natural* to look upon ourselves, human beings, as aspiring to 'godlike existence'. This was in the context of a culture whose gods (if anything about them is clear to intellectual analysis) were clearly not a species separate from the human species.[52] They do not differ from us in anything like the way in which we differ from ants or ants from fishes. There is not only parallel bahaviour, but communication and family relationships and the tribal unity in which all turn towards Zeus as 'father of gods and men'. Even less was the difference between gods and men the difference between finite and infinite. It was the difference between us as we are and as we should be if we were immortal, which is to imply: if we were not afflicted with aging and decline, disease, poverty, toil, frustration, anxiety and exposure to every kind of pain and indignity. The most palpable and pervasive difference between us and brute animals lies not in something called 'rationality', but in our awareness of those miserable conditions as conditions for us to put forever behind us as far as possible. Our rationality (however one interprets the word) is essentially bound up with this awareness, whether as its source or in some way its consequence. Our rationality, therefore, is bound up with our awareness of misery as misery, which is the same as our aspiration to be on a level where we are free of it—free not through death, but *living* free from it—and this is to be living as far as possible 'like the gods'.

It was insane (though, as stories show, not unthinkable) to suppose that one could emulate a god. But emulation meant pretending to divine prerogatives of worship or acclaim. In that sense, to seek to *live like* is not to *emulate*. The desire to live free from misery is not at all the desire to be worshipped oneself or treated by the gods as an equal. Living like the gods would be compatible with observing one's proper position as human, for after all these gods themselves are supposed to respect each other's rights and domains.

What is it to live as a god? It is a life of ease and freedom. But the gods above all are alive and active, so it makes sense to press as Aristotle does the question 'What in their blessedness do they *do?*' The Olympians most vividly come to mind as Homer portrays them: spending their time feasting together, intervening in the affairs of kings and cities, and jockeying with each other for control of historic events. But all this is against a less concretely imaginable background of the performance by gods of regular functions in which they preside over or otherwise run the various branches of nature and universal features of human life: the movement of the sun, the return of the seasons, weather, the sea, childbirth, agriculture and so on. These may be thought of as necessary duties, although within each broadly determined sphere there is room for plenty of wilful variation on the part of the relevant deity. But these permanent features of a god's life are not for them like the bitter necessities which wear us out before we have a chance to realise more than a fraction of our human potential. Now Aristotle's more elevated conception of God provides no easy analogy with the two tiers implied in the traditional picture, according to which the gods carry on their regular cosmic business but also engage in various extraordinary or extracurricular activities. But even so, this two-tiered picture may be relevant to our interpretation presently.

Let me focus first on the formal, then on the concrete aspect of the traditional conception of what I am calling divine extracurricular activity, relating it on both fronts to the substructure of regular cosmic business. This division of tiers is a tool of analysis: it reflects a difference between layers composing the historically complex amalgam which I refer to as 'the traditional view', and it is not meant to depict the view as itself including a deliberate or doctrinal statement of a layered structure. It would be a mistake to assume that the mythology articulates an explicit relation between the tiers or even explicitly recognises their difference. Yet even so we can perhaps follow out some clues suggested by the analytical distinction.

If anyone framed to himself the question 'In virtue of which activities are the gods gods?' the answer would surely have had to refer to the substructural activities. For these correspond to the powers and principles of the cosmos, which, even if it has evolved from something before, seems set to keep going for ever. It is because of their part in this that the gods are deathless, ageless and free like the universe itself which has nothing beyond to constrain it. But the, by comparison, gratuitous activities of the superstructure must also express divinity. They are consequential on godhood, while the others are its basic substance in action. But the activity whereby a god is a god is surely complete and perfect; so how can other activities add anything of significance? We can see how, if we consider a point which a less anthropomorphic view might not so easily permit. The divine life would not be complete without those gratuitous activities, for these are the celebration by the gods of their own freedom and power. However good something is, how can the celebration of it not create a situation still better in beings capable of celebrating their good? And surely it is better to be not merely capable of one's good but capable also of celebrating and knowing it worth celebration—despite the paradox that if celebration adds something, then what is celebrated can never be the supreme good, so that nothing celebrated is ever supremely worth celebrating!

This is not the place to think about resolving this paradox, which I consider to belong with a number of others having to do with the self's relation to itself. But we should not be deterred from seeing in *celebration* a model that might make sense of the following position: there is a kind of activity which is (1) complete and perfect and (2) in some way embeds in itself a different sort of activity which has its own grounds for being considered complete and perfect; and (3) these activities belong to one and the same being; and (4) each is the perfection of the being's nature. On standard and supposedly Aristotelian assumptions about the unity and uniqueness of a thing's essence or nature, and the relation of 'essence' to 'perfection', this claim is self-contradictory. However, those standard assumptions belong in a metaphysical apparatus designed by Aristotle to support the philosophy of nature and the scientific study of living substances in general; perhaps we should not expect them to accommodate the special features of beings essentially self-aware.

Before bringing the model to bear on the problem of the relation of practice to *theōria,* it is helpful to note these points. First, what is celebrated is a necessary condition of the celebration, and the celebration is a kind of consequence; but the former is not undertaken as a means to the latter, and the former is celebrated as something good in itself. Second, the celebratory activity need not be at all similar to whatever is celebrated. Third, the celebratory activity must nonetheless be of a fit nature for celebrating what it celebrates (not anything can celebrate anything). Fourth, the celebratory activity may have its own interest and value as the kind of activity it is, and need not occur only as the celebration of something else. Fifth, the celebratory activity need not, though often it will, be about or refer to what it celebrates. Thus watching a play can celebrate a birthday. Hence, sixth, in many cases, and perhaps in general, what makes an activity celebratory is not its internal character, but the fact that it is engaged in as celebration. The first point recalls the relation, as Aristotle understands it, of pleasure in an activity to the activity enjoyed, where the pleasure is a kind of consequence of the activity, although the activity is not a means to the pleasure. But there is this difference: the pleasure naturally follows from engaging in the activity under the right conditions, but the celebration does not automatically follow or accompany what is celebrated. It has to be engaged in by a separate voluntary act—by arrangement, we might say.

I am suggesting the concept of celebration as the key to the formal structure of what it is to live like a god. The complexity of the structure is not of the teleological type found everywhere in nature, in which one element is a means to another, but reflects the complexity of that self-awareness unique to us and the gods. In our case, that awareness makes its first impact through the drive to lessen the misery of our condition. What powers this drive is not merely the desire to escape the pain of suffering, but a sense that the grind of suffering is a waste of human potential and that we are *fitted* for a different level of life. How else could Thrasymachus' dream of despotism ever have got off the ground? Thus right from the roots we are acting from a kind of ethical vision of ourselves as cut out for a life more than *merely* mortal. The philosopher's task is to shape this dream into a coherent, practicable, ideal worthy of those who dream it.

If the *pain* of suffering were the central issue, ethics, arguably, could shelve the question 'What shall we do in the state of achieved security and leisure—the state from which we engage in the study of ethics?' Or it might give the answer 'Do what you like, it does not matter what, as long as it does not endanger those conditions'; and very likely add 'What matters is not what you do with it (given the proviso), but whether it is available to some without undue cost to others, and how the opportunities for attaining it are distributed'. We may regret that Aristotle does not dig deeply into the problems of social justice and fairness, but should bear in mind that these questions cannot for him be *logically* fundamental, since his ethics must face the prior question 'What shall we do with ease and prosperity, whoever of us attains it?' This is because for him, I take it, the indignity of being ground down by suffering is what is ethically significant—not the unpleasantness. For suffering is an indignity not because it is contrary to freedom from pain, but because it wastes us for something more expressive of what we are; and this cannot simply be freedom from pain, since that is consistent with our being nothing at all or dead. If, however, that sense of indignity, characteristic of our species, is equivalent to an inchoate ethical vision of what human life ideally should be, then the positive content of the universal vision, however uncaptured by concepts initially, cannot be left to individual whim to determine; its clarification must yield a single answer for humanity as such, and we have the right to expect it to be supported by rational argument.

Our formulation of the content will reflect, if not be the same as, our concrete idea of the life of the gods. To picture heaven as a banqueting hall, or a council chamber for debating how to shape momentous human affairs, or even as a place from which the unfolding of those affairs is watched as a spectacle of superlative interest—such picturings do not merely express the feeling of those who indulge in them that this is how they would like to pass their time if they lived a life of blessed leisure. To ascribe those activities to the *lords of the universe* is to hold such employments noble. And this applies to whatever more refined conception may be substituted.

We therefore have to conclude that a judgment that such and such an activity is noble (which is not a mere expression of personal taste, since it holds out a model for human beings) cannot in the end be upheld by the claim that such activity is characteristic of God; for the theological claim turns out to rest on the value-judgment. Thus Aristotle cannot justify *theōria* as a supreme human end by appeal to his notion of God as theorising: the justification must find fresh ground. But even so, his introducing God into the argument has the positive effect of crystallising our deeply human sense that we are meant somehow for better things than the ordinary run of life affords. In acknowledging this universal prereflective intimation, we may wonder what precisely it intimates, but we can hardly suppose ourselves unwise or inhuman for harbouring it. In short, the intimation is now endorsed as an ethical premiss, being couched in culturally conditioned terms of a 'godlike life'. The endorsement works by invoking for Aristotle's audience that part of their tradition which finds it *natural*—hence unselfconsciously demonstrates it *human*—to aspire to 'live as the gods'.

### IX. The Crown of Happiness

According to the interpretation being here advanced, the fully happy life for man, as Aristotle understands it in the *Nicomachean Ethics,* is a life of practical virtue crowned by theoretic activity. This claim has still to be elucidated, but (as I shall argue) it is meant in such a sense that the life in question (1) is properly described as both 'theoretic' and 'practical' and (2) is the supreme human good, complete and perfect, under both descriptions. The ambiguity of 'crowned by' is instructive. A cupola may be said to crown a building, or to crown that part of the building on which it stands. In the latter case, the crowning part is added to another part which it crowns, so that together they compose a complete whole; in the former, what is said to be crowned is the whole itself, and what crowns it is that element in which the rest culminates and which for some reason is regarded as the one above all that renders the whole complete.

But since a whole is incomplete if it lacks any one of its elements, why should one of them in particular be seen as *the* source of completeness? A similar question was raised in connection with happiness in *NE* I.8, and the theme returned later in connection with pleasure as 'perfection'.[53] Though every element of a whole is necessary for its completeness, not all contribute in the same way, and some modes of contribution lend themselves more than others to being thought of as what 'completes' it. Thus (to change the example) a triangle is an area enclosed by an outline, but it is the outline, not the area enclosed, that we think of as that whereby the triangle is complete. Again, the element added last in constructing the whole may be thought of as the one par excellence to which it owes its completeness, especially if that element is such that it has to be added last. The last-added element is more critical than the rest, because when they are already in place and taken for granted, *it* is still an open question. Hence if it fails to be added, more is spoilt than if construction had halted at an earlier stage. Perhaps that in whose absence more would be wasted does most to perfect the whole. From the developmental point of view which pervades Aristotle's ethics, it is not difficult to understand how one of several elements in a whole can figure as *the* one that completes it: whether the whole in question is the best human life for which an account is sought, or whether it is our account itself, slowly built up, of that life.

If *theōria* were, so to say, subtracted from the best human life, what remains would be a life of practical virtue, and it would not be best since what remains would be truncated. It may seem to follow that a life characterised as a life of practical virtue is not the best, on the ground that a life so characterised is inferior to the combination of itself with *theōria*. But that does not follow. Aristotle can hold, and, I believe, does hold, that the life of practical virtue is as such the best; but the mere description 'practical' says less than everything about it. Should we then see this description as a predicate that would have to be conjoined with another predicate in order to give us a term coextensive with the terms 'best life' or 'truly happy life'? Are we to say that although the happy life is a life of excellent practice, a life of excellent practice is not necessarily happy, since happiness requires something more: the addition of *theōria?* This is difficult to reconcile with the fact that at *NE* I.7, 1098 a 3–4, Aristotle *defines* happiness in terms of practical virtue.

If he stands by that definition (even allowing it not to be his fullest and final word), then he cannot regard *theōria*, the crown of the best life, as superimposed on a life of practical virtue as if on something inferior. Let us try considering the relation in terms of the celebration model. *Theōria* (it is supposed) stands to active practical excellence as celebratory activity to what is celebrated. The model's advantage is that it relates the two sides of the happy life without subordinating either to other as means to end. It also allows us the subtlety of applying the general observation that what is celebrated is usually more necessary and *important* than the celebrating, yet the celebration not only makes for a more complete situation, but is that in the whole which par excellence completes or perfects it. So in this important and perfect whole, the element in a sense most important is other than the element most associated with perfection.[54]

But in ordinary cases, the object celebrated is or can be complete and at its best whether celebrated or not. And that it is independently good, and even by the appropriate standards perfect, is the ground for celebration. On the other hand, an act of celebrating has something in common with the act which gave rise to what is celebrated, since each in its way is a valuing of the same thing. And one might say that even if the *object celebrated* is complete without being celebrated, the successful *valuing* of this object—valuing it enough to do or produce it—is incomplete if not consummated by a kind of celebration. This at any rate seems to be so when the agent is the same in both phases, and when the term 'celebration' is allowed to denote what runs through many of our celebrations: namely, pride or gladness in what one has done. The first act calls for such retrospective response; which is the same as saying that to prize, as well as achieve, one's achievement is more human than simply to move on to achieving the next good thing.

These general considerations about complete and incomplete valuing point us to an area where the relations resemble the Eudemian ones between nobility and mere goodness. Having earlier noted the self-reflectional nature of nobility, we should now focus on something distinctive about active practical excellence when this is made an object of celebration. Most objects of celebration, even if they are activities, do not depend for being celebrated on activities like themselves. But it is always a *practical* decision to celebrate something and to arrange for the celebration; hence if the activity of practical wisdom is celebrated, necessarily it celebrates itself. And if we add that virtue is better or more admirable if conscious of its own worth than if always entirely absorbed in its particular ends—and better still if prepared to *do* something, even at some cost, to declare its sense of its worth—then the conclusion begins to emerge that the life of practical virtue is incomplete unless at some level it celebrates itself into completeness by a movement (still practical) into something quite different: for instance, *theōria*. In that case, the life of practical virtue is not something to which, at its best, *theōria* has to be added to form the superlative life and which therefore itself is inferior to the superlative. Instead, it is itself the entire superlative, since it generates within itself the element by which it becomes complete.

I have applied, it may seem too insistently, the celebration-model because this helps to unravel certain well-known difficulties (stemming from assumptions about the relations of whole to parts, and of part to part of a whole) in understanding the position of the *Nicomachean Ethics* taken from beginning to end. According to that position as it emerges here, the good practical life is the supreme human good and not merely a part of this good, even though by itself (i.e., without *theōria*) it would be less good than it can be and less than supreme.

But to clarify in more detail this claim that the Nicomachean ideal is both practical and theoretic and is the human ideal under both those descriptions, I now turn to a notoriously problematic passage, consisting of the last sentence of *NE* X.6 and the first three of 7. In 6, which follows a general discussion of pleasure, Aristotle has been talking about coarse pleasures and trivial amusements, and has been contrasting these ways of spending time with noble and worthwhile practical activities (1176 b 7 ff.). He sums up and continues:

> Happiness does not lie in such occupations, but, as we have said before, in excellent activities. If happiness is activity in accordance with excellence, it is reasonable that it should be in accordance with the highest excellence; and this will be that of the best thing in us. Whether it be *nous* or something else that is this element which is thought to be our natural ruler and guide and to take thought of things noble and divine, whether it be itself also divine or only the most divine element in us, the activity of this in accordance with its proper excellence will be complete [or: perfect] happiness. That this activity is theoretic we have already said. Now this would seem to be in agreement both with what we said before and with the truth. (1177 a 9–19)

The excellent activities mentioned in the first sentence are presumably excellent activities in general. Or at any rate that is how we are to understand them initially, since (notwithstanding his remark in the penultimate sentence[55]) the context has said nothing about *theōria*. But Aristotle thereupon selects from this general excellence one quality which it says is highest, belongs to the best element in us, and is expressed in *theōria*. What is this supreme excellence? Is it theoretic wisdom *(sophia)?* In that case, why is it so casually introduced into a context in which 'excellence', so far, will have been understood as referring to practical excellence? Again, what is the best element in us? Aristotle here calls it *'nous'*, but there is practical as well as theoretical *nous,* and in Book VI (1139 a 5–15) he presented these as distinct elements in the rational soul. So is *nous* here only theoretical, or is it practical too? The latter, I think, because the reference to its 'proper excellence' points to some other excellence of *nous* which is its but less purely its own *(oikeian).* This must be practical wisdom, which is not the exclusive manifestation of *nous,* since virtue of the nonrational part is a necessary dimension of practical wisdom. Hence in this passage *nous,* the 'best thing in us', is the subject of practical and also of theoretic wisdom.[56] However, the virtue here said to be proper (exclusive) to *nous* may not actually *be* theoretic wisdom. It is possible that theoretic wisdom does not figure in these remarks and that what is called 'the highest excellence' is love of and devotion to *theōria*. This quality of soul is most directly expressed in the activity of *theōria* itself, which presumably develops and strengthens this quality, just as it develops the quality called 'theoretic wisdom'.

Love of *theōria* (a nameless virtue) is different from theoretic wisdom, because it unites the two sides of human *nous*. In the human case it is also expressed in practical decisions and actions. The need for such practical expression is not grounded in this virtue's intrinsic nature or in the nature of its object, but in the physical and social aspects of human existence. Consequently, love of *theōria* can also be ascribed to God, even though God is free of all that. Like nobility in the *Eudemian Ethics,* our love of *theōria* is not a species of practical wisdom (since the activity which most perfectly expresses it is not practical deliberation but *theōria*). Rather, it is an evaluative attitude colouring deliberation and helping us hit the mean. Hence from a functional point of view it resembles the familiar moral virtues, and like them can be fostered by predeliberative upbringing. It is, therefore, a virtue of character, and resembles the other virtues of character in that they, too, are aspects of a general willingness to let reason rule. The difference is that the love of *theōria* refers to a rational activity which 'rules' only by being loved and sought, whereas the other virtues of character refer to practical wisdom, which (even though it may be loved for itself) most noticeably rules by prescription. But what is the nature of that mean which love of *theōria* helps us in practice to hit? In the *Eudemian Ethics* it is the mean between excess and deficiency in possession of natural goods beyond what is needed for excellent *praxis*. But in the *Nicomachean Ethics,* it is, I think, a second-order mean between taking practical life too seriously and taking it not seriously enough.[57] More presently on this.

I find it impossible to be sure whether 'the highest excellence' referred to in the passage last quoted is theoretic wisdom or love of *theōria*. (In a broad sense, this passage and what follows it are, of course about both these qualities). I am much more confident that what is here referred to as 'the best thing in us' is *nous* as such, not merely theoretic *nous* (even though its 'proper' activity is *theōria* pure and simple). But with regard to the general interpretation for which I am arguing, the main problem presented by this passage is still to be faced. It is this: the passage does not identify happiness with excellent practice that makes provision for *theōria*. This would be compatible with the earlier tenor of the *NE* and with the ideal recommended in the *EE* (as long as it is here allowed that *theōria* is not the only end which excellent practice serves). Instead, Aristotle says that 'complete happiness' *is theōria* (cf. 1177 b 24), and he speaks of *theōria* as the expression of just *one* excellence which is singled out from the others as supreme. Whether that special excellence is theoretic wisdom or love of *theōria*, the implication is the same: complete happiness is not to be identified with the exercise of the other virtues. So they, presumably, play an inferior part in the ideal life. Since the others, including practical wisdom, are the specifically human virtues, the conclusion seems unavoidable that our true happiness consists not in any exercise of our human nature as such, but in the isolated exercise of the godlike aspect. Since we can never be proper gods, it seems that our best good consists in an imperfect imitation of something other than ourselves and that there is no such thing as truly human happiness.

To weigh this, we must recall what he means by identifying happiness with an *activity* at all. (In Book I, 1098 a 3–4, he identified it with the activity of practical virtue.) This is a technical philosophical position and is not itself the answer to the basic question of the *Ethics*—'What is the truly happy life?'—a question asked by people with no philosophical training. 'Life' in the context of the latter question does not mean vital functioning or vital principle, but life as it is lived from day to day, year to year, in a multiplicity of activities and with inactive periods: a personal history or career. It is this to which Aristotle refers when he answers that basic question by saying that the happiest life *(bios)* is 'theoretic', or 'in accordance with the theoretic part of the soul' (1178 a 5–8): an answer which seems to imply that the happy life as such is not practical.

The happy *life* (in that biographical sense) is the life characterised by whatever *activity* Aristotle sees fit to equate with happiness. The equation does not mean that one is happy only when engaging in that activity, since of course a person can be described as 'happy' even while asleep. It means that the activity is what above all distinguishes the happy life or above all qualifies it to be called 'happy'. Aristotle, we recall, has reasons of logic and metaphysics for applying the term 'happiness' principally to that element *within* the happy life which is the source, principle or substance of its happiness. In the *Metaphysics* the substance of Z comes to be identified with the distinguishing factor whereby Z is Z. Thus substance is form rather than matter, species rather than genus, and (within the form) differentia rather than genus. It follows that the substance of Z can be differently identified depending on the level of analysis or comparison. Within what appears as distinctive on one level it sometimes makes sense to look for something more narrowly distinctive. And whatever is found distinctive on the last analytic level will count as *the* substance of Z in the context of the analysis. So when Aristotle says in *NE* X that happiness is *theōria*, he means, I take it, that the activity of *theōria* is the ultimate differentia of the happy life, since at this point his analysis ends. When he said in *NE* I that happiness is excellent practical activity, he was proposing this as the differentia *at that stage of analysis*. There is no contradiction between the two statements, because 'happiness' in this technical sense, like 'differentia' and 'substance', is a term whose application can shift as inquiry advances.

But does this make sense? It is obvious that the characteristic differentiating a species from a coordinate species may itself turn out to be divisible into more finely differentiated kinds. But how can this apply to the relation of practice to *theōria?* No doubt practical activity distinguishes human lives from the lives of other animals, but *theōria* is not a species of practical activity. Nor, for that matter, is the property of being *two footed* a species of the property of *dwelling on land*. Rather, the animals differentiated by being two footed are a species of the animals differentiated by dwelling on land. And, comparably, I think, the theoretic *life* is a species of the *life* of practical virtue. Hence it is not an alternative kind of life or a rival ideal of happiness.

This can be supported from close at hand in *NE* X. In Chapter 6, Aristotle considers whether happiness is to be equated with virtuous activities or with entertainment of one sort or another. The correct interpretation of this discussion depends above all on our understanding the scope of the question. This will become clearer as we see how Aristotle handles it. The one ground for equating entertainment with happiness is that it, like happiness, is sought only for its own sake. But this also seems to be true of 'actions in accordance with virtue'. The doing of noble and worthwhile actions *(kala kai spoudaia)* is something we value for its own sake—although Aristotle does not say that we value it *only* for its own sake. However, the very characteristic that gives the amusements their momentary candidacy quickly turns into evidence against them. They can only be sought for their own sake, because if we took account of their consequences, we should reject them, since they are mostly harmful to health and prosperity. This is enough to show that they cannot be happiness, since happiness cannot be something which we should ever regret having achieved. Such amusements seem to be a source of happiness because 'people in despotic positions spend their leisure in them', and these and their hangers on are reputedly happy.[58] However, power and the ability to enjoy trivial or coarse pleasures do not constitute someone a good judge of the good and happy life. The good judge is a person of virtue and practical wisdom; he will be known by his worthy *(spoudaiai)* activities and will judge such activities most desirable (1176 b 6–27).

Here, amusement and virtuous activity are competing possibilities for happiness, but we should note in respect of what they compete. It is not for the status of *principle determining all one's actions;* for the amusement seekers presented here are not people who respond to every animal and childish impulse. They are people in power or in good standing with those in power, and amusement is what fills their leisure time. The very existence of that leisure on a stable basis represents an investment of practical wisdom and moral discipline by others and by some of themselves (the founders, at least, of the dynasty). Rulers who engage in unenlightened pleasures stand for a good deal in common with morally refined persons. The difference now is more in the way in which leisure is used than in the way in which it is created. When Aristotle here rejects the vulgar attitude that equates happiness with amusement and not with virtuous activity, he must be referring to opinions about the best employment of leisure, not about the staple activity of the happy life.

This is still clearer in the passage which follows:

> Happiness, therefore, does not lie in amusement; it would, indeed, be strange if the end were amusement, and one were to take trouble and suffer hardship all one's life in order to amuse oneself. For, in a word, everything that we choose we choose for the sake of something else—except happiness, which is an end. Now to exert oneself and work for the sake of amusement seems silly and utterly childish. But to amuse oneself in order that one may exert oneself, as Anacharsis puts it, seems right; for amusement is a sort of relaxation, and we need relaxation because we cannot work continuously. Relaxation, then, is not an end; for it is taken for the sake of activity. (1176 b 27–1177 a 1)

Here amusement as an ultimate end is dismissed as unworthy of serious (*spoudaioi*[59]) people—those who toil for worthwhile ends such as peace, security, order, prosperity, healthy conditions for themselves and others, including future generations. And they also work (surely) to maintain and propagate the considerable virtues by which they live. Amusement cannot be happiness, because hardworking decency owes itself something better than amusement as the crowning glory of the happy life.[60]

It is often the misfortune of individuals and even communities to be living always on or below the edge of hardship. Their best achievement then is to maintain a minimally decent existence. In such conditions the moral virtues and practical wisdom can flourish, these being qualities by which one does one's human best whatever the circumstances. It is possible in a sense to be happy under such conditions, if things go well by the standards which such conditions permit. But what if at the end of the day something is left over: more time, energy, material resources than are needed for sheer carrying on? It is not just a question of the leisure of workers but of, for instance, retired persons, like Cephalus in the *Republic*. This is the question to which Aristotle gives his answer when he says: 'Complete happiness is *theōria*.'[61] by which he means, I am arguing, that *theōria* is the final differentia of the happy life—this happy life (it is taken for granted) being the life of a decent and worthy person, the person of practical excellence.

I may seem to have written as if the proposition that *theōria* is a leisure activity is virtually equivalent to the proposition that *theōria* is an activity that takes place on an infrastructure of active practical virtue. This suggests that leisure for *theōria* is essentially an attribute of virtuous people: a strange description of the facts. Aristotle knows, of course, that worthless people have leisure at their disposal. However, he would surely say that in their case leisure is not a godlike blessed condition, since it is not a condition for happiness. Thus even if *theōria* (say, an interest in astronomy) were added to their leisure, this would not yield them a happy life, so that in this context it would not be true that *theōria is* happiness in the sense explained. The interpretation here developed is consistent, I think, with the whole of the *Nicomachean Ethics;* and it explains why Aristotle does not openly state at an earlier point that happiness is *theōria*. If this means, as some have supposed, that the happy life is one in which *theōria* occupies most of the time or is pursued even at the cost of good practical dealings, the message, though shocking, is simple: so why was it not made clear before? It may be said that Aristotle could not expect to carry his hearers with him. (And those unusual people whom he might have carried with him might not have been willing to spend long hours on the analysis of practical virtues, especially after being warned not to expect the delightful rigour of *theōria* at its most theoretical.) But in this respect the situation down the line is no better than near the beginning. There is no discernible moment in the *Nicomachean Ethics* when '*theōria* is happiness' on one of the above interpretations would have seemed anything but baffling and repugnant to an audience of the character that Aristotle desires in his listeners. And the more he expatiates on practical excellence in the meantime, the more illogical such a message, when it came, would seem. But if *theōria* contributes to the happy life by essentially being the leisure-activity of those whose practical excellence deserves no less (no less, that is, then to be set off by leisure devoted to the activity in which we are most like gods), then the order of Aristotle's exposition makes methodical sense, reflecting the successive layers of differentiation which structure the entire account. We are told first that happiness is an activity of soul; then that it is an activity of the rational practical soul; then that it is an exercise of practical virtue; and finally, since excellent practice aims for and ideally results in at least some leisure from itself, that happiness is the best use of this leisure for a purpose higher than practical. That this purpose is theoretic activity still remains to be clearly established, but it can be seen already that this final stroke, which brings all the rest into focus, was prefigured from near the beginning. *NE* I reread in the light of X affords many clues, especially in its references to happiness as something divine (1099 b 11–18; 1101 b 23–27).[62] We can now see how these in no way jar with the statement, also in I, that *human* happiness is practical (1098 a 3). Studying metaphysics is of course a purely theoretical activity, but studying-metaphysics-rather-than-rolling-dice is not aptly classed as an activity of any kind.[63] Rather, it is a *praxis* or action, and as such it completes the best human life, according to Aristotle's values.

## X. Leisure, Pleasure and Serious Activities

If, as I have argued, *theōria* gracing leisure stands to the life of practical excellence as differentia to genus in the happy life, it must be possible to have the latter without the former. But I have also argued that it belongs to the life of practical virtue to be naturally completed by *theōria*. These claims are not in conflict if the second is understood as referring to the optimal case. There are conditions of existence in which people have nothing to spare, including no margin for general ethical reflection. This is one way in which a life can fall short, and it involves no voluntary defect. There are also good people who do not know what to do with leisure, which again may not be their fault in any simple sense. If they fill the space with amusements— not necessarily gross pleasures, but pastimes that build nothing and go nowhere— they are like that Eudemian good man who on the reflective level misunderstands the value of personal excellence and views it as a means to external goods. The resemblance is in the reflective mistake, since I am suggesting that, for Aristotle, choosing to spend leisure in a certain way is a sort of practical reflection on the value of all the thought and human effort that went into creating conditions for such reflection. To pursue something as a leisure-activity is a way of saying, when so engaged, 'This is what it was all for', even though the particular judgment might have seemed absurd to the very same agent when immersed in the serious business of life. These considerations can be applied across the community and through history; hence the inextricably moral-cum-logical outrage aroused by such images as the drug-peddler dealing with his teenage clients on the steps of the local war memorial.

In such a case, the 'leisure-judgment' would have to have been a practical falsehood (or a practical unthinkable) to the self or selves whose life made possible its utterance at all. Hence the opposed practical truth informing that necessary background is in a way voided by a leisure-response which treats it as if false. This is the 'in vain' of some effort which, however good in itself and successful at the time, is not followed up as it should be, so becomes as if it never had been. For active practical virtue to be thus ineffectual—to have made in the end no good human difference—destroys the all-round success of good agency, though not its moral goodness. Here we should recall that Aristotle takes seriously the curious question whether a person's happiness can be reversed by events in his family after his death (1100 a 18–30; 1101 a 22–b 9).

The argument could be brought to bear on the use not merely of leisure but of all cultural achievements, only that would take us too far. But what should be clear from this limited discussion is that the form in which Aristotle addresses the ethical question of our use of leisure presumes the absolute worth of a life of practical virtue and the priority of its characteristic obligations, even though his answer seems to put that life into the shade. For it seems as if, on his answer, the celebratory activity which good practice deserves is better than the core which is celebrated, and so the latter appears not so worthy after all and our respect is transferred to the former. But this is only an ethical problem if it breeds a problem of choice, whether in particular deliberations or in deciding between models of the good life. If, however, in proposing *theōria* as the acme of happiness Aristotle sees it as essentially framed by leisure, then *theōria* and the nonleisurely staple of the good life are not opposed as competing options, any more than the animal faculties of vision and digestion. The sense in which one is 'higher' than the other rules out exclusionary preference. And however fine *theōria* may be in itself, a theoretic escapist or a glutton for *theōria* is not a fine human being on account of that, if, as the present construction implies, the proper attitude is to give *theōria* due place in our lives as the figure on the ground of day-to-day good conduct.

The diversions of the Homeric deities are all equally unworthy of God: sybaritic pleasures, stirring the pot of mortal affairs, and watching the human soap opera. In respect of the first, they compare with their counterparts at the court of Sardanapallus (1095 b 21–22; cf. 1176 b 16–17); the second wins them the character of 'busybodies', like many mortals in public life (1142 a 1–6); while as to the decency of fascination with human affairs, Aristotle issues this stricture (intended only for human beings!):

> It would be strange to think that the art of politics, or practical wisdom, is the best knowledge, since man is not the best thing in the world. (1141 a 20–22)

> But if the argument be that man is the best of the animals, this makes no difference; for there are other things much more divine in their nature even than man, e.g., most conspicuously, the bodies of which the heavens are framed. (1141 a 33–b 2)

For the divine mind, contemplation of the eternal constituents of the world is the only activity that could suitably engage the eternal leisure. But it is not necessarily the most fitting of the possibilities open to us. Granted that it belongs to virtue to seek noble actions, so that for good people to pass their leisure in idle amusement shows a dangerously unstable set of values, there remains for humans the area of public affairs as an outlet for surplus energy. Political activity even on a moderate scale depends on leisure in the sense of freedom from drudgery and the ability to dispose of one's time, as Aristotle points out in the *Politics* (e.g., 1329 a 1–2). Should this not be the culminating activity of the best life? (The fact of its not being shared by the gods can at best be an auxiliary argument against it, for reasons raised earlier.)

This, the second of the three lives commonly thought to be candidates for happiness, seems the obvious choice now that the question of the best life has been more precisely formulated as the problem of how to use leisure. For so far as leisure represents an investment (already) of practical virtue, the use of leisure as a basis for further noble practical achievements makes for a coherence and thematic unity such as one would expect in a rational picture of the ideal life.

Aristotle, however, argues that the theoretic life is superior on the grounds that its distinctive activity is more continuous (1177 a 21–22), more self-sufficient (1177 a 27–b 1), seeks for nothing beyond itself (1177 b 1 ff.), is more leisurely (1177 b 4 ff.), and has its own proper pleasure (1177 a 22–27). Earlier we raised the question why these attributes considered in the abstract should imply superiority in any ethically relevant sense unless they are assumed to select from activities already designated as humanly appropriate; and with that qualification it seemed far from clear that *theōria* would emerge the winner. But though Aristotle does not point it out, it cannot have escaped his notice that the first two of these characteristics belong to many sybaritic or childish or trivial pastimes (since often they are indefinitely repeatable and need little in the way of equipment or preparation), while the last three apply to all amusements. This answers the earlier question. For the fact that people who know no better gravitate towards such diversions shows a deep-seated desire for something having just those unqualified characteristics. He had already said that amusements are desired only for their own sake since they are often notoriously damaging to health and pocket. The point now is that desire for *them* shows that people long for *something whatever it may be* that is desirable only for its own sake and has the other characteristics. Therefore, if in respect of these characteristics *theōria* is superior even to noble *praxis,* this shows that *theōria* answers to a human need which noble *praxis* is less well able to satisfy, as also to the need for something serious which amusement cannot satisfy either. What proves the first need genuinely human is a human fact which could not apply to the gods: namely, the widespread pathetic error of seeking satisfaction in unconstructive or degrading ways.

That we seek leisure at all shows not only our need to escape the pressure of necessity, but our need for something quite different from the hard work that goes into the escaping. Leisure, properly conceived, is not the contrary of misery, but is withdrawal from the bustle and scattered focus of practical life. Nature must sanction our pursuit of leisure, or she would not have arranged things so that intelligent, practical, social beings, working together as they should, inevitably tend to produce more affluence than they need for basic decent living.[64] It is cancerous, not good, to grow more than you need for normal functioning *by* that same normal functioning, unless the more is needed for a different dimension of good. Hence the very continuity between the gentleman's public involvement and the activities of basic practical goodness is the strongest argument against identifying the former with happiness. Thus Aristotle writes:

> Happiness is thought to depend on leisure; for we are busy that we may have leisure, and make war that we may live in peace. Now the activity of the practical excellences is exhibited in political or military affairs, but the actions concerned with these seem to be unleisurely. Warlike actions are completely so (for no one chooses to be at war, or provokes war, for the sake of being at war; any one would seem absolutely murderous if he were to make enemies of his friends in order to bring about battle and slaughter); but the action of the statesman is also unleisurely, and—apart from the political action itself—aims at despotic power and honours, or at all events happiness, for him and his fellow citizens—a happiness different from political action, and evidently sought as being different. So . . . among excellent actions political and military actions are distinguished by nobility and greatness, and these are unleisurely and aim at an end and are not desirable for their own sake . . . (1177 b 4–18)

This says that political activity is not leisurely, even if it depends on conditions of what would otherwise be leisure. It is therefore to be classed with the struggles by which the conditions are established. The possibility is also suggested that people seeking their outlet in public action may even undo the work of civilization *in order to* fight and win victories. This need not be in terms of battles and killings; we can substitute squabbles and any kind of destructive confrontation. The attitude resembles dedication to coarse or trivial amusements, because it, too, makes practical nonsense of the endeavours which enable it to flourish. But one shows contempt for those endeavours, while the other extols them by repetition or reenactment. Yet true respect for such deeds, this passage implies, would respect their doers' purpose. Though the doing of what they did was noble in itself and their motive (we assume) was simply to do what they felt called upon to do, *what* they were doing or trying to do was to build something up which, being worth the fight, was also worth maintaining. In this sense, practical action aims at an end beyond itself. But if victory becomes a goal only in the sense in which a "goal" in sport is a goal (i.e., a focus whose value lies only in the fact that it gives the activity shape and interest), then striving for victory is no longer serious (however seriously it takes itself) and it cannot command the same respect as before.

There is no difficulty in reconciling the assumption that the good person engages in the right or noble practical action just because it is noble or right, with the supposition that he seeks a result beyond his action; for it is the nature of practical action to be directed to getting something changed. But the above passage also says that admirable political activities (as well as military ones) are not desirable for their own sake; and this does seem to clash with the not much earlier statement that doing noble and excellent actions is thought to be desirable in itself (1176 b 6–9). Political campaigning necessarily is or should be campaigning-for-some-important-ulterior-end, and this is the kind of thing which, according to the passage just mentioned, is supposed to be engaged in for itself as something noble. Otherwise it could not be considered even a possible final differentia of the best life. But that statement of its intrinsic desirability has a normative ring to it. By contrast, the passage just quoted describes, I suggest, a divergent de facto attitude. Good political activity is *supposed* to be desirable for its own sake. That, after all, is what one has to say as long as it seems the only worthy contender for the title of happiness. The question is whether people really see it that way.

In Book I Aristotle said that it is valued because it brings honour, and he called its adherents *'charientes'*—'refined' (or 'genteel') people (1095 b 22–23). The motive of honour is hard to disentangle from the desire to do noble deeds as such. One desires to do and be what deserves to be honoured by worthy people, but the honour, too, is important, even if, as Aristotle says there, mainly as confirmation. However, one can also do what is honourable because it is honourable and not need the reassurance of actual honours. But even in this case one is not entirely drawn by *what* it is that is honourable. Others may honour the person's activity as the kind of activity which it descriptively is, but the agent who engages *because it is honourable* is not choosing it just for the characteristics for which it is rightly honoured. He desires to do the noble thing, but this is not in immediate response to the challenge of the situation itself. It is grounded, rather, in a prior desire that it be true of him that he does what is noble, whether anyone else appreciates that truth or not. To that extent he does not himself directly honour his action or occupation by engaging in it simply for what it is; and so it is as if to him (though, he has to assume, not to other good judges) the occupation in itself is not so honourable after all.

If this is true of those who care more about deserving honour than about getting it, it is even more true of those for whom getting it matters. And in Book X now, in the passage last quoted, Aristotle says that political activity looks beyond itself to power and honours, or anyway to happiness for oneself and the citizens, which happiness is regarded as something of a different nature from that kind of activity.[65] It is important to identify the level of this remark. The point, I think, is not that people active in public life tend to make every particular decision with a view to their own power and honour, but that these figure as motives for engaging in that way of life. Thus one might pursue each particular task disinterestedly (otherwise the action would not begin to be wise and virtuous) but not embrace the life-style entirely for its own sake. As Plato said, good people do not much want to rule and have to be persuaded by honours or in some other way. (We, for our part, speak of 'public *service*'.) This shows that the politically active do not see themselves as enjoying the acme of happiness in doing what they do, even when they do it well and successfully, but rather think of happiness, for themselves and their fellows, as something which lies beyond. This of course brings them dangerously close to identifying happiness with mere possession of some kind of result. Now either their activity itself is indeed the acme of happiness if only they were capable of understanding this to be so, or else their failure to be satisfied shows sound judgment. Aristotle does not consider the first alternative. He probably thinks that if even the best exponents of the political life fail (in significant numbers) to find it totally satisfying, it is hardly up to anyone else to tell them that really they ought to. Since they themselves are good and serious, their attitude cannot be discounted, and their attitude says that their own preferred activity is not the end of ends to the good person. So either nothing is or something else is.

Aristotle's solution, in terms of *theōria,* would have the effect of consolidating familiar values by introducing a new one capable (it is assumed) of bearing the weight of our need of a kind of activity utterly worth living for. Otherwise, too much is expected of practical life, and good *praxis* is no longer loved for its own sake. Our dissatisfaction with it, misdiagnosed, leads us to suppose good *praxis* incomplete without a train of extraneous goods and honours. *Theōria* can restore good *praxis* to its proper place in our affections, not only providing a new outlet for aspirations, but reminding us, by its own uselessness, that even on the practical level the exercise of our rational nature can and should be its own reward.[66] Hence far from recommending a retreat from life on the ordinary, practical level, Aristotle asks that it be lived with a different emphasis. So continuities between *theōria* and everyday existence tell in favour of his enterprise: as, for example, the fact that *theōria* is already a natural human activity, and we engage in it almost all the time without decision and probably without being able to help it. As he says at the beginning of the *Metaphysics,*

> All men by nature reach out for knowledge [or: understanding]. An indication of this is the delight we take in our senses; for even apart from their usefulness they are loved for themselves; and above all others the sense of sight. For not only with a view to action, but even when we are not going to do anything, we prefer sight to almost everything else. The reason is that this, most of all the senses, makes us know and brings to light many differences between things. (980 a 21–27)

This more-than-practical interest in our surroundings and in each other is already *theōria.* It is not yet scientific, responsible, serious, observant of its own principles and standards, issuing in views and arguments which it is confident deserve to be heard, passed on and developed. It cannot become so unless we are persuaded to take it seriously enough to begin realising its possibilities. The best is already under our noses, but it cannot *be* the best for us if we set no store by it and its few eccentric fans. Only by being deliberately cultivated can *theōria* rise from the level of idle impressions and loose ruminations to take on the strength and objective beauty that will place it beyond need of apology.[67]

It is not of the nature of *theōria* to bring about anything beyond itself; hence if we desire it as what it is, this can be only *for itself alone.* The missing step in this part of Aristotle's ethical argument—namely, that we do spontaneously desire and engage in it from the very first—is supplied by those opening lines of the *Metaphysics.* But *theōria* excels its only serious rival in respect of *self-sufficiency,* too, and this in several ways.

That Aristotle even raises this question of self-sufficiency proves beyond doubt that *theōria* and political activity are being viewed against an assumed background of the ordinary business of life. Since human *theōria* needs material conditions but

cannot lift a finger towards obtaining them, human *theōria* in itself i
sufficient activity. But granted the material substructure, lovers of the
independent than would-be politicians, as they need not look out for
sions and resources. The practical virtues need others as partners and
their exercise (1177 a 30–32), whereas the person of theoretic wisdom 'even when by
himself can engage in *theōria,* and the better the wiser he is; he can perhaps do so
better if he has fellow-workers, but still he is the most self-sufficient' (1177 a 32–b 1).
Practical virtue needs contingent possessions and situations, since one cannot be
actively generous without goods to give, or just when lacking the wherewithal to carry
out obligations, or temperate unless there are pleasures at hand to refrain from. Being
effectively good in those ways depends on more than choice and intention, since the
practical virtues make none of the difference they are supposed to make unless one
has the externals of action (1178 a 28–b 3). Whereas *theōria,* Aristotle implies, can
occur whenever we within ourselves are disposed to it, so we never suffer enforced
inactivity on this front. Nor do externals place limits on the quality and scope of the
thought. But for practical actions 'many things are needed, and *more, the greater and
nobler the deeds are*' (1178 b 1–3, my emphasis).

Aristotle could have mentioned further constraints on free expression of the
practical virtues: as, for instance, that if we make a mistake through ignorance we
cannot just revoke our action and start again from a pristine position; and that the
point of our feelings and actions is often unappreciated unless we have friends (a vital
element in the happy life). Real friends are necessarily few, since to be friends they
must 'live together' (1170 b 33–1171 a 11; b 29–1172 a 8). Friends not only share
our values but know at first hand the concrete details of our existence. So, like 'other
selves' (1166 a 31–32; 1169 b 6–7; 1170 b 6–7) they are attuned to all that particularity of our situation which verbal explanations are so often inadequate to convey.
But in *theōria* we can make ourselves clear in universal terms to strangers, and our
'fellow-workers' need not know anything about us as individuals.

As for the question of superiority in point of *pleasure,* this entire comparison
shows, I would say, an unconscious shift from, or at least within, the facile position
that 'the virtuous person takes pleasure in his virtuous actions' (1099 a 15–21). In a
sense the claim still stands, owing to that ambiguity which Aristotle lets go unnoticed.
It can mean (1) 'the virtuous person acts as he does gladly, or with full willingenss'.
It might also be taken to mean (2) 'The virtuous person is satisfied with (we would
say "happy with") his way of life'. Nothing in this latest discussion undermines these
assertions, although the second has been modified so as not to imply that the unmitigated life of practical and political virtue is completely satisfying to the right-minded
person. But taking the claim in the sense of (3) 'The virtuous person enjoys his
actions', we now find it implausible not merely because virtuous actions are sometimes positively unpleasant, but for general reasons which come to our attention
when we try to relate Aristotle's study of pleasure, especially in *NE* X, to the *praxis/
theōria* comparison.

The idea of pleasure was worked out in terms of enjoying some specific activity
which is enhanced and reinforced by enjoyment to the exclusion of other activities.
The more an activity is enjoyed, the more it becomes the kind of activity which it is
supposed to be, and the more decisively it blocks others. A metaphysical connection

.vas drawn between pleasure and being alive, but the reference there was to the acuteness and intensity of an activity, not to life in the biographical sense. But in practical affairs we are judged by the impact of what we do on life in the latter sense, not by our actions considered as vital activities in the sense of 'vital' relevant to the theory of pleasure. *Activity* in that sense is contrasted with *potentiality* and with *state* or *disposition,* and the aliveness of the former corresponds to the quiescence of the latter in the absence of activity. Consequently, there is an activity only where there is a corresponding potentiality or state. Now, the practical virtues are states expressed by particular good responses to perceived situations, but (as Aristotle implies at 1105 b 19 ff.) they are not capacities or dispositions for just those empirical kinds of response, but for whatever would have hit the mean of the type that defines the virtue. Furthermore, we do not multiply potentialities by assuming a potentiality for indignation with *this* person about *that* insult, or for walking *this* mile to *this* destination. There is the potentiality for that kind of anger, and the potentiality for that kind of walking. Thus an activity taken as the vital opposite of mere state or potentiality is taken in isolation from the particular circumstances under which the agent engages in it. Hence if what one enjoys is the activity, what one enjoys may as a matter of fact be a response to particular circumstances, but it is not enjoyed as a response to them. By contrast, the rationally chosen action gladly performed in accordance with the choice is gladly performed *in response to* the particulars, since the choice was formed precisely with a view to *them.*

One enjoys objects by being alive to them in some way, e.g. by looking at them, but this is not quite the same as enjoying one's looking at them, although Aristotle seems not to make this distinction. With the stepping back implied by the latter, the objects themselves swim away from focus. We also enjoy doing things, as distinct from enjoying the objects that inform and instrument our doing. We do not enjoy the ball and racquet, but playing tennis. This complicated area would need careful charting, but the broad division between enjoying an object and enjoying an activity is perhaps enough for the present purpose. In terms at any rate of that division it will not be easy to find a place for the virtuous person's alleged pleasure in virtuous action. We can think of someone as alive to his situation in an ethical and practical way, but we never on that account think of him as enjoying the objects which compose the situation. For one thing, he is too busy seeing through them to their practical implications; and once he has grasped the latter he is busy acting or preparing to act. Should we then say that what he enjoys is responding as he does, whether in feeling, deliberation or action? That is a possible state of affairs, but not one that wins the agent ethical credit, even if his first-level response itself was ethically appropriate. Do we enjoy the activity of helping someone? If so, we pay less attention to the needs of *that* person, so enjoyment lowers the quality of the activity.[68] But really what expresses our ethical nature is not activities *(energeiai)* but actions *(praxeis).* There seems to be no such thing as the *activity* of paying a debt, and if we speak in a more general way of the 'activity of justice' we probably only mean to contrast just *action* with the *disposition* so to act (which we have even when resting). And it is worth considering whether it is appropriate to enjoy, as such, obeying orders or giving orders, since Aristotle's concepts of moral virtue and practical wisdom are worked out in these terms; and whether it is even possible to enjoy, as such, the process of coming to a decision. If activities are what are enhanced by being enjoyed, then activities seem more like exercises of skills than expressions of moral dispositions.

The good person does what he sees as called for without further motive than his sense that it is called for, so in a way he takes on this action for its own sake. But this is quite different from doing it for the pleasure of doing it, although that too looks no further than the action. The practical (as opposed to the hedonic) agent is concerned with doing because he is concerned with getting something done (which is not to say that he is concerned only with having the result). It is the difference between aorist and progressive aspects of the verb. The hedonic agent is concerned with (enjoys) the doing as a doing; thus it makes sense for him to linger over it, savour its every detail, go with the flow of *its* internally suggested ramifications, and shut his mind to everything else. The ethical agent is ready all the time to modify his action in response to new particulars. He cannot afford to get locked into action of a given description, and since a variety of concerns informs his every move, he is always in a sense taking care of many things at once. Thus he cannot isolate his performance of some conspicuously noble practical deed from the business of ensuring the material conditions necessary, and he is watchful of these even while performing. If he reserves for himself the noble deeds and takes for granted that others (or himself in some quite other capacity) have provided the wherewithal, his performance is vulnerable to changes outside his control; and although the same is true of *theōria, theōria* needs no such elaborate set-up. If, on the other hand, he keeps an eye on the conditions, being ready himself to intervene on that level if necessary, he has lost that noble unity of focus, and his performance is not 'leisurely' nor (I have argued) enjoyed.

Getting lost in the minutiae of one's performance when the performance is supposed to be practical; enjoying one's action as 'an exercise of courage' (or one's distress for another as 'an exercise of compassion') as distinct from simply getting on with it; engaging in symbolic or ritual noble actions whose isolation from the rest of life matches their *practical* emptiness—such phenomena confess our human need for a serious *activity* (as well as for serious *actions* and responsibilities). For in the absence of such an activity, pleasure cannot be linked to seriousness as a constituent of the good life.

## XI. The Best Life

Aristotle says; 'Happiness extends as far as *theōria* extends and those to whom *theōria* more fully belongs are more truly happy' (1178 b 28–31); but he lays down no rule for the proportion of time to be spent on *theōria* in the best human life.[69] This is because it depends on the amount of leisure, which varies with people's circumstances. He may have it in mind that *theōria* would not occupy much time, for he writes: 'We ... must, so far as we can, make ourselves immortal, and strain every nerve to live in accordance with the best thing in us; for even if it be small in bulk, much more does it in power and worth surpass everything' (1177 b 33–1178 a 2). Since the soul and its parts are without extension, 'lack of bulk' here probably means that *theōria,* even at its best, need not make heavy demands on time.[70]

So he does not call for a situation in which people would be expected to engage in full-time professional theorising, all their material needs being met by some patron or institution. All the same, the theoretic life as Aristotle understands it affords more leisure than would have been available otherwise, because the theoretically minded individual has reason to turn away from gratuitous practical involvements. And as the value of *theōria* takes hold, presumably some things which previously seemed obligatory to persons of quality or refinement (the *charientes*), on grounds such as 'one owes it to one's station', will begin to seem gratuitous. But nothing suggests that Aristotle's theoretic man will ever be far ahead or far to one side of his society's consensus on what counts as a practical obligation or on its degree of priority. Priorities tend to be decided by urgency, and on that basis *theōria* never has priority, being independent of special opportunities which have to be seized in time. That it is so easily shoved aside, and for good reasons, means that *theōria* has little chance of getting serious prolonged attention unless it is regarded as of *immense* value, too noble to need to prove its claim by comparison with practical necessities, since in any such competition it must be always the loser.[71] If, therefore, we are to make freedom for *theōria* or for any nonpractical activity, we must be prepared on occasion to draw a line between necessary and gratuitous exercises of practical and political virtue. And in case the insistence on due space for *theōria* seems exclusively to the advantage of the latter, we should notice, from what has already been said, that practical activity, even with high standards and the best will in the world, tends towards its own corruption when allowed to dominate leisure. Thus the turn towards *theōria* can even be seen as a gesture of second-order modesty or temperance on the part of practical virtue—its recognition of its own limitation.

In view of the continuity in type between acts of basic practical goodness and conspicuously noble public deeds, it is important to Aristotle to emphasize that it shows no defect not to engage in the latter, and that the former are consistent with a quieter life-style allowing space for *theōria*.

> Self-sufficiency and action do not depend on excess and we can do noble acts without ruling earth and sea; for even with moderate advantages one can act excellently (this is manifest enough; for private persons are thought to do worthy acts no less than despots—indeed even more); and it is enough that we should have so much as that; for the life of the man who is active in accordance with excellence will be happy. (1179 a 3–9)

The notion of leisure is correlative to that of an activity which above all expresses one*self* so far as possible pure and simple, as distinct from oneself in response to unchosen circumstances which partly determine the response. It can be seen from this that the activities most suitable to dignify leisure will not be those that say more about a person's wealth and position than about his quality as a person. But despite this lesson not to be overimpressed by conspicuous noble deeds, Aristotle is far from despising such actions when backed by excellent character. A city needs fine statesmen, administrators, generals; and it needs public figures to exercise the virtue called 'magnificence' in funding and organising projects that represent the city to itself and to others: festivals, athletic or dramatic contests, the entertainment of foreign dignitaries, missions to other cities or to the great religious centres.

Consequently, it is hard to be sure about the reference of the following passage. Aristotle has just said (1178 a 5–8) that the theoretic life is 'best and pleasantest' for a human being, and that it is 'happiest' (or 'supremely happy'). He now goes on:

> But in a secondary way the life in accordance with the other kind of excellence is [happiest];[72] for the activities in accordance with this befit our human estate. Just and brave acts, and other excellent acts, we do in relation to each other, observing what is proper to each with regard to contracts and services and all manner of actions and with regard to passions; and all of these seem to be human. Some of them seem even to arise from the body, and excellence of character to be in many ways bound up with the passions. Practical wisdom, too, is linked to excellence of character, and this to practical wisdom, since the principles of practical wisdom are in accordance with the moral excellences, and rightness in the moral excellences is in accordance with practical wisdom. Being connected with the passions also, the moral excellences must belong to our composite nature; and the excellences of our composite nature are human; so, therefore, are the life and the happiness which correspond to these. The excellence of *nous* is a thing apart [sc. from the compound]. (1178 a 9–22)

What is the life called 'happiest in a secondary way'? According to my general interpretation, this 'life' is not, as some have suggested, the practical side of the theoretic person's existence.[73] For in that case, Aristotle's phrase 'theoretic life' would refer only to the theoretic side of it, whereas in my view it refers to a concrete existence both essentially practical and distinctively theoretic. So the life expressing 'the other kind of excellence' [i.e., practical] is numerically different from the theoretic life, but what sort of life is it? The answer depends on how one interprets the statement that it is 'happiest in a secondary way'. If this means that it ranks second in degree to the theoretic life, the reference should be to the latter's logical competitor (the species coordinate with it), and this is the political life: i.e., the life of basic practical virtue differentiated by 'leisure time' noble practical deeds. I am inclined to think that this is not the reference. The passage does not mention 'the noble', and the textbook summary of the relations of virtues in the 'compound' suggests a compound stripped down to unglamorous human essentials. And 'happi*est* in a secondary way' is a strange, if not impossible, expression for 'second in degree of happiness', although many scholars have taken the phrase in something like that sense.

Instead, the reference is, I believe, to the modest life of practical virtue without significant leisure. Such an existence fits neatly into the amount of resources it commands. These suffice for full and effective expression of the familiar virtues and for necessary relaxations, but leave nothing over for serious extras. However, in view of the continuity in nature between this life and the more conspicuously political life (since practical wisdom is paramount in both and the latter turns out to be not so leisurely after all), this is not a clear-cut issue. So the question is whether (if Aristotle bundles them together, which would be understandable) he thinks of the bundle as 'modest (though going over into conspicuously political)' or as 'conspicuously political (though merging with modest)'.

If the latter, this can be only because he means to state that this life, mainly conceived as political, is second best. However, as we have just noted, on a natural reading the text does not support this interpretation. Aristotle would give high honours to the life of political excellence informed by genuine virtue (not merely showy deeds); but the phrase 'happi*est* in a secondary way' suggests a life in some way super-latively happy, and this accolade is precisely what he is denying to the political life. Now whereas the latter is one admirable way, but not the best, of fulfilling our poten-tial, the modest life without margins to spare represents the unfulfilled and therefore unspoilt potential for the very best.[74] Hence it can be said to *be* the best and happiest in the secondary sense of 'be' in which something potentially F is said to 'be F'[75] (cf. *Metaphysics* 1017 a 35–b 8). If this is the reference and meaning of 'happiest in a secondary way', then Aristotle is not saying that the modest life is second best (and thereby implying that it is superior to the political). He is not ranking it at all. So we are still free to assume that he puts the political life second. On this interpretation, he never actually says so, but that would be because it is already obvious.

Aristotle is pleased that his conclusion accords with what Solon and Anaxagoras said about the happy person:

> Solon, too, was perhaps sketching well the happy man when he described him as moderately furnished with externals but as having done (as Solon thought) the noblest acts, and lived temperately; for one can with but moderate possessions do what one ought. Anaxagoras also seems to have supposed the happy man not to be rich nor a despot, when he said that he would not be surprised if the happy man were to seem to most people a strange person; for they judge by externals, since these are all they perceive. The opinions of the wise seem, then, to harmonize with our arguments. (1179 a 9–17; cf. *EE* 1215 b 6–14)

And it was also Anaxagoras who 'answered a man who was raising problems of this sort and asking why one should choose rather to be born than not by saying "for the sake of viewing the heavens and the whole order of the universe"' (*EE* 1216 a 11–16). Since only a rational *animal,* not a god, could choose to be (be glad to be) *born* rather than not, the judgment expressed is a thoroughly human judgment, though it may not seem so to 'the many'. The many would also have trouble in understanding how the 'strange person' who makes this judgment could possibly be considered a 'good citizen' in any but an incidental sense. 'The life of the good citizen' was how the *Nicomachean Ethics* first presented the supreme good in order to prove (in the statesman argument) that there is some such objective. Since that presentation entered in at the level of the initial claim *that* there is a summum bonum, it might have been intended as no more than a cursory gesture towards *what* the summum bonum should be held to be. In fact, however, Aristotle explains this 'what' without swerving from his original direction. For his theoretic individual, as I understand the case, is indeed a *model citizen:* one who, in addition to making his own good prac-tical contribution, gives due recognition to his and his community's practical achievements by putting the consequent affluence to the highest possible use. In so doing, it is not only that affluence itself that he values as it should be valued, but the human wit and moral dedication that made it all possible. And this is an evaluation not couched in words, but carrying more weight than if it were; for it consists in what we cannot now but regard as a *practical* gesture: the turning away from these things to the realms of the eternal.

Having found confirmation in Solon and Anaxagoras, Aristotle turns to the final court of appeal:

> But while even such things carry some conviction, the truth in practical matters is discerned from what we do and how we live *(ek tōn ergōn kai tou biou);* for these are the decisive factor. We must therefore survey what we have already said, bringing it to the test of what we do and how we live, and if it harmonises with our doings *(tois ergois)* we must accept it, but if it clashes with them we must suppose it to be mere words. (1179 a 17–22)[76]

His audience, like us, would naturally understand 'what we do' to include a reference to his and their own theoretic activity and his life of devotion to it. But if this carries *ethical* authority, it can only be for a reason which he mentioned earlier in connection with the hedonism of Eudoxus: 'His arguments were credited more because of the excellence of his character than for their own sake; he was thought to be remarkably temperate, and therefore it was thought that he was not saying what he did say as a friend of pleasure, but that the facts really were so' (1172 b 15–18). However, 'what we do and how we live' has also a wider reference. We—human beings in general— by seeking and prizing leisure, by then frittering it on idle amusements because they have the shape of free and self-sufficient activity, or by filling it up with grand but wearisome commitments—we show what we are and what we need; and the contradictions inherent in those two courses prove that neither course is the answer.

Aristotle's answer is determined by a disjunctive premiss limiting the field to three traditional candidates. *Theōria,* in the sense of systematic truth-seeking intellectual activity, wins by comparison with the other options presented. But the argument could be recast with a wider field of possibilities, including ones not envisaged by Aristotle. When the we who are Aristotle's modern readers take account of what *we* do and how we live, we know that for us the disjunctive premiss would be longer. Imaginative creativity in all its kinds is an obvious contender and so is philanthropic activity, to name but two. Every age can furnish a disjunctive premiss according to its own intuitions of value and its own conceptions of the divine nature; for instance, as a nature creatorial or ethical. How new candidates fare against the old and against each other can be told only by those historically placed so as to understand the spirit of each. Nor should we assume that an argument of this type is a failure unless one victor emerges to everyone's satisfaction. We can think of Aristotle as intending mainly to eliminate false but deceptive alternatives, thus setting criteria for a better sort of option satisfiable in more than one way or perhaps by a combination.[77] We should also note that the disjunction of options at any given time must be finite, or it is not a practical premiss. Since Aristotle means the *Ethics* to make a practical difference beginning with those around him, and since he does not aim for the finished precision of an Aristotelian science, his assertion that the theoretic life is peerless should be read as meaning 'best of the alternatives recognised *then*'. Whether we classify the *Ethics* as a display of 'practical wisdom' or restrict that term to deliberation about particulars, the *Ethics* is an inquiry by and on behalf of metaphysically 'compound' beings (1177 b 28–29; 1178 a 20). This is shown by the way in which the universality of its arguments and its conclusions is compounded with the openness of the practical.

But *theōria,* too, as practised by Aristotle, has its own flexibility, so in comparing his theoretic ideal with what to us may seem more attractive alternatives, we should not think of *theōria* as a monolithic intellectual juggernaut. When Aristotle says that our theoretic nature is our truest self, he is surely leaving a great deal out, but he is not necessarily leaving out intellectual individuality or what we should call creativity. He believes and in his work demonstrates that philosophy advances by probing what is sound and unsound in the diversely angled positions of extraordinary thinkers, each of whom makes a *distinctive* contribution to the truth.

One such contribution of which I have spoken is Aristotle's ethical solution to the problem posed by the life of Socrates, which Plato could find no way to solve on terms that fit actual conditions of human existence.

In the *Apology* Socrates says to 'the men of Athens':

> If you say to me, Socrates, this time . . . you shall be let off, but upon one condition, that you are not to enquire and speculate any more, and that if you are caught doing so again you shall die; . . . I should reply: Men of Athens, I honour and love you; but I shall obey God rather than you, and while I have life and strength I shall never cease from the practice and teaching of philosophy, exhorting anyone whom I meet and saying to him, after my manner: you, my friend,—a citizen of the great and mighty and wise city of Athens—are you not ashamed of heaping up the greatest amount of money and honour and reputation, and caring so little about wisdom and truth and the greatest improvement of the soul, which you never regard and heed at all? And if the person with whom I am arguing, says: Yes, but I do care; then I do not leave him or let him go at once; but I proceed to interrogate and examine and cross-examine him, and if I think that he has no virtue in him, but only says that he has, I reproach him with undervaluing the greater and overvaluing the less. And I shall repeat the same words to everyone whom I meet, young and old, citizen and alien, but especially to the citizens, inasmuch as they are my brethren. For know that this is the command of God, and that I believe that no greater good has ever happened in the state than my service to the God. (29 c 6–30 a 7)[78]

If the true goods are goods of the soul, and these are the practical virtues, and if these virtues are developed through prerational training of the emotions, what good could be achieved by Socrates' logical cross-examinations? How could Socrates not be utterly wrong in taking his interlocutor's failure under questioning as a sign 'that he has no virtue in him' rather than as showing him lacking the conceptual skill to frame definitions? If God theorises with eternal truths as his objects, then Socrates may have been serving God by imitation; but what had this to do with concern for the welfare of his fellow citizens, and how could it be the greatest good that ever happened *in the state*—except in the eyes of a confused Socrates, who held that we cannot be virtuous unless we understand intellectually what virtue is?

Socrates' self-acknowledged ignorance does not extend to the presupposition informing his practice: he cannot doubt that virtue and happiness depend on philosophy. Aristotle's *Ethics* shows a way in which this position survives Plato's revision of the concept of moral goodness, and his own of practical wisdom, by presenting a picture of the happy life that integrates these with theoretic wisdom while fully respecting the differences. The picture itself is a far cry from Socrates, but the motive inspiring Aristotle's presentation is thoroughly Socratic. For in Aristotle's book, there is at least one virtue of character in which we shall be deficient (because we shall give ourselves no chance to cultivate it) unless *first* we are shown through rational argument what it is, why it is a virtue and how it contributes to our happiness. That virtue is love of *theōria*. By systematic reflection on their existing values, Aristotle's audience is led to see how the leisure which affords them this reflection is leisure for higher activities of reason; and how despite and because of our practical essence such noble occupations are properly ours.

## Notes

1. Cf. the *Philebus,* which starts as a contest between pleasure and wisdom for the title of 'summum bonum', but ends by awarding it to neither.
2. The phrase 'in a secondary *way*' begs fewer questions than the *Revised Oxford Translation*'s 'in a secondary *degree*'.
3. The only earlier passages that might have led one (without hindsight) to expect it are 1143 b 33–34 and 1145 a 6–11 in *NE* VI, which may not originally have formed part of the *NE.* And even they seem hardly consistent with the exclusive emphasis on *theōria* in *NE* X.7–8.
4. Such is the embarrassment in some quarters nowadays over *NE* X.7–8 that one scholar has publicly expressed the wish that these chapters (along with 6) would 'go away', while another has suggested that, although they may have been composed by Aristotle at a different stage from the bulk of the *Ethics,* they were (in that case) inserted in their present position 'by someone else'.
5. It would not, however, follow that the ideal mode of existence would be regarded by Aristotle as a combination of different *lives* (as if 'lives' meant aspects of life). Rather he would regard it as one life having a complex ethical focus. See Cooper [3] against Keyt, and Section XI below, especially note 73.
6. Cf., e.g., *NE* 1096 b 24. On *phronēsis* in *EE,* see Rowe [2]; Kenny [2], Chapter 7. The *Revised Oxford Translation* wrongly has 'practical wisdom' for *'phronēsis'* at 1214 a 32.
7. I am not convinced by the arguments of Rowe [1] that Aristotle fails to distinguish practical from theoretic wisdom in *EE.* He may use the word *'phronēsis'* indifferently for either, but he is clear that (1) moral virtue is not theoretical knowledge (1216 b 3 ff.) and (2) moral virtue is closely bound up with a practical kind of wisdom (see especially VIII.1 = VII.13). From this it is hard to believe that he is not also clear that (3) practical wisdom is not a theoretical accomplishment. For detailed discussion, see Kenny [2], Chapter 7.
8. The *Revised Oxford Translation* has 'standard'.
9. Chapter 4, Section II.
10. And despite the fact that the backward reference at 1249 b 3–4 may be to passages also referred to at *NE* VI, 1138 b 18 ff.
11. If the book on practical wisdom belongs, as now seems more probable, with the *Eudemian* rather than the *Nicomachean Ethics,* we should positively expect the two passages to be making different, though no doubt connected, points. See Kenny [2], 182.
12. Thus Monan [2], 126–29; Rowe [1], 110; Ackrill [2]; Cooper [1], 138 ff.
13. Or alternatively 'definition'.
14. As well as rendering *horos* by 'limit', this departs from the *Revised Oxford Translation* in minor ways.
15. For a valuable account of the evidence on this and later Peripatetic divisions of goods, see

Tuozzo, Chapter 1. For the interpretation of 1248 b 18–20, see Allan [3]; Woods [1], 44 and 186 ad loc.; Tuozzo, 35–37 and 27–28 (note 52).

16. The terms imply a contrast between what is good to or for morally healthy individuals and what is good to or for others. Cf. Chapter 6, Section VII.

17. Woods [1], ad 1248 b 25–37 takes it to be 'the criterion' of the good man that natural goods benefit him. This must be mistaken if 'criterion' means 'mark by which we identify', since in that case the nature of the benefit must be understood in the ordinary sense, and the upshot will be that Aristotle is saying that possession and use of honour, wealth etc. is the sign of moral goodness. (Not that Woods intends this; see 189 ad fin.)

18. This is connected with the fact that Aristotle never suggests that there is an ethical mean for theoretic activity. (Similarly, in *NE* X 7–8, perfect happiness is simply engaging in *theōria*, not engaging in it *well*.) But we should not rush to infer that for him there cannot be too much theoretic activity in the *polis* or in someone's life, whether in general or on some occasion. For parallel reasoning would force him to say that there cannot be too little, whereas he certainly thinks that there can. (Hence the absence in the system of a just limit on *theōria* is not a prescription to maximise it.)

19. At 1248 b 31 he is contrasted with those who are intemperate or unjust. I take this to imply that he has the corresponding virtues.

20. At 1249 a 14–16 the merely good man is said to 'do noble things per accidens'. This is the most difficult passage to accommodate to the interpretation offered here. If the interpretation is correct, the reference is not to particular deeds (since the good man does each for the sake of the noble), but to engaging in the general practice of nobility from a general view of the value of good conduct.

21. The error can be construed as logical or as substantial. If logical, the merely good man is seen as retaining his (correct) view that the qualities normally called 'justice', 'courage' etc. are human virtues, but as speaking as if he had lost grip on the formal identity of *happiness* with *activity in accordance with virtue*. Thus he has moved towards our modern conceptions, on which (1) the phrase 'the virtues' means or is close to meaning 'courage and justice and moderation etc.', and (2) the path of virtue can conflict with that of happiness. If we construe the error as substantial, then we shall see the merely good man as clinging to the Greek formal connections between *well-functioning* and *virtue*, and between these and *happiness*, but as speaking as if he held a view implying that the principal human virtues are love of gain, commercial shrewdness etc.

22. At 1248 b 10 the virtue of nobility is said to arise from the other virtues. I take its connection with them to be natural but not necessary: it arises from them when the virtuous person reflects on his own life-style and draws an accurate reflective conclusion on why virtue matters.

23. See Mackie, Chapter 1, with the comments of Burnyeat [2].

24. Cf. the Spartans, who exhibit what Aristotle must regard as an ironic combination: they are amongst the very few nations sensible enough to have laws controlling moral education (*NE* 1180 a 24–26), but they value virtue because it breeds the natural goods (*EE* 1248 b 37–39).

25. Honour and wealth are said to be 'suitable objects of pursuit in themselves' *(haireta kath'auta)* at *NE* 1147 b 29. Cf. *EE* 1214 b 6–11; 1217 a 35–39; *MM* 1184 a 3–4.

26. But in *On the Soul* only the 'active intellect' seems to be separable, and the theoretic intellect comprises more than this; see Whiting, who makes the point in connection with *NE* X.7–8.

27. That Aristotle takes trouble to reach this (as we would say) 'verbal' result is a measure of his anxiety to accommodate the hallowed tradition (Anaxagoras, Plato) that 'mind (or mental activity) rules' to his own newly found awareness that the theoretical intellect cannot exercise practical control. See Section VI below.

28. Noble practical activity can be said to be 'in accordance with complete excellence' if, besides directly expressing practical wisdom and moral virtue, it also expresses respect for theoretic wisdom; and theoretic activity can be said to be 'in accordance with complete

excellence' if, as well as directly expressing theoretic wisdom, engagement in it represents a noble *use* of natural goods.

29. It may be conjectured that the difference of emphasis reflects a difference in the audiences—the *EE* (it is sometimes supposed) being intended for scholars, the *NE* for budding politicians. Aristotle places the accent where it may be needed to correct their respective predilections.

30. See 1179 a 34, and cf. Plato, *Laws* 803 a–b, for a similar remark in a similar context. See above, Chapter 1, Section V.

31. Cooper [3] rightly sees '*natural* teleology [my emphasis] in the way in which moral virtue in the *polis* helps set the stage for *theōria*'.

32. On this entire topic see the excellent discussion by Natali [2]; see also Dover, 10 ff.

33. Cf. Jaeger, 80–81, and Aubenque, 144. Nussbaum [1], 166, draws the consequence: 'If there can be no science of morals, there may be no place for moral philosophy in the city'. And if not for moral philosophy, how for any other branch of philosophy?

34. On this topic see Jaeger's classic discussion (Appendix II).

35. It seems that he had not always faced it. See the earlier work *Protrepticus* (esp. [B46]–[B51], Düring) for evidence of his holding theoretical knowledge to be practical. For a survey of the evidence and interpretations, see Monan [2], Chapters 1 and 2.

36. *Theōria* makes Plato's rulers fit to rule not only because it leads to the intellectual vision of the good, but also (paradoxically) because their love of *theōria* fosters that dislike of wielding power which Plato sees as a sine qua non of good rulership (*Republic* 347 b–e, with 519 c ff.).

37. Plato's dialogues kept memories fresh of the itinerant sophists. The voice of reason in *Parmenides, Sophist, Statesman* and *Timaeus* is represented by a visitor to Athens. Anaxagoras, for whom Aristotle's respect is evident, was a resident alien at Athens in his time; and so, of course, was Aristotle in his.

38. Cf. *Republic* 497 a, which says that philosophy cannot achieve the greatest things it is capable of until the philosopher finds himself in a city *ready to accept rule by philosophers*. This implies that theoretical studies, which are possible under current conditions (as long as the philosopher keeps out of public life; cf. 496 d–e), do not represent philosophy at its best.

39. Jowett's translation.

40. See especially 'From their youth up they have never known the way to market place or law court or Council Chamber or any other place of public assembly . . . it is really only [the philosopher's] body that sojourns in his city, while his thought, disdaining all such things as worthless, takes wings etc.' (tr. Cornford). Thus there was a real question, brought forward by Aristotle in *Pol.* VII, 1325 a 14–15, whether it is better from the point of view of happiness to be a citizen in one's own *polis* or an alien with no political allegiance. Any argument in favour of the latter is an argument for discarding the idea of the human summum bonum as the prime concern of the statesman.

41. The *Dialogues* do not show a monolithic view on the rôle of the philosopher and the relation of philosophical knowledge to practical life. In *Theaetetus* the philosopher is impractical; in *Republic* he is practical and theoretical combined; in *Meno* philosophic wisdom is not necessary for good practice (97 a–c, 99 a ff.); in *Philebus* it is not sufficient (62 b).

42. This restriction may be implied in *EE*. Defourny argues that in *NE* the field of the *theōria* which is supreme happiness is first philosophy/theology. (This may be the meaning of the restrictive '*theōria tis*' at 1178 b 32.) However, at *NE* VI (= *EE* V) 1141 b 1–3, the objects of theoretic wisdom include fundamental features of the physical cosmos; and 1139 b 18–36 suggests that theoretic wisdom ranges over all the theoretical sciences. Since 1145 a 6–11 says that practical wisdom subserves theoretic wisdom, one is bound to infer that theoretic activity in *NE* VI is of supreme value even when it is concerned with physics rather than theology (not that it is clear what theology includes, for Aristotle; *On the Heavens* 279 a 30 ff. and *Meta.* 1074 a 30–b 4 suggest that astronomy is part of it).

43. As perhaps he does at *Meta.* 1072 b 25.

44. Aristotle assumes that if they were to give, it could only be to each other.
45. Theoretic activity is not 'connected in description' with the body (Hardie [4], 80); it is 'separate in account' (Whiting). The point stands even if it is the same event as a physical process.
46. The author of the *MM* voices such a doubt at 1212 b 34 ff. On the general theme, see Aubenque, 166–69.
47. *Athanatizein:* to an unsympathetic ear the word suggests the adoption of alien manners and alien loyalties.
48. Cf. 1166 a 10–23 and 1168 b 28–1169 a 18 where the self is identified with the best part and with *nous.*
49. By 'individuals' here I mean members of a species. The formulation is meant as no more than adequate for the present. Thus it does not prejudge such metaphysical questions as whether the species is the same as the form or whether form or species is itself in a way individual.
50. See also Plato's sketch, not without sinister overtones, of the standard image of the philosopher at *Sophist* 216 b–d: the philosopher is more than human, comes concealed into the midst of ordinary men, is a destructive critic of human weakness, is not rooted in any city, seems 'of no account to some, and to others above all worth'.
51. Aristotle's awareness of this difficulty is shown by the way in which he recasts the argument 'Oneself is one's highest element; therefore in choosing the theoretic life one is choosing one's *own* best' as follows: 'If the intellect is above all *the human being,* then such a life is best for *the human being*' (1178 a 2–7). He is not denying that the highest element is divine (or at any rate godlike) but now insists that it is (also) human. (On wider and narrower applications of the word 'human' in *NE* I and X, see Kraut [1].)
52. For a concise survey of this topic, see Dover, 75–81.
53. See Chapter 1, Section IV, and Chapter 6, Section V.
54. Cf. *Topics* 118 a 5–15.
55. It refers either to a lost passage or to another work or to passages in *NE* VI (1141 a 18–22; 33–b 2; 1143 b 33–34; 1145 a 6–11) which imply the inferiority of practical to theoretic intellect (or of the former's objects to the latter's).
56. Cf. Gauthier and Jolif, Vol. II, Part 2, ad 1177 a 14–15, and Devereux [1]. The present interpretation is confirmed by comparing *NE* IX, 1166 a 22–23 with 1178 a 2–3. Both passages say that one *is* one's *nous* more than anything, but while the first has to do with *nous* in the context of friendship (hence not with purely theoretic *nous*) the second refers to *nous* as subject of *theōria*. (On continuity between *NE* IX and X, see above, pp. 314 and 325–26). Again, the *nous* (or whatever it is; cf. 1177 a 13–14) whose proper virtue is said to be active in *theōria* is introduced as that which 'is thought to be our natural ruler and guide' (1177 a 14–15). Aristotle says nothing to nudge us away from taking this in the natural sense, i.e., as meaning a *prescriptive* ruler. Similar language is used at 1113 a 6, where the referent is practical *nous*. It is true that at 1177 b 30 and 1178 a 6–7 Aristotle reserves the label 'life in accordance with *nous*' for the theoretic life. But this does not entail that the *nous* referred to is purely theoretic (so that practical *nous* would be, so to say, numerically distinct). I take the label as shorthand for 'the most purely intellectual life'. Since a life featuring *theōria* is distinguished by the exercise of an intellectual virtue which (unlike practical wisdom) is independent of virtues belonging to the nonrational part of the soul, this life more than any other merits the title 'in accordance with *nous*'. For the same reason at 1178 a 21–22 theoretic activity is called 'the happiness of *nous*'. This happiness is said to be 'separate' from the nonrational soul, but it does not follow that the *nous* which is its subject is not also the subject of an 'inseparable' (because practical) type of happiness-activity. *Nous* is subject of the latter only insofar as it is wedded to the nonrational virtues. With this in view Aristotle predicates practical happiness of 'the composite' (1177 b 28–29; 1178 a 20). 'The composite', I suspect, is virtually synonymous here not with a phrase expressing a whole of parts, as, e.g., 'rational element plus nonrational element', but with a phrase that denotes one element but presents it in a metaphysical context, as, e.g., 'reason (or *nous*)-of-an-animal'. But this position would have to be

defended from out of the *Metaphysics,* which I cannot undertake here. Some scholars, e.g., Cooper (at least in 1975) and Kenny, hold (1) that what is contrasted with 'the composite' in *NE* X.7–8 is the ontologically separable *nous* of *On the Soul* III.5, and (2) that this must be exclusively theoretic (Cooper [1], 162, 168–80; Kenny [2], 180). Against (1), see Whiting. As for (2): even if *nous* in *NE* X were ontologically separable (i.e., if it can be active in a way that does not ontologically depend on a body or nonrational soul), then although, if actually separated, it would be entirely theoretic, this does not entail that it, the same *nous,* is not also practical on occasion when it finds itself in charge of a psycho-physical complex. (Aristotle even seems to imply this at *On the Soul* 430 a 22, where he says 'when separated it is alone just what it is', which suggests that it is also operative when *not* separated; i.e., operative in ways that manifest the operation of a nonintellectual principle as well.) Consequently, Aristotle can (and, I believe, does) hold that, when a human being engages in *theōria, what* so engages is *what* deliberated to make this possible (and at other times deliberates with other ends in view than *theōria*).

57. But reference to this mean cannot be definitive of love of *theōria,* or it could not be a divine attitude.
58. On the ancient Greek passion for sports and games (especially dice), see Gauthier and Jolif, Vol. II, Part 2, ad 1176 b 12–13.
59. On the connotation of this key word, see Aubenque, 47–48.
60. Superficially, Aristotle's remarks against trivial and gross amusements can be read as a retort to Plato's statement (*Laws* 803 c–d) that leisure should be spent on the 'playing of games'. But they should not be so read, for Plato's 'games' (described as 'sacrifice, song and dance') are religious rituals. Cf. *Rep.* 372 b–c, where similar activities grace what Glaucon calls the 'city of pigs' (372 d). Aristotle's complaint against the *Laws* ideal would presumably be not that leisure there is filled with unworthy activity, but that for the urbane citizens of a highly developed society, *theōria* offers a better mode of god-ward expression.
61. It is clear from *EE* 1215 a 24–35 and *Pol.* 1337 b 30–1338 a 3 that the question of happiness is the question of how to use leisure. For *theōria* (not without moral virtue) as the answer to that question, cf. *Pol.* 1334 a 22–39. See the excellent notes by Gauthier and Jolif, Vol. II, Part 1, ad 1096 a 5–6, and Part 2, 867–70; see also Keyt.
62. There is also a light reference to leisure as a condition for happiness at 1096 a 5–6. (The money-making life is not happy because its characteristic activity is a response to the pressure of need.)
63. There is no corresponding potentially or capacity. See Section X below.
64. Cf. *Pol.* 1323 a 40–41: 'mankind does not acquire or preserve the virtues by the help of the external goods, but external goods by the help of the virtues'. See also Plato *Statesman* 272 a–d on *theōria* as the only defence against degeneration bred by leisure in the age of Cronus; and cf. *Rep.* 548 e–549 b.
65. This must be the meaning of 1177 b 14–15. The passage is sometimes taken as saying that political activity seeks a result, namely happiness, which lies beyond it. This is, of course, an Aristotelian conceptual truth about political activity, whose defining end is (conditions for) the happiness of the citizens (see *NE* I, with Chapter 1, Section II above). But that says nothing about the motive with which one might engage in political activity. In particular, it lends no support to the proposition that one could not or would not practise politics for the sake of doing just that (rather than for the sake of wealth, honours etc.), even if it would not make sense to do so if one did not set a value on the political end. If, however, the politically active person thinks *both* that (1) he is working to promote happiness *and* that (2) *happiness is of a different nature from the sort of activity that is his work,* then he cannot see himself as already exemplifying happiness, and so he embraces public life not for its own sake.
66. This is well argued by Depew in connection with the *Politics.*
67. Cf. Plato, *Rep.* 528 b–c, for the complaint that a theoretical discipline (in this case, solid geometry) languishes if not honoured in the community and given institutional support.
68. Cf. Rorty [1], Part IV ad fin.
69. Thus he recognizes no automatic inference from '*theōria* is the supreme good' to '*theōria*

should be maximised' (see N. P. White). The language at 1178 b 28–31 is sometimes taken to imply that one man is happier than another if (or if, ceteris paribus) he spends more time in *theōria*. But the context rather suggests that 'more fully belongs' refers to quality, not to duration as such: thus gods are happier than men, and the virtuoso human thinker is happier than one who stumbles or is distracted (cf. Cooper [3]). At 1177 a 21–22 Aristotle prefers *theōria* to *praxis* because the former is more continuous. His point is not that with *theōria* we get longer bouts of good activity than with *praxis,* but that the intermittency of the latter renders it a less perfect kind of good.

70. Cf. *Meta.* 1072 b 15, where the life of God is compared with 'the best that we enjoy only for a short time'.

71. Cf. Wilkes: 'The happiness it brings, being divine, is utterly incommensurable with that resulting from any other activity'. (She, however, concludes that, for Aristotle, theorising must always be preferred to other activities.) Cf. the plight of *theōria* in a practical world with the plight of civilized activities in general vis à vis raw impulses. The former have no chance unless we are prepared on occasion to treat the latter as of no account, rather than weighing the two sides against each other. Aristotle registers the incomparability of the value of *theōria* with that of good *praxis* by denominating the former *'timia'* ('precious'), the latter *'epainetē'* ('praiseworthy').

72. I depart from the *Revised Oxford Translation,* which has 'in a secondary degree the life in accordance with the other kind of excellence is happy'. Many translators and commentators write as if 1178 a 9 had *deuterōs* instead of the MSS' *deuteros.* This qualifies the superlative *eudaimonestatos,* understood from line 8.

73. For example, Keyt, and Engberg-Pedersen, 107 ff. For the contrary interpretation see Cooper [1], 159 ff. and [3]. My view that 'theoretic life' and 'life of the other sort of excellence' refer to alternative concrete lives (rather than to compatible aspects of one concrete life) is not grounded on the semantics of the word *bios* (which seem not to compel a conclusion one way or the other), but on the assumption expounded in Chapter 1, Section IV, that for the purpose of ethics the significant difference between one 'life' and another lies in what is valued most. It is the logical force of 'most', not of *'bios',* that creates an exclusive disjunction. Aristotle does of course sometimes distinguish the different aspects, theoretical and practical, of the ideal life (e.g. at 1178 b 5 and, by implication, at 20–21 [*aphairoumenou*]), but these are not what he means by 'lives' in the ethical context.

74. This interpretation fits one possible translation of *ho kata tēn allēn aretēn* (1178 a 9); namely, 'the life in accordance with the *rest of excellence'*, meaning 'in accordance with what remains of the totality of excellence if we abstract from the finest life the theoretic involvement that distinguishes it'. The concept of the secondarily happiest life is reached by abstraction from the ideal life, even though the former is also instantiated in less-than-ideal lives.

75. For the interpretation of *deuterōs* as contrasted with *prōtos* or *kurios,* see Burnet, and Gauthier and Jolif (Vol. II, Part 2), ad loc.; and cf. 1176 a 29.

76. This departs slightly from the *Revised Oxford Translation.*

77. Thus at *Pol.* 1338 a 13–32 'music' (which includes poetry and dance) is argued to be an honourable leisure activity. See Depew.

78. Jowett's translation.

# Works Cited

## Texts of Aristotle

*Aristoteles Graece,* ed. I. Bekker. Berlin, 1871.
*Ethica Eudemia,* ed. F. Susemihl. Leipzig, 1884.
*Ethica Nicomachea,* ed. I. Bywater. Oxford, 1894.

## Other Works

(Translations and commentaries appear against the name of the translator or commentator. Collections containing three or more cited articles are listed against the editor's name, as follows: J. Barnes [3], P. Moraux, J. Moravcsik, D. J. O'Meara, A. O. Rorty [2].)

J. L. Ackrill [1], *Aristotle's Ethics.* London, 1973.
J. L. Ackrill [2], 'Aristotle on *Eudaimonia*', *Proceedings of the British Academy* 60 (1974); 339–59; also in Rorty [2], 15–33.
J. L. Ackrill [3], 'An Aristotelian Argument about Virtue', *Paideia* (1978): 133–37.
J. L. Ackrill [4], 'Aristotle on Action', *Mind* n.s. 87 (1978): 595–601; also in Rorty [2], 93–101.
J. L. Ackrill [5], *Aristotle the Philosopher.* Oxford, 1981.
D. J. Allan [1], 'Aristotle's Account of the Origin of Moral Principles', *Actes du XIe Congrès Internationale de Philosophie* XII (1953): 120–27; also in Barnes [3], 72–78.
D. J. Allan [2], 'The Practical Syllogism', *Autour d'Aristote,* ed. S. Mansion. Louvain, 1955, 325–40.
D. J. Allan [3], 'The Fine and the Good in the Eudemian Ethics', in Moraux, 63–72.
T. Ando, *Aristotle's Theory of Practical Cognition* (3d ed.). The Hague, 1971.
J. Annas, 'Plato and Aristotle on Friendship and Altruism', *Mind* n.s. 86 (1977): 532–54.
G.E.M. Anscombe, 'Thought and Action in Aristotle', *New Essays on Plato and Aristotle,* ed. R. Bambrough. New York, 1965, 143–58; also in Barnes [3], 61–71.
P. Aubenque, *La Prudence chez Aristote.* Paris, 1963.
J. L. Austin, '*Agathon* and *Eudaimonia* in the Ethics of Aristotle', in Moravcsik, 261–96.
J. Barnes [1], 'Aristotle's Theory of Demonstration', *Phronesis* 14 (1969): 123–52; also in *Articles on Aristotle,* ed. J. Barnes, M. Schofield, R. Sorabji, vol. 1. London, 1975, 65–87.
J. Barnes [2], Introduction to revised edition of *The Ethics of Aristotle,* trans. J.A.K. Thomson. Harmondsworth, 1976.
J. Barnes [3] (ed., with M. Schofield and R. Sorabji), *Articles on Aristotle,* vol. 2. London, 1977.
J. Barnes [4], 'Aristotle and the Methods of Ethics', *Revue Internationale de Philosophie* 34 (1980): 490–511.

J. Barnes [5] (ed.), *The Complete Works of Aristotle, Revised Oxford Translation.* Princeton, 1984.

H. Bonitz, *Index Aristotelicus.* Berlin, 1870.

D. Bostock, 'Pleasure and Activity in Aristotle's Ethics', *Phronesis* 33 (1988): 251–72.

A. Broadie, 'Aristotle on Rational Action', *Phronesis* 19 (1974): 70–80.

S. Broadie [1], 'On What Would Have Happened Otherwise: A Problem for Determinism', *Review of Metaphysics* 39 (1986): 433–54.

S. Broadie [2], 'Nature, Craft and Phronesis in Aristotle', *Philosophical Topics* 15 (1987): 35–50.

S. Broadie [3], 'Necessity and Deliberation: An Argument from *De Interpretatione* 9', *Canadian Journal of Philosophy* 17 (1987): 289–306.

S. Broadie [4], 'The Problem of Practical Intellect in Aristotle's *Ethics*', *Proceedings of the Boston Area Colloquium in Ancient Philosophy* 3 (1987): 229–52.

J. Burnet, *The Ethics of Aristotle.* London, 1900.

M. F. Burnyeat [1], 'Aristotle on Learning to be Good', in Rorty [2], 69–92.

M. F. Burnyeat [2], 'Can the Skeptic Live His Skepticism?' *Doubt and Dogmatism: Studies in Hellenistic Epistemology,* eds. M. Schofield, M. Burnyeat, J. Barnes. Oxford, 1980, 20–53.

M. F. Burnyeat [3], 'Aristotle on Understanding Knowledge', *Aristotle on Science,* ed. E. Berti. Padua, 1981, 97–139.

S. Cashdollar, 'Aristotle's Politics of Morals', *Journal of the History of Philosophy* 11 (1973): 145–60.

D. Charles [1], *Aristotle's Philosophy of Action.* New York, 1984.

D. Charles [2], 'Aristotle: Ontology and Moral Reasoning', *Oxford Studies in Ancient Philosophy* 4 (1986): 119–44.

W. Charlton, *Weakness of Will.* Oxford, 1988.

Cicero, *De Natura Deorum,* ed. A. S. Pease. Cambridge, Mass., 1955.

S. Clark, *Aristotle's Man.* Oxford, 1975.

J. M. Cooper [1], *Reason and Human Good in Aristotle,* Cambridge, Mass., 1975.

J. M. Cooper [2], 'Aristotle on the Goods of Fortune', *Philosophical Review* 94 (1985): 173–96.

J. M. Cooper [3], 'Contemplation and Happiness: A Reconsideration', *Synthese* 72 (1987): 187–216.

F. M. Cornford, *Plato's Theory of Knowledge.* London, 1935.

N. O. Dahl, *Practical Reason, Aristotle, and Weakness of the Will.* Minneapolis, 1984.

P. Defourny, 'Contemplation in Aristotle's Ethics', in Barnes [3], 104–12.

D. J. Depew, 'Politics, Music and Contemplation in Aristotle's Ideal State', in *A Companion to Aristotle's* Politics, ed. D. Keyt and F. Miller. Oxford, 1990.

D. T. Devereux [1], 'Aristotle on the Essence of Happiness', in O'Meara, 247–60.

D. T. Devereux [2], 'Particular and Universal in Aristotle's Conception of Practical Knowledge', *Review of Metaphysics* 39 (1986): 483–504.

F. Dirlmeier [1], *Aristoteles Eudemische Ethik.* Berlin, 1962.

F. Dirlmeier [2], *Aristoteles Nikomachische Ethik.* Berlin, 1964.

K. J. Dover, *Greek Popular Morality in the Time of Plato and Aristotle.* Oxford, 1974.

A. Edel, *Aristotle and His Philosophy.* Chapel Hill, 1982.

T. Engberg-Pedersen, *Aristotle's Theory of Moral Insight.* Oxford, 1983.

J.D.G. Evans, *Aristotle's Concept of Dialectic.* Cambridge, 1977.

W. W. Fortenbaugh [1], '*Ta pros to telos* and Syllogistic Vocabulary in Aristotle's Ethics', *Phronesis* 10 (1965): 191–201.

W. W. Fortenbaugh [2], *Aristotle on Emotion.* London, 1975.

D. J. Furley [1], 'Aristotle on the Voluntary', in Barnes [3], 47–60.

D. J. Furley [2], 'Self-Movers' in *Aristotle on Mind and the Senses: Proceedings of the Seventh Symposium Aristotelicum,* ed. G.E.R. Lloyd and G.E.L. Owen. Cambridge, 1978, 165–179; also in Rorty [2], 55–68.

R. A. Gauthier and J. Y. Jolif, *L'Éthique à Nicomaque* (2d ed). Paris-Louvain, 1970.

A. Gomez-Lobo, 'A New Look at the Ergon Argument in the *Nicomachean Ethics*', *Proceedings of the Society for Ancient Greek Philosophy* (1988).

J.C.B. Gosling, *Plato;* Philebus. Oxford, 1975.

J.C.B. Gosling and C.C.W. Taylor, *The Greeks on Pleasure.* Oxford, 1982.

L.H.G. Greenwood, *Aristotle, Nicomachean Ethics Book Six.* Cambridge, 1909.

W.F.R. Hardie [1], 'The Final Good in Aristotle's *Ethics*', *Philosophy* 40 (1965): 277–95; also in Moravcsik, 297–322.

W.F.R. Hardie [2], 'Aristotle and the Freewill Problem', *Philosophy* 43 (1968): 274–78.

W.F.R. Hardie [3], 'Aristotle's Doctrine that Virtue Is a "Mean"', in Barnes [3], 33–46.

W.F.R. Hardie [4], *Aristotle's Ethical Theory* (2d ed.). Oxford, 1980.

R. M. Hare, 'Plato and the Mathematicians', *New Essays on Plato and Aristotle,* ed. R. Bambrough. New York, 1965, 21–38.

D. Harlfinger (see P. Moraux).

R. Heinaman [1], 'The Eudemian Ethics on Knowledge and Voluntary Action', *Phronesis* 31 (1986): 128–47.

R. Heinaman [2], 'Eudaimonia and Self-Sufficiency in the *Nicomachean Ethics*', *Phronesis* 33 (1988): 31–53.

P. Huby, 'The First Discovery of the Freewill Problem', *Philosophy* 42 (1967): 353–62.

D. Hume [1], *A Treatise of Human Nature,* ed. L. A. Selby-Bigge. Oxford, 1896.

D. Hume [2], *Enquiries,* ed. L. A. Selby-Bigge. Oxford, 1902.

R. Hursthouse [1], 'A False Doctrine of the Mean', *Proceedings of the Aristotelian Society* n.s. 81 (1980–81): 57–72.

R. Hursthouse [2], 'Acting and Feeling in Character: *Nicomachean Ethics* 3.i', *Phronesis* 29 (1984): 252–66.

R. Hursthouse [3], 'Moral Habituation: A Review of Troels Engberg-Pedersen's *Aristotle's Theory of Moral Insight*', *Oxford Studies in Ancient Philosophy* 6 (1988): 201–19.

D. S. Hutchinson, *The Virtues of Aristotle.* London, 1986.

T. H. Irwin [1], 'First Principles in Aristotle's Ethics', *Midwest Studies in Philosophy* 3 (1978): 252–72.

T. H. Irwin [2], 'Reason and Responsibility in Aristotle', in Rorty [2], 117–156.

T. H. Irwin [3], 'Aristotle's Method of Ethics', in O'Meara, 193–224.

T. H. Irwin [4], 'Aristotle's Conception of Morality', *Proceedings of the Boston Area Colloquium in Ancient Philosophy* 1 (1985): 115–143.

T. H. Irwin [5], *Aristotle,* Nicomachean Ethics *(translation and notes).* Indianapolis, 1985.

T. H. Irwin [6], 'Permanent Happiness: Aristotle and Solon', *Oxford Studies in Ancient Philosophy* 3 (1985): 89–124.

T. H. Irwin [7], *Aristotle's First Principles.* Oxford, 1988.

T. H. Irwin [8], 'Disunity in the Aristotelian Virtues', *Oxford Studies in Ancient Philosophy Supplementary Volume,* 1988, 61–78.

W. Jaeger, *Aristotle: Fundamentals of the History of his Development* (2d ed.). Oxford, 1962.

H. H. Joachim, *Aristotle, The Nicomachean Ethics.* Oxford, 1955.

J. Y. Jolif (see R. A. Gauthier).

B. Jowett, *The Dialogues of Plato Translated into English.* Oxford, 1892.

I. Kant, *Groundwork of the Metaphysic of Morals,* trans. and analysed H. J. Paton. New York, 1964.

A. Kenny [1], 'The Practical Syllogism and Incontinence', *Phronesis* 11 (1966): 163–84.

A. Kenny [2], *The Aristotelian Ethics.* Oxford, 1978.

A. Kenny [3], *Aristotle's Theory of the Will.* London, 1979.

D. Keyt, 'Intellectualism in Aristotle', *Paideia* (1978): 138–57.

C. Korsgaard, 'Aristotle and Kant on the Source of Value', *Ethics* 96 (1986): 486–505.

L. A. Kosman [1], 'Understanding, Explanation and Insight in the *Posterior Analytics*', *Exegesis and Argument,* ed. E. N. Lee, A.P.D. Mourelatos, R. M. Rorty. Assen, 1973, 374–92.

L. A. Kosman [2], 'Being Properly Affected: Virtues and Feelings in Aristotle's Ethics', in Rorty [2], 103–116.

R. Kraut [1], 'The Peculiar Function of Human Beings', *Canadian Journal of Philosophy* 9 (1979): 467–78.

R. Kraut [2], 'Two Conceptions of Happiness', *Philosophical Review* 88 (1979): 167–97.

R. Kraut [3], *Aristotle on the Human Good.* Princeton, 1989.

H.D.P. Lee, 'Geometrical Method and Aristotle's Account of First Principles', *Classical Quarterly* 29 (1935): 113–24.

S. R. Leighton [1], 'Aristotle and the Emotions', *Phronesis* 27 (1982): 144–74.

S. R. Leighton [2], 'Aristotle's Courageous Passions', *Phronesis* 33 (1988): 76–99.

J. H. Lesher, 'The Meaning of *NOUS* in the *Posterior Analytics*', *Phronesis* 18 (1973): 44–68.

A. MacIntyre, [1], *After Virtue* (2d ed.). Notre Dame, 1984.

A. MacIntyre [2], *Whose Justice? Which Rationality?* Notre Dame, 1988.

J. L. Mackie, *Ethics: Inventing Right and Wrong.* Harmondsworth, 1977.

G. Matthews, 'Weakness of Will', *Mind* n.s. 75 (1966): 405–19.

J. McDowell [1], 'Are Moral Requirements Hypothetical Imperatives?' *Aristotelian Society Supplementary Vol.* 52 (1978): 13–29.

J. McDowell [2], 'Virtue and Reason', *Monist* 62 (1979): 330–50.

J. McDowell [3], 'The Rôle of *Eudaimonia* in Aristotle's Ethics', *Proceedings of the African Classical Association* 15 (1980): 1–15; also in Rorty [2], 359–76.

A. R. Mele [1], 'Choice and Virtue in the Nicomachean Ethics', *Journal of the History of Philosophy* 19 (1981): 405–24.

A. R. Mele [2], 'Aristotle on *Akrasia* and Knowledge', *The Modern Schoolman* 58 (1981): 137–59.

A. R. Mele [3], 'The Practical Syllogism and Deliberation in Aristotle's Causal Theory of Action', *The New Scholasticism* 55 (1981): 281–316.

A. R. Mele [4], 'Aristotle on the Roles of Reason in Motivation and Justification', *Archiv für Geschichte der Philosophie* 66 (1984): 124–47.

A. R. Mele [5], 'Aristotle's Wish', *Journal of the History of Philosophy* 22 (1984): 139–56.

A. R. Mele [6], *Irrationality: An Essay on* Akrasia, *Self-Deception and Self-Control.* Oxford, 1987.

R. D. Milo, *Aristotle on Practical Knowledge and Weakness of Will.* The Hague, 1966.

J. D. Monan [1], 'Moral Knowledge in the *Nicomachean Ethics*', *Aristote et les problèmes de methode, 2nd Symposium Aristotelicum,* ed. S. Mansion. Louvain, 1961, 247–71.

J. D. Monan [2], *Moral Knowledge and Its Methodology in Aristotle.* Oxford, 1968.

P. Moraux (ed., with D. Harlfinger), *Untersuchungen zur Eudemischen Ethik, 5th Symposium Aristotelicum.* Berlin, 1971.

J.M.E. Moravcsik (ed.), *Aristotle, A Collection of Critical Essays.* New York, 1967.

C. Natali [1], 'Virtù o scienza? Aspetti della *phronēsis* nei *Topici* e nelle *Etiche,*di Aristotele', *Phronesis* 29 (1984): 50–72.

C. Natali [2], '*Adoleschia, Leptologia* and the Philosophers in Athens', *Phronesis* 32 (1987): 232–41.

M. C. Nussbaum [1], *Aristotle's* De Motu Animalium. Princeton, 1978.

M. C. Nussbaum [2], *The Fragility of Goodness.* Cambridge, 1986.

D. J. O'Meara (ed.), *Studies in Aristotle.* Washington, 1981.

M. Ostwald, *Aristotle,* Nicomachean Ethics. Indianapolis, 1962.

G.E.L. Owen, 'Aristotelian Pleasures', *Proceedings of the Aristotelian Society,* n.s. 72 (1971–72): 135–52; also in Barnes [3], 92–103.

J. Owens, 'The *KALON* in Aristotelian *Ethics*', in O'Meara, 261–78.

D. Pears, 'Courage as a Mean', in Rorty [2], 171–88.

Plato, *Opera,* ed. J. Burnet. Oxford, 1900–6.

H. A. Prichard, 'Does Moral Philosophy Rest on a Mistake?' *Moral Obligation.* Oxford, 1949, 1–17.

D. B. Robinson, 'Ends and Means and Logical Priority', in Moraux, 185–94.

R. Robinson, 'Aristotle on Akrasia', *Essays in Greek Philosophy,* London, 1969, 139–60; also in Barnes [3], 79–91.

A. O. Rorty [1], '*Akrasia* and Pleasure: *Nicomachean Ethics* Book 7', in Rorty [2], 267–84.

A. O. Rorty [2] (ed.), *Essays on Aristotle's Ethics.* Berkeley, 1980.

A. O. Rorty [3], 'Where Does the Akratic Break Take Place?' *Australasian Journal of Philosophy* 58 (1980): 333–46.

W. D. Ross [1], *Aristotle* (5th ed.). London, 1949.

W. D. Ross [2], translation of *Nicomachean Ethics* (rev. J. O. Urmson) in *The Complete Works of Aristotle, Revised Oxford Translation* (see Barnes [5]).

C. J. Rowe [1], *The Eudemian and Nicomachean Ethics, A Study in the Development of Aristotle's Thought, Proceedings of the Cambridge Philosophical Society,* Supplement No. 3, 1971.

C. J. Rowe [2], 'The Meaning of *phronēsis* in the Eudemian Ethics', in Moraux, 73–92.

G. Ryle, 'Pleasure', *Dilemmas.* Cambridge, 1954.

G. Santas, 'Aristotle on Practical Inference, the Explanation of Action, and Akrasia', *Phronesis* 14 (1969): 162–89.

M. Schofield (see Barnes [3]).

N. Sherman, *The Fabric of Character.* Oxford, 1988.

F. A. Siegler [1], 'Reason, Happiness and Goodness', *Aristotle's Ethics,* ed. J. J. Walsh and H. L. Shapiro. Belmont, 1967, 30–46.

F. A. Siegler [2], 'Voluntary and Involuntary', *Monist* 52 (1968): 268–87.

J. Solomon, translation of *Eudemian Ethics* in *The Complete Works of Aristotle, Revised Oxford Translation* (see Barnes [5]).

R. Sorabji [1], 'Aristotle on the Rôle of Intellect in Virtue', *Proceedings of the Aristotelian Society* n.s. 74 (1973–74): 107–29; also in Rorty [2], 201–20.

R. Sorabji [2] (see Barnes [3]).

R. Sorabji [3], *Necessity, Cause and Blame, Perspectives on Aristotle's Theory.* London, 1980.

J. A. Stewart, *Notes on the Nicomachean Ethics of Aristotle.* Oxford, 1892.

J. L. Stocks, *Morality and Purpose,* London, 1969.

C.C.W. Taylor (see Gosling).

J.A.K. Thomson, *The Ethics of Aristotle* (rev. H. Tredennick) Harmondsworth, 1976.

T. M. Tuozzo, *'Eudaimonia,* Practical Reason and the Theory of the Good in Aristotle's Ethics'. Ph.D. dissertation, Yale University, 1987.

J. O. Urmson [1], 'Aristotle on Pleasure', in Moravcsik, 323–33.

J. O. Urmson [2], 'Aristotle's Doctrine of the Mean', *American Philosophical Quarterly* 10 (1973): 223–30; also in Rorty [2], 157–70.

J. O. Urmson [3], 'Pleasure and Distress (A Discussion of J.C.B. Gosling and C.C.W. Taylor, *The Greeks on Pleasure)'*, *Oxford Studies in Ancient Philosophy* 2 (1984): 209–22.

J. O. Urmson [4], revised version of W. D. Ross's translation of the *Nicomachean Ethics,* in Barnes [5].

J. O. Urmson [5], *Aristotle's Ethics.* Oxford, 1988.

J. J. Walsh, *Aristotle's Conception of Moral Weakness.* New York, 1963.

S. Waterlow [Broadie], *Nature, Change and Agency in Aristotle's* Physics (2d ed.). Oxford, 1988.

M. Wedin, 'Aristotle on the Good for Man', *Mind* n.s. 90 (1981): 243–62.

M. J. White [1], 'Functionalism and the Moral Virtues in Aristotle's Ethics', *International Studies in Philosophy* 11 (1979): 49–57.

M. J. White [2], 'Aristotle's Concept of *Theōria* and the *Energeia-Kinesis* Distinction', *Journal of the History of Philosophy* 18 (1980): 253–63.

M. J. White [3], *Agency and Integrality.* Dordrecht, 1985.

N. P. White, 'Good as Goal', *Southern Journal of Philosophy* 27, Supplement (1988): 169–93.

J. Whiting, 'Human Nature and Intellectualism in Aristotle', *Archiv für Geschichte der Philosophie* 68 (1986): 70–95.

D. Wiggins, 'Deliberation and Practical Reason', in Rorty [2], 221–40.

K. V. Wilkes, 'The Good Man and the Good for Man', *Mind* 87 (1978): 553–71; also in Rorty [2], 341–57.

M. Woods [1], *Aristotle's* Eudemian Ethics, *Books I, II and III.* Oxford, 1982.

M. Woods [2], 'Intuition and Perception in Aristotle's Ethics', *Oxford Studies in Ancient Philosophy* 4 (1986): 145–66.

# Name Index

# Subject Index

449

# Index Locorum Aristotelis

*Politica*

*Rhetorica*

*Poetica*